The
Humanities

LIBRARY SCIENCE TEXT SERIES

The Humanities: A Selective Guide to Information Sources. 4th ed. By Ron Blazek and Elizabeth Aversa. 1994.

The School Library Media Manager. By Blanche Woolls. 1994.

Systems Analysis for Librarians and Information Professionals. By Larry N. Osborne and Margaret Nakamura. 1994.

Information Sources in Science and Technology. 2d ed. By C. D. Hurt. 1994.

Introduction to Technical Services. 6th ed. By G. Edward Evans and Sandra M. Heft. 1994.

Library and Information Center Management. 4th ed. By Robert D. Stueart and Barbara B. Moran. 1993.

Introduction to Library Public Services. 5th ed. By G. Edward Evans, Anthony J. Amodeo, and Thomas L. Carter. 1992.

Introduction to Library Services. By Barbara E. Chernik. 1992.

Introduction to United States Government Information Sources. 4th ed. By Joe Morehead and Mary Fetzer. 1992.

Introduction to Cataloging and Classification. Bohdan S. Wynar. 8th ed. By Arlene G. Taylor. 1991.

Reference and Information Services: An Introduction. By Richard E. Bopp and Linda C. Smith, General Editors. 1991.

Immroth's Guide to the Library of Congress Classification. 4th ed. By Lois Mai Chan. 1990.

Library Instruction for Librarians. 2d rev. ed. By Anne F. Roberts and Susan G. Blandy. 1989.

The Social Sciences: A Cross-Disciplinary Guide to Selected Sources. By Nancy L. Herron, General Editor. 1989.

Audiovisual Technology Primer. By Albert J. Casciero and Raymond G. Roney. 1988.

The Collection Program in Schools: Concepts, Practices, and Information Sources. By Phyllis J. Van Orden. 1988.

Developing Library and Information Center Collections. 2d ed. By G. Edward Evans. 1987.

Online Reference and Information Retrieval. 2d ed. By Roger C. Palmer. 1987.

Micrographics. 2d ed. By William Saffady. 1985.

Introduction to Library Automation. By James Rice. 1984.

The Library in Society. By A. Robert Rogers and Kathryn McChesney. 1984.

The Humanities
A Selective Guide to Information Sources

FOURTH EDITION

Ron Blazek
Professor
Florida State University
and
Elizabeth Aversa
Dean
School of Library and Information Science
The Catholic University of America

To Jim
great luck and best
wishes for a great future
Ron Blazek

1994
Libraries Unlimited, Inc.
Englewood, Colorado

LIBRARIES UNLIMITED, INC.
P.O. Box 6633
Englewood, CO 80155-6633
1-800-237-6124

Project Editor: Rebecca Morris
Production Editor: Steve Haenel
Copy Editor: Brooke Graves
Proofreaders: Louisa Griffin and Kay Minnis
Typesetter: Pamela J. Getchell

Suggested Cataloging

Blazek, Ron.
    The humanities : a selective guide to information sources / Ron Blazek, and Elizabeth Aversa.--4th ed.
    xix, 504 p. 17x25 cm.--(Library science text series)
    ISBN 1-56308-167-9; ISBN 1-56308-168-7 (pbk.)
    1. Bibliography--Bibliography--Humanities. 2. Humanities--Bibliography. 3. Reference books--Humanities--Bibliography.
4. Humanities--Information services--Directories. I. Aversa, Elizabeth Smith. II. Title. III. Series.
Z6265.B53 1994
[AZ221]
016.0160013--dc20

CONTENTS

PREFACE TO THE
FOURTH EDITION

Librarians, scholars, and teachers of literature and reference sources in the humanities had depended upon the efforts of A. Robert Rogers in producing *The Humanities: A Selective Guide to Information Sources* through its first two editions in 1974 and 1979. The untimely death of Dr. Rogers in 1985 left a wide gap that needed to be addressed. While working on the third edition, issued in 1988, the co-authors became aware of the magnitude of the task in developing the new product. Now it is six years later and they have completed the updating and expansion, embracing new developments in the electronic environment and new emphases on the multicultural and the female influence and accomplishment. The objective of the fourth edition remains the same: to provide a work useful primarily to teachers and students in schools of library and information science, as well as to reference librarians, collection development officers in libraries, humanities scholars, and others who have information needs in the broad discipline.

Permission to incorporate still useful segments of the text from the "Access" chapters of the second edition had been obtained earlier from Mrs. A. Robert Rogers through Libraries Unlimited, Inc., in developing the third edition. Basically, the format utilized originally by Rogers was retained, although there have been several revisions of varying magnitude with respect to organization of the subject disciplines in the "Sources" chapters. The fourth edition, based on its predecessor, grew out of concerns of the authors, both of whom teach advanced-level reference courses in graduate library schools, for a more comprehensive as well as updated guide to humanities information resources. As was true of the third edition, the co-authors divided the task, with Professor Blazek assuming responsibility for revision and updating of the "Sources" chapters and Dean Aversa the "Access" chapters.

"ACCESS" CHAPTERS

The odd-numbered chapters (1-11) relate to accessing information. Each odd-numbered chapter consists of several sections: a "working definition" of the field, a section on "use and users," a section on major divisions of the field, and a "computers" section. Finally, each access chapter has a few pages on important collections, research centers, and organizations. We have retained the "Computers in ..." section for each chapter, because we believe that users vary with the subfields in the humanities, and that electronic information has yet to be fully integrated into library collections and scholars' desks. A new section has been added to each chapter. "Helpful Resources for Students, Librarians, and General Readers," serves to point the user to additional resources to read, acquire, or consider for purchase. These sections will serve as aids to students with limited backgrounds in the fields described. A section on "use and user studies" has also been added to each "Access" chapter. The objective of these sections is to direct the reader to relevant use and user studies for the specific disciplines of the humanities.

Additionally, online databases appropriate to the humanities are mentioned in sections of the "Access" chapters. The coverage here is limited, so the reader will do well to check the various information services' catalogs for new resources and updated years of coverage for the files. (Entries in the "Sources" chapters also include notations of online availability of individual databases so the user of this guide has two ways to find appropriate online sources.) Important Internet sources have also been added. This change in the format from previous editions reflects the present and growing importance of information technology to the fields of the humanities.

"SOURCES" CHAPTERS

The even-numbered chapters (2-12) describe the reference tools, both print and electronic. Bibliographic specialists from various libraries were again contacted for their suggestions on inclusion and deletion in the fourth edition. The co-author wrote to each of the experts, thanking those who had agreed to serve yet another time in this capacity and welcoming those who were doing it for the first time. These specialists are identified in the acknowledgments section. It was clear after examining all their reports that there would be a sizable increase in the total number of entries, along with co-entries or minor entries described in the annotations.

As before, we have attempted to provide in-depth annotations so that this book can serve the needs of students and educators for a textbook, as well as those of librarians and scholars for a literature guide. The fourth edition should better serve the practicing librarian than did its predecessor, because of its more comprehensive coverage. Even so, it remains a selective work; a more comprehensive effort on computer disk is planned for the near future.

Again, titles of periodicals were not considered as entries in this section unless they had reference value. In such cases they were placed in appropriate sections on current awareness or serial bibliography. We made a systematic attempt, however, to identify guides and directories to serial publications in each "sources" chapter. Computerized databases, whether remote, or CD-ROM, are integrated with the books. When any of the print items are available online or in CD-ROM format, this is noted and described. Several of these resources appear only in computerized format rather than print; they are also treated within their appropriate reference category (index, bibliography, etc). Online or CD-ROM availability is indicated by an asterisk (*) in the numbered entries and the author and title index.

All chapters identifying the principal information sources have been completely reworked; all annotations for tools previously included were reviewed and, when necessary, updated, revised, and expanded. Every numbered entry is described in enough detail to provide adequate comprehension of the scope and coverage of the tool covered. In most cases, additional details concerning audience, arrangement, special features, authority, and even history of the work are furnished. Annotations range from 100 to 275 words, with an average of about 150 words each. Similar to the third edition is the inclusion of numerous cross-references linking the entries.

The job of writing annotations for newly added sources was completed in a nine-month period from July 1993 to March 1994. The job of selection, identification, and location of new materials, along with updating of existing entries, had begun two years earlier in Spring 1991 and was continued throughout the writing phase. Emphasis has been given to the need to identify new titles and new editions, and the project was conducted with the assistance of a cadre of interested and energetic young people, students in the humanities reference and advanced reference classes, DIS students, friends, and volunteers. The names composing this talented army are given in the acknowledgments section.

Titles were also added during the editing phase through June 1994, and forthcoming titles and editions have been identified. This relatively compressed writing period (although somewhat brutal for the co-author) was advantageous in terms of recency of material. Criteria for selection involved a trio of considerations, which included the previously explained (1) acknowledgment of value by experts along with (2) favorable reviews, and/or (3) familiarity of the co-author through his experience as instructor of humanities reference for the past twenty-two years.

The final product is a literature guide of 1,250 major entries, as compared to a total of 973 in the third edition. This represents an increase of 277 titles or 28 percent. These entries identify useful or important items for which information is presented in depth and is up-to-date at time of writing. It does not include the hundreds of additional titles actually embraced within the annotations given to the major entries. These co-equal entries, or minor entries as the case may be, were used cautiously in the third edition but more liberally in the current effort.

Proportions of the total number of major entries within the "Sources" chapters remain approximately the same as in the third edition, with slight increases in four of the six major divisions balanced by a slight decline in the other two.

REFERENCE SOURCES

	Third edition #	Third edition %	Fourth edition #	Fourth edition %
General	17	1.3	29	2.3
Philosophy	56	3.7	60	4.8
Religion	138	13.2	188	15.0
Visual Arts	209	22.1	266	21.3
Performing Arts	294	34.0	353	28.2
Language and Literature	259	26.6	354	28.3
Total	973	100.0	1250	99.9

The bibliographic style of the entries has been changed somewhat in the fourth edition to conform to the style now used by the publisher, although the arrangement of entries remains alphabetical by title within the categories. Names of authors, editors, and compilers are placed in the same field position following the edition statement, regardless of Library of Congress designation of their status. This should alleviate certain frustrations in determining whether the title or its editor belongs in the main-entry position. It resolves all difficulties in determining why certain individuals are accorded author status whereas others who do the same type of work are identified as editors or compilers. In any case, the indexes are to be employed to provide access when either a name or title is known. Also, place of publication is included as part of the imprint, and series are identified. For the first time, ISBN and ISSN designations are included for major entries (although not for co-entries or minor entries).

USEFUL SOURCES OF INFORMATION

In the course of preparation of this edition, standard reference works have been of considerable help. Among the most valuable for preparation of the "Access" chapters were *Encyclopedia of Associations; Research Centers Directory; Encyclopaedia Britannica (Macropedia)*, 15th edition. The several volumes of the *Annual Review of Information Science and Technology* and the *Proceedings, International Conferences on Computers and the Humanities, DIALOG's Database Catalog*, the *BRS Brief System Guide*, and the *WILSONLINE Tutorial* provided information for the "Online Resources" sections of the chapters. Previous editions of Rogers provided the format, some text, and guidance on the important issues to cover.

For the "Sources" chapters, the new technology was indispensable in identifying and verifying both old and new material. OCLC was a constant in the lives of the co-author and his bibliographic assistants. DIALOG Information Services, especially the category of "Book Reviews," was used daily. Also important was the print version of *Book Review Digest* (since WILSONLINE was unavailable). Especially fruitful in producing useful reviews was Wynar's *American Reference Books Annual*, Robert Balay's *Guide to Reference Books: Covering Materials from 1985-1990. Supplement to the Tenth Edition* (Sheehy), and such review journals as *Choice, Library Journal*, and the "Reference Books Bulletin" segment of *Booklist*.

ACKNOWLEDGMENTS

Obviously, a work of this kind cannot be completed without the help of others. The co-authors take this opportunity to express their deep appreciation to the bibliographic specialists and experts who took the time to respond to the initial request of Dr. Rogers for evaluation of titles in the second edition and continued their assistance with the third and fourth editions. They are Dr. Hans E. Bynagle, Chief Librarian, Whitworth College, Spokane, Washington (philosophy); Michael A. Keller, formerly head of the Music Library, University of California at Berkeley, California, now Director of Libraries at Stanford University (music); Dale Manning, Bibliographer for English and Linguistics Communication Studies for the library at Vanderbilt University, Nashville, Tennessee (language and literature); and Edmund F. SantaVicca, formerly Humanities Reference Bibliographer, Cleveland State University, Cleveland, Ohio, now Head of Reference Services at Arizona State University at Tempe, Arizona (performing arts). We are also deeply appreciative of the assistance provided by two specialists from the University of Florida for the first time. Edward Teague, University Librarian, Architecture and Fine Arts Library, provided valuable advice regarding not only inclusion of additional new material but also the reorganization of the visual arts chapter. Blake Landor, Bibliographer in Religion and Philosophy, provided excellent input regarding religion.

The co-author also wishes to thank his wife, Genevieve Blazek, for additional input regarding the structure of the visual arts segment. Special mention should go to his graduate assistant, Lori Bell, who proved to be a quick learner in all phases of the search operation and served as the chief bibliographic assistant and word processing person during the critical writing period. Special thanks are given to Dr. Theresa Griffin Maggio for her willingness to provide additional word processing assistance, to David Miner and his "can-do" attitude as manager of the computer laboratory, and to Dr. Maria Chavez as head of interlibrary loan at Florida State University's Strozier Library. Also deserving of recognition are students and former students of Florida State University School of Library and Information Studies—Mari Blanchard, David Blazek, Moss Davis, Mary Kautz, Dr. Maggio, Dr. Anna Perrault, Diane Rider, and Gloria Woody—who provided sound bibliographic advice.

A great debt is owed to the many students at Florida State University who over the past three years participated in the identification of titles and location of reviews: Mari Blanchard, David Blazek, Alphise Brock, Bridgit Broderick, Sandra Brown, Cathy Chapman, Dale Collum, April Dail, Moss Davis, Melanie Duncan, Donnah Dunthorn, Robin Ede, Sharon Estes, Steve Fadel, Jay Frantz, Maria Fullerton, Trudi Green, Katherine Gregory, Vera Gubnitskaia, Elisabeth Gullett, John Hatton, Jennifer Hechtman, Fran Henson, Dusty Hill, Judy Howard, Julie Johnston, Terri Jones, Mary Kautz, Sharon Kelly, Lin Lai-Yin, Amy Larson, Jason LeDuc, Clark Love, Alan Martin, Tim McConaghy, Megan McDonald, John McPhillips,

Denise Mickelson, Gwen Miller, John Miller, Tom Minton, Mary Mlady, Cathy Moloney, Hoi-San Ng, Mary E. Nolan, Claire Olund, Patty Patterson, Kathy Pisapia, Margaret Pugh, Maria Redburn, Diane Rider, Megan Schenk, Kim Smith, Betsy Spearing, Jon Stasko, Willette Stinson, Margo Surovic-Bohnert, Louise Taylor, Carol Travis, Lisa Wagner, Jennifer Wasick, Bob West, Larry White, Mark Williams, Gloria Woody, Michelle Worthington, and He Yu.

Daniel Cabirac, a graduate student at the University of Maryland at College Park, provided valuable material, both in print and in electronic access, on Internet resources. Cabirac's next work should be a "complete guide to the Internet" of his own; the shame of it is that so little of his extensive work could be included in this guide. His "navigational skills" and good humor are most appreciated. William Wilson, Librarian at the College of Library and Information Services, University of Maryland at College Park, provided a continuous "alert" to the second author. Humanities articles, hold notices for new books, and publisher catalogs appeared regularly in the faculty mailbox. These were invaluable. Wilson's assistant, Bill Pitt, until his untimely death, provided helpful advice on electronic resources, and student assistants in the CLIS library were cheerful even in the face of last minute checkouts and copying requests—always just before closing time.

LIST OF ABBREVIATIONS AND SYMBOLS

2/yr.	twice a year
Ann.	annual
Bienn.	biennial
Bimo.	bimonthly
Biwk.	biweekly
Corr.	corrected, corrections
Cum.	cumulative, cumulation
Enl.	enlarged
Exp.	expanded
Mo.	monthly
Pbk.	paperback
Q.	quarterly
Quin.	quinquennial
Repr.	reprinted
Rev.	revised
Semiann.	semi-annual
Trans.	translated
Trienn.	triennial
Wk.	weekly

SYMBOL
* indicates online or CD-ROM availability in both "Sources" chapters and author and title index.

1 ♦ INTRODUCTION TO THE HUMANITIES

WORKING DEFINITIONS OF THE HUMANITIES

What disciplines constitute the humanities? The question of the classification of knowledge, or of scholarly endeavors, into fields, disciplines, research areas, or subjects is itself a humanistic problem. It is also a very practical problem for librarians and information specialists who need to categorize the literature into workable systems for storage, retrieval, and physical access to information sources, and for educators who design curricula and establish the organizational components of schools, colleges, universities, and systems of higher education. Although the Commission on the Humanities suggested, in a 1980 report, that "fields alone do not define the humanities," and that "the essence of the humanities is a spirit or attitude toward humanity,"[1] scholars have, at various times, classified different areas of study as "humanistic disciplines," as opposed to those in the social and behavioral sciences, or those in the physical and life sciences.

In classical and early Christian times, the scope of the humanities seemed very broad. Literature constituted the core, but virtually every discipline relating to the mind of man was considered a part of the humanities. In the Renaissance period, the term *humanities* was used in opposition to the term *divinity* and seemed to embrace all areas of study outside the field of religion. In the nineteenth century, the term was used to include those disciplines that could not be considered part of the natural sciences. By the twentieth century, the fields of study that dealt with social, rather than natural, phenomena had emerged, along with "scientific" methods of investigation in the several social sciences. In the last years of the twentieth century, the humanities remain those fields of scholarship and study which are "dedicated to the disciplined development of verbal, perceptual, and imaginative skills needed to understand experience."[2] The fields of study that we include in this guide are philosophy, religion, the visual arts, the performing arts, and language and literature.

The reader may ask, "What about history?" and that is a worthwhile question. Although many consider history a central humanities field, research methods in history and indications of similarities between information use in that field and in the social sciences lead us to place history closer to the social sciences than to the humanities, at least for the purpose of constructing a guide to bibliographic sources. We believe that this source therefore reflects the past half century's migration of history from a narrative enterprise to one using many approaches that are closely related to those of the social and behavioral sciences. This is not to suggest that the reader should overlook the many studies of information-seeking behavior among historians; these works have contributed considerably to our understanding of how scholars work, and they are indeed required reading for the librarian.

1

The student wishing to explore the nature and scope of the humanities can access many useful resources. For an excellent general overview, the articles entitled "The Humanities" and "The History of Humanistic Scholarship," in the *Encyclopaedia Britannica* (15th edition, v.20, pp. 722-35) should be consulted. Kenneth McLeish's readable *Key Ideas in Human Thought* (Facts on File, 1993) offers brief, signed articles on the many disciplines and subfields that constitute the humanities, with a definite 1990s perspective. Volumes of the *Princeton Studies: Humanistic Scholarship in America* (Princeton, 1963-) provide a reflective look at the field.

The place of the humanities in higher education and the curriculum in general is addressed in Robert E. Proctor's *Education's Great Amnesia: Reconsidering the Humanities from Petrarch to Freud* (Indiana University Press, 1988) and also in Walter Kaufman's earlier work, *The Future of the Humanities* (Crowell, 1977). The former offers a curriculum that incorporates the humanities and suggests what students should be expected to know in the area; the latter suggests the logic behind teaching the humanities in the first place. Kaufman says that, among other reasons, the humanities should be taught to ensure the conservation and cultivation of humanity's greatest works and to teach broad truths and "vision."[3] Other, more recent, popular works have also addressed education, especially as it relates to the humanities. Allan Bloom's *The Closing of the American Mind* (Simon & Schuster, 1987) is one book that continues to provoke discussion and debate.

The previously cited report, *The Humanities in American Life* (University of California Press, 1980) continues to be cited in many articles on the state of the large discipline. Most relevant to librarians will be the chapter on "Cultural Institutions."

Finally, two additional works provide extensive current and retrospective views of the fields of the humanities and the role of the library. Lester Asheim's classic *The Humanities and the Library,* published in 1956 by the American Library Association, is still worthy of the reader's attention; many of the sources and articles have been brought up to date in the recently published, thoroughly revised second edition. See, then, Nena Couch and Nancy Allen, *The Humanities and the Library* (2d ed., American Library Association, 1993).

NATURE OF SCHOLARSHIP IN THE HUMANITIES

The nature of scholarship in the humanities and the literature of librarianship and information services for the fields within the broad discipline are considered in the remainder of this chapter.

At the outset, it should be remarked that humanistic research is differentiated most sharply from that in the natural sciences by the constant intrusion of questions of value. To the scientist *qua* scientist, such considerations are indeed intrusions. They interfere with and damage the quality of research concerned with objective, empirically verifiable data and with experimental results that can be replicated by other researchers. "Informed judgment" might play a part in determining which experiments to conduct, but "refined sensibility" would have no impact on the experimental outcome. Yet these are the bread of life for the humanistic scholar, whether dealing with a poem, a piece of music, a painting, a religious doctrine, or a philosophical theory. Thus, humanistic scholarship has traditionally been intimately intertwined with considerations of value.

One consequence of this connection between scholarship and value systems is the peculiarly personal and individualistic nature of humanistic research. Unlike colleagues in the natural sciences, or even, to a lesser degree, in the social and behavioral sciences, the humanist finds the research to be such an intimately personal matter that it is more difficult than in other disciplines to function effectively as a team. The results of team effort, it is felt, are more likely to be compromise and mediocrity than a productive division of labor. Collaborative efforts are possible, but they require special planning and are not nearly as "normal" as in the natural sciences.

On the other hand, it has also been suggested that it is not necessarily the content of the scholarship in the humanities that leads to independent and solitary work. Instead, it may be that something is different about the training and education of humanistic scholars that leads to the lack of collaborative work. For this new perspective on this aspect of humanities scholarship, see "Knowledge Collaboration in the Arts, the Sciences, and the Humanities—Part 3—The Humanities and Social Sciences," edited by Carla M. Borden, in *Knowledge: Creation, Diffusion, Innovation* 14 (September 1992): 110-32.

Regardless of the reason for humanists working alone, a further result of this is the general lack of ability on the part of the humanities scholar to delegate bibliographic searching to others. The interconnections within the researcher's mind appear to be so subtle or complex that it is necessary to examine personally the index entry or abstract to identify an item of potential relevance, and to see the book or article to determine its actual relevance. The problem continues to be compounded by the relative lack of standard or controlled vocabularies of the sort that are common in the pure and applied sciences. Yet the humanistic scholar needs help in the form of the availability of a wide variety of finding aids and access tools.

Part of the problem faced by the humanistic scholar also relates to the nature of knowledge in the humanities. It is not likely to consist of hard, identifiable facts such as formulas in chemistry, population and income statistics from census data, or the content of genetic matter. Of course there are plenty of facts in the humanities, but their sum total is considerably less than what the humanist is searching for. Knowing the number of times Shakespeare used the word *mince* in *Hamlet* tells us very little about the importance of *Hamlet*. Yet the patient accumulation and analysis of this sort of factual data, now more possible than ever with electronic text and analytical tools, can lay the foundation for knowledge of the order sought by the humanistic scholar.

Closely related to the nature of knowledge is the question of progress. In the natural sciences, knowledge tends to be progressive or cumulative. Each successive finding confirms, modifies, or overturns some piece of existing knowledge. This is true whether the problem is the identification of a new virus that has been detected through more sophisticated laboratory equipment or a far-ranging perception of relationships, such as the replacement of Newtonian physics with Einsteinian. In the humanities, no such "progress" is observable. Sophocles's *Antigone*, Wagner's *Der Ring des Nibelungen*, and Michelangelo's *Pietà* are not superseded as was the "phlogiston" theory of chemistry. This is not to say that works based upon the same or similar themes do not appear and that patterns of influence are not clearly evident. What is not cumulative is our perception of beauty, our insight into the human condition, or our understanding of how humans act in terms of artistic creativity.

The reader should not overlook the fact that, despite the differences previously outlined, the sciences and the arts and humanities actually have many connections. Michael Moravcsik, Eugene Garfield, and others have written of the relationships between the broad disciplines and the shared objectives of practitioners from both cultures.[4] Indeed, a bibliography by D. R. Topper and J. H. Holloway, "Interrelationships Between the Visual Arts, Science, and Technology: A Bibliography" (*Leonardo* 13 [1980]: 29-33), provides a number of resources on the topic.

INFORMATION SEEKING AND USE IN THE HUMANITIES

The factors noted in the previous paragraphs have an effect on patterns of use of information and library materials. They influence how humanities scholars seek information and the nature of the literature in their disciplines. For the humanist, the library is at the heart of the research enterprise. For the natural scientist, by contrast, the laboratory is at the center, with the library providing a supporting role. In this respect, the creative artist, as distinct from the researcher in the humanities, may be more nearly like the scientist—as anyone who has witnessed dialogue between a sculptor and an art historian can testify! Here the library provides support to the studio, just as it supports the lab activities of the scientist. Regardless of the type of work in which the humanist engages, the library is often an important resource.

The centrality of the library for the humanistic researcher is still accompanied by the centrality of the monograph as distinct from the periodical article. Although there have been fewer user studies in the humanities than in other fields, the pattern of preference for books and pamphlets continues to emerge, in contrast to the ongoing preference of the natural and physical scientist for journal articles, reprints, and preprints. This pattern is evident even as scholars, regardless of discipline, turn increasingly to electronic sources of information.

Another characteristic reported in such few user studies as we have is the greater spread of individual titles used by researchers in the humanities. Whereas a relatively small number of journals contain a high proportion of frequently cited articles in fields like chemistry and mathematics, the same high degree of concentration in journal or monographic titles has not been observed in the humanities. This is not to deny that critical studies tend to cluster around certain landmark works, but the spread of titles in which the criticisms appear is greater and the concentration much less intense.

A third use pattern that continues to distinguish humanistic from scientific researchers is a much wider time spread in the materials used. Whereas publications of the past five years seem more crucial to scientific research, with usage dropping off rapidly beyond that, the humanist is likely to be interested in works of twenty, forty, fifty, or a hundred or more years ago. Indeed, if one considers the classics in each field, the range of interest may extend to items 2,000 or 3,000 years old.

A fourth distinguishing use pattern is that the humanist appears to have a greater need to browse than do scientists and social and behavioral scientists. Although little systematic evidence has been collected to support this use pattern, experiential accounts suggest this practice. Additional work is still needed to substantiate this claim, and to determine if the need to browse is inherent in the humanistic researcher's nature and work, or if the lack of systematic organization of the materials in the field makes browsing a necessity. Studies in the use of electronic networks may enable us to collect more data and to analyze it with regard to the browsing issue.

Finally, we must mention citation practices and studies of publication and citation data in the arts and humanities. When the Institute for Scientific Information introduced its *Arts and Humanities Citation Index* in 1978, Eugene Garfield pointed out that inconsistent citation practices, citations to unpublished manuscripts and catalogs, and references to original sources embedded in texts without explicit citation were but three of the problems that were considered in developing the *Index*. The need to "enhance" titles for the Permuterm subject index has also been discussed in Garfield's works. See Eugene Garfield, "Will ISI's *Arts and Humanities Citation Index* Revolutionize Scholarship?" in *Essays of an Information Scientist Volume 3, 1977-1978* (ISI Press, 1980), pages 204-8, and "Is Information Retrieval in the Arts and Humanities Inherently Different from That in Science?" *Library Quarterly* 50 (1980): 40-57.

User studies that will clarify the generalizations about humanists' scholarly practices and information seeking are not plentiful, but their numbers have increased over the recent years. The studies seem to fall into three broad categories: first, there are the broad, comprehensive studies that cut across disciplinary lines; second, there are more limited studies that look at a single aspect of information seeking or at one or just a few users or disciplines; and finally, there are studies that focus entirely on electronic information and how humanists respond to it. The third category has dominated the recent work on humanities information seeking and use.

Among the broad and general reviews, a good starting point remains Sue Stone's "Humanities Scholars: Information Needs and Uses," *Journal of Documentation* 38 (December 1982): 292-313. A good background, as well as a look at key developments in electronic information, is provided by Paul Sturges in "Research on Humanities Information and Communication in Britain," *The Electronic Library* 10 (February 1992): 21-26. A sweeping view of changes in scholarly communications is provided by a series of articles edited by Paula T. Kaufman and Tamara Miller in *Library Hi Tech* 10 (1992): 61-68. Of special interest is Deanna Marcum's contribution, "New Realities, Old Values," on pages 62-67.

Two contributions by Helen R. Tibbo demand special mention because of the wealth of bibliographic information found in them. Tibbo's "Information Systems, Services, and Technology for the Humanities," *Annual Review of Information Science and Technology* 26, edited by Martha E. Williams (1991): 287-346, emphasizes technology, but still provides background as well as an extensive bibliography encompassing all aspects of communication and use of information by humanists and researchers in the subfields of the humanities. (The bibliography alone accounts for more than twenty pages of the review.) The second of Tibbo's contributions is her *Abstracting, Information Retrieval, and the Humanities* (American Library Association, 1993). Although this work is subtitled "Providing Access to Historical Literature," chapters on abstracting and the humanities and on technology and the humanities will prove useful to readers from other disciplines as well. As with the *ARIST* review, the bibliography is exhaustive.

Other general studies should round out the librarian's basic reading. Results of a major study by the Research Libraries Group is Constance Gould's "Information Needs in the Humanities: An Assessment" (RLG, 1988), referenced elsewhere in this guide. "Patterns of Information Seeking in the Humanities," by Stephen E. Wiberley, Jr., and William G. Jones (*College and Research Libraries* 50 [November 1989]: 638-45), reports on sources typically consulted by humanist researchers and suggests further questions for resolution in future studies of humanists' information-seeking behavior. Susan S. Guest's "The Use of Bibliographic Tools by Humanities Faculty at the State University of New York at Albany" (*Reference Librarian* 18 [Summer 1987]: 157-72) confirms the findings of some earlier studies, but also suggests an increased importance of the journal literature and more recent publications than had previously been acknowledged. The medium of research material and attitudes of scholars to remote storage of library material were investigated in Wendy P. Lougee, Mark Sandler, and Linda K. Parker, "The Humanistic Scholars Project: A Study of Attitudes and Behavior Concerning Collection Storage and Technology," *College and Research Libraries* 51 (May 1990): 231-40.

Many specific studies of use and users in individual disciplines are covered in the remaining access chapters of this guide. However, two that are not mentioned elsewhere, because they essentially address the area of history, may be helpful to the reader interested in humanities librarianship. These are both by Donald O. Case: "The Collection and Use of Information by Some American Historians: A Study of Motives and Methods," *Library Quarterly* 61 (1991): 61-82, and "Conceptual Organization and Retrieval of Text by Historians: The Role of Memory and Metaphor," *Journal of the American Society for Information Science* 42 (October 1991): 657-68.

The number of works on use and information seeking in electronic information resources, the impact of electronic information on the humanities, and the future of humanities communication in light of electronic information overwhelmed the literature on humanities scholarship and librarianship during the past five years. Only a few titles can be mentioned here. "The Lonely Scholar in a Global Information Environment," by Donald N. Langenberg (in *New Technologies and New Directions: Proceedings from the Symposium on Scholarly Communication*, edited by G. R. Boynton and Shelia D. Creth [Meckler, 1991], pp. 27-40) provides a good introduction. More specific to librarians are Edward Shreeves, "Between the Visionaries and the Luddites: Collection Development and Electronic Resources in the Humanities" (*Library Trends* 40 [Spring 1992]: 579-95) and James H. Sweetland's "Humanists, Libraries, Electronic Publishing and the Future" (pages 781-803 in the same issue of *Library Trends)*. Another work that comprises many papers on the topic of humanities scholarship and technology is edited by May Katzen and entitled *Scholarship and Technology in the Humanities: Proceedings of a Conference Held at Elvetham Hall, Hampshire, UK 9-12 May 1991* (Bowker/Saur, 1991).

An excellent review is "Scholarly Communication and Information Technology: Exploring the Impact of Changes in the Research Process on Archives," by Avra Michelson and Jeff Rothenberg (*American Archivist* 55 [Spring 1992]: 236-315). Like the Tibbo review mentioned earlier, this one has an extensive bibliography and provides much general background as well as specific observations on information technology.

Finally, "Information Delivery in the Social Sciences and Humanities: The Changing Role of the Library," by Toni Carbo Bearman and Linda H. Schumacher (published in *Databases in the Humanities and Social Sciences 4*, edited by Lawrence J. McCrank [Learned Information, 1987]), gives an overview of some of the issues related to the future of libraries in the technological information environment.

Publishing in the humanities, and especially the new electronic publishing, has been the topic of many articles in recent years. A few "must" readings include: John M. Budd, "Humanities Journals Ten Years Later: Practices in 1989," *Scholarly*

Publishing (July 1991): 200-16; Ann Oklerson, "Electronic Journal Publishing on the Net: Developments and Issues" in *New Technologies and New Directions*, (cited earlier); various articles in *The Public-Access Computer Systems Review* 2 (1991), edited by Charles W. Bailey, Jr., Leslie B. Pearse, Michael Ridley, and Dana Rooks (LITA, ALA, 1992).

COMPUTERS IN THE HUMANITIES

The impact of computers is felt not only in the area of publishing, but also in the immense increase in the number of computerized resources and tools for the humanist scholar. From electronic texts and the tools required to analyze them, to online databases for bibliographic access, to CD-ROM resources for use at the scholar's workstation, computers have had the greatest of all influences since the third edition of this guide appeared. Word processing, database searching, electronic publishing, analytical and statistical packages, graphical software, user-friendly interfaces, and even more topics have been discussed in the literature.

Because of the large number of publications in this area, only a few can be mentioned here. Others, discipline-specific, are mentioned in the "Access" chapters of this guide. Reviews and compilations are increasingly important, because they help the reader to sort through the hundreds of sources that are out there. The only pitfall is that things change so rapidly that even a hastily prepared review is soon obsolete. Nonetheless, a few resources will get the reader started. There have been several reviews in the *Annual Review of Information Science and Technology*, and the most recent review by Helen R. Tibbo (vol. 26, 1991) will bring the reader up-to-date, relatively speaking, and point the reader to publications on a diverse set of topics. McCrank's *Databases in the Humanities and Social Sciences 4* (Learned Information, 1989), its successor *Computers in the Humanities and Social Sciences 5* edited by H. Best, E. Mochmann, and M. Thaller (N. G. Saur, 1991), and the *Volume of Abstracts from the Cologne Computer Conference* (1988) serve as indexes to the vast new literature in this area, as does Ian Lancashire and Willard McCarty's *The Humanities Computing Yearbook* (Clarendon, 1988).

The journal *Computers and the Humanities*, now approaching its thirtieth year, is an invaluable source of articles on all aspects of computing in all areas of the humanities. An informative overview of humanities computing, written by the founding editor on the occasion of the twenty-fifth anniversary of the journal, is Joseph Raben's "Humanities Computing 25 Years Later," *Computers and the Humanities* 25 (1991): 341-50.

Other journals that the librarian should consult on matters of computers and information services in the humanities include *Library HiTech*, *Database*, *Online*, *CD-ROM Professional*, and *Journal of the American Society for Information Science*, to name only a few. Special issues of other journals also offer coverage: a good example is the Spring 1992 issue of *Library Trends*. Edited by Mark Stover, the issue is aptly titled "Electronic Information for the Humanities." Several general articles referenced in this chapter appear in the issue, along with articles by experts on electronic information on most disciplines of the arts and humanities.

Online searching is an area of computer use that has continued to receive attention in the literature. Whereas how-to articles dominated in the early 1980s, the more recent focus has been on search behavior, database choice, and the overall impact of online information on the humanities scholar. The vocabulary used in online searching in the humanities was studied, along with other aspects of search, in Marcia J. Bates, Deborah N. Wilde, and Susan Siegfried, "An Analysis of Search Terminology Used by Humanities Scholars: The Getty Online Searching Project Report Number 1," *Library Quarterly* 63 (January 1993): 1-39. David Everett and David M. Pilachowski looked at searching of personal names in "What's in a Name? Looking for People Online—Humanities," *Database* (October 1986): 26-30. (Names—proper, common, institutional and collective—are also explored from the indexing viewpoint in Stephen E. Wiberley, Jr., "Names in Space and Time: The Indexing Vocabulary of the Humanities," *Library Quarterly* 58 [January 1988]: 1-28.)

The possibilities and realities of hypertext are explored in many articles. Particular projects are described in the reviews and collective titles already mentioned. Of special interest are Karen E. Smith's "Hypertext—Linking to the Future," *Online* 12 (March 1988): 32-42, and Susan K. Kinnell's piece within Smith's article, "Information Retrieval in Humanities Using Hypertext," pp. 34-35. Patrick W. Conner offers a view of the future in "Hypertext in the Last Days of the Book," *Bulletin of the John Rylands Library of Manchester University* 74 (1992): 7-23.

Four additional articles on online and CD-ROM sources should be read by the librarian. These are: Peter Stern, "Online in the Humanities: Problems and Possibilities," *Journal of Academic Librarianship* 14 (July 1988): 161-64; Teresa M. Harrison and Timothy Stephen, "On-line Disciplines: Computer-Mediated Scholarship in the Humanities and Social Sciences," *Computers and the Humanities* 26 (1992): 181-93; Den Ruiz and Daniel E. Meyer, "End-User Selection of Databases—Part III," *Database* (October 1990): 59-64; and Lucy Buck and Paul Travis Nicholls, "Arts and Humanities Sources on CD-ROM," *CD-ROM Professional* (March 1991): 96-91.

Finally, directories of online and CD-ROM databases, as well as vendor literature, should be consulted for the most recent offerings from hundreds of database producers and publishers.

Perhaps the most influential development since publication of the third edition of this guide in 1988 is the accessibility of the Internet and its wealth of sources for librarians, scholars, and teachers in the humanities fields. Because rapid changes occur on the Internet, a description of individual sources is a snapshot reflecting just what is available at the moment. In this guide, we suggest tools to access humanities materials rather than specific offerings.

There are several good print guides that discuss both tools for accessing the Internet and the resources themselves. These include Harley Hahn's *The Internet Complete Reference* (Osbourne McGraw-Hill, 1994), Paul Gilster's *The Internet Navigator* (John Wiley, 1993), and the older *The Whole Internet User's Guide and Catalog* by Ed Krol (O'Reilly, 1992). All three define, as well as can be, the Internet and suggest access methods. Gilster's work provides a fairly comprehensive list of humanities materials available on the Internet. Krol provides a directory of sources, organized by topics and subtopics—such as "Poetry," "Project Gutenberg," "Dante Project"—within the "Literature" section. All include means of accessing and addresses for additional information.

The gopher file server entitled "Clearinghouse of Subject Oriented Internet Resource Guides" archives many detailed guides to the Internet, and provides lists for specific subject areas in the humanities.

Humanists can access and use a wide range of Internet tools, and we are beginning to study who uses what and how. For the present, access to electronic mail, access to library catalogs and reference sources, access to text files, and access to graphical material are among the major tools. USENET newsgroups (discussion groups that can be accessed by the user) enable scholars to communicate with others who share interests in a particular topic.

The most basic Internet tool is electronic mail, which allows researchers to communicate directly with one another, but also to subscribe to electronic discussion groups. After subscribing, messages posted to the group go directly to the user's mailbox. Messages can be archived or deleted after the user digests them. Most of the guides to the Internet give basic instructions on the use of e-mail and the searching of archives.

Gopher is a simple document delivery tool that provides access to documents ranging from mailing lists to full-length monographs. Even multimedia "documents" such as images and sound can be retrieved via gopher. Although gopher files are like menus, a tool that allows easier keyword searching of many gopher files is a tool called Veronica. Gopher and Veronica are both among the most frequently used tools for Internet access.

Another information delivery tool is FTP. FTP is often used by the scholar to obtain full texts of long documents (such as literary works), and materials in the visual arts and music. Archie is an indexing tool that provides keyword searching of files and directories that are archived at FTP sites. Electronic text projects, such as Michael Hart's "Project Gutenberg," are attempting to put major literary works in machine readable form and to provide access over the Internet.

USENET newsgroups, mentioned previously, differ from e-mail membership in discussion groups in that here the user accesses the discussion groups rather than having all messages posted to the electronic mailbox. One user said, "The slight disadvantage of having to learn the use newsreader software is made up for by not having numerous messages clog up your mailbox." The same user went on to say, "One of the most useful newsgroups for researchers is the newsgroup called news.answers. It is a collection of FAQs (frequently asked questions) on a wide variety of topics, usually compiled by knowledgeable individuals who continually update the questions and answers through feedback from others who are familiar with a particular topic."[5]

Telnet enables a user to connect to remote computers. Librarians and scholars alike use Telnet to connect to online library catalogs such as the Library of Congress SCORPIO system, the University of California's Melvyl system, and RLIN (Research Libraries Information Network). There is even a guide to library catalogs available on the network: look in the print guides for information and instruction on how to access Art St. George and Ron Larsen's "library package," which lists hundreds of library catalogs and databases and how to get to them.

The librarian and humanities scholar alike are embarking on a new era of information access, and they will do well to explore the possibilities of Internet access.

OTHER HELPFUL INFORMATION FOR STUDENTS, LIBRARIANS, AND GENERAL READERS

Two additional topics must be mentioned. First, the nature of the materials in the humanities deserves attention. The working scholar in a humanistic discipline tends to perceive the materials with which to work as falling into three broad categories. There are original texts or artifacts, critical literature, and literature designed for specific groups and purposes. Each requires further elaboration.

The heart of humanistic study is the original work, whether a poem, painting, symphony, or discourse on ethics. The creative contribution is what the humanist scholar studies.

The second major category is the critical literature: it takes the form of analysis, interpretation, or commentary on the creative work. It may later be regarded as a creative work in and of itself.

The literature designed for special groups or purposes may be subdivided into popularizations, access tools, and professional literature. These are all of special interest to the librarian or information specialist. Popularizations allow for the dissemination of special-interest material to wider audiences, thus enabling libraries to play a greater educational role. Access tools, of course, are what enables libraries to provide information services; here we think of bibliographies, indexes, abstracts, encyclopedias, dictionaries, handbooks, and the other finding aids needed to access information for scholarship and research.

Finally, the professional literature in each humanities field is comprised of publications by associations and professional societies, with journals, indexes, abstracts, conference proceedings, and current awareness services as typical outputs.

The excellent library collection will include all three categories of humanities-related material, and the librarian will need a familiarity with all types. This guide provides information on the materials required for the major subject areas in the field, but, because no single collection can provide everything, the librarian should also have such tools as *Subject Collections* 7th ed., edited by Lee Ash and William G. Miller (Bowker, 1993), to lead the researcher to special collections of libraries and museums in the United States and Canada.

The second additional topic is funding for the humanities, which, especially as it affects libraries, continues to be discussed in a wide-ranging literature. The annual *ALA Yearbook of Library and Information Services* (American Library Association) reviews the National Endowment for the Humanities and its activities as it aids libraries. See, for example, Thomas Phelps, "The National Endowment for the Humanities," in volume 15 (pp. 173-74). Another informative article that provides a detailed background as well as a discussion of issues involving funding and intellectual freedom is Alvaro Ignacio Anillo, "The National Endowment for the Humanities: Control of Funding Versus Academic Freedom," *Vanderbilt Law Review* 45 (1992): 455-86. The popular press has addressed the same topic, primarily in relation to the funding of artists' works and museum exhibitions.

General reference tools, such as the *Directory of Grants in the Humanities 1993/1994* (Oryx Press, 1993) and the same publisher's annual *Directory of Research Grants*, will lead the scholar or librarian to detailed entries on funding opportunities from both governmental and private sources. Amounts of funding, types of projects, dates for and restrictions on applications, and address information about sponsors are part of each entry, and subject, program type, and sponsor indexes allow for a variety of access methods.

NOTES

[1]Commission on the Humanities, *The Humanities in American Life* (Berkeley, Calif.: University of California Press, 1980).

[2]Ibid.

[3]Michael J. Moravcsik, "Scientists and Artists: Motivations, Aspirations, Approaches, and Accomplishments," *Leonardo* 7 (1974): 255-57.

[4]Eugene Garfield, "Art and Science. Part 1. The Art-Science Connection," in *Essays of an Information Scientist* v.12 (ISI Press, 1989), pp. 54-61. This article contains a list of journals that cover the science-art connection.

[5]Daniel Cabirac, personal communication with Aversa, February 1994.

The authors are grateful to Mr. Cabirac for his contributions on Internet tools and resources; his work is evident in every "Computers in ..." section of this Guide.

2 ◆ SOURCES OF GENERAL IMPORTANCE TO THE HUMANITIES

BIBLIOGRAPHIC GUIDES AND DIRECTORIES

Reference Books and Research Guides

1. **American Popular Culture: A Guide to the Reference Literature**. Frank W. Hoffman. Englewood, CO: Libraries Unlimited, 1994. ca. 250p. ISBN 1-56308-142-3.
   Another in the line of popular culture reference books by Hoffman is this selective reference literature guide to all aspects of the study, from comic books to motion pictures. It is slated for publication in fall 1994, and should be of interest to a wide range of users. Organization of the work is by type of information source, and coverage is given to 1,500 annotated entries placed under categories by type of tool: guides to the literature, general and subject encyclopedias, subject dictionaries, handbooks and manuals, biographical compilations, directories, indexes and abstracts, bibliographies, discographies, videographies, and supplemental sources such as periodicals, research centers, and associations. These segments are then subdivided by topic or subject: general, popular arts (music and fine arts), mass media (radio, computers), folkways/oral tradition, and social phenomena (fads, events, trends). Annotations are informative, providing description and in some cases evaluation of sources.

2. **American Reference Books Annual**. Bohdan S. Wynar et al., eds. Englewood, CO: Libraries Unlimited, 1970- . Ann. ISSN 0065-9959.
   This is the most complete and detailed source of information on reference books published in this country in a single year; the 1993 volume contains 1,792 entries. Reviews are thorough and average about 200 to 225 words in length, although there are variations depending upon the individual reviewer or the tool being reviewed. The work is divided into four major segments, one of which is the humanities and accounts for some 27 percent of the total coverage in ten chapters ("Decorative Arts," "Fine Arts," "Literature," "Music") and more. Access is easily provided through a detailed table of contents and excellent indexes covering author/title, subject, and contributor. Quinquennial indexes are available for 1970-1974, 1975-1979, 1980-1984, and 1985-1989 to facilitate searching.

3. **Guide to Reference Books**. 10th ed. Eugene P. Sheehy. Chicago: American Library Association, 1986. 1560p. ISBN 0-8389-0390-8. **Supp. 1985-1990.** Robert Balay, ed., 1992. 613p. ISBN 0-8389-0588-9.
   The tenth edition of this massive source contains annotations of 14,000 reference books issued up to 1985. Similar to the previous editions, it is divided into five major sections: "General Reference," "Humanities," "Social Sciences," "History and Area Studies," and "Pure and Applied Sciences." Predictably, reference works in the humanities represent approximately one-third of the total number of entries. Although the coverage is international in scope, there is an acknowledged emphasis on both American publications and the English language in general. Arrangement is by subject and type of tool, employing a unique alphanumeric system now familiar to its audience. Annotations tend to be brief and descriptive. It remains the most important reference

literature guide for the majority of American librarians because of its comprehensive nature. Its excellent detailed index expedites the search for titles as well as names of individuals responsible for them. Biennial supplements had supplemented the previous editions, but the tenth edition (the last to be edited by Sheehy), is followed by a 1992 supplement treating 4,668 entries published over a six-year period. *Guide to Reference Books: Covering Materials from 1985-1990. Supplement to the Tenth Edition* is edited by Robert Balay, who apparently will continue the endeavor. A completely revised edition is planned for publication in the mid-1990s.

4.   **Walford's Guide to Reference Material**. 6th ed. A. J. Walford et al., eds. London: Library Association, 1993-1994. 3v. ISBN 1-85604-015-1 (v.1); 1-85604-044-5 (v.2); 1-85365-549-9 (v.3).

The British counterpart to Sheehy (entry 3), Walford is another standard source of information and remains a close second to its American rival among academic reference librarians in the United States. Considered by some to be more balanced in perspective, with better annotations in some respects, there is, indeed, greater international coverage. Both Walford and Sheehy complement each other and generally are found side-by-side. Walford's sixth edition follows an established pattern of publication in three volumes issued at different times, Science and Technology being first (1993). Volume 2, "Social and Historical Sciences, Philosophy and Religion" was issued in 1994. Volume 3, "Generalities, Language & Literature, the Arts" is yet to come, so the fifth edition volume (1991) is still in use. Volumes 1 and 2 provide a sound basis for humanities reference work. Arrangement of entries in all volumes is under categories established by the Universal Decimal Classification. Access is provided by author/title and subject indexes in each volume.

Periodical Guides

5.   **Magazines for Libraries**. 7th ed. Bill Katz and Linda Sternberg Katz, eds. New York: R. R. Bowker, 1992. 1212p. ISSN 0000-0914.

Like its previous issues, the seventh edition of *Magazines for Libraries* seeks to identify and describe the best and most useful magazines for the average primary or secondary school, public, academic, or special library. More than 100 consultants in different subject areas selected and annotated some 6,600 titles from among more than 70,000 possibilities. As in the previous editions, entries are organized by subject and coded according to the appropriate audience. This is an extensive revision with review, modification, or deletion of all entries as well as addition of new titles. About 80 percent of the titles have been returned from the previous edition and 20 percent represent new titles. Humanities areas are well served from the standpoint of reference and collection management through the inclusion of such subject headings as art, music, dance, etc. Titles of indexing and abstracting services are supplied following the full bibliographic description. The annotations show purpose, scope, and audience, with some evaluation provided. Each subject section begins with a short introduction and a recommended list of core periodicals essential for a basic collection.

*6.   **1994 Gale Directory of Publications and Broadcast Media: An Annual Guide to Publications and Broadcasting Stations**. Julie Winklepleck et al., eds. Detroit: Gale Research, 1994. 3v. Ann. ISSN 1048-7972.

Regarded as a standard and issued under a variety of titles since its initial edition in 1869. It was known as *Ayer Directory of Publications* from 1972 to 1982, *IMS/Ayer Directory of Publications* from 1983 to 1985, and *IMS Directory of Publications* in 1986. In 1987, it became *Gale Directory of Publications* and added "Broadcast Media" to the title in 1990, indicating an expanded scope. The complete subtitle following the one used for this entry reads "Including Newspapers, Magazines, Journals, Radio Stations, Television Stations, and

Cable Systems." The 1994 issue is the 126th edition of this useful work, which continues to provide full marketing information on newspapers and periodicals in the United States, Canada, and Puerto Rico. With the addition of the broadcasting media, the work now offers a comprehensive directory of more than 10,000 radio and television facilities as well. Directory information includes address, printing method, advertising rates, and circulation statistics for the print media, with similar identification given for the broadcasting units. Statistical summaries are furnished by state and by type; a master index provides quick access.

*7.   **Ulrich's International Periodicals Directory: A Classified Guide to Current Periodicals, Foreign and Domestic, 1993-1994.** 32d ed. New York: R. R. Bowker, 1993. 5v. Ann. ISSN 0000-0175.
     Begun in 1932 and now in its thirty-second edition, this is the leading guide to world periodical publications in treating some 140,000 serials in 966 subject categories. Irregular serials, annuals, and infrequent periodicals were incorporated within the text after the demise of Bowker's *Irregular Serials and Annuals: An International Directory* following its thirteenth edition (1987-1988). Entries are arranged alphabetically by subject and include title, frequency, publisher, country of publication, and Dewey Decimal Classification number. Additional information such as ISSN, year of inception, circulation, subscription price, etc., is included when known. The new edition adds 11,000 new titles and updates 90,000 entries from the previous issue. Electronic publications are included, with 880 serials on CD-ROM and 3,838 titles issued online. More than 7,000 daily and weekly newspapers are identified in volume 5. *Ulrich's* has set the standard in the field.
     Updating takes place on a quarterly basis since 1992 through *Ulrich's Update*, formerly issued three times per year (1988-1991). Prior to that it was a quarterly known as *Bowker International Serials Database Update* (1985-1988). This had continued an earlier title, *Ulrich's Quarterly* (1977-1985), which in turn had superseded *Bowker Serials Bibliography Supplement* (1972-1976). The initial publication was *Ulrich's International Periodicals Directory Supplement* (1966-1972). The Bowker listings are available online through BRS and DIALOG. The database (same name as entry) is updated monthly. Also available is *Ulrich's Plus Computer File* (1986-), providing CD-ROM quarterly coverage on cumulative compact disks.

Computerized Databases/CD-ROM

*8.   **The CD-ROM Directory with Multimedia CD's.** 9th ed. Matthew Finlay, ed. London/ Washington: TFPL Publishing, 1993. 1072p. Ann. ISBN 1-870889-30-4.
     This British publication provides a selective listing of some 2,500 CD-ROM titles in a variety of fields. About 20 to 25 percent are representative of the humanities, with coverage given to the arts, language and linguistics, and more. Architecture is combined with construction in a separate class. The work is divided into several useful segments, beginning with one on copying information and followed by the main section on CD-ROM titles (arranged alphabetically). Entries supply information on type, language, scope, time span, subject, updating, and system requirements. Following that is a section on multimedia CD-ROMs similar in format and coverage. Subsequent sections treat hardware and software companies, as well as conferences and exhibitions useful for planning sales and marketing. Several indexes supply access. It is available on a semiannual basis in CD-ROM from the publisher.
     CD-ROM Finder: The World of CD-ROM Products for Information Seekers, edited by James Shelton, is now in its fifth edition (Learned Information, 1993). Coverage is similar to the main entry but more selective in its listing of 1,450 titles. This number has been rising at an exponential rate for this annual directory and indicates the emergence of the CD market. Product profiles include a description and identification of scope, system requirements, and market data. Several indexes are supplied. It is available on CD-ROM from the publisher.

*9. **CD-ROMs in Print 1993: An International Guide to CD-ROM, CD-I, CDTV, Multimedia & Electronic Book Products.** 5th ed. Regina Rega, comp. Westport, CT: Meckler, 1993. 736p. Ann. ISSN 0891-8198.

Another British publication distributed through Meckler, this is regarded as the first source to consult for CD-ROM availability. With steady growth of CD-ROM products, it has become a most important tool for librarians. Ms. Rega's first stint as compiler continues the good work of her predecessor. The directory opens with a thematic essay treating the CD-ROM market in Japan and then follows with the major segment, the "Optical Product Directory" covering nearly 3,000 titles (more than doubling the coverage of the fourth edition). Included here are 78 titles that have been discontinued. Products listed are all commercially available, thus offering an excellent purchasing directory for prospective buyers. Entries supply the usual directory-type information, much of which is accessible through the various indexes (provider, publisher, distributor, etc.). The work is available on CD-ROM on a quarterly basis from the publisher.

*10. **Gale Directory of Databases.** Kathleen Young Marcaccio, ed. Detroit: Gale Research, Jan./July 1993- . 2v. ISSN 1066-8934.

This comprehensive directory was formed as a result of a merger of Gale's *Computer Readable Databases* (1979-1992) and Cuadra/Gale's *Directory of Online Databases* (1979-1992) and *Directory of Portable Databases* (1990-1992). The January 1994 issue profiles more than 5,300 online databases in volume 1 and 3,525 portable databases in volume 2. Each volume opens with a state-of-the-art essay describing market conditions of the appropriate product types. Volume 1 is divided into three major sections, the first of which lists alphabetically the online databases and describes them in terms of content, producer, contact, language, year, time span, updating, rates, etc. The second segment describes 2,230 database producers in terms of products, contact persons, and branch offices. The third section provides contact information for some 825 vendors and distributors. Volume 2 treats CD-ROM, diskette, magnetic tape, handheld and batch access database products, and enumerates system requirements as well as details and descriptions of products, producers, and vendors. Both volumes supply excellent indexing through subject and geographic location of producers and distributors. The work is available online through ORBIT, Questel, and planned for DIALOG; and on CD-ROM through the publisher.

Library Collections

11. **Subject Collections: A Guide to Special Book Collections and Subject Emphasis as Reported by University, College, Public, and Special Libraries and Museums in the United States and Canada.** 7th ed. Lee Ash et al., eds. New York: R. R. Bowker, 1993. 2v. ISSN 0000-0140.

The seventh edition of *Subject Collections* provides access to thousands of collections from nearly 6,000 libraries and museums in the United States and Canada, down from 11,000 libraries in the sixth edition. (Many of the subject collections are no longer separate and have been incorporated into the main collection; also a number of the libraries have closed.) As was true of the previous edition, "virtually all libraries included in this book are listed in the *American Library Directory*" (Bowker, 1923-). Libraries are listed under an alphabetical subject arrangement based upon thousands of LC subject headings. There are 65,818 entries in all, with good coverage given to museums as a result of continuing efforts to gain greater participation on their part. This is an important consideration given the relative uniqueness of such collections. This work has become a standard purchase for most libraries. One should use the *Library of Congress Subject Headings* list in order to make full use of available entries. Reviewed as an extremely laudable and much-needed work.

Museums

12. **The Cambridge Guide to the Museums of Europe**. Kenneth Hudson and Ann Nicholls. New York: Cambridge University Press, 1991. 509p. ISBN 0-521-37175-9.

This well-constructed directory of museums in 20 countries of Western Europe provides the traveler and information seeker with a good source of information. Holdings are described briefly, along with information on address, telephone number, dates/hours of opening, admission charges, parking, refreshments, tours, and facilities. Provisions for disabled patrons are enumerated. Arrangement of entries follows the normal directory prescription: first by country, then by city or town, then by name of unit. All types of museums are included, ranging from the major national and regional operations to the smaller, more specialized facilities, including homes of notables and such varied topical phenomena as oysters or firefighters. Emphasis has been placed on sites other than in capital cities, and an attempt is made to include museums furnishing exhibits of cultural or historical relevance within the country. A subject index aids access.

13. **Museums of the World.** 4th rev. and enl. ed. Bettina Bartz et al., eds. New Providence, NJ: K. G. Saur, 1992. 704p. ISBN 3-598-20533-3.

With publication of the first edition in 1973, this directory established a reputation for comprehensive coverage of a variety of museums throughout the world. Included among the various units devoted to the sciences, technology, history, and specialized studies are those devoted to the arts and archaeology. Arrangement is by continent, then by country and city. The museums are listed alphabetically. Names of the museums are in the native language, although the descriptions are in English. The new edition covers thousands of museums in more than 180 countries. Entries supply information on telephone and fax numbers, along with address, date of founding, current director, holdings, special collections, library, and additional facilities. Entries are arranged geographically under 15 major categories such as "Decorative Arts." There is a museum name index along with a personnel index and a comprehensive subject index.

The Directory of World Museums, by Kenneth Hudson and Ann Nicholls (2d edition, Facts on File, 1981) provides similar coverage and lists each museum under the English form of its name.

14. **The Official Museum Directory.** New Providence, NJ: R. R. Bowker, 1961- . Ann. ISSN 0090-6700.

Since it began more than 30 years ago, this work has undergone changes both in title and in frequency, but since 1980 it has appeared annually. Canadian museums were excluded beginning in 1983. Regarded as the standard tool for the identification of museums in the United States, and now in its twenty-fourth edition (1994), it identifies more than 7,000 institutions of various types (museums, associations, zoos, gardens, etc.). Entries include name, address, founding date, key personnel, governing authority, activities, publications, hours, special collections, and admission. Art, history, science, and various other areas are represented among the subject areas. There are four major sections, beginning with an alphabetical listing by state, then city, then name of institution. A second section lists the institutions alphabetically by name; the third section provides an alphabetical arrangement by names of directors and department heads. The final section lists institutions by type or category. It is available on magnetic tape but not on CD-ROM or online.

Annuals and Current Awareness Sources

15. **Black Arts Annual**. New York: Garland, 1988- . ISSN 1042-7104.

This is a useful and well-designed source of information on African-Americans in the arts, performing arts, and literature. Individual segments each summarize the year's activities in photography, literature, popular music, jazz and classical music, dance, theater, and movies and television. Each of these summaries is written by a specialist and provide a good overview of current developments, some of which are ephemeral and others of which are important benchmarks or milestones. Treatment is given to conferences, festivals, concerts, publications, recordings, and exhibitions. The 1989/1990 *Annual* was issued in 1992 and covers the period from 1 September 1988 to 31 August 1989. Commentary is cogent and traces historically the developments preceding the latest innovations, although articles are not signed. New and upcoming personalities are identified and obituaries are provided. Nineteen traveling art exhibitions are identified, along with fifty-eight permanent exhibitions. An index of names aids access.

INDEXES, ABSTRACTS, AND
SERIAL BIBLIOGRAPHIES

16. **The American Humanities Index**. Troy, NY: Whitston Publishing, 1975- . Ann. ISSN 0361-0144.

Designed for the scholar and serious student, this small-circulation work indexes some 400 creative, critical, and scholarly journals in the arts and humanities. All journals indexed are located at the College of William and Mary. From 1975 to 1987, the work was issued quarterly, with annual cumulations, and initially indexed some 100 titles not normally found in other indexing sources. Through the years, the policy has changed and there is some duplication with *MLA International Bibliography* (entry 964), *Arts & Humanities Citation Index* (entry 17), and *Humanities Index* (entry 22). Nevertheless, many of the titles are little magazines devoted to the work of a single author or subject. Published short fiction is listed under "Stories" as well as under the authors' names, as are poetry and poets. Although a number of the entries are currently found in more widely known indexes, the work is useful in identifying titles not otherwise covered.

*17. **Arts & Humanities Citation Index**. Philadelphia: Institute for Scientific Information. 1978- . Semiann. ISSN 0162-8445.

Since it began as the third of the three major citation indexes from ISI, this work has established itself as a leading source for scholars and students. Initially issued in three parts, January/April, May/August, and finally an annual cumulation of six volumes, it changed to semiannual frequency in 1989. It offers unparalleled coverage of journals in the manner of its companion works in the sciences and social sciences. It currently indexes some 1,000 journals fully and another 5,100 titles partially representing all fields of the humanities. Reviews of books and performances are found easily, but novices should read carefully the explanation of the various indexes (source, permuterm subject, citation, and corporate) to exploit the work to its fullest degree. When these are understood properly, the searcher can move in either direction, beginning with an author listing of indexed journal articles in the source index or finding the references in the bibliographies or footnotes of those articles in the citation index. Keywords from the titles can be used to locate the articles in the subject index.

The work is available online as *Arts and Humanities Search* through both BRS and DIALOG, and on CD-ROM as *Arts & Humanities Citation Index Compact Disc Edition* from the publisher. This represents an extensive file from the various fields of the humanities and social sciences dating from 1980 to the present and is updated weekly. The student should not hesitate to use the publisher's *Social Sciences Citation Index* as well, for there are many items of historical and cultural interest relevant to humanities study (philosophy, history, archaeology, etc.). *Social Scisearch* also is available online through both BRS and DIALOG; and in CD-ROM as *Social Sciences Citation Index (Compact Disc Edition).*

18. **British Humanities Index.** London: Library Association, 1962- . Q. with ann. cum. ISSN 0007-0815.

Published under its present title since 1962, this index supersedes, in part, the *Subject Index to Periodicals* (Library Association, 1915-1961). Several hundred British and Commonwealth newspapers and periodicals in the humanities and social sciences are indexed quarterly by subject, with annual cumulations that include author indexes. Beginning in 1993, abstracts are supplied. There is relatively little overlap with *Humanities Index* (entry 22), more with *Arts & Humanities Citation Index* (entry 17), though the latter is much more comprehensive and very different in purpose. The subjects covered are surprisingly varied, and "Humanities" in the title is misleading if construed in a strict and narrow sense. One of the areas treated in depth, for example, is economics; thus, such subject headings as "Marketing," "Advertising," "Product Development," "Stock Exchange," and "Steel Industry" are found, with many others from the social sciences. These seem to go well, however, with the more representative humanities designations ("Theatre," "Protestantism," "Music," "Art," etc.) when the librarian comprehends the nature of the tool.

*19. **Current Contents: Arts & Humanities.** Philadelphia: Institute for Scientific Information, 1979- . Biwk. ISSN 0163-3155.

This biweekly current awareness service provides tables of contents from more than 1,150 leading journals in art and architecture, performing arts, literature, language and linguistics, history, philosophy, and religion on an international basis. Each issue of each journal is covered as often as it is published. A section on current book contents, in which a few recent multiauthored books are highlighted, appears infrequently. A title word index lists the keywords in the titles of every article and book indexed in each issue. There is also an author index, which lists professional addresses along with a directory of publishers. A new pattern has been established for the inclusion of a semiannual cumulative index.

It should be remembered that this is one of several different publications in the series, and others may be useful, especially *Current Contents: Social and Behavioral Sciences* (ISI, 1974-). This covers about the same number of journals and includes titles in linguistics. Of importance to researchers is the availability of all articles indexed through a document delivery service from ISI. Both services are available online through BRS and DIALOG, for which there is weekly updating; the social/behavioral sciences package is also available on CD-ROM through the publisher.

*20. **Dissertation Abstracts International.** Ann Arbor, MI: University Microfilms International, 1938- . Mo. with ann. cum. ISSN 0419-4209(A); ISSN 0419-4217(B); ISSN 1042-7279(C).

The major source of information on doctoral dissertations worldwide, this service appears in two major segments: A, "The Humanities and Social Sciences," and B, "The Sciences and Engineering." Humanities is divided into five major sections covering communications and the arts; education; language, literature, and linguists; philosophy, religion, and theology; and social sciences. Section C, "Worldwide," which initially appeared in 1976 as "European Abstracts," has gradually increased its scope and indexing and is published quarterly. Entries in all sections are arranged by broad subject categories, with the authors choosing the categories that best describe the general content. The abstracts are prepared by the authors and run from 300 to 350 words in length. In most cases, it is possible to order the dissertation from University Microfilms. Each issue contains both a keyword title index and an author index; there is an annual cumulative author index.

It is recommended that one consult *Comprehensive Dissertation Index* to expedite a thorough search over a period of several years. *Dissertation Abstracts Online*, available through BRS and its component services and DIALOG, provides quick access to dissertations from 1861 to date. Full abstracts are provided and updating occurs with the same frequency as the publisher's various offerings (monthly for *DAI*, quarterly for *Masters Abstracts*, etc.). *Dissertation Abstracts Ondisc* offers the file in CD-ROM format.

*21. **Essay and General Literature Index, 1900-1933: An Index to about 40,000 Essays and Articles in 2144 Volumes of Collections of Essays and Miscellaneous Works.** Minnie Earl Sears and Marian Shaw, eds. New York: H. W. Wilson, 1934. 1952p. v.2-7 1934-1969. 1934- . Semiann. with ann. and quin. cums. ISSN 0014-083X.

Although other areas of the humanities are covered in this standard work, literature receives the greatest emphasis. Originally, the work succeeded the *ALA Index ... to General Literature* (2d edition, American Library Association, 1901-1914), which indexed books of essays, travel, sociological matters, etc. up to 1900. A supplement covered the publications of the first decade of the twentieth century. *EGLI* indexes essays in books published since 1900, the initial volume covering the first thirty-three years. The work is kept up-to-date on a semiannual basis, with cumulations annually and quinquennially since 1955-1959. Prior to that it furnished seven-year cumulations. Thousands of collections and anthologies serve as sources of the indexed essays on authors, forms, movements, genres, and individual titles of creative works. The work is available online through WILSONLINE and BRS, and on CD-ROM through WILSONDISC.

Essay and General Literature Index: Works Indexed 1900-1969 (H. W. Wilson, 1972) is a cumulative index to the 10,000 essays covered during that period. It is arranged by main entry and title.

*22. **Humanities Index**. New York: H. W. Wilson, 1974- . Q. with ann. cum. ISSN 0095-5981.

The leading cumulative index to English-language periodicals in the humanities, this work has been published in its present form since 1974, when *Social Sciences and Humanities Index* (1965-1974) was separated into two publications. Since that time, both *Humanities Index* and *Social Sciences Index* have gained an excellent reputation among the other Wilson indexes. *Humanities Index* indexes the contents of nearly 350 periodicals from all areas of the humanities and, in some cases, the social sciences. The same can be said of *Social Sciences Index*, which treats humanist subjects like anthropology. Both should be employed regularly in searching the literature and both are available online through WILSONLINE and BRS, and in CD-ROM on WILSONDISC. *Humanities Index* database was reported to have a file of 167,000 citations at the beginning of 1993, whereas *Social Sciences Index* database had 240,000. Both are updated twice a week. CD-ROM versions are updated on a quarterly basis.

23. **Index to Social Sciences & Humanities Proceedings.** Philadelphia: Institute for Scientific Information, 1979- . Q. with ann. cum. ISSN 0191-0574.

Developed in the same format as its earlier publication in the sciences, ISI has provided an international multidisciplinary access tool for papers presented at conferences, seminars, symposia, colloquia, conventions and workshops, and published as proceedings. Humanities coverage includes art, architecture, classics, dance, film, television, folklore, theater, etc. The entries provide current awareness for the specialist, particularly important because innovations often are introduced when experts convene. For each entry, full bibliographic information is given for the publication, including the publisher and ordering information. This is followed by a list of individual papers with names and addresses of authors. Indexes give access to each main entry by title, authors and editors, category, sponsor, meeting location, and the organizational affiliation of each cited author. Although currency is indicated in the preface, users should be aware that proceedings are often published long after the event. The proceeding publications selected for the work are considered by the publisher to be the most significant ones for which the majority of the material is printed for the first time.

DICTIONARIES, ENCYCLOPEDIAS, AND HANDBOOKS

24. **Great Events from History II: Arts and Culture Series**. Frank N. Magill, ed. Pasadena, CA: Salem Press, 1993. 5v. ISBN 0-89356-807-4.

Following the initial twelve-volume series treating historical events in America and Europe in ancient, medieval, and modern times; this is the third specialized series following after science/technology and human rights. Coverage is given to nearly 500 chronologically arranged topics relevant to cultural and artistic life (art, literature, cinema, music, etc.) from 1899 to 1992, providing a useful study guide for undergraduates. Articles are arranged chronologically in usual Magill format, beginning with ready reference identification of category of event, time, and locale. Then comes a brief summary of the event and its significance, followed by a listing of important relevant personalities. Following that is a detailed essay describing the nature of the event and its impact or significance, along with a brief bibliography and cross-references to related articles. The work is accessed through indexes by broad category, subject/keyword, individual, and place.

25. **The Oxford Guide to Classical Mythology in the Arts, 1300-1990s**. Jane Davidson Reid and Chris Rohmann. New York: Oxford University Press, 1993. 2v. ISBN 0-19-504998-5.

This recent effort should prove to be of immense value to a variety of users seeking to identify modern cultural achievements of the Western world relating to figures in mythology. It represents a topically classified chronology of more than 30,000 artworks of various kinds (painting, literature, drama, sculpture, music, dance, and opera) produced from the fourteenth century to the present day. Arrangement is under names of some 300 mythological figures, with volume 1 covering Auchelous-Leander and volume 2 treating Leda-Zeus. All important beings are treated, from gods and goddesses to heroes, nymphs, and satyrs. Artworks are arranged chronologically within each entry and are identified by title of work, date, publication or first performance, and present location. Subjects are listed under the Greek name with cross-references to the Roman. The work concludes with a list of sources and index of artists.

BIOGRAPHICAL SOURCES

26. **American Cultural Leaders: From Colonial Times to the Present**. Justin Harmon et al. Santa Barbara, CA: ABC-Clio, 1993. 550p. (Biographies of American Leaders). ISBN 0-87436-673-9.

This effort, part of a series covering United States leaders in various areas of endeavor, provides treatment of 360 individuals considered to be cultural leaders. All aspects of the humanities and creative expression are represented, with brief biographical sketches given to both men and women who have made important contributions. Included are personalities prominent in the visual arts, including architecture, theater, dance, film, literature, and music. Essays are well-developed, range from 750 to 1,500 words, and enumerate the careers and achievements of the various personalities. Cross-references aid access.

European Culture: A Contemporary Companion, edited by Jonathan Law (Mansell/Cassell, 1993), provides brief biographical coverage of 1,000 important contributors to world culture since 1945. Although the work is primarily a biographical dictionary, it also treats movements, issues, and genres relevant to sophisticated cultural development in painting, sculpture, architecture, music, literature, theater, and film. Somewhat less emphasis is placed on philosophy, religion, and the sciences. Popular culture is treated only slightly, with emphasis on the creators rather than the performers.

*27. **Biography and Genealogy Master Index.** 2d ed. Barbara McNeil and Miranda C. Herbert. Detroit: Gale Research, 1980. 8v. Ann. supp. with quin. cum. 1981- . ISSN 0730-1316.

The first edition of this compilation, in 1975, had the title *Biographical Dictionaries Master Index*. The second edition indexes the biographies in more than 350 current and retrospective reference works. Prior to the publication of the first edition, it was necessary to consult these works individually. The *Master Index* contains more than 3 million entries from 675 biographical dictionaries, subject encyclopedias, indexes, and works of literary criticism. The emphasis is on Americans, but a number of foreign biographical tools are also included. Names are listed in one alphabetical sequence. For each name, abbreviated citations to biographical listings found for that person are supplied. Variant forms of names have not been reconciled, so personalities may be listed under more than one form of their names. Entries include birth and death dates, and indicate when a portrait is included with the biography. The work is available online through DIALOG as *Biography Master Index* and as a CD-ROM product from the publisher, and can be searched by name, birth or death years, source publication, and year of publication.

A less expensive version of the index is produced in microfiche under the title *Bio-Base*. The database for the master index is used to produce other biographical indexes by occupations and subject fields.

*28. **Biography Index.** New York: H. W. Wilson, 1946- . Q. with ann. and bienn. cums. ISSN 0006-3053.

Biographical articles from periodicals and essays from collected biographical works, as well as monographs dealing with the careers and lives of notables of all types, are identified in this standard source from the Wilson Company. The title provides excellent general coverage of personalities from all over the world, both living and dead, although there is an emphasis on English-speaking individuals. The index is arranged alphabetically by the names of the biographees. A list by occupation or profession is also included. Basic bibliographic information on the monographs indexed is given in a list of those works included in each issue. The number of years this index has been published makes it useful for comprehensive research. It is available online through WILSONLINE and on CD-ROM through WILSONDISC.

29. **Blacks in the Humanities, 1750-1984: A Selected Annotated Bibliography.** Donald F. Joyce, comp. New York: Greenwood Press, 1986. 209p. (Bibliographies and Indexes in Afro-American and African Studies, no. 13). ISBN 0-313-24643-2.

The compiler has been an active contributor to African-American history and has produced a unique source in terms of its scope, covering leading black personalities and their contributions over a wide range of the humanities and creative arts and spanning a period of more than 200 years. The humanities are defined broadly and black involvement is considered in different chapter headings such as art, music, drama, literary criticism, linguistics, philosophy, science, history, and even library science. Coverage is provided for more than 600 monographs, journal articles, and dissertations, offering both students and researchers well-selected and carefully developed listings. Annotations range from brief to very full; entries have been taken from numerous sources (bibliographies, indexes, union lists, encyclopedias, biographical dictionaries, catalogs, textbooks, etc.). Access is provided by both subject and author/title indexes of comprehensive nature.

3 ◆ ACCESSING INFORMATION IN PHILOSOPHY

WORKING DEFINITION OF PHILOSOPHY

Although the term *philosophy* is derived from two Greek words usually translated to mean "love of wisdom," there is reason to believe that the original usage was somewhat broader, connoting free play of the intellect over a wide range of human problems and even including such qualities as shrewdness, curiosity, and practicality. McLeish, in fact, suggests that the definition "love of knowledge acquired by the exercise of the intellect" is more appropriate to the original meaning.[1]

There has been a gradual narrowing of the meaning of the term *philosophy*, beginning in antiquity and proceeding in stages up through the present time. Socrates differentiated his activity from that of the sophists by stressing the raising of questions for clarification in the course of discussion, as distinct from giving answers or teaching techniques for winning arguments. This emphasis on critical examination of issues remained central to philosophic method in the succeeding centuries. Then encyclopedic concepts of philosophy were shattered by the rise of modern science in the seventeenth century. First the natural sciences emerged as separate disciplines, then the social and behavioral sciences effected their separation from philosophy, and eventually the social sciences migrated into distinct scholarly and applied fields. The combination of philosophy and psychology that characterizes some reference tools produced at the beginning of the twentieth century is evidence of the relatively late departure of psychology and the other behavioral sciences from the broad field of philosophy.

Stripped of the natural and social sciences, what remains now of philosophy? First, there are questions about the nature of ultimate reality. Then there is the matter of knowledge as a whole, as well as the interrelationships of its specialized branches. There are questions of methodology and presuppositions of the individual disciplines. (The phrase "philosophy of . . ." is often assigned to this type of endeavor: philosophy of science, philosophy of education, and the like.) Finally, there are those normative issues for which there are no scientifically verifiable answers.

It may be said, then, that philosophy is the discipline concerned with basic principles of reality, methods for investigation and study, and the logical structures, systems, and interrelationships among all fields of knowledge. For additional definitions of *philosophy* and discussions of some of the problems of defining the discipline, the reader should see Alan R. Lacey's *A Dictionary of Philosophy* (Routledge, 1976) and Anthony Flew and Jennifer Speake's *A Dictionary of Philosophy*, 2d. rev. ed. (St. Martin's Press, 1984). A more recent source of a brief description of the field is Kenneth McLeish's *Key Ideas in Human Thought* (Facts on File, 1993).

MAJOR DIVISIONS OF THE FIELD

Philosophy continues to be divided into five broad areas: metaphysics, epistemology, logic, ethics, and aesthetics. Each of these broad areas, in turn, can be further subdivided.

Metaphysics may be further subdivided into ontology and cosmology. Ontology is concerned with the nature of ultimate reality, sometimes referred to as "being." It includes consideration of whether reality has one, two, or many basic components (monism, dualism, or pluralism, respectively). Monistic philosophies consider whether reality is ultimately mental or spiritual (idealism) or physical (materialism). Dualistic philosophies commonly regard both matter and mind as irreducible ultimate components, whereas pluralistic philosophies allow for many possibilities. Pluralistic ideas are most often argued in the political realm.

Cosmology is concerned with questions of origins and processes. The nature of causality has been a frequent topic of debate. Although a few have argued for pure chance, more philosophers have emphasized antecedent causes (i.e., preceding events that cause the event under consideration to happen) or final causes (ends or purposes that exert influence on the outcome of events). Many of the former persuasion are convinced that there is no room for either chance or freedom in the chain of causality. The determinists are called *mechanists* if they also believe that reality is ultimately physical. Those who emphasize final causes are known as *teleologists*. P. F. Strawson's *Individuals* (Methuen, 1959) is a recommended reading.

Epistemology is concerned with the scope and limits of human knowledge. What can we know? With what degree or certainty? Rationalists stress the role of human reason as the source of all knowledge, whereas empiricists believe that knowledge is derived from experience. It is generally agreed that there are two types of knowledge: *a priori*, which is knowable without reference to experience and which alone possesses theoretical certainty (e.g., the principles of logic and mathematics); and *a posteriori*, which is derived from experience and possesses only approximate certainty (the findings of the science, for example). T. E. Burke's chapter "What Can Be Known?" in Davis and Park's *No Way: The Nature of the Impossible* (W. H. Freeman, 1987) provides an example of recent epistemological work.

Logic deals with the principles of correct reasoning or valid inference. It differs from psychology in that it does not describe how people actually think, but prescribes certain canons to be followed for thinking correctly. Deductive logic (sometimes known as Aristotelian or traditional logic) is concerned with the process by which correct conclusions can be drawn from a set of axioms known or believed to be true. Its most familiar form is the syllogism, which consists of three parts: the major premise, the minor premise, and the conclusion.

> Major premise: All men are mortal.
> Minor premise: Socrates is a man.
> Conclusion: Therefore, Socrates is mortal.

Inductive logic is a result of the development of modern scientific methods. It deals with the canons of valid inference, but is concerned with probabilities rather than certainties and often involves the use of statistics. In a sense the opposite of deductive logic, inductive logic attempts to reach valid generalizations from an enumeration of particulars. Although logic arose in antiquity and was summarized in Aristotelian works, few advances were made until the last half of the nineteenth century, when symbolic and Boolean logic provided forms of notation useful in mathematical reasoning and later in computer science and information retrieval.

In ethics, the questions relate to human nature and to matters of conduct. Can certain actions be considered morally right or wrong? If so, on what basis? Should the interests of self have priority (egotism)? Or should the interests of others be the driving principle (altruism)? Or is there some greater good to which both self- and other interests should be subordinate? Ethical theories may be classified by the manner in which criteria for right actions are established or by the nature of the highest good.

Andrew Jack suggests that ethics can be conveniently divided into three parts: "normative ethics, practical ethics, and meta-ethics."[2] The first deals with normative principles or moral rules, such as the "Golden Rule." Meta-ethics considers the nature of metaphysical issues that can arise for any moral principle. Practical ethics considers specific applications of ethical thinking to particular problems.

Discussions in the popular literature have brought the consideration of practical ethics to newspaper readers and viewers of the television evening news. Such issues as euthanasia, assisted suicide, the death penalty, abortion, equality of the sexes or races, and the use of animals for biomedical research are but a few topics at issue. Peter Singer's *Practical Ethics*, first published in 1979 by Cambridge University Press, and thoroughly revised in 1993, is a highly acclaimed work on the subject, which includes chapters on equality and discrimination, treatment of animals, and environmental concerns, as well as an excellent discussion of the nature of ethics.

The nature of beauty is the subject matter of aesthetics. The concerns of the philosopher may be differentiated from those of the psychologist and the critic. The psychologist concentrates on human reactions to aesthetic objects. The critic focuses on individual works of art or on the general principles of criticism, usually within the confines of a particular discipline. The philosopher is broadly concerned with beauty per se, whether in art or in nature. Does beauty adhere in the beautiful object? Are there objective criteria by which it may be determined? Or is beauty a subjective experience, with no universally valid norms? Classical theories stress objectivity, whereas romantic theories emphasize individualism and subjectivity. Further, aesthetics explores the nature of the arts and considers similarities and differences between the visual and performing arts, and questions concerning what art represents and expresses.

HELPFUL RESOURCES FOR STUDENTS, LIBRARIANS, AND GENERAL READERS

The student desiring a concise introduction to philosophy should read "Philosophy" by C. I. Lewis in the *Encyclopedia Americana* (1992 ed., v.21, pp. 925-42) or the G. S. Davis article in *Academic American Encyclopedia* (1992 ed., v.15, pp. 240-48). The latter has color photographs of both individuals and art works. Still highly useful is John Passmore's "Philosophy," in *The Encyclopedia of Philosophy* (Macmillan, 1967, v.6, pp. 216-26). Passmore's "Philosophy, Historiography of," in the same volume of the *Encyclopedia* (pp. 226-30) provides historical perspectives. A more recent work with useful, brief, signed articles on all manner of philosophical topics is Kenneth McLeish's *Key Ideas in Human Thought* (Facts on File, 1993).

Several works are of particular importance to the librarian. Volume 6 of *The Encyclopedia of Philosophy* contains three articles by William Gerber: "Philosophical Bibliographies," "Philosophical Dictionaries and Encyclopedias," and "Philosophical

Journals." The article on philosophy in Lester Asheim's *The Humanities and the Library* (American Library Association, 1956, pp. 61-99), despite its age, is still a valuable description, and Martin Bertman's *Research Guide in Philosophy* (General Learning, 1974) presents the literature of the field in a well-organized, practical way. A more recent perspective is offered by Richard H. Lineback's chapter on philosophy in Nena Counch and Nancy Allen's *The Humanities and the Library*, 2d ed. (American Library Association, 1993), pp. 212-39. Finally, a recommended source for all librarians is Richard T. de George's *Philosopher's Guide to Sources, Research Tools, Professional Life, and Related Fields* (University of Kansas Press, 1980).

Many introductions and histories of philosophy are extremely technical and therefore forbidding to the lay person. Two classic exceptions are Bertrand Russell's *A History of Western Philosophy* (Simon & Schuster, 1945) and Will Durant's ever-popular *Story of Philosophy* (Simon & Schuster, 1926). Bertman's guide, mentioned earlier, contains an easy-to-read history. The reader needing only a synopsis of a particular work in philosophy will find useful *Masterpieces of World Philosophy*, edited by Frank N. Magill (HarperCollins, 1990) or the more exhaustive five-volume *World Philosophy: Essay Reviews of 225 Major Works* (Salem Press, 1982).

Several *Encyclopaedia Britannica* (15th ed., rev. 1990) entries are especially helpful by providing the librarian good introductory reading and basic bibliographic leads. The following articles in volume 25 should be consulted: "Philosophical Schools and Doctrines," and "Philosophy of the Branches of Knowledge." Both offer insights into the divisions of the field, history of philosophical thought, and defining principles. The focus is on Western philosophy. Different sections within the articles are by experts in the field. Andrew D. Scrimgeour, "Philosophy and Religion," in *Selection of Library Materials in the Humanities, Social Sciences, and Sciences*, edited by Patricia A. McClung (American Library Association, 1985), offers information useful to the selector or person responsible for library collection development.

USE AND USERS OF PHILOSOPHY INFORMATION

A thorough search of the literature of use and user studies indicates that very little research has been done on literature use by philosophers. There is other evidence, however, that the literature of the field is widely used and that particular authors are often cited both within the humanities and by writers in the sciences and social sciences.

A listing of the 100 most cited authors from the 1977-1978 *Arts and Humanities Citation Index* (ISI, 1978) includes Plato and Aristotle, with more than 1,200 citations each, as well as contemporary writers like Karl Popper, Paul Ricoeur, and John Rawls. The most cited author was Karl Marx, whose works received more than 1,600 citations in the year under study (1977-1978); half of the citations were in philosophy journals, according to Eugene Garfield, whose article is the source of these data.[3]

More recently, Garfield compiled a listing of the fifty twentieth-century books most cited in the *Arts and Humanities Citation Index* during the period 1976-1983. The field of philosophy is well represented on the list, as are criticism, linguistics, and fiction. In the philosophy area, the works of Wittgenstein, Popper, and Kuhn are among the most cited on the elite list.[4]

Garfield has also identified the arts and humanities journals that were most cited in the entire ISI family of citation indexes in 1981. The second and seventh most frequently cited journals were *Journal of Philosophy* and *Philosophical Review*, with 640 and 435 citations respectively.[5] Because citations in the sciences, the social sciences, and the humanities were combined for the purposes of ranking, the influence of philosophy across all fields of knowledge is apparent.

Although the citation rankings are, of course, dependent on the coverage of ISI's databases, they nonetheless indicate the relative impact of certain works as compared to all others referenced in the ISI-covered publications. Most importantly, citation does represent a quantitative measure of literature use.

Although carried out as a library collection evaluation, a recent study by Jean-Pierre V. M. Herubel at Purdue University provides insight into the literature used by philosophy scholars in preparing dissertations in one university environment.[6] Reflecting Garfield's earlier findings, *Journal of Philosophy* and *Philosophical Review* were among the most frequently cited journals, first and fourth with 63 and 44 citations respectively. The dissertations, which date between 1970 and 1988, reflect the humanist's heavy reliance on monographs (71.3 percent of all references) and lesser use of the journal literature (28.7 percent).[7]

Studies of scholars' information seeking for the Research Libraries Group (Constance Gould, "Philosophy," *Information Needs in the Humanities: An Assessment* [Stanford, CA: RLG, 1988]) suggest that relatively few philosophers use traditional reference sources to stay current in their field, particularly when compared to researchers in other disciplines. As to books, Henry J. Koren, in his still useful *Research in Philosophy—A Bibliographical Introduction to Philosophy and a Few Suggestions for Dissertations* (Duquesne University Press, 1966), divides philosophy books into "popularizing works, text books, and strictly scholarly works"

MAJOR CLASSIFICATION SCHEMES

Utilization of shelf arrangement as a tool for philosophic information retrieval must be considered secondary to other approaches, but some knowledge of the major library classification schemes will be advantageous. The two most frequently used schemes are the Dewey Decimal Classification (DDC) and the Library of Congress Classification (LC).

From the user's standpoint, there are three principal approaches to the arrangement of philosophic writings: by individual philosophers, by specialized branches of philosophy, and by interrelationships and influence groupings. The first approach (by individual philosophers) is particularly helpful if one wishes to study a specific philosopher's thought system or specific works of an individual. It is especially convenient if the library shelves secondary works, such as criticism and commentary, with the primary works. The second approach to organizing philosophical materials (by subdivisions of the discipline) would group works on metaphysics, epistemology, logic, ethics, and aesthetics together. Finally, the interrelationships and influences approach would organize a collection of materials around the work's attributes of temporal period, language, school of thought, nationality grouping, and so forth.

Clearly, no truly useful classification system would follow a single approach to organizing. Hence, both DDC and LC attempt to balance the differing and sometimes conflicting approaches.

The DDC was first devised by Melvil Dewey in 1876 and, although revised and expanded over the years, still reflects a late nineteenth-century view of the world. Its handling of philosophy (100-199) has been frequently criticized for its separation of philosophical viewpoints from the period-specific sections, for placing aesthetics with the arts (in the 700s), and for its inclusion of psychology (150). In spite of these problems, however, the DDC is the most commonly used scheme, especially in public, school, and smaller academic libraries.

The major DDC subject divisions for philosophy and related disciplines are

110   METAPHYSICS
120   EPISTEMOLOGY, CAUSATION
130   PARANORMAL PHENOMENA AND ARTS
140   SPECIFIC PHILOSOPHICAL VIEWPOINTS
150   PSYCHOLOGY
160   LOGIC
170   ETHICS
180   ANCIENT, MEDIEVAL, ORIENTAL PHILOSOPHY
190   MODERN WESTERN PHILOSOPHY

The Library of Congress (LC) schedule for philosophy was first published in 1910 and has also been revised. Although it, like the DDC, includes psychology, it is generally considered to be superior in its handling of philosophy. For example, LC includes aesthetics.

Subclass B is designed to keep the works of individual philosophers together and to place them in relation to periods, countries, and schools of thought. The general pattern for individual philosophers is (1) collected works, (2) separate works, and (3) biography and criticism. LC also has sections for major divisions of the field. The principal divisions are

B   PHILOSOPHY (GENERAL)
          Serials, Collections, etc.
          History and systems
BC   LOGIC
BD   SPECULATIVE PHILOSOPHY
          General works
          Metaphysics
          Epistemology
          Methodology
          Ontology
          Cosology
BF   PSYCHOLOGY
          Parapsychology
          Occult sciences
BH   AESTHETICS
BJ   ETHICS
          Social usages, Etiquette

Although some special philosophy classifications have been developed, their use appears to have been confined to the arrangement of certain bibliographies and special collections.

SUBJECT HEADINGS IN PHILOSOPHY

Searching library catalogs (whether in card, book, or computer form) continues to play an important role in the retrieval of philosophical information. Although many subject indexes in recent years have been constructed on the basis of keywords from document titles, or from text, most library catalogs use a controlled or standardized vocabulary embodied in a list of subject headings. Such lists usually include guidance on choice of main headings, methods of subdividing major topics, and cross-references to lead the user to the headings chosen or to related topics.

The majority of large American libraries today follow the *Subject Headings Used in the Dictionary Catalogs of the Library of Congress* (Library of Congress, 1992), available in print, on microfiche, and on magnetic tape. The subject headings enable the reader looking for a specific topic to go directly to that heading. The disadvantage in this discipline is that philosophic topics are scattered throughout an entire alphabetic sequence. This is true whether the library uses an integrated "dictionary" catalog or a divided catalog (in which the subject portion is separated from the author-title section).

This chapter includes some information that will not be repeated in later chapters of this guide. Examples of Library of Congress subject headings are provided in figure 3.1. The table is followed by a brief discussion of basic principles drawn from sources as diverse as Lois Mai Chan's *Library of Congress Subjects Headings: Principles and Applications* (Libraries Unlimited, 1986), David Judson Haykin's *Subject Headings: A Practical Guide* (Government Printing Office, 1951), *Subject Cataloging Manual: Subject Headings* (Library of Congress, 1984), and *Library of Congress Subject Headings: A Guide to Subdivision Practice* (Library of Congress, 1981).

Philosophers *(May Subd Geog)*
   UF   Philosophy—Biography
   BT   Scholars
   NT   Aestheticians
          Alchemists
          Ethicists
          Hermetic philosophers
          Logicians
          Philosopher-kings
          Platonists
          Women philosophers
   —Relationship with women

GEOGRAPHIC SUBDIVISIONS

—Greece
   NT   Seven wise men of Greece
Philosophers, Ancient *[B108-B708]*
   UF   Ancient philosophers
Philosophers, Islamic
   USE   Philosophers, Muslim
Philosophers, Jewish *(May Subd Geog)*
   UF   Jewish philosophers
Philosophers, Medieval *[B720-B785]*
   UF   Medieval philosophers
Philosophers, Modern
   UF   Modern philosophers
Philosophers, Muslim
   UF   Islamic philosophers
          Muslim philosophers
          Philosophers, Islamic
          Philosophers' egg

   USE   Alchemy
Philosophers in art
Philosophers' stone
   USE   Alchemy
Philosophical analysis
   USE   Analysis (Philosophy)
Philosophical anthropology *[BD450]*
   UF   Anthropology, Philosophical
          Man (Philosophy)
   BT   Civilization—Philosophy
          Life
          Man
          Ontology
   RT   Humanism
          Persons
          Philosophy of mind
   NT   Fallibility
          Femininity (Philosophy)
          Man—Animal nature
          Mind and body
          Soul
          Philosophical grammar
   USE   Grammar, Comparative
          and general
Philosophical literature *(May Subd Geog)*
   RT   Philosophy—Bibliography
Philosophical recreations
   [GV1507.P43]
   UF   Recreations, Philosophical
   BT   Amusements
          Games

Philosophical theology *[BT40]*
   UF   Theology, Philosophical
   BT   Philosophy and religion
          Theology, Doctrinal
Philosophy *(May Subd Geog) [B-BJ]*
   UF   Mental philosophy
   BT   Humanities
   SA   *subdivision Philosophy*
          under topical headings,
          individual and groups
          of Indian tribes, and
          names of individual
          persons, except
          philosophers
   NT   Absurd (Philosophy)
          Accidents (Philosophy)
          Act (Philosophy)
          Aesthetics
          Agent (Philosophy)
          Alienation (Philosophy)
          Analysis (Philosophy)
          Antinomy
          Appearance (Philosophy)
          Atomic swerve (Philosophy)
          Atomism
          Attribute (Philosophy)
          Authenticity (Philosophy)
          Autonomy (Philosophy)
          Axioms
          Banality (Philosophy)
          Becoming (Philosophy)
          Belief and doubt
          Body, Human (Philosophy)

Philosophy *(Continued)*
Causation
Chain of being (Philosophy)
Children and philosophy
Color (Philosophy)
Communism and philosophy
Comparison (Philosophy)
Compensation (Philosophy)
Complexity (Philosophy)
Comprehension (Theory of knowledge)
Consciousness
Consequentialism (Ethics)
Constitution (Philosophy)
Construction (Philosophy)
Constructivism (Philosophy)
Contingency (Philosophy)
Contradiction
Contrast (Philosophy)
Convention (Philosophy)
Criticism (Philosophy)
Cycles
Cynicism
Depth (Philosophy)
Description (Philosophy)
Desire (Philosophy)
Determinism (Philosophy)
Difference (Philosophy)
Disposition (Philosophy)
Dissymmetry (Philosophy)
Distinction (Philosophy)
Division (Philosophy)
Dogs in philosophy
Drunkenness (Philosophy)
Dualism
Eclecticism
Egoism
Emotions (Philosophy)
Ends and means
Engagement (Philosophy)
Entity (Philosophy)
Epiphanism
Essence (Philosophy)
Ethics
Ethnophilosophy
Events (Philosophy)
Evidence
Evolution
Exact (Philosophy)
Expectation (Philosophy)
Experience
Expression (Philosophy)
Extension (Philosophy)
Face (Philosophy)
Facts (Philosophy)
Fate and fatalism
Femininity (Philosophy)
Finalism (Philosophy)
Finite, The
Formalization (Philosophy)
Four elements (Philosophy)
Goal (Philosophy)
Good and evil
Habit (Philosophy)
Harmony (Philosophy)
Hedonism
Heuristic
Humanism
Hylozoism
Idea (Philosophy)

Idealism
Ideals (Philosophy)
Ideology
Illusion (Philosophy)
Image (Philosophy)
Imagination (Philosophy)
Immaterialsim (Philosophy)
Immortality (Philosophy)
Individuation (Philosophy)
Indivisibles (Philosophy)
Infallibility (Philosophy)
Innate ideas (Philosophy)
Instinct (Philosophy)
Instrumentalism (Philosophy)
Intentionality (Philosophy)
Interaction (Philosophy)
Interest (Philosophy)
Interpretation (Philosophy)
Intuition
Irrationalism (Philosophy)
Isolation (Philosophy)
Judaism and philosophy
Justice (Philosophy)
Knowledge, Theory of
Law (Philosophy)
Listening (Philosophy)
Logic
Many (Philosophy)
Materialism
Mean (Philosophy)
Meaning (Philosophy)
Meaninglessness (Philosophy)
Mechanism (Philosophy)
Memory (Philosophy)
Metaphysics
Mixing (Philosophy)
Monadology
Monism
Movement (Philosophy)
Naturalism
Need (Philosophy)
Negation of negation (Dialectical materialism)
Negativity (Philosophy)
Neoplatonism
New and old
Nihilism (Philosophy)
Nominalism
Nonexistent objects (Philosophy)
Norm (Philosophy)
Notions (Philosophy)
Object (Philosophy)
One (The One in philosophy)
Ontologism
Ontology
Operationalism
Opinion (Philosophy)
Opposition, Theory of
Optimism
Order (Philosophy)
Organism (Philosophy)
Panpsychism
Pantheism
Parapsychology and philosophy
Participation
Peace (Philosophy)
Perception
Perception (Philosophy)
Perfection

Performative (Philosophy)
Personalism
Perspective (Philosophy)
Pessimism
Phenomenalism
Philosophy of mind
Place (Philosophy)
Play (Philosophy)
Pluralism
Polarity (Philosophy)
Positivism
Possibility
Power (Philosophy)
Practice (Philosophy)
Pragmatism
Presentation (Philosophy)
Principle (Philosophy)
Priority (Philosophy)
Process philosophy
Psychoanalysis and philosophy
Psychology
Psychology and philosophy
Purity (Philosophy)
Quality (Philosophy)
Quantity (Philosophy)
Reaction (Philosophy)
Realism
Reality
Reductionism
Reference (Philosophy)
Reflection (Philosophy)
Relation (Philosophy)
Relevance (Philosophy)
Renunciation (Philosophy)
Repetition (Philosophy)
Representation (Philosophy)
Right and left (Philosophy)
Schematism (Philosophy)
Scholasticism
Secret (Philosophy)
Self (Philosophy)
Sense (Philosophy)
Separation (Philosophy)
Silence (Philosophy)
Simplicity (Philosophy)
Situation (Philosophy)
Space and time
Specialism (Philosophy)
Spiritualism (Philosophy)
Spontaneity (Philosophy)
Strategy (Philosophy)
Structuralism
Style (Philosophy)
Subject (Philosophy)
Sufficient reason
Surfaces (Philosophy)
Techne (Philosophy)
Teleology
Theory (Philosophy)
Thomists
Thought and thinking
Topic (Philosophy)
Tradition (Philosophy)
Transcendence (Philosophy)
Transcendentalism
Triads (Philosophy)
Truth
Univerals (Philosophy)
Utilitarianism

Philosophy *(Continued)*
    Waiting (Philosophy)
    War (Philosophy)
    Will
    Woman (Philosophy)
    Wonder (Philosophy)
—Bibliography
    RT Philosophical literature
—Biography
    USE Philosophers
—History *[B69-B4695]*
—Introductions *[BD10-BD28]*
—Methodology
    USE Methodology
—Germany
——Awards
    NT Dr. Leopold-Lucas-Preis
—Germany (West)
——Awards
Philosophy, African *[B5300-B5320]*
    UF African philosophy
Philosophy, Afro-American
    USE Afro-American philosophy
Philosophy, American *[B851-B945]*
    UF American philosophy
    NT Aesthetic Realism
        Afro-American philosophy
—18th century
—19th century
—20th century *[B934-B945]*
Philosophy, Analytical
    USE Analysis (Philosophy)
Philosophy, Ancient *[B108-B708]*
    Here are entered works dealing
with ancient philosophy in
general and with Greek and
Roman philosophy in particular.
    UF Ancient philosophy
        Greek philosophy
        Philosophy, Greek
        Philosophy, Roman
        Roman philosophy
    NT Ataraxia
        Atomism
        Cosmology, Ancient
        Cynics (Greek philosophy)
        Diaeresis (Philosophy)
        Eleatics
        Gnosticism
        Manichaeism
        Megarians (Greek philosophy)
        Neoplatonism
        Peripatetics
        Platonists
        Pythagoras and Pythagorean
          school
        Skeptics (Greek philosophy)
        Sophists (Greek philosophy)
        Stoics
—Oriental influences
    BT Civilization, Oriental
—Phoenician influences *[B180]*
    BT Phoenicia—Civilization
Philosophy, Arab *[B740-B753*
    (Medieval)]
    UF Arabic philosophy

Philosophy, Arabic
    NT Philosophy, Islamic
Philosophy, Arabic
    USE Philosophy, Arab
    Philosophy, Islamic

OTHER GEOGRAPHIC AND
ETHNIC SUBDIVISIONS (E.G.,
PHILOSOPHY, GERMAN AND
PHILOSOPHY, BUDDHIST) IN
ADJECTIVE FORM (SEE LCSH)

Philosophy, Modern *(May Subd
    Geog) [B790-B5739]*
    UF Modern philosophy
    NT Critical theory
        Existential phenomenology
        Existentialism
        Humanism—20th century
        Neo-Scholasticism
        Phenomenology
        Positivism
        Pragmatism
        Semantics (Philosophy)
        Transcendentalism
—16th century
    USE Philosophy, Renaissance
—17th century *[B801]*
—18th century *[B802]*
    NT Enlightenment
—19th century *[B803]*
—20th century *[B804]*
Philosophy, Renaissance
    [B770-B785]
    UF Philosophy, Modern—16th
        century
        Renaissance philosophy
Philosophy, Roman
    USE Philosophy, Ancient
Philosophy and civilization *[B59]*
    BT Civilization
    NT Civilization—Philosophy
Philosophy and cognitive science
    (May Subd Geog)
    UF Cognitive science and
        philosophy
    BT Cognitive science
Philosophy and communism
    USE Communism and philosophy
Philosophy and Islam
    USE Islam and philosophy
Philosophy and Judaism
    USE Judaism and philosophy
Philosophy and parapsychology
    USE Parapsychology and
        philosophy
Philosophy and psychoanalysis
    USE Psychoanalysis and
        philosophy
Philosophy and psychology
    USE Psychology and philosophy
Philosophy and religion
    Here are entered works on the
reciprocal relationship and
influence between philosophy
and religion. Works on the

philosophy of religion are
entered under Religion—Philosophy.
    UF Christianity and philosophy
        Religion and philosophy
    BT Religion
    NT Buddhism and philosophy
        Catholic Church and philosophy
        Islam and philosophy
        Philosophical theology
Philosophy and science *(May
    Subd Geog) [B67]*
    BT Science
    NT Science—Philosophy
Philosophy and social sciences *[B63]*
    BT Social sciences
Philosophy and the Catholic Church
    USE Catholic Church and
        philosophy
Philosophy and the Koran
    USE Koran and philosophy
Philosophy in literature *[PN49]*
    NT Existentialism in literature
Philosophy libraries *(May Subd
    Geog)*
    UF Libraries, Philosophy
    BT Humanities libraries
Philosophy of history
    USE History—Philosophy
Philosophy of international law
    USE International law—
        Philosophy
Philosophy of law
    USE Law—Philosophy
Philosophy of literature
    USE Literature—Philosophy
Philosophy of medicine
    USE Medicine—Philosophy
Philosophy of mind *(May Subd
    Geog) [BD418-BD418.5]*
    UF Mind, Philosophy of
        Mind, Theory of
        Theory of mind
    BT Philosophy
    RT Cognitive science
        Metaphysics
        Philosophical anthropology
Philosophy of mind in children
    (May Subd Geog) [BF723.P48]
    BT Child psychology
Philosophy of nature *[BD581]*
    UF Nature—Philosophy
        Nature, Philosophy of
    RT Natural theology
    NT Nature—Religious aspects
        Uniformity of nature
Philosophy of psychiatry
    USE Psychiatry—Philosophy
Philosophy of rhetoric
    USE Rhetoric—Philosophy
Philosophy of teaching
    USE Education—Philosophy

Fig. 3.1. Library of Congress subject headings for philosophy—1992.

To use these headings as a guide in the formulation of a search strategy, it is helpful to understand the basic forms subject headings may take:

1. *Simple nouns as headings.* This form is the most direct, immediate, and uncomplicated. If adequate to the text, it is the preferred method. The most obvious example, in this context, is "Philosophy."

2. *Adjectival headings.* These may be in natural or inverted form. An example of the natural form is "Philosophical anthropology"; an example of the inverted form is "Philosophers, Ancient." The choice is determined by the need to emphasize those search words of greatest importance to the intended user. In the first example, the term "philosophical" is more significant to the philosophy student than the word "anthropology." In the second example, the term "American" would be of significance to the person seeking information on American philosophy, but the natural order would bury the topic among dozens of other entries beginning with "American." Because the prime topic is philosophy, with American philosophy as one variety, the inverted form is chosen.

3. *Phrase headings.* These usually consist of nouns connected by a preposition. An example is "Philosophy in literature." Another type of phrase heading is the so-called compound heading made up of two or more coordinate elements connected by "and." An example from the sample listing is "Philosophy and cognitive science."

It often happens that the approaches described here do not result in headings that are sufficiently specific. In such cases, further division of the topic is required. The techniques most frequently used for division are as follows:

1. *By form.* The plan of division is not based on the content of a work but on its manner of arrangement or the purpose it is intended to serve. Examples include:

   Philosophy—Bibliography;
   Philosophy—Dictionaries;
   Philosophy—Study and teaching.

2. *By political or geographic area.* Generally, this is not a consideration in the field of philosophy, as the need for geographic subdivision is accomplished by use of the inverted form of adjectival headings, such as "Philosophy, French" or "Philosophy, Chinese."

3. *By period.* This technique for subdivision can cause some confusion for the uninitiated, especially in a field like philosophy. This represents a departure from the customary alphabetical approach in that headings for different historical periods are arranged chronologically. In philosophy, the technique is used to divide under separate countries as in "Philosophy, French—17th century," which precedes "Philosophy, French—18th century." (Notice that alphabetical presentation would put *e*ighteenth ahead of *s*eventeenth.) The situation is further complicated by the use of subject heading for broad periods for philosophy (e.g., "Philosophers, Ancient") that are arranged in the customary alphabetical way. The searcher will be wise to double check until thoroughly familiar with the subject matter and the approaches to its headings.

It should also be noted that any formal list of subject headings will not include one very large category of subject entries—that of individual names as subjects. These may be personal (e.g., "James, William") or corporate (e.g., "American Philosophical Association"). In the case of very prolific or prominent writers, entries may be further subdivided. An example would be "Dewey, John—Addresses, essays, lectures."

A subject heading system must make provisions for the user who may choose as the initial search term a word or phrase other than the one used in the system. The necessary connections are customarily made by means of *see* references, which direct readers from terms that are not used to those that are used. Similarly, the user has traditionally been provided access to other headings that might lead to relevant information by *see also* references. More recent subject headings use additional symbols for such cross-references, as are illustrated in figure 3.2.

USE

UF   (Used for)

BT   (Broader term)

NT   (Narrower term)

RT   (Related term)

SA   (See also)

Fig. 3.2. Cross-reference symbols.

This thesaurus-type approach eliminates the need for symbols indicating reverse patterns of *see also* references and other sometimes confusing notation.

Scope notes are sometimes, though not frequently, provided to remove doubt or confusion as to what may or may not be covered by certain subject headings. An example from figure 3.1 is found under the heading "Philosophy, Ancient": "Here are entered works dealing with ancient philosophy in general and with Greek and Roman philosophy in particular."

Comparison of the list in figure 3.1 with the subject catalog of a library of medium or large size will make it apparent that many more subject headings are used in practice than are enumerated on the list. However, the headings are most often formed in accordance with the principles mentioned here and examples can be found by checking a list such as the LCSH.

It should also be remembered that no subject heading list should be static, even in a field as stable as philosophy. New terms are constantly coming into use and older terms are being revised or deleted. A comparison of the subject headings illustrated in the third edition and the present edition of this guide reveals a number of new headings in the philosophy area: "Philosophy and cognitive science" is but one example.

Searching in printed library catalogs and browsing machine-readable catalogs are made considerably easier if the reader understands the filing system used by the particular catalog. The dictionary catalog or subject portion of a divided catalog will most often follow an alphabetical arrangement, but a chronological arrangement may be used wherever a division by date seems more logical than a strictly alphabetical sequence.

Alphabetical filing arrangements usually follow one of two patterns. The first is the letter-by-letter method used by many reference tools, including several indexes and encyclopedias. With this method, all the words in the heading are treated as parts of one unit. Filing proceeds strictly on the basis of the order of the letters in the unit as a whole, regardless of whether they are in separate short words or in a single long word. Thus, "Newark" would precede "New York." Libraries have not favored this method because it tends to scatter closely related topics.

Most libraries, then, have adopted the word-by-word or "nothing before something" approach, in which each word is treated as a separate unit for filing purposes. Using this method, "New York" would precede "Newark" in the catalog.

For the controlled indexing terms used in online and CD-ROM bibliographic databases, the user should consult the thesaurus for the database in question. The use of controlled subject terms will likely improve the search by complementing the use of keywords and enhancing precision. Many online thesauri have print counterparts that can be consulted in advance of the search, in preparation for it. For descriptions of thesauri, including *Philosophers Index* and others relevant to the humanities, the reader should consult Chan and Pollard's *Thesauri Used in Online Databases* (Greenwood Press, 1988). The area of online access is only one of the many areas in which computers are influencing the way the work of the field is carried out in the 1990s.

COMPUTERS IN PHILOSOPHY

It can be reasonably argued that philosophy is the field that has seen the greatest growth and expansion of computer use since the third edition of this guide. This has a great deal to do with the fact that this field lagged so far behind so many other disciplines, including others in the humanities, where computer use was concerned.

The increasing use of computers by philosophy scholars is evidenced by the coverage in reviews of information systems in the humanities. The *Annual Review of Information Science and Technology* (*ARIST*) has included reviews of the situation in the humanities three times: in 1972 (J. Raben and R. L. Widmann, "Information Systems Applications in the Humanities," *ARIST*, v.7, 1972, pp. 439-69); in 1981 (J. Raben and S. K. Burton, "Information Systems and Services in the Arts and Humanities," *ARIST*, v.16, 1981, pp. 247-66); and in 1991 (Helen R. Tibbo, "Information Systems, Services, and Technology for the Humanities," *ARIST*, v.26, 1991, pp. 287-346). In 1972 and 1981, philosophy was neither singled out, nor even mentioned, as a field where computer applications deserved discussion. Tibbo, however, notes several applications of computers to the work of philosophers: word processing, text analysis, and in theorem proving and logic studies and teaching.

Preston K. Covey ("Formal Logic and Philosophic Analysis," *Teaching Philosophy* 4 [July-October 1991]: 277-301) and Larry Wos et al., (*Automated Reasoning: Introduction and Applications* [Prentice-Hall, 1984]) address the applications in logic. Donald Sievert and Maryellen Sievert ("Humanists and Technology: The Case of Philosophers," *Information and Technology: Planning for the Second 50 Years: Proceedings of the American Society for Information*

Science 51st Annual Meeting v.25 [1988]: 94-99) consider philosophy scholars' use of information technology.

Section 21 of *The Humanities Computing Yearbook* by Ian Lancashire and Willard McCarty (Clarendon Press, 1988) suggests a dozen readings on computing in philosophy. The chapter also includes an annotated list of more than fifty computer software packages and databases in the discipline.

Concordances and word indexes, among the primary applications of computers to literature, are also used for the analysis of philosophical works. The development of *The Index Thomisticus*, covering the work of St. Thomas Aquinas, is described in "The Annals of Humanities Computing: The Index Thomisticus," *Computers and the Humanities* 14 (October, 1989): 83-90.

Although there is no evidence that philosophers are heavy users of commercially available online and CD-ROM information resources, it has been reported that they are often aware of such resources as *Philosopher's Index*.[8] The number of machine-readable philosophy indexes and bibliographies is still limited, the audience is relatively small, and great growth in the area is unlikely. A. Robert Rogers's 1985 article, "A Comparison of Manual and Online Searches in the Preparation of Philosophy Pathfinders" (*Journal of Education for Library and Information Science* 26 [Summer 1985]: 54-55), suggesting that manual searching has not been replaced by the use of online services, still holds up today.

Two major online bibliographic resources in the field are *Philosophers Index*, published by the Philosophy Documentation Center at Bowling Green State University, and the philosophy section of FRANCIS (Fichier de Recherches bibliographiques Automatisses sur Nouveautes, la Communication et l'Information Sciences sociales et humaines), which corresponds with the print *Bulletin Signaletique—Sciences Humaines Section 519 Philosophie*. The former is now available on CD-ROM, and was reviewed in C. LaGuardia's "Philosopher's Index OnDisc," in *CD-ROM Professional* 4 (1991): 119-20. Both databases include journals and other forms of publications, and coverage of both goes back to the 1940s.

The Internet is another useful resource for the student of philosophy or the "casual" reader to tap. The many Internet resources related to philosophy, including mailing lists with archives that can be searched and electronic journal titles, can be accessed using the tools outlined in chapter 1. There are several specific resources worth exploring.

The Academic Philosophy mailing list based at York University (listname "philosop") is a popular place for users to post messages about upcoming philosophical conferences, newsletters, journals, and associations, and for them to exchange job announcements and information. Similar information can be gotten from the American Philosophical Association Bulletin Board. The Usenet Newsgroup "alt.philosophy.objectivism" is just one example of a newsgroup in the field. Other "ism"-based groups can be identified through the several Internet guides now in print.

Because of its very nature, philosophy is a field where interactive forms of scholarship appear especially likely to develop as more students and teachers become knowledgeable about communicating on the net. For an overview of interactive scholarship and a list of conferences and bulletin boards in humanities and social science fields (including philosophy), the reader should see Teresa M. Harrison and Timothy Stephen, "On-Line Disciplines: Computer-Mediated Scholarship in the Humanities and Social Sciences," *Computers and the Humanities* 26 (1992):181-93.

For users looking for electronic philosophy texts, there is a list of the texts that are available on the Internet. Leslie Burkholder of Carnegie Mellon University compiled the list, which was later updated by Eric Palmer of the University of Utah, for the American Philosophical Association Subcommittee on Electronic Texts in Philosophy. A few philosophy titles can also be found in general guides and catalogs of Internet resources, such as *The Internet Complete Reference Guide* (Osborne McGraw-Hill, 1994) by Harley Hahn and Rick Stout; Paul Gilster's *The Internet Navigator* (John Wiley & Sons, 1993); and Ed Krol's *The Whole Internet User's Guide & Catalog* (O'Reilly & Associates, 1992).

The gopher server "Clearinghouse of Subject Oriented Resource Guides" lists "Philosophy" among the many Guides on the Humanities. The user may also find "Multiple Subjects—Gopher Jewels," on the same menu, to be helpful.

Finally, the reader should note that the Internet and other network arrangements make it possible for researchers to access remote library catalogs worldwide. The user can explore holdings of Ivy League university libraries like Princeton's or access the Library of Congress catalog of more than 4 million titles. Most Internet guides list library catalogs that are on the network, methods of access, and sources of additional information. If, indeed, the library is the laboratory of the humanities, the Internet expands that laboratory by orders of magnitude.

MAJOR SOCIETIES, INFORMATION CENTERS, AND SPECIAL COLLECTIONS IN PHILOSOPHY

It has become a truism to say that the competent librarian will employ information sources far beyond the collection of a single library. Indeed, since the last edition of this guide, emphasis has increasingly been on access rather than ownership of information resources. The role of bibliographies, indexes, union catalogs, and remote library catalogs is familiar. Still, some discussion of supplementary information sources may be of help to the researcher.

In philosophy, the supplementary resources may be grouped into three categories: philosophical societies, information centers, and special collections. The following paragraphs provide a sampling of major sources of additional information; the list is by no means exhaustive, but is meant to jog the librarian or research's memory and to suggest where to turn when other resources do not provide what is needed.

International philosophical societies and groups outside North America are listed in the latest edition of the *International Directory of Philosophy and Philosophers* (Philosophy Documentation Center, Bowling Green, Ohio). International philosophical congresses are listed in the "chroniques" section of *Revue philosophie de Louvain*.

UNESCO has, over the years, provided support for many international philosophical activities. In 1946, it recognized the International Council of Scientific Unions (The Hague) as coordinating body. One of its branches is the International Union of the History and Philosophy of Science (Paris), which in turn has branches in other countries and maintains affiliations with both national and international organizations. The International Council for Philosophy and Humanistic Studies (1 rue Miollers, F75732, Paris, France), which is composed of many international nongovernmental organizations, is also recognized by UNESCO, and has received funding for activities of its member organizations.

The most comprehensive philosophical society in the United States is the American Philosophical Association, founded in 1900 to promote the exchange of ideas among philosophers and to encourage scholarly and creative activity in the field. Membership is restricted to those qualified to teach philosophy at the college or university level, and national and regional groups elect officers and sponsor annual conferences and meetings. The Association publishes *APA Bulletin*, *Proceedings and Addresses of the American Philosophical Society*, and several newsletters. The reader may learn more by contacting the Association at the University of Delaware, Newark, DE 19716.

Phi Sigma Tau was founded in 1931 to promote ties between philosophy students and departments of philosophy. It is the publisher of *Dialogue* and a newsletter.

The American Catholic Philosophical Association, an example of a more specialized association in the field, was founded in 1926. It publishes *The New Scholasticism* and its *Proceedings*, and has a membership of more than 1,600. Write to the Association at The Catholic University of America, Washington, DC 20064.

Two associations address the interests of persons working in the field as journalists and teachers. The first of these is the Association of Philosophy Journal Editors, Journal of Philosophy, Columbia University, 709 Philosophy Hall, New York, NY 10027. It was founded in 1971 and meets annually in conjunction with the American Philosophical Association. The International Association of Teachers of Philosophy promotes teaching of philosophy at secondary and college levels and sponsors professional training for philosophy teachers. An international association founded in 1975, it holds a biennial conference and publishes its proceedings. The address is Am Schirrof 11, 32427 Minden, Germany.

Some associations are organized around a particular subdivision of philosophy. An example is the International Association of Ethicists, which acts as a clearinghouse for information in ethical studies worldwide and promotes "ethical and moral" studies. The Association publishes in the area of applied ethics. The address is 117 W. Harrison Building, Suite I-104, Chicago, IL 60605.

The C.S. Pierce Society (State University of New York, Philosophy Department, Baldy Hall, Buffalo, NY 14260) is but one example of the many societies organized around the work and influence of a single philosopher. The Pierce Society was founded in 1946 and publishes its *Transactions* quarterly. The Kant Society (Saarstrasse 21, 55122 Mainz, Germany) furthers the study of Immanuel Kant by conducting research and publishing studies of Kant and his work.

Finally, the International Association of Women Philosophers (IAWP), located at Burknerstrasse 24, 12047 Berlin, Germany, is comprised of women philosophers from fifteen countries. The Association holds triennial congresses and publishes a newsletter.

Details of other philosophical societies may be found in the "Societies" section of the latest *Directory of American Philosophers*.

Information centers in the United States and abroad continue to work on publication, indexing, and retrieval of information in philosophy. The Philosophy Documentation Center (Bowling Green State University, Bowling Green, OH 43404) collects, stores, and disseminates bibliographic data in the field. The Center publishes *The Philosopher's Index*, which is available in print and online.

The Philosophy Information Center (University of Dusseldorf, Dusseldorf, Germany) cooperates with the publication of *The Philosopher's Index* and produces other bibliographic indexes as well.

Le Centre Nationale de la Recherche Scientifique, through its center for documentation (54 Boulevard Raspall, Paris VIe, France), contributes the previously mentioned *Bulletin Signaletique—Section philosophie*, a quarterly publication with annual cumulative indexing.

More than twenty-five national centers participate in the work of L'Institut International de Philosophie (8, rue Jean Calvin, F75005, Paris, France), which publishes the quarterly bulletin *Bibliographie de la Philosophie*. L'Institut Superieure de Philosophie de l'universite Catholique de Louvain, like l'Institut International de Philosophie, has received funding from UNESCO; it publishes *Repertoire bibliographique de la philosophie*.

Special collections in philosophy may attempt to cover the discipline as a whole, a period of history, a special topic, or the works of a single philosopher. Many examples are listed in *Subject Collections* 7th edition, compiled by Lee Ash and William G. Miller (R. R. Bowker, 1993). A few special collections of note include:

1. The House Library of Philosophy at the University of Southern California contains more than 40,000 volumes and covers all time periods from medieval manuscripts to contemporary publications. A catalog of this collection was published by G. K. Hall.

2. The Renaissance period is the topic of the Professor Don C. Allen Collection at the University of California, San Diego.

3. The General Library of the University of Michigan has a large collection dealing with Arabic philosophy.

4. The Weston College Library attempts to be comprehensive in collecting works of Catholic philosophy, and the Dominican College Library specializes in Thomist works and attempts to collect all works by Dominican authors.

5. The Van Pelt Library at the University of Pennsylvania holds nearly 3,000 manuscripts of fifteenth-through-nineteenth century Hindu philosophy, religion, and grammar.

6. McMaster University Library in Hamilton, Ontario, holds the papers of Bertrand Russell—more than 250,000 items. Information is disseminated in *Russell: The Journal of the Bertrand Russell Archives*.

NOTES

[1] Kenneth McLeish, ed., *Key Ideas in Human Thought* (New York: Facts on File, 1993), p. 556.

[2] Andrew Jack, "Ethics," in McLeish, op. cit., 248-49.

[3] Eugene Garfield, "Is Information Retrieval in the Arts and Humanities Inherently Different from That in Science ...?" *Library Quarterly* 50 (1980): 40-57.

[4] Eugene Garfield, "A Different Sort of Great-Books: The 50 Twentieth-Century Works Most Cited in *The Arts and Humanities Citation Index*, 1976-1983," in *Essays of an Information Scientist* v.10 (ISI Press, 1989), p. 101.

[5] Eugene Garfield, "Journal Citation Studies. 38. Arts and Humanities Journals Differ from Natural and Social Sciences Journals—But Their Similarities Are Surprising," in *Essays of an Information Scientist* v.5 (ISI Press, 1983): 763.

[6] Jean-Pierre V. M. Herubel, "Philosophy Dissertation Bibliographies and Citations in Serials Evaluation," *The Serials Librarian* 20 (1991): 65-73.

[7] Ibid., p. 67.

[8] Donald Sievert and Maryellen Sievert, "Humanists and Technology: The Case of Philosophers," *Information and Technology: Planning for the Second 50 Years: Proceedings of the American Society for Information Science 51st annual meeting* v.25 (1988), pp. 94-99.

4 ◆ PRINCIPAL INFORMATION SOURCES IN PHILOSOPHY

BIBLIOGRAPHIC GUIDES

General

30. The Philosopher's Guide to Sources, Research Tools, Professional Life, and Related Fields. Richard T. De George. Lawrence, KS: Regents Press of Kansas, 1980. 261p. ISBN 0-7006-0200-3.

A successor to De George's 1971 publication, this title has been reworked and expanded into a more comprehensive offering. In addition to the coverage of philosophy, there are two additional sections, one on general research tools in the related fields of religion, humanities, and fine arts, the other on mathematics, etc. Of course, the major emphasis is on philosophy tools: bibliographies, indexes, dictionaries, encyclopedias, standard histories, etc. These are treated in section 1. This section is divided into general works; sources for the history of philosophy, with subdivisions by both period and individual philosopher; and branches, movements, and geographic regions of systematic philosophy. There are chapters on the serial literature and professional societies as well. Although this work must be considered an important contribution to the bibliography of philosophy, it does not provide annotations for all entries. Some of the existing annotations are relatively meager and are of little help in determining the value of the item.

31. Philosophy: A Guide to the Reference Literature. Hans E. Bynagle. Littleton, CO: Libraries Unlimited, 1986. 170p. ISBN 0-87287-464-8.

The emphasis here is on English-language works and, although it is less comprehensive than De George's work (entry 30), Bynagle has made an important contribution. Especially useful is the emphasis given to description and evaluation of the reference literature. Lengthy annotations make it possible for the user to make an assessment of the content or utility of every item. More than 400 reference tools published up to mid-1985 are included, with separate entries. Separate chapters are given to both general and specialized sources in some cases, with bibliographies receiving especially careful attention through coverage in five chapters. There is a chapter on core journals and one on professional associations, which should be helpful to the individual in locating additional information regarding topics or movements. Standard histories are not included. The guide represents an important source of information regarding reference material in the field.

32. Research Guide to Philosophy. Terrence N. Tice and Thomas P. Slavens. Chicago: American Library Association, 1983. 608p. (Sources of Information in the Humanities, no. 3). ISBN 0-8389-0333-9.

This is part of the series edited by Slavens with the help of specialists in various areas of the humanities. Tice is a philosopher at the University of Michigan and has contributed the major portion of the volume, consisting of thirty bibliographic essays under two categorical headings, "The History of Philosophy" and "Areas of Philosophy." The former includes thirteen chapters covering ancient to modern philosophy, with special emphasis on the nineteenth and twentieth centuries. Each chapter begins with a description of general trends, with excellent bibliographies, followed by coverage of major philosophers and bibliographies. The "areas" segment contains seventeen chapters developed along the same plan and covering both core and peripheral studies (epistemology and logic as well as philosophy of various disciplines). The essays are lucid and well developed and cover the monographic literature up to 1982, identifying more than 4,000 publications. An author-title index is provided. The final section, by Slavens, now a retired professor of library science (and general editor of the series) is a selective listing, with good annotations, of some fifty major reference books.

Periodicals

33. **Philosophy Journals and Serials: An Analytical Guide.** Douglas H. Ruben, comp. Westport, CT: Greenwood Press, 1985. 147p. ISBN 0-313-23958-4.

Although somewhat dated, this work is a thorough and well-designed guide to 335 journals and serials in the English language, and should be of use to those who are seeking information regarding possible purchase or submission of manuscripts. Entries provide full annotations regarding publishers, prices, circulation, acceptance rates, target audiences, and coverage in abstracting and indexing services. There is commentary regarding each journal's point of view and some indication of strengths and weaknesses. Special features are also pointed out. An examination of the journals covered reveals a wide range of subject matter, from the traditional studies of metaphysics to such specialties as learning and behavior and even psychic phenomena. Arrangement is alphabetical by title and access is provided through subject and geographical indexes.

BIBLIOGRAPHIES AND CATALOGS

General

34. **Bibliographia philosophica, 1934-1945.** G. A. de Brie. Bruxelles, Belgium: Editiones Spectrum, 1950-1954. 2v.

Long a standard in the field of philosophy bibliography, this title deals with a very brief, specific time period. The major purpose is to fill the gap in bibliographic control after the war because of the suspension of publication of one of the leading serial bibliographies, *Bibliographie de la philosophie* (entry 48). The first volume covers the history of philosophy and is arranged chronologically; the second volume employs a classified arrangement similar to the *Répertoire bibliographique de la philosophie* (entry 54) in identifying publications dealing with philosophical doctrine. With the avowed purpose of listing all literature (books, reviews, and articles) in the major Western languages for the twelve-year period, the volumes provide access to more than 48,000 entries through a name index.

35. **Bibliography of Philosophy, Psychology, and Cognate Subjects.** Benjamin Rand. New York: Macmillan, 1925. 2v. Repr. Part 1, Bristol, UK: Thoemmes, 1992. 542p. ISBN 1-85-506174-0.

One of the landmark bibliographies in the field, this work was published as volume 3 of James Mark Baldwin's *Dictionary of Philosophy and Psychology*, initially issued at the turn of the century. It attempts to provide comprehensive coverage of the major books and periodical articles up to about 1900. It was published in two parts, sometimes referred to as volumes, although this may confuse the fact that the work itself was considered a single volume of a larger publication. The first volume or part covers bibliography and the history of philosophy and includes individual philosophers listed alphabetically. The second part treats the topics of systematic philosophy, logic, aesthetics, ethics, etc., subdivided by both form and subject. Although criticized for omissions in coverage of philosophy of certain disciplines, the value of this work is understood and it remains an important source of bibliographic information, especially for materials of the nineteenth century.

36. **Grundriss der Geschichte der Philosophie.** Friedrich Ueberweg. 11.-12. Aufl. Berlin: Mittler, 1916-1928; repr., Basel, Switzerland: Schwabe, 1951-1956, 1960-1961. 5v.

An important history of philosophy first appearing in the 1860s, this work has received even more attention through the years for its rich bibliographic coverage. For this reason, it is considered a necessary tool for philosophical study and has often appeared in the bibliographic sections of literature guides (as it does here). The eleventh and twelfth editions were especially important in this regard and several reprintings have taken place over the years. The coverage represents ancient to modern philosophy. Bibliographies include both primary and secondary sources, both periodical and monographic, up to about 1920. It should be noted that the English translation of this work was completed in the nineteenth century from the fourth edition, and lacks the bibliographies. In 1991, the ATLA Monograph Preservation Program produced a microfiche version of the English translation of volume 2, which includes bibliographical references.

37. **Handbuch der Geschichte der Philosophie.** Wilhelm Totok. Frankfurt, Germany: Klosterman, 1964-1990. 6v. ISBN 3-465-01665-3.

Developed as a supplementary history and bibliography to the Ueberweg work (entry 36), this title covers the literature of philosophy from 1920 to the time of the publication of each of the volumes. It is a work of great magnitude and judged to be thorough in its coverage of the history of philosophy, beginning with ancient philosophy in volume 1 and progressing through modern philosophy during the twentieth century in volume 6. The work is international in its coverage of books. Bynagle warns of its forbidding nature through extensive use of abbreviations and its presentation of bibliographic listings in paragraph form. Nevertheless, it must be regarded as an extraordinary vehicle for bibliographic control, especially for writings in the Western languages. Author and subject indexes conclude each volume.

38. **The History of Ideas: A Bibliographical Introduction.** Jeremy L. Tobey. Santa Barbara, CA: ABC-Clio, 1975-1977. 2v. ISBN 0-87436-143-5 (v.1).

These two volumes present a series of well-developed and thoughtful bibliographic essays of importance to both the student and the specialist. Volume 1 covers classical antiquity and volume 2 embraces medieval and early modern Europe. Considered to be a useful resource in its treatment of "important research and reference tools and scholarly works on the history of ideas and its related fields," much of the coverage in both volumes is devoted to philosophy and aesthetics. The philosopher will find much of value also in the treatment given science and religion. There appears to be an emphasis on English-language resources identified in the bibliographic essays, and Tobey's ideas are expressed clearly. These are welcome because they give evidence of his depth of understanding of the issues and clarify certain alternatives for the reader. There is an index of periodicals and an author-title index.

39. **A History of the Bibliography of Philosophy.** Michael Jasenas. New York: George Olms, 1973. 188p. ISBN 3-487-04666-0.

Informative essays describe bibliographies of philosophy published in Western languages between 1592 and 1960. Concentrating on bibliographies that cover the whole of philosophy, the content is divided into five major chapter headings or phases of bibliographic growth ("Renaissance," "Modern," "German Aufklarung," "Post-Kantian," and "Twentieth Century"). The essays are useful not only in describing the bibliographies themselves, but also in providing insight into the historical influences regarding their production and development. In describing these influences, attention is given to major figures. Appendix 1 arranges the bibliographies both chronologically and alphabetically, thus providing a handy bibliography of bibliographies. A second such listing covers bibliographies not described in the text. Appendix 2 is a short-title list of major philosophical works. Finally, there is a name index.

40. **Manuel de bibliographie philosophique.** Gilbert Varet. Paris: Presses Universitaires de France, 1956. 2v.

Another of the standard works in the field, this is a selective bibliography of approximately 20,000 books and articles published primarily from 1914 to 1934. This emphasis on World War I and the postwar era complements the coverage of de Brie's *Bibliographia philosophica* (entry 34), completed just two years earlier. Volume 1 treats the subject historically, beginning with Oriental philosophy and moving forward to the present. There are subdivisions by period and by individual. Works in all languages are included. For prolific authors, the most important editions are mentioned. Volume 2 is concerned with the development of systematic thinking. One section covers philosophy of art, religion, and history; another, philosophy of the sciences; and a third, political philosophy, educational psychology, etc. There are many brief annotations. A general index of names is given at the end of volume 1.

41. **Philosophy Books 1982-1986.** Thomas May, ed. Bowling Green, OH: Philosophy Documentation Center, 1991. 211p. Trienn. ISBN 0-912632-89-5.

In beginning what was intended to become a triennial publication furnishing current awareness of recently published books of importance in the field of philosophy, May has produced a selective convenience tool for both students and scholars. Criteria for inclusion require previous treatment in *Philosopher's Index* (entry 53), multiple reviews in philosophy literature, and frequent mention in *Arts & Humanities Citation Index* (entry 17). This weeding process assures a certain stature to any books that meet such reviewing criteria and has resulted in a selection of 600 titles (culled from a pool of some 3,500). Additionally there are fifty books of similar "quality" that were not treated in *Philosopher's Index*. As is true of any convenience tool, one must judge whether the cost is worth the convenience when one is a subscriber to the original sources of the information.

A recent, less restrictive work is *World Philosophy: A Contemporary Bibliography*, edited by John R. Burr and Charlotte A. Burr (Greenwood Press, 1993), which provides listings of the most important books and monographs on philosophy published all over the world between 1976 and 1992. Nearly 4,000 entries are arranged into geographical regions such as Africa, Asia, the Americas, etc., then into countries. Many of the entries are annotated briefly with indication of special features as well as content. Author and subject indexes provide access.

Specialized by Topic, Region, or Period

42. **A Bibliographic Guide to the Comparative Study of Ethics.** John Larman et al., eds. New York: Cambridge University, 1991. 811p. ISBN 0-521-34448-4.

Sponsored by the Berkeley-Harvard Program in Comparative Religion, this collaborative effort of scholars and specialists seeks to address questions of morality of a cross-cultural nature. These questions are examined and analyzed through bibliographic listings designed to furnish enlightenment on individual traditions and to address differences and similarities with others. This global approach to topical considerations, such as friendship, spirituality, and various other ingredients of moral behavior, represents a unique and valuable approach for scholars and serious students as well as practitioners in the areas of business or government. Listings emphasize primary documents from various traditions, both Eastern and Western, concerned with the topics.

Ethics: An Annotated Bibliography by John K. Roth et al. (Salem Press, 1991) is an introductory guide to the topic, which furnishes a well-annotated bibliography of a selective nature for undergraduates. Listings include both primary source documents and books on current issues of concern. Most of the books listed were published within the past decade.

43. **Bioethics: A Guide to Information Sources.** Doris Mueller Goldstein. Detroit: Gale Research, 1982. 366p. ISBN 0-8103-1502-5.

The field of bioethics continues as a topic of importance within the discipline of philosophy, and this guide retains its prominence in terms of usefulness and value to current inquiry. The most important feature is an annotated bibliography of about 1,000 important documents based on the collection of the Bioethics Library at the Kennedy Institute, where Goldstein has served as library director. This segment is part 3 of the guide and is organized under such topics as abortion, behavior control, and death and dying. Organizations, programs, and special collections are enumerated in part 1, whereas the second part considers general sources (periodicals, bibliographies, encyclopedias, etc.). Authors, titles, and subjects are combined in a single index for quick access.

44. **Business Ethics and Responsibility: An Information Sourcebook.** Patricia Ann Bick. Phoenix: Oryx Press, 1988. 204p. (Oryx Series in Business and Management, no. 11). ISBN 0-89774-296-6.

This is an interesting example of specialized bibliography devoted to a field of growing interest. There are more than 1,000 annotated entries arranged under 13 subject divisions, which themselves are divided into more specific topics. These divisions or sections cover such areas as corporate social responsibility, employee rights, and international aspects. It is important to note the specialized section on South Africa in view of contemporary interest in socially responsible investments. Various types of literature are treated, but represent primarily business publications and dissertations rather than periodicals of the legal profession or social services. Most helpful to librarians is the "Core Library Collection" that identifies useful reference sources and the listings given to research centers, major journals, and relevant organizations. Omissions have been noted, such as AIDS in the workplace and ethical standards of major business schools. Author, title, and subject indexes aid access.

45. **Encyclopedia of Indian Philosophies: Bibliography.** Rev. ed. Karl H. Potter. Princeton, NJ: Princeton University Press, 1983. 1023p. ISBN 0-691-07281-7.

This is a revised and much expanded version of the 1970 publication originally published as the initial volume of *Encyclopedia of Indian Philosophies* (entry 73). The earlier edition listed more than 9,200 sources in an attempt to present the concepts of Indian philosophy and the content of Indian philosophical texts to a wider public. The bibliography was the initial volume of the projected encyclopedia and helped establish its scope. Meanwhile, the revised edition of the bibliography has added more than 4,000 items incorporating the supplementary lists published in the *Journal of Indian Philosophy* (Dordrecht, Holland: D. Reidel, 1970-), as well as new material. Three of the four main sections deal with Sanskrit texts, authorship, and dates; section 4 presents secondary literature in Western languages. Several indexes (name, title, subject) provide access.

Guide to Indian Philosophy by Potter and others (G. K. Hall, 1988) is part of the same series as *Guide to Chinese Philosophy* (entry 46), and furnishes an annotated bibliography of nearly 900 books and articles published during the twentieth century up to 1985, with emphasis on the past decade prior to publication. Primarily intended for the undergraduate or interested layperson, all works are in English with the articles being at least ten pages in length. All areas of Indian philosophy are covered, from metaphysics to politics. Arrangement of entries is alphabetical by author; there is both a name index and a subject index to aid access.

46. **Guide to Chinese Philosophy.** Charles Wei-Hsun Fu and Wing-tsit Chan. Boston: G. K. Hall, 1978. 262p. ISBN 0-8161-7901-8.

This is an annotated bibliography mainly of English-language sources useful to the student or nonspecialist, and of peripheral interest to the serious scholar who would be more interested in Chinese-language texts. The guide is divided into sixteen sections, beginning with "History of Chinese Philosophy," which covers the various schools in sequence from pre-Confucian to Marxist. Topics such as ethics and human nature are treated in the next twelve chapters, whereas the final three chapters concern analytical sources, comparative philosophy, and significant texts. There is an author and title index. Prepared as part of the Asian Philosophies and Religions Project of the Council for Intercultural Studies and Programs, this work supersedes Chan's *An Outline and an Annotated Bibliography of Chinese Philosophy* (Yale University, 1969).

Guide to Buddhist Philosophy by Kenneth K. Inada (G. K. Hall, 1985) is another of the publisher's resource guides in both Eastern religion and philosophy geared to the undergraduate level. It serves as a companion volume to Frank E. Reynolds's *Guide to Buddhist Religion* (G. K. Hall, 1981) for purposes of providing a thorough study of Buddhism. More than 1,000 books, articles, and dissertations are listed, most of which are in English. Arrangement of entries is under categories similar to those employed in other works of this series, such as history, metaphysics, etc. Annotations are brief but informative; there are detailed author-title and subject indexes.

47. **Resources in Ancient Philosophy: An Annotated Bibliography of Scholarship in English 1965-1989.** Albert A. Bell and James B. Allis. Metuchen, NJ: Scarecrow Press, 1991. 799p. ISBN 0-8108-2520-1.

This is an excellent resource bibliography to more than 7,000 scholarly books and articles on the subject of ancient philosophy written over a twenty-five-year period. The philosophers are analyzed through introductory narratives that highlight accomplishments. Major contributions are noted. Annotations for entries tend to be brief but informative in furnishing a clear understanding of the topic. Arrangement of entries is under chapter headings that treat the subject chronologically e.g., "Thales to Augustine." Schools of thought are then treated alphabetically by authors of the secondary source material listed. In establishing this order, the authors have enabled us to search a particular document such as Plato's *Republic* to find what specifically has been done by contemporary scholars. This book should prove useful to all levels of inquiries although the subject index is less than precise. There is no author index.

A more recent effort is *The Presocratic Philosophers: An Annotated Bibliography* by Luis E. Navia (Garland, 1993), identifying and describing 2,700 books and articles from the international scholarly literature. Various points of view are embraced, giving a well-rounded perspective to the individual philosophers and their accomplishments. The materials, cited from nearly 450 journals, represent diverse levels of inquiry and sophistication. Coverage is given to bibliographical works, source collections, and general studies, followed by single chapters for each of the eleven major philosophers treated. Entries are in the language of the original, with English translations supplied.

INDEXES, ABSTRACTS, AND SERIAL BIBLIOGRAPHIES

48. **Bibliographie de la philosophie.** Paris: Vrin, 1937-1953. ISSN 0006-1352.

A now-defunct serial bibliography published under the auspices of the Institut Internationale de Philosophie, this work provides listings without annotations of philosophical books and articles. A multilingual quarterly publication, it covered philosophy in an exhaustive manner, identifying both well-known and obscure publications. During the postwar period, it reviewed more than 700 journals for relevant articles. It was suspended during the war years (mid-1939-1945), creating the need for the subsequent publication of de Brie's *Bibliographia philosophica* (entry 34). Each issue of the *Bibliographie* had two major divisions, an alphabetical author listing and a systematic subject index. The latter included a chronological/geographical section; an index of philosophers who were the subjects of books and articles in the first part; and an index of concepts and terms, with books and periodical articles identified under each term. Coverage of periodical articles was dropped in a change of editorial policy by its successor (entry 49).

49. **Bibliographie de la philosophie/Bibliography of Philosophy.** Paris: Vrin, 1954- . Q. ISSN 0006-1352.

A dual-language title accompanied the change in editorial policy of this work (entry 48). Published under the sponsorship of several international organizations, including the Institut Internationale de Philosophie and the International Federation of Philosophical Societies, it receives aid from UNESCO and the French National Centre for Scientific Research. Now published as an abstract journal for books only, the abstracts appear in the language of the original work if in English, French, German, Italian, or Spanish. Abstracts of books written in other languages are provided in either English or French. There is a classified arrangement under ten broad divisions of philosophy. Indexes appear only in the final issue of each volume, in which access is provided through authors, titles, and keywords. An "Index of Names" is also given which gathers all publishers, translators, and individuals mentioned in titles and in abstracts.

A selective but worthy source is *Philosophical Books* (Oxford: Blackwell, 1960-), providing in-depth reviews of high quality of a variety of philosophical books. Many of these have not been reviewed extensively and thus are more elusive. The tool is presently issued on a quarterly basis and furnishes about twenty reviews per issue. *Cumulative Index of Philosophical Books: Volumes 1-15 (1960-1974)* compiled by Julius Ariail (Statesboro, GA: Sweet Bay, 1980) furnishes access to the first fifteen years of reviews. After 1974, the reviews are indexed in **Philosopher's Index* (entry 53).

*50. **Bibliography of Bioethics.** Detroit: Gale Research (publisher varies), 1975- . Ann. ISSN 0363-0161.

Presently sponsored by the Kennedy Institute of Ethics at Georgetown University, this annual bibliography has taken on added importance in the past few years owing to the increased publicity and volatility of ethical and public policy issues relating to medicine, health care, and related research. Abstracts have appeared since the ninth volume (1983). The coverage includes several forms of material, primarily journal articles, but also books, newspaper articles, and monographs all in the English language. Entries are arranged by numerous subject headings such as abortion, contraception, etc.; an annual thesaurus has been issued since 1984. Author, title, and subject indexes facilitate access. *Bioethics Thesaurus* has been issued as a section of this work since 1984, and is also published separately. It furnishes a controlled vocabulary to aid the searcher.

Corresponding to the printed work is the computerized database **BIOETHICSLINE* (Kennedy Institute of Ethics), which provides cumulative coverage online of the entire file from the beginning to the present. Although not issued through any vendor service, access is possible through searching of MEDLARS/MEDLINE and also through Questel. Direct searches are available to authorized individuals and organizations such as selected academic, medical, and special libraries.

*51. **Francis bulletin signalétique. 519, Philosophie.** Nancy, France: Institut de l'Information Scientifique et Technique (INIST), 1947- . Q. Ann. cum. ISSN 1157-3694.

Having undergone several name changes, this work continues as part of the large-scale FRANCIS computerized operation to provide quarterly coverage of philosophy periodical literature from all over the world. It started out as *Bulletin analytique: Philosophie (1947-1955)*, then became *Bulletin signalétique*, with a variety of subtitles. From 1970 until 1990, it was **Bulletin signalétique: 519* and was produced by the Centre National de la recherche scientifique (CNRS). After 1990, INIST took over the major responsibility from CNRS. The work employs a classified arrangement to embrace articles from more than 4,000 periodicals. Brief abstracts are given in French regardless of the language of the original article. Book reviews are cited and abstracts given, although books are not listed routinely. Separate author and subject indexes appear in each issue, as does an index of journals covered. All three indexes cumulate annually.

The database, *Philosophie (CNRS-INIST), is available online and in CD-ROM as part of the ongoing indexing and abstracting program (FRANCIS) of the French Centre National de la Recherche Scientifique now being conducted with INIST. Coverage of philosophy is available from 1972 to the present. *Philosophische Dokumentation (University of Dusseldorf, 1968-) is a German-language abstracting and indexing service for 250 current philosophical and historical periodicals. Presently, it is published and distributed on a quarterly basis in print form by Kraus Thomson Organization. It is available online from the University of Dusseldorf and covers the period from 1970 to the present.

*52. **The Philosopher's Index: An International Index to Philosophical Periodicals and Books.** Bowling Green, OH: Philosophy Documentation Center/Bowling Green State University, 1967- . Q. Ann. cum. ISSN 0031-7993.

Today considered the most important source for philosophers in the Anglo-American tradition, this work provides abstracts in English for articles from all major philosophy journals in English, French, German, Spanish, and Italian, with selective inclusion from journals in other languages. Originally limited to articles from British and American periodicals, the scope expanded as it matured, and books were added in 1980. Book material is limited to that in the English language only, but includes monographs, translations, bibliographies, biographies, textbooks, dissertations, dictionaries, and anthologies. There are both subject and author listings for all entries, with the abstracts appearing in the author section. There is a separate index for book reviews.

A corresponding database, *PHILOSOPHER'S INDEX, is available online and in CD-ROM. It is updated on a quarterly basis and includes abstracts from the retrospective publications (entry 53) as well. Book reviews are not included online. The service is available through DIALOG and EasyNet gateway system. There is an aid to the database written by Richard H. Lineback and Lynn Walkiewicz, entitled The Philosopher's Index Thesaurus (Philosophy Documentation Center, 1992), which furnishes a brief introduction and description of the database along with some practical advice for searching both CD-ROM and DIALOG versions.

*53. **The Philosopher's Index: A Retrospective Index to U.S. Publications from 1940.** Bowling Green, OH: Philosophy Documentation Center/Bowling Green State University, 1978. 3v. ISBN 0-912632-12-7.

Developed to expand the coverage of the ongoing current index, which began in 1967, this retrospective effort covers the journal literature from 1940 to 1966, and books published from 1940 to 1926. (Books were not picked up in the current series until 1980, so a small gap still exists.) Total coverage is of some 15,000 articles and 6,000 books. Developed in the style of the current index (entry 52), the first two volumes represent the subject index, and volume 3 contains the author listing with abstracts.

A complementary work edited by Richard H. Lineback, *The Philosopher's Index: A Retrospective Index to Non-U.S. English Language Publications from 1940 (Philosophy Documentation Center, 1980, 3v.) follows a similar format and arrangement. It includes approximately 12,000 articles from 70 periodicals published between 1940 and 1966, and some 5,000 books published between 1940 and 1978. Entries from both retrospective publications are available online.

54. **Répertoire bibliographique de la philosophie.** Louvain, Belgium: Institut Superieur de Philosophie, 1949-1990. Q. ISSN 0034-4567.

This important serial bibliography has an interesting and varied past beginning as an appendix to Revue néo-scholastique de philosophie from 1934 to 1948. Since 1939, it also was issued under the title Bibliografisch repertorium as a supplement to the Dutch Tijdschrift voor filosofie. It continued in this manner even during World War II when the Revue néo-scholastique was suspended. From 1949 to 1990, it operated as an independent supplement to Revue philosophique de Louvain, and gained an excellent reputation for providing exhaustive coverage of books and articles in Catalan, Dutch, English, French, German,

Italian, Latin, Portuguese, and Spanish. There was a single classified listing, aided by a name index that was issued in November of each year.

Its past associations helped shape its present status, since in 1991 it was merged with the still-active *Bibliografisch repertorium van de wijsbegeerte* to form a new quarterly English/French language publication, *International Philosophical Bibliography-Repertoire bibliographique de la philosophie-Bibliografisch repertorium van de wijsbegeerte*, published jointly by the Institut and by Universite Catholique de Louvain.

DICTIONARIES, ENCYCLOPEDIAS, AND HANDBOOKS

General

55. **A Dictionary of Philosophy.** 2d ed. Anthony Flew, editorial consultant, and Jennifer Speake, ed. New York: St. Martin's Press, 1984. 380p. ISBN 0-312-20924-X.

Considered by some to be the best dictionary in the field, this book provides concise treatment of the subject. Good, lucid definitions for the most part are easily understood by the layperson, although some articles tend to be more technical. It is not clear as to what degree Flew, the well-known British philosopher, now retired from the University of Reading, participated in the revision. His name, however, establishes authority for the work, and Rogers found precious little change from the earlier edition in his ARBA 1985 review. The dictionary includes biographical articles on philosophers which, although brief, serve to identify the individuals cited. There is some coverage of Oriental philosophy, but the emphasis is definitely Anglo-American, with coverage of continental European subject matter secondary in importance.

56. **Dictionary of Philosophy.** Ivan Timofeevich Frolov et al., eds. New York: International Publishers, 1984. 464p. ISBN 0-7178-0604-9.

This is an English translation of a standard Soviet dictionary and represents philosophy from the perspective of Marxism-Leninism. Non-Western philosophy and ancient philosophy are treated objectively, but modern thought and its various exponents are described in relation to the development of communism. Thus the definitions and identifications are sprinkled with a variety of labels such as "bourgeois." Stalin is not mentioned here, which reflects the position of the Soviet state subsequent to Khrushchev. The work is valuable, historically, in light of recent developments and for its inclusion of many Russian philosophers who are unfamiliar to those with a Western orientation. It is interesting to consider what type of "de-communized" editions might be issued in the future in view of the breakup of the Soviet Union.

57. **A Dictionary of Philosophy.** 2d ed. Alan Robert Lacey. London: Routledge & Kegan Paul, 1976; repr. 1990, 266p. ISBN 0-4150-5872-4.

Designed for the layperson or student, this dictionary does an excellent job in describing the problems and questions of the discipline through its brief but informative definitions. The emphasis is on Anglo-American philosophy, particularly that which concerns epistemological or logical topics. It covers all periods, branches, and schools of ancient, medieval, and modern philosophy in Western thought, but no coverage is given to Eastern philosophy. There are numerous entries for individual philosophers. It is regarded as being especially strong in bibliographies, some of which are extensive for a work of this size. These are provided for many of the entries and are extremely useful for the intended audience in suggesting related works. There are numerous cross-references as well.

Dictionary of Philosophy by Dagobert D. Runes (Philosophical Library, 1983) is a revised edition of an old standard, first published in 1942, meant to furnish clear and concise definitions and descriptions in comprehensive fashion. This it succeeded in doing, and still does, despite the fact that revision has been minimal. Entries are signed by the seventy-five contributors, and the work is of value now for its historic character as well as its comprehensive and accurate nature in treating various thinkers, issues, and ideological systems of the past. Less sophisticated is the recent effort by Peter A. Angeles, *The HarperCollins Dictionary of Philosophy* (2d ed. HarperCollins, 1992). It supplies some 3,000 definitions of major philosophical concepts suitable for the beginning student or layperson in his or her study of Western philosophy. Definitions are brief and uniform in style; there are no references to sources consulted. Biographical treatments are included.

58. **Dictionary of the History of Ideas: Studies of Selected Pivotal Ideas.** Philip P. Wiener, ed.-in-chief. New York: Scribner's, 1973-1974. 4v. plus index; repr. 1980. 5v. ISBN 0-684-16418-3 (pbk).

Considered to be a significant contribution to the reference literature of philosophy and related fields, this encyclopedic work contains more than 300 lengthy articles, all signed, on a wide array of subjects in intellectual history. Distinguished scholars from various disciplines have served as contributors to "establish some sense of unity of human thought and its cultural manifestation in a world of ever-increasing specialization and alienation." Not restricted to philosophical material in its interdisciplinary, multicultural coverage, the work offers a rich body of information for philosophical inquiry. Broadly, the areas of coverage embrace the sciences and the external order of nature; anthropology, psychology, religion, philosophy, and human nature; literature and the arts; attitudes toward the historical sciences; economic, legal, and political institutions and ideologies; religious and philosophical ideas; and mathematics and logic. Bibliographies are included and the articles are arranged alphabetically. A separate index volume provides access.

59. **Enciclopedia filosofica.** 2d ed. Florence, Italy: Sansoni, 1968-1969. 6v. Repr. and rev. Rome: Lucarini, 1982. 8v.

Prior to the publication of *The Encyclopedia of Philosophy* (entry 60), the earlier edition of this Italian work in four volumes was the most comprehensive tool of its kind. Always considered to be a scholarly encyclopedia, it contains signed articles and good bibliographies. Arrangement is dictionary-style, with individuals, places, ideas, schools, movements, and other topical material in one alphabet. There is an emphasis on Continental European philosophy, and the coverage of Italian thought and thinkers is especially strong, although the work is respected for its international coverage too. Eastern philosophy is treated, but, as one might expect, much less fully than Western thought. The volumes are arranged in columns rather than pages, and the final volume has three major indexes (theoretical concepts, historical development, and terms and personal names for which entries do not appear but which received references in the text).

60. **The Encyclopedia of Philosophy.** Paul Edwards, ed.-in-chief. New York: Macmillan, 1967. 8v. Repr. 1972, 8v. in 4.

The compilers of this monumental set tried to cover the whole realm of philosophy (Eastern and Western) and its points of contact with other disciplines. The *Encyclopedia* contains nearly 1,500 articles, some monographic in length and most with copious bibliographies. There are excellent articles on philosophical movements, major ideas, the philosophy of various subject fields, the history of philosophy in different countries, and biographies of major philosophers. Coverage of ancient, medieval, and early modern philosophers is generally good. Coverage of contemporary philosophers is better for Western Europe, North America, and India than for what was the Soviet Bloc and the People's Republic of China. There are good articles on philosophical bibliographies, dictionaries, encyclopedias, and journals. The editor has tried to minimize editorial bias, but favors an Anglo-American tradition. The monographic approach has been preferred to a series of short articles, and smaller topics can be located by means of a detailed index in volume 8. More than 1,500 philosophers from all over the world contributed, and 150 scholars from the United States,

Great Britain, and Europe served on the editorial board. This is likely to remain the definitive encyclopedia of philosophy for many years to come.

61. **Historisches Wörterbuch der Philosophie**. Joachim Ritter, ed. Basel, Switzerland: Schwabe, 1971- . v.1-8. ISBN 3-7965-0115-X.

More than 1,200 scholars contributed to this revision of Rudolf Eisler's *Worterbuch der Philosophischen Begriffe* (Berlin: Mittler, 1910). Some subjects covered in the earlier work (e.g., psychology) have been dropped and new materials added. Other topics are revised and updated. The articles, ranging in length from a few sentences to several pages, treat the historical development of philosophical terms and concepts in a very scholarly manner. Documentation is abundant and up-to-date. An index and list of abbreviations are included in each volume. "It should be noted that articles on individual philosophers are not within the scope of this dictionary, although schools of thought based on the teachings of a single man are described." Work had slowed perceptibly since Ritter's death in 1974, but recent years have renewed the quest to complete the projected ten volumes by 1995. Volume 7 was issued in 1990 and volume 8 in 1992, bringing the set through "R" in alphabetical sequence.

62. **Talking Philosophy: A Wordbook**. A. W. Sparkes. New York: Routledge, 1991. 307p. ISBN 0-415-04222-4.

This extraordinary tool furnishes useful information to a variety of users, ranging from the specialist to the interested layperson, in providing a thematic and conceptual awareness of the meanings of terms and their position with respect to other related words. Similar to *Roget's International Thesaurus* (entry 943) in its structure, words are first located through the detailed alphabetical index, where references are made to the proper chapters, which cover such categories as "saying things" and "relations." Words defined in a section have parallels or similarities in context or previous use, which are supported with references to sources listed in a bibliography of 800 entries at the end. These sources are varied in nature and range from the philosophical to the literary; therefore, not all definitions are accepted within the field of philosophy. The advantage or importance of such an approach is obvious to the philosopher-linguist. Entries contain numerous cross-references.

63. **Vocabulaire technique et critique de la philosophie.** 17th ed. André Lalande, ed. Paris: Presses Universitaires de France, 1992. 2v. ISBN 2-13-044512-8.

This is an old standard in the field, the first complete edition having been published in 1926. It has been consistent and predictable in its revisions and retains a position of importance as a reference tool. Prior to the first complete edition, it appeared in twenty-one segments published in the *Bulletin de la Societe Française de Philosophie* between 1902 and 1923. Definitions are good; additional coverage is given to examples of use by philosophers, along with etymologies and bibliographic notes. German, English, and Italian equivalents are provided as well. The emphasis is on clarification of terms and ideas; therefore, there are no biographical entries.

64. **World Philosophy: Essay-Reviews of 225 Major Works.** Frank N. Magill, ed. and Ian P. McGreal, assoc. ed. Englewood Cliffs, NJ: Salem Press, 1982. 5v. ISBN 0-89356-325-0.

This is an expansion of Magill's earlier *Masterpieces of World Philosophy in Summary Form* (Salem Press, 1961), in which 200 philosophical classics were summarized in a manner similar to other works by the noted editor. The new set retains the summaries or essay reviews of the earlier edition and adds twenty-five more, but with a new feature considered by the editors to be its major purpose. The inclusion of a section on pertinent literature supplies at least two critical commentaries for each essay-review. These critical studies are as detailed as the essay-reviews (600 to 1,000 words) and are significant additions. Following the critical commentaries are annotated lists of relevant English-language secondary sources for additional reading. The work is meant to appeal to a wide audience, with emphasis on the needs of laypersons, high school students, and undergraduates.

A more recent publication is Magill's *Masterpieces of World Philosophy* (HarperCollins, 1990) which is simply an abridged edition of the five-volume work. About 100 documents ranging from those of Confucius to those from the twentieth century have been selected by John Roth from the earlier effort and arranged chronologically. Entries contain essay-reviews followed by brief listings of additional secondary sources to consult.

Specialized by Topic, Region, or Period

65. **Blackwell Companions to Philosophy** series. Cambridge, MA: Blackwell, 1991- . ISBN 0-631-16211-9 (v.1).

This recent series has already produced three volumes devoted to either a specific area or an historical period: *A Companion to Ethics*, edited by Peter Singer (volume 1, 1991; repr. with corr. 1993); *The Blackwell Companion to the Enlightenment*, edited by John W. Yolton (volume 2, 1992); and *A Companion to Epistemology*, edited by Johnathan Dancy and Ernest Sosa (volume 3, 1992). The series is of generally high quality and appears to be carefully supervised by the eminent scholars and bibliographers who serve as editors of the individual volumes. Included in each are brief biographical and topical essays by an array of contributors. The selective bibliographies furnished for each entry make the volumes useful to a variety of potential users, from scholars and serious students to interested laypersons. The series appears to fulfill a need for treatment of specific areas of philosophy within a comprehensive planned program of publishing.

66. **The Concise Encyclopedia of Western Philosophy and Philosophers.** New ed. completely rev. James O. Urmson and Johnathan Ree, eds. Boston: Unwin Hyman, 1989. 331p. ISBN 0-04-445379-5. Repr. London: Routledge, 1991, 1993. ISBN 0-41-507883-0 (pbk).

Long a popular reference tool, this work was written for the intelligent layperson or nonspecialist. Numerous distinguished contributors participated in the effort, and the work continues as a useful source of information on Western philosophers and their contributions. In addition to the biographies, there is coverage of trends and, of course, definition of terms. Articles are brief to moderate in length and favor the contributions and individuals associated with Anglo-American thought. Additional new articles furnish coverage of important developments subsequent to publication of the second edition in 1975, and needed corrections have been made. No bibliographies are provided, which limits the volume's use to identification purposes.

A Dictionary of Philosophical Quotations, edited by A. J. Ayer and Jane O'Grady (Blackwell, 1992) identifies quotations from nearly 350 philosophers representing the Western European tradition. Emphasis is placed on modern philosophers of the late nineteenth or twentieth centuries, providing a useful perspective on contemporary thought. Quotations are thorough in providing analysis of topical nature; they vary from a single line to a full page but average a paragraph in length. A glossary is included, along with a subject index.

67. **Dictionary of Asian Philosophies.** St. Elmo Nauman, Jr. New York: Philosophical Library, 1978; repr., London: Routledge, 1989. 372p. ISBN 0-4150-3971-1 (pbk).

This work in the past has helped provide a corrective to the bias toward Western philosophy found in most tools and in most library reference collections. With the appearance of newer titles such as *Encyclopedia of Eastern Philosophy and Religion* (entry 71), it has diminished somewhat in importance. "Asian philosophies" is interpreted to include the thinkers of the Middle East as well as the Far East, and it covers philosophers, schools, texts, terms, and concepts. Entries vary considerably in length, from one sentence to monographic proportions. A number of omissions have been pointed out by Bynagle in his annotated bibliography (entry 31), such as lack of a survey article on Islamic philosophy, even though such articles exist for Indian philosophy and for Jewish philosophy. One would have to agree with the judgment that the work is not as useful as it could be. It is also true, however, that there are precious few one-volume works focused on Eastern philosophy in this manner.

68. **A Dictionary of Marxist Thought.** 2d ed. Tom Bottomore, ed. Cambridge, MA: Blackwell, 1991. 647p. ISBN 0-631-16481-2.

The initial edition of this work (1983) established itself as a useful work, although it has been criticized for uneven quality in the array of topics and subjects presented. As a product of Anglo-American scholarship, it examined the essence of contemporary Marxist thought in such areas as aesthetics, ethics, and theory of knowledge. The second edition updates its predecessor and similarly goes beyond Marxist philosophy in its analysis of the concepts involved. New treatments include "analytical Marxism," "crisis in socialist society," and "market socialism." Continued excellent coverage is given standard elements like "alienation and dialectics." Philosophical schools and movements within Marxism are treated and individual philosophers are identified and described. In light of current events leading to the dismantling of the U.S.S.R., this tool provides a needed Western perspective on Marxist thought. Because of the timeliness of the topic and the nature of the ongoing debates regarding Marxism, it remains an important source.

69. **Encyclopedia of Bioethics.** Warren T. Reich, ed.-in-chief. New York: Free Press, 1978. 4v. Repr. 1982. 2v. ISBN 0-02-925910-X.

This is a comprehensive work on the important field of bioethics, treating the ethical and social issues of life sciences, medicine, health care, and the health professions. Philosophical perspectives are provided, among others, as the work is interdisciplinary in nature. The elements included embrace the study of history, theology, science, law, and the social sciences. For the philosopher, there is value not only in the specialized area of bioethics but in the excellent coverage given general ethical theory under "Ethics." The twelve articles in this segment can be used to supplement and update the coverage in *The Encyclopedia of Philosophy* (entry 60). Entries are arranged alphabetically from "Abortion" to "Women and biomedicine," and in many cases are composed of several writings from different authors. There is an attempt to avoid technical language and to achieve a universal perspective, with 15 countries represented by 285 contributors. The work has a comprehensive index and cross-references are supplied. An update or supplement to this work would be useful, to have more recent views on the topics.

70. **Encyclopedia of Cosmology: Historical, Philosophical, and Scientific Foundations of Modern Cosmology.** Norriss S. Hetherington, ed. New York: Garland, 1993. 686p. ISBN 0-8240-7213-8.

This one-volume compendium examines the whole realm of cosmology with all its ramifications, from philosophical to scientific, through a well-developed collection of scholarly articles. Such diverse aspects as Aristotle's cosmology, anthropic principle, creation, multiple universes, and plurality of worlds, and philosophical elements within the origins of modern cosmology are treated along with aspects of particle physics, dark matter, deceleration of the universe, and galaxy formation. In addition to Aristotle, the ancient theories of Ptolemy and Plato are analyzed, together with such illustrious Renaissance personalities as Copernicus, Kepler, Descartes, and Newton. Modern figures such as Einstein and Hubble receive scrutiny as well. Numerous scholars have contributed to the volume, producing well-developed, cogent exposition. An important characteristic of this work is its inclusion of debates, contested issues, and alternative theories along with the accepted version. All entries contain suggestions for additional readings; an index is furnished.

71. **The Encyclopedia of Eastern Philosophy and Religion: Buddhism, Hinduism, Taoism, Zen.** Ingrid Fischer-Schreiber et al., eds. Boston: Shambhala, 1989. 468p. ISBN 0-87773-433-X.

This is considered an indispensable recent source for information on Eastern traditions that previously had been treated only by highly specialized sources and Nauman's *Dictionary of Asian Philosophies* (entry 67). It is an English translation of a German work, *Lexikon der östlichen Weisheitslehren* (Bern, Switzerland: Barth, 1986), and furnishes some 4,000 definitions and biographical sketches. Arrangement is alphabetical and narratives vary in length according to importance of topic. Entries furnish cross-references, which are helpful in linking associated subjects and issues. Some of the lengthy entries furnish expositions of doctrines and examine their culture and historical impact. There are bibliographical references to relevant studies as well as a final detailed bibliography identifying both primary and secondary sources. No index is furnished, but the cross-references within entries are useful for access. A good feature is the lineage chart which furnishes insight into the transmission of the Eastern traditions.

72. **Encyclopedia of Ethics.** Lawrence C. Becker and Charlotte B. Becker, eds. New York: Garland, 1992. 2v. (Garland Reference Library of the Humanities, v.925). ISBN 0-8153-0403-X.

Recognized by experts as one of the best of the specialized information sources in the field, this work furnishes more than 400 signed articles dealing with ethics on a broad scale. Emphasis is given to perceptions of the English-speaking world, but it also includes moral concepts as viewed by other cultures. From general to the level of serious inquiry as practiced by scholars and university students, the work is well-written. Essays vary from 500 to 9,000 words, with most articles ranging between 1,000 and 5,000 words depending upon the significance of the topic. Essays are thorough and informative in enumerating the various aspects of theories and alternatives regarding issues. Covered here are individual philosophers, ethics of specific fields such as business or government, theories, values and traits, and so on. Useful bibliographies are furnished within each entry. There is an extensive subject index and an index to authors cited in the bibliographies.

73. **Encyclopedia of Indian Philosophies.** Ram Shankar Bhattacharya et al. Princeton, NJ: Princeton University, 1977- . v.1- .

Originally begun as a monumental project of an Indian publishing house in 1970, the work has been continuing under the auspices of Princeton University since 1977. Produced by teams of scholars, each volume furnishes another segment of what is considered to be a definitive encyclopedia of the various systems of classical Indian philosophy. Much of the work has been done by Karl H. Potter, whose initial bibliographic volume has been revised on two occasions (entry 45). The first six volumes have been issued, with volume 5 appearing in 1990 and volume 6 in 1992.

A Concise Dictionary of Indian Philosophy: Sanskrit Terms Defined in English, by John A. Grimes (State University of New York, 1989), is designed to provide a basic introduction to the terminology of the major schools of Indian philosophy. Because Sanskrit is basic to the understanding of various concepts and themes, this dictionary of some 2,500 terms should prove useful to users at all levels of inquiry. Definitions vary in length from simple translations of a phrase to thorough descriptions and interpretations of usage and doctrine. Arrangement of entries is by roman alphabet; special features include fourteen charts showing relationships of works, categories, and sourcebooks for the various schools. There is an index of important terms.

74. **Handbook of Metaphysics and Ontology.** Hans Burkhardt and Barry Smith, eds. Philadelphia: Philosophia Verlag, 1991. 2v. ISBN 3-88405-080-X.

Considered to be an excellent source of information on the ancient study of metaphysics and ontology, this work furnishes excellent coverage of the issues and debates that have endured over thousands of years. Conversely, systematic treatment is given to more recent developments of the past four decades. All periods are treated, along with schools of various thought systems, although the central framework resides within the Aristotelian traditions. There are nearly 500 articles, furnished by specialists, varying from one page to more than ten pages in length. Essays are highly technical; contributors have been straightforward and objective in their descriptions. In a highly selective work of this kind, questions inevitably follow regarding inclusions and exclusions, but generally speaking the work is well-conceived. Bibliographies to secondary sources accompany each entry. There is a detailed index which has been criticized for certain difficulties in locating relevant articles.

75. **Handbook of World Philosophy: Contemporary Developments since 1945.** John R. Burr, ed. Westport, CT: Greenwood Press, 1980. 641p. ISBN 0-313-22381-5.

A collection of twenty-eight essays grouped by six regions (Western Europe, Australia, and Israel; Eastern Europe; the Americas; Africa and the Republic of South Africa; Islamic Countries; and Asia), this work provides an international survey of philosophical directions, tendencies, and cross-currents since 1945. The essays describe thoughts, work, and activities up to about 1977. Within the regions, there are many subdivisions by country, and each essay/article is accompanied by a substantial bibliography. The work has been criticized for a certain unevenness of coverage; for example, "France receives twice as much space as any other country." Nevertheless, this is a worthwhile tool, because much of the coverage by country is not duplicated elsewhere, not even in the multivolume encyclopedias. There are both subject and name indexes, as well as a directory of philosophical associations and a list of congresses and meetings in the appendices.

DIRECTORIES AND BIOGRAPHICAL SOURCES

76. **Dictionnaire des philosophes antiques.** Richard Goulet, ed. Paris: Editions du Centre national de la recherche scientifique, 1989. v.1- . ISBN 2-222-04042-6 (v.1).

Volume 1 of this multivolume biographical encyclopedia was issued in 1989 and gave indication of what is to become a comprehensive biographical encyclopedia of early philosophers. Time span ranges from the beginning of philosophy to about the sixth century. Articles vary considerably in length depending upon the importance of the subject; more than 100 pages are given to Aristotle, whereas others receive only a single paragraph. The biographical essays contain references to other sources dating from all time periods and furnish exposition of the subject's influence and thought systems. There is a listing of textual histories and standard editions for each philosopher. Volume 1 contains indexes of subjects, Greek words, and names.

A one-volume biographical dictionary of contemporary philosophy is *Dizionario dei filosofi del Novecento* (Firenze, Italy: L. S. Olschki, 1985), which furnishes some 1,500 biographical sketches. Included here are philosophers, scholars, writers, historians, linguists, and others who have either utilized or influenced twentieth-century philosophy in some way. Emphasis is given to Western thought, with a number of the writings taken from the *Enciclopedia filosofica* (entry 59).

77. **Directory of American Philosophers, 1994-1995.** 17th ed. Archie J. Bahm et al., eds. Bowling Green, OH: Philosophy Documentation Center/Bowling Green State University, 1993. 506p. ISBN 0-912632-95-X.

The recent edition of this biennial work basically continues the familiar format of the previous publications. The main body is composed of a directory of American college and university departments of philosophy, arranged alphabetically by state, then by name. There is a listing of faculty members for each entry, along with the address and telephone number of the department. Canadian colleges and universities receive similar treatment in a separate listing and are arranged alphabetically by province, then name. Additional information is provided in separate sections on assistantships, societies, institutes, publishers, and journals in the field. Separate indexes provide ready access through names of philosophers (primarily the faculty members), institutions, publishers, journals, centers and institutes, and societies. The final section provides statistics on size of philosophy departments, number of philosophers, etc. A complementary source is *International Directory of Philosophy and Philosophers* (entry 81).

78. **Essays on Early Modern Philosophers: From Descartes and Hobbes to Newton and Leibniz**. Vere Chappel, ed. New York: Garland, 1992. 12v. ISBN 0-8153-0573-7.

This magnificent multivolume sourcebook provides some 300 essays by various scholars and specialists on early modern philosophers of the seventeenth century and their work. These articles were written over a period of sixty-three years, from 1926 to 1989, and were published in fifty different sources. The work provides a near-definitive examination of the philosophical influences of that important time period as shaped by modern science, politics, religion, and commerce. Volume 1 treats Descartes; volume 2, Grotius to Gassendi; volume 3, the Cartesians; volume 4, Port-Royal to Bayle; volume 5, Hobbes; volume 6, British philosophers; volume 7, natural scientists; volumes 8 and 9, Locke; volume 10, Spinoza; volume 11, Malebranche; and volume 12, Leibniz. Each volume supplies from thirteen to thirty-seven articles dealing with some aspect of the subject's work and thought. Relevant connections between the philosopher's various thought systems are explored, synthesized, and evaluated by the different writers.

79. **Fifty Major Philosophers: A Reference Guide**. Diane Collinson. New York: Routledge, 1987. 170p. ISBN 0-4150-3135-4.

This modest effort was written primarily for nonspecialists or students, to enable them to understand the views of fifty of the most important philosophers from Thales to Sartre. It represents a highly selective collective biography which provides a good read. As is true of any other work of similar nature, the major criticism relates to the judgment or decision with respect to which philosophers are to be omitted. All those selected are deceased, and are major thinkers who have had some influence on the Western tradition. Biographical sketches are clearly written and easily digested and are accompanied by a brief exposition of the philosopher's thought system and chief directions. Each entry contains a brief bibliography of suggested readings designed to aid further inquiry. Arrangement of entries is chronological; there is a glossary of some fifty terms.

80. **Great Thinkers of the Western World: The Major Ideas and Classic Works of More Than 100 Outstanding Western Philosophers**. Ian P. McGreal, ed. New York: HarperCollins, 1992. 572p. ISBN 0-06-270026-X.

Written for the undergraduate level, this work provides a useful perspective on the thoughts and thought systems of 116 thinkers from various fields of philosophy, the sciences, and the social sciences. Thinkers range from ancient Greek philosophers to twentieth-century scientists. All are major in terms of their importance and influence on Western culture. The work is similar to the Magill publication (entry 64) in its arrangement and narrative treatment. Entries are arranged chronologically by birthdate of subjects and begin with a summary of the individual's principal ideas, followed by a biographical and descriptive commentary on writings and contributions. Entries conclude with a brief bibliography of secondary sources. Thirty-five contributors, specialists in the field, have signed their essays and furnished a total package which successfully conveys the subject matter with clarity and lucidity.

81. **International Directory of Philosophy and Philosophers, 1993-1994.** 8th ed. Ramona Cormier and Richard H. Lineback, eds. Bowling Green, OH: Philosophy Documentation Center, Bowling Green State University, 1993. 451p. ISBN 0-912632-94-1.

A companion and supplementary work to *Directory of American Philosophers* (entry 77), this publication excludes the United States and Canada. A pattern has emerged in which a new edition appears every three to four years (7th ed. 1990), an improvement over its earlier irregular frequency (1st ed., 1966; 2d ed., 1972). There is expanded coverage with more than 100 pages over its predecessor. Like its companion work, the format is predictable. Part 1 covers international organizations of philosophy, while part 2 remains the major contribution, listing college and university philosophy departments alphabetically by country or region and providing listings of faculty members. Part 3 contains the indexes, which permit access by name of philosopher, university, center, society, journal, or publisher.

82. **The Library of Living Philosophers.** Paul A. Schilpp, ed. Evanston, IL: Northwestern University, 1939-1949 (v.1-7); Open Court, 1952- . v.8- . ISSN 0075-9139.

Considered a major series in contemporary philosophy, each volume is devoted to a bio-bibliographical study of a single philosopher. The format of the series has remained constant, and one can generally expect the following sequence of information: a philosophical autobiography which emphasizes the philosophical position of the individual; a series of critical, expository essays on the philosopher by well-known scholars; and a reply by the philosopher. Bibliographies are provided. A slight departure occurred in the case of Sartre (v.16, 1981), whose failing eyesight did not permit him to read and respond to the essays. The format has worked well through the years in facilitating discussion and airing of viewpoints of prominent philosophers. By early 1993, 21 volumes had been completed, the most recent one being on A. J. Ayer (1992). Two philosophers have been covered twice: a second edition appeared for Jaspers in 1981, and for John Dewey in 1982.

A useful online source is *Living Philosophers*, which provides bio-bibliographies of living philosophers. Produced by the University of Dusseldorf, it is written in German. It is available from the University through contact with Professor Dr. Norbert Henrichs.

83. **Philosophen-Lexikon: Handwörterbuch der Philosophie nach Personen.** Werner Ziegenfuss. Berlin: de Gruyter, 1949-1950. 2v.

A standard biographical dictionary in the field, this work covers philosophers of all countries from all periods of time. There is an emphasis on nineteenth- and twentieth-century individuals. For each entry, there is a biographical sketch, a critical and analytical commentary of the person's contribution or impact, a listing of the major publications (*Schriften*), and an index-listing of works (both monographs and articles) that evaluate his or her contributions (*Literature*). Known for its extensive bibliographies, which in many cases make up the bulk of the entries, this work has stood the test of time. Despite a definite bias toward German philosophers (Kant gets thirty-four pages to Plato's ten), it remains a useful source of information.

Metzler Philosophen Lexikon: dreihundert biographisch-werkgeschichtliche Portrats von den Vorsokratikern bis zu den Neuen Philosophen, produced under the direction of Mitarbeit von Christel Dehlinger et al. (Stuttgart: Verlagsbuchhandlung, 1989), furnishes nearly 300 biographical essays of philosophers from all time periods, along with a picture and brief bibliography for each entry. Essays are signed by contributor-specialists. There is an index of names.

84. **Thinkers of the Twentieth Century.** 2d ed. Roland Turner, ed. Chicago: St. James Press, 1987. 977p. ISBN 0-912289-83-X.

An excellent biographical dictionary that first appeared in 1984 and then was considerably expanded through recommendations of librarians and reviewers for more mathematicians and scientists. With the addition of 50 individuals, 480 persons are now covered. About 100 of these are philosophers in the strict sense (Sartre, Buber, Wittgenstein, etc.), but many others were known for their philosophical impact (Gandhi, Durkheim, C. S. Lewis, etc.). Most of the thinkers were writers whose contributions influenced our times. There is a biographical sketch for each individual, accompanied by a listing of his or her books. Also, a list of biographies and a list of critical studies are included. An excellent feature is the interpretive essay of approximately 2,000 words, written by an informed contributor, which analyzes the individual's life and influence. The lack of a subject index is the main drawback to an otherwise extraordinary research tool.

85. **Women Philosophers: A Bio-Critical Sourcebook.** Ethel M. Kersey and Calvin O. Schrag, eds. New York: Greenwood Press, 1989. 230p. ISBN 0-313-25720-5.

This work opens with an excellent informative essay furnishing a useful thematic perspective on the historical influence of women in philosophy. Included here are some 150 biographical sketches of women who have been identified as having written or taught in the field. All traditional areas of philosophy, such as metaphysics and logic, are represented and the work is of historical nature because most biographees were born before 1920. All or nearly all are contributors to the Western tradition, and their major ideas are examined in clear fashion. Both primary and secondary sources are listed in bibliographies for each entry. There is a useful table of quick reference in the appendix identifying dates, countries, and so on for women in the field; there is a name index.

A bibliographic effort that seeks to help establish the work of women philosophers within the corpus of the field is Else M. Barth's *Women Philosophers: A Bibliography of Books Through 1900* (Philosophy Documentation Center, 1992). Listings include books both by and about women philosophers. Arrangement is by category, and there are cross-references to related works. Most of the books are products of the twentieth century. The works are not evaluated critically. There is a name index.

HISTORIES

86. **A History of Greek Philosophy.** William Keith Chambers Guthrie. Cambridge: Cambridge University Press, 1962-1981; repr. 1986. 6v. ISBN 0-521-05160-6 (v.2).

Since the appearance of the first volume in 1962, this work has been extolled by scholars for its erudition, technical accuracy, and insight, while at the same time remaining lucid and readable. Beginning with the pre-Socratics of early vintage in volume 1, it progresses to the later pre-Socratics in volume 2, and to the fifth century in volume 3. Plato is covered in his earlier period in volume 4, and his later period in volume 5. The final volume is devoted to Aristotle. The six volumes comprise a monumental contribution to the study of classical philosophy, even though Guthrie died before fulfilling his intention to provide a complete link to neo-Platonism. Each volume is thoroughly documented with references, and provides a strong bibliography and an index.

Although technically not a series, Cambridge later began to publish single-volume histories, through the efforts of influential scholars, that provide excellent perspective for students and specialists. *The Cambridge History of Later Greek and Early Medieval Philosophy*, edited by Arthur H. Armstrong (1970) established the pattern for this sequential coverage through a collaborative effort of eight scholars. Historical exposition is excellent in treating the development of variations of Platonic-Aristotelian systems and their impact over a 1,400-year period from 300 B.C. to 1100 A.D. Cogent thinking, historical accuracy, and excellent documentation have been continued in subsequent publications. *The Cambridge History of Later Medieval Philosophy: From the Rediscovery of Aristotle to the Disintegration of Scholasticism, 1100-1600*, edited by Norman Kretzmann et al. (1982), continues the coverage another 500 years. *The Cambridge History of Renaissance Philosophy*, edited by Charles B. Schmitt et al. (1988), covers the historical development of the Renaissance from 1500 to 1600 A.D. In all these volumes, bibliographies of primary and secondary sources are recognized for their value to students and specialists.

87. **The History of Philosophy.** Emile Brehier. Trans. by Joseph Thomas and Wade Baskin. Chicago: University of Chicago Press, 1963-1969. 7v.

Originally published in France during the period 1926-1932, this work went through eight editions before it was translated into English. Through the years it has become a standard history, known for its clarity and comprehensive nature. The bibliographies for each chapter are selective and considered of high quality. Volume 1 covers the Hellenic Age; volume 2, the Hellenistic Age and Roman Age; volume 3, the Middle Ages and the Renaissance; volume 4, the seventeenth century; volume 5, the eighteenth century; volume 6, the nineteenth century, period of systems, 1800-1850; and volume 7, contemporary philosophy since 1850. The translation, mainly the work of Baskin, is highly readable and informative, and its presence will be appreciated in any philosophy collection.

88. **A History of Philosophy.** Frederick Charles Copleston. New York, Image Books, 1985. 9v. in 3. ISBN 0-385-23031-1 (v.1); 0-385-23032-X (v.2); 0-385-23033-8 (v.3). Repr. in progress, 1993- . v.1- . ISBN 0-385-46845-8 (v.1).

Written from the standpoint of a scholastic philosopher (Copleston was a Jesuit priest and Professor of the History of Philosophy at Heythrop College, Oxford), this work first appeared in 1945. It has become a standard history of philosophy in the English language through frequent additions and reprints. Beginning with ancient times (Greece and Rome), the coverage progresses through the various schools of Western philosophy—Neoplatonism, Scholasticism, Rationalism, Empiricism, Romanticism, and Utilitarianism—using representative philosophers as labels for each of the volumes. The ninth volume (the most recent) covers French philosophy through Existentialism and Sartre. Each volume was published with a good bibliography and index. This edition employs a compact format that combines three volumes in one for the entire set. The current reprint treats the single volumes individually; three volumes have been issued, bringing coverage through the early Renaissance.

89. **A History of Western Philosophy.** 2d ed. Bertrand Russell. New York: Simon & Schuster, 1961; repr. 1984, London: Unwin. 895p. ISBN 0-04-100045-5 (pbk).

Originally developed as a series of lectures for presentation at the Barnes Foundation in Pennsylvania, the purpose of this work is to portray the philosophy of the West as an "integral part of social and political life." That Russell achieved this purpose was a point of question among reviewers at the time. Criticized for a superficial treatment of both history and philosophy and a highly opinionated style that gave short shrift to thinkers whose positions he found politically disagreeable, Russell's work is still regarded as one of the important popularizations. There is an emphasis on social, economic, and political conditions reflecting the author's progressive leanings. Coverage is given to all major philosophers and many minor ones. It is certainly one of the more interesting works in the field.

5 ◆ ACCESSING INFORMATION IN RELIGION

WORKING DEFINITION OF RELIGION

The word *religion* is thought to derive from the Latin *religare*, which means "to bind," thus offering two alternative explanations for the general use of the term: either as a set of beliefs to which the follower is devoted or bound, or, as McLeish suggests, "that which binds things together ... and which enables mankind to live in harmony with the animal world and with the gods."[1]

More broadly stated, the study of religion includes both the beliefs and the behaviors that, according to John F. Wilson and Thomas P. Slavens, "express as a system the basic shape or texture of the culture or subculture under observation."[2] Lester Asheim suggested a more familiar definition: religion being "the study of man's beliefs and practices in relation to God, gods, or the supernatural."[3] Either definition allows for the more traditional concept of religion as well as more recent New Age concepts of spirituality.

Religion influences other disciplines of the humanities and the social sciences in a way no other discipline, with the possible exception of language, does. Every student will be able to identify religious influences and themes in art, music, literature, drama, history, anthropology, law, sociology, and psychology. Walter Kaufmann's chapter on religion in his *The Future of the Humanities* (Crowell, 1977, pp. 126-53), suggests that the only appropriate way to teach religion in higher education is to use an interdisciplinary approach. In recommending that mode, he says, "Religion is far too important to be left to theologians."[4]

There are many approaches to the study of religion. The most prevalent include the historical approach, the social science approach, and the study of the spiritual/phenomenological aspects. A discussion of these is found in John Macquarrie's article "Religion," in *Academic American Encyclopedia* (rev. 1992, v.16, pp. 137-41). The article includes a map of the world's religions. A broad perspective on religion and its literature is offered by Jaroslav Pelikan in the introductory chapter of a compendium entitled *The World Treasury of Modern Religious Thought* (Little, Brown & Co., 1990). The articles on religion in the latest *Encyclopaedia Britannica* (15th edition) offer excellent background reading for the librarian. J. Gordon Melton's *New Age Encyclopedia* (Gale, 1990) identifies New Age spiritual issues as well as information on other related concepts.

MAJOR DIVISIONS OF THE FIELD

Religions are commonly classified as being predominantly sacramental, prophetic, or mystical. Sacramental religions place great emphasis on the observation of ritual and on the sacredness of certain objects. Eastern Orthodoxy and Roman Catholicism are familiar examples. Prophetic religions emphasize the communication of the Divine Will in verbal form, often with strong moralistic emphasis. Islam and Protestantism reflect this approach. Mystical religions stress direct encounter with God and view words, rituals, and sacred objects as auxiliary at best, or hindrances at worst, to the full communion that is seen as the ultimate goal of all religious striving. Certain branches of Hinduism and Buddhism are example of this type of religion.

The literature generated by the religions of the world may be conveniently analyzed under four predominant headings: (1) personal religion; (2) theology; (3) philosophy of religion; and (4) science of religion.

Personal religion is the primary and most direct source of religious writing. It is intimately related to the experiences of the individual and reflections about their significance. A major class of documents in this category is the sacred scriptures of the world's great religions. Closely related to the sacred writings are those documents of explication and interpretations commonly known as commentaries. Finally, there is a much larger body of literature that does not have the same authoritative standing as the sacred scriptures and their commentaries. Works in this category may be devotional, autobiographical, or biographical. In this group are also included a large number of popularizations.

Theology is an attempt to express in intellectually coherent form the principal doctrines of a religion. It is the product of reflection upon the primary sources of religion. It differs from philosophy in that the basic truth of the religious position is accepted, and attention is given to its systematic and thoughtful exposition. The field has many subdivisions. Within the Christian tradition, systematic (or topic-oriented) theology and biblical theology have been especially important, but there is also a substantial body of literature on moral, ascetic, mystical, symbolic, pastoral, philosophical, liturgical, and natural theology as well.

The philosophy of religion is an attempt to relate the religious experience to other spheres of experience. It differs from theology in that it makes fewer assumptions about the truth of a religious position, at least in the beginning. It differs from philosophy in its selection of religion as the area for speculative investigation. Perhaps it is best described as a bridge between philosophy and theology. The article in the *Encyclopaedia Britannica* (v.15, pp. 592-93) treats philosophy of religion in a direct and informative way.

The science of religion has also generated a substantial body of literature. Here, emphasis is placed on comparative and historical methods, with no presuppositions about (and possibly no interest in) the truth or falsity of the religions being examined. Whereas the locus of interest in the first three categories is usually one of the world's living religions, this is not always the case in the scientific study of religion, where a purely objective approach to the description and comparison of religious phenomena represents the ideal.

HELPFUL RESOURCES FOR STUDENTS, LIBRARIANS, AND GENERAL READERS

The student wishing to read more about religion and its subfields will find it helpful to go back to *Religion: A Humanistic Field*, by Clyde A. Holbrook (Prentice-Hall, 1963); *Religion*, edited by Paul Ramsey (Prentice-Hall, 1965); and *Religion in America*, by Winthrop S. Hudson (4th ed., Scribner's, 1987). (Unfortunately, the first two titles, still excellent despite their age, are now out of print.)

More recent guiding material specifically for the librarian and serious researcher are Edward D. Starkey's *Judaism and Christianity: A Guide to the Reference Literature* (Libraries Unlimited, 1991) and *Religion and the American Experience, 1620-1900, A Bibliography of Doctoral Dissertations* by Arthur P. Young and E. Jens Holley (Greenwood Press, 1992). The latter is one in Greenwood's extensive series of more than 25 titles, "Bibliographies and Indexes in Religious Studies," a series that should be consulted for other useful titles. In the same series, Michael A. Fahey's compilation *Ecumenism: A Bibliographical Overview* (Greenwood Press, 1992) will lead the user to more than 1,300 books and journal titles on ecumenism. Another useful title for the librarian and scholar of religion is the third edition of James P. McCabe's *A Critical Guide to Catholic Reference Books* (Libraries Unlimited, 1989).

E. T. Thompson's "Religious Records," in *Researcher's Guide to Archives and Regional History Sources* (Library Professional Publications, 1988, pp. 74-77), addresses the use of archival materials in religious studies. The student should not overlook entries in the literature indexes under headings like "Religious Archives" for help in locating guides and finding tools for special collections. See, for example, *Researching Modern Evangelism; A Guide to the Holdings of the Billy Graham Center, with Information on Other Collections*, by R. D. Schuster and others (Greenwood Press, 1990).

A general perspective for the librarian is still well represented by Lester Asheim's chapter on religion in *The Humanities and the Library* (American Library Association, 1956). Gary Ebersole and Martha S. Alt's chapter "Religion," in the second edition of *The Humanities and the Library*, edited by Nena Couch and Nancy Allen (American Library Association, 1993), adds up-to-date profiles of religion librarianship and references to readings for specialists and generalists as well. The anthology of works previously mentioned, edited by Jaroslav Pelikan (*The World Treasury of Modern Religious Thought* [Little, Brown & Co., 1990]) offers the broadest coverage of carefully selected representative authors, from Karl Marx to Mahatma Gandhi, Martin Luther King, and Paul Tillich. The anthology, along with Edward Lundin and Anne H. Lundin's forthcoming and equally thought-fully prepared *Contemporary Religious Ideas Bibliographic Essays* (Libraries Unlimited, 1995), will prove of great help in working with all types of users: ministers and rabbis, religious educators, library selection committees, and students at all levels, from high school to seminarians.

Religious scholar John F. Wilson has contributed a great deal to the librarian's understanding of religious studies. With Paul Ramsey, he edited *The Study of Religion in Colleges and Universities* (Princeton University Press, 1970), a report that places the evolving area we call religious studies in the context of the seminary, the graduate school, and the full service university. More recently, he contributed the survey of religious literature portion of *Research Guide to Religious Studies*, co-authored with Thomas P. Slavens (American Library Association, 1982).

Bibliographic guides by Cyril J. Barber, including his *Introduction to Theological Research* (Moody Press, 1982), reflect the more conservative religious viewpoint. His *Introduction* includes information on how to use the library, useful material for the intended audience of beginning Bible students.

The librarian has a wide range of journal articles, brief publications, and chapters to consult on religious material, though a good many of the sources are older. A search of the index *Library Literature* (H. W. Wilson) for the period 1988 through 1993 reveals a considerable emphasis on acquisitions and on machine-readable material. The latter topic is discussed in a later section entitled "Computers in Religion."

Collection development and evaluation are served well by W. Griffin's bibliographic essays and reviews in *Library Journal* and *Publishers Weekly*; *PW* regularly features semiannual listings (for example, "Spring 1992 Religious Books, " in the February 10, 1992, issue) as well as periodic coverage of religious bestsellers. Reviews are also featured regularly in the journal *Catholic Library World*. With religion being a large and diverse area of publishing, religious books are well represented in the library and publishing literature.

Selection and acquisition of religious material for libraries are addressed in B. E. Deitrick's *A Basic Book List for Church Libraries* (Church and Synagogue Library Association, 1988). A special issue of *Library Acquisitions* (v.15, no. 2 [1991]: 145-227) is devoted to collection development of religious material. R. Singerman edited the issue, which includes articles on such diverse materials as Liberation theology in Latin America and obtaining and preserving Buddhist materials. The issue also includes W. J. Hook's "Approval Plans for Religious and Theological Libraries" (pp. 215-27).

Collection development in specialized areas is also addressed in David H. Partington, "Islamic Literature: Problems in Collection Development," *Library Acquisitions: Theory and Practice* 15 (1991): 147-54, and, in the same journal issue, S. Peterson, "From Third World to One World: Problems and Opportunities in Documenting New Christianity" (pp. 177-84).

The special area of children's books in religion is thoroughly covered in the periodical literature. Both *Publishers Weekly* and publications of the Church and Synagogue Library Association offer recommendations for teachers and librarians who work with children.

Finally, Charles Harvey Arnold's bibliographical essay, "Philosophy and Religion" (*Library Trends* 15 [January 1967]: 459-77), is still useful.

Organizing religious materials is another important area for the librarian. "The Classification of Philosophy, Religion, and the Occult," in D. W. Langridge's *Classification and Indexing in the Humanities* (Butterworth's, 1976, pp. 59-77) remains useful, but the user will also want to see *Classifying Church or Synagogue Library Materials*, 2d revised edition, by D. B. Kersten (Church and Synagogue Library Association, 1989). Specific issues concerning the organization of religious materials are also discussed in articles such as W. P. Collins, "Classification of Materials on the Baha'i Religion: Expansion of Library of Congress BP300-395," *Cataloging and Classification Quarterly* 8 (1987): 99-133; and A. R. Carr and N. S. Strachan, "Development of a System for Treatment of Bible Headings in an OPAC

Catalog at Aberdeen University," *Catalogue and Index* no. 95 (Winter 1989): 5-6. The librarian involved with cataloging will need to keep up-to-date by consulting any ongoing revisions of both Dewey Decimal and Library of Congress schemes.

USE AND USERS OF INFORMATION IN RELIGION

There continues to be a distinct lack of use and user studies in the area of religion. This may be the result of the very diverse nature of religious literature and the multiple viewpoints represented, along with the wide audience served by this literature. Users of historical materials, for example, are unlikely to be users of devotional and inspirational literatures; indeed, few libraries will include devotional, informative, historical, and the wide range of doctrinal-interpretive works. The difficulty of investigating uses of literature through citation studies, a method useful in some other fields in the humanities, is compounded by the fact that many uses of the religious literature do not result in publication, that many references made to scriptural works are not formally cited, and that religious publications have a remarkably low rate of citation in general. Indeed, David P. Hamilton, in an article entitled "Research Papers: Who's Uncited Now?" (*Science* 251 [January 4, 1991]: 25), notes that 98.2 percent of published papers in religion are uncited five years after publication. There is a continuing need for further investigation into the use of religious materials; Gleason and Deffenbaugh called for such studies in their *Collection Management* article "Searching the Scriptures ..." (vol. 6 [Fall/Winter 1984]: 107-17), cited in the last edition of this guide.

Two religious periodicals were among the humanities journals sampled for the age of references cited in Derek J. de Solla Price's now-classic "Price's Index" paper ("Citation Measures of Hard Science, Soft Science, Technology and Non-Science" in *Communication among Scientists and Engineers,* edited by C. E. Nelson and D. K. Pollock [Heath, 1970, pp. 3-22]). Both journals (*Anglican Theological Review* and *Journal of the American Academy of Religion*) cited more references, and more recent references, than any other humanities journals among the seventeen studied. The Price study suggests a methodology that could be fruitfully used to look closer at citation, a measure of use, in the religious literature. John W. Heussman's "The Literature Cited in Theological Journals and Its Relation to Seminary Library Circulation" (Ph.D. dissertation, University of Illinois, 1970) provides a broader view of the use of theological journals in a specific setting, but it is evident that use and user studies in religion are still needed to give further direction in publishing and librarianship.

COMPUTERS IN RELIGION

Until recently, concordancing and word index construction were the primary focuses for computing in the area of religion. D. M. Burton has written extensively on the subject in the journal *Computers and the Humanities.* John Hughes's *Bits, Bytes and Biblical Studies* (Zondervan, 1987) also addresses all aspects of computers in religious and biblical studies, and provides descriptive annotations of research projects and products. Since the late 1980s, there have been scores of articles on topics related to computers in religion: subjects addressed include the use of online databases, methods and tools for text analysis, Internet resources, new electronic archives for scholarly use and, still, concordance construction methods and programs.

Online databases serving the field of religion include *Religion Index One* and *Two*, produced by the American Theological Library Association and available through multiple vendors. Newer on the online horizon are numerous Bible versions, some available on the Internet. Scholars in religion will also find the following databases to be of importance: *Dissertation Abstracts Online*, *Arts and Humanities Search*, *SocialSciSearch*, *Magazine Index*, *Books in Print*, and *Philosophers Index*. General history and periodical indexes will also be helpful for some topical searches.

CD-ROM databases have become widely available in libraries and scholars' workstations. Lucy Buck and Travis Nicholls provide a list of humanities resources on CD-ROM in "Arts and Humanities Sources on CD-ROM," *CD-ROM Professional* (March 1991): 96-100. Their list includes: *CD Word*, *Die Bibel*, *The Bible Library*, *Fabs Electronic Library*, *Fabs Reference Bible System*, *Master Search Bible*, and *Religion Indexes* (WilsonDisc). *R&TA* on CD-ROM, then known as *REX* on CD-ROM, is also on the list. *Religion Indexes on CD-ROM* and *R&TA on CD-ROM* are both described there, and articles about them are identified in Mark Stover's "Religious Studies and Electronic Information: A Librarian's Perspective," *Library Trends* 40 (Spring 1992): 687-703. Stover has also published "Optical Bibles: A Review of Three Bible Concordances and Full-Text Theological Reference Sources on CD-ROM," in *Laserdisk Professional* 3 (January 1990): 56-60.

David L. Mealand, of the University of Edinburgh, argues persuasively for increased use of computers in the field of biblical research. In "On Finding Fresh Evidence in Old Texts: Reflections on Results in Computer-Assisted Biblical Research," *Bulletin of the John Rylands University Library of Manchester* 74 (Autumn 1992): 67-88, Mealand states that the electronic availability of large texts gives the religious and literary scholar "something far, far more useful than index or concordance. We can discover all that such invaluable tools can tell us, and far more." W. T. Claassen's "Databases and Information in Biblical Studies: Current State and Future Prospects," in *Databases in the Humanities and Social Sciences 4*, edited by Lawrence J. McCrank (Learned Information, 1989), pp. 164-75, provides similar promise along with some cautions.

Electronic texts enable scholars to study grammar, syntax, and semantics, as well as to investigate authorship, influences, and relationships between various texts and authors. Text archives held at several American institutions support biblical and religious studies: Duke University holds the Duke Data Bank of Documentary Papyri; the Center for Computer Analysis of Texts (University of Pennsylvania) has materials for Septuagint studies; and the Thesaurus Linguae Graecae (TLG) at the University of California at Irvine contains texts of Greek literature from 750 B.C. to about 600 A.D. Other electronic publication projects in the classics which are of interest to religious scholars include Chadwyck-Healey's *Patrologia Latina Database*, and the *Perseus Project*, a hypertext text and image database of classical Greece. The evaluation of the latter is the subject of Delia Neuman's "Evaluating Evolution: Naturalistic Inquiry and the Perseus Project," *Computers and the Humanities* 25 (August 1991): 239-45.

The most prevalent electronic text in the area of religious studies is, of course, the Bible. Several dozen computer "versions" have been reported in the literature, and they are available online from commercial vendors (DIALOG, for example, offers the King James Version as File 297), on diskettes and CD-ROMs, and from various Internet resources. For more on electronic Bibles and biblical texts, see J. A. Wilderotter, *Electronic Bibles and Electronic Texts in Biblical Studies* (Georgetown University, Center for Text and Technology, 1991). Hughes's newsletter *Bits and Bytes Review* updates his compendium reference work mentioned earlier in this section. Mark Stover's "Religious Studies and Electronic Information: A Librarian's Perspective," *Library Trends* 40 (Spring 1992): 687-703, and "Biblical Studies" in Lancashire and McCarty's *The Humanities Computing Yearbook* (Clarendon, 1988), describe additional electronic texts, research projects involving machine-readable texts, and software products that serve varied purposes in religious studies.

The Internet resources on religious subjects are numerous and diverse, and include the full text of many major religious works that can be searched with keywords. A guide to resources is Michael Strangelove's "Electronic Mystic's Guide," which Gilster describes as "an intriguing and exhaustive compendium of Internet sites with a religious theme."[5] Access the Guide via FTP at panda1.uottawa.ca in the directory/pub/religion.

WAIS databases include the following at the access addresses indicated: Australian National University's *Asian Religions Bibliography* (WAIS ANU-Asian-Religions.src); *The Koran* (WAIS Quran.scr); *The Book of Mormon* (WAIS Book_of_Mormon.src); *the Bible* (WAIS Bible.src).

Other Internet offerings in religion that are listed in two or more Internet resource guides include Religious Studies Publications Journal—CONTENTS, a current awareness electronic publication (contents@acadvm1.uottawa.ca) and various news groups (soc.religion.) Software to aid in religious studies is also available over the Net via FTP. Examples include *Bible Browser for Unix*, Bible search programs, and study aids for particular versions. Hahn and Stout's *The Internet Complete Reference* (Osborne McGraw-Hill, 1994) has an extensive list with access addresses. Finally, the gopher file server "Clearinghouse of Subject Oriented Internet Resource Guides" includes several guides in the area of religion.

MAJOR RELIGIOUS ORGANIZATIONS, INFORMATION CENTERS, AND SPECIAL COLLECTIONS

Religious organizations, whether denominational, ecumenical, or academic, are major sources of information. The number of denominational organizations is immense. Certain useful generalizations can be made about the larger religious groups. Generally, they maintain national offices and have extensive publishing programs. Much of their publishing is designed to serve the needs of local congregations for devotional and educational materials. However, a number of the denominational groups do maintain research staffs at the national level, and nearly all of them gather such basic statistics as size of membership, number of congregations or suborganizations, and attendance at religious education programs. Most also issue directories as well as reports of proceedings of national, regional, or state conferences and other activities. Many support theological seminaries and some have parochial schools and colleges as well. A good number of the national offices also maintain collections of historical materials pertaining to the denomination, and some actively promote church libraries among local congregations. Although the Lutherans, Southern Baptists, and United Methodists have such organizations, the Catholic Library Association (461 West Lancaster Avenue, Haverford, PA 19041) probably has the widest range of activities, including a publishing program that includes *Catholic Library World* and the *Catholic Periodical and Literature Index.*

Ecumenical cooperation is exemplified by the work of the National Council of the Churches of Christ in the U.S.A. (575 Riverside Drive, New York, NY 10115). The work of the Council includes the collection of data for and publication of the *Yearbook of American and Canadian Churches.* The Church and Synagogue Library Association (Box 19357, Portland, OR 97280-0357), supportive of library activities regardless of denominational affiliation, publishes *Church & Synagogue Libraries* bimonthly.

The oldest of the academic organizations is the Association for the Sociology of Religion (Lebanon Valley College, Annville, PA 17003-0501), which was founded prior to World War II and which publishes the quarterly journal *Sociological Analysis* as well as a newsletter and biennial directory. A larger academic group is the Society for the Scientific Study of Religion (Purdue University, Pierce Hall #193, West Lafayette, IN 47907). Their publication is *Journal for the Scientific Study of Religion.* A more recently founded organization, the Religious Research Association (Marist Hall #108, The Catholic University of America, Washington, DC 20064), publishes the quarterly *Review of Religious Research.*

Very specialized organizations serving the religious community may also have useful information on very focused topics. Examples of these organizations include the nonprofit Religious Conference Management Association (One Hoosier Dome, Suite 120, Indianapolis, IN 46225), the Religious Education Association (409 Prospect Street, New Haven, CT 06511-2177), and the Religious Public Relations Council (357 Righters Mill Road, Box 315, Gladwyne, PA 19035). These organizations publish quarterly newsletters or journals and hold periodic meetings.

An organization that developed in response to the need for greater coordination of research and improved dissemination of religious information is ADRIS, the Association for the Development of Religious Information Systems. They publish *ADRIS Newsletter* and, irregularly, a directory (ADRIS, c/o Department of Social and Cultural Sciences, Marquette University, 526 North 14th Street, Milwaukee, WI 53233). In Europe, the source of coordination is the International Federation of Institutes for Social and Socio-Religious Research at Louvain, Belgium.

There are far too many educational organizations to mention them all here. However, a good starting point on a search for information in the area is the Council of Societies for the Study of Religion (Valparaiso University, Valparaiso, IN 46383), publisher of the *Directory of Departments of Religion* (annual) and less frequently, *Directory of Faculty of Departments of Religion.* The latter appeared most recently in 1992. Encouraging communication among religious scholars is the goal of the American Society for the Study of Religion (Department of Religion, Duke University, Durham, NC 27108-0964).

Only a few major information centers can be mentioned here. The Office of Research, Evaluation and Planning of the National Council of Churches is noteworthy for its extensive research efforts and its computerized inventory of more than 2,000 documents in the H. Paul Douglass Collection of research reports. The American Theological Library Association (820 Church Street, Suite 300, Evanston, IL 60201) publishes *Religion Index One*, the index available online, in print, and now on CD-ROM, *Religion Index Two*, and many other monographs, bibliographies, and a newsletter.

A major Catholic research effort is conducted by the Center for Applied Research in the Apostolate (3700 Oakview Terrace, Washington, DC 20017). The Centre Protestant d'Etudes et de Documentation (8, Villa du Parc Montsouris, Paris 14e, France) publishes a bulletin and cooperates closely with a similar research center in Strasbourg. IDOC/North America (145 East 49th Street, New York, NY 10017) is part of an international religion documentation network that operates in more than thirty countries.

The subject of special collections in the field of religion would provide material sufficient for an entire book. The best starting point for a search is under "Religion" in *Subject Collections*, 7th ed. (R. R. Bowker, 1993), by Lee Ash and William G. Miller. For more specialized inquiries, look under names of denominations, individual religions, and personal names of religious leaders. G. K. Hall has published library catalogs of some outstanding collections, including the American Jewish Archives (Cincinnati), the Pontifical Institute of Medieval Studies (Toronto), Union Theological Seminary (New York), the Klau Library of Hebrew Union College (Cincinnati), and Dr. Williams' Library (London) and Institut des Etudes Augustiniennes (Paris). Thomas Slavens's *Theological Libraries at Oxford* (Saur, 1984) will also be of interest to students of special collections and religious libraries.

NOTES

[1] Kenneth McLeish, ed., *Key Ideas in Human Thought* (New York: Facts on File, 1993), p. 626.

[2] John F. Wilson and Thomas P. Slavens, *Research Guide to Religious Studies* (Chicago: American Library Association, 1982), p. 4.

[3] Lester Asheim, *The Humanities and the Library* (Chicago: American Library Association, 1956), p. 2.

[4] Walter Kaufmann, *The Future of the Humanities* (New York: Crowell, 1977), p. 152.

[5] Paul Gilster, *The Internet Navigator* (New York: John Wiley & Sons, 1993), pp. 393-94.

6 ◆ PRINCIPAL INFORMATION SOURCES IN RELIGION, MYTHOLOGY, AND FOLKLORE

BIBLIOGRAPHIC GUIDES

General

90. **Church and State in America: A Bibliographic Guide. The Colonial and Early National Periods.** John F. Wilson, ed. New York: Greenwood Press, 1986-1987. 2v. ISBN 0-313-25236-X (v.1). ISBN 0-313-25914-3 (v.2).

This is a collection of bibliographical essays prepared by young scholars in the field. Following each essay is a bibliography of recent writings (the past twenty-five years), although some of the very important older studies are also included. Wilson explains the work in the introduction, in which he describes his preference for the listing of references which are broadly based rather than narrow in scope and are critical rather than prescriptive in tone. Volume 1 covers the colonial and early national periods and volume 2 covers the Civil War to the present. Each volume furnishes eleven bibliographic essays prepared by young scholars covering historical periods, geographical divisions, or topical elements. Each essay is accompanied by a listing of 250 publications. This work is a product of the Project on the Church-State Issue in American Culture at Princeton University, where Wilson has held an endowed chair. It represents an important attempt to enumerate books and articles of comparative and historical nature that examine the early relationships between religious and political interests in our country. There is an author-subject index.

91. **Judaism and Christianity: A Guide to the Reference Literature**. Edward D. Starkey. Englewood, CO: Libraries Unlimited, 1991. 251p. (Reference Sources in the Humanities Series). ISBN 0-87287-533-4.

This is a handy guide to reference sources in religion, furnishing descriptive, and in some cases evaluative, annotations to more than 750 titles. The author is an experienced librarian with a master's degree in religious studies who has focused on what is called the Judeo-Christian tradition. Choice of entries is excellent in providing a fundamental listing of the most important English-language resources, with coverage given to numerous dictionaries as well as bibliographical sources. Annotations vary in length, with a number receiving in-depth commentary. Biblical sources are included and represent a substantial portion of the total. Arrangement of entries is by format or type of source within twenty-one chapters, such as bibliographies or encyclopedias. A useful and informative introduction furnishes some insight into the nature of research and acquisition of resources. An author-title index along with a subject index furnish access.

92. **Reference Works for Theological Research: An Annotated Selective Bibliographical Guide.** 3rd ed. Robert J. Kepple and John R. Muether. Lanham, MD: University Press of America, 1992. 250p. ISBN 0-8191-8564-7.

Developed originally as a textbook for students of his course on theological research methods, the author's third edition represents an enlargement and expansion of the earlier offerings. It now provides annotated entries for some 800 titles arranged within 39 chapters.

Similar to the second edition in format, the first section is given to chapters containing general reference works and religious/theological works of general nature (encyclopedias, handbooks, directories, bibliographies, etc). A newly added chapter on computer-assisted research identifies online and CD-ROM databases as well as their guides. The second section furnishes a topical approach and covers reference literature for research on subjects such as practical theology, worship and liturgy, biblical studies, and various aspects of church history. The scope is limited for the most part to the Christian religion, with only brief coverage of Catholic materials, because they are covered by McCabe's *Critical Guide to Catholic Reference Books* (entry 104). Nevertheless, Kepple and Muether's work is extremely useful for the number of reference items listed. There is an index to authors, editors, titles, and variant titles.

93. **Religious Information Sources: A Worldwide Guide.** J. Gordon Melton and Michael Koszegi. New York: Garland, 1992. 569p. (Garland Reference Library of the Humanities, v.1593; Religious Information Systems Series, v.2). ISBN 0-8153-0859-0.

Melton, a prolific writer in the field of religion, has combined with Koszegi to produce a handy guide to reference books, bibliographies, databases, microform materials, and other publications. The work also serves as a directory of such resource units as oral history collections, professional associations, and research centers. There are more than 2,500 entries arranged in various segments, beginning with the general concept of religion and proceeding to particular religions organized geographically. Christianity is treated in a separate section, with chapters on the various denominations as well as church history. Scope is broad and sweeping (atheism and the occult are not overlooked). The breadth of the work may be faulted in its superficial treatment of any particular element, denomination, or tradition, although certain areas are more thoroughly covered than others. The tool is convenient, however, and will find favor among reference librarians and their patrons.

94. **Research Guide to Religious Studies.** John F. Wilson and Thomas P. Slavens. Chicago: American Library Association, 1982. 192p. (Sources of Information in the Humanities, no. 1). ISBN 0-8389-0330-4.

The first in a series of study guides to various disciplines within the humanities in which Slavens served as general editor and co-author with a noted authority in the field. The intent is to help librarians, students, and other interested persons to use the resources. Wilson, a noted scholar and professor of religious studies at Princeton University, contributed the major part of the work, part 1, "Introduction to Religious Scholarship." His contribution is a group of bibliographic essays in which the field is surveyed and the important sources identified. The second part, by Slavens, a professor of library science at the University of Michigan, is a fifty-page annotated listing of important reference sources. The annotations are detailed, although the listings are somewhat dated. More breadth is found in Kepple (entry 92), who provides more tools but less information about each one. The guide is useful for the intended audience, and the essays enlighten the reader about the state of the literature.

95. **Theological and Religious Reference Materials.** G. E. Gorman and Lyn Gorman. New York: Greenwood Press, 1984-1986. 3v. (In progress, projected 4v.). (Bibliographies and Indexes in Religious Studies). ISBN 0-313-20924-3 (v.1). ISBN 0-313-24779-X (v.2). ISBN 0-313-25397-8 (v.3).

The objective of this series of guides is to introduce students to the complete range of reference sources likely to be encountered in a program of religious studies. At present, three of the projected four volumes have been published, which when completed will approximate the generally accepted divisions of theology. Volume 1 represents general theology; volume 2 establishes coverage of doctrine and church history; and volume 3 embraces practical theology. The final volume, still in progress, will deal with comparative theology, and will also cover non-Christian religions. Each volume is meant to be used separately and provides several thousand annotated entries on the subject matter. There is useful introductory material regarding the nature of the topic in volume 1. Each volume is indexed separately by author, title, and broad subject.

Periodicals

96. **Religious Periodicals Directory.** Graham Cornish, ed. Santa Barbara, CA: ABC-Clio, 1986. 330p. (Clio Periodicals Directories). ISBN 0-87436-365-9.

Religion is interpreted in a broad manner for purposes of inclusion in this directory, and it embraces periodical titles from a variety of related fields (history, anthropology, art, literature, etc.). The scope is international and includes periodicals from a range of denominations and sects. Periodicals are arranged alphabetically under one of six geographic regions: Canada and the United States; Latin America; Europe; Africa; the Middle East; and Asia and the Pacific Region. Countries are listed alphabetically within the regions, and entries include title, publisher, language, frequency, and years of publication. Coverage by indexing and abstracting services is also indicated. There are both title and subject-geographic indexes. More than 1,700 periodicals are covered.

A more recent, but more restrictive, title is *Religion Journals and Serials: An Analytical Guide*, compiled by Eugene C. Fieg, Jr., as part of a series for Greenwood Press (1988). It serves as a very selective guide to some 330 English-language serials selected from a pool of 1,900 on the basis of importance. Entries are arranged alphabetically by title under various subject headings, such as history of religions, denominations, modern faiths, etc. Reviewers have criticized both the quality of annotations and selections for inclusion.

97. **Religious Periodicals of the United States: Academic and Scholarly Journals.** Charles H. Lippy, ed. Westport, CT: Greenwood Press, 1986. 607p. (Historical Guides to the World's Periodicals and Newspapers). ISBN 0-313-23420-5.

This is a highly selective but useful guide for those who seek to identify scholarly and academically oriented journals in the field of religion and religious studies. It is the only guide of its type to provide a complete focus on journals published in this country. It is likely to be the only one to treat the topic in such detail. Slightly more than 100 journals are covered. Each entry is described in terms of its subject matter, publishing history, and extraordinary features. Indexing services are identified. Information regarding title changes, volumes, publication, circulation, and editors are included. Appendices provide material of interest such as a chronology of the periodicals covered and a listing of denomination. A comprehensive index by titles and authors concludes the work.

BIBLIOGRAPHIES AND CATALOGS

General

98. **A Critical Bibliography of Religion in America.** Nelson R. Burr. Princeton, NJ: Princeton University Press, 1961. 2v. ISBN 0-691-07107-1. Repr., University Microfilms, 1976. Microfilm.

Although getting on in years, this work remains important in the field because it provides an excellent bibliographic commentary on the history of religion in the United States. Published as volume 4 (in two volumes) of *Religion in American Life* by James Ward Smith and A. Leland Jamison, the bibliography is often listed separately and is the most important contribution of the set. The bibliography is comprehensive and provides the best coverage of the topic to date, with the inclusion of both primary and secondary sources. It begins with a general introductory section on bibliographic guides, followed by sections covering the evolutionary development of American religion, religion and society, religion in the arts and literature, and intellectual history and theology. Christianity receives the most emphasis, reflecting its prominent position in this country, but other religions are not overlooked. Author and title indexes provide access.

Coverage is continued through *American Religion and Philosophy: A Guide to Information Sources*, by Ernest Robert Sandeen and Frederick Hale (Gale, 1978). This is a general survey of recent secondary and key primary sources which have appeared subsequent to Burr. It emphasizes books and articles published since 1961, and supplies 1,650 entries grouped into 21 different chapters representing chronological periods. A recent effort is *Religion and American Life*, edited by Anne T. Fraker (University of Illinois, 1989), which provides detailed and critical annotations of nearly 250 books and articles. These were selected as part of a project conducted at Indiana University. *Religion and the American Experience, 1620-1900: A Bibliography of Doctoral Dissertations*, compiled by Arthur P. Young and E. Jens Holley (Greenwood Press, 1992), supplies listings for 4,240 doctoral dissertations treating religion in this country. Dissertations have been drawn from *Dissertation Abstracts International* (entry 20), resulting in a well-constructed convenience tool divided into a segment of specific denominations and movements and one of more generic or thematic nature. Author and subject indexes are provided.

*99.   **World Council of Churches Catalogues.** Geneva, Switzerland: World Council of Churches Library, 1989- .

Available since 1989 as an online database, this work identifies the holdings of the library of the World Council of Churches, the international membership organization. Representing one of the well-developed collections of global perspective, the emphasis is on ecumenical history and theology. The work is divided into three major files: the Archives Catalogue, the Library Catalogue, and the Documentation Service Catalogue. Languages employed in the database are English, French, and German. Coverage begins with 1910 and continues to the present day. Updating occurs on a daily basis. The database is available from the World Council of Churches in Geneva, through payment of an annual subscription fee.

Christian

100.   **American Evangelicalism: An Annotated Bibliography.** Norris A. Magnuson and William G. Travis. West Cornwall, CT: Locust Hill, 1990. 495p. ISBN 0-933951-27-2.

Both this bibliography and the following co-entry appeared at the same time and cover much of the same ground. This one has twice the number of books and articles, however, and is the more extensive. Even so, there is a surprising lack of duplication in areas touched by both works, such as "The Bible." One is able to detect a greater emphasis on monographic literature as compared to periodical literature in this title. Also, there is a greater focus on the literature of evangelicalism rather than literature on the topic of evangelicalism. Although the scope of this work is primarily focussed on the twentieth century, the nineteenth century is surveyed as well. Annotations are brief, and there is an author index.

Twentieth Century Evangelicalism: A Guide to the Sources by Edith L. Blumhofer and Joel A. Carpenter (Garland, 1990) is another offering of Garland Reference Library of Social Science (v.521). More selective than the preceding effort, it serves as a useful complementary vehicle with a helpful introductory segment and a good subject index. Annotations are slightly longer than are those of Magnuson and Travis. Another useful tool is *Holy Ground: A Study of the American Camp Meeting*, by Kenneth O. Brown (Garland, 1992), which furnishes good bibliographical coverage of the literature as well as an informative history of the phenomenon, which originated in the South during the late eighteenth and early nineteenth centuries.

101. **Bibliography of Published Articles on American Presbyterianism, 1901-1980.** Harold M. Parker, Jr. Westport, CT: Greenwood Press, 1985. 261p. (Bibliographies and Indexes in Religious Studies, no. 4). ISBN 0-313-24544-4.

Students and scholars of American Protestantism will find this recent work to be of great value in revealing the development of Presbyterianism in this country through a variety of published articles. This work includes but does not limit itself to national and regional secular reviews of a historical nature. Church reviews are also used, but house organs of churches are excluded. The author has compiled an excellent bibliography of nearly 3,000 articles, some of which would most assuredly be overlooked because of their nondescriptive or misleading titles or their surprising presence in certain journals. Entries are arranged by author and indexed by topic. Library locations are indicated, as much of the material is difficult to obtain.

102. **Black Theology: A Critical Assessment and Annotated Bibliography.** James H. Evans, comp. Westport, CT: Greenwood Press, 1987. 205p. (Bibliography and Indexes in Religious Studies, no. 10). ISBN 0-313-24822-2.

Evans has provided a broadly developed, annotated bibliography of the black church in all its aspects. There are 461 books and periodical articles, primarily from religious journals. Three major divisions or sections comprise the work, beginning with the origin and development of black theology, followed by liberation, feminism, and Marxism, and concluding with cultural and global discourse. Within the sections, the entries are arranged alphabetically by author under classifications by denomination and geographical region. A well-developed, cogent essay opens the work and furnishes insight into the nature of black theology. Annotations are informative in providing an awareness of the scope of the selected items. There is an index of names, along with a title index and subject index.

Black Holiness: A Guide to the Study of Black Participation in Wesleyan Perfectionist and Glossolalia Pentecostal Movements, by Charles E. Jones (Library Association/Scarecrow Press, 1987), furnishes a listing of 2,400 books and articles on the Holiness Movement. Existing on the periphery of mainstream religion, these charismatic movements influenced the lives of blacks even before their impact was felt on whites around the turn of the century. Jones has furnished historical and biographical commentary and notes that precede the various sections. This title represents a commendable effort to organize material that is elusive and difficult to locate, and is appreciated by scholars and students.

103. **Christian Communication: A Bibliographical Survey.** Paul A. Soukup. New York: Greenwood Press, 1989. 400p. (Bibliography and Indexes in Religious Studies, no. 14). ISBN 0-313-25673-X.

The author acted on a perceived need to provide a comprehensive bibliography treating all aspects of communication used by Christian churches or utilized in a style consistent with Christian ethics or practices. The work opens with a bibliographic essay identifying issues within a historical framework. Chapter 2 lists general resources: periodicals, directories, bibliographies, and catalogs. Chapters 3 to 9 furnish the topical approach, covering communication theory, history, rhetoric, interpersonal communication, intercultural communication, and mass communication. There are 1,311 entries; all are numbered in sequence. Annotations are thorough, reflecting the author's expertise in both theology and communications; books, articles, and dissertations are treated. The work is indexed by author, title, and subject.

A specialized tool is *Speaking in Tongues: A Guide to Research on Glossolalia*, edited by Watson E. Mills (Eerdmans, 1986), which supplies a collection of essays, commentaries, and research studies written between 1954 and 1980 along with a bibliography of relevant writings. The work opens with an introductory essay providing a historical overview of the topic. The essays are written by theologians, scholars, historians, and psychologists, and provide divergent opinions on the nature of this widespread phenomenon. There are indexes of names and of Bible references.

104.   **Critical Guide to Catholic Reference Books.** 3d ed. James Patrick McCabe. Englewood, CO: Libraries Unlimited, 1989. 282p. (Research Studies in Library Science, no. 20). ISBN 0-87287-621-7.

Both of the earlier editions (1971 and 1980) were considered meritorious efforts in their thorough coverage of the subject, furnishing well-written descriptive and evaluative annotations of about 1,000 reference works expressing Catholic perspectives on both theological and secular issues. The new edition has been expanded somewhat in its inclusion of older titles excluded in previous editions as well as new titles. It retains its basic format of five major chapters dealing with general reference works, theology, the humanities, the social sciences, and history. The main emphasis continues to be on English-language titles, although foreign-language works are given ample coverage if available on this continent. Annotations are cogent, and access is provided through a comprehensive author, title, and subject index.

105.   **Liberation Theologies: A Research Guide**. Ronald G. Musto. New York: Garland, 1991. 581p. (Garland Reference Library of Social Science, v.507). ISBN 0-8240-3624-7.

With the increasing interest in freedom of individuals, there has been an impetus to what is called liberation theology, emphasizing the liberalizing influences and emancipation from oppression. Musto, an acknowledged advocate of these reforms generally opposed by conservative and fundamentalist theologians, begins with an informative introductory essay describing the meaning and significance of liberation theology. Nearly 1,300 books are listed along with full and detailed annotations. Some contain vigorous emotional description—for instance, Cardinal Ratzinger is labeled a "witch hunter." Entries are arranged in nine chapters by time period, geographical area, and topic. In perceiving that liberation theology originated almost as a grass-roots Christian response to oppression (poverty, sexism, racism), Musto has represented the works of gay theology, black theology, and feminist theology in fair manner, along with the writings of conservative opponents. There is an index of authors and one of titles.

106.   **Women and Religion: A Bibliographic Guide to Christian Feminist Liberation Theology**. Shelley D. Finson, comp. Buffalo: University of Toronto Press, 1991. 207p. ISBN 0-8020-5881-7.

As part of the increasing vigor with which the new liberation theology is being pursued, comes this listing of books, articles, dissertations, reports, and other materials published during a thirteen-year period from 1975 to 1988. Feminist theology, along with gay and black theology, represents part of the reform movement forcing changes in mainstream religion and language usage within the Bible. The writings included here are recognized for their liberation perspective and critical interpretation of the female experience within the church traditions. Arrangement of entries is by subject (e.g., Bible, history, ministry, spirituality, and so on). This tool is of value to students and teachers who wish to examine the various issues surrounding feminism and the church, and serves as an excellent resource for women's studies. Of course, one must consult current indexes for the large amount of material that has appeared subsequent to this guide's publication.

Non-Christian

107.   **Bibliography of English-Language Works on the Babi and Baha'i Faiths, 1844-1985**. William P. Collins. Oxford: G. Ronald, 1990. 521p. ISBN 0-85398-315-1.

The author had served as the director of the International Baha'i Library at the Baha'i World Centre in Haifa, Israel, from 1977 to 1990 and was well-prepared to take up this task. This is the most comprehensive bibliography of the subject in its attempt to identify all books, pamphlets, theses, and journal articles published in the English language on the Babi and Baha'i faiths. Approximately 7,400 entries are furnished within 13 sections. The first six cover Baha'i writings of Baha'v'llah, the Babi 'Adbu'l-Baha, and others. The remaining sections treat the secondary sources. There is a well-developed introduction that outlines the Baha'i literature. Each section contains explanatory notes with annotations for the most important entries. This has become the standard work in the field, and there are plans to continue the coverage with supplements for the period subsequent to 1985. There are detailed indexes by name, title, and subject.

108. **Guide to Buddhist Religion.** Frank E. Reynolds et al. Boston: G. K. Hall, 1981. 415p. (The Asian Philosophies and Religions Resource Guides). ISBN 0-8161-7900-X.

One of the initial publications in a projected seven-part series to provide basic resources for the study of Asian religions and philosophies (entries 109 and 110), the guide provides an annotated listing of 4,000 items. Categories, which are used in all volumes, are general history, religious thought, sacred texts, popular practices, religious involvement in social life and politics, ritual and practice, etc. Particular attention is paid to the inclusion of appropriate articles from research journals. It has been noted that there is no annotated listing of journals used in this particular guide. There is an emphasis on English-language materials, and access is provided through author-title and subject indexes.

The most recent addition to the series is David C. Yu's *Guide to Chinese Religion* (1985) which is complementary to the Reynolds work, as it excludes Buddhism. Instead, Yu identifies books and articles on Taoism, Confucianism, Lao Tzu, and even Maoism. Ancient superstitions are included within the format, which is similar to others in the Hall series.

109. **Guide to Hindu Religion.** David J. Dell et al. Boston: G. K. Hall, 1981. 461p. (The Asian Philosophies and Religions Resource Guides). ISBN 0-8161-7903-4.

An annotated bibliography of 2,000 items, this work follows the procedure and pattern for the series (entries 108 and 110). There is an excellent breadth in terms of coverage, with consideration given to art and anthropology. Annotations are well developed and descriptive of the topic under which the entry appears. Singled out for special praise by reviewers is this guide's section on bibliographies and research aids. An attractive special feature for this work is its annotated listing of journals. An unfortunate circumstance is the author's oversight in providing adequate access. There is neither a subject nor a title index, but only an author approach. Happily, this inadequacy is not shared by other volumes in the series. Still, the work is extremely important for what it does.

110. **Guide to Islam.** David Ede et al. Boston: G. K. Hall, 1983. 261p. (The Asian Philosophies and Religions Resource Guides). ISBN 0-8161-7905-0.

Following the pattern of other volumes in the series (entries 108 and 109), this guide is intended to provide the English-language reader with a sufficient choice of significant publications in order to learn about Islam as a religion and a civilization. Intended for students at both graduate and undergraduate levels, the guide provides an annotated bibliography of nearly 3,000 items, mostly English-language books and articles. Most were published prior to 1977, a drawback for those expecting more recent coverage. As is true of all guides in the series, any of the publications listed may be obtained through the Institute for the Advanced Study of World Religions in photocopy or microformat when not available elsewhere. It is reported that a supplement is being prepared to update the coverage. Like others in the series, this is a useful and welcome effort.

111. **Judaica Americana: A Bibliography of Publications to 1900.** Robert Singerman, comp. New York: Greenwood Press, 1990. 2v. (Bibliographies and Indexes in American History, no. 14). ISBN 0-313-25023-5.

Sponsored by the Center for the Study of the American Jewish Experience at Hebrew Union College, Singerman, a librarian of Judaica at the University of Florida, has produced an extensive new bibliography on the topic. In so doing, he has incorporated all the entries from the standard resource, *An American Jewish Bibliography ...* by A. S. W. Rosenbach (American Jewish Historical Society, 1926), and its three supplements published in 1954,

1958, and 1971. He has extended the coverage to 1900 (from 1850) and has added hundreds of titles. The present effort lists more than 6,500 books, pamphlets, and serials written by both Jews and non-Jews examining the American Jewish experience. Entries are arranged chronologically, and library locations are supplied when known. This is a significant work with appeal to a wide audience ranging from scholars to interested laypersons. A detailed general index provides access by authors, titles, publishers, printers, and subjects.

Jewish Heritage in America: An Annotated Bibliography, by Sharad Karkhanis (Garland, 1988), volume 467 of the Garland Reference Library of Social Science, presents a good array of nearly 325 books and 800 articles of both popular and scholarly literature. The author is the librarian of a community college in New York City and drew his entries from nearly ninety journals spanning a period of more than sixty years from 1925 through 1987. Selection was based on the perceived significance of the topic and its treatment, with recognition of the need to furnish a balanced listing. Excluded are autobiographies, biographies, poetry, and fiction. Availability was a factor, with some emphasis on access through medium-sized libraries. Arrangement of entries is under seven broad categories, all of which are further divided by subcategories. Descriptive annotations are lengthy. Author, title, and subject indexes are furnished.

112. **Sikhs in North America: An Annotated Bibliography**. Darsan Singh Tatla. New York: Greenwood Press, 1991. 180p. (Bibliographies and Indexes in Sociology, v.19). ISBN 0-313-27336-7.

As an authority on Sikh culture in the West, Tatla furnishes an excellent listing of books, articles, dissertations, reports, newspaper articles, and even audiovisual materials. Annotations tend to be brief, but vary considerably in size, with conferences and symposia treated in greater depth. Arrangement of entries is within topical chapters covering such aspects as employment, education, and family life. These follow an initial chapter on general sources which includes useful listings of special libraries and archives, as well as newspapers and journals. There is an index of names but not subjects. The work follows the pattern set in Tatla's earlier effort, *Sikhs in Britain* (Coventry, UK: Centre for Research in Ethnic Relations, 1987).

Sikhism and the Sikhs by Priya M. Rai (Greenwood Press, 1989) provides an annotated listing of English-language books and articles published since 1965. Entries are topically arranged and represent scholarly effort. There are author, title, and subject indexes.

113. **2,000 Books and More: An Annotated and Selected Bibliography of Jewish History and Thought.** Jonathan Kaplan, ed. Jerusalem: Magnes Press, Hebrew University, 1983. 483p. ISBN 965-223-444-3.

This annotated bibliography of books on Jewish history and thought proposes to furnish students, teachers, and librarians with a basic list of sources of major importance in the study of the topic. International in scope, it includes works in Hebrew, English, German, Spanish, Portuguese, and French. It has proven to be a useful tool both in book selection and in Jewish studies. Major divisions are historical periods, subdivided into smaller time segments or topics. There is also a listing of publications by Jewish communities. Cross-references are employed to link editions published in different languages. Annotations are brief. The introduction is in both English and Hebrew, as is a name index.

A Critical Bibliography of Writings on Judaism, by David B. Griffiths (Mellen, 1988) furnishes a comprehensive two-volume annotated listing of books and articles published in the English language. Most are relatively recent publications and cover the period from ancient to early modern times in part 1. Part 2 treats modern Jewish history, including the Holocaust.

114. **The Yogacara School of Buddhism: A Bibliography**. John Powers. Metuchen, NJ: Scarecrow Press, 1991. 257p. ISBN 0-8108-2502-3.

Sponsored by the American Theological Library Association, Powers has produced a unique specialized bibliography on the Yogacara school of Mahayana Buddhism. As an esoteric study, this work will appeal to a limited number of users primarily from the ranks of academe. The purpose is to list all writings on Yogacara in any languages of the world.

The work is divided into two major segments, the first dealing with the primary sources of scripture written in Sanskrit, Tibetan, and Chinese. The second segment treats secondary sources or studies by modern authors and represents all languages, both Oriental and Occidental. Five separate indexes furnish access to authors and titles of modern, Indian-, Tibetan-, Chinese-, and Japanese-language publications.

A specialized bibliography of more popular nature is *Zen Buddhism: A Classified Bibliography of Western-Language Publications through 1990*, by James L. Gardner (Wings of Fire Press, 1991). This is a comprehensive listing of more than 2,800 books, articles, dissertations, and essays written in various languages. Entries cover the concepts, functions, philosophy, people, and movements and are classified by topic. The work opens with a brief introduction explaining the purpose and composition of the bibliography. There are well-constructed indexes to authors and subjects.

New Alternatives: New Age, Occult, Etc.

115. Bibliography of New Religious Movements in Primal Societies. Harold W. Turner. Boston: G. K. Hall, 1977-1992. 6v. ISBN 0-8161-7927-1 (v.1).

Planned as a series of four volumes initiated in 1977, only volume 1, "Black Africa," and volume 2, "North America," had appeared prior to 1990. Then, with a burst of productive energy following delays caused by relocation and the need to microfilm the documentation, Turner issued volume 3, "Oceania," in 1990; and volumes 4, "Europe and Asia," and 5, "Latin America," both in 1991, and volume 6, "Caribbean," in 1992. This appears to have completed the project, for which the focus has been to represent religious movements "which arise in the interaction of a primal society with another society where there is great disparity of power or sophistication." The volume on Black Africa was designed to correct, supplement, and update *A Comprehensive Bibliography of Modern African Religious Movements*, by Turner and Robert Cameron Mitchell (Northwestern University Press, 1966; repr., University Microfilms, 1985). The second volume on North America emphasizes the United States, with subdivisions of Indian tribes, cults, etc., with smaller sections for Canada and northern Mexico. The additional volumes continue in the same tradition and now provide an important resource for study and scholarship. All volumes contain indexes of authors and sources.

Diane Choquette treats the emergence of new religious movements in this country in *New Religious Movements in the United States and Canada: A Critical Assessment and Annotated Bibliography* (Greenwood Press, 1985). She lists and describes nearly 740 books, articles, and papers housed mainly in the collection of the Graduate Theological Union Library at Berkeley. These movements began to emerge in the 1960s; they are accessed by author-title and subject indexes.

116. Channeling: A Bibliographic Exploration. Joel Bjorling. New York: Garland, 1992. 363p. (Garland Reference Library of Social Science, v.589). ISBN 0-8240-5691-4.

A salient characteristic of New Age religious activity is *trance channeling*, or the transmission of a message from the spirit world through a selected human being. This work is the most extensive bibliography of its kind, identifying more than 2,700 items dealing with the activity. They are listed in several chapters dealing with the history of channeling, channel revelations as found in books, UFO-contactee channeling (including messages from extraterrestrials), and contemporary channeling treating personalities and groups. An important feature is the introductory essay that precedes the chapters and furnishes exposition of various aspects, such as the literature of channeling, mediums, history of different movements, and so on. These essays furnish references that are linked to the entry numbers of listed works, affording a handy guide to especially relevant materials.

The Palmist's Companion: A History and Bibliography of Palmistry, by Andrew Fitzherbert (Scarecrow Press, 1992), is an up-to-date guide to the history and literature of palmistry. There are essays on various aspects of the art preceding an annotated bibliography of 560 entries. A title index provides access.

117. **Magic, Witchcraft, and Paganism in America: A Bibliography.** 2d ed. J. Gordon Melton and Isotta Poggi. New York: Garland, 1992. 408p. (Religious Information Systems, v.3; Garland Reference Library of Social Science, v.723). ISBN 0-8153-0499-4.

In this, the second edition of what has become a standard bibliography in the field, the authors have produced an updated and important volume. The magical community in this country has increased greatly during the past decade, and revision was needed since publication of the first edition took place in 1982. The work is divided into eight major segments, the first seven of which identify relevant topics such as ceremonial magic and traditional Earth religions. These sections supply 2,540 entries representing relevant books and articles. Secret works of various groups are excluded. The eighth section identifies current periodicals from all over the world. Appendices contain a listing of titles on witchcraft found in the New York Public Library in 1908 as well as the curriculum of the A.A. (*Argenteum Astrum*) employed by magical lodges. A name index of authors, editors, compilers, and translators provides access.

118. **Parapsychology: New Sources of Information, 1973-1989.** Rhea A. White. Metuchen, NJ: Scarecrow Press, 1990. 699p. ISBN 0-8108-2385-3.

With this work it would appear that White has established herself as the leading bibliographer on the topic of parapsychology, a field employing scientific methodology in examining unexplained phenomena. This useful bibliographic guide is a continuation and expansion of White's earlier effort issued in 1970, *Parapsychology: Sources of Information*. The present effort covers a period of more than 16 years of published writings. More than 480 books are arranged under 27 subject headings in the chapter on books. These subjects represent content, publication, format, or scope. Entries are numbered in sequence beginning with 343 (since the 1970 work ended with 342). In addition to the books, another 300 entries are furnished in chapters on periodicals, organizations, general sources, government reports, and theses. Entries are arranged alphabetically by author within each section. Annotations for books and organizations are detailed and in some cases are evaluative. There is a glossary along with various listings in the appendices. There are indexes by author, title, and subject.

INDEXES, ABSTRACTS, AND
SERIAL BIBLIOGRAPHIES

*119. **Bulletin signalétique 527: Histoire et Sciences des religions.** Nancy, France: Institut de l'Information Scientifique et Technique (INIST); Paris: Centre National de la Recherche Scientifique (CNRS), 1970- . v. 24- . Q. ISSN 0180-9296.

This important abstracting journal is part of the massive indexing effort undertaken by the Centre National, now taken over to a great degree by INIST. The Centre began indexing periodical literature of the sciences in 1940, then added humanities coverage in 1947. Philosophy and religion were covered together in *Bulletin analytique: Philosophie* (vols. 1-9); *Bulletin signaletique: Philosophie. Science humaines* (vols. 10-14); *Sciences humaines: Philosophie* (vols. 15-22); and *Philosophie, sciences religieuses* (v.23). They were separated in 1970, with each discipline retaining the volume number in its new journal title. From 1970 to 1978, this title was known as *Bulletin signaletique 527: Sciences religieuses*.

Now many disciplines have been added, including journals in the social sciences. All are covered by separate indexes bearing a number and subtitle. Thousands of international journals are covered on a quarterly basis in the humanities and social sciences and monthly in the sciences. The information is stored in a computerized database identified by a collective acronym *FRANCIS*. This particular index is available online and in CD-ROM as part of *FRANCIS*. *Histoire et Sciences des Religions* which (as of 1992) contains about 156,000 citations, half of them with abstracts, dating from 1972 to the present. It adds about 2,500 records per quarter and is available through INIST.

120. **Catholic Periodical and Literature Index.** Haverford, PA: Catholic Library Association, 1967/1968- . v.14- . Bi-mo. with bienn. cum. ISSN 0008-8285.

The leading current index of the Catholic faith, this work was created from a combination of two earlier efforts. *Guide to Catholic Literature, 1888-1940* (Romig, 1940) provided an author-subject-title approach in identifying books and booklets pertinent to the Catholic faith or by Catholic authors. This was continued as an annual publication with four-year cumulations until 1967. *Catholic Periodical Index* (Catholic Library Association) indexed periodicals in the English language from 1939 to 1967 on a quarterly basis, with coverage back to 1930. The present work covers both books and articles. It provides annotations and an author-title-subject approach to several thousand adult books either by Catholics or on subjects of interest to Catholics, published during each calendar year. It regularly indexes some 150 periodicals, primarily in the English language. Articles are indexed by author and subject.

121. **Index to Jewish Periodicals.** Cleveland Heights: The Index, 1963- . Semiann. ISSN 0019-4050.

Beginning as a publication of the College of Jewish Studies in Shaker Heights, Ohio, this small index has held its own through the years. It generally indexes forty to forty-five periodicals relating to the Jewish faith or regarding Jewish life. It is considered an excellent source of information in identifying the thoughts and writings especially of American Jewry. All periodicals are in the English language, and book reviews are indexed. The material is indexed by author and subject and represents a wide range of interests and scholarship. Both popular and scholarly journals are included. The work is numbered as a quarterly, with each of the two issues receiving two numbers (1-2, July-December, and 3-4, January-June).

LC MARC: Hebrew is the quarterly computerized tape version from the Library of Congress which furnishes its cataloging copy of all monographs in Hebrew and Yiddish. It is part of the MARC (machine-readable cataloging) operation and is available through membership in Research Libraries Information Network (RLIN, p. xxi) or from the Library itself. Listing began in 1989.

122. **The Quarterly Index Islamicus.** London: Mansell, 1977-1993. Q. with quinquenn. cum. ISSN 0308-7395.

This index provided good coverage of books, articles, and essays on Islamic subjects. More than 1,300 periodicals are examined, as are anthologies and festschriften. There has been an increased coverage of social science issues in the past few years. This serial grew out of an earlier monographic publication, *Index Islamicus*, 1906-1955, by J. D. Pearson (London University School of Oriental Studies Library, 1958). This provided a catalog of some 26,000 articles in many languages on Islamic subjects. After issuing four supplements (1956-1960, 1961-1965, 1966-1970, and 1971-1975) in which 33,000 additional articles were identified, Pearson began his editorship of the *Quarterly*. The fifth supplement (1976-1980) is in two volumes, with both monographs and articles receiving separate treatment. It cumulates the contents of the first five volumes or twenty issues of the *Quarterly*. Bowker-Saur began to issue *Index Islamicus*, an annual bound volume, for the first time at the end of 1994; for each volume there will be four advance fascicles providing up-to-date information. This replaces the *Quarterly Index Islamicus*.

Islam is an annual index of books, journals, and newspapers available on CD-ROM. Coverage begins with the year 1991, and it is published and distributed by Hassan. The software is produced by Computerland.

*123. **Religion Index One: Periodicals.** Chicago; Evanston, IL: American Theological Library Association, 1949/1953- . Semiann. with bienn. cum. ISSN 0149-8428.

Beginning in 1953, with indexing from 1949, the *Index to Religious Periodical Literature* established itself as the leading current index representing the Protestant viewpoint. With the title change in 1977, this tradition has continued and *RIO* has expanded its coverage to embrace more than 300 titles in Western languages. Book reviews are listed separately, as always. Although concentrating primarily on Protestantism, the index has traditionally demonstrated an ecumenical outlook and still selectively includes several Jewish and Catholic periodicals. It is indexed by subject and author, with a separate index for book reviews. *Religion Index Two: Multi-Author Works* (1976-) first appeared in 1978. *RIT* represents an index of composite works (compilations, anthologies, festschriften, proceedings, etc.) published during the year covered.

The entire file of this very important family dating back to 1949 is available online through DIALOG. *RELIGION INDEX* database is updated each month and has more than 600,000 records. CD-ROM versions are available from ATLA. * *Religion Index One on CD-ROM* has provided coverage of both *RIO* and *Index to Book Reviews in Religion*, with coverage beginning in 1980. A newer offering (April 1993), *Religion Indexes:RIO/RIT/IBRR 1975-on CD-ROM*, furnishes coverage of *RIO*, *RIT*, and *IBRR* from 1975 to the present.

*124. **Religious and Theological Abstracts.** Myerstown, PA: Religious and Theological Abstracts, 1958- . Q. ISSN 0034-4044.

Highly regarded as a nonsectarian abstracting service which covers 300 journals on an international basis. Abstracts are in English and average about 100 words in length. Journals represent a wide range of interests and beliefs and include representative titles of Christian (primarily Protestant), Jewish, and Muslim origins. There are five major categories or topical divisions: biblical, theological, historical, practical, and sociological. Each section is further subdivided, with numbers being given to each entry. Subject, author, and scripture indexes appear on an annual basis in the final issue of each volume. A list of abstractors accompanies each issue and abstracts are generally signed with initials. The work is available from the publisher on CD-ROM as *R&TA on CD-ROM*; it is updated on an annual basis.

125. **Science of Religion: Abstracts and Index of Recent Articles.** Amsterdam: Free University, and Leeds, England: University of Leeds, 1980- . v.5- . Q.

This provides a continuation of an earlier bibliography which enjoyed an excellent reputation in the field. *International Bibliography of the History of Religions* (Leiden, Netherlands: Brill, 1952/1954-1979) was published under the auspices of the International Council for Philosophy and Humanistic Studies by the International Association for the History of Religions and received UNESCO support. An annual publication, it listed books, articles, and reviews for the year covered on the history of the various religions of the world. International in coverage, listings appeared in the language of the original document in a classified arrangement. An author index was provided. The present work retains the same sponsorship, with volumes 1-4 appearing under the title *Science of Religion Bulletin*. It covers approximately 250 journals representing all religions and time periods. Each issue is indexed by author and subject, both of which cumulate in the final issue of each volume.

Répertoire Bibliographique des Institutions Chretiennes (Strasbourg: Centre de Recherches et des Documentation des Institutions Chretiennes) is a semiannual publication that furnishes bibliographic listings of books and articles from more than 1,400 journals and 3,000 books and monographs. It covers all topics related to Christian institutions, from organization and governance to their relations to ethical and theological concepts and actions. The work is available on magnetic tape from the producer.

DICTIONARIES, ENCYCLOPEDIAS, AND HANDBOOKS

General

126. **Contemporary Religions: A World Guide.** Ian Harris et al., eds. Harlow, Essex, UK: Longman; distr., Detroit: Gale Research, 1992. 511p. ISBN 0-582-08695-7.

This is a comprehensive information resource for all faiths and religious branches existing today throughout the world. Coverage is handled through three major segments, beginning with a collection of seven essays on "Major Religious Traditions." These provide background information of the contextual framework of the various entries. Section 2, "Religious Groups and Movements," is the major segment, incorporating more than 800 articles on an array of faiths, cults, and denominations ranging from specific churches to movements and organizations. Included in this directory segment are survey-length articles on such topics as Native-American religions. Entries vary in length from brief overviews of 100 words to lengthier expositions of 2,000 words. Coverage is distributed fairly, with approximately equal representation of denominations within and outside the Judeo-Christian tradition. Part 3 is a "Country by Country Summary" showing the distribution and influence of the different religions. There is a glossary but no bibliography, a serious deficiency for serious students.

127. **A Dictionary of Comparative Religion.** S. G. F. Brandon. New York: Scribner's, 1970; repr. Macmillan, 1988. 704p. ISBN 0-684-15561-3.

Considered a standard in the field, this work of British scholarship covers the beliefs, rituals, important personalities, schools, councils, and sacred books of the various religions of the world. Articles are brief, signed by the contributor, and generally have bibliographies. There is a certain degree of complexity associated with comprehension of some of the articles, which is not true of *Abingdon Dictionary of Living Religions* (Abingdon, 1981). Unlike *Abingdon*, however, this work includes religions not extant and provides a strong focus on intellectual history in its efforts "to treat the various religions proportionately to their significance in the history of human culture." Coverage of the Eastern religions is very strong and sectional editors describe Buddhism, Hinduism, Islam, China, and the Far East. There are no illustrations. The work has a synoptic index which groups all relevant entries under the name of the religion, as well as a general index of names and subjects. For optimal reference service, both Brandon and *Abingdon* should be used.

128. **A Dictionary of Judaism and Christianity**. Dan Cohn-Sherbok. Philadelphia: Trinity Press International, 1991. 181p. ISBN 0-281-04538-0.

The author is a rabbi and known advocate and promoter of Christian-Jewish relations who has succeeded in producing a useful comparative dictionary. Its format and style present a brief treatment of terms, concepts, topics, and issues spanning a wide segment of theology and religion. The design of the work is to represent these matters and furnish an explanation of how they are treated or accommodated by the two religious faiths. Such elements as anointing, education, original sin, and racism (which includes anti-semitism) are juxtaposed in such a way that commonalities are readily seen and appreciated. The treatment of ecumenicism, for example, furnishes an excellent comparison of efforts within each faith and with each other. Few personalities are singled out for separate articles: Abraham, Adam, David, Elijah, and Jesus. The tone of the work is fair, and written in a spirit friendly toward Christianity.

129. **Eerdmans' Handbook to the World's Religions.** R. Pierce Beaver et al., consulting eds. Grand Rapids, MI: Eerdmans, 1982; repr. 1991. 448p. ISBN 0-8028-3563-5.

Another fine product from this reputable publishing house is this handbook treating the world's religions. History, scriptures, worship, and customs are described in an easy-to-use and convenient fashion. Generally brief in coverage, there is great breadth in the scope of this effort, which includes religions both living and dead. Some 300 photographs, 100 in color, add to the attractiveness and appeal of this volume. Development of religion is handled through descriptions of the nature of religious study, personalities and places of major importance, and origins and history. Unlike Brandon (see entry 127), this volume treats Christianity separately, and ancient religions account for about one-third of the text. The "Rapid Fact-finder" is a glossary of terms and personalities. Subject access is provided through a general index.

130. **The Eliade Guide to World Religions**. Mircea Eliade et al. San Francisco: Harper-SanFrancisco, 1991. 301p. ISBN 0-06-062145-1.

Begun shortly before his death in 1986, the work bears Eliade's name as his final publication. Like other products and projects with which he was connected, this guide is an excellent and authoritative handbook to the study of religions. Following a brief introductory essay, there are thirty-three chapters on different religious traditions, both living and defunct. Emphasis has been given to the major traditions (Christianity, Buddhism, Judaism, and Islam). Described in concise but thorough fashion are the histories and doctrines, which are accompanied by useful bibliographies.

The Facts on File Dictionary of Religions, edited by John R. Hinnells (Facts on File, 1984) is a similar product from a noted scholar and authority, in which an attempt has been made to provide an exposition of all religions of the world in relatively compact format. It has succeeded as a reference tool of convenience and covers the various aspects associated with religious bodies. Good coverage is given to astrology, magic, and the occult. Technical terms, leading figures, and deities are covered in a lucid and learned manner.

131. **Encyclopaedia of Religion and Ethics**. A. J. Hastings et al., eds. New York: Scribner's, 1910-1927; repr. 1961, 1969, 1980. 13v. ISBN 0-567-06501-4 (v.1).

Through the years, this work has been recognized as an outstanding example of scholarship and erudition. It remains the most comprehensive religious encyclopedia in the English language and has never been superseded or equalled in its treatment. Although old, it is not outdated, and provides long, scholarly articles on belief systems, customs, various religions, and national characters of religious movements in various countries of the world. Most impressive are the comprehensive articles on various social topics relating to ethical or religious matters, and the depth provided for exposition of various abstractions such as happiness. Anthropology, mythology, folklore, biology, psychology, and economics are among the elements considered in this expansive work. Articles range from brief (personalities get only a few lines of identification) to monographic in length. The final volume has an analytical index, an index to foreign words, an index to scripture passages, and an index to authors of articles. Although the work is of liberal, Protestant authorship, there is little sectarian bias.

132. **Encyclopedia of African American Religions**. Larry G. Murphy et al., eds. New York: Garland, 1993. 1006p. (Religious Information Systems, v.9; Garland Reference Library of Social Science, v.721). ISBN 0-8153-0500-1.

With the emphasis in the past few years on the black experience comes this comprehensive one-volume encyclopedia on African-American religious traditions. There are some 1,200 entries, two-thirds of which are devoted to personalities. In addition to people, coverage is given to churches, organizations, topics, and issues dating from the eighteenth century to the present. All predominantly black denominations are included, along with participation in mainstream traditions. The Nation of Islam is treated in depth, with exposition of black Muslim developments of the twentieth century. Opening the work is a well-constructed introductory essay that provides a detailed summary of black religion. This is followed by a chronology of major events. There are about thirty survey-length entries on major topics and issues such as the civil rights movement and abolitionism. An appendix lists organizations, and there is a comprehensive bibliography. Indexes of names, subjects, and organizations furnish access.

133.   **The Encyclopedia of American Religions.** 4th ed. J. Gordon Melton. Detroit: Gale Research, 1993. 1217p. ISBN 0-8103-6904-4.

The initial edition of this important work was issued in 1978 by McGrath Publishing and later by Gale Research. The second edition appeared nine years later in 1987, and was followed by the third edition in 1989. It may have settled on a four-year freqency with publication of the present effort. The title has established itself as a solid source of information, and the new edition resembles its predecessor in scope and format. The present effort treats approximately 1,600 religious bodies on the North American continent, similar to its predecessor. Canadian groups continue to receive good coverage. A categorical arrangement embraces the different religious families under various chapter headings. Both essays and listings furnish insight and perspective on traditional groups such as Lutheran and Reformed Presbyterian, along with more modern systems like the Communal, Metaphysical, Psychic, and New Age families. Information is provided on the various bodies (history, development, organizational aspects), as well as bibliography and bibliographic notes.

A recently published companion work is Melton's *Encyclopedia of American Religions: Religious Creeds* (Gale, 1993), which enumerates more than 460 religious creeds, confessions, statements of faith, summaries of belief, and articles of religion associated with all types of religions practiced in America. There are indexes by creed/organization name and by keyword. Another useful source with a fine reputation is Frank S. Mead's *Handbook of Denominations in the United States*, revised by Samuel S. Hill for its ninth edition (Abingdon, 1990). Although not as detailed as the Melton effort, information is well developed in furnishing history, doctrine, governance, and statistics for 225 religious groups. Useful listings are given in an appendix; glossary, bibliography, and index are provided.

134.   **The Encyclopedia of Native American Religions**. Arlene Hirschfelder and Paulette Moulin. Facts on File, 1992. 367p. ISBN 0-8160-2017-5.

This one-volume encyclopedia is the only reference tool devoted to Native American religions and will be a welcome resource for libraries serving a variety of students, from junior high school to undergraduate. It furnishes easily comprehended descriptions of spiritual and religious traditions and personalities associated with Native American observance. Included here are ceremonies, rituals, terminology, and biographies of Native American healers, Christian missionaries and others, relevant court cases, religious sites, and mythology. All entries are alphabetically arranged, vary in length from a few sentences to several pages, and furnish dates and tribal affiliations. Most entries run one or two paragraphs. To facilitate learning, there are photographs, line drawings, and maps. Hirschfelder is a prolific writer who has worked for the Association on American Indian Affairs for more than thirty years; Moulin is a member of the Ojibwa (Chippewa) tribe.

135.   **The Encyclopedia of Religion.** Mircea Eliade, ed.-in-chief. New York: Macmillan, 1987; repr. 1993. 16v. ISBN 0-02-897135-3.

Eliade's comprehensive encyclopedia represents an extraordinary project furnishing more than 2,700 entries by 1,400 eminent scholars. Entries generally consist of broad descriptive narratives on religious traditions, individuals, and themes. Its coverage is worldwide, with especially good treatment of Eastern religions and cultures. Emphasis is on detailed examination of individual traditions and comparative study of religions with each other. Articles provide an overview of the topic, details on particular aspects of the topic, and some bibliography (although this is not complete). Biographical and narrow topics occasionally receive briefer treatment. The work is aimed at the student or nonspecialist, but the great amount of information provided makes it valuable to the serious scholar as well. The final volume, issued a year after the encyclopedia was first published, provides a thorough topical index along with a synoptic outline of contents.

An Encyclopedia of Religion, by Virgilius Ture Anselm Ferm (Philosophical Library, 1945; repr. 1981) retains a place in the minds of reference librarians and on the shelves of reference collections. It represents a broad coverage of all religions even though it is written from a Protestant point of view. Entries are generally brief and cover a variety of topics: terms are identified; feast names are identified; and persons, movements, and institutions are explained. It is particularly good in the coverage of Oriental religion. It furnishes brief treatment of various denominations, theologies, and personalities associated with all faiths. Bibliographies are included.

136. **Encyclopedia of the American Religious Experience: Studies of Traditions and Movements.** Charles H. Lippy and Peter W. Williams, eds. New York: Scribner's, 1988. 3v. ISBN 0-684-18062-6.

This three-volume encyclopedia is a throwback to an earlier period of encyclopedia production which featured monographic-type essays of substance and depth. There are 100 essays averaging about 17 to 18 pages each; these are produced by young scholars writing in a clear and readable style. Each essay concludes with a summary paragraph and a bibliography of books and articles. Considered to be a scholarly effort in terms of breadth and depth of coverage, both historical and contemporary conditions are covered. Entries are organized into nine major segments dealing with approaches to religion, principal religious groups, movements, the arts, politics, education, and so on. The work is exhaustive in nature and includes coverage of the most pertinent topics. It serves as both a reference tool for students and scholars and an agreeable reading experience for those interested. There is an excellent detailed index.

137. **The New Westminister Dictionary of Liturgy and Worship.** J. G. Davies, ed. Philadelphia: Westminster, 1986. 544p. ISBN 0-664-21270-0.

Published in both Great Britain and the United States, this excellent reference tool first appeared in 1972. The new edition represents a revision and slight expansion of the earlier publication, with about sixty new entries as well as modification of existing ones. It has been described by reviewers as having a greater spirit of ecumenicism, which provides an attitude more receptive to ethnic pluralism and greater participation by the laity in church ritual. Treatment of women is timely, with articles on ordination of women, the Feminist Liturgical Movement, and women and worship. Emphasis is on conceptual awareness rather than definitions of precise terms, and it is quite possible that a person unfamiliar with terminology may not come away with a precise meaning. Articles vary in length and cover both Christian and non-Christian religions. The tool provides a necessary ingredient to the religion collection.

A more recent but somewhat less authoritative and less exhaustive publication is *The ABCs of Worship: A Concise Dictionary*, by reform Presbyterian pastor Donald Stake Wilson (Westminster/John Knox Press, 1992). This handy work provides generally useful definitions of 176 terms, both historical and contemporary. Definitions average close to a page in length, although some are much briefer.

138. **Die Religion in Geschichte und Gegenwart. Handwörterbuch für Theologie und Religionwissenschaft.** Tubingen, West Germany: Mohr, 1957-1965; repr. 1986. 7v. ISBN 3-16-145098-1.

One of the outstanding multivolume sets, this work has earned a reputation for excellence in scholarship. Known and identified simply as *RGG*, it features signed articles and bibliographies of considerable length. Coverage is given to all religions, and it remains an important contribution of German Protestant scholarship. This authoritative tool includes biographical sketches of living as well as dead persons. Biographical notes on the more than 3,000 contributors are found in volume 7, the "Registerband." There is an extensive subject index.

139. **Religions of the World.** 3d ed. Niels C. Nielsen et al. New York: St. Martin's Press, 1993. 536p. ISBN 0-312-05023-2.

The third edition continues the excellent tradition of its predecessors in furnishing a first-rate aid for students at all levels. Each of the sections is compiled by an eminent scholar in the field. Although an introductory tool, it is a useful resource for those with an advanced interest as well. The initial section explores the basic questions and concepts that all religions share and also treats the important extinct religions of the past (Middle East, Greece, and Rome). The remaining segments describe the major living religions from both East and West; Hinduism; Buddhism; Judaism; Christianity; etc. There are many illustrations and there is balanced treatment of the various faiths. Bibliographical notes for each chapter as well as an annotated bibliography are included at the end; chronological tables provide useful overview.

Religions on File is a recent offering of the Diagram Group (Facts on File, 1990), designed to provide a visual format for understanding the great religions of the world. Held in a looseleaf binder, the various charts, diagrams, chronologies, maps, listings, specifications, etc. can be removed for easy reproduction. Because all materials are free of copyright restrictions, libraries will find this a useful tool.

140. **This Day in Religion.** Ernie Gross. New York: Neal-Schuman Publishers, 1990. 294p. ISBN 1-55570-045-4.

Developed in the tradition of the "book of days," this religious chronology provides a needed comprehensive and easy-to-use reference tool. Each day of the year is given coverage through a tabular format supplying one or two sentences identifying the religious events that occurred on that particular day. Emphasis has been placed on the western Christian tradition, although important dates from the Jewish and Eastern faiths have been included. Coverage ranges from about 300 CE (A.D.) to the time of publication, providing an up-to-date source of information. The greatest limitation of the tool is its emphasis on mainstream religion, with little attention given to smaller sects and religious bodies. In other respects, it is a solid effort and represents a good source of information for a variety of uses. Also included are a glossary and bibliography along with an extensive general index.

Religious Holidays and Calendars: An Encyclopedic Handbook, by Aidan Kelly et al. (Omnigraphics, 1993), is a slender volume providing identification of some 300 religious holidays. The work is divided into two segments, the first of which supplies a relatively detailed introductory history of religious calendars, followed by the main text describing the various holidays and their dates of observance. There is a general bibliography and several indexes.

141. **Treasury of Religious Quotations.** Gerald Tomlinson, comp. and ed. Englewood Cliffs, NJ: Prentice-Hall, 1991. 341p. ISBN 0-13-276429-6.

This is a unique tool in its focus on religious quotations, which draws from a wide array of talent and perspective. Philosophers from Martin Buber to Woody Allen are included, along with religious leaders from all faiths and denominations. Stature and status vary among the quoted personalities, and source material includes the Bible, Book of Mormon, Koran, ecclesiastical writings, and more. There are more than 2,000 quotations, preceded by an introductory section explaining the purpose and method of selection. Arrangement of entries is alphabetical by subject, beginning with "achievement" and concluding with "zeal." A useful feature is the segment of brief biographies of the personalities quoted, which follows the main body. This is followed by an exposition of 30 religions and philosophies, then a bibliography of some 250 basic sources. A general index concludes the work.

Christian

142. **Christian Symbols Ancient and Modern: A Handbook for Students.** Heather Child and Dorothy Colles. New York: Scribner's, 1971. 270p. ISBN 0-684-13093-9.

One of the standard tools in iconography is this highly regarded exposition of the use of Christian symbols in the conduct or services of the Church. There are numerous illustrations, including line drawings and photographs accompanying descriptive passages, which make the work a useful item to a variety of readers. Artists and craftspersons may well be enlightened in their search for thematic material in producing their own work, and students will be informed of the rich heritage of visual symbolism found in the Christian religion. Symbols included are those found in the decorative or applied arts of carving, embroidery, stained glass, etc. The work is divided into categories of representation, with chapters on the cross, the trinity, images of Christ, the Virgin Mary, the Holy Spirit, angels, etc. There is an index and a brief bibliography.

More recent is *Outward Signs: The Language of Christian Symbolism*, by Edward N. West (Walker, 1991), which is a concise but informative handbook identifying and defining origins and meanings of Christian symbols. More than 450 drawings accompany the text, along with a glossary and bibliography. A subject index furnishes access.

143. **The Coptic Encyclopedia**. Aziz S. Ataya, ed.-in-chief. New York: Macmillan, 1991. 8v. ISBN 0-02-897025-X.

This is a monumental source of information on the Coptic people and their representation in culture, history, and religious tradition, and will be the standard for years to come. Some 2,800 articles in the first seven volumes provide comprehensive coverage of movements, doctrines, rites, canonical literature, art, history, geography, customs, and personalities of this Eastern branch of Christianity that developed in Egypt during the late classical and early medieval periods. Today the Coptic church represents a small but spiritually active segment for which reference tools were noticeably lacking. The present effort has filled the void with its authoritative treatment; articles have been signed by more than 260 specialists and scholars. There are numerous photographs and line drawings to illustrate points and provide insight. Volume 8 furnishes maps, technical articles on Coptic linguistics, and an index to the set.

144. **Dictionary of Christian Lore and Legend**. J. C. J. Metford. New York: Thames & Hudson, 1983. 272p. ISBN 0-500-11020-4.

This work succeeds in its purpose to provide a guide to the major elements of the Christian tradition as represented in the arts, music, and literature. There are more than 1,700 generally brief definitions cover architectural features of church buildings as centers of worship, the liturgy, symbols and symbolism, biblical characters, saints, and tales of the Christian religion. *Lore* is interpreted to be knowledge relating to Christian culture, whereas *legend* represents narrative that should be read regardless of belief in its veracity. Developed as a resource for the nonspecialist, the work is written in a clear, readable style, and provides numerous illustrations in black-and-white. There are cross-references but no bibliographies.

Another title of popular interest is *The Dictionary of Bible and Religion*, by William H. Gentz (Abingdon, 1986), which provides clear exposition not only of the Bible, but also of the history and doctrine of Christianity. Various religions are lucidly explained. The text is accompanied by photographs, illustrations, and colored maps. The work is the product of twenty-eight ecumenically Christian contributors whose viewpoints range from conservative to liberal.

145. **Dictionary of Christianity in America**. Daniel G. Reid et al., eds. Downers Grove, IL: Intervarsity Press, 1990. 1305p. ISBN 0-8308-1776-X.

This one-volume dictionary furnishes comprehensive coverage of Christianity in English-language countries of North America by providing 2,400 articles embracing some 4,000 topics contributed by 500 scholars. Reed and his team begin the work with an introductory essay on the history of Christianity in America and supply a guide to use of the book as a reference tool and source of information. The publisher is generally associated with evangelical materials, but has succeeded in producing an objective, descriptive work giving insight to and enlightenment on American traditions. Included here is clear treatment of denominations, movements, events, institutions, and personalities; all are alphabetically arranged and easy to read. Emphasis has been placed on historical development rather than contemporary conditions, although popular living personalities (Billy Graham, Jerry Falwell, Jimmy Swaggart, and others) are included. Bibliographies accompany many of the entries.

146. **A Dictionary of Hymnology Setting Forth the Origin and History of Christian Hymns of All Ages and Nations.** John Julian. New York: Scribner's, 1907; repr., Grand Rapids, MI: Kregel, 1985. 2v. ISBN 0-8254-2960-9.

The years have continued to add to the reputation of this work, which is still the standard in the field for information on the history of Christian hymns in the Western languages. First appearing in 1892, it has gone through several printings, including an initial revision to correct some typographical errors in 1907. Coverage is universal in terms of time and place, but there is an emphasis on hymns of English-speaking countries. To use the work to best advantage, one should become familiar with the composition. The first part is the dictionary, with separate entries on history, biography, and topical matters. This is followed by a cross-reference index to first lines, then an index of authors, translators, etc., followed by two appendices providing additions and corrections to articles in the dictionary. The last two segments comprise another supplement and set of indexes to the appendices and supplement.

Another helpful, but older work, is Katharine Smith Diehl's *Hymns and Tunes: An Index* (Scarecrow Press, 1966), which indexes tunes from seventy-eight hymnals.

147. **Dictionary of Pentecostal and Charismatic Movements.** Stanley M. Burgess et al., eds. Grand Rapids, MI: Zondervan, 1988. Repr. with corr., Regency Reference Library, 1993. 914p. ISBN 0-310-44100-5.

The segment of evangelical Christianity treated here represents the fastest growing Christian movement in the world, a fact that justifies the specialized treatment of this one-volume effort. There are some 800 entries providing description and awareness of denominations, issues, topics, and personalities important to the understanding of the Pentecostal and Charismatic movements. They furnish bibliographies also. Personalities range from the famous to the obscure, and represent a wide array of intellect and advocacy. Reviewers have pointed out a bias in favor of born-again individuals. Entries are supplied by more than sixty contributor-specialists from seminaries, pastorates, and university religious departments. A good five-page introduction opens the work by providing a historical perspective; a general bibliography concludes the effort. There is no index, but access is aided through cross-references within the entries.

148. **Dictionary of the Ecumenical Movement.** Nicholas Lossky et al., eds. Eerdmans, 1991. 1196p. ISBN 0-8028-2428-5.

Produced under the auspices of the World Council of Churches, this dictionary supplies more than 600 entries relevant to the understanding of the ecumenical movement. This twentieth-century phenomenon has sought to provide a unity among the diverse Christian groups on matters of doctrine, worship, and organization. It has proved to be a controversial issue inspiring heated debate and fierce criticism that has not been fully addressed within the entries. Entries furnish awareness of important ecumenical themes, events, activities, topics, and personalities. Different regions of the world and various denominations are considered in terms of their ecumenicism. Entries contain bibliographies, and in some cases are accompanied by illustrations. Articles vary in length, with detailed treatment of doctrinal topics and brief coverage of personalities. Various scholars have contributed. Access is aided by a detailed index and cross-references within the entries.

149. **Dictionnaire d'archeologie chretienne et de liturgie.** Fernand Cabrol and Henri Leclercq. Paris: Letouzey, 1903-1953. 15v.

A standard in the French language, this excellent and profound treatment of Christian liturgy and archaeology is without peer. Originally published as the third multivolume set in a series of sets collectively entitled *Encyclopédie des sciences ecclesiastiques* (Letouzey, 1907-), it remains the most important and unique work of the series. There are excellent articles, all signed, with good bibliographies on all aspects of liturgy and archaeology of the early Christian religion to the time of Charlemagne. Coverage includes monuments, iconography, epigraphy, designs, diagrams, rites and ceremonies, numismatics, and symbols. Latin terms are defined as well. No other compendium of antiquities rivals this work for depth of coverage.

150. **Encyclopedia of Biblical and Christian Ethics**. Rev. ed. R. K. Harrison, gen. ed. Nashville, TN: Nelson, 1992. 472p. ISBN 0-8407-3391-7.

This is a paperback offering a "modest revision" of the first edition published in 1987, with only slight changes. Two new entries have been added treating AIDS and homelessness, the irrepressible societal phenomena of the past decade. Only nine entries have been updated; some are understandable but others provoke some curiosity as to their selection. Revised entries appear for abortion, addiction, civil rights, contraception, euthanasia, fetal rights, Kinsey report, nuclear warfare, and population control; such topics as apartheid remain unchanged. There are the expected corrections of inaccuracies or errors in the previous issue, and greater emphasis on cross-references within the entries. Even now, the work has been criticized for omission of needed cross-references, however. It remains a solid effort, although relatively unchanged from its 1987 publication date.

151. **Encyclopedia of Early Christianity**. Everett Ferguson et al., eds. New York: Garland, 1990. 983p. (Garland Reference Library of the Humanities, v.846). ISBN 0-8240-5745-7.

There are nearly 1,000 entries contributed by 135 specialists relating to the doctrines, practices, art, liturgy, heresies, schisms, places, and personalities of early Christianity. This covers a period of some 600 years beginning with the life of Jesus and proceeding through the formative centuries of Christian development. Entries vary in length but tend to be brief, running from a few sentences to a half-page. Many obscure figures are treated, which adds greatly to the value of the work for academic libraries. Although the scholarship is primarily U.S. and Canadian, there is good representation from abroad. Entries are arranged alphabetically and supply definitions, background, and historical development during the early period. There is a detailed subject index providing excellent access.

Supplementing the *Encyclopedia*, from the same publisher, is an eighteen-volume set of writings and research studies by members of the North American Patristic Society. *Studies in Early Christianity* is also edited by Ferguson et al. and was published in 1993. Personalities, literature, worship, art, various doctrines, missions, acts of piety, and more are covered in the 18 individual volumes standardized at 400 pages each.

*152. **Encyclopedia of Mormonism: The History, Scripture, Doctrine, and Procedure of the Church of Jesus Christ of the Latter Day Saints**. Daniel H. Ludlow, ed. New York: Macmillan, 1992. 4v. ISBN 0-02-879605-5.

This is a detailed and comprehensive compendium of the Mormon Church edited by a well-known professor of religion. Entries are well-written and organized under five major topics: history of the Church, scriptures of the Church, doctrines of Mormonism, organization of the Church, and practices of Church members in society. Certain controversial topics, such as feminism, abortion, and racism, are treated in a frank and forthright but succinct and nonjudgmental manner. Doctrinal concepts may be difficult to grasp. The first four volumes furnish more than 1,100 signed articles with bibliographies and cross-references. The optional fifth volume contains the sacred scriptures of Mormonism, including the *Book of Mormon*. Numerous illustrations accompany the text. Contributors to the encyclopedia are religious scholars of various affiliations. The CD-ROM version is available through Infobases of Orem, Utah; it does not contain the sample Mormon hymns.

153. **Encyclopedia of the Early Church**. Institutum Patristicum Augustinianum; Angelo Di Berardino, ed. New York: Oxford University Press, 1992. 2v. ISBN 0-19-520892-7.

This is a well-developed, informative work covering the history of early Christianity up to the eighth century CE (A.D.). It is a translation of an Italian effort that was issued in 1983, and represents the combined scholarship of 167 specialists from 17 countries and diverse Christian traditions. Entries vary in length, but tend to be brief. They cover aspects of archaeology, philosophy, linguistics, theology, and geography, with attention given to the influence of various personalities. Especially noteworthy is the excellent coverage given to the interrelationships and interactions of Christianity with the pagan beliefs of the time.

Lengthy coverage is given to certain philosophical systems such as Aristotelianism and Platonism. The work is well illustrated with black-and-white photographs, along with color maps and a synoptic table of various events correlated with cultural/doctrinal elements. Bibliographies are up-to-date; a detailed index provides access.

154. **Encyclopedia of the Reformed Faith**. Donald K. Mckim, ed. Louisville, KY: Westminster/John Knox Press, 1992. 414p. ISBN 0-664-21882-2.

The Reformed faith is viewed as the Calvinist perception of Christian faith based in the Protestant reformation along with that of the Swiss Reformation. Due to the impact of the Reformed tradition on Christianity in the United States, this work fills a void and represents an important acquisition. Although not detailed, it supplies a comprehensive effort with contributions from 200 scholars, mostly from the United States, but representing international scholarship as well. Most important, these contributors represent the full range of thinkers from liberal to conservative persuasion and provide a balanced perspective for the work as a whole. There are some 600 entries, ranging in length from several lines to several pages according to the significance of the subject. Coverage is given to personalities, institutions, events, movements, issues, concepts, and topics. A brief bibliography of both modern and historical writings accompanies most of the entries.

155. **New Catholic Encyclopedia.** New York: McGraw-Hill, 1967-1979; repr. Palatine, IL: Publishers Guild, 1981. 17v. Palatine, IL: Jack Heraty, 1989. v.18. ISBN 0-07-010235-X.

Prepared under the supervision of an editorial staff from the Catholic University of America, this represents a completely new work rather than a revision of *The Catholic Encyclopedia* (1907-1922, 17v.). The older work continues to be used because of its excellent in-depth coverage of topics in medieval literature, history, philosophy, art, etc., as well as matters of Catholic doctrine. *New Catholic Encyclopedia* represents a timely and clearly written exposition from the perspective of the Catholic faith in the twentieth century. There are approximately 17,000 articles, all signed, on the Catholic Church in the world today, with an emphasis on the United States and the English-speaking world. Biographies are limited to deceased persons. Bibliographies are given for most articles. Volume 15 is an index; volume 16 is a supplement covering developments from 1967 to 1974; volume 17 includes supplementary coverage of change in the Church; and volume 18 furnishes an update of developments during the 1978-1988 period. All supplementary volumes reflect a certain freedom of thought in the articles on abortion, contraception, women as priests, etc., which are handled in an objective and impartial manner.

A work which serves to supplement the encyclopedia is *The Catholic Fact Book*, by John Deedy (Mercier, 1992). It contains much information on Church history, basic tenets, personalities, events, and documents, as well as definitions of terminology. Smaller libraries may use it as an alternative to the more costly encyclopedia. *Dictionary of the Liturgy* by the Catholic priest, Jovian Lang (Catholic Book, 1989), provides details of the history of the development of Catholic liturgy since Vatican II. A bibliography of additional readings is included.

156. **New Dictionary of Theology.** Joseph A. Komonchak et al., eds. Wilmington, DE: Michael Glazier, 1987. 1112p. ISBN 0-89453-609-5.

This is the first of a trilogy of refined works designed to provide exposition of the Catholic faith in the modern world. Subsequent to Vatican II, there has been a review of theological positions held by many thinkers. In this work, one finds both the traditional and the more contemporary perspectives with regard to the significance of the Bible as well as the various elements that combine to produce a prevailing theology. Issues and topics such as sin, sexuality, justice, and mercy are examined within such perspectives as held by the contributor. Traditional, liturgical, and biblical positions are reviewed and explored by a group of Catholic scholars from English-language-speaking countries. Summations of contemporary thought are supplied. Bibliographies accompany the signed articles.

The New Dictionary of Sacramental Worship is the second of the publisher's offerings in this series and is edited by Peter E. Fink, S.J. (1990). The work seeks to inform the reader of the nature of liturgical reform since Vatican II. Most of the 300 entries examine the Latin rite of the Roman church, although Eastern rites are included. Entries are long and represent detailed essays of the current scholarly position on large topics rather than specific terms.

157. **The Oxford Dictionary of the Christian Church.** 2d ed. F. L. Cross and E. A. Livingstone. New York: Oxford University Press, 1974. 1518p. Repr. with corr. 1983. 1520p. ISBN 0-19-211545-6.

This is a standard, comprehensive, one-volume compendium on religious subject matter. There are more than 6,000 entries from nearly 250 contributors. It is especially useful for its biographies, definitions, and coverage of theologies and heresies. Doctrines, movements, church bodies, events, and holidays are included. Bibliographies are routinely provided for most articles, though articles are not signed. Intended for the intelligent layperson, this work provides little coverage of American Christianity and emphasizes treatment of British aspects. Special attention has been given to the councils and policies that have undergone change. The Eastern Church is given more detailed treatment in this edition than was true of the earlier work.

158. **Schaff-Herzog Encyclopedia. The New Schaff-Herzog Encyclopedia of Religious Knowledge.** New York: Funk and Wagnalls, 1908-1912. Repr. Grand Rapids, MI: Baker, 1949-1950. 13v; 1977. 15v. ISBN 0-8010-7947-0.

Based on the third edition of the monumental German work by J. J. Herzog, *Realencyklopadie für Protestantische Theologie und Kirche* (Hinricks, 1869-1913), this remains one of the most important works from a Protestant perspective in the English language. It provides excellent, in-depth coverage on a variety of topics (historical, biographical, theological, etc.) relevant to Christianity. Some treatment is given to non-Christian religions and religious leaders of various affiliations. Much of the material from the German work has been revised and abridged to make it a more readable but no less authoritative effort. Considered to be weak in its treatment of biblical aspects, it furnishes a useful source of information on doctrine, practical theology, sects, denominations, churches, organizations, missions, and religious controversies.

A new work, *New Twentieth Century Encyclopedia of Religious Knowledge*, edited by J. D. Douglas (2d ed. Baker, 1991), is a major revision of the 1955 supplement to the *Encyclopedia*. It furnishes a useful tool in its own right with biographical sketches, articles on issues and topics of more recent interest, and revision of outdated entries. There are more than 2,000 entries by 250 contributors. An example of ongoing in-depth German Protestant scholarship is *Theologische Realenzyklopäedie* (de Gruyter, 1976-), which is projected to fill thirty volumes. So far, eighteen volumes have been completed, with volume 18 issued in 1988. The work contains long signed articles of a profound nature, complete with bibliographies. The focus is on theological issues with detailed exposition by specialists. It is less regimented to the strictly Protestant point of view than the *Realencyklopadie* mentioned previously.

159. **The Westminster Dictionary of Christian Ethics.** James F. Childress and John Macquarrie, eds. Philadelphia: Westminster, 1986. 678p. ISBN 0-664-20940-8.

In this extensive revision of Macquarrie's *Dictionary of Christian Ethics* (Westminster, 1967), only about 40 percent of the entries were retained, and these were updated if necessary. Contributors from different parts of the English-speaking world, representing the various elements within the Judeo-Christian tradition, have provided a modern approach in examining the relevant issues of contemporary society. Not limited to theologians, this work presents the perspectives of philosophers, lawyers, and physicians in analyzing developments in science, health care, medicine, etc. Such sensitive bioethical subjects as abortion, euthanasia, and human experimentation are considered. Traditional concepts are covered, as are biblical ethics. There are no entries for individual thinkers; rather, a thematic approach is taken in which individuals' values are described. A name index provides access within this context. Like its predecessor, this work should become a standard source.

160. **The Westminster Dictionary of Christian Theology.** Alan Richardson and John Bowden, eds. Philadelphia: Westminster, 1983. 614p. ISBN 0-664-21398-7.

Although based on Richardson's earlier work (Westminster, 1969; repr. London, S.C.M., 1972), which was recognized as the standard for Protestant theology, Bowden has produced an important new tool. Some 175 contributors from Europe and the United States, representing Protestant, Anglican, Catholic, and Orthodox traditions, provide an emphasis on theological thought in a historical context. There are nearly 600 signed articles, with bibliographies covering theology in a variety of settings: biblical, patristic, medieval, reformation, and modern. Biographical sketches have been eliminated in the same manner as in the other Westminster publication, *The Westminster Dictionary of Christian Ethics* (entry 159). More important is the lack of bibliographic coverage for about one-fourth of the entries, which may be regarded as a deficiency of serious proportions.

161. **World Christian Encyclopedia: A Comparative Study of Churches and Religions in the Modern World, AD 1900-2000.** David B. Barrett, ed. New York: Oxford University Press, 1982. 1010p. ISBN 0-19-572435-6.

Based on an extensive survey and twelve years in the making, this work represents a major accomplishment in providing a detailed exposition of the entire realm of Christianity. Covering nearly 21,000 different denominations representing the beliefs of nearly 9,000 different groupings of people speaking more than 7,000 languages, it is far and away the most comprehensive statistical reference work on churches and missions. Many non-Christian religions are covered as well. The volume is divided into fourteen major segments, beginning with a status report on Christianity in the twentieth century, followed by a chronology, methodology of the survey, a cultural classification of peoples, etc. Of major importance is the seventh part, which presents the survey (arranged country-by-country), providing demographic and cultural information as well as narratives of the non-Christian religions and analyses of Christian history and current status. The remaining sections include statistics, a dictionary, a bibliography, an atlas, directories of individuals and organizations, and a set of indexes.

Non-Christian

162. **The Blackwell Dictionary of Judaica**. Dan Cohn-Sherbok. Cambridge, MA: Basil Blackwell, 1992. 597p. ISBN 0-631-16615-7.

Designed by the author to provide students with single-volume, comprehensive coverage of basic information regarding the Jewish people and their religion, it is conceded that this text affords no substitute for the multivolume encyclopedia. Scope is broad and encyclopedic, however, in its treatment of all aspects of Jewish civilization. There are about 7,000 entries, arranged alphabetically, covering terms, personalities, organizations, events, issues, topics, and objects relevant to the Jewish faith. Cross-references are well designed and useful in revealing related entries. There is a chronology of Jewish history, along with two maps.

Encyclopedia of Jewish History, edited by Joseph Alpher (Facts on File, 1986) is a one-volume effort designed to appeal to the popular interest in providing a comprehensive history of world Jewry. Information is brief and clearly presented with respect to Jewish history and culture. Personalities are included. *The Encyclopedia of Jewish Symbols*, by Ellen Frankel and Betsy Plakin Teutsch (Jason Aronson, 1992), is more specialized in its focus on some 250 ceremonial objects, concepts, and motifs as well as personalities, places, and events symbolic of Jewish culture. Description is lucid, and detailed indexing and cross-referencing facilitate access.

163. **Dictionary of Non-Christian Religions.** 2d ed. Geoffrey Parrinder. Amersham, Bucks, England: Hulton, 1981. 320p. ISBN 0-7175-0972-9.

A slight revision, but not an expansion, of the author's earlier edition in 1971, this remains an important and useful work for its rather unique general coverage of non-Christian faiths. The belief systems, practices, gods, heroes, cults, and observances of non-Christian religions are covered. There is an emphasis on the systems of Hinduism, Buddhism, and Islam, because they represent the largest non-Christian faiths, but other parts of the world are not neglected. Postbiblical Judaism, the Americas, Australasia, and Africa are covered in ample fashion. Entries are generally brief but informative, and include cross-references when necessary. There are numerous illustrations, both photographs and drawings. Entries lack bibliographies, but a general reading list is supplied at the end. Also included are lists of dynasties from different regions.

164. **Encyclopaedia Judaica.** New York: Macmillan, 1972. 16v. Repr. Jerusalem: Keter, 1982. 17v. ISBN 0-685-36253-1.

A comprehensive and authoritative treatment of all aspects of Jewish life is provided in approximately 25,000 articles, most of which are signed by a panel of some 1,800 international contributors and 300 editors. Most entries conclude with bibliographies that stress English-language materials. An interesting point worth noting is the placement of the index in volume 1, in order to assure its use to exploit the resource to its fullest degree. Biographical sketches are included and represent universal coverage of both living and deceased persons. A yearbook series was begun the year following publication of the encyclopedia, but its frequency varies.

The work never succeeded in replacing its equally massive twelve-volume predecessor, *The Jewish Encyclopedia* (Funk and Wagnalls, 1901-1906), which remains an excellent scholarly resource for historical interpretation of the customs, cultural traditions, and practices of Jewish life to a Christian audience. An important publication in 1982 was the *Encyclopedia Judaica Decennial Book, 1973-1982* (Jerusalem: Encyclopedia Judaica) which covers the ten-year period 1972-1981 and includes updates, revisions, etc., complete with cross-references to the major work.

165. **Encyclopaedia of Islam.** New ed. H. A. R. Gibb et al., eds. Leiden, Netherlands: Brill, 1954- . v.1- ; London, Luzac, 1960- . 5v. and supp. and fascicles.

The original 1913 edition of this work served as a dictionary of the geography, ethnography, and biography of the Islamic peoples and was regarded as a scholarly and authoritative publication. Revision began in 1954 and has proceeded slowly but steadily since that time, with the publication of separate fascicles which later become parts of bound volumes. Five volumes have been completed, with several fascicles to volume 6 placing it in the M's in terms of coverage. Supplements 1 to 6 accompany the volumes at present. The new work, when completed, will have succeeded in providing a more current exposition of the Islamic tradition with greater attention given to history, geography, and culture. Arrangement is alphabetical, but includes terms from the Arabic which in translation may not be as familiar as English expressions. Cross-references are provided in many cases. Articles vary in length from a paragraph to several pages, depending upon the topic. An index produced in 1989 covers the first five volumes and supplements.

Shorter Encyclopaedia of Islam, edited by Gibb and J. H. Kramers (Brill, 1953; repr. 1991) is a one-volume abridgment of the earlier edition, which contains only articles dealing with law and religion. *The Concise Encyclopedia of Islam*, by Cyril Glasse (Harper, 1989), is the most recent compendium on Islamic culture and religion. It is an excellent one-volume reference work that provides brief but lucid definitions and well-developed expositions of religious forms, ideologies, observances, and important personalities. Appendices include maps showing the spread of Islam, genealogical tables, and a chronology.

166. **Harper's Dictionary of Hinduism: Its Mythology, Folklore, Philosophy, Literature, and History.** Margaret Stutley and James Stutley. San Francisco: Harper & Row, 1977. 416p. Repr. 1984. 372p. ISBN 0-06-067767-8.

Critically acclaimed at the time of its publication as the major dictionary of Hinduism, this work was a product of twenty years of research. It represents an excellent blend of scholarship and readability and fulfills its mission to meet the requirements of both the student and the general reader. There are 2,500 entries, most of which are fairly brief, although some are quite long. The coverage is of classical Hinduism from its beginnings well before the dawn of Christianity to the fifteenth century. Entries include rites, practices, concepts, myths, places, and events of importance. There are references to library texts and sources are frequently identified. There is a fifteen-page bibliography.

A Glossary of Indian Religious Terms and Concepts, by Narenda Nath Bhattacharyya (South Asia Books, 1990), is a compact and handy volume providing definitions and explanations of Hindu, Jain, and Buddhist terms. Distinctions are noted and nuances and subtle differences are described. Definitions tend to be brief and are intended to aid the beginner, but users at all levels will profit from the comparative approach. The work begins with a useful introduction covering philosophical aspects of meanings and examines the history of Sanskrit lexicography developed within a Western perspective. A bibliography is included, along with an index of words for which definitions have been provided under a variant term.

167. **Historical Dictionary of Buddhism.** Charles S. Prebish. Metuchen, NJ: Scarecrow Press, 1993. 387p. (Historical Dictionaries of Religions, Philosophies, and Movements, no. 1). ISBN 0-8108-2698-4.

This is a well-designed and important reference tool initiating a new series of historical dictionaries from this publisher. The author is a well-known scholar in the field and has done an excellent job not only in selection of terms, issues, personalities, events, texts, doctrines, practices, institutions, and movements for inclusion but in their accurate represenatation and exposition. Slightly more than 250 pages of the text are used for the dictionary proper, whereas nearly 100 pages are given to a fine classified bibliography of real value to students and specialists. The remainder of the work is introductory material, including preface, foreword, and pronunciation guide as well as an overview of Buddhist scriptures, map, and chronology. Most important is the excellent introductory history describing the origin and spread of the religion. Although the entries contain cross-references, an index would have been a desirable feature.

168. **Islam in North America: A Sourcebook.** Michael A. Koszegi and J. Gordon Melton. New York: Garland, 1992. 414p. ISBN 0-8153-0918-X.

Up to now there has been a dearth of information sources regarding the development of the Islamic religion in this country and region of the world. The *Sourcebook* furnishes a carefully selected array of documents that otherwise might not be found by students and researchers. There is a good mix of articles, bibliographies, and directories based on the holdings of the specialized collections at the University of California. The articles are written by Arab Islamic scholars, many of which are useful to black studies as well (Nation of Islam, African-American Muslim community, and more). Certain articles have been written for this work, and others are reprints of historical value (Muhammad A. R. Webb's 1893 address on the spirit of Islam). The work is divided chronologically into eighteen chapters: most furnish relevant articles along with bibliographies. The last two chapters supply a directory of Islamic organizations and centers in North America, and a listing of nonprint sources.

Islam and Islamic Groups: A Worldwide Reference Guide, edited by Farzana Shaikh (Longman; distr., Gale, 1992), treats the political focus rather than the doctrine of Islam. Coverage is given to Islamic political presence in more than 100 countries, describing the origins and developments, demographic representations, relationships to the government, and modern political activity. Arrangement of the work is by country, with narrative text followed by listings of organizations and publications.

169. **Jewish-American History and Culture: An Encyclopedia.** Jack Fischel and Sanford Pinsker, eds. New York: Garland, 1992. 710p. (Garland Reference Library of the Social Sciences, v.429). ISBN 0-8240-6622-7.

This is considered by reviewers to be a groundbreaking work in presenting a well-designed and clearly written one-volume source of information of comprehensive nature revealing the richness and depth of contribution of the Jewish experience in America. Entries are alphabetically arranged and describe all aspects of life such as arts, economics, history, humanities, military, sciences, social institutions, organizations, popular culture, etc. Personalities are covered in liberal fashion. Entries range in size from brief to detailed survey length, and furnish not only description, but also, in many cases, critical evaluation. Useful bibliographies accompany most entries, allowing the reader to research the topic further. Contributors to the work are specialists in the field of Jewish studies who provide an enlightening and fair-minded exposition. Useful listings include Jewish Nobel prize winners and libraries with extensive collections on the subject.

170. **The New Standard Jewish Encyclopedia**. 7th ed. Geoffrey Wigoder, ed. Facts on File, 1992. 1001p. ISBN 0-8160-2690-4.

Now in its seventh edition, this well-known and frequently used one-volume information source was edited initially by Cecil Roth. Wigoder, the editor-in-chief of *Encyclopaedia Judaica* (entry 164) has continued the tradition of an easy-to-use reference tool furnishing definitions of terms and exposition of institutions, organizations, and personalities. Arrangement of entries is alphabetical and articles have been updated to include such elements as German reunification and the dissolution of the U.S.S.R. Population figures are up-to-date as of 1991, as are death dates of personalities. The work continues to serve as a useful source of brief exposition and identification.

Also edited by Wigoder is *The Encyclopedia of Judaism* (Macmillan, 1989), that in similar fashion supplies definitions, identifications, and brief biographies arranged alphabetically. Organizations, associations, and issues are treated in more than 1,000 brief but effective articles. U.S. coverage is excellent, with treatment of both Conservative and Reform movements. The work is well illustrated, and is accessed through an index along with useful cross-references.

New Alternatives: New Age, Occult, Etc.

171. **Dictionary of Cults, Sects, Religions and the Occult**. George A. Mather and Larry A. Nichols. Grand Rapids, MI: Zondervan, 1993. 384p. ISBN 0-310-53100-4.

This work provides informative description of cults, sects, and other forms of alternative religion judged to be the most popular, interesting, and influential in this country. The authors write from an admittedly evangelical Christian perspective in treating groups, movements, topics, issues, and personalities. Terms are defined and doctrines explained. For each group or personality, there is fairly detailed exposition of history and teachings as well as concluding commentary. Arrangement of entries is alphabetical and cross-references are provided. Four appendices and a bibliography are classified by major group or movement.

The Illustrated Encyclopedia of Active New Religions, Sects, and Cults, by Benjamin Beit-Hallahmi (Rosen, 1993), provides comprehensive treatment with more than 2,200 entries relevant to the study and comprehension of elements of new religons. These are defined by their age of less than 200 years, an avowed new claim to divine truth, and belief in a supernatural setting with deities, dead souls, angels, or devils. Sects are generally thought to have developed out of a schism or separation from an earlier religious organization, whereas cults have arisen without previous connections. Included in this work are Mormons and Second Day Adventists along with Krishna groups, "Moonies," and Scientologists. Entries are alphabetical and range from a single sentence to several hundred words in length.

172. **The Encyclopedia of Ghosts and Spirits.** Rosemary Ellen Guiley. New York: Facts on File, 1992. 374p. ISBN 0-8160-2140-6.

One of the increasing number of resources appearing on the supernatural or pseudoscientific is this well-constructed, one-volume encyclopedia. It is a handy tool furnishing a great deal of information on the supernatural. Scientific explanations for certain phenomena are rendered along with legend and folklore. Topics vary from ouija boards to apparitions and famous hauntings. There are more than 400 entries accompanied by some 70 illustrations. They treat not only events and happenings but personalities associated with spiritualistic endeavor or serious research. Brief bibliographies accompany each entry; a topical index provides access.

Another effort by Guiley is *The Encyclopedia of Witches and Witchcraft* (Facts on File, 1989), considered to be a solid and informative piece. All aspects of the subject are treated, again furnishing more than 400 entries on animals, beliefs, myths, personalities, practices, and so on. Entries are straightforward and vary in size from brief to lengthy. There is a good general bibliography and a thorough index.

173. **Encyclopedia of Occultism & Parapsychology: A Compendium of Information.** 3d ed. Leslie Shepard, ed. Detroit: Gale Research, 1991. 2v. ISBN 0-8103-4907-8.

This is an update and extension of a work issued first in 1978 and conceived as a combination of 1,000 modern entries with entries from two old standards in the field, *Encyclopaedia of Psychic Science*, by Nandon Fodor (Arthurs Press Limited, 1933) and *Encyclopaedia of Occultism*, by Lewis Spence (G. Routledge, 1920). The second edition, issued in 1984 in three volumes, represented an updating and extension of the earlier effort developed within an improved format. The third edition retains that format, provides corrections of errors, and updates the entries. Hundreds of new entries have been added in response to interest in recent phenomena, concepts, cults, personalities, organizations, and publications. The complete title identifies this work as "a compendium of information on the occult sciences, magic, demonology, superstitions, spiritism, mysticism, metaphysics, psychical science and parapsychology with biographical notes and comprehensive indexes." It is considered the most comprehensive of its type and represents an important purchase.

174. **The Encyclopedic Handbook of Cults in America.** Rev. ed. J. Gordon Melton. Hamden, CT: Garland, 1992. 407p. ISBN 0-8153-0502-8.

With the continuing interest in the topic, this work replaces the earlier edition published in 1986. It remains a timely and informative handbook of alternative religions and represents an extensive revision and expansion. Melton, long an authority on religion in American life and founder of the Institute for the Study of American Religion, presents an objective treatment of thirty-three different groups, ranging from the more established Rosicrucians to the more recent Unification Church and the Krishna affiliates. Especially useful are opening essays defining cults and their opposition in the United States. Each group is described in terms of leading figures, belief systems, organizational structure, and controversies. Bibliographies are provided. A name index and a detailed table of contents facilitate access.

175. **Harper's Encyclopedia of Mystical & Paranormal Experience.** Rosemary Ellen Guiley. San Francisco: Harper, 1991. 666p. ISBN 0-06-250365-0.

As part of the increased representation of the occult in libraries and bookstores, this effort is designed to provide the general audience with information and insight. Articles are brief and arranged alphabetically for easy access. They are clearly written and cover a variety of topics, including the New Age movement, psychical research, astrology, and so on. Personalities are included, but in a selective manner, as emphasis is placed on topical material. Entries supply cross-references that link related items; there are references to more than 1,100 books and almost as many articles. The strength of this effort lies in its recency and coverage of contemporary issues.

Dictionary of Mysticism and the Occult, by Nevill Drury (Harper & Row, 1985), supplies nearly 3,000 entries describing elements of magic, spiritualism, parapsychology, mysticism of both East and West, folklore, divination, tarot, and astrology. Rites, terms, personalities, and topics are treated in an informative fashion with relevant research findings. The author is a recognized authority in the field.

176. **New Age Encyclopedia: A Guide to the Beliefs, Concepts, Terms, People, and Organizations.** J. Gordon Melton et al. Detroit: Gale Research, 1990. 586p. ISBN 0-8103-7159-6.

Melton, the well-known author and editor of religion reference tools, has embraced the New Age movement, defined as "the new global movement toward spiritual development, health and healing, [and] higher consciousness." There are nearly 335 entries identifying beliefs, concepts, terms, personalities, and organizations related to the New Age, made popular by such personalities as Shirley MacLaine. This work provides thorough coverage and furnishes a useful introductory essay explaining the origin, development, and conceptual basis of the belief system. Seven contributors have joined with Melton to supply an objective and systematic explanation of important aspects; the work is not judgmental but descriptive in its approach. All major topics have been treated, although there are the usual number of controversial omissions and inclusions. Entries contain bibliographies; there is a chronology, a listing of educational institutions, and a general index.

DIRECTORIES, ANNUALS, AND
CURRENT AWARENESS SOURCES

177. **American Jewish Yearbook.** Philadelphia: Jewish Publication Society; New York: American Jewish Committee, 1899- . Ann. ISSN 0065-8987.

Designed by the Jewish Publication Society to review events of the year relating to Jewish affairs in the United States and other countries of the world, this tool has been published by the American Jewish Committee since 1950. Feature articles appear at the beginning of the work, followed by signed articles on a variety of subjects regarding developments in the American Jewish community. These are treated in some detail, followed by briefer treatment of conditions in other countries. Also included are directories of various organizations in the United States and Canada, biographies, necrologies, and bibliographies. Among these resource items is a useful listing of Jewish periodicals and a summary Jewish calendar. Volume 92 (1992) has feature articles on intermarriage patterns and population trends which should be especially useful for reference service. Each volume is approached through a detailed name and subject index.

*178. **Catholic News Service.** Washington: Catholic News Service. 1988- (database).

Available online since 1988 is this database of news and miscellaneous information regarding the activities of the Catholic Church, both in the United States and around the world. The Service's satellite newswire acts as the supplier for those who wish to be informed on a continuing or continuous basis. Coverage begins with January 15, 1988, and continues to the present day with daily updates. Regular features include "Washington Letter" and "Vatican Letter" columns, along with reviews of books, motion pictures, and television previews.

Catholic Trends is another online product of the Catholic News Service; it targets the current news and furnishes analysis of Church activities as they relate to public policy, ecumenicism, court decisions, education, and the ministries. Coverage begins with April 2, 1988, and continues to date. The database is updated on a biweekly basis. Both the *Catholic News Service* and *Catholic Trends* databases are available through NewsNet, Inc.

179. **Directory of African-American Religious Bodies: A Compendium by the Howard University School of Divinity.** Wardell J. Payne, ed. Washington: Howard University Press, 1991. 363p. ISBN 0-88258-174-0.

This represents a thorough and comprehensive reference tool devoted to the African-American religious experience. The work comprises a series of directories with historical essays and a full set of appendices. Four categories of religious units are treated: African-American religious bodies; African-American religious councils, ecumenical organizations, and service agencies; African-American religious education institutions; and white religious bodies and agencies with significant African-American membership. Another directory identifies more than 150 African-Americans with scholarly interest in religion. Arrangement of entries is alphabetical within five groupings; the entries furnish basic description of history, purpose, composition, and location of units and name, title, affiliation, education, and address of personalities. The sixth segment contains historical essays on various religious groups. There are places by name, publication, category, state, and grouping, along with an introductory essay and a selective bibliography.

180. **Directory of Departments and Programs of Religious Studies in North America.** David G. Truemper, ed. Macon, GA: Mercer University Press, 1987- . Ann. ISBN 0-86554-283-X (1987); ISBN 1-88313-500-1 (1993).

This annual directory was issued first in 1987 and edited then by Watson E. Mills. It furnishes a useful listing of schools, as well as departments and programs offering at least a bachelors degree. Information on both graduate and undergraduate programs in religious studies at American and Canadian four-year colleges, universities, and specialized theological schools is furnished in a clear and easy-to-assimilate fashion. Entries include contact persons, and supply profiles of faculty, programs, facilities, degrees, and financial aid. Descriptive data are based on responses to a questionnaire resulting in coverage of some 20 to 30 percent of the total number of schools in the various categories. This coverage of more than 1,200 institutions represents a more comprehensive treatment than is true of other sources.

Another directory of this type is *Guide to Schools and Departments of Religion and Seminaries in the United States and Canada: Degree Programs in Religious Studies* (edited by Modoc Press [Macmillan], 1987). This work furnishes more in-depth treatment of just over 700 regionally or nationally accredited schools. Arrangement is alphabetical by state or province, then by name of institution. Indexes furnish access.

181. **Directory of Religious Organizations in the United States.** 3d ed. J. Gordon Melton and Amy Lucas, eds. Detroit: Gale Research, 1993. 728p. ISBN 0-8103-9890-7.

A classified listing of nearly 2,500 religious and lay organizations in the field of religion, this is an update of a work published eleven years earlier. Its reception has been excellent, and the tool is well developed, with information presented in a handy and useful manner. The new edition adds nearly 1,000 organizations to the total covered in the previous effort, not surprising with respect to the amount of time and degree of religious activity subsequent to the earlier work. All organizations listed are regarded as having a religious purpose. Representative organizations are departments of national churches, professional associations and societies, volunteer groups of various types, government agencies, businesses, and fraternal societies. Information given includes religious affiliation, address and location, fax and telephone numbers, officers, purpose, activities, founding date, publications, and membership. Information is supplied by the organization. Many of these organizations are not easily found elsewhere; therefore, the work represents a desirable addition to the collection. It is indexed by personal name, function, affiliation, and keyword.

182. **Fund Raiser's Guide to Religious Philanthropy.** 7th ed. Bernard Jankowski, ed. Rockville, MD: Taft Group; distr. Detroit: Gale Research, 1993. 412p. ISSN 1042-0053.

As one of several titles in the field of religious philanthropy, the seventh edition of this well received, useful source continues in the same tradition, furnishing profiles of several hundred philanthropic sources. This provides excellent articles for fund seekers and units needing support in the area of religion. Arrangement of entries is alphabetical by state, then by foundation name. Entries furnish name, address, telephone number, officers, and description of purpose, activities, limitations of support, and application process. There are numerous indexes (donors, officers, places, subjects, types of support, and more).

National Guide to Funding in Religion, edited by Stan Olson and others (Foundation Center, 1993), is the second edition of a similar publication intended to be a beginning point for grant seekers looking for financial support. More than 2,800 foundations and programs are listed; these were culled from the Center's general publications, *National Directory of Corporate Giving* (Foundation Center, 1989-) and *The Foundation Directory* (Russell Sage Foundation, 1960-). Another effort is the third edition of *Foundation Guide for Religious Grant Seekers*, edited by Francis J. Butler and Catherine E. Farrell (Scholars Press, 1987). This is a revised and enlarged issue of what is considered a useful source of information on Christian, Jewish, and interfaith foundations. More than 400 such organizations are treated.

*183. **Methodists Make News.** Nashville, TN: United Methodist News Service, 1983- . Wk. (database).

Another of the online databases available through NewsNet, Inc. is this file of news and features of interest to the United Methodist Church. Formerly known as *United Methodist Information*, the service provides the full text of the weekly print newsletter of the same name. Information is given concerning members, activities, projects, issues, and related matters. Coverage ranges from May 1983 to the present.

The *Lutheran News Service*, published by the Evangelical Lutheran Church in America, is a database supplying the complete text of the *Lutheran News*, a print weekly. Articles cover social issues, theology, and miscellaneous news from the Evangelical Lutheran Church in America and the Lutheran World Federation. Similar to the Methodist offering, it covers the time period from January 10, 1986, to date, with the file updated on a weekly basis. It also is available through NewsNet, Inc.

184. **National Directory of Churches, Synagogues, and Other Houses of Worship.** J. Gordon Melton, ed. Detroit: Gale Research, 4v. 1993- . Trienn. ISSN 1070-3314.

Melton is a prolific writer and editor who has a knack of providing needed reference sources for the study of religion. This comprehensive directory, projected as a triennial publication, lists more than 350,000 churches, synagogues, mosques, etc. representing 35 primary religious traditions in the United States. Entries are presented in four volumes, each treating a different region of the country (Northeastern States, Midwestern States, Southern States, and Western States). The intent is to provide identification of worshipping congregations, both urban and rural, throughout the country. Within each volume, listings are given by state, then city, then denomination, then by church and congregation name. Entries supply name, address, telephone number, date established, size of congregation, and name of church leader. There is a guide to denominational locations and an index to churches and congregations in each volume.

185. **The Official Catholic Directory.** New York: P. J. Kenedy/Reed Reference Publishing, 1886- . Ann. ISSN 0078-3854.

Although there have been some variations in title through the years, this directory has been a predictable commodity and represents a standard reference tool. Developed with the purpose of providing up-to-date, accurate information on a yearly basis, it serves an important function in disseminating the reports of statistical and institutional information as provided by diocesan authorities. The 1993 issue represents the 176th edition of this reputable work. Coverage includes the organization, clergy, missions, schools, churches, and religious orders of the Catholic Church in the United States, and its affiliates and territories, as well as Canada and Mexico. Arrangement is by hierarchical order of the Church under countries and subdivisions of countries. Dioceses are listed by states and detailed information is provided regarding names of individuals serving in various positions. Traditionally, the index has appeared at the beginning of the volume. Numerous classified advertisements help subsidize the costs of the publication..

186. **Religious Bodies in the United States: A Directory.** J. Gordon Melton. New York: Garland, 1992. 313p. (Religious Information Systems Series, v.1; Garland Reference Library of Humanities, v.1568). ISBN 0-8153-0806-X.

From the time of its initial publication under a slightly different title in 1977, this directory has earned the respect of librarians and their patrons for its excellent brief coverage of hundreds of religious bodies in this country. The present effort continues the excellent tradition with a needed update. Unlike the earlier effort, there is no attempt to classify the denominations under families. Chapters are given to the various religions (Hindu, Jewish, Christian, Buddhist, Occult/Magical, etc.). Arrangement is alphabetical by name of the body in the directory sections, and information is provided regarding origin, history, address, and telephone number. Publications are treated, as are interfaith organizations. There is a bibliography of materials relating to American religious groups at the end.

187. **Yearbook of American and Canadian Churches.** Nashville, TN: Abingdon, 1916- . Ann. ISSN 0195-9034.

Although its title, publisher, and frequency of appearance have varied in the past, this work has assumed an important position as a reporting tool for statistics and developments of major religious bodies in the United States and Canada. Originally limited to Protestant religious bodies, it has changed character through time and now covers the organizations and activities of all faiths. Consisting of three major sections plus an index, greatest coverage is in the second segment, "Directories," which is classified by categories. Separate listings are given for American and Canadian groups, but each entry provides a brief historical overview, listing of officers, organizational information, and a list of periodicals. The first part provides "a calendar with a four-year projection of major religious dates for all faiths," and the third section presents statistics regarding financial conditions and membership. The index groups denominations under generic headings such as "Baptist Bodies."

BIOGRAPHICAL SOURCES

188. **Biographical Dictionary of American Cult and Sect Leaders.** J. Gordon Melton. New York: Garland, 1986. 354p. ISBN 0-8240-9037-3.

Melton has had a great deal of success in reading the desires of the marketplace, and this title was developed in response to a clear need for material on leaders of divergent, nonmainstream groups and their leading figures. Both scholars and students should profit from the focus on what has come to be called alternative religions.

This is a comprehensive biographical dictionary of 213 founders and major leaders of American cults and sects. Coverage is limited to deceased persons. A *sect* is considered to be a group in protest of the mainstream church, and a *cult* is defined as a more radical new spiritual option. Some of the groups have become mainstream, such as the Mormon church. The biographies are well written and informative, from 300 to 500 words in length, and include bibliographies by and about the personality. Appendices provide classification of the personalities by tradition, birthplace, and religious influences. A good general index is given.

189. **The Book of Saints: A Dictionary of Servants of God.** 6th ed., entirely rev. and reset, 1st American ed. Benedictine Monks of St. Augustine's Abbey, Ramsgate, comps. Witton, CT: Morehouse Publishing, 1989. 605p. ISBN 0-8192-1501-5.

This new edition of a standard biographical dictionary was issued twenty-three years after its predecessor and has updated and enlarged its coverage. There are nearly 10,000 entries, doubling the number treated in the fifth edition, and at the same time extending the scope to embrace a greater proportion of non-English saints. Those entries for saints removed from the General Calendar in 1969 are noted as having questionable authenticity. Recently canonized saints are treated. Entries are brief but informative and furnish name, appellation, feast day, dates, liturgical group, and religious order, along with a biographical sketch. They are arranged alphabetically and in many cases are accompanied by illustrations of Christian art. The work supplies a brief bibliography along with an index of emblems, a list of patron saints representing the various professions and activities, and a list of the twelve sibyls or prophetesses of the pre-Christian world.

190.   **Butler's Lives of the Saints**. Herbert Thurston and Donald Attwater, eds. New York: P. J. Kenedy, 1956. Repr. Westminster, MD: Christian Classics, 1990. 4v. ISBN 0-87061-0457.

In Attwater's revision and abridgment of Thurston's earlier twelve-volume edition (1926-1938), which itself was a revision of the eighteenth-century effort by Butler, much of the original material has been included without change. Some brief treatments were deleted and some biographies of recently canonized saints have been added. The homilies have been omitted. The purpose of the work is to present information on the principal saints familiar to English-speaking Catholics. The saints are listed by months and days, which requires in many cases the use of the index to locate the entry. A good biography of the individual's life is followed by a listing of sources. Each volume is indexed, and a general name index for the set appears in volume 4. A one-volume concise edition, revised and updated, was issued by HarperSanFrancisco in 1991.

191.   **Dictionary of American Catholic Biography**. John J. Delaney. Garden City, NY: Doubleday, 1984. 621p. ISBN 0-385-17878-6.

In this volume, an attempt has been made to provide factual information regarding the lives and activities of Catholics who have been influential in this country. The work covers about 1,500 individuals, all of whom are deceased, but whose dates range from the colonial period to the present. In addition to theologians, the entries include a distinguished listing of performers, artists, athletes, and politicians. Such persons as Bing Crosby, Arturo Toscanini, Babe Ruth, and John F. Kennedy are included, as well as those of more controversial nature such as Joseph McCarthy. Each entry covers birth information, education, activities, achievements, and date and place of death. This appears to be a useful source for its stated purpose.

A useful eight-chapter narrative history, providing detailed bibliographical notes on periods and topics along with biographical sketches, is Patrick W. Carey's *The Roman Catholics* (Greenwood Press, 1993). Included here are brief biographies of 145 major personalities who influenced the Catholic faith in this country. Bibliographies accompany each of the sketches. For coverage on an international basis, see the earlier work *Dictionary of Catholic Biography*, by Delaney and James Edward Tobin (Doubleday, 1961) which covers nearly 15,000 individuals from earliest times to the time of publication.

192.   **Dictionary of American Religious Biography**. 2d ed. rev. and enl. Henry Warner Bowden. Westport, CT: Greenwood Press, 1993. 686p. ISBN 0-313-27825-3.

A retrospective biographical dictionary which is limited to religious figures who died before 1 July 1992, expanding the first edition that provided coverage to 1 July 1976. Detailed treatment is given to religious leaders who represent a wide range of denominations and belief systems. Of the 425 treated in the first edition, all have been retained, with most having been updated and revised. About 125 names have been added for a total of 550 persons. Included are such diverse figures as Increase Mather and Martin Luther King, Jr. Each entry begins with a brief career overview and personal and educational data. Following this is a detailed narrative sketch which includes both expository and evaluative commentary. A special attempt has been made to include women and minorities as well as dissidents from mainstream activity. Bibliographies providing references by and about the biographee are included with each entry. A selected general bibliography has been added at the end of the new edition. There are name and subject indexes.

193. **Jewish Profiles: Great Jewish Personalities and Institutions of the Twentieth Century.** Murray Polner, ed. Northvale, NJ: Jason Aronson, 1991. 410p. ISBN 0-87668-793-1.

This is a selective biographical and informational tool furnishing forty articles taken from *Present Tense*, a now-defunct Jewish magazine of liberal persuasion. Most articles are reports of interviews held with the subjects, who figure prominently in the affairs of the day. Featured are artists, politicians, educators, and others wielding influence (Elie Wiesel, Teddy Kollek, Betty Friedan, and so on). Also covered are certain institutions such as Brandeis University and the *Jewish Daily Forward*. A detailed index provides access.

Who's Who in American Jewry (Standard Who's Who, 1980) is a useful and informative publication providing coverage of over 6,000 notable Jewish men and women in the United States and Canada. This work is recognized for its comprehensive treatment of both individuals and institutions. The first part includes the biographical coverage of those who have achieved distinction in a particular field or area of human endeavor as well as those who hold positions of leadership either in the Jewish community or on the national scene. The second segment incorporates the "Directory of American Jewish Institutions," supplying information regarding more than 9,000 Jewish institutions. This is arranged by state. *Reform Judaism in America: A Biographical Dictionary and Sourcebook*, edited by Kerry M. Olitzky of Hebrew Union College and others (Greenwood Press, 1993), provides first-rate coverage of the American reform movement in treating the lives and achievements of the most influential leaders. Rabbis, cantors, scholars, and volunteers are profiled in biographical sketches, along with bibliographies of primary and secondary sources. Several essays provide historical perspective of important organizations.

194. **The Oxford Dictionary of Popes.** J. N. D. Kelly. New York: Oxford University Press, 1986; repr. 1988, 347p. ISBN 0-19-213964-9.

A fairly recent biographical dictionary which covers all 264 popes who followed Peter up to 1981, this work is a useful source of information. Entries for each pope are arranged chronologically and cover family, social and educational background, life prior to becoming the head of the Church, and career activities while shouldering the responsibility of office. In general, the bibliographies are considered to be impartial and informative, although at times gossip and innuendo find their way into the descriptions. There is an appendix on "Pope Joan" which explores the myth of a female pope. Each entry provides a bibliography of source materials for each pope's life and official acts. An excellent detailed index provides easy access.

195. **The Oxford Dictionary of Saints.** 3d ed. David Hugh Farmer. New York: Oxford University Press, 1992. 512p. ISBN 0-19-283069-4.

The initial edition of this informative biographical dictionary treating the lives of the saints of Great Britain was published in 1978, and was updated with the second issue in 1987, covering more than 1,000 saints. The third edition provides updated, and in some cases, revised accounts of more than 1,100 saints. Like those in the previous efforts, some were native to England, others are considered important by the British, and still others died in England. Entries are concise and supply useful facts for all the saints recorded in English place names, in the calendar of the Book of Common Prayer, the Sarum Rite, and the Calendar of the Roman Catholic church. It also includes coverage of the leading saints of Ireland, Scotland, and Wales. Arrangement is alphabetical by Christian names for those who lived prior to the sixteenth century and by surname for those who followed. There are selective bibliographies which provide references to official sources. An index of places associated with particular saints is also included.

196. **The Presbyterians.** Herbert Randall Balmer and John R. Fitzmier. Westport, CT: Greenwood Press, 1993. 274p. (Denominations in America, no. 5). ISBN 0-313-26084-2.

This is a comprehensive history and biographical dictionary of the Presbyterian church in this country, and it fills a void in the library collection. Part 1 provides a detailed historical account of the European origin of the Church and the influence of Zwingli, Calvin, and Knox in the creation of Reformed and Presbyterian theology. The Church's development and growth in the United States is lucidly described, and the immigration of the Scottish-Irish Presbyterian in the late eighteenth century is explained. The Church later was to split over the issue of slavery, and the two factions were not reconciled until recent years as part of the ecumenical movement. Part 2 supplies a biographical dictionary of Presbyterian leaders to complement the historical survey. This must be considered an important tool for academic and religion libraries.

197.   **Religious Leaders of America: A Biographical Guide to Founders and Leaders of Religious Bodies, Churches, and Spiritual Groups in North America.** J. Gordon Melton. Detroit: Gale, 1991- . Trienn. 604p. ISSN 1057-2961.
   This most recent effort by the prolific author represents a biographical dictionary of nearly 1,050 personalities, all of whom made their contributions subsequent to the Civil War. Coverage extends over a wide range of figures representing both the traditional Judeo-Christian heritage and the alternative or fringe areas as well. Included are minority figures, females, blacks, and Native Americans, in a purposeful attempt to be inclusive. Although most of the entries are deceased, there is a good representation of living persons. Thus, we have Pat Robertson along with Jesse Jackson and Billy Graham; Mother Cabrini along with Madalyn Murray O'Hair. Entries furnish birth and death dates, birthplaces, and religious affiliations, together with a well-developed biography. There is an appendix of religious affiliation classifying the subjects into various groups. A comprehensive index identifies individuals, organizations, publications, and more.
   Twentieth Century Shapers of American Popular Religion, edited by Charles H. Lippy (Greenwood Press, 1989), is a most unusual and welcome tool for both scholars and students in its detailed biographical essays on the leading figures, both living and dead, who represent some form of popular religion. Religions of this type are considered to be outside the mainstream and focussed on a charismatic leader utilizing (or exploiting) the media. Television evangelists of today along with the capable spokespersons of the past are represented. Coverage is highly selective and is limited to just over 60 men and women creating a unique presence (Harvey Cox, Marcus Garvey, Amy Semple McPherson, Malcolm X, and Pat Robertson). Others have been included for their influence, such as Sinclair Lewis for his *Elmer Gantry*. Entries include an evaluation, critical summary, and bibliography. A detailed index is given.

198.   **Who's Who in Religion, 1992-93.** 4th ed. Wilmette, IL: Marquis Who's Who, 1992. ISBN 0-8379-1604-6.
   Beginning with what appeared to be a yearly or possible biennial publication with the first two editions published between 1975 and 1977, then followed a hiatus which happily ended with the publication of the third edition in 1985. The earlier editions covered individuals in a much more extensive fashion (16,000 in the first edition and 18,000 in the second edition), whereas the third issue limited itself to around 7,000 religious and lay leaders, church officials, clergy, and educators. The fourth edition continues the tradition of its predecessor in treating those who achieved a position of prominence in the United States, and selections for inclusion were aided by a special advisory board of Marquis. Biographies provide information on occupation, family, creative works, activities, memberships, etc. The work covers all denominations and represents a valuable resource tool.

199.   **Who's Who in the Old Testament: Together with the Apocrypha.** Joan Comay. New York: Oxford University Press, 1993. 398p. ISBN 0-19-521029-8.
   Initially issued in 1971 by a different publisher, this is for the most part a reprint without the illustrations of the original issue. It provides well-developed and informative entries for every character who appears in the Old Testament. These entries are arranged alphabetically and describe in detail the lives and activities of biblical personalities, with more extensive treatment given to the major figures. In this work, some 3,000 men and women are covered, beginning with Adam and Eve, through the great prophets such as Isaiah, to influential rulers

such as David and Solomon. Entries are developed within the context of modern biblical scholarship and recent research. A separate section treats the Apocrypha.

Who's Who in the New Testament, by Ronald Brownrigg (Oxford University Press, 1993), is a reprint of a companion piece, also published initially in 1971 by a different publishing house. It offers comprehensive coverage, treating every character who appears in the New Testament in a detailed and informative manner. Exposition of the various versions of the gospels is provided in light of recent biblical scholarship, with special attention given to sites of major events in Jesus's life.

200. **Who's Who of World Religions.** John R. Hinnells, ed. New York: Simon & Schuster, 1992. 560p. ISBN 0-13-952946-2.

This is one of the few biographical dictionaries to attempt a balanced coverage between the Christian and non-Christian religions of the world. All regions and all time periods are covered in this universal approach that embraces such diverse personalities as Sun Myung Moon, Pope John Paul II, and the Ayatollah Khomeini. Both men and women are included, and founders such as L. Ron Hubbard are positioned with creative artists and poets such as J. S. Bach or Giotto. The majority of figures are Christian, as might be expected, but the 1,500 entries represent a good mix with coverage given to twenty-six religious groups. Some sixty scholars contributed to this effort; bibliographies, maps, and indexes are included.

Religious Leaders, by Jacques Brosse (Chambers, 1988; repr. 1991), is a highly selective biographical dictionary of leaders (those concerned solely with guiding others to the truth). Selflessness, along with a lack of interest in worldly status, is the primary characteristic shared by the 163 personalities (Socrates, Joseph Smith, George Whitefield) and groups (Sikhs, Neoplatonists). Entries run from one to two pages and are accompanied by illustrations along with a glossary and index.

HISTORIES AND ATLASES

201. **The Cambridge History of Judaism.** W. D. Davies and Louis Finkelstein, eds. New York: Cambridge University, 1984- . v.1- . ISBN 0-521-21880-2 (v.1).

Projected for completion in four volumes, this authoritative work presents a scholarly history of the Jews from the destruction of the temple in 586 B.C. to the period of the closure of the Mishnah in 250 A.D. The two volumes that have been completed examine not only the developments in Israel but in Babylonia and Egypt as well. Volume 1 presents an introduction in its coverage of the geography of Palestine and the Levant and is termed the "Persian Period." This consists of a series of sixteen essays, erudite but readable, related to the development of Jewish culture in this period. Volume 2 (1989) continues the exposition with cogent coverage of the Hellenistic Age. New data are utilized in the inquiry, which represents a work of ecumenical proportions because the contributors are of various backgrounds and national origins. As is true of other Cambridge efforts, the bibliographies are full and of value to those who would research further. There are chronological tables and an index.

The Origins of Judaism: Religion, History, and Literature in Late Antiquity, edited by Jacob Neusner with William Scott Green (Garland, 1990), is a scholarly thirteen-volume compilation of articles and essays providing detailed examination of all aspects of early Judaism. More than 300 writings of classic importance completed during the past fifty years are organized in thematic volumes covering such elements as "Normative Judaism," The Pharisees and Other Sects," and "Controversies in the Study of Judaic Religion and Theology," along with historically sequenced volumes.

202. **Christian Spirituality: Origins to the Twelfth Century.** Bernard McGinn and John Meyendorff, eds. New York: Crossroad, 1985; repr. 1992, 502p. (World Spirituality: An Encyclopedic History of the Religious Quest, v.16). ISBN 0-8245-0681-2.

Although this is numbered volume 16 in a projected twenty-five-volume set, it was the first to reach the marketplace. Since then, McGinn and Meyendorff have collaborated with Jill Raitt to produce *Christian Spirituality: High Middle Ages and Reformation* (v. 17, 1987). Meyendorff has continued his efforts in behalf of the Christian perspective in joining Louis Dupre and Don E. Saliers to publish *Christian Spirituality: Post-Reformation and Modern* (v. 18, 1989). *Spirituality* is generally defined as "that inner dimension of the person called by certain traditions, the spirit." The general editor of the series is Ewert Cousins, and the issuance of these volumes indicates the magnitude of the entire effort once completed. Attempting to respond to an increased consciousness on the part of the world's citizenry and increasing intercourse between Eastern and Western religions, the multivolume history should have no equal in this field of endeavor. The volumes are comprised of a series of essays, each of which can be used alone or in context with others. The contributors and the editorial board are distinguished scholars of ecumenical character who have generated an outstanding narrative on early church spirituality in a variety of contexts (iconography, art, literature, Monasticism, etc.). An index is provided at the end.

203. **The Cultural Atlas of Islam.** Ismail R. al Faruqi and Lois I. al Faruqi. New York: Macmillan, 1986. 512p. ISBN 0-02-910190-5.
       Considered by the authors (who unfortunately met with a violent death prior to publication date) to be a "first production" in the exposition of the Islamic culture, this is an important work combining informative narrative along with maps, charts, diagrams, tables, line drawings, and photographs. Sources utilized were chosen carefully on the basis of historical and cultural integration; the result was a collection of seventy-seven maps illustrating various aspects and phenomena of the Islamic tradition. The work is divided into four major parts: "Origin," "Essence," "Form," and "Manifestation," without regard to national or regional boundaries. Within these segments one is able to read of the history, art, and cultural identity of Islam. As part of the new phenomenological approach employed in the development of contemporary cultural atlases, it represents an impressive and useful work for both researchers and students. There is an index to aid access.

204. **Eerdmans' Handbook to Christianity in America.** Mark Noll et al. Grand Rapids, MI: Eerdmans, 1983. 507p. ISBN 0-8028-3582-1.
       The work is divided into four sections, chronologically sequenced: "God and the Colonies," "Christianity and Democracy," "The Era of Crisis," and "Christianity in the Secular Age." It provides an exposition of the entire Christian experience in a historical context, beginning with the early Puritans and bringing the reader to the modern evangelicals. There are numerous graphs, charts, and diagrams illustrating the points made in the text. The work is both interesting and useful in its interpretation of the Christian experience in this country. For purposes of enlightenment, quotations help the reader comprehend the thoughts of those being studied. There is a detailed table of contents, but no index.

205. **Handbook of Church History.** Hubert Jedin and John Dolan, eds. New York: Herder & Herder, 1965-1981. 10v.
       Translated from Jedin's *Handbuch der Kirchengeschichte* (3d ed., New York, Herder, 1962-1979; 7v. in 10), this represents a major contribution to church history from a Roman Catholic viewpoint. The purpose is to examine both the Church's external career in the world and its inner life. Major events and personalities are described and explained with respect to their impact on or relationship to such elements as church doctrine, liturgy, dogma, organization, and literature. Beginning with volume 1, "From the Apostolic Community to Constantine," by Karl Baus, the sequence of events is presented in scholarly fashion. Each volume is a work of separate authorship, with three written by Roger Aubert. The final volumes treat the church in the modern age and provide an appropriate capstone to an erudite, well-conceived effort.
       Compact but comprehensive in coverage is *Catholicism in Early Modern History; A Guide to Research*, by John W. O'Malley (Center for Information Research, 1988). It is comprised of sixteen different state-of-the-art reviews, by various scholars, which treat geographical areas

such as Germany and France and topical aspects such as spirituality and preaching. The essays examine current scholarship in lucid manner. There is an excellent bibliography.

206. **Historical Atlas of the Religions of the World.** Isma'il Ragi al Faruqi. New York: Macmillan, 1974. 346p. ISBN 0-02-336400-9.
Developed by the editor with an international team of scholars, this work provides not only excellent and authoritative historical maps, but also scholarly narratives on the histories of religion. These are integrated with the graphic material, which in addition to maps includes photographs, tables, and charts describing the links of religion to cultural and geographic locations. Past religions are covered first, contemporary ethnic and universal religions next, and finally specific areas and religions. There is an appendix of chronologies of the various religions treated, with the current religions being subdivided by the particular denominations that constitute them. There is a detailed table of contents, and subject and name indexes provide access.

207. **The Macmillan Atlas History of Christianity.** Franklin Hamlin Littell. New York: Macmillan, 1976. 176p. ISBN 0-02-573140-8.
Arranged by historical periods, this work illustrates the development of Christianity through graphic representation of its encounters (and in some cases its disputes) with other ideologies and belief systems. Developed with a Protestant perspective, it provides chronological coverage of the emergence and growth of Christianity in considering such topics as the Jewish matrix, the Carolingian Empire, and the age of the Colonialism. Nearly 200 maps and more than 100 separate illustrations are linked to the textual description, providing a useful framework for comprehension of the material presented. There is some variation in size and detail among the maps, but in general they are quite adequate. Access is provided through a general index.

208. **The Oxford Illustrated History of Christianity.** John McManners, ed. New York: Oxford University Press, 1990. 724p. ISBN 0-19-822928-3. Repr. in pbk 1992. ISBN 0-19-285259-0.
McManners, an acknowledged authority and professor emeritus of ecclesiastical history at Oxford University, has produced an attractive, well-illustrated (350 pictures with 32 color plates) reference and browsing source. In addition, eighteen other specialists and scholars also contributed to the development of this highly readable and informative history. The work is divided into three segments, the first (and lengthiest) of which covers the earliest period "From the Origins to 1800." The articles in this section are arranged chronologically, beginning with an essay by Henry Chadwick on the early Christian community. The second segment, "Christianity Since 1800," supplies six chapters representing different regions of the world. The final section with briefest coverage, "Christianity Today and Tomorrow," treats contemporary theological doctrine and also trends of the future. There are a chronology of events and an annotated bibliography. A detailed subject index furnishes access.

THE BIBLE

The books of the Old Testament were written in Hebrew at various times between 1200 and 100 B.C. Final decisions as to which ones should be included in the Jewish canon (list of divinely inspired books) appear to have been made around 100 A.D. A notable translation into Greek, known as the Septuagint, was made in the third and second centuries B.C. It included some books not officially accepted as part of the Jewish canon. The books of the New Testament were written in Greek, mainly in the last half of the first century A.D. By the end of the second century, the contents of today's New Testament were fairly clear. The first complete list of the twenty-seven books accepted today appeared in the Easter Letter of Athanasius in

367 A.D. A major translation of the Bible into Latin (known as the Vulgate) was completed by Jerome in 404 A.D.

In the recent past, the great efforts have been in both modernization of language and treatment as well as interpretation. While retaining the accuracy of intent of the earlier translations, the modern versions have successfully negotiated the difficult passage to clear, nonsexist language and treatment. These modern Bibles are more precise in language and lack the "elaborate eloquence" of their predecessors in making the important points. Of course, they are well suited to the temper and tempo of our times.

The most detailed general description of Bible origin and development is found in *The Cambridge History of the Bible* (entry 256). A more up-to-date resource is *The English Bible from KJV to NIV: A History and Evaluation*, by Jack P. Lewis, now in its second edition (Baker Book, 1991). The chapter on Bibles and related texts in *The Reader's Adviser*, volume 4 in "The Best in the Literature of Philosophy of World Religions" (13th ed., R. R. Bowker, 1986-1987, 6v.), describes various versions and editions. For a comparison of the New Revised Standard Version and the Revised English Bible, one should consult the "Symposium" section of *Theology Today*, October 1990.

Recently, much effort has gone into computerization of files and creation of various databases leading to the development of either online or CD-ROM products for biblical studies. The King James Version especially has received the attention of such publishers. In reality, the large-scale efforts identified and described as entries in the section on multiple versions have rendered most major Bible editions accessible in this manner.

Only the principal English-language versions are listed here, and they are listed in chronological order of initial publication.

Versions and Editions

CHRISTIAN

*209. **King James or Authorized Version** (1611).

Because of the majestic beauty of its language, this version is still a favorite among Protestants. Numerous editions are in print. It remains possibly the most frequently used of all Protestant Bibles. As stated in the introduction to this segment, KJV has been computerized and is available online through DIALOG. A CD-ROM version, *CD-ROM Bible Database* (Nimbus Information Systems), has been discontinued.

A recent edition, The New King James Version (Nelson, 1990), has introduced modern language "where necessary." It has updated archaic terms and replaced seventeenth-century verb forms, but retains its lyrical style. It appears to follow the original text more closely than the other contemporary Bibles, although its language is simpler than either the Revised Standard or the New American Standard versions.

210. **Douay Bible** (1582-1610, rev. by Challoner in 1749-1750).

Translated from the Vulgate, this version has been for Roman Catholics what the King James has been for Protestants. Differs from Protestant versions inasmuch as the Apocryphal books are accepted as canonical and integrated in the text.

211. **American Standard Version** or **American Revised Version** (1901).

Published shortly after the English Revised Version (1885), it has been widely used by American Protestants since its publication at the turn of the century. It has been favored by the American evangelical population, and the subsequent revision was a product of that community. A revision first appeared in 1971 as the New American Standard Bible from World Publishing Company. Other publishers followed suit. In comparison to the new versions of the past few years, it is somewhat more complex and difficult to negotiate. It is generally considered a successful attempt to furnish a more modern version of ASV.

212. **Revised Standard Version.** Nashville, TN: Nelson, 1952.

This revision into modern English by a group of American scholars from many denominations attempts to follow the style of the King James Version. There is both a Protestant edition and a Catholic edition with the Apocrypha.

The Reader's Digest Bible, edited by Bruce Metzger, which reduced the RSV by some 40 percent by tightening the rhetoric and shortening the genealogies and listings, was issued in 1982. The New Revised Standard Version (NRSV) (Zondervan, 1990) is a truly contemporary offering in nonsexist language, with references to *humankind* rather than *man*. It is precise in wording and easily understood, while remaining true in terms of message being delivered.

213. **The Jerusalem Bible.** Garden City, NY: Doubleday, 1966.

Preceded by a French edition (1956) prepared by the Dominicans at L'Ecole Biblique in Jerusalem, the English version is a direct translation from the original languages, with references to the French edition. It won the Thomas More Association Medal for "the most distinguished contribution to Catholic literature in 1966." A new edition appeared in 1985, entitled The New Jerusalem Bible.

214. **The New English Bible.** New York: Oxford University Press, 1971.

The result of more than twenty years of work by a group of scholars to translate the Bible into clear, modern English, this one differs from the Revised Standard Version in that no effort was made to follow the style of the King James Version. Representatives from the various Protestant churches of the British Isles combined to provide a faithful rendering of the available texts in a fluid, idiomatic, but still elevated prose and poetry.

The Revised English Bible (Oxford University Press, 1989) is a substantial revision of the NEB in further reducing passages of exaggerated prose, but also in eliminating the use of sexist language. REB represents a fresh and clearly developed version which has eliminated many inconsistencies with respect to translation of original Greek words and phrases as well.

215. **The New American Bible.** New York: P. J. Kenedy, 1971.

Sponsored by the Bishops' Committee of the Confraternity of Christian Doctrine, this is a thoroughly modern translation for American Catholics, including the deuterocanonical books. It includes textual books on Old Testament readings and an encyclopedic dictionary of biblical and general Catholic information. A revised edition was issued by Eerdmans in 1988; notes and introductory passages have been expanded.

216. **New International Version** (NIV). Grand Rapids, MI: Zondervan, 1978. ISBN 0-310-90000-X.

Based on a thirteen-year effort, initially begun by the Committee on Bible Translation in 1965, the work was sponsored by the New York Bible Society International in 1968. Participating in the process were more than 100 scholars from various evangelical denominations representing various countries. It represents a successful modern approach in its use of current English, and is much more easily read and understood than the ASV. A useful device is the inclusion of quotation marks around quotes. Initially, the Bible Society issued the New Testament version as The Great News in 1973.

NON-CHRISTIAN

217. **The Holy Scriptures.** Jewish Publication Society, 1908; latest repr. 1988. ISBN 0827602529.

Various editions of the Old Testament Bible have appeared in English since this work was published. The most recently completed revision is a three-volume edition of a new translation of the Holy Scriptures According to the Masoretic Text, done over a twenty-year period, 1962-1982. It includes volume 1, The Torah; volume 2, The Prophets; and volume 3, The Writings. In 1985, a single volume was issued, Tanakh: A New Translation of the Holy Scriptures According to the Original Hebrew Text.

There has been activity in computerization with the issuance of Computerized Torah Treasure on CD-ROM from the publisher with the same name as the title. It contains rabbinic literature in Hebrew and covers Tanakh, Mishnah, and various Talmudic interpretations, along with commentaries. Global Jewish Database furnishes the complete text of 252 volumes of rabbinical responses covering over 1,000 years and more than 30 countries. It includes the Bible and various commentaries and collected works; it is available online from the Institute for Computers in Jewish Life in Israel.

218. **Koran. al-Quran: A Contemporary Translation.** 2d rev. ed. Ahmed Ali. Princeton, NJ: Princeton University Press, 1988. 572p. ISBN 0-691-07329-5.

The first edition of the English-Arabic translation of the Koran was issued in 1984 and was warmly received in libraries and college teaching departments as a needed resource. The Ali translation is considered first-rate in style and accuracy and furnishes parallel columns of the Arabic and English text to allow for quick comparison. The corrected second edition furnishes explanatory notes with informative material by its eighty-year-old author and translator. The lack of a contemporary English translation prior to publication of the first edition was considered a serious deficiency to Islamic studies. The work is indexed by subject and also by names of prophets, for which both the English and Arabic name forms are furnished.

MULTIPLE VERSIONS

*219. **The Bible Library.** Oklahoma City: Ellis Enterprises, 1992. (CD-ROM).

This is an enormous tool furnishing access to nine versions of the Bible as well as various concordances, word-studies, dictionaries, commentaries, sermon outlines, and illustrations (including hymn stories). It is an excellent example of a class of computer-accessed comprehensive religious sources enhancing the library collection in a modestly priced manner ($600 or so). Bible versions treated are American Standard Version, Hebrew-Greek Transliteration, King James Version, Literal English Translation, Living Bible, New King James Version, New International Version, Revised Standard Version, and Simple English New Testament. The CD-ROM operates on an IBM system and is available for purchase through the Faxon Company. As reference librarians begin to explore their complete systems of Bible information, they will appreciate the "one-step shopping" convenience in the host of informational tools available. Updates are issued when needed.

The *CDWord Interactive Biblical Library, produced by CDWord Library in 1990 in cooperation with the faculty of the Dallas Theological Seminary, is another of these CD-ROM publications of comprehensive nature selling for about the same price as the previously cited work. It furnishes access to sixteen of the world's most used Bible texts and reference sources. These have been carefully selected by scholars and specialists; updates are issued on an annual basis. Included here are two complete Greek versions, four English texts, two dictionaries, three Greek word books, three commentaries, and parsing for each Greek word.

*220. **FABS Reference Bible System.** Foundation for Advanced Biblical Studies (FABS International), 1988. (CD-ROM).

This is another of the computerized systems, comprehensive in nature, producing convenient access to information from a variety of sources for the librarian and the patron. It provides eight English translations of the Bible, the Greek New Testament, the Greek Septuagint, six volumes of aids to language study, concordances, Apocryphal translations, Josephus and Apostolic Fathers. The company has been developing such software for several years and is regarded as a major supplier of computer-accessible software in the field. It sells for around $400.

Another source from the same company is *FABS Electronic Bible System*, priced at less than half of the preceding source. This one furnishes the text of five English-language versions along with a concordance for each version. It represents an excellent reference source for the librarian in accessing information for frequently asked queries.

Bibliographies, Indexes, and Abstracts

221. **The Bible Study Resource Guide, Revised**. 2d ed. rev. Joseph D. Allison. Nashville, TN: Nelson, 1984. ISBN 0-8407-5927-4.

This work has gone through several revisions in seeking to fulfill its intent to provide an easy-to-follow-and-understand guide for the layperson in making decisions regarding the choice of Bibles and study aids. It represents a handy information piece which should be of use to both librarians and students, although exposition tends to be brief. Explanations are given of Bible versions, concordances, commentaries, dictionaries, atlases, etc. Historical origins and development of these tools are explained.

More detailed for serious students and researchers is the revised and expanded edition of *Multi-Purpose Tools for Bible Study* by Frederick W. Danker (Fortress, 1993). The new issue continues the tradition of the earlier edition, which was acknowledged as the best literature guide to the study of the Bible. It provides excellent coverage of standard reference tools which, of course, should be supplemented with a more recent bibliographic aid such as the one just cited.

222. **New Testament Abstracts: A Record of Current Periodical Literature.** Cambridge, MA: Weston School of Theology, 1956- . 3/yr. ISSN 0028-6877.

Now in its thirty-eighth year, this is the oldest continuing abstract service on Bible studies in the English language. The abstracts cover the literature on the Bible which has appeared in a variety of Western languages from periodicals of varied extraction. Catholic, Protestant, and Jewish periodicals all contribute the source material. Each volume contains indexes of scripture texts, authors, book reviews, and book notices published in the third issue. All abstracts appear in English regardless of the language of the original publication. The work indexes more than 500 periodicals and lists more than 500 books per year. There is a broad classified arrangement with Gospels, Acts, Epistles, Revelation, etc.

A recently published bibliography considered to be an extraordinary achievement is *New Testament Christology: A Critical Assessment and Annotated Bibliography*, compiled by Arland J. Hultgren (Greenwood Press, 1988). More than 1,900 books, articles, and essays representing the twentieth-century theological scholarship of numerous countries and languages are identified, described, and frequently evaluated with clarity and precision. Arrangement of entries is under major categories that are then subdivided by orientation. There are indexes by name, book title, and subject.

223. **Old Testament Abstracts.** Washington, DC: Catholic Biblical Association of America, 1978- . 3/yr. ISSN 0364-8591.

Developed on the model of *New Testament Abstracts* (entry 222) in terms of its thrice-yearly frequency and its style of coverage, this newer work has also made a significant contribution in an area not previously covered by an abstracting service. Each year more than

200 journals from various denominations and geographic regions provide the source material for nearly 1,000 abstracts in English. These articles cover all aspects of Old Testament study (Pentateuch, the historical books, the writings, etc.). Like the earlier service, this one provides a separate listing of book reviews, and indexes of authors and scripture texts in the third issue. In addition, there is an index of semitic words.

*224. **Old Testament Commentary Survey.** Tremper Longman III. Grand Rapids, MI: Baker Book House, 1991. 160p. ISBN 0-8010-5670-5.

Commentaries are among the most frequently consulted reference tools in the area of religion, furnishing explanation of the meaning of Bible passages. This work furnishes a useful guide to their selection in treating those commentaries focussed on the Old Testament. Longman represents an evangelical tradition, but furnishes objective evaluation in terms of ratings based on a five-point system recognizing merit rather than brand of theology. Included here are introductions, theologies, histories, and atlases, along with commentaries that make the tool especially valuable in developing a collection.

A more broadly developed source is *A Guide to Selecting and Using Bible Commentaries*, by Douglas Stuart (Word Books, 1990). Not limited to Old Testament sources, Stuart furnishes an excellent guide to more than 1,100 commentaries of various types produced in the English language. The work opens with an exposition of the nature of commentaries with attention given to such requisites as size, detail, level of readership, and theological perspective in their classification. The last chapter provides personal recommendations.

Concordances and Quotations

225. **Complete Concordance to the Bible (Douay Version).** Newton Wayland Thompson and Raymond Stock. St. Louis, MO: Herder, 1942; repr. 1945, 1953, 1964; Woodbridge, CT: Research Publications, 1992 (microfilm). 1914p.

The Douay version is the old edition (still revered by many) which has occupied a prominent place in the rites of Catholics through the years. A parallel can be drawn to the King James Version in its remarkable longevity and appeal in the light of many subsequent discoveries, revisions, and new translations. Therefore, this concordance retains an important position in libraries that serve the needs of Catholic patrons. First published in 1942, the concordance was revised and expanded only three years later with the addition of many words and references. Citations to passages with excerpts from them are found after each listed word. Provides a good coverage of words in the Bible except for those of very common, nondistinctive character.

226. **Cruden's Complete Concordance to the Old and New Testaments.** Grand Rapids, MI: Zondervan, 1976. Repr. McLean, VA: MacDonald, 1984. 783p. ISBN 0-917006-31-3.

This most famous of the concordances was first published in 1737 and has achieved a classic position among reference books of this type. It has been revised, reedited, and published under a variety of imprints since that time. A paperback edition was published in 1976. It presents about 250,000 English words from the King James Version in alphabetical order. Not nearly as complete as some of its successors in coverage of the canon, it remains useful for its treatment of the Apocrypha. The work is divided into three sections: common words, proper names, and apocryphal words. It provides definitions for proper names and for common words with obscure meanings. Some of the modern reprints omit the Apocrypha section, which greatly affects its value as a reference tool.

227. **The Eerdmans' Analytical Concordance to the Revised Standard Version of the Bible.** Richard E. Whitaker. Grand Rapids, MI: Eerdmans, 1988. 1548p. ISBN 0-8028-2403-X.

Whitaker and his associates at the Institute for Antiquity and Christianity have prepared an important analytical concordance of the whole Revised Standard Version; it identifies the words being translated from the original language within their context. The Revised Standard Version is considered to be a more authoritative translation than the King James, and the analysis of the English and original Greek wording makes it an important vehicle for both students and scholars. Personal pronouns and certain prepositions and conjunctions are omitted as being nonessential. In addition to the major text, there are listings of proper nouns and of numbers, along with indexes in Hebrew, Aramaic, Greek, and Latin.

An Analytical Concordance to the Revised Standard Version of the New Testament by Clinton Morrison (Westminster, 1979) is an attempt to treat the RSV (entry 212) as did Young the KJV (entry 209). It has proven to be a successful effort in creating a needed reference source. The concordance is divided into two parts, the concordance itself and an index-lexicon. The concordance provides, for each English word, references to scripture as well as definitions, Greek phraseology, and English transliterations. The index-lexicon identifies the transliterated Greek words with the English words used in the Bible, thus serving as an index to the concordance.

228. Nelson's Complete Concordance of the New American Bible. Stephen J. Hartdegan, gen. ed. Nashville, TN: Nelson, 1977. 1274p. ISBN 0-8407-4900-7.

The Nelson Company has been an early and active force in developing new concordances with the aid of the computer. This work on the New American Bible (a translation by Catholic scholars issued six years earlier), presents 300,000 entries grouped under 18,000 key terms. These major terms are arranged alphabetically and are subdivided by entries that are listed in order of their occurrence in the Bible. Keywords are set off in boldface capitals to facilitate their use. Frequency of appearance is indicated for keywords as well. References are provided for exact locations in the Bible. A list of omitted words representing nonsignificant descriptors is given in the preface.

229. The NIV Exhaustive Concordance. Edward W. Goodrick and John R. Kohlenberger III. Grand Rapids, MI: Zondervan, 1990. 1853p. ISBN 0-310-43690-7.

This is an expanded offering of a 1981 publication with a slightly different title. Because of the increasing influence and popularity of the New International Version (entry 216), this concordance has become an important purchase and common feature of reference departments. It is a computer-produced concordance of exhaustive proportions, covering all words in the Bible and furnishing easy access to required passages and phrases for both the scholar and the layman. There are numerous special features, such as frequency counts, related word lists, cross-indexing to Strong's classic work (entry 231), and a listing of variant terms for British and American usage. The present edition identifies original Hebrew, Aramaic, and Greek words in separate indexes; articles, conjunctions, prepositions, and pronouns are treated also, with their biblical citations.

230. The NRSV Concordance Unabridged: Including the Apocryphal/Deuterocanonical Books. John R. Kohlenberger III. Grand Rapids, MI: Zondervan, 1991. 1483p. ISBN 0-310-53910-2.

This concordance, published one year after the issue of the New Revised Standard Version, is a computer-produced effort divided into four sections. The main concordance lists every major word and about 630 phrases also, with a frequency count, related words, and cross-references to the King James Version (entry 209). In addition, there is an index of articles, conjunctions, pronouns, and particles; an index to NRSV footnotes; and a topical index identifying such elements as animals, athletics, and musical instruments of the Bible. The work is thorough and well constructed, with good contextual information for each word.

NRSV Exhaustive Concordance, published by Thomas Nelson in the same year, is a competitor and provides similar coverage to the preceding work. In similar fashion, it furnishes a main concordance with a new identical listing of words, but only about thirty phrases. Other parts are similar to the Kohlenberger effort, although the topical index is much more detailed in this title. There are some additional special features, such as listings of laws of the Bible, Jewish calendar, Jewish feasts, prayers of the Bible, and more.

231. **Strong's Exhaustive Concordance of the Bible with Key-word Comparison.** Rev. ed. James Strong. Nashville, TN: Abingdon, 1980; repr. 1986, variant paging. ISBN 0-687-40033-3.

This is a reprint of one of the classic concordances, originally published in 1894, embellished with keyword comparisons. Strong's work is regarded as the most complete in terms of its coverage of every word of the King James Version (entry 209) (including article adjectives and other nondistinctive types). These are listed alphabetically in two places, with the important words in the main text and the forty-seven common words in the appendix. In addition, there is a comparative treatment of selected words and phrases to those found in five leading contemporary translations. There are brief dictionaries of the original Hebrew and Greek terms with references to the English words. The apocryphal books are not covered. The cover title identifies it as *Abingdon's Strong's Exhaustive Concordance of the Bible.*

The New Strong's Exhaustive Concordance of the Bible (Nelson, 1984) is one of the modern computer-generated concordances which has produced a pleasant, new format. This involves changes in sequence of information presented in the entries, simplified instructions, and the addition of some helpful new features. A complementary effort is *NKJV Exhaustive Concordance: New King James Version* (Nelson, 1992) providing coverage similar to that of the recent NRSV efforts (entry 230). It treats every word in the new translation; articles, possessives, and prepositions are found in extensive listings at the back of the volume. Words are cross-referenced with the King James Version. There are no charts or explanatory articles as in the NRSV works.

232. **Young's Analytical Concordance to the Bible.** Newly rev. and corr. Robert Young. Nashville, TN: Nelson, 1982. 1428p. ISBN 0-8407-4945-7.

The subtitle reads: "Containing about 311,000 references, subdivided under the Hebrew and Greek originals, with the literal meaning and pronunciation of each: based upon the King James Version, including index-lexicons to the Old and New Testaments." Names of people and places are included. The main text consists of the word listings (nouns, adjectives, verbs, and adverbs) in alphabetical order. These are identified with scriptural passages as well as definitions and indications of original forms in Greek, Hebrew, and Aramaic, when necessary. The analytical coverage of words in the ancient languages has given this work a reputation for comprehensiveness and has established it as a landmark effort for study and reference with the King James Version (entry 209).

A simplified edition was issued recently as *Analytical Concordance to the Bible on an Entirely New Plan ...* from Hendrickson Publications in 1992. It is designed for the "simplest reader of the English Bible."

Dictionaries, Encyclopedias, and Handbooks

233. **The Anchor Bible Dictionary.** David N. Freedman et al., eds. New York: Doubleday, 1992. 6v. ISBN 0-385-19360-2 (v.1).

This is a monumental effort designed to provide a reference source for serious Bible study. It can be used specifically with the Anchor Bible or generally with all versions. There are nearly 1,000 contributors (scholars and specialists in the field) who furnished 6,200 entries over the period of six years which it took to bring the title to fruition. Articles are full and detailed with each of the contributors providing his or her own perspective. Unfortunately, in many cases they have not provided indication of alternative theories. It would appear that this work will replace *Interpreter's Dictionary of the Bible* (entry 242) in those areas in which the *IDB* is outdated, although certainly not in all respects. It was originally planned in five volumes, but as work progressed it became obvious that a larger set was necessary. Although there are cross-references, the work suffers somewhat from lack of an index.

234. **Dictionary of Jesus and the Gospels.** Joel B. Green and Scot McKnight, eds. Downers Grove, IL: Intervarsity Press, 1992. 933p. ISBN 0-8308-1777-8.

This recent effort serves to supplement the earlier classic title by Hastings, *Dictionary of Christ and the Gospels* (Scribner's, 1906-1908). Such an update was necessary because of the vast amount of inquiry and investigation into the topic in previous decades. Numerous scholars have contributed to this work, an evangelical effort from an evangelical publisher. They have written in a manner that is both informative and critical, but are focussed on the authority of scripture and the accuracy of the Gospels in furnishing perspective on Jesus Christ. The work is noted as being easy to use and relatively free of needless jargon, enabling it to be employed with a wide-ranging audience in terms of scholarship and seriousness of purpose. Articles furnish cross-references as well as current bibliographies of useful reading materials.

235. **Dictionary of Proper Names and Places in the Bible.** O. Odelaine and R. Seguineau. Garden City, NY: Doubleday, 1981. 479p. Repr. Robert Hale, 1991. 528p. ISBN 0-7090-4400-3.

Translated from the French and adapted by Matthew J. O'Connell, this has proved to be a useful dictionary of proper names identified in the Jerusalem Bible (entry 213). Although the majority of these words can be found in other Bible dictionaries, it is unique in its coverage of this modern version. Coverage is provided of words in both the Old and New Testaments, and entries include the English form of the name, transliteration of the Hebrew or Greek form as originally used, frequency of occurrence in the Bible, and definition and etymology, as well as an indication of its importance. There is an introductory essay explaining the purpose of the work and the importance of biblical names. There are name listings and chronological tables. A word of caution: indexing may not be complete for each word, and it may appear more frequently than the number of references provided.

236. **Dictionary of Qur'anic Terms and Concepts.** Mustansir Mir. New York: Garland, 1987. 244p. (Garland Reference Library of the Humanities, v.693). ISBN 0-8240-8546-9.

An excellent supplementary resource to *Encyclopaedia of Islam* (entry 165) and *Shorter Encyclopaedia of Islam* (entry 165n) is this dictionary of some 500 terms drawn from the Qur'an (entry 218), the Bible of the Islamic faith. Entries are generally brief, ranging from a few sentences to about two pages depending upon the significance of the topic. Arrangement is alphabetical by English translation, and coverage includes definition and explanation of the significance of the various terms with references to passages in the Qur'an. The work appears to fulfill its purpose of providing concise and methodical treatment of both major and minor terms and concepts. It is especially useful to a beginning student or to a general reader. No bibliography or index is provided, but entries have cross-references. Concluding the work is a twenty-page listing of terms included.

237. **The Eerdmans' Bible Dictionary.** Rev. ed. Allen C. Myers. Grand Rapids, MI: Eerdmans, 1987. 1094p. ISBN 0-8208-2402-1.

This is an important revised and expanded English translation of the reputable Dutch dictionary, *Bijbelse Encyclopaedie*, first published in 1950 under F. W. Grosheide and later revised in 1975, 1979, and 1982. Representing the evangelical Protestant tradition but presenting a fair perspective and treatment, it has nearly 5,000 entries contributed by nearly fifty North American scholars of various denominations. The work has been updated with the addition of current topics and recent archaeological studies, and is based on the Revised Standard Version (entry 212), although other modern translations are incorporated. Articles are not signed, but scholarship is evident in the treatment given to every person and place named in the Bible, and the exposition of theological concepts and cultural aspects. Some entries contain bibliographies, and there are a number of photographs, line drawings, and color maps by Hammond. There is a list of abbreviations along with a transliteration scheme and a pronunciation guide.

238. **Encyclopedia of Biblical Theology: The Complete Sacramentum Verbi.** 3d ed. Johannes B. Bauer. New York: Crossroad, 1981. 1141p. ISBN 0-8245-0042-3.

This work was translated from the German language and represents the combined efforts of biblical experts from West Germany, Austria, France, and Switzerland. It is a high point of erudition and consistency for Roman Catholic scholarship and covers important words, their changes of meaning, and significance. Articles are cogent and well written, and provide an analysis of the reasoning behind Catholic theological beliefs. Although of scholarly quality, the tool can be used by the laity. Entries range from a few paragraphs to several pages in length, depending upon the importance or significance of the topic. Articles are signed and provide bibliographies of both English- and foreign-language sources. There are indexes of biblical passages and of Hebrew and Greek words, among others.

*239. **Harper's Bible Dictionary.** Paul J. Achtemeier et al., eds. San Francisco: Harper & Row, 1985; repr. 1993. 1178p. ISBN 0-06-069863-2.

Taking a cue from the nonsectarian production of the 1976 supplementary volume of the *Interpreter's Dictionary of the Bible* (entry 242), this unique effort employs the talents of 180 members of the Society of Biblical Literature. Contributors represent all elements of western traditions, Catholic, Protestant, and Jewish, mostly from the United States but also from the United Kingdom and Israel. Although not noted in the bibliographic statement, this is the ninth edition of this Harper & Row publication, first issued in 1952 and last revised in 1973. It has disengaged from conventional piety and represents the concepts and personalities in a matter-of-fact fashion characteristic of historical scholarship. Such elements as the Shroud of Turin are categorically dismissed. Current topics are treated along with all important personalities and places named in the Bible. There are numerous illustrations (maps, photographs, drawings), some in color. A general index furnishes access. It is available on CD-ROM as a file in *CDWord Interactive Biblical Library* (entry 219n).

Its sister publication is *Harper's Bible Commentary* (entry 251). The publisher prepared a two-volume set combining the two efforts in 1991, entitled *Harper's Bible Dictionary and Harper's Bible Commentary.*

240. **The Illustrated Bible Dictionary.** Wheaton, IL: Tyndale, 1980. 3v.

A complete revision and expansion of the popular *New Bible Dictionary* (Tyndale, 1962; rev. 1965), this work has been prepared by a distinguished group of editors. Contributions from 165 scholars from the United States, Great Britain, Australia, and other countries makes this a work of international significance for English-speaking people. Articles cover the *Revised Standard Version* in terms of its books, people, major words, and doctrines. Coverage also is given to background information on the history, geography, customs, and culture of Israel and surrounding countries. There are more than 1,600 photographs, some of which are in color, as well as maps, charts, diagrams, and tables. Bibliographies are also provided. The work is impressive in depth, quality, and physical format and should be considered on the same level as the *Interpreter's Dictionary of the Bible* (entry 242).

A more recently issued work intended for the same audience is *The Illustrated Bible Handbook,* by Edward P. Blair (Abingdon, 1987), which is a revision of Blair's *Abingdon Bible Handbook* (1975). Blair is a conservative but presents an impartial summary of both liberal and conservative views, Catholic and Protestant perspectives, and various Bible versions. It may well be a first choice for libraries with small collections.

241. **The International Standard Bible Encyclopedia.** Rev. ed. Geoffrey W. Bromiley, gen. ed. Grand Rapids, MI: Eerdmans, 1979-1988. 4v. ISBN 0-8028-8160-2.

Since its original edition in 1915 and revision in 1930, the *ISBE* has been regarded as a standard for library purchase and a classic in the field. Indications are that the recent issue has assumed a similar position of importance. Volume 1 (A-D) was published in 1979, followed by volume 2 (E-J) in 1981. Volume 3 (K-P) was completed in 1986 and volume 4 (Q-Z) was issued in 1988. Designed for teachers, students, pastors, and interested laypersons, it covers all persons and places mentioned in the *Revised Standard Version* (entry 212), along with references to similar words in the *King James Version* (entry 209), the *American Standard Version* (entry 211), and the *New English Bible* (entry 214). Entries include pronunciation, etymology, and evolution of meaning through both the Old Testament and New Testament. There are numerous illustrations, some in color. Also covered are terms relating to theology. Cross-references are supplied.

242.   **The Interpreter's Dictionary of the Bible: An Illustrated Encyclopedia.** Nashville, TN: Abingdon, 1962. 4v. **Supps.** 1976, 1982. ISBN 0-687-19270-6.
     Considered the leading scholarly encyclopedic dictionary, it covers both the *King James Version* (entry 209) and the *Revised Standard Version* (entry 212). Its full subtitle indicates its purpose in "identifying and explaining all proper names and significant terms and subjects in the Holy Scriptures, including the Apocrypha, with attention to archaeological discoveries and research into the life and faith of ancient times." It is a work of modern scholarship which includes references to the Dead Sea Scrolls and other recently investigated ancient manuscripts. Developed for the use of preachers, scholars, students, teachers, and general readers, it has met the needs of this diverse grouping in an extraordinary manner. Each important article receives a bibliography, and the work provides maps and illustrations, some of which are in color. An indispensable source, it proves to be an excellent companion to *The Interpreter's Bible* (entry 252). The supplements represent a departure from the past in adding new articles of ecumenical nature as well as updating material needing revision.

243.   **Mercer Dictionary of the Bible.** Watson E. Mills et al., eds. Macon, GA: Mercer University Press, 1990. 987p. ISBN 0-86554-299-6.
     This work was designed to serve the needs of college students of religion and Bible classes. It represents an important effort, reflecting the more conservative orientation but with a balanced perspective. It is a product of the scholarship of 225 specialists, all members of the National Association of Baptist Professors of Religion. Entries furnish exposition of the full range of possible topics; books of the Bible, characters, places and geographical features, theological concepts, history, and culture. They are well developed, utilize current scholarship, and reflect a broadly informed and somewhat worldly view. There are 1,450 signed articles alphabetically arranged. For the most part, they furnish bibliographies of both liberal and conservative writings, and vary in length from a few sentences to several pages. There are sixty-four pages of color maps and photographs; black-and-white photographs appear throughout.

244.   **The New International Dictionary of Biblical Archaeology.** Edward M. Blaiklock and R. K. Harrison, eds. Grand Rapids, MI: Zondervan, 1983. 485p. ISBN 0-310-21250-2.
     Considered to be an outstanding, comprehensive scholarly dictionary which covers all aspects of biblical archaeology. Entries are provided for personal names, place names, deities, texts, languages, animals, architecture, archaeological techniques, furniture, etc. There are more than 800 articles from twenty contributors from all over the world. Articles are signed and include bibliographies and cross-references. They vary in length from a few columns to a dozen pages or more. There are more than 200 photographs, including a sixteen-page section in full color. Maps are incorporated, although possibly not as frequently as needed. Emphasis is on providing facts of interest to a wide audience; theological interpretation is left to the reader.

245.   **The New Unger's Bible Dictionary.** Rev. ed. Merrill F. Unger, R. K. Harrison et al., eds. Chicago: Moody Press, 1988. 1400p. ISBN 0-8024-9037-9.
     The third edition of Unger's reputable work was published in 1966, and since then has provided a serious and scholarly source of information based on a conservative perspective of the *New American Standard Bible* (entry 211n). The present effort continues the excellent coverage, and includes certain passages of the *King James Version* (entry 209) and the *New International Version* (entry 216). Unger was a semitic scholar and prolific contributor to

religious studies. Similarly, the present work is guided by the well-known scholar R. K. Harrison, who now serves as editor. Emphasis has been placed on several areas of inquiry: archaeological treatment based on important recent scholarship; historical and geographical scrutiny of biblical lands of the Near East; the influence and activities of various personalities associated with biblical events; and thorough exposition of common doctrines and beliefs. The work is profusely illustrated with photographs, drawings, and maps. An index provides access.

The New Unger's Bible Handbook, revised and updated by Unger (Moody, 1984), has held a respected position among reference tools. It has a conservative orientation based on the evangelical tradition. The new edition continues in the same vein and has appeal for the layperson. Attractive in format, the descriptions provided are brief and to the point, with little identification of scholarly source material. There are numerous illustrations, including photographs, drawings, maps, charts, diagrams, and colorful chronologies. The books of the Bible are explained in regard to their place in canonical literature, authorship, and themes. Brief background articles cover related aspects of Bible study, such as history and archaeology.

246. **The Oxford Companion to the Bible**. Bruce M. Metzger and Michael D. Coogan, eds. New York: Oxford University Press, 1993. 874p. ISBN 0-19-504645-5.

Another of the excellent one-volume handbooks in the *Oxford Companion* series, this recent effort furnishes more than 700 signed entries describing and interpreting all aspects of Bible development and use. Unlike other Bible dictionaries, it is designed to track the continuing significance of the work in cultural developments relating to the law, arts, politics, and literature. More than 250 international scholars are listed as contributors, and they have provided a variety of insights and important perspectives. Entries vary in length from a few lines to extensive essays, and treat personalities, books of the Bible, events, and rites. Coverage is given to religious concepts such as the Holy Spirit and immortality as well as contemporary social issues such as homosexuality and anti-Semitism. There are a number of well-constructed full color maps to illustrate locations and sites, along with an index to aid access.

247. **Papal Pronouncements: A Guide, 1740-1978.** Claudia Carlen. Ann Arbor, MI: Pierian Press, 1990. 2v. ISBN 0-87650-266-4.

This is a complementary work to an earlier title by Carlen, *The Papal Encyclicals 1740-1981*, described later. *Papal Pronouncements* lists and describes all types of pronouncements, both formal and informal, beginning with Benedict XIV, who revived the encyclical. In addition to encyclicals, coverage is given to letters, apostolic constitutions, homilies, addresses, allocutions, and more. A total of sixteen popes are covered; volume 1 treats Benedict XIV to Paul VI and volume 2 covers Paul VI to John Paul I. Not included are the decrees from the two Vatican Councils. Identification is made by form and content with entries supplying dates, titles, audience, type of pronouncement, length, summary, and sources where they can be found. There is a directory of collection of such material, a general bibliography, and a general index.

The Papal Encyclicals, 1740-1981, completed by Carlen for the same publisher in 1981 and reprinted in 1990 as a five-volume set, provides the complete text in English of 280 encyclicals issued over a span of 240 years. The encyclical is described in an introductory essay as an instrument of papal teaching. Arrangement is chronological under the name of the pontiff; the encyclicals are numbered consecutively. The reign of each pope is described historically; the encyclical follows, then a listing of sources. References appear in endnotes.

*248. **Theological Dictionary of the New Testament.** Gerhard Kittel and Gerhard Friedrich, eds. Grand Rapids, MI: Eerdmans, 1985. 1356p. ISBN 0-8028-2404-8.

This is an abridgment of the author's monumental ten-volume work of the same name (Eerdmans, 1964-1976), translated from the German by Geoffrey W. Bromiley, who also was responsible for this shorter version. The earlier, major work brought contributions from many specialists. It defined in great length the Christian meanings of 2,300 Greek terms, with some articles reaching monographic proportions. Known as *Kittel* or as *TDNT*, the multivolume work is regarded as an indispensable aid for scholarship. The recent one-volume *Kittel* retains the same number of entries as does the original, but shortens them drastically. Entries still cover history, variant meanings, and connotations, but the emphasis is on biblical usage, with far less attention given to original context. Designed to appeal to a wide range of users, from beginning students to scholars and specialists in need of a convenient information source who do not mind the deletion of bibliographical references. It is available on CD-ROM as part of the package provided by *CDWord Interactive Biblical Library* (entry 219n).

Less detailed and thorough is *Exegetical Dictionary of the New Testament* (Eerdmans, 1990-1993), the three-volume translation of a German work edited by Horst Balz and Gerhard Schneider. It represents a useful tool in its exposition of the meaning of biblical text for its first audience. Coverage is given to all words in the Greek New Testament, enabling the user to comprehend the original intent. It is convenient and readable, and offers a solid source of information to both student and specialist.

249. **Theological Dictionary of the Old Testament.** G. Johannes Botterweck and Helmer Ringgren. Grand Rapids, MI: Eerdmans, 1974- 6v. (In progress). ISBN 0-8028-2330-0 (v.6).

Projected as a twelve-volume set, *TDOT* is a translation of a German work also in progress. The English translation is progressing at a rate that closely matches its initial production in German. Volume 6 was issued in 1990. Considered to be an extremely valuable resource for students and scholars, it provides lengthy, technical articles on important words, tracing the etymology in ancient languages. Definitions are given, as are expositions of semantic relations and the word's social, cultural, and historical context. There is a liberal provision of footnotes and bibliographies, and students will appreciate the discussions of the theological importance of the words. Articles are signed by contributors who are noted scholars. It should be considered a companion to the full set of Kittel's *Theological Dictionary of the New Testament* (entry 248), and is sometimes referred to as *OT Kittel*.

Commentaries

250. **Encyclopedia of Biblical Interpretations: A Millenial Anthology.** Menahem M. Kasher. New York: American Biblical Encyclopedia Society, 1953- . 9v. (In progress).

This is a translation by Rabbi Harry Freedman of an extensive thirty-five-volume set that is being shortened somewhat in the process of translation. About half of the original edition has been covered in the nine volumes produced thus far. It presents a collection of Jewish interpretations of and commentaries on the Bible from the time of Moses to the Talmudic-Midrashic period. Each verse of the Bible is covered and the sources are identified. Included among the commentary are both exegetical works and parables, with careful documentation of the sources both modern and ancient. Bibliographies and indexes are included in each volume.

251. **Harper's Bible Commentary.** James L. Mays et al., eds. San Francisco: Harper & Row, 1988. ISBN 0-06-065541-0.

This is a Bible commentary appearing twenty-six years after its predecessor from the same publisher. Sponsored by the Society of Biblical Literature, its purpose is to make available the fruits of current scholarship to an audience of general readers. As such, it represents a companion volume to *Harper's Bible Dictionary* (entry 239) and furnishes cross-references to relevant entries in that work. In its focus on mainstream scholarship, it has been considered by some to be the natural successor to *Peake's Commentary on the Bible* (Nelson, 1962). Worthy of mention are the well-constructed introductory essays both on the entire Bible and on each of its parts or books, including the Apocrypha. There are black-and-white illustrations along with color plates and maps. More than eighty contributors have joined the six editors in producing a useful and up-to-date work. In 1991, Harper prepared a two-volume set of its two works entitled *Harper's Bible Dictionary and Harper's Bible Commentary*.

252. **The Interpreter's Bible.** New York: Abingdon-Cokesbury, 1951-1957; repr. 1988-1989. 12v.

An outstanding work in every way, the subtitle states "The Holy Scriptures in the King James (entry 209) and Revised Standard (entry 212) versions, with general articles and introduction, exegesis and exposition for each book of the Bible." A product of the combined energies of some of the best minds in the area of biblical scholarship, most of the large Protestant denominations were represented among the consulting editors. Some 125 contributors were involved in providing both exegesis and exposition. (The former provides awareness of the setting and the meanings of words in the phrases, whereas the latter provides the present-day meanings of the passages.) The work also provides introductory material, maps, and topical articles. Developed for the general reader as well as the specialist, this is an indispensable tool for Bible study.

253. **Interpreter's Concise Commentary.** Nashville, TN: Abingdon, 1983. 8v. ISBN 0-687-19232-3 (v.1).

This is a revision of *The Interpreter's One-Volume Commentary on the Bible*, edited by Charles Laymon (Abingdon, 1971), and similarly is based on the Revised Standard Version (entry 212). It has been divided into eight paperback volumes, each of which deals with a different aspect or issue. The volumes cover "The Pentateuch," "Old Testament History," "Wisdom Literature and Poetry," "The Major Prophets," "The Minor Prophets and the Apocrypha," "The Gospels," "Acts and Paul's Letters," and "Revelation and the General Epistles." The contributors represent a wide range of scholars from different parts of the world. Commentary is generally lucid, with information given regarding historical, literary, and linguistic study of the Bible. Each volume has an introduction, bibliographies, and maps. In general, the set represents a good purchase at a reasonable price.

254. **The New Jerome Biblical Commentary.** Raymond E. Brown et al. Englewood Cliffs, NJ: Prentice-Hall, 1990. 1484p. ISBN 0-13-614934-0.

About two-thirds of the material is new, making this extensive revision of the initial 1968 publication a noteworthy new tool, and it continues to be recognized as an important work. It provides a brief but informative commentary by some seventy Roman Catholic scholars from North American universities on each book of the longer canon identified and defined at Trent as the various parts of the Bible. Numerous articles provide exegesis and interpretation of high quality and sophistication in expressing the range of varying belief within the Church today. Bibliographies are also provided. The perspective in which the work was undertaken reflects the ecumenicism developed through the Second Vatican Council, and, like the initial edition, it has been issued as a result of the emphasis on the part of the Roman Catholic Church on biblical scholarship. The same editors produced a more concise tool based on this work, entitled *The New Jerome Bible Handbook*, for Liturgical Press in 1992.

255. **The Oxford Study Bible: Revised English Bible, with the Apocrypha**. M. Jack Suggs et al., eds. New York: Oxford, 1992. 1597p. ISBN 0-19-529001-1.

This aid to Bible study treats analytically the *REB* (entry 214n), the revision of the New English Bible which had been issued through the publisher three years earlier. The work is a truly ecumenical product that included seven Catholic and six Jewish scholars among the various contributors. There are more than twenty expository articles placing the Bible within a historical and cultural context. These essays are comprehensive in their coverage and topical approach. Notes and annotations to Bible passages are thorough and well developed, aiding interpretation. As is the case with other study Bibles, this work combines the Bible version with study materials designed to help distinguish the nuances of meaning within the passages, and to help provide a general perspective. There are twenty-eight pages of plates and fourteen color maps.

Histories and Atlases

256. **Cambridge History of the Bible.** Cambridge, UK: Cambridge University Press, 1963-1970. 3v. ISBN 0-521-29018-X.

An important standard in the field, this is an authoritative and scholarly record of the development of the Bible. The volumes appeared at different times, with number 1 being the last to appear. Volume 1 covers the period from the beginning to Jerome and provides exposition of both the Old Testament and the New Testament and the Bible in the early Church. Volume 2 covers the Western world to the time of the Reformation, providing descriptions of book production and Bible illustration in early times. Volume 3, the first published, treats the most recent period, from the Reformation to the present day. Each volume has a table of contents, bibliography, an index of biblical references, and a detailed, general index. There is no comprehensive index to the entire set.

257. **The Harper Atlas of the Bible.** James B. Pritchard, ed. New York: Harper & Row, 1987. 254p. ISBN 0-06-181883-6.

This atlas presents a well-developed, understandable graphic/narrative description of the land, events, and personalities associated with biblical times. The historical periods from the time of the Old Testament through the period of the New Testament and Byzantine Palestine are treated through maps, charts, graphs, illustrations, and informative commentary. There is a detailed chronology from prehistoric times to 150 CE (A.D.) providing an overview of the contextual coverage of the work. Cogent narrative supplies insight into the customs, beliefs, practices, scriptural styles, crafts, and military equipment of the period. Some fifty specialists (linguists, historians, archaeologists, and theologians) representing different parts of the world contributed their expertise to produce this excellent work. Also included is a glossary providing biographical data and an extensive place-name index.

The Harper Concise Atlas of the Bible (1991) is a product of the same editor and international team of contributors. They have rewritten the narrative in more concise form and eliminated certain areas of study, such as crafts and city planning, and special features such as the chronology and the biographical glossary. Documentation of biblical times remains excellent in terms of scope and treatment; it is a carefully constructed and successful abridgment.

258. **The Macmillan Bible Atlas.** Completely rev., 3d ed. Yohanan Aharoni and Michael Avi-Yonah. New York: Macmillan, 1993. 215p. ISBN 0-02-500605-3.

Always considered a work of sound scholarship and skillful cartography, this atlas continues in the tradition of the earlier editions and remains an outstanding Bible atlas. Since publication of the second edition in 1977, there have been great strides in biblical study of ancient documents that have been incorporated into what now is a timely and up-to-date source of information. In keeping with modern theory, there has been greater interest in the ecology of the lands, especially the Ancient Near East and Greco-Roman world. It contains a large number of maps that are well developed and carefully presented. The atlas covers the period from 3000 BCE (B.C.) to 200 CE (A.D.), just as it did previously, and continues to geographically depict social and political events pertaining to the influence of religious, political, economic, and military events during the periods of the Old and New Testaments. The commentary in the Old Testament section has been thoroughly revised, along with parts of the New Testament section. There are many useful charts and drawings. The scholarship and fruitful yield are acknowledged by all.

259. **New Bible Atlas.** J. J. Bimson et al., eds. Wheaton, IL: Tyndale, 1985. 128p. ISBN 0-8423-4675-9.

A recent effort which has made an impact on the field, this atlas was developed out of the same research activity that created *The Illustrated Bible Dictionary* (entry 240). A product of British scholarship, it provides some eighty maps, which compares favorably with other biblical atlases except for *The Macmillan Bible Atlas* (entry 258). Most of the maps are in color and illustrate a variety of events in biblical history. Cartographically, it is as good as or better than other current atlases, and it is superior to *Macmillan* in clarity and visual interest. Topography, geological features, vegetation, climate, and trade routes are depicted. There are numerous photographs and ample expository narrative providing summaries of biblical history. In general, it is a far more attractive publication than most of the older atlases and should be welcomed by both laypersons and serious students.

260.   **Oxford Bible Atlas.** 3d ed. Herbert G. May, ed. New York: Oxford University Press, 1984. 144p. ISBN 0-19-143452-3.

As part of the new breed of recently produced Bible atlases, much attention has gone into the physical appearance of this volume. It is a well-illustrated, attractive effort which has emphasized the recent findings in biblical scholarship and archaeological study. Beginning with an introduction that describes the climate and geographic features of the area around Palestine, the story of the Israelites is graphically presented through maps and illustrative material from the time of Saul in 1025 B.C. to the fall of Jerusalem in 70 A.D. Both topographical and historical maps are used to enlighten the reader about the context in which biblical history was made. There is not as much textual narrative as is found in other atlases.

261.   **Zondervan NIV Atlas of the Bible.** Carl G. Rasmussen. Grand Rapids, MI: Regency Reference Library, 1989. 256p. ISBN 0-310-25160-5.

Based on the New International Version (entry 216), this clear and well-constructed atlas supplies excellent maps, charts, diagrams, and pictures along with lucid text. The work is divided into two major segments, the first of which is the geographical section providing insight into the geography of Israel and Jordan. Longitudinal zones are enumerated and such elements as weather patterns, roads and routes, and geographical regions are examined. Subsections are given to coverage of Egypt, Syria, Lebanon, and Mesopotamia. The second segment is the historical section and presents a historical overview from the prepatriarchal period to the fall of Jerusalem. There is a total of 121 maps, along with 33 charts and 61 plates, furnishing useful insight into biblical times. The work concludes with a grouping of appendices supplying endnotes, bibliography, glossary, historical timeline, as well as indexes of scripture references and personalities. Also included is a gazetteer with index.

MYTHOLOGY AND FOLKLORE

Bibliographies, Indexes, Abstracts, Etc.

262.   **A Bibliography of North American Folklore and Folksong.** 2d ed. rev. Charles Haywood. New York: Dover, 1961. Repr. New York: Peter Smith. 2v.

Since its original edition in 1951, this work has achieved an enviable reputation as a comprehensive, classified bibliography which covers printed music and recordings as well as books. The more recent edition was a corrected revision of the initial effort, and added an index of composers, arrangers, and performers to the author and subject index. Title entries for individual songs are included. There are some descriptive and evaluative annotations. Volume 1 covers the American people north of Mexico, including the Eskimos.

Another work of importance is Katherine Smith Diehl's *Religions, Mythologies, Folklores: An Annotated Bibliography* (Scarecrow Press, 1962), which includes nearly 2,500 numbered items in a classified arrangement with an author and title index. *American Folklore: A Bibliography, 1950-1974*, by Cathleen C. Flanagan and John T. Flanagan (Scarecrow Press, 1977), provides brief annotations.

263. **Folklore and Folklife: A Guide to English-Language Reference Sources.** Susan Steinfirst. Hamden, CT: Garland, 1992. 2v. (Garland Folklore Bibliographies, v.16). ISBN 0-8153-0068-9.

This is a comprehensive guide to reference material in folklore written in the English language, and represents a needed tool in the field. With the increasing interest in and growth of the study in recent years, there has been much more interdisciplinary effort embracing a variety of fields such as sociology, psychology, folk art, architecture, and literature. Targeted to the needs of students and beginning folklorists, the entries are arranged by subject such as folk literature or folk belief systems. Journals and societies are treated as well. Annotations describe the scope of each item; there are indexes of authors, titles, and subjects.

Folklife Sourcebook: A Directory of Folklife Resources in the United States and Canada, 2d ed. by Peter T. Bartis and Barbara C. Fertig (Library of Congress, 1994), is another effort to control resources in the field of American folklore. It is a directory of library collections and organizations that house materials, offer programming, or publish resource material on folklife. These include federal agencies, state folk cultural programs, societies and other organizations, institutions, and foundations. Serial publications are listed. All receive treatment in separate sections of the work, with the Archives of Folklore, Folklife, and Ethnomusicology being described in section 6. Entries provide address, initial year, telephone number, regulations regarding access and services, research facilities, collection size and format with special collections noted along with publications.

264. **Index to Fairy Tales, 1949-1972: Including Folklore, Legends and Myths in Collections.** Norma Olin Ireland. Westwood, MA: F. W. Faxon, 1973. 741p. ISBN 0-8730-5101-7. **Supp. Four 1973-1977.** 1979. 259p; **Supp. Five 1978-1986.** 1989. 575p. Metuchen, NJ: Scarecrow Press, 1989. 575p. **Supp. Six 1987-1992.** 1993. ISBN 0-8108-2750-6.

Compiled as a continuation of Mary Huse Eastman's *Index to Fairy Tales, Myths, and Legends* (F. W. Faxon, 1926, supps., 1937, 1952), this work indexes more than 400 anthologies under titles and subjects. Collections of fairy tales, folklore, legends, and myths from all over the world are included in the coverage. Authors are identified only if their names appear in the titles, but the subject index is detailed, facilitating access. Because this volume presents itself as the third supplement to Eastman, its own supplements, which cover the periods 1973-1977 and 1978-1986, are considered the fourth and fifth supplements to Eastman. An additional 130 collections are indexed, most of which were published during this time period, in *Supp. Four*, and another 261 anthologies are indexed in *Supp. Five*.

265. **Jewish Folklore: An Annotated Bibliography.** Eli Yassif. New York: Garland, 1986. 341p. (Garland Folklore Bibliographies, v.10). ISBN 0-8240-9039-X.

This is an annotated bibliography of international proportions on 100 years of contributions to the study of Jewish folklore. Textbooks and anthologies of folklore are not included. Annotations are both descriptive and evaluative and provide detailed information on the important and representative studies. The period ranges from 1872 to 1980 and represents more than 1,300 numbered entries. The bibliography is arranged alphabetically by author and is selective in the entries that were chosen for inclusion. Areas of study excluded are East European Jewish culture and Judeo-Spanish folklore. A general index provided for access covers themes, motifs, names, and approaches. The compiler is a professor at Ben-Gurion University in Israel and is a recognized authority in the field of Hebrew literature.

266. **Recent Studies in Myths and Literature 1970-1990: An Annotated Bibliography.** Bernard Accardi et al., comps. New York: Greenwood Press, 1991. 251p. (Bibliographies and Indexes in World Literature, no. 29). ISBN 0-313-27545-9.

This volume may serve as a supplementary vehicle within the reference collection on literary criticism and serves a specialized audience of students and scholars. Mythic criticism in the vein of Frazer's *Golden Bough* (3d ed. Macmillan, 1990) is identified within a twenty-year span. More than 1,000 entries are furnished, representing modern mythical scholarship, and demonstrating that the genre is one of continuing interest to researchers. Entries are located within seven chapters, beginning with studies of mythic personalities such as Orpheus and Faust, continuing with classical literature, then dividing into periods of British and American literature, with subsections on certain authors. Shakespeare, Milton, Melville, Joyce, and others are treated. Annotations are well developed and informative. Providing access to mythical figures, themes, and theories is a good subject index, along with an index of authors.

Dictionaries, Encyclopedias, Handbooks, Etc.

267. **Brewer's Dictionary of Phrase and Fable.** 14th ed. Ivor H. Evans, ed. London: Cassell, 1989. Repr. New York: Harper Perennial, 1220p. ISBN 0-06-272022-8.
Since its initial appearance in 1870, Ebenezer Brewer's work has undergone frequent revision and has come to be regarded as a standard in the field. Arranged alphabetically are allusions, heroes of mythology and fiction, popular colloquial and proverbial phrases, titles, and linguistic oddities of various sorts. Because of its eclectic character and expansive scope, it is considered a work of value both for general reference and for purposes of entertainment relating to the interest or curiosity of the user. (Brewer himself referred to it as a "treasury of literary bric-a-brac.") The most distinctive consideration of this particular edition is not only the 300 new entries that have been added, but the presence of an index for the first time. In the past, the work had relied on an excellent system of cross-references to furnish access to related terms. The new keyword (headword) index aids the process considerably.
Brewer's Dictionary of 20th-Century Phrase and Fable (Houghton, 1992) focusses on interesting and evocative words and phrases introduced during this century. Inclusion of contemporary fable or myth results in the coverage of famous events of sometimes sensational nature, such as murders, military disasters, political scandals, and even legendary stars of the cinema. Adhering to the style of the original work, the new offering is a useful reference to British slang and idiom.

268. **Dictionary of Celtic Mythology.** Peter Beresford Ellis. Santa Barbara, CA: ABC-Clio, 1992. 232p. ISBN 0-87436-609-7.
This dictionary is a companion work to a previous title on Irish mythology by the same author, described later. The present effort provides a handy introduction to Celtic mythology for a wide audience. Irish and Welsh influences and culture are examined in this alphabetical listing of entries describing places, events, gods, heroes, weapons, and fantastic creatures. Irish and Welsh origins are identified by symbols for each entry. The work opens with a fine introductory essay on the cultural history of the Celts and their descendants (Bretons, Irish, Cornish, Manx, Scots, and Welsh). A number of the entries are taken from the compiler's earlier publication; they vary in length from a single sentence to a full page. There is a useful bibliography to sources, but no index is provided.
Ellis's *A Dictionary of Irish Mythology* (ABC-Clio, 1987) is more narrowly focused on the Irish culture, and established the pattern of coverage employed by the more recent work. The earlier effort is similar to the other in being a concise and convenient title volume for a general audience. Entries vary in length from one or two lines to two pages and treat terms, events, personalities, and so on. There is an introductory essay and a select bibliography.

269. **Dictionary of Classical Mythology: Symbols, Attributes, and Associations.** Robert E. Bell. Santa Barbara, CA: ABC-Clio, 1982. 390p. ISBN 0-87436-305-5.
Considered an important contribution for a number of reasons, one of which is the topical arrangement given to the entries. Classical mythology is interpreted to be that of Greece and Rome, with references to other ancient belief systems (Assyrian, Egyptian, Etruscan, and Phoenician) when they relate to Greco-Roman topics. Subject entries are diverse and represent a good share of minor points and features, such as "wine." There are

numerous cross-references with citations to source material. The volume makes an excellent tool for authors in finding classical allusions. A list of surnames and a guide to persona appears at the end of the book.

Although it is out-of-print, librarians will continue to use *Crowell's Handbook of Classical Mythology*, by Edward Tripp (Crowell, 1970; repr. Collins, 1988), which presents an alphabetical arrangement of characters and events with descriptions ranging from brief to extensive in length. Other related sources include *The Concise Dictionary of Greek & Roman Mythology* (Harper & Row, 1986) and *The Dictionary of Classical Mythology* (Basil Blackwell, 1986).

More recent is *Athena: Classical Mythology on CD-ROM*, an extensive sourcebook and encyclopedia to be issued by Macmillan/Hall in mid-1994. It contains full text of 20 classical works, including the *Iliad*, *Aeneid*, *Odyssey*, etc.; 1,200 myth summaries; and identification of mythological figures, along with 500 illustrations and genealogical tables. Searching system is convenient and the tool should meet the needs of a variety of users.

270. **A Dictionary of World Mythology.** Rev. and exp. ed. Arthur Cotterell. Oxford: Oxford University Press, 1986. 314p. ISBN 0-19-217747-8.

A revision and expansion of the 1980 edition, this work continues to be an important and useful source of information for the reference librarian. Unlike many of the other efforts in this category, this one provides excellent coverage of the more exotic and difficult-to-locate geographic locales. Although Europe is also covered, the major contribution is the inclusion of Asia, the Americas, Africa, and Oceania, as this material is more unique and less duplicated in other sources. Sections are divided along geographic lines and each section is given an introductory overview of the historical development of myth and religion in that area. Under each section, entries are arranged alphabetically and include deities, place names, and terms. An index and maps have been added to the new edition. Also included are a bibliography and illustrations.

271. **The Facts on File Encyclopedia of World Mythology and Legend.** Anthony S. Mercatante. New York: Facts on File, 1988. 807p. ISBN 0-8160-1049-8.

This work may serve both reference and browsing purposes, as it is a well-constructed and clearly written information tool with some 3,000 entries. Entries furnish plot descriptions of titles, definitions of terms, and identification of characters both fictitious and real, from saints and rulers to fantastic creatures. Most entries run less than a page, but are informative regarding origins, significance, and background. Numerous cross-references are utilized to reveal related entries. The work is valuable for its comprehensive coverage of the various elements associated with mythology. There is a useful bibliography along with an extensive general index and a cultural and ethnic index.

Adrian Room's *NTC's Classical Dictionary: The Origins of the Names of Characters in Classical Mythology* (National Textbook, 1990) is a reprint of his *Classical Dictionary* published in 1983. It furnishes more than 1,200 entries alphabetically arranged, providing information regarding the origin and meaning of names of mythological characters. There are several appendices furnishing name listings of various kinds. This is a good tool for serious students.

272. **Funk & Wagnall's Standard Dictionary of Folklore, Mythology, and Legend.** Maria Leach, ed. and Jerome Fried, assoc. ed. New York: Funk and Wagnalls, 1972. Repr. San Francisco: Harper & Row. 1984. 1236p. ISBN 0-06-250511-4.

Originally published as a two-volume work in 1949-1950, this has become the basic tool for reference in the field. The present effort is a reprint of that original edition. It has been repackaged into one volume with the addition of a key to the 2,045 countries, regions, cultures, areas, people, tribes, and ethnic groups described in the text. Entries are arranged alphabetically. Coverage is comprehensive and includes lengthy, signed survey articles of an authoritative nature on individual regions and major topics, complete with bibliographies, as well as concise articles on beliefs, customs, gods, heroes, songs, tales, dances, motifs, proverbs, games, etc. The dictionary is known for its richness of material.

273. **Guide to the Gods**. Marjorie Leach. Santa Barbara, CA: ABC-Clio, 1992. 980p. ISBN 0-87436-591-0.

This is a highly useful reference tool, comprehensive in its inclusion of mythological gods from all parts of the world and developed within the current orientation to multiculturalism. Gods from the legend and myth of the Greeks are treated with those from other parts of Europe, Asia, Africa, and Polynesia. Entries are arranged alphabetically within chapters falling under eight major sections: cosmogonical, celestial, atmospheric, terrestrial, life-death cycle, economic associations, sociocultural concepts, and religion. More than 20,000 gods are covered in double-column format. Identifications are brief and include country, place, or culture. Within each section, the chapters present different attributes or functions. Commonalities of the various cultural deities are easily determined in this manner, a useful strategy to benefit students. Entries provide references to a lengthy bibliography at the end of the work. A detailed name index provides access.

274. **Man, Myth and Magic: The Illustrated Encyclopedia of Mythology, Religion, and the Unknown.** New ed. Richard Cavendish, ed.-in-chief and Yvonne Deutch, comp. and ed. New York: Marshall Cavendish, 1983. 12v. (Ref. ed., 1985). ISBN 0-86307-041-8.

Originally published in Great Britain in weekly installments, the first edition of this work appeared in 1970 in twenty-four volumes and was criticized for presenting certain material that was not needed or irrelevant. This edition has eliminated those segments. Coverage embraces a wide variety of topical matter, alphabetically arranged from volume 1 to volume 11. The twelfth volume is an index that refers to main articles and to topics. There is a bibliography with classified subject guides. Cross-references are used throughout. Illustrations are plentiful and appear on almost every page; some are in color. Coverage is given to such topics as alchemy, sorcery, witchcraft, etc., with long survey articles on the religions of the world. Among the many contributors who have provided signed articles are some of the very distinguished scholars of our time. This should prove to be a useful source of information. A revised edition is to be issued in 1994.

275. **Mythical and Fabulous Creatures: A Sourcebook and Research Guide.** Malcolm South, ed. Westport, CT: Greenwood Press, 1987. 793p. ISBN 0-313-24338-7.

This important work provides detailed studies by South and seventeen colleagues on twenty different creatures. Part I of the work is divided into four segments, beginning with "Birds and Beasts" (unicorn, dragon, phoenix, roc, griffin, chimera, and basilisk). The coverage continues with "Human Animal Composites" (manticora, mermaids, sirens, harpies, gorgon medusa, sphinx, minotaur, satyr, and centaur). "Creatures of the Darkness" covers vampires and were-wolves, and the work concludes with "Giants and Fairies." The essays provide in-depth information on each creature and cover its origin as well as its treatment in literature, film, and art from ancient to modern times. A useful bibliography is furnished at the end of each essay. Part II contains a bibliography of general works on the subject as well as on individual creatures that do not fit into any of the four categories established in part I. This is considered a top-notch reference book for both students and interested laypersons.

Another good title is *Encyclopedia of Things That Never Were: Creatures, Places, and People*, by Michael Page and Robert Ingpen (Viking Penguin, 1987). This is a handy and practical work for identification of fictional and fantastic characters. More than 400 entries from over 100 different source titles of witchcraft, mythology, astrology, and classic adventure fiction are furnished. Entries are ample and range from 150 to 2,000 words in length. The work is well illustrated in color.

276. **Who's Who in Classical Mythology**. Michael Grant and John Hazel. New York: Oxford University Press, 1993. 352p. ISBN 0-19-521030-1.

With information drawn from a number of ancient literary sources, this represents an important tool for identification of all Greek and Roman mythological figures. Included here are all the gods and all the mortal heroes, both familiar and relatively obscure. Entries furnish well-developed, cogent description and exposition of these personalities and treat events associated with them. These articles are written in an interesting and even entertaining fashion that will appeal to all types of library users. Grant and Hazel are both well-known classical scholars who have combined their expertise to produce a readable and authoritative work.

A companion effort, *Who's Who in Non-Classical Mythology* (Oxford, 1993), represents a revision by Alain Kendall of *Everyman's Dictionary of Non-Classical Mythology* by Egerton Sykes (4th ed., Dutton, 1968). It is important in its focus on the personalities from the mythology of cultures other than Greek and Roman. Contributors to the coverage are the Celts, Teutons, Slavs, Basques, the Americas, Africa, Australia, China, Japan, and Indonesia, providing a fresh and much-needed perspective on world mythology.

277. **Women of Classical Mythology: A Biographical Dictionary.** Robert E. Bell. Santa Barbara, CA: ABC-Clio, 1991. 462p. ISBN 0-87436-581-3.

This is an interesting and useful reference tool for students and the general public in its coverage of 2,600 female personalities from mythology. Treated here are all types of goddesses, heroines, and monstrous beings. Entries vary in length from a single sentence to about four pages, and are written in clear and lucid manner. They provide excellent insight developed within a perspective sensitive to the social position of women. Both famous and obscure figures are included. Arrangement of entries is alphabetical, providing simple access to the personalities. Both Greek and Roman mythology serve as the basis for this work. Entries furnish references to ancient sources where the characters have been treated, a useful feature for student users. Another special feature is a listing of male figures cited in the various entries, entitled "The Men in Their Lives."

7 ◆ ACCESSING INFORMATION IN THE VISUAL ARTS

WORKING DEFINITION OF THE VISUAL ARTS

The term *art* is derived from the Latin word *ars*, which means skill or ability. At the time of the Italian renaissance, the craft guilds were known as *arti*, and the word *arte* denoted craftsmanship, skill, mastery of form, or inventiveness. The phrase *visual arts* serves to differentiate a group of arts that are generally nonverbal in character and that communicate by means of symbols and the juxtaposition of formal elements. Michael Greenhalgh and Paul Duro suggest a definition of *visual arts* as "the practice of shaping material, such as wood or stone, or applying pigment to a flat or other surface, with the intention of representing an idea, experience, or emotion."[1]

The representation is communicated by the creation of emotional moods and through expansion of the range of the aesthetic experience. "Beauty," as such, is not an integral part of art, but more a matter of subjective judgment. The difficulty here is that aesthetics deals with individual taste—a subjective issue from the outset. Nevertheless, certain concepts of balance, harmony, and contrast have become a part of our way of thinking about art as a result of Greek speculation about the nature of beauty.

Style normally refers to the whole body of work produced at a given time in history; however, there may be regional and national styles as well as one basic style for a period. In modern times, attention has even been given to the *styles* of individual artists. Style, like taste, is a subjective phenomenon.

Iconography is the use of symbols by artists to express universal ideas; the Gothic style of architecture, for example, symbolized humanity's reaching out toward God. On a more recent note, designers of graphical software have used icons to denote certain functions and messages; an example is the use of a timepiece (clock, hourglass, or wristwatch) to communicate that the user should wait and that processing is taking place.

MAJOR DIVISIONS OF THE FIELD

The visual arts may be conveniently divided into four main groups: (1) pictorial arts, (2) plastic arts, (3) building arts, and (4) minor arts.

The pictorial arts employ flat, two-dimensional surfaces. The term is most often applied to painting, but it can also include drawing, graphic arts, photography (including moving pictures and video), and mosaics. Painting may be done with a variety of materials: oil, tempera, water color, or other media. Drawing is most often done with pencil, pen and ink, wash, crayon, pastel, or charcoal.

The graphic arts are produced by the printing process, with three basic methods employed. *Intaglio*, in which the design is hollowed out of a flat surface and the ink is gathered in the hollows for transmission to the paper, is exemplified by etching or engraving. *Cameo*, or *relief*, in which the design is on a raised surface (as in woodcut, mezzotint, aquatint, or drypoint) and only the raised surface is inked, is the second method. Finally, there is the *planographic method* in which a completely flat surface is used and the design is created by using substances that will either attract or repel ink. *Lithography* is the term often used for the method, as the flat surface was frequently made of stone.

The pictorial arts employ one or more of three basic forms: murals, panels, or pages. *Murals* involve pictures directly applied to walls of buildings or painted on canvases and permanently attached to the walls. *Panels* are generally painted on wood or canvas—these are sometimes known as *easel paintings*. *Pages* may be illuminated manuscripts or, more often, produced via the printing process. The basic problems of the pictorial artist, regardless of the form used, include surface, design, movement, space, and form. These are commonly solved by the use of line, color, values (light and dark), and perspective.

In the plastic arts, of which sculpture is the most obvious example, ideas are expressed by means of three-dimensional objects. This type of art is perhaps the oldest form, predating even cave painting. The materials used include stone, metal, wood, plaster, clay, or synthetics (such as plastic). Tools of the artist may include chisels, mallets, natural and chemical abrasives, and punches. The techniques used are determined primarily by the materials and tools available, and include carving, casting, modeling, or welding. The finished product may be free-standing or bas relief (part of a wall or planar surface). In sculpture, the human figure has traditionally provided the most common subject matter, although the twentieth century has seen increased use of abstractions.

In the building arts (architecture), spaces are enclosed in such a way as to meet certain practical needs (as in schools, homes, offices, or factories) and to make some kind of symbolic statement of basic values. These values may be utilitarian and the symbolic statement very pedestrian, or they may be related to the highest aspirations of the human spirit. Factories and gasoline stations are frequently examples of the former; Gothic cathedrals are often cited as examples of the latter. Architects design buildings of three basic types: *trabeated*, in which a lintel is supported by two posts; *arcuated*, in which arches support rounded vaults and domes; and *cantilevered*, in which only one post is required to support a lintel or beam. The materials used in the construction will determine the type used. Wood is useful for trabeated construction, but brick and stone can be better adapted to the requirements of arcuated building. Structural steel and reinforced concrete make possible large-scale cantilevered construction.

The minor arts are a special group, often classified on the basis of the materials used: ceramics, glass, metals, textiles, ivory, precious gems, wood, reeds, synthetics, and the like. Ordinarily, they follow the same styles as the major art forms. The end products may be useful everyday objects, such as coins, clothing, baskets, utensils, and furniture, or they may be ornamental items, such as jewelry, stained glass, and many items of interior decoration. The minor arts are often referred to as *crafts*, *decorative arts*, or *collectibles*, or some combination of the 50 terms.

The topic of technology must be addressed as part of any discussion of the visual arts. The application of science to problem solving in all four divisions of the arts is obvious. In the paragraphs on the major divisions of the field, we have addressed aspects of the more traditional technologies: materials and tools. Just as the areas of sculpture and architecture have changed as new tools and materials have evolved, so too do all the visual arts change. Two good examples of where technology and art are melded are photography and computer art. The former has been around for over 100 years, whereas the latter is a creation of recent decades. Nonetheless, both depend heavily on technology—so much, in fact, that it is hard to distinguish between the technology and the art, except in the final product.

More information on the divisions of the visual arts can be found in the *Encyclopaedia Britannica* article "Arts, Classification of the" (15th rev. ed., v.14, pp. 98-102). This and the related articles are intended for the general reader, though they are more advanced treatments than one finds in many other encyclopedias. For briefer articles and shorter histories of various divisions of the arts, see McLeish's *Key Ideas in Human Thought* (Facts on File, 1993). Entries on "Art(s), Visual" (pp. 47-49) and on "Christian Art" (pp. 119-20), "Computer Art" (p. 149), "Architecture" (pp. 44-45), and "Aesthetics" (pp. 13-14) provide both introductions to the topics and suggestions for further reading. *The Encyclopedia of World Art* (Publishers Guild, 1959-1988) contains signed articles by experts on the topics, and it should be consulted by the student or librarian looking for more technical, detailed encyclopedic coverage on art, its subfields, and related subjects. Finally, for histories of the visual arts, a recommended source is the newer *Encyclopedia of Visual Art* (Encyclopaedia Britannica Educational Corp., 1989). A ten-volume set, the *Encyclopedia* covers the area fully, includes illustrations as well as text, and points the user to other material. An overview of the field of art history is found in *Research Guide to the History of Western Art*, by W. Eugene Kleinbauer and Thomas P. Slavens (American Library Association, 1982). A highly regarded guide to research methods is the recently revised *Art Research Methods and Resources: A Guide to Finding Art Information* 3rd ed., by Lois S. Jones (Kendall/Hunt, 1990). Besides providing background material on different aspects of visual arts, both guides are also intended to help the reader find published information in the arts.

HELPFUL RESOURCES FOR STUDENTS, LIBRARIANS, AND GENERAL READERS

Unlike philosophy and religion, where conventional techniques of librarianship and library research will cover most situations, the visual arts pose several distinct problems. As a result, art, or visual arts, librarianship has emerged as a specialized branch of the field. The chapter "Fine Arts" in Lester Asheim's now-classic text *The Humanities and the Library* (American Library Association, 1956, pp. 100-150) suggests some basic tenets that still hold. First, different types of art libraries serve differing purposes, although the subject matter contained in them may be similar. Museum, art school, and departmental public and university libraries serve diverse, though sometimes overlapping, clienteles, and hence the institutions will have varying policies and practices in terms of management, collection development, user education, public services, and organization. Not only librarians, but also users of the libraries will benefit from awareness of the differences and similarities.

An article on art libraries appears in each annual *ALA Yearbook of Library and Information Services* (American Library Association, 1975-), and each one- or two-page entry summarizes the year's developments in the field. An old, but still helpful, encyclopedic treatment of art libraries and special collections is Wolfgang Freitag's article in *Encyclopedia of Library and Information Science* (v.1, pp. 571-621). Philip Pacey's *A Reader in Art Librarianship* (Saur, 1985) is a standard source.

An important consideration is the different types of materials found in an art library collection. In "How to Research a Work of Art," in *Guide to Basic Information Sources in the Visual Arts* (repr. 1980, ABC-Clio, 1978), Gerd Muehsam outlined several distinctive types of art catalog publications. The *catalogue raisonné* is defined as

> a systematic, descriptive, and critical listing or catalog of all known, or documented, authentic works by a particular artist—or of all his known works in one medium. Each entry aims at providing all ascertainable data on the work in question: (1) title, date, and signature, if any, as well as size and medium; (2) present location or owner and provenance (previously recorded owners and history of the work); (3) description, comments, analysis, or literary documentation; (4) bibliographical references to books and periodicals; (5) listings of exhibitions and reproductions. Usually there is also an illustration. The entries are numbered consecutively. These catalog numbers are often referred to in scholarly literature about the artist and permanently identify a particular work.[2]

The *oeuvre catalog* is similar but may omit documentation and provenance. *Museum catalogs* are catalogs of a museum's permanent collection; *exhibition catalogs*, in contrast, include works from many museums or owners' private collections that are brought together for a particular exhibition. *Corpus catalogs* attempt to do for an entire category of art what the catalogue raisonné does for an individual artist. Because of their scope, these often depend on international collaboration.

Catalogs are first-rate sources of art information, but the researcher must understand the difficulties of bibliographic control prior to publication of the ongoing *Worldwide Art Catalogue Bulletin* (1963/1964-). The subject of catalogue collecting is addressed in B. Houghton and G. Varley, "A Local Approach to National Collecting: A UK Feasibility Study for the Cooperative Collection of Exhibition Catalogues," *Art Libraries Journal* 14 (1989): 38-43, and in Houghton's earlier article, "Acquisition of Exhibition Catalogues," *Art Libraries Journal* 9 (1984): 67-78. S. D. Mount's award-winning paper, "Evolutions in Exhibition Catalogues of African Art," *Art Libraries Journal* 14 (1988): 14-19, and J. Robertson's "The Exhibition Catalog as Source of Artists' Primary Documents," *Art Libraries Journal* 14 (1989): 32-36 also address this special research resource. The chapter by Susan Wyngaard on "Fine Arts" in the second edition of *Humanities and the Library*, edited by Nena Couch and Nancy Allen (American Library Association, 1993), covers exhibition and sales catalogs in considerable depth. Artists' books and ephemera are also discussed in the same chapter.

Another special type of document for the art library is the so-called art book. Elizabeth Esteve-Coll discusses the medium in her provocative keynote paper, presented at the European Conference of the IFLA Art Libraries Section and published as "The Art Book: The Idea and the Reality," *Art Libraries Journal* 17 (1992): 4-6. Nikos Stangos's article addresses the issues in art book publishing in the same issue ("Art Book Publishing: Minority Issue, Popular Entertainment, or Kudos?" on pp. 31-33).

Planning and developing visual art collections are covered from a management orientation in Nancy Shelby Schuller's book *Management for Visual Resources Collections* 2d ed. (Libraries Unlimited, 1990). For the librarian, there are many sources on selecting and acquiring materials to be found in the journal literature . The journals *Art Documentation* and *Art Libraries Journal* are the most specific to art library collection development, but *Library Journal* also covers art books on a regular basis. *AB Bookman's Weekly* is also a good resource: see F. L. Kurtz, "Publishing Roundup: Recent Books on Fine Art and Illustration," in volume 85 (April 2, 1990): 1422-27, for example.

Special materials are discussed in the following articles: sales at auction sources in C. H. Backlund, "The Cutting Edge: New Auction Sources and Computer Projects," *Art Documentation* 9 (Winter 1990): 175-78; special problems with eastern European materials in E. Kasinec and R. H. Davis, "Materials for the Study of Russian/Soviet Art and Architecture: Problems of Selection, Acquisition, and Collection Development for Research Libraries ...," *Art Documentation* 10 (Spring 1991): 19-22; Native American art in "Balance and Harmony: Books on American Indian Art," by D. Seaman, in *Booklist* 90 (October 1, 1993): 238-39; and other special items in M. R. Hughston's "Preserving the Ephemeral: New Access to Artists Files, Vertical Files, and Scrapbooks," *Art Documentation* 9 (Winter 1990): 179-81. The sixth edition of *Slide Buyers' Guide: An International Directory of Slide Sources for Art and Architecture* 6th ed. (Libraries Unlimited, 1990), edited by Norine D. Cashman, addresses all aspects of this nonbook form. Daniel Lombardo's "Focus on Art Instruction Books," *Library Journal* 116 (August 1991): 65-68; Don Stave's "Art Books on Approval: Why Not?" *Library Acquisitions: Practice and Theory* 7 (1983): 5-6; and Anne H. Lundin's "List-Checking in Collection Development: An Imprecise Art," *Collection Management* 11 (March-April 1989): 103-13, add to the librarian's knowledge in the area of collection development. The topic is also addressed in various occasional papers issued by ARLIS/NA; see, for example, "Current Issues in Fine Arts Collection Development: Occasional Paper #3," published in 1984.

Other aspects of art libraries and librarianship that are especially important include the special security problems presented by art materials, the education and training of art librarians and information specialists, and art library facilities. The first of these areas is discussed in articles in the Winter 1991 *Art Documentation* (vol.10, pp. 175-87). Training and education are addressed by Robertson in "Survey of Library Schools in North America: Educational and Training Opportunities for Careers in Art Libraries and Visual Resources Collections," *Art Documentation* 10 (Fall 1991): 141-43. "Museum, Arts, and Humanities Librarians: Careers, Professional Development and Continuing Education," by E. G. Bierbaum in *Journal of Education for Library and Information Science* 29 (Spring 1988): 127-34 also relates to professional careers. The "Profile of Fine Arts Librarianship," in the chapter by Wyngaard, referenced earlier, also provides advice regarding qualifications and training for the field.

As to the issue of facilities, Betty Jo Irvine edited *Facilities Standards for Art Libraries and Visual Resources Collections,* published by Libraries Unlimited (1991) for ARLIS, the Art Libraries Society of North America. Irvine's book includes an excellent bibliography on the subject of art and architecture library facilities (pp. 105-108). "Space Planning for the Art Library" was also the topic of ARLIS/NA Occasional Paper no. 9, published by the Society in 1991.

In the technical areas of librarianship, two titles dealing with the organization of materials should be mentioned. The first is Carolyn Frost's *Media Access and Organization: A Cataloging and Reference Sources Guide for Nonbook Materials* (Libraries Unlimited, 1989). The second is *Nonprint Cataloging for Multimedia Collections*, 2d ed., by JoAnn V. Rogers and Jerry D. Saye (Libraries Unlimited, 1987).

The articles in volume 37, issue 2 of *Library Trends* (1988) are of interest, too. These include N. S. Allen's "The Museum Prototype Project: A View from the Library" (pp. 175-93), which describes similarities and differences between libraries and museums in sharing research data and in serving the art field; J. F. Vanderwateren's "Achieving the Link Between Art Object and Documentation: Experiences of the British Architectural Library" (pp. 243-51); and others. *The Architecture Library of the Future—Complexity and Contradiction*, edited by Peggy Ann Kusnerz (University of Michigan Press, 1989), is a compendium of articles covering user needs, resources, administration, and the librarian's role in architectural libraries. The journal *Visual Resources: An International Journal of Documentation* (1981-) should be checked periodically by the art librarian for coverage of special topics of interest. The journal is published by Gordon and Breach.

USE AND USERS OF
ART INFORMATION

Users of visual arts information can be categorized as art professionals (art historians, artists, art educators, critics, curators, and architects); students of the visual arts who are enrolled in art schools, colleges and universities, and secondary schools; and the interested public (museum goers, collectors, and others for whom art is a hobby or avocation). The article "Art Libraries and Collections" in the *Encyclopedia of Library and Information Science*, cited earlier, covers the myriad needs of visual art information users.

Interest in use and users of art materials is not a new phenomenon: an early article on use of art materials was "The Use of Art Books," by Katherine Patten (*Bulletin of the American Library Association* 1 [July 1907]: 183). More recent works include Phillip Pacey's enduring contribution, "How Art Students Use Libraries—If They Do," *Art Libraries Journal* 7 (Spring 1982): 33-38; and Deidre Corcoran Stam's "How Art Historians Look for Information," in *Art Documentation* 3 (Winter 1984): 117-19. Stam's contributions in this area have continued with "Tracking Art Historians: Information Needs and Information Seeking Behavior," *Art Libraries Journal* 14 (Fall 1989): 13-16. The latter paper describes three prevalent methods for generating data on information needs: bibliometric tracking, autobiographical methods or participant observation, and user studies.

Several chapters in Kusnerz's *The Architecture Library of the Future* (Univ. of Michigan Press, 1989) address user needs. See especially Kurt Brandle, "What Do Researchers Want from the Architecture Library?" (pp. 21-26) and Hemalata Dandekar, "What Do Planners Want? What Do Planners Need?" (pp. 27-34). The Getty Art History Information Project investigated information-seeking practices of art historians and published the report entitled *Object, Image, Inquiry: The Art Historian at Work* (Getty Art History Information Program, 1988), by Elizabeth Bakewell, William O. Beeman, and Carol M. Reese. J. Cullars has investigated citation practices in the arts, and published "Citation Characteristics of Monographs in the Fine Arts," *Library Quarterly* 62 (July 1992): 325-42. Cullars is referenced elsewhere in this volume for other citation studies in the humanities. Despite the increase in use and user studies over the past decade, more information is needed—especially about users other than art historians—and users of other than traditional print materials. The next decade may see expansion of our present definition of use and user studies.

COMPUTERS IN THE VISUAL ARTS

The literature of computer applications in the visual arts is large and continues to expand rapidly. The computer is used in a wide variety of ways, from computer-assisted design in architecture to computer graphics and computerized information retrieval in museums and libraries.

The historical development of computer applications in art can be traced by referring to several review sources. *The Annual Review of Information Science and Technology* is a good starting point. "Information Systems and Services in the Humanities," by Joseph Raben and Sarah K. Burton, covers arts information systems through 1980 (vol.16, ASIS, 1981, pp. 254-56), and the review entitled "Visual Arts Resources and Computers," by Karen Markey in volume 19 (ASIS, 1984, pp. 271-309) is specifically directed to the visual arts and brings the reader up to a decade ago. An early book on the subject is worth a look if it is history that is of interest: see Jasia Reichardt's *The Computer in Art* (Van Nostrand, 1971).

Subject access is the topic of Karen Markey's *Subject Access to Visual Resources Collections: A Model for Computer Construction of Thematic Catalogs* (Greenwood Press, 1986).

The Art and Architecture Thesaurus Project of the J. Paul Getty Trust has been the subject of many articles. For a description, see "Architectural Projects of the J. Paul Getty Trust," by Marilyn Schmidt in Kusnerz's book. Other articles on the project and its output are C. Whitehead, "Faceted Classification in the Art and Architecture Thesaurus," *Art Documentation* 8 (Winter 1989): 175-77; and J. Stanley, "Symposium: Implementing the Art and Architecture Thesaurus—Controlled Vocabulary in the Extended MARC Format," *Art Documentation* 9 (Fall 1989): 121 ff.

R. Skinner's "Networking from the Ground Up: Implementing Macintosh Networks in a Newly Constructed Arts Library," in *Library LANs* (Meckler, 1992, pp. 50-62), describes a system at Southern Methodist University.

Information technology and its applications in architecture libraries are discussed in Part 2, "Information Resources in the Architecture Library," in Kusnerz's *The Architecture Library of the Future*, referenced earlier. Archivist David Bearman addresses the necessity of organizing architectural drawings for interdisciplinary access in "Buildings as Structures, as Art and as Dwellings: Data Exchange Issues in an Architectural Information Network," in *Databases in the Humanities and Social Sciences 4*, edited by Lawrence J. McCrank (Learned Information, 1989). The work of Bearman was supported by the Getty Trust. Ronald Stenvert suggests computer-aided design (CAD) in study of the construction of buildings illustrated in two-dimensional drawings. (Stenvert's paper was part of a series of art history presentations at the 1988 Cologne Computer Conference, a conference held September 7-10, 1988, at Cologne University. The papers are abstracted in *Cologne Computer Conference 1988 Volume of Abstracts*, pp. A.7 1-14.)

The number of online and CD-ROM databases of bibliographic information in the visual arts continues to grow, but the literature in this area has more recently focused on both bibliographic and new image databases rather than the "how to search" articles that were typical in the early to mid-1980s. Among the most important bibliographic databases is Art Literature International (*International Repertory of the Literature of Art*), which includes all entries in the print *RILA* database since 1975. Art Literature International covers all aspects of Western art from late antiquity to the present and is file 191 on DIALOG's service. RILA's contents were merged with that of *Repertoire d'Art et d'Archeologie* to form the newly titled *Bibliography of the History of Art* (J. Paul Getty Trust, 1991 ff.). The *Repertoire d'Art et d'Archeologie* was produced from 1910 through 1990 in Paris by the Centre de Documentation Sciences Humaines.

ArtBibliographies Modern, another online bibliographic file, covers nineteenth- and twentieth- century art and design, as well as nineteenth-century themes begun in the eighteenth century. Updated semiannually, the database covers the literature from 1974 on. It is produced by ABC-Clio.

Two online files in architecture are available on DIALOG Information Services: *Architecture Database* and the *Avery Architecture Index*. The former is provided by the British Architectural Library at the Royal Institute of British Architects and is comprised of records from the *Architectural Periodicals Index* (from 1978 on) and the *Architectural Book Catalogue* (1984 to the present). The *Avery Architecture Index* is produced at the Avery Architectural and Fine Arts Library of Columbia University. It is part of the Getty Art History Information Program, and utilizes terms from the Art and Architecture Thesaurus, also sponsored by the Getty. All areas of architecture, including technical aspects, are included in the database, which covers from 1979 to the present.

The Cologne Computer Conference 1988 featured several papers on databases for museums and libraries. In the conference abstracts, see, for example, "ArtQuest and the ASI Art Reference Library," by Richard Hislop. This particular paper addresses the Art Sales Index information service, which stores auction sales information gathered from art sales catalogs worldwide. Another paper abstracted in the "data banks" group is Gunther Baum's "The Database of Dusseldorf's Cultural Institutions," a description of marketing plans for the cooperative catalog of the largest art institutions in Dusseldorf. Ultimate goals include making the data available on CD-ROM. (See pp. E4-1 to E4-14 in the *Cologne Computer Conference 1988 Volume of Abstracts.*)

Sales catalogs are indexed in *SCIPIO* (*Sales Catalog Index Project Input Online*), a tool that leads the user to libraries holding particular sales catalogs. Like the *Avery Index*, this tool has been sponsored by the Getty Art Information Project.

H. W. Wilson's *Art Index* (available in print, online, and on CD-ROM) continues to be one of the most used databases in fine arts. Available in machine-readable form from 1984, *Art Index* serves as a good starting point for searching art periodicals and museum publications. Although it does include foreign-language materials, its scope and coverage will seem limited to the most scholarly art historian because of the omission of valuable art history materials such as books, theses, and dissertations.

The automation of visual arts information has had unparalleled support from the Getty Art History Information Program. Besides support of database access and the Art and Architecture Thesaurus project, two additional projects deserve mention here. The development of Synoname[TM] answers the problem of variant names for individual artists; the software is available on diskette. It is an extension of the development of the *Getty Union List of Artist Names.* An extensive article on the name variant problem and various solutions, including Synoname[TM], is "Getty's Synoname[TM] and Its Cousins: A Survey of Applications of Personal Name-Matching Algorithms," by Christine L. Borgman and Susan L. Siegfried, in *Journal of the American Society for Information Science* 43 (August 1992): 459-76. A second project addresses the problem of place names, the *Thesaurus of Art Historical Place Names.* Information on these tools is available from the Getty Art History Information Program. Both have implications for online searching in the arts.

There are several articles that will lead the reader to additional online and CD-ROM resources in the visual arts. Nadine Walter's "Computerization in Research in the Visual Arts," *Art Documentation* 10 (Spring 1991): 3-12 is an excellent source: it lists computerized projects in art history with specific examples of many types: art object cataloging projects, national inventory projects, databases of museum collections, photo archives projects, provenance projects, and image databases are identified and briefly described. Marcia Reed's "Navigator, Mapmaker, Stargazer: Charting the New Electronic Sources in Art History," *Library Trends* 40 (Spring 1992): 733-55, is a thorough bibliographic essay on the sources and the projects that developed them. A good list of CD-ROM offerings in art and art history is included in Lucy Buck and Paul Travis Nicholls's "Arts and Humanities Sources on CD-ROM," *CD-ROM Professional* (March 1991): 99. Augusta Maria Paci and co-authors Paola Castellucci and Lucina Ferraria provide a European perspective on art information: they list Italian information products in the visual arts in "Electronic and Optical Sources of Information in the Humanities: A Survey of Library Users, Products and Projects in Italy," *Online Review* 14 (1990): 390-400.

Museum automation and the development of multimedia approaches to information management have been addressed in both the arts management literature and the literature of library and information science. Only a few examples can be mentioned here. "The Changing Museum," by Howard Besser (*ASIS '87 Proceedings of the 50th ASIS Annual Meeting*, edited by Ching-Chih Chen, ASIS, 1987), provides background on image digitization in museum information management. Judi Moline's "Designing Multimedia Systems for Museum Objects and their Documentation," *Microcomputers for Information Management* 8 (June 1991): 69-86, discusses hypertext and multimedia approaches to providing curators and art historians needed access to museum objects. Knowledge representation in the arts and humanities is addressed in several other publications by the same author.

Jonathan Moffett's article, "The Beazley Archive: Making a Humanities Database Accessible to the World," in *Bulletin of the John Rylands University Library* 74 (Autumn 1992): 39-52, details examples of applications of information technology in the visual arts. Moffett considers diverse aspects of providing access to a specialized text and image database, from the relational structure of the database to problems of providing images to remote locations to data security and copyright considerations.

Deidre C. Stam describes the Clearinghouse on Art Documentation in "Automating Art and Museum Information," *Art Documentation* 11 (Winter 1992): 181-84. The clearinghouse, according to Stam, "collects and disseminates information on the development and application of computer technology and the documentation of that development, particularly in the art research and museum environments. Included in that definition is information related to reproductive visual resources" (p. 181).

The final topic involving computers in visual arts information is the expanding availability of materials on the Internet. The growth in the field of visual arts is rapid even when compared to the explosive growth of the Internet as a whole. Not only do we have text- and resource- finding tools available, but a variety of image files are now accessible through the network. The images are especially easy to access for those using workstations with hypermedia browsers such as Mosaic. Even for those with only dialup access, images can be viewed and downloaded to the personal computer.

Several guides that will make Internet use easier have appeared. The "Gopher Jewels" list, compiled by David Riggins and accessible via Veronica, lists many gophers under the heading "Arts and Humanities." Other guides include Diane Kovac's "Listservs in Art" and "SURAnet Guide to Selected Internet Resources." These guides can also be found at the gopher file server called "Clearinghouse of Subject Oriented Internet Resource Guides."

Among the resources listed in these guides are several locations where images and accompanying text files are archived. These include two electronic art galleries: the OTIS gopher server at the University of North Carolina, Chapel Hill; and the AMANDA gopher server at the University of Wisconsin, Madison. Information for users of OTIS specified that "OTIS is here to distribute original, creative images over the world's computer networks for public perusal, scrutiny, and retransmission ... to facilitate communication, inspiration, critique, and to set the foundations for digital immortality." Instructions for putting artwork in the "gallery" follow the introduction. Access OTIS by anonymous ftp: sunsite.unc.edu. The University of Wisconsin's Archigopher provides access to many architectural images and also serves as a gateway to related gophers containing images and text on such as the highly acclaimed Vatican exhibition at the Library of Congress.

On a less scholarly, but still useful note, ASCII cartoons are available on the Internet, and include the Simpsons, among other characters. Access is via Gopher: Universitaet des Saarlandes. See Harley Hahn and Rick Stout, *The Internet Complete Reference* (Osborne McGraw-Hill, 1994), p. 541, for details and other art sources.

An essential source of information for anyone interested in image files is Jim Howard's "The 'What/Where/How' for Pictures," a FAQ (frequently asked questions file) on news.answers. Other FAQs that may be useful to users of visual arts materials range from one on historical costumes to one on bonsai. Users can expect to see still greater increases in the number of Internet sources in the visual arts, at least for the next few years.

MAJOR ART ORGANIZATIONS AND SPECIAL COLLECTIONS IN VISUAL ARTS

At the international level, much of the impetus for the collection and dissemination of art information has come from projects aided by UNESCO. For example, since 1949 UNESCO and its national commissions have worked with art publishers to establish a central archives service of art reproductions. In this undertaking, UNESCO had the assistance of the International Council of Museums. Other organizations that have been active on the international scene include the Artists International Association, International Association of Art Critics, and the International Union of Architects. Another major influence in the area of art information is the Getty Trust, of which the Art History Information Program, the Getty Center for the History of Art and the Humanities, and of course, the Getty Museum in Malibu, California, are part. Projects as diverse as Art and Architecture Thesaurus, the Census of Antique Art and Architecture Known to the Renaissance, and the Program for Art on Film, based at various locations in the United States and abroad, are all supported by the Getty organizations. The J. Paul Getty Trust public affairs office is located at 1875 Century Park East, Suite 2300, Los Angeles, CA 90067.

Within the United States, the variety of national, regional, and state organizations concerned with art information is too large for an exhaustive listing, but several national organizations should be mentioned. The American Federation of Arts (41 East 65th Street, New York, NY 10021) was founded in 1909 to broaden public art appreciation, especially in areas of the country not served by large museums. Its membership includes 500 art institutions and 3,000 individuals. The program of the organization includes circulating museum collections and preparing curricula on visual arts education. The Federation advises on the publication of the *American Art Directory*, *Sources of Films on Art*, and *Who's Who in American Art*.

The National Art Education Association (1916 Association Drive, Reston, VA 22091) was founded in 1947 to promote study of the problems of teaching art as well as to encourage research and experimentation in the visual arts. Affiliated with the National Education Association, the National Art Education Association has 8,000 art teachers, supervisors, and students as members.

Other national organizations include the American Association of Museums (1225 Eye Street NW, Washington, DC 20005), the College Art Association (275 7th Avenue, New York, NY 10001-6708), and the American Arts Alliance (1319 F Street NW, Suite 500, Washington, DC 20004). There is also the American Art Association.

Of special interest to librarians and information specialists are the Art Libraries Society, with headquarters in Coventry, England, which publishes *Art Libraries Journal*, and its American counterpart Art Libraries Society/North America (c/o Pamela J. Parry, 3775 Bear Creek Circle, Tucson, AZ 85749), publisher of *Art Documentation*.

The Museums, Arts, and Humanities division of Special Libraries Association (SLA) was established in 1929 (as the Museum Group) and is now the fifth largest SLA division, with over 1,000 members. The American Society for Information Science (ASIS) also has a special interest group (SIG) on Arts and Humanities. According to the 1994 directory of ASIS, members of the SIG are "interested in retrieval of text, images, sound and humanistic implications of information technology."

There is also the Association of Architectural Librarians (1735 New York Avenue NW, Washington, DC 20006), which publishes a newsletter for the membership.

There are also many special associations that will have information for the interested librarian or information specialist. General directories will give the particulars on organizations like the Glass Art Society, Handweavers Guild of America, the National Sculpture Society, National Watercolor Society, the American Pewter Guild, and the Art Dealers Association of America, to name just a few.

Collections in the fine arts are numerous and can be found in public, academic, and special libraries. Examples of public library collections of note include the Art and Architecture Division of the New York Public Library and the Fine Arts Library of the Westminster City Libraries (UK). Among university libraries, we have the Avery Architectural Library at Columbia University (New York), the Fine Arts Library of Harvard University (Cambridge, Massachusetts), and the Marquand Library of Princeton University (Princeton, New Jersey).

Other notable United States library collections include the Dumbarton Oaks Research Library in Washington, D.C., the Frick Art Reference Library in New York; the libraries of the Art Institute of Chicago; and the Archives of American Art in Washington, D.C.

Art Information: Research Methods and Resources, by Lois Swan Jones (Kendall/Hunt, 1990), has a section on research centers which should be consulted for other library and research collections. *Subject Collections* 7th ed., by Lee Ash (R. R. Bowker, 1993), is also a valuable source of information on special resources.

NOTES

[1] Kenneth McLeish, ed., *Key Ideas in Human Thought* (New York: Facts on File, 1993), pp. 47-49.

[2] Gerd Muehsam, *Guide to Information Sources in the Visual Arts* (Santa Barbara, CA: ABC-Clio, 1978), p. 12.

8 ◆ PRINCIPAL INFORMATION SOURCES IN THE VISUAL ARTS

ARTS IN GENERAL

Bibliographic Guides and Periodical Directories

278. **Art Research Methods and Resources: A Guide to Finding Art Information.** 2d ed. Rev. and enl. Lois Swan Jones. Dubuque, IA: Kendall/Hunt, 1984. 332p. ISBN 0-8403-3237-8.

A useful and informative literature guide on the various reference tools in the field; coverage includes both the broad and general reference materials and also those that are highly specialized for scholars and specialists. The earlier edition in 1979 was commended for its attention to methodology as well as sources, although the resources section was considered more successful than either the section on methodology or the one on obtaining the material. This edition has enlarged the coverage to four sections, the first of which is intended for the novice and serves as a manual of preparation. The second section describes methodology for doing art research projects, whereas the third section provides an annotated listing of 1,500 tools (including online databases). The fourth section covers the procedures on obtaining materials and describes research library collections. Appendices include multi-language glossaries of art terms; indexes are provided.

Visual Arts Research: A Handbook, by Elizabeth B. Pollard (Greenwood Press, 1986), covers information sources of both the fine and applied arts, with chapters devoted to separate categories of information.

279. **Fine Arts: A Bibliographic Guide to Basic Reference Works, Histories, and Handbooks.** 3d ed. Donald L. Ehresmann. Englewood, CO: Libraries Unlimited, 1990. 373p. ISBN 0-87287-640-3.

This is a welcome edition, as its predecessor (1979) had begun to show its age. The title remains a useful source of information regarding reference literature in the arts. Having incorporated all relevant titles from Chamberlin (entry 282n) in past editions, it continues to furnish a blend of older standard works, both articles and books of reference value, along with recent titles. Treatment is accorded to 2,051 entries representing the major body of reference literature published in the Western languages between 1830 and September 1988. Only tools that treat two or more of the three major media (painting, sculpture, or architecture) are included. Part I contains seven chapters representing reference types such as bibliographies or directories, but also includes iconography. Part II adds six chapters of histories and handbooks classified by historical period (prehistoric and primitive art) or by geography (Oriental Art). Annotations are relatively brief and descriptive for the most part, but evaluative comments are found in some entries. There are detailed author-title and subject indexes.

280. **Fine Arts Periodicals: An International Directory of the Visual Arts.** Doris Robinson. Voorheesville, NY: Peri Press, 1991. 570p. ISBN 1-879796-03-1.

This large-type, handy dictionary was developed in response to a need to control the periodical literature of art in a comprehensive and manageable way. The work identifies nearly 2,800 art periodicals, newsletters, and newspapers, a number of which are not found in *Ulrich's International Periodicals Directory* (entry 7). All media and fields of art are represented through inclusion of both major and minor sources, providing an excellent overview of publishing in the field. Entries are arranged under broad topical headings such as "Information Sources," "Visual Arts," "Decorative Arts and Crafts," "Buildings and Interiors," "Photography," etc. These are subdivided by more specific or specialized aspects. Entries furnish current information regarding address, publisher, editor, subscription, audience, summary of content, and pointers for authors and advertisers. The work is adequately indexed by title, publisher, organization, ISSN, and subject.

281. **Guide to Research in Classical Art and Mythology**. Frances Van Keuren. Chicago: American Library Association, 1991. 307p. ISBN 0-8389-0564-1.

Designed to provide students and specialists with a guide and manual to conducting research in the area of classical art and mythology, this excellent work by a professor of art history is divided into three principal segments. Coverage is given to "General Research," "Mythology," and "Media Studies," which in turn are subdivided into seventeen chapters. The three chapters under "General Research" cover Greek, Etruscan, and Roman art and architecture. The segment on "Mythology" supplies five chapters on mythology as treated in ancient art and literature, and the nine chapters in "Media Studies" each treat a particular art form such as Etruscan mirrors or Athenian vases. Each chapter opens with a description of the major source or sources and their applications for study and research, followed by annotated listings of complementary and supplementary sources. Emphasis is on English-language sources when possible. Author-title and subject indexes provide access.

282. **Guide to the Literature of Art History.** Etta Mae Arntzen and Robert Rainwater. Chicago: American Library Association, 1980. 616p. ISBN 0-8389-0263-4.

An extremely comprehensive work that covers more than 4,000 reference and research items in the field. The emphasis is on the needs of advanced researchers, but the coverage, featuring chapters on art history, proves useful to a general audience as well. The four main sections treat general reference sources, general primary and secondary sources, specific art forms (such as painting or sculpture), and serials. This work represents a complete revision of the old standard in the field by Mary Walls Chamberlin, *Guide to Art Reference Books* (American Library Association, 1959). It retains 40 percent of Chamberlin's materials, but annotations are revised and rewritten.

The Chamberlin effort, long considered a landmark publication, annotates more than 2,500 titles ranging from ready-reference to highly specialized, topical materials. Annotations are descriptive and frequently provide critical commentary.

283. **Research Guide to the History of Western Art.** W. Eugene Kleinbauer and Thomas P. Slavens. Chicago: American Library Association, 1982. 229p. (Sources of Information in the Humanities, v.2). ISBN 0-8389-0329-0.

Another in the series of literature guides edited by Slavens, a now-retired professor of library science at the University of Michigan, in which he collaborates with an authority in the field. This work is designed for library school students and librarians. It covers first the work of Kleinbauer, which consists of a series of bibliographic essays on the field of art history. This is the major segment, and presents interpretations of topical material such as "psychological approaches" and "studying the art object." The second segment is by Slavens and covers reference works. This is an annotated list of major reference tools. Although the annotations are full and informative, the entries represent standards in the field rather than newer reference books.

Bibliographies and Catalogs

284. **Action Art: A Bibliography of Artists' Performance from Futurism to Fluxus and Beyond.** John Gray, comp. Westport, CT: Greenwood Press, 1993. 343p. (Art Reference Collection, no. 16). ISBN 0-313-28916-6.

The compiler serves as the Director of the Black Arts Research Center, and has been a published bibliographer of the performing arts. He brings expertise and understanding to the development of this work. The result is a comprehensive bibliography of international proportions, and a successful first effort to document performance art as a modern art form. There are more than 3,600 entries identifying both print and media materials issued from 1914 to 1992. The history of performance art is well treated here, with coverage given to its origins in various early twentieth-century movements such as Futurism, Dada, Russian Constructivism, and Bauhaus. The peak decades from the 1950s to the 1970s are identified through references to such developments as Fluxus, Guerilla Art Action, and Situationism. Individual artists and groups are included. Appendices supply useful listings of reference sources, archival collections, country, and group.

285. **Art and Architecture in Canada: A Bibliography and Guide to the Literature to 1981. Art et Architecture au Canada ...** Loren R. Lerner and Mary F. Williamson. Toronto: University of Toronto Press, 1991. 2v. ISBN 0-8020-5856-6.

A well-developed introductory essay establishes the purpose of this important and unique work documenting the art history literature of Canada. There are now more than 9,500 entries identifying the most important publications issued between 1825 and 1981 relating to Canadian art and architecture, regardless of place of publication. Arrangement of entries is by topical subject and geographical categories subdivided chronologically. Abstracts are furnished for each entry and written in the language of publication, either French or English. The authors bring expertise to the task from their professional positions as art librarians in academic libraries. Volume 1 treats the arts: painting, graphic arts, photography, decorative arts, sculpture, and so on is the first section, and architecture in all its aspects is the second section. Volume 2 supplies detailed indexes to authors and subjects.

286. **Art Books: A Basic Bibliography of Monographs on Artists.** Wolfgang M. Freitag. New York: Garland, 1985. 351p. (Garland Reference Library of the Humanities, v.574). ISBN 0-8240-8763-1.

This is a listing of 10,543 monographs on 1,870 individual artists representing all time periods and geographic locations. There is an emphasis on European and North American artists, and the work is based on the collection of the Harvard Fine Arts Library, where Freitag served as librarian. The bibliography was produced with a grant for aiding the study of art history from the Getty Trust, and begins with a list of 150 bibliographical sources. The major segment of the text is an alphabetical listing by artist of monographs which include biographies, bibliographies, catalogs, and *catalogues raisonnés*. Of course, major artists receive more entries than do lesser-known ones. There is an author index, and the bibliography includes titles in various languages. This effort draws on the previous work by Edna Louise Lucas, *Art Books: A Basic Bibliography on the Fine Arts* (New York Graphic Society, 1968), which contains 4,000 entries, including many on individual artists.

287. **The Arts of Africa: An Annotated Bibliography. 1986- .** Janet L. Stanley, comp. Atlanta, GA: Crossroads Press/African Studies Association, 1989- . ISSN 1044-8640.

Volume 1 furnishes coverage of the 1986-1987 period and was issued in 1989 to initiate this biennial publication based on the monthly library acquisition lists from the National Museum of African Art Branch of the Smithsonian Institution. The compiler serves as head librarian of the facility and has succeeded in producing a useful guide to the literature of African art. Volume 1 is a 268-page effort identifying books, articles, reviews, and exhibition catalogs. There are two major sections dealing with general studies, divided into twenty-one different geographical regions of the Continent. Entries represent the various art forms, along with treatment of African culture and black imagery in the Western world. Entries are full and informative and include OCLC numbers for the serials. Detailed author and subject indexes furnish access.

288. **Card Catalog of the Manuscript Collections of the Archives of American Art.** Wilmington, DE: Scholarly Resources, 1981. 10v. **Supp. 1981-1984**, 1985. 542p. ISBN 0-8420-2235-X.

Originally housed in the library of the Detroit Institute of the Arts, and now part of the Smithsonian Institution in Washington, the Archives was started in 1954 to provide documentation of all areas and aspects of American art history. The reproduction of its master catalog provides an excellent source of information on manuscripts in the collection. There are nearly 6 million items in 5,000 different collections. All items are available on microfilm either through interlibrary loan or at the regional centers in Boston, Detroit, New York, Washington, and San Francisco; thus, the work furnishes complete bibliographic control. Most items are biographical and much of the information is accessed through names of artists. There is no subject approach. The supplement furnishes listings for an additional 1,000 new collections acquired during the early 1980s, along with modifications for some of the earlier entries.

289. **Dictionary Catalog of the Art and Architecture Division, the Research Libraries of the New York Public Library**. New York Public Library, Art and Architecture Division. Boston: G. K. Hall, 1975. 30v. ISBN 0-8161-0061-6. **Supp. 1974.** 1976. 556p. **Ann. Supp.** 1976- .

This is another of the G. K. Hall publications providing photoreproduction of the catalog entries of a major research collection. This specialized tool lists the holdings of the Art and Architecture Division, regarded as one of the most significant resource collections in the visual arts. It consists of material cataloged through December 1971, representing painting, drawing, sculpture, the applied arts, and architecture. It is estimated to cover about 200,000 items treating all periods of art history on an international basis. Included also are those relevant volumes from other departments, such as the Cyrillic, Hebrew, and Oriental collections, as well as the Local History and Rare Books Divisions, and even indexing of related articles from journals in all parts of the library. A 1974 supplement was published in 1976 and covered material added from January 1972 to September 1974. Since 1972 all additions to the collection have been listed in the major general catalog of the library, *Dictionary Catalog of the Research Libraries*. Annual supplements have been issued since 1976 as *Bibliographic Guide to Art and Architecture* (entry 298).

290. **Dictionary Catalog of the Library of the Freer Gallery of Art. Smithsonian Institution.** 2d enl. ed. Boston: G. K. Hall, 1991. 252 microfiche. ISBN 0-8161-1791-8.

Another in the G. K. Hall line of catalog reproductions, this, like the others, has reproduced the cards of a notable library. The Freer Gallery has excellent depth in Oriental, Near Eastern, and nineteenth-century American art and its library resources are useful to people with a serious interest. Now on microfiche, this new edition represents an expansion of the six-volume print edition issued in 1967. The work is divided into two parts or sections; one for books in Western languages and the other for books in Oriental languages. More than 40,000 publications are represented, including books, pamphlets, and periodicals. An important feature is the inclusion of analytics for relevant periodical articles. Each section (Eastern and Western languages) is accessed individually through its authors, subjects, and titles in a unified, alphabetical arrangement.

291. **Feminist Art Criticism: An Annotated Bibliography.** Cassandra Langer. Boston: G. K. Hall, 1993. 250p. (A Reference Publication in Art History). ISBN 0-8161-8948-X.

Developed by a well-known specialist, art historian, and critic, this effort marks the first attempt to provide extensive documentation to the field of feminist art and its culture, theory, and criticism. More than 1,000 publications are identified; these include books, pamphlets, articles, periodicals, exhibition catalogs, newspapers, and even unpublished manuscripts. These vary from scholarly monographs to brief expositions in both mainstream and alternative press publications. Publication dates embrace the past 100 years and the Western tradition, but emphasis is placed on British and American scholarship over the past twenty-five years. An entry supplies the title, author, and imprint along with Langer's appraisal of its significance. Bibliographic references are included for some. Most valuable overall is the variety of perspectives offered by the listed titles, revealing a lack of systematic theory in their disagreements and contradictions concerning the feminist position.

292. **From Museums, Galleries, and Studios: A Guide to Artists on Film and Tape.** Susan P. Bessemer and Christopher Crosman, comps. Westport, CT: Greenwood Press, 1984. (Art Reference Collection, no. 6). 199p. ISBN 0-313-23881-2.
    A timely and useful source of information on more than 600 films, videocassettes, and audiocassettes which are currently available for loan, rental, or purchase. Educators, students, historians, and interest groups or professional organizations can use this guide to identify filmed and taped interviews with artists. This has been a useful tool at a time when oral history has been playing an increasingly important role in the planning of research and resource collections. For the most part, the work is restricted to the visual arts and includes painters, sculptors, architects, photographers, film and video artists, craftspeople, folk artists, and graphic artists. Annotations vary in length but complete bibliographic identification is provided for all entries.
    Another fine source, although older, is *Films on Art: A Source Book* from the Canadian Film Institute in association with Watson-Guptill (1977). This lists more than 450 films available in the United States and Canada alphabetically by title with complete bibliographic information.

293. **Library Catalog of the Metropolitan Museum of Art.** 2d ed. Rev. and enl. Metropolitan Museum of Art. Boston: G. K. Hall, 1980. 48v. **Supp. 1-4.** 1982-1989. ISBN 0-86291-862-6 (Supp. 4).
    Since the appearance in 1960 of the initial edition of this major source, it has been recognized as one of the chief bibliographic tools in the field. The new edition incorporates all holdings from the first edition still part of the collection, along with material from the eight supplements that followed it. (The supplements are still being produced for libraries that do not wish to invest in this new edition.) This dictionary catalog of author, subject, and title cards of the library holdings is in the style familiar to users of G. K. Hall products. Much recataloging was done to update terminology and spelling and to include new art developments. Sales catalogs are accessed by subject and by collector or auction house in the final three volumes. The new edition has supplements of its own that have appeared since its publication. The *Third Supplement* covers the period 1983 to 1986 in three volumes, while the *Fourth Supplement* treats materials added between 1987 and 1989, also in three volumes.

Indexes, Abstracts, and Serial Bibliographies

294. **Smithsonian on Disc: Catalog of the Smithsonian Institution Libraries on CD-ROM.** Boston: G. K. Hall, 1994. (CD-ROM)
    Through the wonders of the electronic age, users are now given "instant access to a national treasure." G. K. Hall, the longtime publisher of catalogs in print format, has introduced CD-ROM versions in what must be a prototype for future activity. The entire holdings of the Smithsonian Institution Libraries embrace 19 major collections and several affiliates. Relevant to the humanities are the holdings of Cooper Hewitt/National Museum Design Branch, National Museum of African Art Branch, National Museum of American Art Library, National Portrait Gallery Library, and numerous others with collections in architecture, textiles and tapestries, decorative arts, etc. Important also is the ability or opportunity to combine searches on the art objects with information on the ethnic or historical significance

obtained through materials from other collections (Anthropology Branch, National Museum of American History, Museum Reference Center Branch, etc.). Searching by keyword, name, or subject should be effective.

295. **Annual Bibliography of Modern Art.** The Museum of Modern Art Library, New York. Boston: G. K. Hall, 1987- . ISSN 0898-7300.

Compiled for the RLIN records of both recent and earlier publications acquired by the Museum Library, this work is available in print and microfilm and has proven to be a useful source for identification and verification of published materials. It documents the materials cataloged by this library and it affords bibliographers and specialists the opportunity to identify a wide range of materials. The collection at MOMA is one of the most comprehensive of its kind and treats modern art in all aspects and phases. As one might expect, this collection is international in scope and embraces a number of languages, although emphasis is given to the United States, Europe, and Japan. Books, periodicals, exhibition catalogs, manuscripts, and rare documents, as well as books created as art objects, are treated. Entries are arranged alphabetically by author, title, and subject and furnish cross-references. Main entries provide full information.

*296. **Art Index.** New York: H. W. Wilson. 1929- . Q. with ann. cum. ISBN 0-685-22229-2 (v.1-8); 0-685-22230-6 (v.9-28); 0-685-22231-4 (v.29-34).

This major indexing tool in the field covers approximately 225 periodicals, yearbooks, and museum bulletins in all fields related to the arts (archaeology, architecture, art history, city planning, crafts, graphic arts, industrial design, interior design, landscape architecture, museology, photography, and film, as well as the fine arts). Coverage is international, with periodicals in five languages; it represents the most comprehensive source of bibliographic information on periodical literature. Listings of articles appear under both author and subject, whereas book reviews are listed separately under the author of the book being reviewed. Exhibitions are listed under the artist or appropriate form heading, and the tool now indexes reproductions of art works. Illustrations without accompanying text are indexed under the artist's name. It is available online through WILSONLINE and in CD-ROM through WIL-SONDISC from September 1984 to the present. The discs are updated quarterly; the database is updated twice a week. Each is cumulative and contains well over 200,000 records.

Ethnoarts Index (Data Arts, 1987-) is a useful quarterly tool indexing the periodical literature related to art of the American Indian. Initially published as *Tribal Arts Review* from 1984 to 1987, it supplies a geographical arrangement and a quinquennial cumulation. Unfortunately, the publication appears to be on shaky ground, as no issues have appeared since 1991.

*297. **ARTbibliographies MODERN.** Santa Barbara, CA: ABC-Clio, 1973- . v.4- . Semiann. ISSN 0300-466X.

This work indexes and abstracts books, periodical articles, theses, and exhibition catalogs related to art and design of the nineteenth and twentieth centuries. Entries are arranged alphabetically and include artists' name and subjects. There is both an author index and an index of museums and art galleries. Online coverage is available through DIALOG with a database of the same name from 1974 to date. It is updated twice a year (the same as the print volume); there are well over 100,000 records, with about 12,000 added each year. Recently it has become available on CD-ROM as *ARTbibliographies MODERN on DISC* also on a semiannual basis. With the demise of *LOMA: Literature of Modern Art* (Lund Humphries, 1971-1972), this title established itself as the heir apparent and assumed the *LOMA* numbering system. The 1969-1971 volumes of *LOMA* are considered to be volumes 1-3 of the present effort. This left the 1972 period without coverage.

A competing publication, now defunct, *Art, Design, Photo* (Idea Books, 1973-1977), also regarded itself as the successor to *LOMA*—with the same editor. It began its coverage in 1972, thus providing uninterrupted access. It was unable to survive beyond the coverage of the 1976-1977 season, however.

298. **Bibliographic Guide to Art and Architecture.** Boston: G. K. Hall, 1976- . Ann. ISSN 0360-2699.

Although this work serves as an annual supplement to the *Dictionary Catalog of the Art and Architecture Division* of the New York Public Library (entry 289), it has gained recognition as a serial bibliography in its own right. Providing comprehensive coverage of the field, it reflects the broad collection development scheme of the library. It is not limited to the cataloging done for the division, but also includes entries from the MARC tapes of the Library of Congress. Coverage includes materials from the fields of painting, drawing, sculpture, architecture, and the applied arts. Entries are listed under authors, titles, and subjects in a dictionary arrangement and represent a variety of formats (monographs, serials, and nonbook materials).

*299. **Bibliography of the History of Art: BHA=Bibliographie d'histoire de l'arte.** Santa Monica, CA: J. Paul Getty Trust, Getty Art History Information Program, 1991- . ISSN 1150-1588.

Beginning with the 1990 volume, BHA emerged as the successor of *RILA (entry 302) and *RAA (entry 301). Sponsored as a cooperative enterprise of the International Committee for the History of Art, Comite français d'histoire de l'arte, College Art Association of America, and Art Libraries of North America, it operates as part of the J. Paul Getty Trust and of the Centre National de la Recherche Scientifique/Institut de l'Information Scientifique et Technique in Nancy, France. It represents an important abstracting service of international dimensions, with coverage given to some 4,000 periodical titles along with books, exhibition catalogs, and dissertations relating to the history of art. The initial 1990 volume (published in 1991) includes the 1989 period so as to continue the coverage of *RILA and *RAA. Coverage is given to European art from late antiquity and American art from the period of European discoveries. Eastern art is included only when it has influenced the West. All media are included, and each issue furnishes author, subject, and journal indexes. A fifth issue supplies a cumulative annual index. The work is available online through DIALOG as a continuation of the *RILA file and through QUESTEL as part of FRANCIS.

Art and Archaeology Technical Abstracts started initially in 1955 as an abstracting service sponsored by the International Institute for Conservation of Historic and Artistic Works and for the first ten years was produced in London. Beginning in 1966, it was published through the Institute of Fine Arts at New York University, and since 1986 it has operated as a part of the Conservation Information Network as a joint project of the Getty Conservation Institute and the Department of Communication, Canada. Throughout its existence, it has continued to provide abstracts of technical studies of conservation and restoration drawn from monographs, journals, and technical reports. It is available online through the Conservation Information Network.

*300. **Francis bulletin signalétique 526: art et archeologie, Proche-Orient, Asie, Amerique.** Paris: Institut de l'Information Scientifique et Technique, 1971- . Q. ISSN 0007-5612.

This quarterly abstracting service is part of the large-scale program of the Centre National de la Recherche Scientifique, now joined by the Institut in taking over the publishing activities of the CNRS Centre des Sciences Humaines et Sociales. This work covers international books and articles on the art of Asia, the Near East, and pre-Columbian America. These areas initially had been picked up by the *Bulletin* from the *Répertoire d'art et d'archeologie* (entry 301) after that publication narrowed its coverage. Online availability is through FRANCIS; the database is *Francis: Art et Archeologie. 526.* The complete file of about 35,000 citations dates from its beginning as a print resource in 1972, and adds about 2,800 records per year.

*301. **Répertoire d'art et d'archeologie.** Paris: Morance, 1910-1989. Ann. ISSN 0080-0953.

This was a highly regarded, classified, annotated bibliography of books, pamphlets, and periodical articles recognized for its extensive coverage of materials on an international basis. Books were covered beginning in 1920, and classifications tended to be broad, generally by period and country. It ended when it merged with *RILA* (entry 302) to form *Bibliography of the History of Art* (entry 299). Since its inception in 1910, it had undergone several changes in sponsorship and in scope and had appeared under the auspices of the Comite Français d'Histoire de l'Art with the aid of UNESCO. Since 1965, a new series begins with Early Christian art, eliminating the coverage of antiquity, Islamic art, and Eastern art. These areas were taken by the massive CNRS FRANCIS biblographic project (entry 300) and the Repertoire was issued as a quarterly publication by the Institut de l'Information Scientifique et Technique beginning in 1971. There is an index of artists as well as an author index and a subject index. The work is available online from 1973 to 1989 as *Francis bulletin signalétique 530: Répertoire d'art et d'archeologie* through the FRANCIS system (CNRS and the Institut de l'Information Scientifique et Technique). There are about 200,000 records.

*302. **RILA, Répertoire international de la litterature de l'art/International Repertory of the Literature of Art.** Williamstown, MA: Clark Art Institute/Getty Art History Information Program, 1975-1989. Semiann. ISSN 0145-5982.

This work ended with its merger with *Répertoire d'art et d'archeologie* (entry 301) to form *BHA* (entry 299). It began with an introductory or demonstration issue in 1973, providing initial exposure to what turned out to be an important and comprehensive international abstracting tool treating books, periodical articles, newspaper articles, festschriften, congress reports, exhibition catalogs, museum publications, and dissertations relating to post-classical European and post-Columbian American art. Its scope complemented *Francis Bulletin signalétique 526: art et archeologie* (entry 300). The abstracts were arranged alphabetically by author under topical headings representing forms such as reference works, or subjects and periods such as medieval art. An exhibition list and an author-subject index were included. The file of *RILA* is available online through DIALOG as *Art Literature International*. Coverage is complete from 1975 to 1989. It contains more than 133,000 records.

Art Work and Reproductions—Catalogs, Etc.

303. **The Black Artist in America: An Index to Reproductions**. Dennis Thomison, comp. Metuchen, NJ: Scarecrow Press, 1991. 396p. ISBN 0-8108-2503-1.

This is a useful and comprehensive index to the reproductions appearing in books, magazines, and exhibition catalogs of the work of nearly 1,000 African-American painters, sculptors, printmakers, illustrators, and others in the visual arts. The compiler is a university librarian who brings both expertise and familiarity with abundant resources to his treatment of artists dating from the mid-eighteenth century (Joshua Johnson) to the present (Richard Hunt and Faith Ringgold). The work is divided into three principal sections, beginning with a list of publications and institutions cited in part 2, the main body of the effort. Part 2 supplies entries alphabetically arranged by artist and gives personal information and references to biographical sources, reproductions, and additional readings. The final section contains several bibliographic listings, including audiovisual materials and doctoral dissertations. A subject index is provided.

*304. **Electronic Library of Art: A Survey of Western Art**. Milpitas, CA: EBook, 1992. 4v. (CD-ROM).

The study of art is aided immeasurably by the appearance of the new technology. CD-ROM, especially, may be used for identification, exposition, and interpretation of art works. This effort supplies a variety of images along with exposition of artists and time periods. Thousands of pictures in full color help the student appreciate the nature of the work. Exposition is well-developed. The work embraces the various art forms: painting, sculpture, architecture, and photography. Text is culled from theater dictionaries and other information tools. The work is indexed by artist, title, medium, school, and subject and represents a comprehensive survey of Western art. Each volume is issued on a separate disc, with all four volumes appearing in 1992.

The *International Art Catalog* is an extensive set of 22 discs produced by Artificial Intelligence Publishing and selling for more than $20,000. It supplies full-color reproductions of paintings and sculptures from all parts of the world and various time periods. Indexing is thorough and access is possible by artist, period, title, pseudonym, subject, and school.

305.   **The Fine Art Index**. North American ed. Chicago: International Art Reference; distr., New York: Distributed Art Publishers, 1991. 660p. ISBN 0-962816-0-5.

Not really an index, but more a catalog of illustrations of some 1,000 examples of North America's finest artwork, this tool furnishes reproductions by some 350 artists. Illustrations are excellent, in full color, and provide awareness of the work of both established and aspiring artists. The effort is divided into the broad general categories of paintings, drawings and prints, conceptual and installed artwork, sculpture, and photographs; crafts are excluded entirely. Omissions and inclusions remain a problem for any title that attempts to treat "the finest." Entries are brief and range from one to three photographs, with no prices or accompanying text other than basic identification information. Directory listings include galleries, museums, and business services; exhibition schedules along with maps of gallery communities are given. Indexes furnish access by galleries, artists, appraisers, associations, auction houses, and conservators.

306.   **Harvard University Art Museums: A Guide to the Collections.** Kristin A. Mortimer with William G. Klingelhofer. New York: Abbeville, 1985. 344p. ISBN 0-89659-600-1.

Harvard's is one of the most distinguished university art collections, and this catalog presents a sampling of the many objects held by the three museums now designated The Harvard University Art Museums. The tool was produced in celebration of the opening of the Arthur M. Sackler Museum, which joins the William Hayes Fogg and the Busch-Reisinger museums in providing an excellent and well-balanced study of the visual arts. The guide has nearly 400 reproductions of art objects, of which 80 are in color, and represents a diversified collection scheme. The Sackler Museum contains ancient, Islamic, and Oriental art; the Fogg has Western, European, and American; the Busch-Reisinger is limited to European, with an emphasis on German, art. Objects are identified by title, artist, date, medium, source, and acquisition number. Arrangement is generally by time period, medium, or country, and most items are given brief description and historical coverage.

Since 1987, Chadwyck-Healey has issued *The Artists File* of the New York Public Library on over 11,000 microfiche. This is mainly the clipping file of some 1.5 million items treating 76,000 painters, sculptors, architects, and craftspeople and represents the most comprehensive source of biographical information available in the art world. It is also the single largest collection of reproductions ever issued. Files include brochures, newsletters, book jackets, and more, constituting an important pictorial resource.

307.   **Historical Art Index, A.D. 400-1650: People, Places, and Events Depicted.** Mercedes Rochelle. Jefferson, NC: McFarland, 1989. 217p. ISBN 0-89950-449-3.

This is a unique and valuable tool for those seeking art work representing events, personalities, and places in Western history. It serves first to locate art objects of various kinds (paintings, woodcuts, tapestries, manuscripts, engravings, miniatures, etc.) in museums and galleries and second to identify reproductions in books. Emphasis is on the topic rather than the artist, with entries arranged alphabetically by subject of the artwork. Although topical coverage is restricted to a period of 1,250 years, there are no limitations on the date of the art, with some entries created as recently as the early twentieth century. Most coverage is given to European nobility and portraiture. Entries furnish brief description of subject, date, artist, and medium along with indications of location and reproduction. Works are listed chronologically under each heading. There is a directory of collections and a bibliography of books cited.

308. **Illustration Index.** 2d ed. Lucile E. Vance and Esther M. Tracey. Metuchen, NJ: Scarecrow Press, 1966. 527p. **Supps. III-VII.** 1973-1991. ISBN 0-8108-2659-6. (VII).

This has become a standard tool for identification of photographs, maps, and drawings in eight to ten popular periodicals as well as a selective listing of books. This second edition replaces the initial effort in 1957 and its 1961 supplement by including their content together with additional material in an expanded volume supplying coverage to July 1963. Several supplements have followed to provide continuous coverage, and have been labeled as editions. *Illustration Index III,* by Roger C. Greer (Scarecrow Press, 1973), covers the period July 1963 to December 1971, whereas *Illustration Index IV,* by Marsha C. Appel (Scarecrow Press, 1980), embraces a five-year period, 1972-1976. *Illustration Index V,* also by Appel (Scarecrow Press, 1984), treats the period 1977-1981. *Illustration Index VI* (Scarecrow Press, 1988) identifies some 35,000 illustrations in nine magazines between 1982 and 1986. A variety of subjects, such as animals, architecture, plants, Indians, furniture, personalities, and more, are covered. Thousands of entries provide references, with description of type and illustration. Arrangement is by subject. Appel's most recent issue is *Illustration Index VII* (Scarecrow Press, 1993) providing access to more than 28,000 illustrations appearing in the media between 1987 and 1991. They are indexed under some 19,000 subjects.

309. **Mythological and Classical World Art Index: A Locator of Paintings, Sculptures, Frescoes, Manuscript Illuminations ...** Mercedes Rochelle. Jefferson, NC: McFarland, 1991. 279p. ISBN 0-89950-566-X.

The complete title of this effort goes on to say "Sketches, Woodcuts and Engravings Executed 1200 B.C. to A.D. 1900, with a Directory of the Institutions Holding Them." It complements the coverage of Rochelle's earlier effort, *Historical Art Index, A.D. 400-1650* (entry 307). The Greek and Roman world, as depicted in paintings, sculpture, mosaics, and drawings over a period of more than 3,000 years, provides the focus. Personalities, places, and events, including those relating to the gods and goddesses, are listed as topics or subject headings. Under these topics come the artworks, ranging from a single listing to around 250 in the case of Venus. Included for each is a brief description of the art, medium, artist, and museum location, along with references to one or more books to locate reproductions. There is a directory of museums, bibliography of cited works, and an index of artists and art works.

310. **Picture Sources 4.** 4th ed. Ernest H. Robl. New York: Special Libraries Association, 1983. 180p. ISBN 0-87111-274-4.

This is an interesting directory of picture collections that has earned a place in the hearts of those who have an interest in picture research. The new edition has listings for nearly 1,200 collections, of which 200 have been added since the third edition in 1975. Information is gathered through a survey of existing facilities that house pictures, maps, art reproductions, and news photographs. Although entries in earlier editions were arranged by subject, the present effort lists all collections in one alphabetical sequence. Helping to provide access is a detailed subject index. Entries supply the usual directory-type information, including collection size and scope. An important tool for general reference, with special value for the art librarian.

A similar effort is *Picture Researcher's Handbook: An International Guide to Picture Sources and How to Use Them,* now in its fifth edition (Blueprint, 1992) and compiled by Hilary Evans and Mary Evans. This is a well-conceived directory of more than 1,000 commercial sources of illustrations. Arranged alphabetically under broad categories (general, regional, national, and specialist), entries furnish address, telephone, telex, historical period of coverage, special subject collections, information on use, and access. The British slant is complementary to the emphasis on North America in *Picture Sources 4.*

Art Sales and Exhibitions—Catalogs, Etc.

311. **American Art Auction Catalogues, 1785-1942: A Union List.** Harold Lancour. New York: New York Public Library, 1944. 377p.

An old friend to those involved with the retrieval of information regarding the sale of art is this union checklist of more than 7,000 catalogs of auction sales of art objects. Covering a span of 157 years, it represents material originally published in the *Bulletin of the New York Public Library* between 1943 and 1944. This tool identifies locations of the catalogs listed in twenty-one libraries. Art objects represent a broad spectrum and include paintings, drawings, sculpture, furniture, rugs, jewelry, textiles, musical instruments, and curios. Not covered are books, maps, bookplates, stamps, and coins. There is a list of auction houses and an index of owners.

A comprehensive source of information on European sales is *Repertoire des catalogues de ventes publiques interessant l'art ou la curiosite, tableaux, dessins ...* by Frits Lugt (The Hague: Nijhoff, 1938-1987) which in four volumes provides a chronological list of more than 70,000 catalogs of art sales held between 1600 and 1925.

312. **Art and Antique Auctions World-Wide, 1982/83.** 2d ed. Janny Stuurman-Aalbers and Reinold Stuurman. New York: Facts on File, 1982. 320p. ISBN 0-317-57972-X (1987-1988).

This was the first issue of what was planned to be an annual review of art sales of nearly 200 auction houses located all over the world. Providing comprehensive coverage of the various fields of art, it includes paintings, drawings, and sculpture, as well as extensive listings of antiques and collectibles of decorative or hobbyist nature. Tiles, jewelry, classic automobiles, musical instruments, icons, rugs, and photographs are included, as well as numerous other components of the collector's art. Indexed by name of the artist are paintings, drawings, and etchings only. Subsequent issues have appeared biennially in the same format.

Art Prices Current (Art Trade, 1908-1973) provided an annual record of sales at European and American auction houses over a period of sixty-five years, except for a brief suspension of publication during World War I. Its focus was narrower and was limited to paintings, drawings, miniatures, engravings, and prints. *SCIPIO (Sales Catalog Index Project)* is a database begun in 1980 and available online through RLIN (Research Libraries Information Network). Citations are given to thousands of international auction catalogs held by eight major art libraries, including the National Gallery of Art, the Art Institute of Chicago, and the Getty Center for the History of Art and the Humanities. There are over 100,000 entries dating from 1600 to the present day.

313. **Art at Auction in America.** Silver Spring, MD: Krexpress, 1989- . Ann. ISSN 1046-4999.

Unlike the Sotheby Parke Bernet effort (entry 317), this is primarily an annual price guide for the art trade in this country. A total of sixteen American auction houses are treated each season, furnishing information on over 5,000 artists and 20,000 art works. Coverage is limited to paintings, water colors, and drawings, but embraces all periods and artists, reflecting the wide variety of purchases in American auction houses. Only works identified with a particular artist are presented; works of anonymous creators or from a certain school are excluded. Entries furnish artist name, medium, size, title, date of creation, auction house, date of sale, and price (beginning with $25). Intended for a wide audience, the work includes valuable advice and suggestions regarding value and pricing. Because of the low threshold price, it serves as an excellent survey of the entire market.

*314. **Art Sales Index: Oil Paintings, Drawings, Water Colours, and Sculpture.** Poughkeepsie, NY: Apollo Book, 1968/1969- . Ann.

The title of this work has changed several times, in line with a change in scope in which two of the publisher's serials (one covering oils, the other watercolors) were merged. Later, sculpture was added to the field of coverage. The text is written in both English and French, with the summaries given in English. The index provides listings of thousands of art items sold at auction throughout the world. Details of the sales include prices (given in pounds and dollars), currency of the sale, and a physical description of the art work. Name, nationality, and dates of artists are provided. Dates of sales are revealed, as are references to illustrations in auction catalogs.

315. **Frick Art Reference Library Sales Catalogue Index.** Boston: G. K. Hall, 1992. 230 microfiches. ISBN 0-8161-1794-2.

Since its beginning in 1920, the Frick Art Reference Library in New York has been one of the leading research centers for the history of art and has developed one of the largest collections of photographic reproductions of artworks. In its desire to document the photographs, there was an emphasis on the acquisition of sales catalogs, which continues to this day. The collection of 60,000 auction catalogs is recognized as the most valuable and comprehensive of its kind. Nearly 1,200 of that number were issued prior to the nineteenth century; more than 2,100 are unique to the United States or to the world. Emphasis is on Western art; paintings, drawings, sculpture, and illuminated manuscripts sold in Europe and the United States from the seventeenth century to the present. The index is organized in three sections, providing access by date of sale, auction house or place of sale, and by owner or collector.

Another important collection of exhibition catlaogs is held by the Arts Library of the University of California at Santa Barbara. Chadwyck-Healey has issued an excellent access tool on 13 microfiche. *Subject Index to Art Exhibition Catalogues on Microfiche* was issued initially in 1982. It now cumulates all entries in one sequence up to 1984. The work is valuable because of the international scope of the collection.

316. **Leonard's Annual Price Index of Art Auctions.** West Newton, MA: Auction Index, 1981- . Ann. ISSN 0747-6566.

Because of the immense size of the art market, a number of serial indexes of sales have been issued. *Leonard's Index of Art Auctions* was established initially as a quarterly publication to provide a record of original works of art sold at the major auction houses in this country. Because the season runs from September to the end of August, this annual cumulation appears in October or thereabout. Unlike some of the other guides, there are no illustrations here; instead, listings identify sales from more than thirty major American auction houses. Purchases are arranged by artist in alphabetical order, and listings are by price, with the most expensive items first. Art work includes oils, water colors, pastels, gouache, mixed media, drawings, and sculpture. There is a good annual review of paintings sold at auction for the year, a description of trends, and a brief bibliography.

317. **Sotheby's Art at Auction: The Art Market Review**. London: Sotheby Publications, 1967- . Ann. ISSN 0084-6783.

Sotheby's is now approaching its 260th season, having joined with Park Bernet to become one of the major art auction houses in the world. Offices and facilities are located in both London and New York, as well as other metropolitan areas. For a number of years, librarians and art devotees have anxiously awaited the appearance of its annual review of the preceding season, *Art at Auction: The Year at Sotheby's*, as it was formerly called. With its 1986-1987 issue, it changed its name, but retained its essential character as a generally slick and beautiful catalog, handsomely illustrated with photographs of objects sold. The sections with color may be described as lavish in appearance. The work is arranged according to medium, country, or style, with chapters on various topics. The format has changed at different times but generally some of the prime items sold are highlighted in expository essays, which sometimes embrace historical topics as well. All forms of art are sold at Sotheby; therefore, it provides an excellent record of notable sales.

Christie's Review of the Season (Phaidon; distr., Salem, NH: Salem House) is also a yearly record of an international auction house that provides a slick, detailed catalog with some illustrations of art objects to illustrate the sale of notable items. Its coverage dates back to the 1920s.

318. **The Worldwide Bibliography of Art Exhibition Catalogues, 1963-1987.** Millwood, NY: Kraus International Publications, 1992. 3v. ISBN 0-527-98004-8.

After twenty-four years, *The Worldwide Art Catalogue Bulletin* (Worldwide Books, 1963-1987), the quarterly publication valued by art librarians and specialists, ended with its fourth issue in 1987. It served to inform the user of the availability of exhibition catalogs, an important but elusive resource, from the leading jobber in the field, Worldwide Art Catalogue Centre, created in 1962 and supported by the major national art bodies. This cumulation furnishes information on the 17,500 exhibition catalogs treated during that twenty-four-year period. These catalogs are of immense value for their detailed descriptions of art objects contained in these exhibitions held throughout the world. Each catalog is described in detail and was available through the Centre. The cumulation is divided into four major sections; geographic, media, topic, and monographic (listing the catalogs of a single artist). Entries include title, English translation, first exhibiting institution, stock numbers, and references to the issue of the *Bulletin* in which the particular catalog was described.

An important work from the Archives of American Art is the *Collection of Exhibition Catalogs* (G. K. Hall, 1979), which gives the catalog cards for about 15,000 exhibition catalogs identified through a survey of libraries in both the public and private sectors. Arrangement is by name of gallery or museum and under the artist's name. Material covers the nineteenth and twentieth centuries, with an emphasis on the latter.

Dictionaries, Encyclopedias, and Handbooks

319. **American Artists: Signatures and Monograms, 1800-1989.** John Castagno. Metuchen, NJ: Scarecrow Press, 1990. 826p. ISBN 0-8108-2249-0.

This is a useful identification tool prepared by a creative artist-art representor who has identified some 5,100 artists with 10,000 signatures, monograms, and estate stamps. Entries are arranged alphabetically and furnish facsimile signatures of 4,500 Americans and 600 Canadians and Latin Americans. Many of the nineteenth-century and late twentieth-century artists have not been treated elsewhere. Also included in the entries are dates, nationality, and references to various sources of biographical, bibliographical, and pictorial information. Citations to relevant auction catalogs from more than twenty major galleries are supplied. A similar effort is Peter H. Falk's *Dictionary of Signatures and Monograms of American Artists: From the Colonial Period to the Mid-Twentieth Century* (Sound Vien Press, 1988), developed as a companion volume to *Who Was Who in American Art* (entry 358). It also identifies some 10,000 signatures arranged in three major segments; "Signatures and Monograms," "Initials and Monograms," and "Shapes and Symbols."

Castagno has also produced a companion effort, *European Artists: Signatures and Monograms, 1800-1990, Including Selected Artists from Other Parts of the World* (Scarecrow Press, 1990). Like the American version, it provides reference source material along with some 9,000 facsimile signatures of 4,800 European and 400 Australian, South African, and Japanese artists.

320. **Artists' Monograms and Indiscernible Signatures: An International Directory, 1800-1991.** John Castagno. Metuchen, NJ: Scarecrow Press, 1991. 538p. ISBN 0-8108-2415-9.

Signature and monogram sourcebooks for artists received a big boost with publication of the Castagno efforts the year prior to this work (entry 319). This is the first title devoted to identification of difficult or illegible signatures. It furnishes around 5,200 monogram and signature facsimiles for some 3,700 artists worldwide active within a period of nearly 200 years. As is true of the author's other efforts, signatures are drawn from reference books, catalogs, and magazines. Included here are painters, cartoonists, poster artists, and illustrators. There are chapters on initials, symbols and Oriental signatures, Cyrillics, Hebraic, and more. This is an important title for its emphasis on contemporary American artists, and places it along with the other Castagno efforts as supplementary to the massive Goldstein work described here.

Monogramm-Lexikon: Internationales Verzeichais der Monogramme bildender Kunstler seit 1850, by Franz Goldstein (de Grunter, 1964), is the standard source for identification of monograms of artists active since 1850. Entries give dates, media, and references to various information sources, such as Thieme and Becker (entry 343) and Benezit (entry 350). Arrangement is alphabetical by letters of the monogram. It complements the earlier five-volume title by George Kaspar Nagler, *Die Monogrammisten und diejenigen bekannten und unbekannten Kunstler aller Schulen ...* (Franz, 1858-1879; repr. de Graaf, 1966). This is a comprehensive dictionary of monograms and marks on all types of artwork by artists up to the 1850s. Arrangement is by dominant letter of the monogram.

321. The Artist's Handbook of Materials and Techniques. 5th ed. Ralph Mayer. Rev. and updated by Steven Sheehan. New York: Viking, 1991. 761p. ISBN 0-670-83701-6.

This is one of the established sources in the field that has gained an excellent reputation for depth of coverage and accuracy beginning with its initial appearance more than fifty years ago. Librarians have recognized this title as a vital work for both the practitioner and the librarian serving his or her needs. Originally published in 1940, the fourth edition was issued in 1981. The purpose of the tool has been and continues to be to provide the artist with a fully integrated, up-to-date account of both materials and procedures. The new edition by Sheehan (the director of the Ralph Mayer Center at Yale University) continues in the style of its predecessors in providing in-depth coverage of with new information on pigments, oil painting, tempera painting, watercolor, solvents, new materials, conservation practices, and so on. Outdated material has been deleted. Included also are notes, bibliographies, and an index.

322. The Classified Directory of Artists' Signatures, Symbols & Monograms. Enl. and rev. ed. H. H. Caplan. Detroit: Gale Research, 1982. 873p. ISBN 0-8103-0977-7.

Originally appearing in 1976, this tool gained a reputation as a solid piece of work in helping to identify artists by their signatures or monograms. Several thousand artists are covered, with the first section alphabetically arranged by name and providing facsimile signatures. The second section treats monograms arranged under the first letter; section 3 provides a listing of illegible signatures, which are arranged under the first recognizable letter. The final segment presents symbols arranged by general shape, such as circle or star. Preceding the text is an introductory section written in five different languages, evidence of the international character of this work. In general, this edition includes a greater number of lesser-known British artists than did the original.

This emphasis is continued by Caplan's supplementary effort, *The Classified Directory of Artists' Signatures, Symbols, & Monograms: American Artists with New U.K. Additions* published in London by P. Grahame in 1987.

323. The Color Compendium. Augustine Hope and Margaret Walch. New York: Van Nostrand Reinhold, 1990. 360p. ISBN 0-442-31845-6.

This work has provoked mixed reactions from its reviewers; it was felt in some quarters that it did not live up to its expectations as a comprehensive illustrated encyclopedia entirely devoted to color. Others have praised its scholarly yet popular approach in combining profound essay-length articles with brief descriptive pieces. In all, there are 1,100 entries arranged alphabetically, touching on every facet, some of peripheral nature, relating to the exposition of color. This breadth is admired by certain critics and lamented by others, but the work represents a panoramic view of the meaning, impact, and influence of color as it affects the world today. Computer technology, food preparation, advertising, fashion, architecture, and the arts are treated. There are good color plates to illustrate points, and useful appendices that provide listings of international color organizations, color specific systems, and a well-developed bibliography.

324. **Contemporary Masterworks**. Colin Naylor, ed. Chicago: St. James Press, 1991. 933p. (Contemporary Art Series). ISBN 1-55862-083-4.

As part of the Contemporary Art Series, this title represents a change in direction from previous issues, as it emphasizes the artworks rather than the artists. Coverage is given to 450 pieces of art recognized as having made an important contribution to twentieth-century culture. They are arranged alphabetically by artist in four segments, beginning with "Art" (painting, sculpture, performance work, etc.) and progressing through "Architecture," "Photography," and "Design" (automobiles, posters, fashions, etc.). Entries furnish a critical essay, catalog data, bibliography, and a full-page, black-and-white illustration for each work. There are 160 specialists who served as contributors in preparing the signed articles. Selections were made by an advisory board of twenty distinguished experts. The effort is noteworthy for its inclusion of a variety of artworks ranging from pop art to serious artistic productions. There is a brief general bibliography and an index to individuals, studios, and manufacturers.

325. **A Dictionary of Art Quotations**. Ian Crofton, comp. New York: Schirmer Books, 1989. 223p. ISBN 0-02-870621-8.

First published in the United Kingdom by Routledge in 1988, this is the first American edition of this compact little volume targeted to quotations concerning Western art. The bulk of the text is given to the fine arts of painting, drawing, and sculpture, although there are separate segments addressing architecture and photography. It has been criticized for being somewhat whimsical in its approach to the subject and its selection of quotations and for being uneven in its coverage. The value of the work lies in its unique focus on art quotations and the variety of perspectives offered. Entries are arranged under numerous topical sections, including artists' names (architects and photographers are excluded). Quotations are drawn from a variety of written sources in a rather arbitrary manner. Bibliographic references are brief, and the work is geared to the interests of the curious rather than the needs of the scholarly. A general index provides access.

326. **Encyclopedia of World Art**. New York: McGraw-Hill, 1959-1987; 17v. ISBN 0-07-019467-X.

Considered to be the cornerstone of every reference collection in art, this magnificent work was published simultaneously in Italian and in English. Providing treatment of considerable length, the signed articles represent the best scholarship on an international level. Bibliographies are extensive and are regarded as a real strength. Entries are alphabetically arranged, but the emphasis on monographic-length articles makes use of the index (volume 15) mandatory. Biographies of artists, although numerous, tend to be brief, with the major emphasis on the articles regarding various schools, movements, and national characteristics in which the personalities are mentioned. The scope is broad and covers the entire field of visual arts in all countries and periods. Each volume contains about 500 plates, some of which are in color. The index volume is detailed and provides access through some 20,000 entries. Volumes 16 and 17 serve as supplements providing coverage of contemporary art and new perspectives.

Slated for publication in 1996 is the monumental 34-volume edition of *The Dictionary of Art*, published by Grove's Dictionaries, Inc. It will serve as the definitive counterpart to its sister publication in music (entry 612) in supplying some 41,000 articles of varying length, written by 6,700 art historians and specialists from all over the world. In production for more than a decade and a half, the finished product will contain 15,000 illustrations integrated with the text, providing treatment of the entire realm of the visual arts on an international basis.

327. **Glossary of Art, Architecture, and Design Since 1945**. 3d ed. Rev., enl., and ill. John A. Walker. London: Library Association Publishing; distr., Boston: G. K. Hall, 1992. 500p. ISBN 0-8161-0556-1.

This has been one of the standard tools in the field since its initial publication in 1973 and its subsequent revision in 1977. At that time, its subtitle read "terms and labels describing movements, styles and groups derived from the vocabulary of artists and critics." The third edition represents an effort augmented by the inclusion of 173 illustrations, all in black-and-white. There are 700 entries, each providing a concise but up-to-date and informative definition. A bibliography is furnished for each one, adding to the value of the work both for the curious information seeker and the more serious inquirer. The Library Association of Great Britain has produced an attractive tool with a wide appeal. Access is assured through use of cross-references within entries and provision of a detailed general index.

328. **The HarperCollins Dictionary of Art Terms and Techniques**. 2d ed. Ralph Mayer. Rev. and ed. by Steven Sheehan. New York: HarperPerennial, 1991. 474p. ISBN 0-06-271518-6.

One of the standard art dictionaries in the field, the earlier edition of this work had been reprinted several times since its initial appearance. Sheehan, the director of the Ralph Mayer Center at Yale University, has updated this effort along with *The Artist's Handbook of Materials and Techniques* (entry 321). Using the Mayer pattern, the work continues to provide coverage of the terminology and techniques representing a broad spectrum of art activity. It contains several thousand entries providing cogent and well-developed definitions and identifications. The purpose remains the definition of those terms encountered by the student or specialist in the literature of the field. This work is not as technical in nature as the more detailed *Artists' and Illustrators' Encyclopedia* (McGraw-Hill, 1972) by John Quick, although technical expertise is evident. There are entries on schools, styles, and periods, with some illustrations provided. The emphasis is on the procedures and materials of the artist.

329. **An Index-Dictionary of Chinese Artists, Collectors, and Connoisseurs with Character Identification by Modified Stroke Count** ... Nancy N. Seymour. Metuchen, NJ: Scarecrow Press, 1988. 987p. ISBN 0-8108-2091-9.

The full title goes on to say "Including over 5,000 Chinese names and biographies from the T'ang Dynasty through the Modern Period." This gives an idea of the broad coverage and scope of this important reference work. It addresses the need for a source of identification for artists and other personalities related to the world of Chinese art. They are listed alphabetically using the Wade-Giles romanization system, but entries also furnish alternative spelling through the Pinyin system of romanization. Included in the entries are brief biographical sketches, number of strokes in the character of the surname, full script characters for each name, and references to additional biographical sources listed. The second section of this work presents a useful instructional approach to identifying and explaining Chinese characters and signatures. It supplies a methodology for identifying characters by a stroke-counting system, as well as a chronology of Chinese dynasties. There is a character index of Chinese names.

330. **The Oxford Companion to Art.** Harold Osborne, ed. Oxford: Clarendon, 1970; repr. 1984, 1986, 1989. 1277p. ISBN 0-19-866107-X.

Another useful tool in the Oxford Companion series, this one has been reprinted several times. There are about 3,000 entries, arranged alphabetically. The major focus is on painting and sculpture, although other aspects of the visual arts, such as architecture and ceramics, are covered. Applied arts and handicrafts receive little attention. Articles vary in length from a brief paragraph to a number of pages on broad topical categories such as "perspective." Although they are not signed, the authors' expertise is evident in the exposition given the various elements covered: national and regional schools of art, movements, concepts, styles, techniques, themes, iconography, biographies, and museums. Articles are introductory in nature and include cross-references but no bibliographies. An extensive bibliography in the appendix provides additional references.

331. **The Oxford Companion to Twentieth-Century Art.** Harold Osborne, ed. New York: Oxford University Press, 1981; repr. with corr. 1985, 1988. 656p. ISBN 0-19-866119-3.

One of the strong features of the earlier work, *Oxford Companion to Art* (entry 330) is the coverage given to contemporary art movements and artists. This newer title provides more timely information on the nature of the modern art scene. There are numerous biographies of individual artists as well as informative treatments of styles, movements, and schools. Terms are defined in a lucid fashion, in the manner of the previous works in this series. The tool is intended to serve as a handbook or guide for students and interested laypersons seeking enlightenment on the subject of modern art. Such recent aspects as computer art and body art are treated, along with the more standard manifestations of dada and art deco. Living artists are covered, with their achievements summarized to the mid-1970s. Illustrations are included and a selective bibliography is appended.

332. **The Oxford Dictionary of Art.** Ian Chilvers and Harold Osborne, eds. New York: Oxford University Press, 1988. 548p. ISBN 0-19-866133-9.

Another of the useful one-volume Oxford efforts, this one based on *The Oxford Companion to Art* (entry 330), *The Oxford Companion to Twentieth Century Art* (entry 331), and *The Oxford Companion to the Decorative Arts* (entry 496). Much of the material has been revised and updated, and about 300 new entries have been produced for the first time. The lengthy survey articles in the larger works, treating art in the various countries, architecture, and Oriental art, have been omitted. In all, some 3,000 entries provide brief but informative descriptions of various aspects of Western art, including personalities, periods, schools, techniques, paintings, graphics, and sculpture. Architecture is excluded. Coverage begins with antiquity and continues to the present.

The Concise Oxford Dictionary of Art and Artists, edited by Chilvers (Oxford University Press, 1990) supplies a condensed version of the principal work annotated here. It provides some 2,000 entries on painting, sculpture, and graphic arts. The new title retains the essential character of the parent effort, while having deleted one-third of its entries.

Directories

333. **American Art Directory.** New York: R. R. Bowker, 1898- . Bienn. ISSN 0065-6968.

With publication of the fifty-fourth edition (1993-1994), this directory remains the acknowledged standard in the field. Originally entitled *American Art Annual* (vols. 1-37, 1898-1945/1948), it is now published biennially. The frequency has varied in the past, but it seems to have established its pattern in terms of both frequency and format. The most recent edition provides information on more than 7,000 art museums, libraries, associations, schools, and studios within the U.S. and Canadian sphere of influence. Major emphasis is given to treatment of museums, libraries, and associations, with geographical arrangement by state and city. Entries include address, key personnel, sources of income, description of collections, and publications. Coverage also includes art councils, periodicals, scholarships, exhibitions, and booking agencies, as well as schools and academic departments. Access is provided by three indexes: organization, personnel, and subject.

Art in America Annual Guide to Galleries, Museums, Artists is compiled by the editors of the well-known monthly periodical, *Art in America*. The *Guide* is regarded as a solid piece of work, identifying individuals as well as institutions of importance and interest to artists in this country. It has been issued since 1982.

334. **American Art Galleries: The Illustrated Guide to Their Art and Artists.** Les Krantz, ed. New York: Facts on File, 1985. 304p. ISBN 0-81600-089-1.

This is a comprehensive directory of nearly 1,100 art galleries of importance to art patrons, collectors, and dealers. Galleries are defined in terms of their activities, which include both selling and exhibiting, thus eliminating museums and exhibition centers that do not provide opportunity for purchase. Arrangement is alphabetical by state, then by city, with the galleries then arranged alphabetically under the city. Galleries from all fifty states and the District of Columbia are represented. Each entry provides a history of the gallery, identification of its leading artists and their media, and enumeration of any specializations in art styles or group exhibits. Addresses, telephone numbers, key personnel, and business hours are included. There are excellent illustrations of selected art objects, some of which are in color. An important feature is an extensive artist index.

335. **American Artists' Materials Suppliers Directory.** Alexander W. Katlan. Park Ridge, NJ: Noyes Press, 1987-1992. 2v. ISBN 0-815550-64-2 (v.1); 0-932087-19-1 (v.2).

Katlan, a painting conservator, prepared the initial volume to facilitate the identification and dating of unsigned American paintings of the nineteenth century through listings of some 3,700 art supply firms in the Boston and New York area during that time. Unique stencil marks and labeling on the canvases prepared by these firms serve as excellent clues to their origin. Entries supply addresses and dates of the supply houses. In addition, there are brief histories of eight major firms and black-and-white photographs of the marks and labels. Volume 2 emphasizes the actual art materials, with entries furnishing exposition along with illustrations of stretchers, panels, artist boards, and canvas. Included are listings of stretcher patents from 1849 to 1949, segments of original trade catalogs, and a directory of art supply houses in Philadelphia and Baltimore. Case histories are given on the materials used by three artists.

336. **Art on Screen: A Directory of Films and Videos About the Visual Arts**. Program for Art on Film; Nadine Covert, ed. Boston: G. K. Hall, 1991. 283p. ISBN 0-8161-7294-3.

This is a useful directory or catalog of more than 900 films and videos related to the study, enjoyment, appreciation, or understanding of the fine arts, decorative arts, archaeology, crafts, and so on. Its intent is to draw a selective listing from the 17,000 entries in the *Art on Film Database* compiled by the Program for Art on Film and sponsored by the Getty Trust and the Museum of Modern Art. It does not duplicate the listings in *Films on Art* (Canadian Center for Films on Art, 1977), but rather treats favorably reviewed items issued between 1976 and 1990. Entries are listed under one of two major categories treating documentaries and shorts, and feature films. Entries supply series title, running time, format, year of release, agency, etc., along with a synopsis and evaluation. There are several informative introductory essays; five indexes furnish access.

337. **IFLA Directory of Art Libraries.** Jacqueline Viaux, comp. New York: Garland, 1985. 480p. (Garland Reference Library of the Humanities, v.510). ISBN 0-8240-8913-8.

A group effort of art librarians of the International Federation of Library Associations, this directory is of value to researchers and scholars as well as librarians in the field. Art libraries from all over the world, with the exception of the United States and Canada, are listed. The title of this work appears in four languages (English, French, Spanish, and German) that, together with Russian, represent the official languages of IFLA. Coverage is given to the holdings of art libraries in nearly fifty countries listed in alphabetical order. The index identifies all countries in each of the five languages and provides cross-references. Entries include telephone number, policy of access, hours, loan policies, founding date, and services. Size of holdings is given by subject and type of format. There is a subject index. Information on U.S. and Canadian libraries is found in *Directory of Art Libraries and Visual Resource Collections in North America* (Neal-Schuman, 1978), by Judith A. Hoffberg, compiled for ARLIS/NA. A supplement was published in 1979.

338. **International Directory of Arts. 1993-1994.** 21st ed. Frankfurt: Art Address Verlag; distr., Detroit: Gale Research, 1993. 2v. Bienn. ISBN 3-59823-07-2.

This is the most comprehensive international directory in the art field, identifying a host of representative organizations and personalities associated with the arts. The twenty-first edition of what has turned into a regular publication, like its predecessor, is in two volumes and provides information on more than 140,000 addresses and related facts. Information is gathered through a survey of organizations and individuals throughout the world. Volume 1 covers museums and institutional galleries, universities, academies and art schools, associations, and artists. Volume 2 identifies dealers and their galleries, publishers, periodicals, book dealers, restorers, auctioneers, and collectors. Arrangement is generally alphabetical by country, then by city. Frequency of publication has varied in the past, but the pattern of biennial appearance has been established in recent years. The tool is especially useful for museums, research libraries, and specialized collections. It has been criticized for its lack of indexing.

339. **Looking at Art: A Visitor's Guide to Museum Collections.** Adelheid M. Gealt. New York: R. R. Bowker, 1983. 609p. ISBN 0-8352-1730-2.

Different from most catalogs and guides to specific collections, this work provides background knowledge and insight into the nature of the types of art produced through time. It is a good information piece on the thoughts and influences that have shaped the styles and developments. The book is divided into two major sections, the first of which covers the history of collecting and the growth and practices of art museums. The second part contains a number of chapters devoted to the history of art in the Western world from ancient times to the present. There is also coverage of Asian, pre-Columbian, and tribal arts. There are lists of major museums and lists of artists which identify their media as well as dates. The volume also provides a concluding bibliography and a detailed comprehensive index.

A selective survey of collections is *Art Museums of the World*, edited by Virginia Jackson (Greenwood Press, 1987. 2v.). It covers some 200 museums, with a lengthy historical essay for each. Directory-type information, such as directors, departments, and telephone numbers, is not given.

340. **Slide Buyers' Guide: An International Directory of Slide Sources for Art and Architecture.** 6th ed. Norine D. Cashman, ed. Englewood, CO: Libraries Unlimited, 1990. 190p. (Visual Arts Resources Series). ISBN 0-87287-797-3.

Since its initial edition in 1972, this directory has established a solid reputation for its comprehensive coverage of sources of slides on a worldwide basis. Originally a biennial with a different publisher, the work has settled into a less frequent but more viable pattern of four to five years between editions (5th edition, 1985; 4th edition, 1980; 3d edition, 1976). It remains an extremely important tool for those who work with this medium, for there is nothing else like it. Listings emphasize U.S. and Canadian sources in the first section, and the second section provides coverage of Asia, Australia, Great Britain, Europe, Ireland, and the Middle East. Commercial sources are grouped separately from museum sources for each country. The evaluative commentary is slight but helpful. Appendices supply listings of vendors who did not reply to the questionnaire and of sources of textbook slide sets. Both name and detailed subject indexes provide access.

341. **The Visual Resources Directory: Art, Slide, and Photograph Collections in the United States and Canada**. Forthcoming. Carla Conrad Freeman and Barbara Stevenson, eds. Englewood, CO: Libraries Unlimited, 1995. ca.200p. ISBN 1-56308-196-2.

To be published in 1995 is this important resource tool for librarians and specialists, the first comprehensive directory of visual resources to be published in years. Coverage is given to more than 500 individual collections housed in the United States and Canada. These represent the broad expanse of the visual arts through all media, including architecture and design. Entries are arranged under state or province, then city and institution, and identify contact persons, telephone and fax numbers, electronic mail addresses, borrowing privileges, hours, size of collection and staff, and type of visual media in collection. Also of value to the user is the description of the manner of cataloging and classification utilized in the organization of modern collections, and identification of imaging projects underway. Access is assured through indexing by subject, institution, and personnel.

342. **World Museum Publications: A Directory of Art and Cultural Museums, Their Publications and Audio-Visual Materials, 1982.** New York: R. R. Bowker, 1982. 711p. ISBN 0-8352-1444-3.

The first issue of what purports to be a serial directory, this work provides the most comprehensive information to date on museum publications. Developed through a survey of nearly 10,000 museums in 111 countries, it presents listings of more than 30,000 publications in various formats (books, catalogs, bulletins, journals, newsletters, pamphlets, posters, and picture books). Audiovisual titles, such as films, filmstrips, slides, recordings, and videotapes, are also included. Material is presented in five different indexes: geographic guide to museums, museum publications and audiovisual materials by title. A listing of publishers and distributors completes the volume. This should prove to be a valuable resource for academic libraries and for specialized art libraries.

Biographical Sources

343. **Allgemeines Lexikon der bildenden Kunstler von der Antike bis zur Gegenwart.** Ulrich Thieme and Felix Becker. Leipzig, Germany: Seeman, 1907-1950; repr. 1970-1971, 1978. 37v.

This is considered the most complete and scholarly biographical reference work in the entire art field. It includes nearly 50,000 artists from all countries and all time periods. The emphasis is on painters and engravers, but architects and sculptors are also covered. Articles vary in length but generally provide good depth of coverage, with the longer ones signed by the contributors. Locations are provided for works of art, and this title is known for the bibliographies accompanying the majority of the entries. These include references to books, catalogs, and periodical articles. Entries are arranged alphabetically by names of personalities.

The work is continued by a supplementary effort by Hans Vollmer entitled *Allegemeines Lexikon der bildenden Kunstler des XX Jahrunderts* (Seeman, 1953-1962, 6v.). Although there is some overlap with Thieme (that included a few living persons at time of publication), the concentration on twentieth-century artists is for the most part unique. It includes about 6,000 brief biographies with bibliographical references.

344. **Artists of the American West: A Biographical Dictionary.** Doris Ostrander Dawdy. Athens, OH: Swallow Press, 1974-1985. 3v.; repr. v.1, 1990. ISBN 0-8040-0607-5.

A comprehensive biographical source that covers more than 4,000 artists who worked and lived in the western part of this nation. Limited to artists born before 1900, there is excellent coverage given to twentieth-century art, as many of the individuals achieved their greatest success during this period. Limited to painters, illustrators, and printmakers for the most part, entries are arranged alphabetically and include dates and places of birth and death, primary area of residence, location of works, and references to additional sources of information in books and periodical literature. Biographical information is brief. There is a classified bibliography of source materials relating to all three volumes and a general index to the set in volume 3.

345. **Biographical Dictionary of Japanese Art.** Yutaka Tazawa, ed. Tokyo: Kodansha International; distr., New York: Harper & Row, 1981. 825p. ISBN 0-87011-488-3.

Developed as the final volume of a three-volume dictionary on Japan, this should prove to be of value to the reference collection in its focus on the art and artists of the East. Coverage is broad, as it should be in a general-purpose tool intended to represent the multifaceted artistic production of the Japanese. Included are biographical sketches grouped by media and type of art (painting, printmaking, architecture, sculpture, calligraphy, graphic design, tea ceremony, gardens, ceramics, swords, metalwork, textiles, and lacquer). Heaviest emphasis is placed on figurative artists. Arrangement is alphabetical by names in English transliteration and entries are adequate (in some cases anecdotal). Appendices are varied and useful and include a glossary, maps, bibliography, and historical charts and tables.

346. **Contemporary Artists.** 3d ed. Colin Naylor, ed. Chicago: St. James Press, 1989. 1059p. ISBN 0-912289-96-1.
    The first edition of this work appeared in 1977 and covered more than 1,300 artists worldwide. The second edition deleted 450 of those artists while adding 150 new names, for a total of 1,000. This weeding and reduction process continues, with the third edition having deleted 200 and added 50 new ones for a total of 850. Generally, artists who died before World War II have been excluded; the deletion of 200 personalities who died before 1960 signals a narrowing selection policy. Artists from various media in the fine and applied arts are covered if they have exhibited their work in important art galleries, have been included in museum shows, or are exhibited in the permanent collections of major museums. Entries include a brief biography, references to exhibitions and collections in which the artist has been represented, a bibliography by and about the artist, name of agent or dealer, and a signed critical essay. Photographs are included along with comments by the artists themselves. It is recommended that libraries retain the previous editions together with this revision, to provide fuller coverage.

347. **Creative Canada: A Biographical Dictionary of Twentieth Century Creative and Performing Artists.** Toronto: University of Toronto, 1971-1972. 2v. ISBN 0-8020-3262-1.
    A good example of a specialized biographical dictionary, this work is published in association with the McPherson Library at the University of Victoria. Each volume covers about 500 artists "who have contributed as individuals to the culture of Canada in the twentieth century" and whose contributions have been described in print. The rationale is that artists have not really achieved status if their works have not been praised in books, periodical articles, or newspapers, and the coverage is intended to be limited to significant artists. Excluded from coverage are architects and practitioners in the applied arts, although musicians, dancers of various types, and radio, television, and film performers, as well as producers, directors, and designers, join painters and sculptors in the listing. Arrangement is alphabetical by name, with entries varying in length according to the amount of documentation available. A general index provides access.

348. **Dictionary of Contemporary American Artists.** 6th ed. Paul Cummings. New York: St. Martin's Press, 1994. 738p. ISBN 0-312-08440-4.
    This biographical dictionary is recognized as a standard for identification of American artists, about three-quarters of whom are still living. The present edition treats some 900 artists who have attained a certain stature or status, for which brief information is provided regarding education, teachers, teaching career, scholarships or prizes, address, dealer, exhibitions, collections, special commissions, and notes on the artist's specialty. A bibliography of books by and about the subject is included. More than 100 black-and-white illustrations are scattered throughout the work. There is much more detail here than in *Who's Who in American Art* (entry 359), although Cummings is much more selective in terms of number of artists covered. Emphasis is on painters, but sculptors and printmakers are included as well. There is an index of artists with a pronunciation guide for difficult names, and a key to museums and galleries in which the artists are represented.

349. **Dictionary of Women Artists: An International Dictionary of Women Artists Born before 1900.** Chris Petteys et al. Boston: G. K. Hall, 1985. 851p. ISBN 0-8161-8456-9.

More than 21,000 female artists are covered, making this the most comprehensive source of information to date. Painters, printmakers, illustrators, and sculptors are included, but photographers, architects, craftswomen, and designers are not. Although this is one of several publications recently dedicated to the identification of women artists, it is unequalled in terms of its utility in identifying elusive or obscure names. Entries provide full name, married name, pseudonyms, birth and death dates, medium, subject or thematic matter, residence, education, exhibitions and awards, and references to source material from which the biographies are derived. Bibliographic references to additional material are also included. This is of major value in art reference work.

350. **Dictionnaire critique et documentaire des peintres, sculpteurs, dessinateurs, et graveurs de tous les temps et tous les pays.** New ed. Emmanuel Benezit. Paris: Grund, 1976. 10v. ISBN 2700001494.

In the past, this multivolume biographical dictionary has been rated by art librarians as a vital source. It has retained its reputation through the years since its initial appearance in three volumes (1911-1923). The present edition is a complete revision of the 1948-1955 effort of eight volumes, although the format is the same and similar information is given. Coverage includes artists from the fifth century B.C. to the mid-twentieth century, and represents both Eastern and Western cultures. Entries vary in length from a few lines to several columns, but generally provide a list of the artist's chief works and museums where they are displayed. Reproductions of symbols and signatures, including those of anonymous artists, are placed at the end of each key letter of the alphabet. There is a brief bibliography of sources in volume 10.

351. **Guide to Exhibited Artists.** Santa Barbara, CA: ABC-Clio, 1985. 5v. ISBN 0-90345-095-X.

Each volume of this important multivolume set covers a different medium, and each can be purchased separately. The most extensive volume is the one on European painters, but the most unique—and therefore important—are the volumes on printmakers and on craftspeople. The remaining volumes cover sculptors and North American painters. The set as a whole provides listings of 16,000 contemporary artists for whom information is given on nationality, address, type of work, medium, date and place of birth, gallery representation, and recent exhibits. Information is relatively up-to-date and should be welcomed by librarians, students, and collectors, as well as critics and writers. Each volume is indexed separately.

352. **Index to Artistic Biography.** Patricia Pate Havlice. Metuchen, NJ: Scarecrow Press, 1973. 2v. ISBN 0-8108-0540-5. **Supp.**, 1981. ISBN 0-8108-1446-3.

A valuable index to the biographies of about 70,000 artists representing all time periods and all geographic regions, this work covers sixty-four art publications. Primarily biographical dictionaries and works of collective biography, these sources appear in ten different languages and were published between 1902 and 1970. Entries in this index include artists' names, dates of birth and death, nationality, medium, and coded references to the source book with volume number. A one-volume supplement issued in 1981 provided references to an additional seventy titles.

353. **International Dictionary of Art and Artists**. James Vinson, ed. Chicago: St. James Press, 1990. 2v. ISBN 1-55862-001-X (Art); 1-55862-000-1 (Artists).

The volume on artists supplies a biographical dictionary of the most important European and American artists ranging from the thirteenth to the twentieth centuries. Entries treat 500 personalities chosen by a panel of specialists and provide a biographical sketch highlighting the careers and achievements of painters, sculptors, and engravers who have earned recognition as master artists. Following a detailed critical essay on the consequence of the artist's work, there is a listing of the most important collections of the artist's works, along with bibliographic references. The volume on art treats 500 individual works of art in a chronological arrangement. Information regarding artist, location, size, and date are given along with a signed critical essay. Articles are written by specialists, primarily art historians; for the most part, the same scholar contributes both the article on the artist and the one on his or her work. There is an index of artists and of artwork locations.

354.   **Mallett's Index of Artists, International Biographical: Including Painters, Sculptors, Illustrators, Engravers, and Etchers of the Past and Present.** Daniel Trowbridge Mallett. New York: R. R. Bowker, 1935. 493p. **Supp.** 1940. 319p. Repr., Detroit: Gale Research, 1976; Editions Publishers, 1986. 2v. ISBN 0-317-57518-X.

Another of the standard biographical sources along with Thieme (entry 343) and Benezit (entry 350), this work covers more than 25,000 artists whose works are exhibited in leading galleries or who are subjects of inquiry of modern students. Artists represent many different phases and media of the art world, and come from all countries and time periods. As this is primarily an index, limited biographical information is provided in each entry (name, pseudonym, nationality, period of productivity, residence, and dates). There are references to 22 general reference works and more than 1,000 specialized sources providing fuller biographical treatment. The supplement provides entries for artists of all countries and periods not covered in the main edition, with a necrology from 1935-1940. Although criticized for certain inaccuracies, it remains a likely first source for biographical information.

355.   **Mantle Fielding's Dictionary of American Painters, Sculptors, and Engravers.** 2d ed., rev. and enl. Mantle Fielding. Glenn B. Opitz, ed. Poughkeepsie, NY: Apollo Book, 1986. 1081p. ISBN 0-938290-04-5.

There have been several reprints and revisions of this standard biographical tool since its appearance in 1926. The 1965 work was a reprint with addenda containing corrections and new material, whereas the 1983 effort is a complete revision that doubled the coverage from about 5,000 to over 10,000 names. The present edition provides information on nearly 13,000 American artists of all time periods. They are arranged alphabetically and the volume is by far the most attractive in terms of typeface. Material has been updated and corrections have been made. (Although Fielding had a good reputation for inclusiveness, the work has been criticized for inaccuracies in the past.) Nevertheless, it provides a comprehensive source of information on both major and minor artists of the United States.

356.   **Modern Arts Criticism: A Biographical and Critical Guide to Painters, Sculptors, Photographers, and Architects from the Beginning of the Modern Era to the Present**. Joann Prosyniuk et al., eds. Detroit: Gale Research, 1991- . ISSN 1052-1712.

Another of the biocritical tools from Gale, this title emulates the publisher's *Literary Criticism* series in providing thorough and well-developed treatment of visual artists from all media. A volume was issued annually in 1991 and in 1992; both the third and fourth volumes appeared in 1993, giving indication that the series is alive and well even in these days of diminished purchasing budgets. Each volume treats around twenty-five painters, sculptors, architects, photographers, etc. active from the latter part of the nineteenth century to the present. These are major figures such as Ansel Adams, Frank Lloyd Wright, Dali, van Gogh, and so on. Entries furnish biographical sketches, along with excerpts from critical appraisals drawn from books and periodical articles. Also included are reading lists and reproductions of works for each artist. The title is indexed by individual artwork and by medium.

357.   **Spanish Artists from the Fourth to the Twentieth Century: A Critical Dictionary**. Frick Art Reference Library. New York: G. K. Hall, 1993- . v.1- . ISBN 0-8161-0614-2.

The first volume of this projected three-volume work indicates that the complete set will be a real asset to students and scholars alike. In citing biographical sources on this little-documented target group, the tool fills a real void. Volume 1 treats the artists alphabetically from A-F and provides an introductory guide for use of the work in English, Spanish, German, and French. Volume 2 will treat the "G-M" segment and is expected in 1994; volume

3, anticipated in 1995, will conclude the coverage "N-Z" along with a comprehensive index, chronological list, and complete bibliography. Some 10,000 personalities who were born in Spain or worked there are to be treated. Artistic endeavors vary and include architecture, painting, sculpture, printmaking, drafting, and the applied arts. Entries supply dates, medium, and variant names as well as listings of biographical sources.

358.   **Who Was Who in American Art.** Peter Hastings Falk, ed. Madison, CT: Sound View Press, 1985. 707p. ISBN 0-932087-00-0.

This work is compiled from the original thirty volumes of *American Art Annual* (entry 333n) between 1898 and 1933 that included biographies, and the four subsequent volumes of *Who's Who in American Art* (entry 359) between 1936 and 1947. It represents an excellent source of information on 25,000 deceased persons associated in some way with American art. Included among the entries are painters, sculptors, printmakers, illustrators, photographers, cartoonists, critics, curators, educators, and craftspeople whose creative activity spanned a fifty-year period from the 1890s to the 1940s. Entries include name, profession, last known address, dates of birth and death, education, location of works, exhibitions, awards, memberships, and references to the volume of either of the two source works in which the artist was last covered.

359.   **Who's Who in American Art 1993-1994.** New York: R. R. Bowker, 1936/1937- . Bienn. ISSN 0000-0191.

Originally published as part 2 of the *American Art Annual* (entry 333n) in volumes 1-4, 1936-1947, this work has appeared irregularly in the past, but has settled into a biennial pattern since 1953. A standard in the field, the twentieth edition (1993-1994) represents a comprehensive biographical dictionary of living personalities from some seventy-five related disciplines from all spectra of the arts in the United States as well as Canada and Mexico. Media represented are painting, sculpture, graphic arts, illustration, design, and various crafts. In addition to artists, there are important educators, administrators, collectors, critics, historians, curators, and dealers. There are more than 11,500 entries, alphabetically arranged, with each entry given about 200 words. Entries include birthdate, education, publications, collections, commissions, professional affiliations, honors and awards, style and techniques, media, dealer, and mailing address. The work is indexed by geographic location and professional classification.

360.   **Who's Who in Art: Biographies of Leading Men and Women in the World of Art Today.** Havant, Hants, UK: Art Trade Press, 1927- . Bienn. ISBN 0-900083-15-8 (1994).

The frequency of this comprehensive biographical directory of primarily British artists has varied widely in the past (including a hiatus of fourteen years between the third and fourth editions). It is one of the oldest continuing reference tools in the field, and has established itself as a predictable two-year offering during the past decade. The twenty-fifth edition (1992) provides a comprehensive listing of living artists working in a variety of media in the United Kingdom, with a few other "representative" (outstanding) artists included. It has been decided to restrict this inclusion of foreign artists to those already listed, and eventually produce an all-British listing. Presently, about 3,000 artists are covered, of which less than 10 percent are not British. Entries vary somewhat but are generally one paragraph in length. They provide birthdates, education, memberships in professional societies and organizations, list of exhibitions, and a list of collections in which the subjects are represented. Also included are present addresses and manner of signing their work.

361.   **Women Artists in the United States: A Selective Bibliography and Resource Guide on the Fine and Decorative Arts, 1750-1986.** Paula L. Chiarmonte. Boston: G. K. Hall, 1990. 997p. ISBN 0-8161-8917-X.

This is a comprehensive work of substance in terms of breadth and depth. It serves as an excellent bibliography and resource guide treating female American artists of all types with the exception of needlework. (This is to receive its own volume in the future.) An important contribution is the set of introductory essays by sixteen specialists in the field explaining the criteria used in selection. The work is divided into two segments, with the first providing essays on feminist critics and organizations, directories of manuscript repositories, and special collections. The second cites the literature: books (including biographical tools), catalogs, and articles. This section supplies some 4,000 references covering more than 2,500 female artists, with special attention given to blacks, Native Americans, Asian-Americans, and Latinas. Author/title and artist indexes furnish access.

The two-volume effort by Eleanor Tufts, *American Women Artists, Past and Present: A Selected Bibliographic Guide* (Garland, 1984-1989) is another useful resource. Volume 1 identifies monographs and journal articles on 500 artists of all media but excluding the crafts. These range from the eighteenth century to contemporaries born before 1950. Volume 2 adds another 700 figures supplementing the first volume.

362. **World Artists 1950-1980.** Claude Marks. New York: H. W. Wilson, 1984. 912p. **Supp. 1980-1990.** ISBN 0-8242-0707-6.

The Wilson Company offers a line of fine biographical dictionaries, and editor Marks provides a useful source of information for any library collection. Biographies of more than 300 artists who achieved some prominence in the years following World War II are included. Painters, sculptors, and graphic artists from many countries and representing numerous styles and movements are listed. These are generally the important personalities who influenced the field in some fashion. Entries provide full names, dates of birth and death, and a detailed biographical-critical essay of two to five pages (identifying locations and dates of exhibitions and museums and galleries showing the subject's work). There is also a brief bibliography of books and articles about each artist. Pictures generally accompany the entries.

Marks has produced a supplementary volume, *World Artists 1980-1990* (H. W. Wilson, 1991), that continues the coverage of the work noted here. Some 120 new artists that have been influential during the 1980s are featured, with biographical coverage averaging four pages in length. Many countries are represented and photographs are supplied.

Histories and Chronologies

363. **African Art: An Introduction.** Rev. ed. Frank Willett. New York: Thames & Hudson, 1993. 288p. ISBN 0-500-20267-2.

This represents a revision of an old favorite, first issued in 1971 and reprinted on several occasions. Coverage is the same in providing a comprehensible introduction to African art. The work represents a successful survey and excellent overview of the development of African art in its social and historical context. There are 261 illustrations, with 61 in color, that highlight the various art forms and their distinctive character. Willett served as a professor of African art at Northwestern University and brings a high level of expertise and understanding to this work. He provides useful and informative description and commentary on the geography, culture, and social conditions in which African art developed. He is able to provide exposition of such elements as ancient sculpture, rock drawings and paintings, masks, and decoration. There is a useful seven-page bibliography; an index provides access.

364. **American Art: Painting, Sculpture, Architecture, Decorative Arts, Photography.** Milton W. Brown et al. New York: Abrams, 1979; repr. 1988. 616p. ISBN 0-8109-0658-9.

An authoritative and comprehensive history of the whole spectrum of American art, this tool is based on two earlier works, *American Art to 1900*, by Brown (Abrams, 1977) and John Jacobus's *American Art of the 20th Century* (Abrams, 1973). The content of the two titles has been combined, revised, and expanded to provide a comprehensive yet cohesive survey of the development of American art from the earliest times to the present day. There are more than 750 illustrations (104 in color) that help provide insight into the nature of artistic expression in the eight periods covered. Coverage begins with the colonial period and is followed with sections on the Jackson years, the Civil War to 1900, and so on, with the final segment treating the arts subsequent to 1960. There are extensive bibliographies and a detailed index.

365. **Art: A History of Painting, Sculpture, Architecture.** 4th ed. Frederick Hartt. Englewood Cliffs, NJ: Prentice Hall, 1993. 1127p. ISBN 0-1305-2432-8.

This comprehensive history by a distinguished expert was first issued in 1976, and since then has earned the respect of both librarians and art students. The text is well written and the composition is well developed, with nearly 1,300 illustrations. The second edition appeared in 1985, but since then the frequency has been every four years. Currently, this now-standard work has been modernized, with more emphasis on women artists as well as a change in chapter sequence. The first part treats the period from prehistoric to the late Gothic, whereas the second part embraces the period from the Renaissance to the present day. Considered by reviewers to be a valuable item combining erudition with lucidity. Events and achievements are described and schools and movements are explained. Serving as the basis for the revision are the results of the latest research in the field. Similar to the initial effort, the present work has a glossary, bibliography, and detailed index.

366. **Art Censorship: A Chronology of Proscribed and Prescribed Art.** Jane Clapp. Metuchen, NJ: Scarecrow Press, 1972. 582p. ISBN 0-8108-0455-7.

A work that retains a large measure of its value even with the passage of time, this chronology of censorship begins with the year 3400 B.C. and ends with 1970. *Censorship* is broadly defined as restrictions upon art or artists imposed by state, church, individuals, or society for economic, social, political, moral, or aesthetic reasons. Thousands of such incidents are recorded, with listings arranged by century, year, month, and day. As one might (or might not) expect, more than half of the events took place during this century. The events are documented with good bibliographical references and represent a wide spectrum (painting, sculpture, graphics, architecture, and decorative arts). There is a detailed index to names, titles, and subjects.

367. **Art of the Mediterranean World, A.D. 100 to 1400.** Hugo Buchthal. Washington, DC: Decatur House, 1983. 207p. ISBN 0-916276-11-2.

Developed as a tribute to the author, a renowned art historian and teacher, the book contains a selection of his articles written over a thirty-five-year period from 1940 to 1975. As such, they provide insight and greater-than-usual depth in describing significant developments on the topic. There are four major segments: Islamic and Indian art, Sicilian manuscript illumination, Byzantine manuscript illumination, and iconography. Great care is evident in the representation of illustrations and the attractive format, as one might expect of a work of this type. The four editors (art historians and former students) have contributed commentaries or postscripts and provided additional bibliography. Although not a history in the real sense, this work has utility in its depth of coverage regarding the artistic developments in the Mediterranean world.

368. **The Arts of China.** 3d ed. Michael Sullivan. Berkeley, CA: University of California, 1984. 278p. ISBN 0520049179.

Developed from an earlier work (1973), this title has been recognized for its broad coverage of the development of Chinese art from its beginnings to the present. Each edition has added new insights through material recently identified through research and study. The work retains its scholarly tone and character. It is well illustrated. Background information useful to students at all levels of understanding is presented in the introductions to the various ages. Art trends are described and examples of both typical and monumental nature are given. It remains an important source of information, especially for its up-to-date coverage of contemporary art developments. There is a bibliography as well as additional special features, with an index to facilitate access.

369. **The Arts of Mankind.** Andre Malraux and George Salles, eds. London: Thames & Hudson, 1960- . Repr., New York: Golden Press, 1961- . v.1- . ISSN 0066-815X.

Originally planned in forty volumes, only eighteen volumes have been issued thus far. Each volume has been prepared by noted scholars and supplies a detailed history of the periods covered. Most of the completed works have summarized development in the ancient or medieval periods (e.g., Archaic Greek Art). There are numerous illustrations and maps, some of which are in color. Each volume is cataloged separately by the Library of Congress, although a series-added entry is provided. For a list of titles in the series, consult the OCLC terminals. Largely a work of French scholarship, the series has been issued in both British and American editions and in some cases the titles have varied slightly. Progress has come to a halt, with the last volume appearing in 1973.

370. **5,000 Years of the Art of India.** Mario Bussagli and Calembus Sivaramamurti. New York: Abrams, 1971. 335p. ISBN 0-8109-0118-8.

Heavily illustrated with about 400 color reproductions, this is an attractive work on Asian art. It should be pointed out that the quality of color has been criticized by reviewers in the past, as has the unevenness in style of writing. Although both authors have excellent credentials in art history, Bussagli's writing is much more stylistic and eloquent, whereas sections by Sivarama-murti are stiff and pedestrian. Coverage is given to Indian art through the Mughal period, but also embraces developments in Southeast Asia, Tibet, Ceylon, and Indonesia. Although the tool can be recommended for its content, there is no bibliography or index.

371. **The Formation of Islamic Art.** Rev. and enl. ed. Oleg Grabar. New Haven, CT: Yale University Press, 1987. 232p. ISBN 0-300-03969-7.

The first edition of this work in 1973 established Grabar as a leading interpreter of Islamic art. The revised and enlarged edition continues to furnish a lucid theory of the development of Islamic art and architecture in terms of its origin and subsequent development over a 400-year period from the sixth to the tenth century. Designed as a text for college students, it provides an excellent perspective on the nations under Muslim control during this period of Islamic expansion, in examining the social forces that fashioned the style and contributions of artists. The work is scholarly in nature and places greatest emphasis on the design and ornamentation of architectural structures. There are 131 illustrations in black-and-white that provide further insight into the artistic elements. Each chapter has a bibliography and there is a chronology of important dates.

372. **Gardner's Art Through the Ages.** 9th ed. Horst De la Croix et al. San Diego, CA: Harcourt Brace Jovanovich, 1991. 1135p. ISBN 0-15-503769-2.

If a single work can be called a classic in the field, it must surely be this one-volume encyclopedic history of art originally produced in 1926 by Helen Gardner. Since then, it has served the needs of both high school and college students, as well as reference librarians, in their search for information on schools, movements, art forms, and developments from ancient to modern times. Planned as a college text, it has undergone constant change and revision, ever increasing its scope of coverage. There are many illustrations, and bibliographies are provided at the ends of the chapters. Gardner was a professor of art history at the school of the Art Institute of Chicago and designed the original scheme in line with her teaching responsibilities. The present authorship continues Gardner's excellent treatment, with expanded narrative and illustrations. Coverage is brought up to date.

373. **History of Art: A Survey of the Major Visual Arts from the Dawn of History to the Present Day.** 4th ed. Horst Woldemar Janson. Rev. and exp. by Anthony F. Janson. New York: Abrams, 1991. 856p. ISBN 0-8109-3401-9.

One of the standard histories in competition with *Gardner's Art Through the Ages* (entry 372), this work is now in its fourth edition. Since Janson's death, the work has been carried on by his son. Always regarded as a solid and comprehensive description of the development of Western art, it emphasizes painting, sculpture, and architecture. Some attention is given to Oriental and pre-Columbian periods, with coverage brought to the present day. Although a separate chapter on sculpture since 1900 has been added, the contemporary segment has been judged to be the weakest element of otherwise strong historical coverage. The fourth edition contains more color illustrations and more diagrams and architectural drawings than previous editions. It is one of the top choices as a textbook for art history classes. The bibliography is up-to-date, and a good index is included. The fifth edition is scheduled for publication in 1995.

374. **History of Italian Renaissance Art: Painting, Sculpture, Architecture.** 4th ed., Frederick Hartt. Edited by David G. Wilkins. Englewood Cliffs, NJ: Prentice-Hall, 1993. 696p. ISBN 0-81-093417-5.

The expanded and revised third edition, retained the excellent readable qualities of this exceptional effort issued since 1969. The fourth edition continues the tradition which has made it the first choice of American university professors in selecting a textbook for undergraduates on the Italian Renaissance period. Much of its utility continues to lie in the integrated treatment given to painting, sculpture, and architecture, in its exposition of the technical and stylistic qualities of that very creative era. There are numerous reproductions, and hundreds of individual works are described and analyzed in clear fashion. The illustrations enhance these analyses. Coverage of Florentine art is excellent as in the past, and the work remains a good survey of the period from about 1250 to 1575. A bibliography is provided, along with a glossary, chronology, and an index to works and subjects.

375. **History of Modern Art: Painting, Sculpture, Architecture, Photography.** 3d ed. H. H. Arnason. Rev. and updated by Daniel Wheeler. New York: Abrams, 1986. 744p. ISBN 0-8109-1097-7.

Another standard in the field that has been revised is this well-known survey of modern art covering developments in Europe and America from 1850 to the present day. The present edition represents the most timely history of what may be referred to as the current art scene, describing the origins and influences that have shaped the styles and fashions in painting, sculpture, and architecture. The work is arranged chronologically and designed to appeal to college students and interested laypersons. There are hundreds of attractive illustrations—so many, in fact, that earlier editions were criticized for a somewhat limited text. Biographical sketches of major artists are included. A bibliography is provided.

The Museum of Modern Art Artists Files (Chadwyck-Healey, 1986) is an immense sourcebook of material on nearly 5,700 microfiche taken from the library holdings of the Museum. Some 200,000 items of diverse nature (announcements, magazine clippings, postcards, excerpts from anthologies, reviews, newspaper articles, and more) are presented in full text, with an index of names to provide access. *The Museum of Modern Art Artists Scrapbooks*, issued by Chadwyck-Healey in four looseleaf volumes and in 642 microfiche also in 1986, presents the scrapbooks of forty-four major artists of this century. Again, there is much diversity in the holdings, which include newpaper and magazine articles, invitations, catalogs, and more.

376. **The Oxford History of English Art.** T. S. R. Boase, ed. Oxford: Clarendon Press, 1949-1978. 11v.

This large-scale project was designed as an eleven-volume comprehensive history of British art from its beginnings to 1940, and took nearly thirty years to complete. Each volume of this work is written by a different authority, who covers a time period in his or her area of expertise. Like the other Oxford multivolume sets, it represents a grand attempt to provide in-depth coverage of a scholarly nature, complete with bibliographies. With Boase's death in 1974, future writing activity was uncertain, and completion of the set represents an important achievement for the publisher and the specialists involved. Coverage begins with volume 1, treating the period up to 871 A.D., and concludes with volume 11 (1870-1940).

Outstanding scholars like Boase, Joan Evans, Peter Brieger, D. T. Rice, Eric Mercer, and Joseph Burke authored the individual volumes.

377. **Pelican History of Art.** Nicholas Pevsner et al., eds. New York: Penguin, 1950-1987. v.1-46. ISSN 0553-4755. Yale University Press Pelican History of Art. 1993- .

Initially projected as a fifty-volume set by Penguin, the individual titles of this work cover time periods and/or nations of the world (largely Western Europe) with respect to history of art and architecture. Volumes vary considerably in scope and cover a wide spectrum of topics and trends. From 1953 to 1987, forty-six volumes have appeared, some in their second or third revisions. Individual titles are by authorities and are highly regarded for both depth of coverage (e.g., the volume on Italian painting from 1500-1600), and useful surveys (e.g., the volume on Japanese art and architecture). Only two new titles were issued by Pelican in the 1980s, one covering the Indian subcontinent, the other Islam. In 1992, this useful series was purchased by Yale University, which agreed to issue the fifteen titles contracted by Penguin beginning in 1993. There are plans to redesign the series, placing more emphasis on regions other than Western Europe.

378. **The Visual Arts: A History.** 3d ed. Hugh Honour and John Fleming. Englewood Cliffs, NJ: Prentice-Hall, 1992. 765p. ISBN 0-13-950494-X.

With its initial appearance in 1982, this work quickly developed a reputation for excellent coverage in certain areas considered weak in both Gardner (entry 372) and Janson (entry 373). Beginning with the earliest civilizations, this chronological survey of world art provides a descriptive narrative accompanied by 1,100 illustrations, some of which are in color. Each chapter is introduced with a chronology of events in art history along with other historical developments. It is considered to be stronger than both Gardner and Janson in its treatment of modern art, with an excellent writing style that makes vivid the concepts and developments covered. The purpose is to be exploratory rather than critical in providing an idea of the visual arts in a historical and aesthetic context. Included are a glossary and bibliography, as well as an index to provide access. The work has been issued in the United Kingdom as *A World History of Art* through Macmillan and others. The fourth edition is scheduled for publication in 1995.

379. **Women Artists in the Modern Era: A Documentary History**. Susan Waller. Metuchen, NJ: Scarecrow Press, 1991. 392p. ISBN 0-8108-2405-1.

This documentary history supplies extracts and selections from sixty-one sources comprising artists' correspondence, journals, and memoirs as well as minutes and reports of professional associations and schools. These documents are selected to help explore the experience of women artists and their relationship with men. Also included are critical reviews of the artists' work as reported by the artists' contemporaries, both male and female. Time period ranges from the mid-eighteenth century to the mid-twentieth century, and the work embraces a variety of media from painting and sculpture to ceramics and textiles. The emphasis is on well-known artists, but amateurs are treated as well. Included here are such personalities as Harriet Hosmer, Angelica Kaufmann, and Berthe Morisot. The title serves as a useful convenience tool for undergraduates in beginning their research on these individuals; what is missing, of course, is the more complete picture contained in the whole documents rather than the snippets presented here.

PAINTING, DRAWING, AND PRINT

Bibliographic Guides and Bibliographies

380. **American Drawing: A Guide to Information Sources.** Lamia Doumato. Detroit: Gale Research, 1979. 246p. (Art and Architecture Information Guide Series, 11). ISBN 0-8103-1441-X.

The Gale series has been recognized as one of the best reference sources for bibliographic information, having achieved a high standard in coverage of the literature of the field. This work by Doumato, a former reference librarian at the Museum of Modern Art, maintains the high quality in the series. She provides an annotated bibliography of books, parts of books, exhibition catalogs, and periodical articles on American artists working from the 1890s to the present day. Several prominent illustrators are also included as subjects, although cartoonists are excluded. There is coverage of important library research collections as well. The initial effort in the series was Sidney Starr Keaveney's *American Painting* (Gale, 1974) in which he identified source materials published between 1946 and 1973.

381. **American Popular Illustration: A Reference Guide.** James J. Best. Westport, CT: Greenwood Press, 1984. 171p. (American Popular Culture). ISBN 0-313-23389-6.

A recent work of much value to the field due to its treatment of illustration, a more elusive field not generally the subject of bibliographic coverage. With the spread of popular culture studies in the past few years, this has proved to be a useful tool in both public and academic library settings. The author is an instructor in the field of American illustration and designed the bibliography to reflect his course coverage. There is a brief history of the topic from 1800 to the present day which should prove enlightening for those who need to research its origins. Then follows a critical analysis of the significant titles in a number of categories: histories, illustrated works, biographies, technique, social context, etc. Appendices list periodical titles, research collections, and illustrated books. The bibliography is well conceived and useful.

382. **Central Italian Painting, 1400-1465: An Annotated Bibliography.** Martha Levine Dunkelman. Boston: G. K. Hall, 1986. 351p. (A Reference Publication in Art History). ISBN 0-8161-8546-8.

Although limited in scope, the fifteenth century in Italy is an era rich in art history and is extremely important for study purposes. Accordingly, there is a large body of literature, making this annotated bibliography an appropriate addition to the reference collection of an academic library. As part of a series on the Italian Renaissance, coverage is given to the region composed of Tuscany, Umbria, the Marches, and Lazio, which has attracted more study and publication than any other period or place in Western art. There are more than 2,000 references to books, documents, and articles culled from the major indexing and abstracting services. Coverage begins with early publications, but emphasis is placed on English-language writing of the past half-century. Additionally, there are references to Italian, French, and other European writings. The work is indexed by authors, editors, reviewers, and artists.

383. **Old Master Print References: A Selected Bibliography.** Lauris Mason et al. White Plains, NY: Kraus International, 1986. 279p. (Print Reference Series). ISBN 0-527-62196-X.

This is a selective bibliography on eminent printmakers, similar to the earlier volume in the series (entry 384). It provides a listing of artists, with birth and death dates, followed by a chronological listing of references. This particular volume covers printmakers from the fifteenth through the seventeenth centuries, with slight representation of eighteenth-century artisans. Bibliographic references range from seventeenth-century writings to 1984 publications. The book is international in coverage; foreign-language titles are translated into English. References include books, journal articles, exhibit catalogs, and book reviews. Mason has been a solid contributor to the bibliography of printmaking and has served as editor of *Print Collectors Quarterly* (KTO, 1977-), which publishes essays on eminent printmakers.

384. **Print Reference Sources: A Selected Bibliography, 18th-20th Centuries.** 2d ed. rev. and enl. Lauris Mason and Joan Ludman. Millwood, NY: Kraus Publishing, 1979. 363p. ISBN 0-527-62190-0.

The first edition of this work appeared in 1975 and covered 1,300 printmakers listed alphabetically. Entries listed both primary and secondary sources about them. It is a useful tool, as information on printmakers tends to be difficult to obtain. This edition was enlarged to cover an additional 500 printmakers, with a total of some 5,000 citations. The purpose remains the same: to provide a selective listing of source material on the printmakers of the eighteenth and nineteenth centuries. Sources identified represent a variety of types and forms, including catalogues raisonnés, oeuvre catalogues, museum and dealer publications and checklists, and essays from both book and periodical literature. Both out-of-print and currently available items are identified, of importance to a varied audience ranging from librarians to print collectors and dealers.

A complementary work is *Old Master Print References* (entry 383), covering the period from the fifteenth through the seventeenth centuries.

Artwork and Reproductions—Catalogs, Etc.

385. **American Paintings in the Metropolitan Museum of Art.** Metropolitan Museum of Art. Kathleen Luhrs, ed. New York: The Museum, 1956-1980. 3v. ISBN 0-87099-244-9 (v.3).

Volume 1 of a projected three-volume set was issued in 1956 as *American Paintings: A Catalogue of the Collection of the Metropolitan Museum of Art*, by Albert Ten Eyck Gardner and Stuart P. Feld. This effort covers American painters born by 1815. Following its publication, there was a hiatus, until Ms. Luhrs was authorized to serve as editor. Volume 2, by Natalie Spassky and others, treats the paintings by artists born between 1816 and 1845. Volume 3, by Doreen Bolger Burke, supplies the paintings by artists born between 1846 and 1864. Volumes 2-3 (1980) cover paintings accessioned by the Museum prior to January 1979. There are references to artists' biographies and sources of quotations. Works mentioned but not illustrated are identified by museum location or source of reproduction. This is an indication of the potential magnitude of the effort, and there is the possibility that it might continue to become a complete catalog of the paintings of American artists in the museum.

A similar coverage of paintings in British museums is *Subject Catalogue of Paintings in Public Collections*, published by Visual Arts Publishing. Volume 1, issued in 1989, treats the collections of London's National Gallery, the Wallace Collection, and the Wellington Museum in providing precise information on each work. Volume 2 (1990) continues the coverage of London collections by treating the Old Masters collection at the Tate Gallery. Entries supply names and dates of artist, school, title, year, size, and medium along with detailed description of the painting. Several indexes are furnished, providing access through artist, subject, subjects of portraits, and location.

386. **American Paintings in the Museum of Fine Arts, Boston.** Boston Museum of Fine Arts. Boston: The Museum; distr., Greenwich, CT: New York Graphic Society, 1969. 2v. ISBN 0-87846-005-5.

A standard item in art reference, this scholarly catalog lists all American paintings in the excellent collection held by the Museum. The first volume contains the text and provides coverage of artists alphabetically arranged. Pictures are listed in chronological order, and each entry provides description, measurements, and provenance. There are brief biographies of the artists, with good bibliographical references, and references to exhibitions in which the paintings have been displayed. The catalog furnishes a listing of more than 1,000 paintings, with more than 600 reproductions, some in color. Reproductions are in volume 2 and are arranged chronologically, with paintings by individual artists grouped together. The catalog was published in celebration of the Museum's centenary and is representative of the attractive published catalogs of the leading museums of the world.

387.   **American Prints in the Library of Congress: A Catalogue of the Collection.** Karen F. Beall, comp. Baltimore, MD: Johns Hopkins University Press, 1970. Repr., San Francisco: Alan Wofsy Fine Arts, 1991. 568p. ISBN 1556600887.

This is considered to be an outstanding reference book in the field of graphic arts, because it identifies approximately 12,000 American prints from 1,250 different artists. These works span the complete history of our country dating from the colonial period to the year of publication. The Library of Congress has one of the truly outstanding collections in this area, and the catalog provides documentation difficult to find elsewhere. The arrangement is alphabetical by artist's name, under which are listed the prints in the Library's collection. Information includes date of execution, imprint, medium, and size. The analytical notes are useful. There are indexes for iconography, names, and also for print series. A seven-page bibliography is included. The work was copied and made available by University Microfilms in 1981.

*388.   **Coates Art Review: Impressionism.** Quanta Press, 1990, 1993. CD-ROM.

With the increasing importance of computerized products, the study of art is benefited immensely by the ability to furnish graphic images in CD-ROM format. From Quanta Press comes this resource to more than 600 images of Impressionist art. Designed for both VGA and Super VGA viewing, and compatible with both IBM and Macintosh equipment, this catalog and tutorial on Impressionism provide well-developed images. Brief identification information is included, making this title a useful educational device for both high school and undergraduate students as well as an information source for the general public. Entries supply the title of the work, artist, medium, date, size, and location. Biographies of artists are included, along with a chronology of important events.

389.   **Finder's Guide to Prints and Drawings in the Smithsonian Institution.** Lynda Corey Claassen. Washington, DC: Smithsonian Institution, 1981. 210p. ISBN 0-8747-4317-6.

This was the first in a series of guides planned to enumerate the collections of the Smithsonian Institution in order to make these resources available or accessible to students and scholars. Individual prints and drawings in a total of forty-nine collections are indexed. Information provided includes artists, subjects, historical periods, and locations. Media and formats treated are water colors, pastels, posters, scientific and engineering drawings, and books with original illustrations. General information regarding the collections includes availability of catalogs or directories, publications, photo-duplication services, exhibition programs, loan policy, hours, and type of public access. A special feature of value is a location guide to graphic artists that identifies more than 10,000 artists whose works are owned by the eight major Smithsonian art collections. The text has an index to facilitate access.

390.   **Fine Art Collections.** Greenwich, CT: New York Graphic Society, 1986. ISBN 0821216449. **Supp.** 1988- .

First published in 1946, this title, known initially as *Fine Art Reproductions, Old and Modern Masters,* has gone through numerous editions and has become a fixture in art reference departments, where its use varies widely from one library to another. This catalog of the reproductions available for purchase from the New York Graphic Society has itself become an attractive collection of reproductions. Arranged by groupings such as Old Masters, twentieth-century painting, and American painting, the catalog gives a historical overview while providing color illustrations for each work. Although they are small in size, they are extremely attractive and provide a good idea of how the reproductions will look. The society has high-quality prints and is considered a useful source for libraries. Included are names and dates of artists; nationality; title with date and location of the original; and catalog number, size, and price of reproduction. There are indexes of artists and subjects. A periodic looseleaf supplement, begun in 1988, provides an updated master price list.

391. Index to Reproductions of American Paintings: A Guide to Pictures Occurring in More Than Eight Hundred Books. Isabel Stevenson Monro and Kate M. Monro. New York: H. W. Wilson, 1948; repr. 1972. 731p. **First Supp.** 1964. 480p. ISBN 0-8242-0025-X.

An old standard in the field of art reference, this work will retain its value as long as its source materials (books that it indexed) remain in libraries. Especially useful for libraries through the years because of the great number of sources covered, the work indexes pictures of American paintings in 520 books and more than 300 exhibition catalogs. Alphabetically arranged by name of artist, title of the work, and in some cases by subject, entries include dates of artist, dates and locations of paintings, and references to books that provide reproductions. A supplement appeared in 1964 indexing more than 400 books and catalogs published between 1948 and 1961. A more recent update is by Smith and Moure (entry 392).

A companion work is *Index to Reproductions of European Paintings: A Guide to Pictures in More Than Three Hundred Books* (H. W. Wilson, 1956; repr. 1967), by the same authors. It follows the same plan, except for its concentration on books with no listings from catalogs. A supplementary item is *World Painting Index*, by Havlice (entry 395).

392. Index to Reproductions of American Paintings Appearing in More Than 400 Books, Mostly Published Since 1960. Lyn Wall Smith and Nancy Dustin Wall Moure. Metuchen, NJ: Scarecrow Press, 1977. 931p. ISBN 0-8108-1084-0.

Commended for their thoughtful selection of source material, the authors have provided a useful continuation to the Monros' indexes (entry 391). The arrangement is somewhat similar to the original, with artists listed alphabetically, followed by titles of paintings with references to reproductions in books. There are indications of ownership in permanent collections. Much of the source material is highly specialized in nature, making it more useful in libraries with more extensive art collections. The subject index makes access possible on a wide range of topics such as allegories, animals, and architectural subjects, as well as portraits of individuals. There is no index by title alone.

*393. The National Portrait Gallery, Smithsonian Institution: Permanent Collection of Notable Americans on CD-ROM. Washington, DC: Smithsonian Institution; Cambridge, MA: Abt Books, 1991. 3093 images. ISBN 0-8901-1618-0.

Since 1973, the National Portrait Gallery has been issuing a pictorial account of its collection. Its *Checklist of the Permanent Collection* has appeared at different intervals ranging from two to five years in 1973, 1975, 1982, and 1987. During that period it has grown from a slender 72-page effort to a volume of 461 pages documenting the continued growth of the collection. Illustrations during that time were in black-and-white in the *Checklist*. During the 1990-1991 period, the *Checklist* was converted to machine-readable form and made available in CD-ROM. The new catalog has begun to supply color images and convenient access to the holdings such as the Hall of Presidents, the Meserve Collection (Mathew Brady), and others. Searching is possible through title of portrait, occupation, artist, medium, and dates of birth and death.

394. Print Index: A Guide to Reproductions. Pamela Jeffcott Parry and Kathe Chipman, comps. Westport, CT: Greenwood Press, 1983. 310p. (Art Reference Collection, no. 4). ISBN 0-313-22063-8.

Another work from Parry useful in the art reference area is this index to the prints of more than 2,100 graphic artists. These prints appeared in more than 100 English-language publications. With the focus on the graphic arts, rather than the more customary painting and sculpture, the tool is somewhat unusual. This uniqueness, of course, is its strength and makes it a good purchase for a reference department. Publication dates of the sources vary over a long span of time, from the late nineteenth century to several published during the 1980s. Artists are identified with birth and death dates and nationality. There is an index of subjects and titles.

395. **World Painting Index.** Patrice Pate Havlice. Metuchen, NJ: Scarecrow Press, 1977. 2v. ISBN 0-8108-1016-6. **First Supp. 1973-1980**, 1982. 2v. ISBN 0-8108-1531-1.

This work was intended to supplement and update both works by Monro and Monro (entry 391), as it covers both European and American paintings, among others. The basic edition covers reproductions in nearly 1,200 books and catalogs published from 1940 to 1975. Volume 1 is alphabetically arranged by name of artist and provides references to the books that contain the reproductions. Volume 2 is a title list that refers the user back to volume 1. Criticized for a noticeable bias in favor of Western art and lack of cross-references for variant names, it is still an important reference tool. The supplement covers more than 600 art books and catalogs published between 1973 and 1980. Arrangement and style are similar to the initial offering, including the feature of separate title listings of paintings by unknown artists. There is an increased emphasis on the work of lesser known Western painters as well as female and Third World artists. No subject approach in Havlice approximates the one by the Monros.

396. **The World's Master Paintings from the Early Renaissance to the Present Day: A Comprehensive Listing of Works by 1,300 Painters and a Complete Guide to Their Locations Worldwide.** Christopher Wright. New York: Routledge, 1992. 2v. ISBN 0-4150-2240-1.

This is an identification tool and locator of what has been termed the master paintings of the world. It is a comprehensive source of information supplying coverage of some 120,000 paintings by 1,300 artists. More than 4,000 locations are identified. Described by a reviewer in the *Times Literary Supplement* as "awesome" in scope, the work represents a magnificent effort and an extremely valuable purchase for all types of users. Serious students and researchers will find it an excellent source of information on the products of certain artists who as yet have not been documented well in the literature. Members of the general public will use it to identify the locations of paintings they would like to see or the holdings of a museum they plan to visit. Brief biographies are included for each artist. Indexing is by subject, artist, and title of painting.

Sales and Exhibitions—Catalogs, Etc.

*397. **Gordon's Print Price Annual.** New York: Martin Gordon, 1978- . Ann. ISSN 0160-6298.

Another of the useful indexes to sale items developed during the past two decades is this record of sales of prints, issued on an annual basis. Covering auction sales for the year, entries are listed alphabetically and include title, medium, size, date, references, measurements, notes, and remarks, as well as margins and conditions. Naturally, auction houses and prices are enumerated. Prints are of various combinations and represent not only individual pieces, but also sets, pairs, groupings, and artists' portfolios. Coverage is provided of sales from about twenty-five leading auction houses worldwide. Useful information regarding exchange rates is given, along with the addresses and telephone numbers in a listing of auction houses. It treats about 30,000 entries each year. The work is available online from the publisher.

398. **A Guide to Collecting Fine Prints.** J. H. U. Brown. Metuchen, NJ: Scarecrow Press, 1989. 152p. ISBN 0-8108-2228-8.

In the field of print collecting, as with any other collectible, it is important that one be apprised of the important considerations and factors in determining value. This tool is designed to provide such guidance to the fledgling collector by describing the various conditions relevant to the buying, selling, and collecting of prints. Consideration is given to the purchase of prints both at auction and from dealers, and to the optimal ways to sell prints. There are sections on determining price and authenticity. Also treated are such concerns as conservation, framing, and tax factors when selling or donating prints. A brief and informative history of prints and printing opens the work. There are nearly fifty black-and-white illustrations. Appendices supply listings of art journals and print dealers as well as a glossary and bibliography. A detailed index provides access.

Artist's Market: Where and How to Sell Your Artwork (Writer's Digest Books, 1979-) is another of the annual professional guides to the market offered by this publishing house. The 1991 edition identifies market opportunities available to painters, illustrators, and cartoonists. Treatment is given to advertising agencies, studios, galleries, publishers, the greeting card industry, and more, with new inclusions for the performing arts and record companies. Entries furnish address, telephone, and fax numbers along with contact information and company descriptions. There is a directory of organizations as well as a glossary and index.

399. **Index of American Print Exhibitions, 1882-1940**. Raymond L. Wilson. Metuchen, NJ: Scarecrow Press, 1988. 906p. ISBN 0-8108-2139-7.

This is an important reference effort for identification and location of American prints. It provides a chronological listing of exhibition catalogs treating exhibits and exhibitions at the annual showings of the most important print societies in this country over a period of nearly sixty years. Included here are the New York Etching Club, Chicago Society of Etchers, California Society of Etchers, Printmakers Society of California, and Brooklyn Society of Etchers, as well as the New York World's Fair of 1939 and the Panama-Pacific International Exposition of 1915. Also included are the works treated in the major publications *Fine Prints of the Year* and *Fifty Prints of the Year*, altogether providing an excellent perspective of high-quality print production. Artists are listed alphabetically under each catalog; title of print along with medium is given. There is an index of artists but not of titles.

400. **Print Price Index '93: 1991-1992**. Madison, CT: Sound View Press, 1991- . Ann. ISSN 1058-2339.

Another useful annual guide to the season's sales of prints from auction houses is this recently created price catalog. Included here are the records from nearly 450 auctions held in North America and Europe during the 1991-1992 season. This is only the second issue of this title, and the present effort has been expanded considerably over its predecessor. Prints derived from etchings, engravings, and lithographs are featured, but acquatints, wood engravings, woodblock prints, screenprints, and more are also included. More than 40,000 entries, listed alphabetically by artist, identify nationality, birth and death dates, auction price, title, medium, date of print, edition number, presence of signature, stamp or annotation, auction house and date, lot number, etc. There are listings for different categories of prints, such as books with original prints, natural history, Japanese and Oriental, posters, and so on. A well-developed bibliography is provided, along with a directory of print dealers, glossary, and a listing of catalogues raisonnés by artist.

401. **The Printworld Directory: Contemporary Prints & Prices**. Bala-Cynwyd, PA: Printworld; distr., Poughkeepsie, NY: Apollo Book, 1982- . Ann. ISSN 0734-2721.

Another recent entry in the field of art sales reporting is this useful directory of the world of printmaking. More than 1,200 contemporary artists are identified in the more than 1,000 pages of the fifth edition (1991-1992). Biographical information is provided and gallery affiliations are enumerated. The directory is developed through surveys of the artists, who are listed alphabetically. They find it to their advantage to provide information regarding their works that have sold out as well as those currently available. Criteria for listing the prints are their price, signature (must be signed), and number (not more than 300). Emphasis is on today's artist, and most illustrations are of works from the past two or three years. There are indexes of the artists and of the print publishers and workshops. The work also contains a listing of galleries specializing in original graphics.

402. **World Collectors Annuary.** Voorburg, Netherlands: World Collectors Publishers, 1950- . Ann. ISSN 0084-1498.

Since its beginning in the years following World War II, this work has come to be recognized as an authoritative and well-developed selective listing of sales from nearly forty important auction houses in the art world. It has a reputation for reporting the most important and valued items sold during the year in Europe and the United States, with the range of prices somewhere between five and seven figures for each entry. Paintings, water colors, pastels, gouaches, and drawings are represented, for which stylistic information is given along with description, provenance, place and date of sale, price, and bibliographic references. To facilitate access to individual items, a cumulative index to the first twenty-four volumes was compiled and published as *World Collectors Index 1946-1972* and later replaced with *World Collectors Index 1946-1982*. *World Collectors Index* (Voorburg, Netherlands, World Collectors, 1977-) began with coverage of the 1973-1974 season, the intent being to publish biennially thereafter.

Dictionaries, Encyclopedias, and Handbooks

403. **Artists as Illustrators: An International Directory with Signatures and Monograms, 1800-the Present.** John Castagno. Metuchen, NJ: Scarecrow Press, 1989. 625p. ISBN 0-8108-2168-0.

Another of Castagno's efforts in providing coverage of artists' signatures and monograms (entries 319 and 320), this is a somewhat unusual tool in targeting illustration as a medium. The interesting aspect is that treatment includes many from the fine arts who at some time have crossed the line to create illustrations for books, magazines, record labels, and posters. Thus, we have not only professional illustrators but also painters and even sculptors identified with their signatures as used on illustrations. There are more than 14,000 entries on nineteenth- and twentieth-century figures from all over the world. Unfortunately, of this number, only about 4,000 facsimile signatures are furnished, with most entries containing the artist's name, nationality, dates, and references to biographical sources. Sources indexed include standard biographical tools and magazines, but only three museum publications, a real flaw for serious study. Supplements are planned for the future.

404. **Encyclopaedia of Oil Painting: Materials and Techniques.** Frederick Palmer. Cincinnati, OH: North Light/Writers Digest Books, 1984. 288p. ISBN 0-89134-078-5.

This handbook is considered to be a useful reference work that succeeds in its objective to explain in lucid fashion the purposes of the implements, equipment, and materials, as well as the rationale and basic concepts, of painting. Palmer is both an artist and a teacher and offers sound advice in his commentary. Such elements as easels, palettes, brushes, rags, and pigments are described in terms of their utility, and color is explained in thorough fashion. Techniques of glazing, collage, toning, encaustic, serigraphy, and painting from photographs are treated. Generally intended for the beginner rather than the advanced art student, the work is aided by the inclusion of more than 250 illustrations, most of which are in black-and-white. There is an index of painters as well as a general index.

405. **Encyclopedia of Painting: Painters and Painting of the World from Prehistoric Times to the Present Day.** 4th rev. ed. Bernard S. Myers, ed. New York: Crown, 1979. 511p. ISBN 0-517-53880-6.

This is a comprehensive, one-volume effort supplying numerous illustrations well integrated with the textual description. With an eye toward economy and balanced coverage,

Myers has produced another work which has been found to be useful in libraries. Painters, movements, and styles are covered in one alphabetical dictionary-type arrangement. The work has kept its format since the initial edition in 1955, with each revision having added some new material. This edition continues in that vein with its incorporation of new entries on contemporary artists and styles. Considered to be strong in biographical coverage, much of the total information is provided through the treatment of personalities.

406. **Encyclopedia of Themes and Subjects in Painting: Mythological, Biblical, Historical, Literary, Allegorical, and Topical.** Howard Daniel. New York: Abrams, 1971. 252p. ISBN 0-8109-0099-8.
    This attractive handbook is quite distinctive and has been regarded as a useful reference source for the last decade and a half. Arranged alphabetically are the themes derived from the source elements identified in the title and used in European painting from the early Renaissance to the mid-nineteenth century. There are about 400 topics or themes, most of which are illustrated with reproductions of adequate size and quality. The largest proportion of the themes or subjects represents mythological or religious events; thus, the work has value for students in the areas of religion and literature. There is a list of illustrations, but the main weakness is the lack of an index.

407. **Looking at Prints, Drawings and Watercolors: A Guide to Technical Terms.** Paul Goldman. London: British Museum Publications; distr. Santa Monica, CA: J. Paul Getty Book Distribution Center, 1988. 64p. ISBN 0-89236-148-4.
    This slender, authoritative, and readable wordbook, compiled by a staff member of the British Museum and co-sponsored by the J. Paul Getty Museum, is a useful information piece on certain elements of two-dimensional artwork. Coverage is given to about 100 terms used by art critics, curators, and historians in describing prints, drawings, and watercolors. Techniques like metalpoint and squaring are defined, as are processes like etching, materials like gum arabic, and instruments like stylus and roulette. Terms represent traditional collections rather than modern or contemporary new techniques. British spelling is used (*watercolours*) and certain Americanisms may be found buried within entries more common to English usage. Treatment tends to be detailed and provides exposition of such aspects as manufacture, qualities, components, and utilization by professionals. About seventy illustrations accompany the entries.

408. **The Thames and Hudson Encyclopaedia of Impressionism.** Bernard Denvir. New York: Thames & Hudson, 1990. 240p. ISBN 0-500-20239-7.
    This slender little work has apparently succeeded in its purpose to furnish a brief and up-to-date information tool relating to Impressionism in all its aspects and its practitioners. Included are entries on models, dealers, and critics as well as artists, and on techniques as well as locations and sites. Well-constructed articles treat general themes and furnish background information on social, political, and cultural conditions. A number of the entries are illustrated in black-and-white, although there is some use of color. Bibliographies are included that provide useful references for additional readings, and cross-references are given to related entries. A unique feature is the subject index that precedes the entries and groups them into broad topical categories such as "The Art Market," "Patrons and Collectors," and "Dealers." There is a general bibliography, along with a chronology of the Impressionist period, and a directory of top collections of Impressionist art.

Biographical Sources

409. **The Dictionary of British Artists, 1880-1940; An Antique Collectors' Club Research Project Listing 41,000 Artists.** Jane Johnson and A. Greutzner. Suffolk, UK: Antique Collectors Club, 1976; repr. 1990. 567p. ISBN 0-902028-36-7.

This dictionary provides an excellent source of information on British painters following the Victorian period, as it lists every artist who exhibited in any one of forty-seven selected representative galleries during this time period. Entries are brief and provide dates of birth and death, residence, memberships and honors, places and frequency of exhibitions, and sometimes, art schools attended. The introduction consists of a descriptive essay on the groups, movements, societies, and galleries that developed during this time period. In each entry, there is an indication when one of the artist's pictures brought more than 100 pounds at an auction during 1970-1975.

410. **Innovators of American Illustration.** Steven Heller, ed. New York: Van Nostrand Reinhold, 1986. 224p. ISBN 0-442-23230-6.

An interesting introductory work provided by a distinguished authority in the field. The editor has served as art director for several periodicals, including *New York Times Book Review.* He presents a collection of interviews conducted between 1984 and 1985 with twenty-one American illustrators. Such individuals as Maurice Sendak, Milton Glaser, and Edward Sorel are questioned about their careers from the beginning to the present. They describe their working habits, motivations, and philosophical views on the role of illustration, as well as their education, training, and the personalities who were influential in their lives. Although not necessarily part of the reference collection, this book will have value for both teachers and students.

411. **Larousse Dictionary of Painters.** New York: Larousse, 1981. Repr., New York: Mallard Press, 1989. 467p. ISBN 0-7924-5132-5.

Like other reference books bearing the Larousse name, this one is profusely illustrated with hundreds of reproductions, many of them in color. Unfortunately, they are somewhat cramped in the page layouts, and not of the highest quality. The dictionary is a useful biographical tool providing coverage of the principal figures in painting in both Europe and North America. Information is given regarding the artist's life and contributions to the world of art, in a depth adequate to provide a reasonable awareness of his or her prominence. An important element is the inclusion of locations where the artist's works are displayed. Many nations are represented, including some that generally are not considered important for their artistic influences.

412. **The Lives of the Painters.** John Canaday. New York: Norton, 1969; repr. 1972. 4v. ISBN 0-393-00664-6.

One of the standard biographical dictionaries in the field is this multivolume effort by a distinguished art historian. Volume 1 covers the late Gothic to the Renaissance; volume 2, the Baroque period; and volume 3, Neoclassicism to post-Impressionism. Coverage is given to 450 painters born before 1840. The style employed is a narrative essay linking the commentary throughout. Historical insight is provided as well as a good understanding of the individual's contribution in relationship to others in the art world. The emphasis is on style and achievement rather than biographical description. Volume 4 contains reproductions, both in color and black-and-white, of the artists who are represented in the contents of volumes 1 to 3.

413. **Painting of the Golden Age: A Biographical Dictionary of Seventeenth-Century European Painters.** Adelheid M. Gealt. Westport, CT: Greenwood Press, 1993. 770p. ISBN 0-313-24310-7.

About 300 major painters from all parts of Europe are treated in this well-constructed biographical dictionary. Essays are informative and provide an excellent overview of the career achievements and important contributions of each artist. In the past, the majority of titles covering artists of this time period (Brueghel, Caravaggio, Rubens, etc.) have been issued in French, German, or Italian, making this work of particular importance to English-speaking students and librarians. Entries vary in length from several pages to less than a page, and are accompanied by listings of paintings not covered in the text along with a selective bibliography. Appendices supply listings of painters by geographical area, a detailed bibliography, and a thorough index.

Nineteenth Century Painters and Painting: A Dictionary, by Geraldine Norman (University of California, 1977), is an old favorite that opens with a brief but useful description of the major movements within the art world during the nineteenth century, such as Romanticism and Impressionism. Color reproductions illustrate the stylistic features. The major body of the text is given to biographies of about 700 artists of the period, along with entries for schools, practices, and techniques. Many of these articles are illustrated in black-and-white. Entries vary in length, with some of the longer articles dedicated to less prominent individuals for whom in-depth information is generally not available. Considered a strength is the coverage given to Hungarians, Russians, and others who have escaped attention in the past.

Histories

414. **American Painting.** Jules David Prown and Barbara Rose. New York: Rizzoli, 1979-1987. 2v. ISBN 0-8478-0308-2.

Originally published in 1969, this history of American painting gained recognition as a detailed description of the events and happenings, with excellent exposition of the work of individual artists. Volume 1 is by Prown and covers the colonial period to the Armory Show. Fine treatment is provided of individuals such as West, Copley, Stuart, Cassatt, Sargent, and Whistler. It ends with the emergence of the Ashcan School and the Armory Show, a landmark in modern art. Volume 2 is by Rose, and continues the coverage to the present day, embracing the important as well as the faddish elements and movements that characterize contemporary art. Both volumes contain color reproductions and are handsome works. They were revised in 1979; Rose's volume was updated in 1986 and Prown's in 1987.

415. **Chinese Painting: Leading Masters and Principles.** Osvald Siren. London: Lund Humphries, 1956-1958. Repr., New York: Hacker, 1974. 7v.

This multivolume work has been considered a vital source of information since its appearance thirty-five years ago. It covers the history of Chinese painting, a complex and many-faceted subject, from the earliest times to the end of the Ch'ing dynasty in 1912. Siren's scholarship remains foremost in Chinese art, and the coverage given to individuals and developments is authoritative and complete. Generally considered a necessary purchase for academic libraries, the reprint edition has been criticized for a lower quality of reproduction of the 900 black-and-white prints. The provision of the lists of works by Chinese painters is an asset to scholars and students; bibliographies are international in scope and include materials in the Chinese languages.

416. **A Concise History of Modern Painting.** 3d ed. enl. and upd. Sir Herbert E. Read. New York: Praeger, 1974. 392p. ISBN 0-50020-141-2. Repr., New York: Oxford University Press, 1985. ISBN 0-19-519940-5.

Considered in most quarters to be a fine one-volume history of the origins and development of modern art, this work made its initial appearance in 1959. Since then it has achieved popularity and wide distribution in libraries and is regarded as a staple in the reference department. Beginning with Cezanne, it clearly traces the elements, influences, and styles of modern painting. It includes quotes from the artists themselves, and is well served in number of illustrations, though at times they have been criticized for poor quality. Errors that appeared in the first edition have been corrected, and presently it is a useful tool for those needing a lucid and informative survey work.

417. **The Development of the Italian Schools of Painting.** Raimond van Marle. The Hague: Nijhoff, 1923-1938. Repr., New York: Hacker, 1970. 19v. ISBN 0-87817-048-0.

An extensive and comprehensive treatment of Italian art, this survey of painting covering from the sixth century has no equal in the English language. Scholarly in nature, it provides many references and includes bibliographies for each chapter. Each volume has an index of artists, iconography, and places. The work has been criticized for certain instances of misleading information and obsolete commentary. Until Venturi's *Storia dell'arte italiana* (Hoepli, 1901-1940, repr., Kraus, 1983) is translated, however, this is the best work available for those who must use the English language. An important feature is the total of more than 5,500 illustrations, which suffer somewhat in the reprint version. The final volume is a general index to the whole set.

418. **Painting in the Twentieth Century.** 2d ed. Werner Haftmann. New York: Praeger, 1965. 2v.

A translation from an earlier German work from the mid-1950s, this work provides a good survey of painting in the twentieth century. Volume 1 provides an analysis of the artists and their work, and volume 2 gives a pictorial survey that includes more than 1,000 reproductions, some of which are in full color. Volume 1 is a profound examination of the psychological and philosophical elements associated with contemporary painting and the personalities who engaged in it. About 500 artists are covered, with short biographies, each of which contains a number of bibliographical references. Although it has been criticized for a bias toward German and Italian art, Haftman's work provides enough information on other areas to be recommended as a general source. There are both name and subject indexes in volume 1.

ARCHITECTURE, INTERIOR DESIGN, AND LANDSCAPE ARCHITECTURE

Bibliographic Guides and Periodical Directories

419. **Architecture: A Bibliographic Guide to Basic Reference Works, Histories, and Handbooks.** Donald L Ehresmann. Littleton, CO: Libraries Unlimited, 1984. 338p. ISBN 0-87287-394-3.

A companion piece to other guides by Ehresmann in the fine arts (entry 279) and in the decorative arts (entry 485), this is an essential tool for both collection development and reference. It provides an annotated bibliography of books that have proved to be useful and informative. Books listed are primarily in the English language, but there is coverage of foreign titles in Western European languages. Emphasis is on a practical bibliography and the titles listed are generally available in American libraries. There are 1,350 entries; arrangement is by form or type, such as reference books; by chronological coverage (prehistoric), or by geographic coverage (Oriental). There are both author-title and subject indexes.

420. **Directory of International Periodicals and Newsletters on the Built Environment.** 2d ed. Frances C. Gretes. New York: Van Nostrand Reinhold, 1992. 442p. ISBN 0-442-00792-2.

Considered to be an outstanding resource item for its audience of specialists when published initially in 1986, the second edition of this directory of serial literature is greatly augmented and updated. More than 1,500 publications are placed within 14 sections similar to those used in the first edition. They deal with subjects relevant to the built environment (architecture, office practice, building types, historic preservation and architectural history, urban design, fine arts, planning, landscape design and gardening, building and construction, engineering, real estate development, and so on). Entries are arranged alphabetically within each topical division, and they include complete bibliographic information as well as description of the content. This is a welcome aid to the librarian who serves architects, engineers, designers, planners, and contractors, as the number of documents in these fields has increased dramatically over the past few years. Included are a listing of indexes and abstracts, title index, and a geographical index of countries where the serials are published.

Bibliographies and Catalogs

421. **American Architectural Books: A List of Books, Portfolios, and Pamphlets on Architecture and Related Subjects Published in America before 1895.** New exp. ed. Henry Russell Hitchcock. New York: Da Capo, 1976. 150p. ISBN 0-3067-0742-X.

The first edition of this standard bibliography appeared in 1938-1939 and was recognized as a valuable asset for those doing research on American architectural history. The 1962 edition reprinted the third edition (1946), which had supplied a listing of more than 1,450 documents. These publications were described with notes of important editions, and locations were identified from among more than 130 libraries where copies could be found. Errors were corrected and a few titles added. The most recent edition in 1976 is largely a reprint of the 1962 edition, with a new introduction by Adolf K. Placzek and an appendix representing a short title list in chronological order of Hitchcock's entries, originally issued as a separate publication by the AIA.

422. **Catalog of the Avery Memorial Architectural Library of Columbia University.** 2d ed. enl. Boston: G. K. Hall, 1968. 19v. **Supp. 1-5.** 1972-1982. ISBN 0-8161-0397-6 (Supp 5).

In addition to the extensive holdings of the Avery Library, one of the outstanding architectural collections in the country, this catalog contains all books on the subject of architecture and art held anywhere in the university in any of its libraries. Through the years, this has come to be recognized as one of the most comprehensive sources of bibliographic information in the field. A catalog was first issued in 1895, in printed form, and G. K. Hall produced the first catalog of this type in 1958, a six-volume work received warmly by librarians in the field. The supplements continue to update the coverage.

For listings of films and videos, there is the recent *Architecture on Screen: Films and Videos on Architecture ...* produced as part of the Program for Art on Film under the joint sponsorship of the Metropolitan Museum of Art and the J. Paul Getty Trust in 1994. It supplies detailed information including synopses, references to reviews, production and release information, and more. Some 900 films and videos on architecture are treated in a manner similar to Art on Screen (entry 336). Several indexes supply access.

423. **Early Christian and Byzantine Architecture: An Annotated Bibliography and Historiography.** W. Eugene Kleinbauer. Boston: G. K. Hall, 1992. 779p. (A Reference Publication in Art History). ISBN 0-8161-8316-3.

An extensive introductory section to this work describes the origins and development of the study of early medieval architecture; useful narrative is given to the development of photography of Byzantine architecture in the appendix. Between these expository pieces there lies a well-constituted bibliography of more than 2,000 books, articles, and catalogs representing fifteen different languages. Arrangement of entries is by some 200 topical headings reflecting specific interests or needs of researchers, such as basilicas, aqueducts, catacombs, sculptured decoration, and so on. Christian architecture is treated from its beginning to the sixth century, whereas Byzantine work is examined from the third century until the fall of the Empire in 1453. Publication dates of sources listed run through 1990. There is a subject index containing geographic locales, along with an index to authors.

424.　**The Literature of British Domestic Architecture 1715-1842.** John Archer. Cambridge, MA: MIT Press, 1985. 1078p. ISBN 0-262-01076-3.

A thorough and detailed bibliography of 360 titles printed in Great Britain and Ireland during the eighteenth and nineteenth centuries, this item will be of interest to bibliographers all over the world. Three major essays precede the bibliography and provide coverage of the relationship of architecture to the book trade, describe the elements of format and content, and discuss the development of architectural theory in Great Britain. The bibliography is detailed in its coverage of the early publications, and variant editions are noted, as are library locations. Another 150 titles or so in the appendices join those in the main body of the work to provide excellent coverage of this elusive, albeit important, topic. Many of the works described are of landmark importance. The book is illustrated in black-and-white and contains an index as well as notes and references.

425.　**Romanesque Architecture: A Bibliography.** Martin Davies. Boston: G. K. Hall, 1993. 340p. (A Reference Publication in Art History). ISBN 0-8161-1826-4.

This recent publication is the most comprehensive bibliography on the study of Romanesque architecture, providing an important tool for both students and specialists. All elements of Romanesque architecture are treated, the general decorative and ornamental aspects as well as the specific features incorporated within the style. There are more than 1,600 entries identifying lengthy studies and graphic documentation; no periodical articles are treated, but rather coverage is given to monographs, theses and dissertations, guidebooks, series, maps, audiovisual materials, and atlases. These sources are in all languages. All related styles are embraced; Carolingian, Pre-Romanesque, later Romanesque, and Transitional, as well as Romanesque. Entries are placed in geographically divided chapters treating Europe in both general and distinct regions; these are subdivided chronologically. Maps are provided, along with indexes to ease access.

Indexes, Abstracts, and Serial Bibliographies

*426.　**Architectural Periodicals Index.** 2d ed. rev. and enl. London: Royal Institute of British Architects, 1972/1973- . Q. Ann. cum. ISSN 0266-4380.

A subject index to architectural periodicals found in the British Architectural Library of the Royal Institute of British Architecture (RIBA), this work covers about 450 titles, the majority of which are British. Subjects are assigned through headings utilized in *Architectural Keywords*, a vocabulary control device developed by RIBA in 1982. Arrangement is classified by those subjects, with alphabetical arrangement of titles within the categories. Foreign titles are identified, with indication of language and presence of English abstracts or summaries. There is a name index as well as a topographical and building name index. The *Index* is also available online through DIALOG, covering the period from 1978 to the present (articles) and 1984 to the present for books. It is updated monthly with an additional 1,000 items. There are some 150,000 records in the file at this time.

Comprehensive Index to Architectural Periodicals, 1956-1970 (London: World Microfilms, 1973) offers the card catalog file of the library on twenty reels of microfilm. This represents a retrospective index of some 200 periodicals in an arrangement similar to *Architectural Periodicals Index*. The majority of these listings first appeared in the quarterly issues of *RIBA Bulletin*.

*427.   **Avery Index to Architectural Periodicals.** 2d ed. rev. and enl. Columbia University. Avery Architectural Library. Boston: G. K. Hall, 1973. 15v. **Supp. 1-13**, 1975-1993. ISBN 0-8161-0615-0 (Supp. 13).

One of the leading architectural collections in this country belongs to the Avery Library of Columbia University. G. K. Hall initiated the excellent service by reproducing the card file containing analytics of periodical articles in titles received at the library. The 1973 edition superseded the original 1963 work by absorbing all its entries and those of its supplements. Since then, supplements have appeared that continue to update the listings. Since 1984, the work has been supported by the Getty Art History Information program. The most recent supplement was issued in four volumes in 1993, and is now computer-generated. This set and its supplements include periodical titles not only in architecture but also in decorative arts, sculpture, city planning, and archaeology. There is good coverage of writings on individual architects. With about 700 periodicals indexed, this is the most comprehensive periodical source, although it is limited to periodicals in the Western languages. The index is available online through a database by the same name covering the period from 1979 to date. It is available through RLIN and is updated daily. There are some 115,000 records in the file, with 15,000 added each year.

428.   **World Architecture Index: A Guide to Illustrations**. Edward H. Teague, comp. New York: Greenwood Press, 1991. 447p. (Art Reference Collection, no. 12). ISBN 0-313-22552-4.

Some 7,000 illustrations of buildings and plans culled from 108 important books are indexed in this convenient source. Indexing is detailed and access is possible by site, architect, architectural type, and variant names of the structures depicted in the reproductions. All books are English-language sources, and there is emphasis on Western architecture, although scope and coverage are global. The work is divided into four major segments, arranged alphabetically. Part 1 is the site index, with entries listed under the city. This is the major segment, with approximately half the text. Part 2 is an index of architects listing both individuals and firms responsible for the works portrayed. Brief biographical information is included in some of the entries. Part 3 is an index of building types (dwellings, waterworks, military structures, etc.) and Part 4 lists the names and alternate names of the structures. This work is well organized and handy to use.

A more specialized source compiled by Teague is *Index to Italian Architecture: A Guide to Key Monuments and Reproduction Sources* (Greenwood Press, 1992), which is number 13 in the same series. It identifies illustrations of some 1,800 Italian monuments and buildings in eighty books. Teague is an art and architecture librarian in academe; his expertise is evident in the excellent access provided by site, architect, chronology, type, and work.

Dictionaries, Encyclopedias, Handbooks, Etc.

429.   **Atlas of European Architecture.** Brian Sachar. New York: Van Nostrand Reinhold, 1984. 369p. ISBN 0-442-28149-8.

An attractive and practical handbook for the study of European architecture is this country-by-country exposition of notable buildings. Each of the twelve chapters is devoted to a specific country (arranged alphabetically), in which towns and cities are also listed alphabetically. Entries for each of the 3,500 buildings covered are listed under cities, in chronological order by date of construction. The book is sure to please individuals involved with architectural studies, such as architects, students, art historians, and preservationists, as well as laypersons with an active interest in architecture. Entries provide name, date, address, architect, photograph, and some notes of special features. Also listed when available is information regarding the tourist information office, architects' institute, and major museums with special collections. There is a bibliography, along with an index of architects and artists, and index of cities and towns.

Another richly illustrated source, more comprehensive in scope, is *World Atlas of Architecture* (G. K. Hall, 1984; repr., New York: Portland House, 1988), the English edition of a French title, itself derived from Mitchell Beazley's *Great Architecture of the World* (Random House, 1975). Fully 100 pages of this 408-page effort are devoted to non-Western architecture (China, Japan, Korea, Southeast Asia, India, Black Africa, and so on). The remainder is divided into historical periods beginning with the ancient world and ending with the modern era.

430. **Concise Encyclopedia of Interior Design**. 2d ed. A. Allen Dizik. New York: Van Nostrand Reinhold, 1988. 220p. ISBN 0-442-22109-6.

This slender volume represents an update of the 1976 publication *Encyclopedia of Interior Design*, and is intended to provide a source of information for homeowners, interior designers, students, and teachers. In appealing to such a diverse audience, it employs a popular approach, furnishing articles ranging from one-sentence definitions and identifications to survey essays running two to four pages on such topics as color, lighting, and draperies. Coverage is broad and includes furniture, furniture periods, room arrangements, fabrics, and wall coverings along with the fine arts, architecture, antiques, and construction. Entries provide numerous cross-references (although some have been found to be defective). There are useful charts and tables helping to clarify the treatment given to such considerations as wallpaper coverage, tile coverage, types of carpet fibers, and so on. Four pages of line drawings treat room arrangements.

Entourage: A Tracing File for Architecture and Interior Design Drawing by Ernest Burden, now in its second edition (McGraw-Hill, 1991), provides a compilation of architectural and design renderings that may be traced to complete the various projects undertaken by specialists or students. All types of renderings are supplied (people, vehicles, plants, benches, flags, birds, etc.) and are shown in different perspectives and positions.

431. **Dictionary of Architectural and Building Technology**. Henry J. Cowan and Peter R. Smith. New York: Elsevier Applied Science, 1986. 287p. ISBN 0-85334-402-7.

This is an up-to-date and informative new volume on the technical terminology of modern architecture and related areas. It contains about 5,000 terms, 1,500 of which have been added since publication of an earlier work by Cowan in 1973. The emphasis is on the science of architecture and building, with fine coverage provided of elements such as structures, materials, acoustics, lighting, thermal environment, building services, solar heating, and more. Definitions are brief but informative and are enhanced by more than 120 illustrations, including diagrams and charts. This title is useful to those who are active in the construction of buildings or its study (teachers, students, architects, engineers, consultants, and contractors).

A well-known and important source, now in its second edition, is *Dictionary of Architecture & Construction*, edited by Cyril M. Harris (McGraw-Hill, 1993). The second edition has been expanded by some 2,300 entries to contain 22,500 terms in more than 75 working areas of architecture and construction. Previous entries have been updated when necessary. Illustrations have been enhanced in size and detail; their number has been increased to about 2,000. Modern construction terminology embracing tools, techniques, equipment, etc. is included with the more traditional terms of architectural history.

432. **A Dictionary of Landscape Architecture**. Baker H. Morrow. Albuquerque, NM: University of New Mexico Press, 1987. 378p. ISBN 0-8263-0943-7.

This wordbook received mixed reviews at best, having been criticized for its inclusions of such terms as *biology* and *sidewalk cafe* and for its frequency of errors, such as the dates given to Charles Platt. Nevertheless, it is commended for its attempt to clarify a body of knowledge on which little has been published. The purpose of the work is to identify the many aspects, details, and components of landscape architecture, while at the same time providing exposition of its essential wholeness. Entries vary in length from brief technical definitions of a few words or sentences to longer narratives such as a four-page description of English landscape architecture. There are cross-references that aid access to related articles, along with numerous black-and-white illustrations of drawings, plans, and some photographs. Unfortunately, these illustrations are of poor quality and do little to enhance the work.

433. **Encyclopedia of American Architecture.** William Dudley Hunt. New York: McGraw-Hill, 1980. 612p. ISBN 0-07-031299-0.

A practical and informative reference book for the layperson is this compendium of miscellaneous facts and definitions. Written in nontechnical language, definitions and identifications are clear and adequate. There are more than 200 articles on history, building types, systems and structures, materials, and preservation, with about 50 on prominent architects. There is a special attempt to include women and minorities in the various articles when appropriate. The work is considered to be a useful tool for the general reader, although not as technical as the advanced student might want or need. Comprehensive coverage is provided from the pre-Columbian period to the present. The encyclopedia contains an index, uses cross-references, and provides brief bibliographies. A second edition is scheduled for publication in 1994.

For the specialist in the field is the eleventh edition of *The Architect's Handbook of Professional Practice*, edited by David S. Haviland for the American Institute of Architects (1987-). Volume 1 supplies an architect-firm index; volume 2 identifies the projects; volumes 3 and 4 identify the documents concerned with building contracts and specifications in this country. *The Newsletter of the AIA Document Supplement Service* was issued in 1990 as a monthly looseleaf supplement to the *Handbook*.

434. **Encyclopedia of Architecture: Design, Engineering & Construction.** Joseph A. Wilkes and Robert T. Packard, eds. New York: John Wiley & Sons, 1989-1990. 5v. (A Wiley-Interscience Publication). ISBN 0-471-63351-8.

This five-volume encyclopedia was prepared over a period of six years, issued over a two-year period, and represents an up-to-date and comprehensive information tool. Included in the alphabetically arranged body of entries are architects, firms, types of buildings, materials, and various features, topics, and issues relevant to the comprehension of architecture and construction. Along with the processes and technical elements, there is excellent coverage of both the historical influences and the philosophical aspects, such as aesthetics. This substantial tool has gained recognition as a standard in the field and the first source of information for those who need enlightenment in this area. Some 500 signed articles are contributed by specialists (architects, architectural historians, and academicians). There are 3,000 high-quality illustrations along with 500 tables. Volume 5 (T-Z) contains the index of subjects, personal names, and buildings, along with a 219-page supplement of additional topics.

435. **The Illustrated Encyclopedia of Architects and Architecture.** Dennis Sharp, ed. New York: Whitney Library of Design/Watson-Guptill, 1991. 256p. ISBN 0-8230-2539-X.

Sharp serves as the editor of *World Architecture*, an international journal in the field, and has secured the services of a highly qualified group of contributors in producing this work. It is divided into two parts, the first one being a biographical dictionary treating the lives and careers of 350 architects from both the historical past and contemporary times. The entries are brief and include a summary evaluation of the individual's work along with a bibliography for additional reading. In some cases, photographs of important achievements are supplied. The second section presents a historical overview of architecture through a series of brief essays illustrated with some 400 black-and-white and color photographs. In this way, one is able to comprehend the development of the styles and the nature of the movements and their influences in architectural history. There are cross-references to architects in part 1, along with a general index. A glossary also is furnished.

436. **Time-Saver Standards for Building Types.** 3d ed. Joseph De Chiara and John Hancock Callender, eds. New York: McGraw-Hill, 1990. 1413p. ISBN 0-07-016279-4.

This is the third edition of the initial title in this important series from the publisher. First published in 1973 and revised in 1980, the work continues to provide a standard source of information on all major building types arranged under ten broad categories: residential, educational, cultural, health, religious, governmental and public, commercial, transportation, industrial, and recreation and entertainment. Also included is a miscellaneous category treating farm buildings, nature centers, etc. The editors are practicing architects who have provided information on vital details within each section. Dimensions, facility needs, space criteria, layouts, schematics, arrangements, etc. are supplied for all types of construction, thus providing a starting point in the design process. A detailed index is furnished.

Two other titles have been issued in this series. *Time-Saver Standards for Interior Design and Space Planning*, also by De Chiara and others (McGraw-Hill, 1991), is divided into five parts, the first four covering various types of buildings and construction details. The final section provides general reference data. *Time Saver Standards for Landscape Architecture: Design and Construction Data*, edited by Charles W. Harris and Nicholas T. Dines (McGraw-Hill, 1988), also provides a comprehensive exposition of important data, along with illustrations organized in various sections such as historical landscapes and outdoor accessibility. A similar source is *Ramsey/Sleeper Architectural Graphic Standards*, now in its ninth edition (John Wiley & Sons, 1994). Sponsored by the American Institute of Architects and initiated by Charles George Ramsey and Harold Reeve Sleeper, both of whom died in the early 1960s, this continuing effort is now edited by John Ray Hoke, Jr. It represents a standard source of information regarding standards for building design and construction and is arranged in chapters according to principles established by the Construction Specifications Institute. Recently added chapters treat historic preservation and energy design.

Directories

437. **Landmark Yellow Pages; Where to Find All the Names, Addresses, Facts, and Figures You Need**. 2d ed. Pamela Dwight, ed./National Trust for Historic Preservation. Washington, DC: Preservation Press, 1993. 395p. ISBN 0-89133-169-7.

Originally published as *The Brown Book: A Directory of Preservation Information* (Preservation Press, 1983), this useful directory-handbook has been enlarged and revised and now replaces the first edition published three years earlier. The work is designed to aid the National Trust for Historic Preservation in fulfilling its responsibility to inform and advise states and local agencies that desire to preserve old buildings of historical or architectural significance. Part 1 provides practical information in topical chapters, alphabetically arranged, covering architectural styles, lists of books, bookstores, cities with major programs, libraries, periodicals, etc., along with a glossary and information on tax incentives. Entries supply brief bibliographies. Part 2 treats the preservation network with a directory of several thousand preservation agencies, listed by state and including national, statewide, and local organizations. Territorial and foreign organizations also are included when they are members of the National Trust. There is a general index of sites, names, and publications.

*438. **National Register of Historic Places, 1966-1991: Cumulative List Through June 30, 1991**. Nashville, TN: American Association for State and Local History Press; Washington, DC: National Park Service, 1991. 893p. ISBN 0-942063-21-X.

This is the latest edition of this cumulative listing, replacing the 1989 issue that covered the period 1966-1988. There are nearly 58,000 entries, representing an increase of 6,000 over its predecessor. Included here are all properties listed in the National Register over a period of twenty-five years. Arrangement of entries is directory-fashion, alphabetical by state, then county. Coverage is thorough for the United States and embraces the territory of District of Columbia as well as American Samoa, Guam, Puerto Rico, the Virgin Islands, and Micronesia. This official listing is maintained by the National Park Service and published in cooperation with the American Association for State and Local History. It has been expanded to include properties of local and state significance as well as those of national importance. The work is available online through the National Park Service and on CD-ROM from Chadwyck-Healey.

439. **ProFile: The Directory of U.S. Architectural Design Firms**. American Institute of Architects. Washington, DC: American Institute of Architects, 1993- . Annual. ISSN 0190-8766.

This directory of architectural firms, published under the auspices of the AIA, actually began in 1978 and has appeared irregularly. The 1993 edition bears a slight change of subtitle and a firm new commitment to annual publication. Member firms are listed alphabetically by name within a geographical arrangement, in typical directory fashion. Each entry provides addresses of all offices of the firms and indication of types of practice, as well as the name of the present company. Also included are names of personnel, analyses of work distributions by gross income percentages, geographical work distributions, and awards. There are indexes of both companies and individuals.

The AIA also sponsored *American Architects Directory* (R. R. Bowker, 1955-1970), which furnished biographical information along with names and addresses of members and other prominent architects. Included were a geographical index and lists of fellows and award winners.

Biographical Sources

440. **American Architects from the Civil War to the First World War: A Guide to Information Sources**. Lawrence Wodehouse. Detroit: Gale Research, 1976. 343p. (Art and Architecture Information Guide Series, v.3). ISBN 0-8103-1269-7.

The author, a British architect, has rendered an important bibliographic guide to the study of architectural history that has stood the test of time. It represents a selective annotated biographical bibliography treating the most important American architects from 1860 to the second decade of the twentieth century and continues the coverage initiated by Frank J. Roos, Jr.'s *Bibliography of Early American Architecture* (University of Illinois Press, 1968) that covered the field up to 1860. An annotated listing of 46 general reference books on American architects precedes the major section treating 175 important architects and partnerships. These entries are arranged alphabetically by surname and supply a brief biographical sketch along with a listing of the personality's publications, locations of his or her drawings, and a bibliography of books and articles offering biographical or critical commentary. There is a general subject index and a building location index.

Wodehouse continued his efforts with a similar work on major architects in his native land. *British Architects, 1840-1976: A Guide to Information Sources* is number 8 in the publisher's series and was issued in 1978. It treats 288 important architects from England, Wales, Ireland, and Scotland. Indexing as well as treatment is similar to the annotated work.

441. **Contemporary Architects**. 2d ed. Ann Lee Morgan and Colin Naylor, eds. Chicago: St. James Press, 1987. 1038p. ISBN 0-912289-26-0.

Another good source is this biographical dictionary, now in its second edition. This work furnishes biographical coverage of 575 of the greatest living architects, landscape architects, and structural engineers, along with coverage of some of the acknowledged masters from an earlier part of this century. Entries include a biographical sketch, list of major works, references to books by and about the architect, a photograph of a representative work, and an evaluative essay. In some cases there is commentary from the architects about their work.

Avery Obituary Index of Architects (2d ed., G. K. Hall, 1980) provides some 17,000 references to obituaries contained in about 500 periodicals covered in the *Avery Index to Architectural Periodicals*, along with a selection of newspapers such as the *New York Times*. The work was initiated in 1934, and was last issued in 1963 as *Avery Obituary Index of*

Architects and Artists. The indexing of artists ceased in 1960, however, accounting for the change in title. There is additional indexing of obituaries in four leading U.S. architectural periodicals to their beginnings along with selective inclusion of English, French, and German periodicals.

442. **International Dictionary of Architects and Architecture**. Randall Van Vynckt, ed. Detroit: St. James Press, 1993. 2v. ISBN 1-55862-089-3.

This two-volume guide identifies and describes the lives and careers of 525 master architects and provides exposition of 464 major architectural works. Enhancing the work are numerous illustrations, 900 photographs, and 200 floor plans. Volume 1, "Architects," supplies an alphabetical arrangement of major architects dating from ancient Greece to the present. Entries begin with a biographical sketch and listing of the personality's architectural triumphs. An extensive bibliography of books and articles by and about the figure then precedes a detailed critical essay of up to 2,000 words in length, signed by one of the contributor-specialists. Volume 2, "Architecture," presents important architectural projects dating from the Middle Ages to the present. Included in each entry are the architect's name, location, size, and dates and a signed expository essay on historical, stylistic, and critical aspects. An index of locations is furnished.

443. **Macmillan Encyclopedia of Architects**. Adolf K. Placzek, ed. New York: Free Press/Macmillan, 1982. 4v. ISBN 0-02-925000-5.

This is a comprehensive biographical dictionary of 2,400 prominent architects from all countries and all time periods who either were born prior to 1931 or are deceased. The biographies were selected by an editorial board and approved by specialists of international stature. In addition to architects, there are engineers, bridge builders, landscape architects, and town planners, as well as a few patrons and writers. Criteria imposed upon the biographees were their influence, the importance of their work, and their productivity. Articles generally are of essay length and may be 10,000 words long, although some personalities are covered in less than 100 words. There is also a glossary of terms, as well as indexes of names and architectural works.

444. **Master Builders: A Guide to Famous American Architects**. Diane Maddex, ed. Washington, DC: Preservation, 1985. 203p. (Building Watchers Series). ISBN 0-89133-111-5.

This detailed exposition of the lives of forty American architects is a biographical dictionary of a selective nature. Although in paperback, this is a useful tool and should be purchased by reference departments for the attention it gives to major characteristics, important developments, and resulting influences of the architects' work. A portrait is provided for each individual and, even more importantly, illustrations of his or her major contributions are included. The arrangement of entries is chronological, beginning with William Thornton, who designed the U.S. Capitol, and ending with Venturi, Rauch, and Scott Brown. In addition to the basic text, there are short entries on another seventy architects who are identified by business firms and representative projects. There is a bibliography as well as an index of architects.

445. **Who's Who in Architecture from 1400 to the Present**. J. M. Richards, ed. New York: Holt, Rinehart & Winston, 1977. 368p.

Since its publication, this work has been used consistently in reference departments, and in the minds of most librarians represents a vital source of information on 600 architects, engineers, town planners, and landscape architects. It covers the accomplishments of those who were involved in the creative development of buildings from the time of the Italian Renaissance to the present throughout the Western world. It also includes individuals from outside the West if their cultures have developed as a result of Western influences. About fifty major architects are treated in great depth with lengthy expository essays, whereas the remainder are treated briefly. Many articles have bibliographies, and cross-references are given. There is a classified bibliography at the end.

446. **Who's Who in Interior Design**. Laguna Beach, CA: Barons Who's Who, 1988- . Bienn. ISSN 0897-5914.

This title began with the 1988-1989 edition and has shown promise of becoming a useful source of information on current practitioners. The initial edition contained biographical sketches of 2,300 designers, mostly from the United States. The subsequent issue (1990-1991) takes on an international perspective and treats 3,300 designers active in sixty-one countries, republics, and principalities. Included here are designers in architecture, contract health care, and industry, as well as residential and transportation design. To accommodate the greater scope, the number of U.S. designers was reduced by some 500 personalities. Coverage is given to 550 Japanese designers, 200 French figures, and somewhat fewer British or Italian subjects. About 10 percent of the entries represent Africa, the Middle East, South America, and inner Asia. Entries are arranged alphabetically and supply the usual directory-type information. Also included is a directory of organizations; a geographical index aids access.

Histories

447. **History of World Architecture** series. New York: Rizzoli, 1985- .

This is the most recent of several series that treat the entire history of world architecture. More than fifteen volumes have been issued thus far. Now produced by Rizzoli, the series originated in the 1970s and was published in Italian by Electa of Milan, Italy. The present series has translated these works and, in addition, has incorporated the English-language series of the same name published by Harry N. Abrams, also produced during the 1970s. Rizzoli continues the tradition of its predecessors in selecting architecture of different regions and/or historical periods for individual treatment in the volumes. The Rizzoli efforts cover each major period, beginning with primitive and progressing to modern architecture. Each volume is written by a specialist in the field and presents a narrative history, along with bibliography, in slender volumes of some 200 pages. Indexes are provided.

448. **Sir Banister Fletcher's A History of Architecture.** 19th ed. John Musgrove et al. Boston: Butterworths, 1987. 1621p. ISBN 0-408-01587-X.

Upon his death in 1953, Fletcher left a trust fund to the Royal Institute of British Architects and the University of London for the revision and updating of his well-illustrated history. First published in 1896, the tool set a standard in the field for its excellent coverage of architectural styles and features of various historical periods. The present edition has incorporated several important changes, the most important of which is the increased coverage given Asian, African, Australian, Oceanic, and American cultures from the pre-co-lonial period to the present. The organization is roughly chronological, in seven major parts or segments beginning with ancient Egypt and Greece and concluding with the twentieth century. It continues as an essential reference book for the amount of information it contains; this revision is the product of a distinguished group of contributors from various parts of the world.

SCULPTURE

Bibliographic Guides and Bibliographies

449. **American Sculpture: A Guide to Information Sources.** Janis Ekdahl. Detroit: Gale Research, 1977. 260p. (Art and Architecture Information Guide Series, v.5). ISBN 0-8103-1271-9.

This is an especially useful resource in view of the lack of bibliographic coverage on the topic of American sculpture. Compiled by a college art librarian with a knowledge of the needs of both students and specialists, the work opens with a general section of research materials covering bibliographies, catalogs, indexes, biographical sources, encyclopedias, dictionaries, and directories. The second section treats the history and aesthetics of American culture in seven chapters, and the final section provides listings of sources for nearly 220 American sculptors. Books, parts of books, periodical articles, and exhibition catalogs are identified and described in terms of their principal features. There are author, title, and subject indexes, and a list of institutions with extensive collections of sculpture in the appendix.

450. **Fifteenth Century Central Italian Sculpture: An Annotated Bibliography.** Sarah Blake Wilk. Boston: G. K. Hall, 1986. 401p. (A Reference Publication in Art History). ISBN 0-8161-8550-6.

One of a series of twenty Renaissance bibliographies, most of which are in the planning stages at G. K. Hall, this work provides listings of 2,000 documents. Most entries are annotated and represent excellent bibliographic coverage of Florentine sculpture, with the inclusion of figures such as Donatello, Ghiberti, Brunelleschi, and Luca della Robbia. One section is given to modern scholarship, whereas others identify early sources and studies of technique and materials. There are surveys of a general nature as well as treatments of specific or specialized topics reported in monographs and articles in several Western languages. Also included are theses and other unpublished works. Most coverage is given to works on individual sculptors. Unlike its subject matter, the tool is unattractive, with a typescript appearance, but it is a useful vehicle for both students and specialists.

451. **French Romanesque Sculpture: An Annotated Bibliography.** Thomas W. Lyman and Daniel Smartt. Boston: G. K. Hall, 1987. 450p. (Reference Publications in Art History). ISBN 0-8161-8330-9.

This is a comprehensive bibliography intended to capture all material published in books, periodicals, and catalogs on the topic of Romanesque sculpture in France and its earlier possessions, Corsica and Alsace. This artistic period embraces the late tenth century to the early fourteenth century, and the work is divided into three major chronological periods of publication: 1700-1900, 1900-1944, and 1945 to the present. Of the 2,173 entries, more than 1,200 were issued in the most recent period, reflecting an increased interest among scholars since World War II. Each segment opens with an introductory essay providing historical perspective in terms of publication and research. There are separate listings for each of the three types of sources; entries are arranged chronologically within their form category. There is an extensive detailed index of authors, reviewers, subjects, places, and names in annotations.

Italian Romanesque Architecture: An Annotated Bibliography, by Dorothy F. Glass, is a 1983 publication in the same series. It contains 1,550 briefly annotated entries representing books and periodical articles based on the holdings of the Biblioteca Hertziana in Rome. Entries are arranged within topical sections identifying specific locales and art forms such as wood sculpture.

Artwork and Reproductions—Catalogs, Etc.

452. **Earth Scale Art: A Bibliography, Directory of Artists, and Index of Reproductions**. Patricia Pate Havlice. Jefferson, NC: McFarland, 1984. 138p. ISBN 0-89950-072-2.

Despite being of diminutive size, this is a most useful bibliography and index to reproductions in its unique coverage of earth-scale art. Sometimes termed *earthworks, earth art,* or *land art,* the medium uses the land itself within the context of the art form to produce the finished work. Some of its practitioners have achieved international acclaim or attention, such as Christo, who is one of thirty-two artists treated here. The work opens with a general bibliography of some 100 articles from magazines, placing land art in perspective. Next is the major segment, supplying entries to artists. These contain birth/death dates, training, awards, films about the artist, list of shows, relevant bibliography, and a listing of reproductions both in color and black-and-white. The final segments contain an author index and a title index to the earthworks.

453. **Renaissance Artists & Antique Sculpture: A Handbook of Sources**. Phyllis Pray Bober and Ruth Rubinstein. New York: Oxford University Press, 1986; repr. 1987, 1991. 522p. ISBN 0-19-921029-2.

This standard tool has now been issued as a new impression with the assistance of the J. Paul Getty Trust. It treats more than 200 pieces of monumental sculpture, primarily statues and reliefs, executed prior to the Sack of Rome in 1527. Selections are culled from the enormous catalog begun in 1949 under the sponsorship of the Warburg Institute and New York Institute of Fine Arts, *Census of Antique Works of Art Known to Renaissance Artists.* The purpose is to provide documentary evidence of the influence of ancient artworks on the work of Renaissance artists. The work is organized into two segments, one on Greek and Roman Gods and Myth, and one on Roman History and Life. Entries furnish title, description, and history of the various subjects along with the identification of representations, especially drawings from sketchbooks of Renaissance artists. Appendices furnish an index of artists and sketchbooks and an index of Renaissance collectors.

454. **Romanesque Sculpture in American Collections**. Walter Cahn and Linda Seidel. v.1 New England Museums. New York: B. Franklin, 1979. 344p. ISBN 0-89102-131-0. v.2 New York, South Atlantic, Midwest, and West. Walter Cahn et al. Boston: G. K. Hall, 1994. 500p. ISBN 0-8153-0656-3.

When volume 1 was first published in 1979, it was to initiate a series of critical catalogs published under the sponsorship of the International Center of Medieval Art. Articles were based on studies published earlier in *Gesta,* the Center's journal, and revised and updated by specialists in the field. Stone and wood sculpture of monumental nature is treated; selections are excellent and description is well developed. An illustration is furnished for each work treated. This is an important source for identification of Romanesque sculpture in the eastern United States. The second volume, also edited by Cahn with the assistance of others, did not appear until fifteen years later in 1994. Like the earlier effort, it furnishes a critical inventory of Romanesque sculpture housed in public collections in the United States. Items are described and analyzed in terms of origin, meaning, and significance. Citations to the literature are supplied in both volumes, along with photographs.

French Sculptors of the 17th and 18th Centuries, the Reign of Louis XIV: Illustrated Catalogue, by Francois Souchal et al. (Oxford University Press, 1977-1987), was issued as a three-volume catalog in English translation. Entries are arranged alphabetically and treat the artists' lives and careers, along with a chronologically arranged listing of their work with brief identification. Bibliographic sources are supplied. There is a general index of sites, names, and subjects.

455. **Sculpture Index.** Jane Clapp. Metuchen, NJ: Scarecrow Press, 1970-1971. 2v. in 3. ISBN 0-8108-0249-X.

This excellent index to pictures of sculpture in 950 publications is a staple in the reference departments of art libraries. Listings are dictionary-style under names of artists, titles, and subjects, adding greatly to ease of use. Sources include art histories, collection and exhibition catalogs, and art reference books, and are generally available in public, school, college, and special libraries. Although the emphasis is on modern sculpture after 1900, all periods are represented. The sculpture of Europe and the contemporary Middle East is covered in volume 1; volume 2 embraces the Americas, the Orient, Africa, the Pacific area, and the classical world. Locations of original sculptures are given, and there is an excellent list of both private and public collections by country and city. Entries include nationality and dates of sculptors, materials, size, museum identification numbers, and references to documents. All types of sculpture are included.

Dictionaries, Encyclopedias, Handbooks, Histories

456. **The Encyclopedia of Sculpture Techniques.** John Mills. New York: Watson Guptill, 1989. 239p. ISBN 0-8230-1609-9.

The author is a well-known English sculptor and academic who has utilized his expertise to produce a useful handbook and guide to sculptural techniques and processes. Arrangement of entries is alphabetized, with coverage given to an array of topics and considerations. Text is clear and concise; terms are defined, processes are explained, and instruments are described. Enhancing the articles are some 260 black-and-white illustrations, which include photographs and line drawings presenting step-by-step sequences of activity and instructions as well as finished results. There is liberal use of formulas, charts, and diagrams. All aspects of sculpture are treated, with comprehensive coverage of the terminology that embraces both common and obscure terms. Techniques covered represent the traditional and the contemporary as well as experimental and innovative applications. A selective bibliography identifies titles of practical value.

457. **A History of Western Sculpture.** John Pope-Hennessy. Greenwich, CT: New York Graphic Society, 1967-1969. 4v.

These four volumes are truly monographic works in their own right and are brought together under the collective title with the aid of a consultant editor. Volume 1, *Classical Sculpture*, is by George M.A. Hanfmann; volume 2, by Robert Salvini, is *Medieval Sculpture*. Herbert Keutner has contributed volume 3, *Sculpture: Renaissance to Rococo*; volume 4, by Fred Licht, is entitled *Sculpture: 19th and 20th Centuries*. In all volumes, the connection between sculpture and the social, political, and economic forces is described and carefully analyzed. Historical lines are traced and developed in a manner that provides insight into the reasons behind creative development in different eras. A good survey of sculpture is furnished through the four volumes, each of which has fine illustrations, a bibliography, and an index.

458. **An Introduction to Italian Sculpture.** 3d ed. John Pope-Hennessy. New York: Vintage Books, 3v. ISBN 0-394-72933-1.

An important work in the field, first published in 1955, this is now in its third edition. Titles for the individual volumes have remained unchanged over the years, although succeeding editions have incorporated additional elements, modifications, and corrections when needed. Volume 1 covers Italian Gothic sculpture roughly from Pisano to Ghiberti; volume 2 treats the Italian Renaissance from Donatello to Tullio Lombardo; volume 3 describes the High Renaissance and Baroque. Typically, the volumes include introductory chapters on leading sculptors and trends, plates, notes on sculptors, an index of sculptors, and an index of places. Works are treated chronologically in each volume and biographies of artists are included.

Roman Sculpture, by Diane E. E. Kleiner (Yale University Press, 1993), is one of the few tools to focus exclusively on the sculpture of classical Rome while placing it in the context of cultural development and political and social events. The text is well developed and informative and is enhanced by black-and-white illustrations of high quality. Organization of chapters is chronological in treating the historical influences. Chapters contain bibliographies; the index follows a glossary of Greek and Roman terms.

459. **The Sculpture and Sculptors of the Greeks.** 4th ed. Rev. Gisela Richter. New Haven, CT: Yale University Press, 1970. 317p. ISBN 0-300-01281-0.
     Richter died at the age of ninety, two years after publication of the fourth edition of her work (first issued in 1929). As curator of classical art at the Metropolitan Museum prior to her retirement, she brought expertise and authority as well as a skillful writing style to the production of this important edition. Many additions and corrections were incorporated because of new discoveries and modern perspectives. The first part of the book describes the course of events in sculpture through a chronological survey and exposition of technical considerations. Part 2 covers individual sculptors, in chronological order from the archaic period through the first century B.C. This work can be used and appreciated by a wide range of readers, from those with a general interest to the serious student.

460. **Sculpture in America.** New and rev. ed. Wayne Craven. Newark, NJ: University of Delaware Press; distr., New York: Cornwall Books, 1984. 788p. ISBN 0-87413-225-8.
     For many years, the author's name has been familiar to those who work with the bibliography of art, and this particular effort has been regarded as a solid contribution to the field since its initial publication in 1968. This edition supplies a new chapter on sculpture of the 1960s and 1970s, with good treatment of the formalists and the representationalists. The work provides a fine overview of the relationship between sculpture and the other arts in different art periods in this country. Individual sculptors from colonial times to the present are treated. Most commendable in the view of critics is the excellent treatment given to the sculpture and sculptors of the nineteenth century, as this period has been generally overlooked in the past. The work represents a good blend of scholarship, judgment, and professional expertise, and has been regarded as a must purchase for libraries.

Biographical Sources

461. **Contemporary American Women Sculptors.** Virginia Watson-Jones. Phoenix, AZ: Oryx Press, 1986. 664p. ISBN 0-89774-139-0.
     A useful reference tool with an emphasis on the contribution of female artists, this biographical dictionary covers more than 300 American sculptors. A quick check reveals good coverage of those who have earned recognition, such as Louise Nevelson, Nancy Grossman, and Lee Bontecou. The inclusion of less prominent persons represents a real service in helping to identify our contemporary artists. Much of the information appears for the first time and was gathered through questionnaires mailed to art historians, museums, and art associations. Each entry provides brief biographical information, professional accomplishments, and a statement from each artist. There is a black-and-white reproduction of one of each artist's works.

462. **Dictionary of American Sculptors: 18th Century to the Present.** Glenn B. Opitz, ed. Poughkeepsie, NY: Apollo Book, 1984. 656p. ISBN 0-938290-03-7.
     This title covers more than 5,000 American sculptors from the eighteenth century to the present, although emphasis is on nineteenth- and twentieth-century figures. Those working in this area are aware of the difficulty in finding any detailed commentary on individual sculptors of this period; therefore, the work fills a real need for documentation of obscure

and even more prominent individuals. Many living and recently deceased biographees submitted data directly. These entries join those for which data were gathered from sources such as *American Art Annual* (entry 333n). The work has been criticized for failure to include information subsequent to the 1970s, and a subsequent volume is planned that may address this oversight. Bibliographical references are provided in some cases.

463.   **New Dictionary of Modern Sculpture.** Robert Maillard, ed. New York: Tudor, 1971. 328p. ISBN 0-8148-0479-9.

Although it is getting older, this is still considered a useful biographical dictionary in libraries that need information on modern sculpture. A translation of a French work, it first appeared in English in 1960. It is strictly biographical, with no entries for the description of art movements, countries, or topical coverage. Articles are signed with the initials of the contributors and about 600 sculptors are treated. Each entry provides brief biographical information about the sculptor; highlights accomplishments; and describes the medium, style, and characteristics of his or her work. Best known works are identified, and generally each entry is accompanied by a reproduction of one or two of them. No bibliographical references are provided.

PHOTOGRAPHY

Bibliographies and Catalogs

464.   **History of Photography: A Bibliography of Books.** Laurent Roosens and Luc Salu. New York: Mansell, 1989. 446p. ISBN 0-7201-2008-X.

This is an enormous project, twenty-five years in the making, that provides comprehensive coverage of books issued between 1839 and 1914, and selective coverage of those published from 1915 to the mid-1980s. Some 11,000 books are listed under 3,000 alphabetically arranged subject headings and subheadings. Subject headings treat topics, personalities, and types of publications; citations are arranged chronologically under these subject headings. Photographers treated are limited to those born prior to 1914. A dozen languages of the Western world are represented; broad subjects are subdivided by language. Included here are monographs, dissertations, company literature, and exhibition catalogs; juvenile literature is excluded. Entries supply authors/editors/contributors, title and translation, imprint, pagination, number of illustrations in black-and-white and in color, and edition statements. Entries for photographers identify nationality and dates. There is a detailed comprehensive index of photographers and authors.

465.   **Library Catalog of the International Museum of Photography at George Eastman House.** International Museum of Photography. Boston: G. K. Hall, 1982. 4v. ISBN 0-8161-0294-5.

The International Museum of Photography at George Eastman House was created in 1949 as an independent, nonprofit institution under the joint sponsorship of the Eastman Kodak Company and the University of Rochester. It has amassed an enormous research collection of images, films, photographic equipment, and print publications. Included in this four-volume catalog are more than 43,000 cards that identify 11,000 monographic titles treating the social, historic, cultural, and aesthetic qualities of photography and cinematography. Included are more than 2,700 rare and unique books. Neither periodical publications nor unpublished manuscripts are included. Volumes 1 and 2 treat authors and titles, whereas volumes 3 and 4 identify subjects. All volumes are alphabetically arranged. The work is available from the publisher on sixty-six microfiche as well as four reels of microfilm.

466. **Nineteenth Century Photography: An Annotated Bibliography, 1839-1879**. William Johnson. Boston: G. K. Hall, 1990. 962p. ISBN 0-8161-7958-1.

This is a comprehensive annotated bibliography of an important forty-year period of development and innovation in photography. The author is a well-known researcher in the field who has spent more than twenty years studying this topic. The result is a listing of more than 20,000 books and articles in the English language, the most thorough bibliography ever produced on this subject. Obscure photographers and much documentation are revealed for the first time in this effort. Entries are in two sections, the major one being author or artist. Here, the entries are alphabetically arranged and include biographical information ranging from substantial description in some cases to indication of dates and nationality in others. The other segment treats broad special topics (bibliography, prehistory, history, country, apparatus or equipment, application or usage). Some of these broad topics are subdivided further. An author index completes the work.

467. **Photography and Literature: An International Bibliography of Monographs**. Eric Lambrechts and Luc Salu. New York: Mansell, 1992. 296p. ISBN 0-7201-2113-2.

This is a bibliography unique in its purpose to study the relationship between photography and literature. Nearly 3,900 titles of books, exhibition catalogs, dissertations, and special issues of magazines in twenty different languages are identified. Books are of various types, from those providing monographic studies of the topic to those that treat photographic work produced by writers of literature, as well as those that furnish portraits of writers by credited photographers. Excluded from coverage are magazine articles, pictorial biographies, fiction, and biblical texts. Entries supply the bibliographic data and indicate language of publication. Arrangement of entries is alphabetical by author or photographer; numerous cross-references are included. Because of its unique approach and its theoretical slant, the work is best utilized by researchers, specialists, and serious students. A broad subject index completes the effort.

468. **Photography and Photographers to 1900: An Annotated Bibliography**. Robert S. Sennett. New York: Garland, 1985. 134p. (Garland Reference Library of the Humanities, no. 594). ISBN 0-8240-8728-3.

This is a useful selective bibliography for the specialist and for the student. Its purpose is to identify early books of merit in the field. The author is an academic librarian who utilizes his expertise to supply annotated entries of 408 books of international origin. These were thought to be important for their impact, influence, literary quality, or innovative approaches. Arrangement is within four chapters treating technical treatises, theoretical treatises, monographic works on personalities, and photographic surveys. These chapters are further divided by specific subjects. Although the subject matter represents historical coverage, publication dates of entries run to the mid-1980s. Annotations are brief but informative in describing content; English-language editions are identified for foreign titles. There is a general index providing access by authors and subjects.

Collections, Reproductions, and Sales—Catalogs, Directories, Etc.

469. **Index to American Photographic Collections: Compiled at the International Museum of Photography at George Eastman House**. 2d enl. ed. Andrew H. Eskind and Grey Drake, eds. Boston: G. K. Hall, 1990. 701p. ISBN 0-8161-0500-6.

The first edition of this directory and guide was published in 1982, compiled by James McQuaid, who had a longtime professional interest in the indexing of photographic collections and identification of photographers. The enlarged second edition extends this coverage from 400 to 540 collections open to the public in museums, public and university libraries, art galleries, newspaper and magazine archives, historical societies, and other institutions.

The number of photographers identified has increased from about 19,000 to about 20,000 individuals. All previous listings have been updated where necessary. This large-scale comprehensive coverage is thought to embrace all photographers who have inspired others to collect their works. Entries for collections include alphabetical listings of photographers as well as name of contact person. Name listings include cross-references, dates, and nationality.

470. **The Photographic Art Market: Auction Prices, 1990.** Robert S. Persky, ed. New York: Photographic Arts Center, 1991. 68p. ISBN 0-913069-27-2.

This is a small but informative continuing publication serving as a guide to the sales of important photographs in the large auction houses of Butterfield's, Christie's, Phillips, and Sotheby's. Published at various intervals since its inception, it has become an annual catalog, attesting to the increasing popularity of photography as a collecting medium. Arrangement is alphabetical by names of photographers, under which are listed the titles of photographs. Entries include price, auction house, lot number, physical description, and date of negative or print. Prices for individual prints are listed in a chronological sequence by date of auction. The work is plain in appearance, with listings provided without benefit of illustration. It represents a useful resource item for collectors and dealers.

Holography Market Place: HMP, the Reference Text and Directory of the Holography Industry, edited by Brian Kluepfel and Franz Ross and now in its third edition (Ross Books, 1991), provides specialized treatment of this recent technology. The work consists of thirteen chapters, most of which are topical in covering the various aspects of holography. The final chapters supply listings of businesses and related elements (distributors, wholesalers, retailers, distributors, personalities, copyright holders, etc.). Businesses are organized by category, and individuals are covered. There is a bibliography and an index.

471. **Photography Books Index: A Subject Guide to Photo Anthologies.** Martha Moss. Metuchen, NJ: Scarecrow Press, 1980. 286p. ISBN 0-8108-1283-5. **Supp.** 1985. 261p. ISBN 0-8108-1773-X.

This important work identifies and locates thousands of photographs by indexing twenty-two major titles of photography anthologies. The work is organized into three major sections comprised of a listing of photographers alphabetically arranged, a subject listing based on Sears list of subject headings revealing topical matter contained in the photographs, and a listing of portraits of named individuals, identifying children, men, and women alphabetically by name of model or sitter. These entries include dates, photographers, and source of pictures. *Photography Books Index II* ..., published in 1985, serves as a supplement to the initial effort and continues the process of identification. The same format is followed in the indexing of an additional twenty-eight titles published between 1955 and 1982. Hundreds of personalities and classic photographs by masters of the camera are revealed along with photographic records of events and developments.

*472. **PhotoNet.** Coral Gables, FL: VMSI/PhotoNet. 1983- .

This online database has been available since 1983 and furnishes information useful to professional photographers, photo agencies, and purchasers. Requests for photographs are entered into the system by subscribers; buyers and sellers interact on the electronic bulletin board set-up. Also included are travel itineraries of photographers, stocking information of photoagencies, a photosources directory of photographers and agencies, professional services from Nikon, airline guides, and newswire services. The world of commercial photography is covered in all phases, from equipment to services. General news of interest to the field is provided. Updating is continuous.

The Photoletter is a monthly newsletter available online through Newsnet since 1982. It is published by PhotoSources International of Osceola, Wisconsin, and identifies photo needs of magazines as received from editors of U.S. publications. Descriptions, prices, deadlines, and contacts are specified for photographers to market their wares. *Photomarket* (1984-) also comes from the same publisher and similarly identifies the types of photographs needed by middle-range magazine and book publishers. Both databases are updated biweekly.

Dictionaries, Encyclopedias, Handbooks, Etc.

473. International Center of Photography/Encyclopedia of Photography. William L. Broecker, ed. New York: Crown, 1984. 607p. ISBN 0-517-55271-X.

Designed for a more advanced and sophisticated audience, this encyclopedia contains 1,300 entries providing technical awareness, biographical coverage, and aesthetic understanding. Many cross-references appear in the entries and there are numerous illustrations to augment the exposition provided. Biographies cover prominent individuals over a 100-year period from 1840 to 1940 and are illustrated with examples of the biographees' work. Trends in the field are identified and described, and a bibliography is furnished.

A work similar in content and form is *The Photographer's Bible: An Encyclopedic Reference Manual* by Bruce Pinkard (Arco, 1982). Techniques, equipment, and personalities are covered alphabetically in articles of varying length. There are numerous illustrations as well. Appendices furnish listings of associations and societies, grants, schools and workshops, services, and equipment manufacturers.

474. International Guide to Nineteenth-Century Photographers and Their Works: Based on Catalogues of Auction Houses and Dealers. Gary Edwards. Boston: G. K. Hall, 1988. 591p. ISBN 0-8161-8938-2.

This is a unique and valuable information source for identifying photographers and their works from the historical past. Edwards's intent is to emphasize the finding of basic information on obscure photographers rather than obscure information on famous or well-known photographers. As a result, the work is functional in two ways; it serves both as a catalog of auction sales and as a directory of some 4,000 photographers both obscure and well-known. It opens with a listing of the fifty auction catalogs that provide the source material, along with indication of auction dates. The main body of the work then places entries for all photographers in alphabetical order. Entries supply nationality, dates, principal subject matter, date of activity (earliest to latest known photographs), processes and formats (portraits, genre, etc.), geographical range for topographic and documentary photographers, and locations of photographs in sales catalogs.

475. Looking at Photographs: A Guide to Technical Terms. Gordon Baldwin. Malibu, CA: J. Paul Getty Museum with British Museum Press, 1991. 88p. ISBN 0-89236-192-1.

This slender volume produced by the Getty Museum in cooperation with the British Museum Press is designed to provide an up-to-date wordbook for specialists, scholars, students, and collectors. All technical terms of some magnitude are included in what amounts to a surprising amount of information, considering the diminutive size of the work. All important details concerning the words are treated, with coverage in most cases ranging from one to three paragraphs in length. Arrangement of entries is alphabetical; some of the technical terms are not included in other, more general photography information sources. Entries are enhanced in many cases with illustrations designed to clarify the topic being treated. Alternative terms are identified for the various processes, and cross-references are noted within the entries.

476. Photographers: A Sourcebook for Historical Research. Richard Rudisill et al., ed. by Peter E. Palmquist. Brownsville, CA: Carl Mautz, 1991. 103p. ISBN 0-96219-402-6.

Because of the increased interest in historical figures and their work in photography, Palmquist (a well-known scholar in the field) has created a manual for historical research. There are two major sections, with the first consisting of six essays on research and writing of regional history, each by a different specialist. The second segment presents a briefly annotated listing of directories of photographers developed by Rudisill, a curator of a photographic history collection in New Mexico. Arrangement is geographic by country, region, or state. Rudisill contributed one essay of the six in the first section, describing his ruminations related to the compilation of his bibliography of directories. Another of the essays is written by Palmquist, a personal narrative on researching California photographers and regionalism in practice. Methods and techniques are further explained by writers of the other essays. There is an index of authors.

477. **Price Guide to Antique and Classic Cameras, 1992-1993**. 8th ed. James M. McKeown and Joan C. McKeown, eds. Grantsburg, WI: Centennial Photo Service, 1992. 512p.

The eighth edition of this guide to appear in the last twenty-two years remains an excellent source of information on the specialized interest of antique cameras. One of several guides in this field, it affords a useful and convenient source of information on a subject that has received increased attention on the part of collectors. Arranged alphabetically by manufacturer and chronologically within that category, both still and motion-picture cameras are treated separately. Several thousand cameras from all over the world and all periods of time are listed, making it a useful source for identification. It is illustrated with some 2,500 black-and-white photographs. Each entry provides valuation and brief description (including dates and history whenever possible) and is accessed through a detailed index. Photographic accessories and novelties are included as well.

Biographical Sources

478. **American Photographers: An Illustrated Who's Who Among Leading Contemporary Americans**. Les Krantz, ed. New York: Facts on File, 1989. 352p. ISBN 0-8160-1419-1.

This is a comprehensive and attractive biographical dictionary treating more than 1,000 living photographers representing all areas of the field. Information on the well-known personalities appears to have been culled from standard reference books; others have supplied much of their data through mail questionnaires. Treated in this volume are some of the most prominent names in fashion and advertising media as well as prize-winning photojournalists; the majority of entries, however, represent little-known commercial photographers who at times have contributed what might be called exaggerated descriptions of their competencies. Entries furnish brief mention of type of work, address, telephone number, situations, awards, and education. Personalities have at least five years experience and are expected to have had their work reproduced in at least five media in 1988. Whether this standard is enforced or not is difficult to judge.

479. **Contemporary Photographers**. Colin Naylor, ed. Chicago: St. James Press, 1988. 1145p. ISBN 0-912289-79-1.

As a biographical dictionary of 750 prominent photographers, either living or recently deceased, this work provides a distinctive and useful source on what is generally elusive information. Planned as a quinquennial publication, this edition was issued six years after the initial effort (1982) and adds 100 new names. It covers photographers from all over the world, including a good representation of those from Eastern Europe and the former Soviet Union. Selection was determined by an advisory board composed of distinguished authorities. Entries provide the usual biographical information as well as listings of exhibitions, group expositions, galleries, and museums that display the subjects' work, and a bibliography of books and articles by and about them. An important feature is the critical essay on the style and quality of the photographers' work, as well as statements from them on the topic.

480. **Encyclopedie internationale des photographs de 1839 a nos jours = Photographers Encyclopedia International 1839 to the Present**. Michele Auer and Michael Auer. Hermance, Switzerland: Editions Camera Obscura, 1985. 2v. ISBN 2-903671-04-4.

This bilingual biographical dictionary represents a herculean effort on the part of the authors to identify and describe the life and work of some 1,600 photographers over a period of 145 years. The great value of the work lies in its excellent coverage of contemporary photographers and the nature of their work, because, in most cases, only the well-known early photographers are treated. Information was obtained through actual visits with 600 of the personalities as well as contact with agencies and use of published sources. All entries receive a full page of coverage, opening with a biographical sketch in both English and French, accompanied by photographs of the artists and reproductions of their signatures, along with listings of exhibitions, collections displaying their work, and bibliography. There is also an illustration of their craft. There is a list of abbreviations and a chronology, along with indexes of photographers by country and by other names.

481. **Macmillan Biographical Encyclopedia of Photographic Artists and Innovators.** Turner Browne, ed. New York: Macmillan, 1983. 722p. ISBN 0-02-517500-9.

An extensive biographical dictionary of 2,000 photographers and photographic artists, this volume includes individuals both living and dead. The major photographers are covered, of course, but more important is the utility of the tool in identifying individuals who are less prominent and relatively difficult to find. About 25 percent of the personalities date from the nineteenth and early twentieth centuries, and selection for inclusion is generally based on contribution to the field. Coverage is international and those included have generally had works shown or have had publications or awards. There are nearly 150 reproductions of representative works and separate listings of museums and galleries. This is a valuable resource because of the number of individuals covered.

482. **World Photographers Reference Series**. Anne Hammond and Amy Rule, eds. Boston: G. K. Hall, 1992- . ISBN 0-8161-0577-4 (v.1).

This is an important new series of volumes, each of which treats an individual photographer in a standard format running about 200 pages. Volumes supply a brief chronology of the photographer's life and work and a biocritical essay. Also included is a listing of texts written by and about the artist, an annotated critical bibliography or bibliographic essay utilizing both primary and secondary sources, and a selection of twenty-five to thirty reproductions illustrating the nature of the subject's art. The volumes are beautifully illustrated and combine the appeal of "coffee table" items with good scholarship. The general editors are professionals in the field and have assisted the authors in producing useful works. Ms. Hammond authored the first volume in the series on Frederick H. Evans; subsequent volumes have treated Imogen Cunningham, Henry Fox Talbot, Carleton Watkins, Bill Brandt, and James Craig Annan.

APPLIED DESIGN AND DECORATIVE ARTS

General

BIBLIOGRAPHIC GUIDES, BIBLIOGRAPHIES, AND INDEXES

483. **American Decorative Arts and Old World Influences: A Guide to Information Sources**. David M. Sokol. Detroit: Gale Research, 1980. 294p. (Art and Architecture Information Guide Series, v.14; Gale Information Guide Library). ISBN 0-8103-1465-7.

Like others in this Gale series, this is a well-developed and carefully constructed selective bibliography on the topic. That the subject is the decorative arts makes the work highly desirable for libraries, because the area has not been well documented in the past. More than 1,300 published works are organized within eleven topical and format chapters. The first two chapters treat bibliographies and general reference books, followed by three chapters surveying time periods and geographic regions. Six chapters deal directly with the decorative arts, beginning with a general overview and progressing through specialized treatments of ceramics, furniture, glass, metalwork, and textiles. Entries represent books and articles, with good coverage of exhibition catalogs. Concluding the effort are three separate indexes providing access by author, title, and subject.

484. **American Graphic Design: A Guide to the Literature**. Ellen Mazur Thompson, comp. Westport, CT: Greenwood Press, 1992. 282p. (Art Reference Collection, no. 15). ISBN 0-313-28728-7.

This is a unique effort developed by a specialist/librarian in cooperation with the American Institute of Graphic Arts. It furnishes an annotated listing of 1,100 publications relevant to the field of graphic art and commercial design in this country. All types of publications are included: reference books, textbooks, manuals, sourcebooks, catalogs, periodical articles, films, and online databases. Materials are placed within eighteen sections, opening with one on general reference sources. Following are topical sections dealing with subjects like design education, computer technology, visual resources, advertising, color, comics, photography, etc. Excluded are the book arts, cartography, and commercial printing. Each section treats various types of materials (reference sources, online databases, etc. useful to the topic) with cross-references to separate listings of some 200 annuals and serials in the appendix. Also included is a directory of associations and organizations.

485. **Applied and Decorative Arts: A Bibliographic Guide**. 2d ed. Donald L. Ehresmann. Englewood, CO: Libraries Unlimited, 1993. 629p. ISBN 0-87287-906-2.

A companion volume to the author's other publications on the fine arts (entry 279) and architecture (entry 419), this is a useful and needed literature guide in the broad field of the decorative arts. The new edition doubles the number of entries of the previous issue (1977) and triples the number of pages. Basically, it is a classified and annotated bibliography of 2,482 books in the Western languages published between 1875 and 1991. It embraces the various fields in twenty separate chapters, beginning with a general section on applied and decorative arts, followed by ornaments, folk art, arms and armor, ceramics, clocks and watches, costumes, enamels, furniture, glass, ivory, jewelry, lacquer, leather and bookbinding, medals and seals, metalwork, musical instruments, textiles, toys and dolls, and wallpaper. Excluded are drawing, graphic arts, and mosaic, as they are considered adjuncts to the fine arts. There are author and subject indexes.

486. **Decorative Arts and Household Furnishings in America, 1650-1920: An Annotated Bibliography**. Kenneth L. Ames and Gerald W. R. Ward, eds. Winterthur, DE: Henny Francis du Pont Winterthur Museum; distr., Charlottesville, VA: University Press of Virginia, 1989. 392p. ISBN 0-912724-19-6.

This useful bibliographic guide covers a period of 270 years of involvement with the decorative arts in this country, and represents the efforts of twenty-two specialist/contributors. It opens with an excellent introductory essay linking the decorative arts to cultural history and tracing the nature of interdisciplinary research in the area. There are nine major sections, each beginning with an introductory essay: domestic architecture, furniture, metals, ceramics, glass, textiles, timepieces, household systems, and finally, artisans and culture. The Arts and Crafts Movement is well covered in this country. There are twenty-one individual bibliographies within these segments, each beginning with an introduction and furnishing well-constructed, descriptive annotations of useful and important books and articles published to the mid-1980s. Research needs are identified within the essays. The work is indexed by author and by title.

487. **Design & Applied Arts Index**. Burwash, UK: Design Documentation, 1988- . Semiann. with trienn. cum. ISSN 0953-0681.

Beginning with the 1987 publication year, this work indexes nearly 100 periodicals from the fields of design and the applied arts in order to fully cover related design elements and issues within the areas of art, engineering, and technology. Entries are arranged in a single alphabetical sequence, incorporating both broad and specific topics along with names of personalities. Documentation is thorough and includes articles, news reports, conference reports, reviews of books and exhibitions, obituaries, and illustrations. Entries are selected for inclusion based on their treatment of current topics of interest and/or research value. Because of its interdisciplinary and thorough nature, as well as its international scope, this work shows great promise in achieving recognition as an important indexing source in the field. Computerized access is a likely possibility in the future.

DICTIONARIES, ENCYCLOPEDIAS, HANDBOOKS, ETC.

488. **The Arco Encyclopedia of Crafts.** H. E. Laye Andrew. New York: Arco, 1982. 432p.

As one might expect, a variety of information is included in this work, and coverage ranges over a wide spectrum of craftwork from the very traditional to the very new. Emphasis is on techniques employed in the crafts rather than on specific projects. More than 120 crafts are enumerated, with 850 illustrations to enhance the text. Historical information is given for a number of the crafts described. There are many useful charts and diagrams included in the appendices to facilitate the successful completion of projects, such as conversion charts and diagrams (metric) and color charts. There are lists of suppliers, craft associations, and museums organized by countries.

489. **Design on File.** The Diagram Group. New York: Facts on File, 1984. 320 leaves. ISBN 0-87196-270-5.

As part of the publisher's "On File" series, about 275 designs are presented in loose-leaf format and individually treated. The leaves are of heavy paper stock and suitable for reproduction by students at the high school or college level. Permission to reproduce the designs is granted to purchasers of the work involved in educational or nonprofit activity. Entries are organized under nine design categories: geometry, patterns, projections, diagrams, scales, maps, planning, lettering, and human forms. Like others in the series, this work provides excellent background source material for instructional purposes; it would be especially useful for studying the concept of design in the arts and applied arts as well as mathematics or science. Lost or worn-out leaves can be replaced at small cost, an important consideration for library purchase. A general index aids access.

490. **Dictionary of the Decorative Arts.** John Fleming and Hugh Honour. New York: Icons Editions/Harper & Row, 1977; repr. 1986. 896p. ISBN 0-06-430164-8.

This is a reprint of the well-known and popular *Penguin Dictionary of Decorative Arts*, which has been recognized as a useful and comprehensive source of information. The authors are well known in the field of art history, have published extensively in the past, and furnish impeccable authority for a work of this kind. The emphasis is on furniture and accessories found in both European and American homes past and present. There are about 4,000 entries that include definitions, expositions, and descriptions of materials, techniques, manufacturers, and individual personalities associated with the decorative arts. Bibliographies are furnished for a number of the entries to enable the user to pursue additional readings on the subject. The work is well illustrated and represents a welcome addition to the reference collection.

491. **Dictionary of 20th-Century Design.** John Pile. New York: Facts on File, 1990. 312p. (A Roundtable Press Book). ISBN 0-8160-1811-1. Repr. Da Capo Press, 1994. ISBN 0-3068-0569-3.

This is a broad-based, comprehensive information source by an academic and specialist in the field who has defined *design* as that which determines the form of a functional object. Thus, information related to shape, size, color, texture, and pattern of a variety of objects is treated (furniture, tableware, glass, silver, graphics, etc.) as those objects relate to interiors or industrial design on an international level. There are more than 1,000 entries, all alphabetically arranged for easy access. Styles, periods, movements, firms, individuals (critics, designers, writers, and instructors), journals, schools, museums, and dealers, as well as technical terms, all are presented. Entries vary in length but tend to be brief (60 to 100 words). Illustrations in black-and-white accompany a number of the articles. A bibliography of frequently used sources, along with a detailed index, concludes the work.

492. **The Encyclopedia of Crafts.** Laura Torbet, ed. New York: Scribner's, 1980. 3v. ISBN 0-684-16409-4.
This is a detailed and comprehensive encyclopedia that provides in-depth information on about fifty different crafts. There are approximately 12,000 entries for specific terms associated with these crafts. Designed as a basic tool for the craftsperson as well as the fledgling operative, coverage is given to such activities as basketry, mosaics, block printing, fabric printing, jewelry, ceramics, stained glass, metalworking, batik, and so on. Articles vary in length from a short paragraph to several pages. Many cross-references are provided, with indication given in boldface type within an article to a routine that has its own entry. Considered an excellent source book, the arrangement is alphabetical, and 2,500 illustrations are furnished. There is no index.

493. **Encyclopedia of Design.** New York: Hart, 1983. 399p. ISBN 0-8055-1276-4.
Artists and craftspeople who need designs of various kinds benefit from this title, with its provision of more than 4,000 illustrations from different cultures throughout the world. The illustrations appear in the twenty-nine chapters devoted to various cultures of the world, such as Assyrian, Celtic, Chinese, Coptic, and so on. Most important is the fact that the pictures belong in the public domain and are freely available for reproduction without seeking permission or paying fees. Chapters vary considerably in depth of coverage and range from two to ten pages in length. Numerous designs are furnished in different media, including pottery, masks, tapestry, furniture, and stained glass. There is a bibliography of source material, with precise references given.

494. **Graphic Arts Encyclopedia.** 3d ed. George A. Stevenson; rev. by William A. Pakan. New York: Design Press, 1992. 582p. ISBN 0-8306-2530-5.
The third edition has been increased by about 100 pages and represents an augmented and updated effort of the previous issue, published in 1979. It remains an excellent source of information supplying comprehensive coverage of the graphic arts. Arrangement is alphabetical and entries vary in length from brief identifications to essays. Terminology, technical applications, equipment, and processes embrace a variety of activities such as copy preparation, art reproduction, copying, and printing. The coverage of equipment is brought up-to-date with treatment given to electronic and computer applications as well as traditional processes. Machinery covered includes word processors, keyboard equipment, video display terminals, typesetters, printing presses, microfilm equipment, process cameras, and color copiers. The writing is clear and free of technical jargon and the definitions are still accompanied by a number of black-and-white illustrations. There are numerous tables and charts, but no index.

495. **Graphics, Design, and Printing Terms: An International Dictionary.** Ken Garland. New York: Design Press, 1989. 248p. ISBN 0-8306-1048-0.
This is an up-to-date and handy wordbook, needed in the world of graphic arts with the recent emergence of the new technology in the field. Covered here are the terms utilized in such important new developments as desktop publishing, computer graphics, and photocomposition. Some 2,800 terms are covered relating to typography, advertising, printing, computers, publishing, photography, and film. Older terms have been updated where necessary and technical terms are lucidly defined. Important is the inclusion of recent slang expressions, abbreviations, and acronyms. Also included in many of the entries are charts and diagrams (more than 300 in number) to illustrate features, and numerous cross-references to related

terms. Both British and American usages are clearly indicated by Garland, an Englishman, with work experience in the United Kingdom.

496. **The Oxford Companion to the Decorative Arts.** Harold Osborne, ed. New York: Oxford University Press, 1975; repr., 1985. 880p. ISBN 0-19-281863-5 (pbk).

Basically a reprint of the earlier edition, which was well received by librarians as another useful source of information in the Oxford Companion series, this new edition provides a bibliography on the final page for the article on decorative papers. The decorative arts as a study embraces those fields and crafts not covered in *The Oxford Companion to Art* (entry 330), and may be defined as "creations that are valued primarily for their workmanship and beauty of appearance." These include leather working, ceramics, furniture, jewelry, costume, glassmaking, landscape gardening, clockmaking, enamels, lacquer, toys, lace, embroidery, and so on. Entries vary in length from brief to survey-type, and articles are unsigned. The emphasis is on Western arts, with the countries of the East and Eastern Europe receiving less coverage.

497. **The Thames and Hudson Encyclopaedia of Graphic Design and Designers.** Alan Livingston and Isabella Livingston. New York: Thames & Hudson, 1992. 215p. (World of Art). ISBN 0-500-20259-1.

Another of the volumes of the publisher's "World of Art" series, this, like the others, is for the most part clearly written and informative. The danger of presenting an encyclopedic work on such an extensive topic is apparent, however, and results in a product that functions in part as a catalog, in part as a directory, and also as a dictionary and fact book. Included here are biographies of important personalities, definitions of various technical processes, and descriptions and identifications of journals, magazines, and design organizations. Information tends to be brief, with broad coverage of historical developments treated within a European emphasis and perspective. The tool has been criticized as being too limited in its treatment of certain major elements such as typology. Special features include a chronology covering the development of graphic design from 1840 to 1990 and an eight-page color section.

DIRECTORIES AND ANNUALS

498. **Artist's Market: Where and How to Publish Your Graphic Arts.** Susan Conner, ed. Cincinnati: Writer's Digest Books, 1975- . Ann. ISSN 0161-0546.

Another of the Writer's Digest publications that has become standard fare for those seeking to market their wares. This annual guide is intended primarily for those in the graphic arts. Each issue supplies several thousand entries identifying relevant purchasers; these are arranged under one of fourteen types of markets such as advertising, audiovisual and public relations firms, art/design studios, magazines, book publishers, etc. Prefatory notes are given for each section. Each year there are several hundred new listings and previous entries are updated, making these efforts timely and representative of the current market. Entries generally supply address, telephone number, contact person, brief description, and type of client, along with an indication of needs, terms of contract, and contact person. "Tips" are sometimes included. Illustrations are sometimes furnished as examples of desired products. A glossary and general index are furnished.

499. **The Crafts Supply Sourcebook: A Comprehensive Shop-By-Mail Guide.** Rev. ed. Margaret A. Boyd. Cincinnati: Betterway Books, 1992. 286p. ISBN 1-55870-262-8.

Using the same format—indeed, the same number of pages—as its predecessor in 1989, the revised edition continues to provide directory listings of more than 2,500 merchants and suppliers of materials and equipment. Because many of these crafts dealers are small suppliers, there is less longevity than would be true of other segments of the manufacturing and trade industries; the new edition is needed to provide up-to-date listings. The work is divided into three major sections, the first of which covers the general arts, crafts and hobbies (stained glass, jewelry making, photography, cake decorating, Indian crafts, etc.). The second section treats needlecrafts, including batik, costume, and weaving. All entries receive the usual directory treatment of address, telephone number, etc., along with description of supplies available. The final section covers resources and identifies aids, publications, and associations.

A useful source of purchasing information is *Graphic Design Materials and Equipment* by Jonathan Stevenson (Studio Vista/Cassell, 1987). This slender volume of 192 pages provides a comprehensive listing of suppliers, distributors, manufacturers, and sellers of all types of equipment and supplies needed by graphic artists, photographers, and printers. A more recent publication is *Directory to Industrial Design in the United States ...* by Charles Burnette (Van Nostrand Reinhold, 1992). It provides listings for independent consulting firms, corporate design departments, schools with degree programs, institutions, organizations, and publications in the field.

500. **The Guide to Arts & Crafts Workshops**. Coral Gables, FL: Shaw Associates, 1990. 253p. ISBN 0-945834-05-5.

This is a well-designed guide and directory to instructional offerings for those interested in the creation and sale of fine and decorative arts. Coverage is comprehensive for short-term programs held throughout the world and treating all types of media. Arrangement is alphabetical, using the title of the sponsoring agency in listing seminars, workshops, retreats, and residencies for artists, near-artists, and aficionados. Media covered include painting, drawing, sculpture, and crafts of all kinds (fiber, metal, wood, glass, ceramics, and gems). Entries supply descriptive information on the program, faculty, costs, accommodations, and locations. Student-teacher ratios are enumerated in the style of college directories. Indexing is excellent, with access furnished by a detailed general index as well as specialty and geographical indexes. In addition, there is a listing of workshops for youngsters.

BIOGRAPHICAL SOURCES

501. **Contemporary Designers**. 2d ed. Colin Naylor, ed. Chicago: St. James Press, 1990. 641p. ISBN 0-912289-69-4.

The first edition of this work was issued in 1984 and provided information on the lives and careers of 600 contemporary figures in the world of design. The second edition treats about the same number of individuals, having deleted some and added others. Previous entries have been updated and in many cases expanded to reflect recent activities and accomplishments. Coverage is international and includes important personalities for the many and varied fields of design (architecture, interiors, display, textiles, fashion, film, stage, costume, industry, etc.). A panel of international specialists have recommended the personalities as major figures; more than 120 critics, historians, and designers contributed articles. Entries furnish a detailed biography, listings of major works, bibliography of publications by and about the personality, and a critical-evaluative essay. The work is well illustrated in black-and-white with examples of artwork; no indexes are furnished.

502. **Contemporary Graphic Artists: A Biographical, Bibliographical, and Critical Guide to Current Illustrators, Animators, Cartoonists, Designers, and Other Graphic Artists**. 3v. Maurice Horn, ed. Detroit: Gale Research, 1986-1988. 272p. ISSN 0885-8462.

Developed on a plan similar to that of *Contemporary Authors* (entry 988), the important serial biography by the same publisher, this title was initially projected as a semiannual publication but became a short-lived annual instead. Prior to its termination, three volumes had been issued. Each provides bio-critical coverage in the Gale Research manner to about 100 graphic designers, editorial and magazine cartoonists, book illustrators, animators, and comic strip artists. Arrangement is alphabetical by name. There appears to be an emphasis on cartoonists that was justified because biographical information on cartoonists is, at best, difficult to find. The definition of *contemporary* is broad; several of the artists are nineteenth-century figures. Biographies are brief but informative and the bibliographical references are good. There is no index for the volumes.

503.   **The Facts on File Dictionary of Design and Designers.** Simon Jervis. New York: Facts on File, 1984. 533p. ISBN 0-87196-891-6.

This dictionary has been recognized as a fine reference tool on design and has earned the respect of those who work in the field of art reference. It is useful in its treatment of personalities, with biographies of designers, patrons, and historians from the mid-fifteenth century to the present, and is important for its coverage of obscure individuals as well as prominent ones. Biographies are brief and provide dates, place of birth, training, and influences upon the personalities as well as their achievements. The terminology of design and designing is also covered, with entries given to the various types such as ceramics, furniture, glass, interior decoration and metalwork. Generally the emphasis is on the styles and techniques of Europe and North America. Many cross-references are provided in the entries.

504.   **Folk Artists Biographical Index: A Guide to over 200 Published Sources of Information on Approximately 9,000 Folk Artists.** George H. Meyer et al., eds. Detroit: Gale Research, 1987. 496p. ISBN 0-8103-2145-9.

The editor is Director of the Museum of American Folk Art, and brings his expertise to bear in creating this comprehensive index to information on over 9,000 folk artists found in more than 200 biographical dictionaries and collective works. It is of substantial benefit to librarians, as biographies of folk artists tend to be elusive and difficult to locate. As one might expect, the variety of media represented in the folk arts is great and covers such activity as sculpture, furniture making, carving, weaving, pottery making, and quilting, and such products as samplers, coverlets, decoys, and canes. Individuals are listed alphabetically and entries include birth and death dates, type of work, period, and citations for source materials. The work provides excellent access through the indexes of museums in which the artists' works are displayed, ethnic origin, medium, and type of work.

505.   **Museum of American Folk Art Encyclopedia of Twentieth-Century American Folk Art and Artists.** Chuck Rosenak and Jan Rosenak. New York: Abbeville, 1990. 416p. ISBN 1-55859-041-2.

The authors are serious collectors and enthusiasts who have traveled widely in this country to cultivate their collection and enrich their knowledge. Folk art as the expression of the feelings of common people, largely unschooled, embraces a wide range of media and applications, including painting and sculpture as well as pottery and other decorative arts. This work treats the lives and artwork of 257 contemporary folk artists who have been identified by the Rosenaks. Most of the artists were interviewed and photographed by the authors, resulting in a rich and full treatment. Several well-known specialists also contributed segments. Entries treat biographical data, general background, artistic background, subjects and sources, and media and processes, as well as recognition and popularity. Individuals vary from from the famous to the lesser-known. Appendices list major exhibitions from 1924 to 1990, and supply a bibliography and detailed general index.

Furniture and Woodcraft

BIBLIOGRAPHIES, INDEXES, AND ABSTRACTS

506.   **American Furniture Craftsmen Working Prior to 1920: An Annotated Bibliography**.
Charles J. Semowich, comp. Westport, CT: Greenwood Press, 1984. 381p. (Art Reference
Collection, no. 7). ISBN 0-313-23275-X.
        This is a comprehensive annotated bibliography of value to a variety of users from
specialists and researchers to dealers and the general public. More than 2,000 entries are
supplied, representing secondary sources treating furniture crafters in the early years. Biographical coverage, critical interpretation, and exposition are presented. The work is divided
into four major sections, with the first segment identifying titles dealing with the lives and
work of individual craftspersons and the second section citing those that cover groups of
furniture makers. The third part supplies reference works of general nature, whereas the
fourth lists furniture trade catalogs. Annotations vary in length and quality, with some being
too brief. The appendix contains a listing of trade publications from 1880 to 1930 and one
of manuscript archives. Indexes furnish access by author-title, subject, and name of crafters.

DICTIONARIES, ENCYCLOPEDIAS, HANDBOOKS, ETC.

507.   **American Furniture, 1620 to the Present.** Elizabeth Bidwell Bates and Jonathan L.
Fairbanks. New York: Richard Marek/Putnam, 1981. 561p. ISBN 0-399-90096-9.
        An extraordinary reference work providing comprehensive coverage of the development
of American furniture styles from the colonial period to the present day. Furniture is treated
chapter-by-chapter in different periods, which are illustrated with reproductions of both
paintings and photographs. About 1,400 reproductions (100 in color) show the pieces in their
museum settings, and diagrams are provided of the structure of the furniture. Informative
commentary helps the reader understand the place of the furniture within the social and
historical context. Fairbanks is curator of American decorative arts at the Boston Museum of
Fine Arts, and together with Bates brings expertise and authority to the topic. Included also
are a glossary of cabinetry terms, a bibliography, and an index.

508.   **The Antiques Directory: Furniture.** Judith Miller and Martin Miller, eds. Boston:
G. K. Hall, 1985. 639p. ISBN 0-8161-8748-7. Repr., New York: Portland House, 1988. ISBN
0-5176-6190-X.
        One of the Miller publications, this work maintains the quality and informative content
of the others. Furniture from all over the world is treated, and more than 7,000 photographs
help to illustrate the differences in style and appearance. Intended as a guidebook for those
who seek profit or collect in the field, the work accommodates the needs of its intended
audience in a country-by-country arrangement, subdivided by form or type (tables, chairs,
and so on). As with most guidebooks, the commentary at the beginning of each section is
brief and serves only to introduce the reader to the furniture of a particular country. Pictures
are described in terms of styles, dates, sizes of objects, and periods represented. The emphasis
is on British furniture. There is a useful outline chronology of developments by country from
1450 to 1920. The work contains an index but no bibliography.

509.   **Dictionary of Furniture**. Charles Boyce, ed. New York, Facts on File, 1985. Repr.,
New York: Henry Holt, 1988. 331p. ISBN 0- 8050-0752-0.
        An up-to-date, comprehensive source of information on furniture and furniture making
in all countries and time periods, this work was readily accepted by librarians in the field.
Furnishing brief entries, alphabetically arranged, coverage is given to numerous topics,
issues, styles, personalities, and terms. These are explained in an informative and lucid

manner, in enough detail to satisfy most queries. Both Western and Eastern influences and individuals are treated. The tool is especially helpful in its treatment of modern furniture and designers, as biographical information on twentieth-century furniture makers is elusive.

One of the more recent offerings is the revised and expanded edition of John Gloag's *A Complete Dictionary of Furniture* by Clive Edwards (Overlook, 1991; distr. Viking Press). First published in 1952, this work contains approximately 3,000 terms from the initial effort, and has added an appendix containing some 15 pages of mostly American terms not included by Gloag.

An old standard, first published in 1938, is *The Encyclopedia of Furniture*, by Joseph Aronson (Cronson, 1965). This older work can be used to supplement the coverage of the newer one, as each contains material not found in the other.

Jewelry and Metalcraft

DICTIONARIES, ENCYCLOPEDIAS, HANDBOOKS, ETC.

510. **American Silversmiths and Their Marks IV**. Rev. and enl. ed. Stephen Guernsey Cook Ensko; comp. by Dorothea Ensko Wyle. Boston: D. R. Godine, 1989. 477p. ISBN 0879237783.

Since this work was first issued in 1948 (and reprinted in 1984), it has been recognized as an important and unique source for identification of American silversmiths over a 200-year period from 1650-1850. This revised and expanded edition was compiled by Ensko's daughter. Little is known of individual artisans plying a craft in a unique style for those formative years. American silversmiths had chosen a more simple but elegant execution of American pieces in comparison to the flourishes and ornamentation of their European counterparts. Included in the new edition are entries for thousands of gold and silversmiths, with identification of their marks. There are numerous illustrations, along with a set of maps identifying location of silversmith shops. The bibliography is up-to-date; there is an index of silversmiths located in the maps.

511. **Answers to Questions about Old Jewelry: 1840 to 1950**. 3d ed. Jeanenne Bell. Florence, AL: Books Americana, 1992. 445p. ISBN 0-89689-087-2.

A detailed table of contents provides access to the wealth of information contained in this volume; there is no index. A growing interest in the collection of jewelry has made a guidebook of this type a necessity in most libraries. The current issue replaces the second edition published in 1985 in much the same format. Section 1 provides the historical background and describes the different motifs and personalities associated with the creation of jewelry in five different periods: 1840-1860 (Victoria and Albert); 1861-1889 (Victorian); 1890-1915 (Edward and Art Nouveau); 1920-1930s (Art Deco); and 1940-1950s (Modern). Section 2 treats the materials used in making jewelry, and section 3 identifies simple tests to determine the authenticity of the composition of these materials. Section 4 provides a catalog of marks and a biographical dictionary of prominent designers and craftsmen. Valuations are given, along with small black-and-white pictures of the pieces.

512. **Collector's Dictionary of the Silver and Gold of Great Britain and North America**. 2d ed. Michael Clayton. Ithaca, NY: Antique Collectors Club, 1985. 481p. ISBN 0-907462-57-X.

Those individuals for whom silver and gold play an important role in their collecting habits will appreciate the comprehensive nature and breadth of coverage of this fine dictionary. First published in 1971, it has come to be recognized as a standard item in reference departments for its excellent treatment of gold and silver work from the Middle Ages to the nineteenth century. Entries are generally short, ranging from one to two paragraphs in length, but they cover a wide variety of topics and include cross-references. General topics such as

"American silver" are explained and defined along with specific artifacts, objects, personalities, styles, and techniques. Formerly associated with Christie's Auction House, the author brings expertise and authority to the descriptions and interpretations he provides. There is a bibliography of books and catalogs on selected topics at the end.

513. **Encyclopedia of American Silver Manufacturers**. 3d ed. rev. Dorothy T. Rainwater. West Chester, PA: Schiffer, 1986. 266p. ISBN 0-88740-046-9.

This is another standard tool in the field, with publication of the first edition in 1966 and the second edition in 1975. The third edition has updated and embellished the previous issues with additional entries and revision where necessary. It continues to supply the names of some 1,500 silver manufacturers operating in this country. This comprehensive coverage is enhanced with illustrations of more than 2,000 silver trademarks. Sources utilized were old company catalogs and records from the U.S. Patent Office, as well as current manufacturers and antique shop owners. Reproductions are clear and adequate in terms of detail. Entries are arranged alphabetically by manufacturer's name, supplying location, trademark, and narrative description of the firm's activity. A brief glossary defines terms. Unfortunately, the bibliography has not been updated.

514. **An Illustrated Dictionary of Jewelry: 2,530 Entries Including Definitions of Jewels, Gemstones, Materials ...** Harold Newman. New York: Thames & Hudson, 1981; repr. 1987. 334p. ISBN 0-500-27452-5.

This is a paperback reprint of an earlier edition considered to be a unique and important work with its comprehensive coverage of jewelry. The complete title indicates its vast scope, for it goes on to say "Processes, and Styles, and Entries on Principal Designers and Makers, from Antiquity to the Present Day." Indeed, there is an abundance of information within the more than 2,500 entries, all alphabetically arranged for easy access. Included here are definitions of terms, descriptions of processes and styles, and biographical narratives of designers and craftspeople from the beginning of such artwork to modern-day practice and practitioners. Important gems are identified and locations are indicated. There is a conscious effort to avoid technical terminology; bibliographies accompany certain entries. Articles are well constructed and informative. Both color and black-and-white illustrations are utilized to enhance many of the entries.

515. **Professional Goldsmithing: A Contemporary Guide to Traditional Jewelry Techniques**. Alan Revere. New York: Van Nostrand Reinhold, 1991. 226p. ISBN 0-442-23898-3.

The author is a well-known figure and a master goldsmith who has issued an excellent manual to smithing technique. The work opens with several short chapters on the composition of metals, types of tools, and nature of the craft. Then follows step-by-step sequenced activities, all described in clear fashion and accompanied by color illustrations for purposes of clarification. Thirty projects involving a wide range of smithing techniques are described and illustrated. Intricate processes involve the creation of forged rings and bracelets, mesh chains, and necklace clasps. These techniques have been handed down for generations and represent the traditional approaches so highly prized today. This work may be used as a shop text or as a manual for self-learning. Appendices treat relevant information such as weights and measures. There is a general index.

516. **The Sotheby's Directory of Silver, 1600-1940.** Vanessa Brett. London: Sotheby's Publications; distr., New York: Harper & Row, 1986. 432p. ISBN 0-85667-193-2.

Although there is no shortage of reference works on silver, this survey of 2,000 elegant pieces sold at auction by Sotheby's spans a period of sixty years of auctioneering from the 1920s to the mid-1980s. It is regarded as an important tool not only for the record it provides of prices and costs over the years, but for identifying the work of high-quality silversmiths from both Europe and the United States. Each piece is illustrated, and information is given on category, manufacture, size, and weight as well as sales. Additional information is furnished regarding the silversmith. Unfortunately, makers' marks and monograms are not included, which may be regarded as a deficiency in an otherwise useful work. The arrangement is by country and then by maker, in a sequence that is roughly chronological. An index facilitates access.

Ceramics, Pottery, and Glass

BIBLIOGRAPHIC GUIDES AND BIBLIOGRAPHIES

517. **Pottery and Ceramics: A Guide to Information Sources**. James Edward Campbell. Detroit: Gale Research, 1978. 241p. (Art and Architecture Information Guide Series, v.7). ISBN 0-8103-1274-3.

Designed for use by students, practitioners, and collectors, this is another useful tool from this Gale series. The author is a specialist in the field and has rendered a well-constructed, selective literature guide to the study of ceramics and pottery. All the clay arts are embraced for documentation in primarily English-language books, articles, pamphlets, and catalogs. Annotations are useful and informative, and range from purely descriptive to evaluative in nature. Opening chapters treat reference works of general nature, with subsequent chapters organized within a historical framework. Publications of more than 700 authors are treated, with possibly too little inclusion of government documents when considering the historical context. There are useful listings of periodicals, organizations, societies, and museum collections. Access is provided through author, title, and subject indexes.

518. **Stained Glass: A Guide to Information Sources**. Darlene A. Brady and William Serban. Detroit: Gale Research, 1980. 572p. (Art and Architecture Information Guide Series, v.10; Gale Information Guide Library). ISBN 0-8103-1445-2.

This is a comprehensive guide and bibliography supplying more than 1,700 annotated entries treating English-language books and articles relating to both American and European traditions in stained glass and its manufacture. It continues the coverage begun initially by George Sang Duncan's *A Bibliography of Glass (From the Earliest Records to 1940)* (Dawsons of Pall Mall, 1960). The present effort extends the period to 1976, with the idea of providing a source useful to a variety of individuals, from general readers and hobbyists to art historians and practitioner-specialists. Entries are arranged under format categories such as reference works, bibliographies, dissertations, periodicals, etc. In addition, three specialized periodicals are indexed for the first time. Specialized chapters supply information on conducting library research and furnish directory listings of collections, museums, organizations, and supply houses. There is a general subject index as well as specialized indexes by author, title, name of artist, and location of artwork.

DICTIONARIES, ENCYCLOPEDIAS, HANDBOOKS, ETC.

*519. **The Collector's Encyclopedia of Heisey Glass 1925-1938.** Neila Bredehoft. Paducah, KY: Collector Books; distr., Newark, OH: Heisey Collectors of America, 1989; repr. with upd. 1993. 463p. ISBN 0-89145-307-5.

This encyclopedia furnishes a detailed record of the Heisey lines and the thousands of desirable items produced by the factory. It begins with a historical overview of the fortunes of the Heisey Company. The major segment of the text is catalog material based on information contained in Heisey catalogs of the period covered. All photographs are taken from these sales catalogs and are mostly black-and-white. Each color in the line is illustrated, however, with representative pieces from that line. Entries contain pattern numbers, names, dates, decorations, and indication of marks. Included with the purchase of the encyclopedia but also selling as a separate item is a price guide which provides price ranges for all items and lines described in the encyclopedia. The present edition provides values updated to 1989. It has been available on CD-ROM through the publisher since 1991. The 1991 issue contains values updated that year.

520. Encyclopedia of Pottery and Porcelain 1800-1960. Elisabeth Cameron. New York: Facts on File, 1986. 366p. ISBN 0-81601-225-3.

An important work is this compendium of the world of pottery and porcelain operating over a period of 160 years. The approximately 9,500 alphabetically arranged entries include decorators, designers, factories, materials, styles, techniques, and basic terminology as well as individual potters. Marks are described within the context of the entries for individuals or firms, although they generally are not illustrated. The emphasis is on European (especially English) and American pottery, although Japanese ceramics are not overlooked. There are 450 black-and-white reproductions, with 32 illustrations in color, providing a good indication of nature or character of the representative forms and styles. Considered to be the best single guide available for its coverage of major personalities and elements within this important time span, the encyclopedia provides bibliographic references as well.

A standard source for identification of potters' marks is William Chaffers's *Marks and Monograms on European and Oriental Pottery and Porcelain* (William Reeves, 1965). This two-volume tool was last issued in its fifteenth edition and treats the whole field of European and Oriental pottery in scholarly fashion; adequate illustration of objects is furnished. Volume 2 is geared specifically to British porcelain.

521. An Illustrated Dictionary of Ceramics ... Rev. ed. George Savage and Harold Newman. New York: Thames & Hudson; distr., Boston: Little, Brown, 1985. 319p. ISBN 0-500-27380-4.

This is a paperback reprint of a hardcover edition published in 1974, issued with a warning that the paperback edition should not be lent, resold, hired out, or otherwise circulated without the publisher's consent. The hardcover edition is still preferred by art departments because the paperback does not contain the color reproductions. Other than that, there is not much difference between them, and the black-and-white illustrations are of good quality. The definitions are brief but informative and will be useful for those seeking to define the terminology of the field. Many cross-references are furnished. The subtitle aptly describes the scope as "Defining 3,054 Terms Relating to Wares, Materials, Processes, Styles, Patterns, and Shapes from Antiquity to the Present Day." The emphasis is on English ceramics.

522. An Illustrated Dictionary of Glass. Harold Newman. London: Thames & Hudson, 1977. 351p. ISBN 0-500-23262-8.

The title page of this comprehensive dictionary, now a standard in the field, goes on to say "2,442 entries, including definitions of wares, materials, processes, forms, and decorative styles, and entries on principal glassmakers, decorators, and designers, from antiquity to the present." Scope is universal in terms of international coverage, but emphasis is placed on American and European influences. The entries are arranged alphabetically in dictionary fashion and vary in length from a single sentence to a half-page. Bibliographic references are given in only a small proportion of the entries—an unfortunate decision because there is no bibliography of additional readings. An excellent introductory essay by Robert J. Charleston surveying the history of glassmaking opens the work. Then follows the text, with its brief entries of counties and regions, as well as technical terms and related aspects.

523. The Illustrated Guide to Glass. Felice Mehlman. Englewood Cliffs, NJ: Prentice-Hall, 1982. Repr., London: Peerage, 1985. 256p. ISBN 1-85-052020-8.

This was originally published as *Phaidon Guide to Glass* and earned a reputation as a concise but solid information source. It opens with an excellent introduction describing the materials and processes utilized in the making of glass objects, along with various stylistic and technical features. Popular decorative styles are explained in reviewing the history of glass as it has evolved in different parts of the world. Objects are categorized by type or function and include drinking glasses, jewelry, mirrors, and paperweights. Both color and black-and-white photographs accompany the narrative. Emphasis is placed on historical development throughout the text, with treatment given to important events and developing influences. The exposition is handled well and enables both collector and student to gain a better understanding and appreciation of the craft. There is a brief bibliography and a general index.

524. **The Potter's Dictionary of Materials and Techniques**. 3d ed. Frank Hamer and Janet Hamer. Philadelphia: University of Pennsylvania Press, 1991. 384p. ISBN 0-8122-3112-0.

The third edition of this well-known, now standard, work in the field was issued four years after its predecessor and has added some 100 new photographs as well as revised material identifying new developments in such processes as raku and salt glaze. Recently identified environmental and safety hazards are explained fully. The remainder of the work is essentially the same, with continued emphasis on information relevant to potters in the performance of their craft. Coverage is comprehensive, with entries describing technical terms, processes, techniques, and important concepts. Formulary is included where necessary. Cross-references are supplied within the entries, and tabular data are included in the appendices. The authors are Welsh potters who have the experience and insight to provide cogent and practical commentary. Spelling generally follows British conventions.

Textiles, Weaving, and Needlecraft

BIBLIOGRAPHIC GUIDES AND BIBLIOGRAPHIES

525. **Embroidery and Needlepoint: An Information Sourcebook**. Sandra K. Copeland. Phoenix, AZ: Oryx Press, 1989. 150p. ISBN 0-89774-442-X.

This slender bibliography supplies access to more than 1,700 books and more than 150 periodical titles treating the subject of needlework. Publications range from 1950 to the mid-1980s and represent English-language titles. Foreign-language publications are included when their illustrations are useful even without the text. Entries are placed within chapters by form, such as the initial chapter on general information sources and the second chapter devoted to periodical titles, or by topic, as in subsequent chapters treating specialized techniques: applique, blackwork embroidery, stumpwork, samplers, shisha mirror work, etc. The author is both a librarian and a needlework artist who has used her expertise to produce brief but informative annotations for a majority of the entries. She has also rendered a service with a useful segment of ninety-one works serving as the core library collection. Author, title, and subject indexes are furnished.

526. **Handweaving: An Annotated Bibliography**. Isabel Buschman. Metuchen, NJ: Scarecrow Press, 1991. 250p. ISBN 0-8108-2403-5.

This is a well-developed bibliography of more than 550 books and periodical titles published over a sixty-year period from 1928 to 1989. Coverage is given to basic texts for students, as well as monographs on looms and equipment, patterns, fabrics, historical development, Native American influences, etc. Emphasis is given to technical applications and projects. Publications are placed within five major chapters examining important broad topical and format areas. Covered first are the materials, tools, techniques, and products of handweaving, followed by chapters on history, reference works, and journals. In addition, a full chapter is given to Native American weaving methods. Entries are arranged alphabetically by author within the various chapters. Annotations vary in length but are lucid and informative. There are author, title, and subject indexes.

DICTIONARIES, ENCYCLOPEDIAS, HANDBOOKS, ETC.

527. **The Batsford Encyclopaedia of Embroidery Techniques**. Gay Swift. London: B. T. Batsford, 1984; repr. 1990. Distr., North Ponfret, VT: Trafalgar Square/David & Charles. 240p. ISBN 0-7134-6781-9.

This useful information source was initially published in 1984, and because of its success was reprinted in 1990. It represents a unique source in its description of technical terms, concepts, styles, and applications in such comprehensive manner. All aspects of the embroidery arts are included, with coverage given to applique, quilt making, buttons, lace, etc. Excellent illustrations accompany the text and enable the users to gain a sense of perspective with regard to breadth and patterns of composition. Use of color is exceptional and places this work among others suitable for coffee table display. In addition, there is a listing of the most important embroidery collections, with emphasis on those in the United Kingdom in the bibliography section at the end. There is no index, but access is aided by italicized cross-references within the entries.

528. **The Complete Stitch Encyclopedia.** Jan Eaton. Woodbury, NY: Barron's Educational Series, 1986. 173p. ISBN 0-8120-5731-7.

This is a detailed and comprehensive manual to the various forms of stitchery that have been popular through the years. Identification is furnished for more than 450 different stitches, arranged by type. Categories are organized according to degree of difficulty, with the simplest techniques listed first. There are numerous illustrations in full color for each stitch and detailed instructions given for successful application. The photographs are integrated with the narrative, and sequence photographs are provided for the more complicated techniques. Advice is given regarding such matters as choice of thread, along with brief historical information on some of the older techniques.

529. **Encyclopedia of Batik Designs.** Leo O. Donahue. Philadelphia: Art Alliance; distr., East Brunswick, NJ: Associated University Presses, 1981. 630p. ISBN 0-8453-4729-2.

Batik as a form of textile decoration employing wax resist methods emerged in the eighteenth century, having been introduced by the Dutch East India Company. It very quickly became high fashion and through the years has enjoyed a steady popularity marked by spurts of increased interest. In this volume, exposition is given not only to the creation of the batik but also to the block on tjap for printing on cloth. The processes are explained in detail and many photographs enhance the descriptions provided of the routines and the creation of various effects. There is a glossary of terms, along with a bibliography and an index.

530. **Encyclopedia of Textiles.** Judith Jerde. New York: Facts on File, 1992. 260p. ISBN 0-8160-2105-8.

A recent resource for information on textiles, this relatively compact volume furnishes a broad view of the topic with coverage of design, manufacture, care, and utilization of fabric. Fiber types, patterns, and weaves are explained and illustrated, as are dyes, printing techniques, and technical processes. Entries furnishing definitions, descriptions, and explanations vary in length, with the various fibers receiving the most detailed narrative. The title should be useful to a wide audience ranging from the novice to the skilled artisan. Personalities are also treated with brief biographical sketches.

An earlier work, *The A F Encyclopedia of Textiles* (Prentice-Hall, 1980), is now in its third edition and provides a fine exposition of various fibers, designs, and processes involved in the manufacture of textiles. Brief chapters cover the various topics and include numerous illustrations.

531. **The Illustrated Dictionary of Knitting.** Rae Compton. Loveland, CO: Interweave Press, 1988. 272p. ISBN 0-934026-41-6.

This well-constructed information source is more a handbook of knitting technique and process than simply a dictionary of terms. Of course, terms and relevant topics are described, and historical information is included, along with narrative of stylistic differences among ethnic and cultural groups. Such coverage is brief and of secondary importance, however, and the book should be considered a manual of practice. When entries deal with a technique or process, the activity is generally defined briefly at the outset, followed by a more detailed exposition of the manner in which it is performed, along with possible variations of the application. Specific parts of clothing and apparel, such as zippers, gloves, or socks, are handled individually. The work is well illustrated in color and black-and-white, enabling the user to examine the sequence of steps as well as the finished products.

532. **The Macmillan Atlas of Rugs and Carpets.** David Black, ed. New York: Macmillan, 1985. 255p. ISBN 0-02-511120-5.

A useful and detailed expository work on the history and development of the craft of carpet-making, this atlas furnishes information on the individual countries involved in the practice. Beautiful illustrations (200 in color and 150 in black-and-white) show the various designs and techniques. The work begins with a description of the methods of weaving and carpet design and provides general guidelines for analyzing carpets. The next chapter covers the history of carpets and examines and compares developments in countries considered most desirable for their products (Turkey, Persia, India, and so on). The largest portion of the work covers individual countries with maps, and detailed information is given for each style produced. Included are the braided, hooked, and embroidered rugs of the United States, as well as Navaho blanket weaving.

Fashion and Costume

BIBLIOGRAPHIES AND INDEXES

533. **Costume Index: A Subject Index to Plates and to Illustrated Texts.** Isabel Stevenson Monro and Dorothy E. Cook. New York: H. W. Wilson, 1937. 338p. Supp., 1957. 210p.

An old standard in the field, this work indexes plates appearing in more than 600 titles providing coverage of costume. These sources were rated in terms of their priority, a useful feature at the time of publication but less important with the passage of time. Any full-page illustration has been defined as a *plate*, and occasionally illustrations without accompanying text are included in cases where such reproductions are unique. No titles without illustrations are included. Coverage is broad and historical costumes from any period (with the exception of biblical times) are identified under geographic locations, classes of persons, or details of costume. The supplement covers nearly 350 books published between 1936 and 1956 in a manner similar to the basic edition.

A continuation of coverage may be found in Jackson Kesler's *Theatrical Costume: A Guide to Information Sources* (Gale, 1979), a bibliography of materials dating from 1957 to the 1970s.

DICTIONARIES, ENCYCLOPEDIAS, HANDBOOKS, ETC.

534. **American Costume, 1915-1970: A Source Book for the Stage Costumer.** Shirley Miles O'Donnol. Bloomington: Indiana University Press, 1982; repr., 1989. 270p. ISBN 0-253-30589-6.

An essential work for any costumer is this exposition of American costume over a period of fifty-five years. Beginning with the era of World War I, it provides separate chapters in chronological sequence: "World War, 1916-1919"; "The Twenties (1920-1929)"; "Depression (1930-1939)"; "World War (1940-1946)"; "The 'New Look' (1947-1952)"; "Space Age

(1953-1960)"; and the "Sixties (1960-1970)." The background of each period is described, along with general information on dress, then specific coverage is accorded men's, women's, and children's fashions. Also included are details on grooming, hair styles, and accessories, as well as colors and motifs. There are suggestions for costumers and lists of plays for the different time periods. Illustrations are provided.

535. **The Chronicle of Western Fashion: From Ancient Times to the Present Day.** John Peacock. New York: Harry N. Abrams, 1991. 224p. ISBN 0-8109-3953-3.

This is a useful chronology of fashion and dress ranging over a period of 4,000 years from antiquity (Egypt, 2000 B.C.) to the year 1980. Major historical periods (ancient civilizations, Middle Ages, and Renaissance) lead into sequential, century-by-century coverage from the sixteenth through twentieth. A work such as this depends on its illustrations, and there are more than 1,000 detailed full-color drawings. Illustrations number about ten per page and furnish examples of a variety of styles, with emphasis on the dress of the upper and middle classes. Also shown are the garb of royalty, military, sports, and various occupations from the lower working classes to the professions. Outfits from formal to sleepwear are depicted. Descriptions of each illustration appear at the end of each segment. Included is a glossary of fashion terms, along with a bibliography of sources.

536. **The Dictionary of Costume.** R. Turner Wilcox. London: B. T. Batsford, 1969; repr. 1992. 406p. ISBN 0-7134-7026-7.

This reprint of a standard tool in the field provides a convenient source of information on all aspects of costume on a broad-based international basis. More than 3,200 entries are arranged alphabetically for easy access and present the technical terminology, major personalities, articles of apparel, jewelry, cosmetics, hair and even beard styles, instruments and equipment, and fabrics and materials. The author is an acknowledged authority and writer; this effort is useful to a variety of audiences, from fledgling students to accomplished specialists, in its treatment of all periods of history. Entries vary from precise explanations of particular terms to lengthy survey articles on such topics as "eighteenth century." Numerous illustrations accompany the text and illustrate the apparel and accessories described. Cross-references are provided, a useful practice as there is no index. A brief bibliography concludes the effort.

537. **The Encyclopaedia of Fashion: From 1840 to the 1980s.** Georgina O'Hara. London: Thames & Hudson, 1986; repr. 1989. 272p. ISBN 0-500-27567-X.

This is a well-developed source of information on terms, personalities, styles, articles of apparel, fabrics, movements, trends, furs, and even media that have influenced the fashion world over a period of 140 years. A variety of individuals is treated: designers, jewelers, milliners, hairdressers, illustrators, artists, and more. There are more than 1,000 entries, arranged alphabetically, with numerous cross-references. The text is accompanied by more than 350 illustrations, some in color.

The Fashion Encyclopedia: An Essential Guide to Everything You Need to Know about Clothes, by Catherine Houck (St. Martin's Press, 1982), is an interesting, revealing, and highly readable survey of the field of fashion providing much information from a variety of sources. Coverage is given to style, personalities, production, care, and purchasing of a variety of material, clothing, and accessories. Arrangement is alphabetical by topic and there are many black-and-white illustrations. Among other things, such topics as furs, jewelry, discount houses, mail order, and thrift shops are treated. An especially useful feature is the list of trademarks, copyright, and certification marks of the various products, firms, and processes. Although not scholarly, the tool will prove useful for the variety of information it provides.

538. **Essential Terms of Fashion: A Collection of Definitions.** Charlotte Mankey Calasibetta. New York: Fairchild Publications, 1986. 244p. ISBN 0-87005-519-4.

This dictionary is especially useful for its inclusion of contemporary terminology. It also provides good coverage of the traditional terms of the field, and has been commended for its historical precision. Arrangement is by broad categories of articles of clothing, accessories, or style, such as boots, robes, and pleats. These are subdivided by specific types. Definitions are brief for the most part, but adequate, and cross-references are furnished. Illustrations in the form of line drawings are useful and accompany many of the entries. The terms are those used in the fashions of men, women, and children, and the work has been received well by both librarians and designers.

539. **Fairchild's Dictionary of Fashion.** 2d ed. Charlotte Mankey Calasibetta. New York: Fairchild Publications, 1988. 749p. ISBN 0-877005-635-2.

Designed as a comprehensive source of information on the world of fashion from the time of antiquity to the present, the second edition of this useful and well-known source supplies more than 15,000 entries. These are arranged alphabetically and provide brief definitions and explanations of terminology relevant to costume, including nationalist, cultural, stylistic, and artistic expression. Nearly 100 of these terms are given to broad categorical representation, such as "cuffs," "shoulders," "heels," etc., under which are grouped numerous related terms, which themselves are listed alphabetically in the main text along with cross-references back to the categories. These broad categories are indexed separately. About 500 black-and-white illustrations are integrated within the text, in addition to a section of color illustrations. About 170 biographical entries on important fashion designers are included in the appendix with more than sixty photographs. No bibliography is given.

540. **The Illustrated Encyclopedia of Costume and Fashion 1550-1920.** Jack Cassin-Scott. Poole, UK: Blandford; distr., New York: Sterling, 1986. 160p. ISBN 0-7137-1811-0.

This tool supplies 150 color reproductions providing excellent images of more than 300 costumes. Detail is clearly shown and reveals the styles worn by lords and ladies, children, military figures, peasants, and musicians. Costumes are described briefly and dates are furnished. In most cases, type of fabric is given and country of origin established. The work has been criticized for certain oversights among the illustrations provided, such as cropping of the lady's train in one plate and a portion of a skirt in another. It remains a worthwhile addition to the reference department, however, for its comprehensive coverage and attractive format.

541. **A Visual History of Costume: The Twentieth Century.** Penelope Byrde. London: B. T. Batsford; New York: Drama Book Publishers, 1987. 144p. ISBN 0-89676-100-2.

This is the final volume in a highly stylized five-volume series on costume; each volume is done in the exact same format with the same number of pages. An English publication from Batsford, it is sold in the United States by Drama Book Publishers. Sequentially, the series begins with *A Visual History of Costume: The Sixteenth Century* by Jane Ashelford (1984), followed by ... *The Seventeenth Century* by Valerie Cumming, ... *The Eighteenth Century* by Aileen Ribeiro (1983), and ... *The Nineteenth Century* by Vanda Foster (1984). The volumes are considered useful sources of information on the styles of costume, and are illustrated through a series of reproductions of the artwork of the time. Illustrations are chronologically arranged, appear both in color and black-and-white, and depict men and women dressed in fashions of the day. These are mostly English, and captions describe the costume features. Each volume begins with an introduction surveying the world of fashion in that century, and provides an index and a selective bibliography.

BIOGRAPHICAL SOURCES

542. **Costume Design on Broadway: Designers and Their Credits, 1915-1985.** Bobbi Owen. New York: Greenwood Press, 1987. 254p. (Bibliographies and Indexes in the Performing Arts, no. 5). ISBN 0-313-25524-5.

Only since 1936 have costume designers in theater been granted recognition by the union; thus, there has been relatively little documentation or consideration of their achievements. The author is a scholar in the field who has produced a well-constructed and useful source of information for specialists and students. More than 1,000 designers who contributed at least one costume to a Broadway production within a seventy-year period from 1915 to 1985 are treated. Entries are alphabetically arranged and supply a biographical sketch along with a listing of Broadway credits. Following this is a segment of black-and-white sketches of selected costumes. Three appendices identify award-winning designers, with separate listings for Tony, Marharam, and Donaldson winners. Finally, there is an index of 7,000 plays checked, along with their designers if available.

543. **Who's Who in Fashion. A Biographical Encyclopedia of the International Red Series Containing Some 6,000 Biographies.** Karl Strute and Theodor Dolken, eds. Zurich, Switzerland: Who's Who the International Red Series; distr., New York: UNIPUB, 1982. 3v. in 2. ISBN 0-87005-574-7.

This is the first edition of what was to be a triennial directory of important personalities and institutions related to fashion from Western European countries. Also treated are the related areas of cosmetics and jewelry; altogether, about 6,000 individuals are identified and described. These people represent all phases or elements of the fields (artistic or creative, economic, and even scientific interests). They include costume designers, beauty operators, and jewelers. Entries vary in length, but furnish birthdates, parents, spouses, children, home and work addresses, education, career information, current job, publications, memberships, awards, specialties, and hobbies. The appendices provide useful listings of national and international organizations, schools and training institutes, museums, fairs, societies, prizes, and journals. A number of photographs of individuals are included. Volume 1 covers fashion, and volumes 2 and 3 cover beauty and jewelry.

Who's Who in Fashion, by Anne Stegemeyer (Fairchild, 1988), now in its second edition, provides an alphabetical listing of some 200 influential and established designers from all over the world. Illustrations (some in color) are furnished for designers and their work. Entries vary in length from a few paragraphs to three pages and treat background, career, education, and achievements of the personalities. A sixty-one-page supplement was issued in 1992.

9 ◆ ACCESSING INFORMATION IN THE PERFORMING ARTS

WORKING DEFINITION OF THE PERFORMING ARTS

The term *performing arts* has not become standardized in its usage. It is used to differentiate the arts or skills which, by their nature, require public performance, as opposed to those whose beauty is appreciated through the sense of sight or some surrogate, as in the visual arts. McLeish says that "In the performing arts ... the performer, the intermediary, is a crucial part of the process."[1] Generally, three elements are necessary for consideration as a performing art: there must be the piece or work performed, the performer or performers, and an audience hearing, viewing, or experiencing the performance. Sometimes the three elements originate in the same individual, as is the case when a songwriter composes a work and performs it for himself or herself in the privacy of the practice room or studio, for example. Most often, however, the entities are different individuals or groups, and we treat the performing arts accordingly in this guide.

MAJOR DIVISIONS OF THE FIELD

As used in this guide, the performing arts include music, dance, opera, the theater, film, radio, television, and video. An interesting, though slightly different approach, is taken in the second edition of *The Humanities and the Library*, edited by Nena Couch and Nancy Allen (American Library Association, 1993). In that update of Asheim's earlier work, the editors present music and performing arts as separate chapters. Both are useful for the librarian and student; the music chapter is by Elizabeth Rebman (pp. 132-69) and Couch and Allen provide the performing arts section (pp. 173-211). Here, however, we maintain the arrangement of previous editions and include music within the performing arts chapter.

Music is commonly defined as the art of organizing sound. Its principal elements are melody (single sounds in succession), harmony (sounds in combination), and rhythm (sounds in a temporal relationship). The two major divisions are vocal music and instrumental music. Vocal music includes songs, opera, oratorios, etc., whereas instrumental music includes solos, chamber music, and orchestral music. Musical instruments may be classified as stringed (violin, harp, or guitar, for example), woodwind (flute, bassoon, oboe, English horn), brass (trumpet, cornet, bugle, trombone), percussion (drums, bells, gongs, chimes), keyboard (piano, organ, electronic keyboard), and others (accordions, harmonica, bagpipes, concertina, to name a few). The modern system of musical notation came to be used in about 1700.

The librarian responsible for a music collection will need to keep in mind three major elements: (1) the music itself, which follows to some degree the divisions just outlined; (2) the literature about music, which divides more along the conventional lines for all disciplines, but with some special characteristics; and (3) the vast array of recordings on records, discs, tapes, cassettes, and video which are a part of any modern music library and which pose problems in terms of organization, preservation, retrieval, and use.

The dance may be defined as movement of the body to a certain rhythm. There are three major division of the field: folk dancing, ballroom dancing, and theater dancing. Folk dancing, which originated in open-air activities, is characterized by great vigor and exuberance of movement. Ballroom dancing had its origin in the European courts of the Renaissance and is an indoor participant activity. Theater dancing is a spectator activity that may be traced to religious dances in the ancient world and to performances known as masques in the courts of Renaissance Europe. Its most characteristic form is the ballet. The dance is usually (though not always) accompanied by music.

Theater is the art of presenting a performance to a live audience. In modern usage the term is restricted to live performances of plays. A distinction is sometimes drawn between theater and drama; theater is restricted in meaning to those matters having to do with public performance, whereas drama includes the literary basis for the performance (i.e., the text of plays). The texts are often classed with literature in libraries, leading to the seemingly illogical separation of the texts of plays from works about performance of those plays. Topics that are closely related to theatrical performance, and that help to differentiate it from drama, are acting, costume, makeup, directing, and theater architecture.

Film may be divided into two types: feature-length (an hour or longer) and shorts. Many feature-length films are fictional, often based on books of some popularity. Others, known as documentaries, are prepared for informational purposes. The fictional and documentary form may be combined to make colorful travelogues or the so-called docu-dramas in which real situations are presented in fictional, or partly fictional, form. Two other forms of film are animated cartoons and puppet features. Recent technology has allowed for the melding of live action and animated cartoons, so that cartoon characters mix with live casts. Shorts are often filmed by independent producers and sold to distributors of feature-length films or video to complete an "entertainment package" for viewing in theaters or homes.

Films are widely used in schools, universities, churches, and other institutions for informational, educational, and training purposes. Films of this type are likely to constitute the bulk of many library collections.

Video is a relative newcomer to the performing arts field, particularly as a form available to most of the public. Feature-length films, educational films, "how-to" instructions in a variety of fields, and music performance are all widely distributed on tape for home consumption. The inclusion of the tapes in public library collections, although attracting some new users to libraries, may pose problems from the standpoint of preservation, censorship, and fees for services.

Radio, which depends entirely on sound for its effects, and television, relying on sound and pictures, can be presented either live or in prerecorded form. For libraries, it is the residual audio and video tapes that may be included in collections. These materials share with the other performing arts some of the problems of organization and preservation.

Coverage of music, dance, theater, and film is reasonably good in many general encyclopedias. The pivotal article on music in the fifteenth edition of *Encyclopaedia Britannica*, entitled "Music, Art of" (v.24, pp. 493-552), can be followed up by looking up such topics as "musical forms and genres." Similarly, the dance article ("Dance, Art of") can be followed by articles such as the one on "Dance, Western" or "Dance and Theatre, East Asian." Articles in the same encyclopedia on theater and motion pictures are also excellent, especially if an historical perspective is wanted.

The reader can obtain a psychiatrist's view of music, and the role of audience and listener, in Anthony Storr's *Music and the Mind* (Ballantine, 1992).

For divisions of the field of music and related performing arts, the reader should not overlook the monumental *New Grove Dictionary of Music and Musicians* 6th edition, edited by Stanley Sadie (Groves, 1980). Articles are accompanied by highly authoritative bibliographies that will lead the reader to additional publications on all aspects of music and related fields.

HELPFUL RESOURCES FOR STUDENTS, LIBRARIANS, AND GENERAL READERS

There are many helpful resources for students, librarians, and general readers who wish to understand more about performing arts materials, how they are selected for libraries, and how they are organized for both preservation and retrieval. Some of the readings are older, but the basic information is still useful if the reader overlooks references to specific bibliographic sources that have been updated or revised. Of course, if an historical perspective is needed, the older sources will serve the reader well.

The music chapter in Lester Asheim's *The Humanities and the Library* (American Library Association, 1956, pp. 151-98) remains a good introduction to the basic organization and use of a music collection. It is supplemented and somewhat updated by "Music Libraries and Collections," by Guy A. Marco, in *Encyclopedia of Library and Information Science* (Dekker, 1976, v.18, pp. 328-493). A classic in the field is *Music Libraries*, by Jack Dove (Deutsch, 1967), a revision of the 1937 work of the same title by L. R. McColvin and H. Reeves.

More recent entries in the music librarianship literature include E. T. Bryant and Marco's *Music Librarianship: A Practical Guide* (2d ed., Scarecrow Press, 1985) and *American Music Librarianship: A Biographical and Historical Survey*, by Carol J. Bradley (Greenwood Press, 1990). The former title was written for general librarians and students, and gives more than an introduction to such topics as administration, reference, cataloging and classification, and recordings. A long bibliography is also a useful feature. Michael Och's *Music Librarianship in America* (Harvard, 1991) is a set of papers presented at a symposium in honor of the first music library chair in the United States, the Richard F. French Chair in Librarianship at Harvard. The publications were also published as the *Harvard Library Bulletin* 2 (Spring 1991).

Frank P. Byrne's *A Practical Guide to the Music Library: Its Function, Organization, and Maintenance* (Ludwig Music, 1987) is another general title in music librarianship that will be helpful to the student reader as well as specialist.

Guides to the literature of music are numerous, but among the best is *Music Reference and Research Materials: An Annotated Bibliography* 4th edition, compiled by Vincent Duckles and Michael A. Keller (Schirmer, 1988). The guide, referred to by librarians as simply "Duckles," consistently received high ratings because of the quality of the annotations. Duckles (1913-1985) contributed much more to music librarianship and music scholarship; a bibliography of his publications appeared in *Notes*, the journal of the Music Library Association, as a memorial tribute from his colleagues in the field. (See "Vincent Duckles: A Bibliography of His Publications," compiled by Patricia Elliott and Mark S. Roosa, *Notes* 44 [December 1987]: 252-58.)

Other guides that will be helpful to the librarian or student are *Music: A Guide to the Literature*, by William Brockman (Libraries Unlimited, 1988); and Robert Michael Fling, *Basic Music Library: Essential Scores and Books* (2d ed., American Library Association, 1983). The latter title is current only through 1980, but the notations for essential titles remain timely.

Many special topics in music librarianship and research have been addressed in special reports (Technical Reports Series) issued by the Music Library Association. These have focused largely on cataloging and processing issues in terms of contents, but some recent reports have addressed space use in music libraries (report no. 20, 1992, by James Cassaro and "Careers in Music Librarianship," report no. 18, 1990, by Carol Tatian).

Besides the special issues published by the Association, the journal literature and recent books have covered the topics of technical services and the organization of materials. Richard P. Smiraglia, who has written and spoken extensively on the topic, has published *Music Cataloging: The Bibliographic Control of Printed and Recorded Music in Libraries* (Libraries Unlimited, 1989). The text includes a historical summary of music cataloging and subject access. Subject headings are the topic of *Music Subject Headings*, compiled from the Library of Congress Subject Headings by Perry Bratcher and Jennifer Smith (Soldier Creek Press, 1988). The MLA publication entitled *Music Cataloging Bulletin* should be consulted regularly for changes in subject headings.

Articles addressing other technical aspects of handling and organizing music materials include: Michelle Koth and Laura Gayle Green, "Workflow Considerations in Retrospective Conversion Projects for Scores," *Cataloging and Classification Quarterly* 14 (1992): 75-102; "ARIS Music Thesaurus: Another View of LCSH," *Library Resources and Technical Services* 36 (October 1992): 487-503; Annie F. Thompson, "Music Cataloging in Academic Libraries and the Case for Physical Decentralization: A Survey," *Journal of Academic Librarianship* 12 (May 1986): 79-83; and "A Use Study of Card Catalogs in the University of Illinois Music Library," by Jeanette M. Drone, *Library Resources and Technical Services* 28 (July-September 1984): 253-62. J. Krantz offers "The Music Uniform Title: Sources for the Novice Cataloger," *Cataloging and Classification Quarterly* 9 (1988): 73-80. The role of nonprofessional staff in music cataloging is addressed in J. Kranz, "Paraprofessional Involvement in Music Cataloging: A Case Study," *Cataloging and Classification Quarterly* 10 (1990): 89-98.

Linda Crow addresses physical arrangement of materials in "Shelf Arrangement Systems for Sound Recordings: Survey of American Academic Music Libraries," *Technical Services Quarterly* 8 (1991): 1-24. "Preservation Policies and Priorities for Recorded Sound Collections," by Brenda Nelson-Strauss, in *Notes* 48 (December 1991): 425-36 is one of many works addressing the physical preservation issue. C. D. Jerde's "Technical Processing of Popular Music at Tulane University Library's Hogan Jazz Archive," *Technical Services Quarterly* 4 (Summer 1987): 49-56, is another.

Finally, rounding out the large selection of materials focused on technical services aspects is an article on instruction for users of online catalogs: A. Hall and G. J. Sonnemann published "Establishing an Instructional Program for Music Users of Online Catalogs: Concepts, Options, and Priorities," *Fontis Artis Musicae* 37 (April-June 1990): 138-49.

Collection development in music and performing arts libraries is discussed in *Selecting Materials for Libraries* by Robert Broadus (2d ed., H. W. Wilson, 1981, pp. 352-63) and in numerous journal articles. Collecting popular music is the subject of the Winter 1983 issue of *Drexel Library Quarterly*; the issue, in volume 19, was edited by Tim LaBorie. The same issue contains Sheldon Lewis Tarakan, "Classical Pop: Documenting Popular Musical Culture in Library Audio Collections," pp. 123-50. Also, F. Hoffman's "Popular Music Periodicals in the Library," *Serials Librarian* 12 (1987): 69-87, is concerned with journal collection building. An extensive bibliography accompanies the latter article.

William F. Coscarelli and Anna H. Perrault authored "Music Collections in ARL Libraries: A Report of a Survey at Louisiana State Universities," *Collection Management* 16 (1992): 13-59, in which results of a 1986 survey of 60 ARL libraries are reported. Verna Fond Ritchie's "A Burgeoning in the World of Discography," *RQ* 21 (Spring 1982): 254-67, provides a listing of discographical resources.

There are many sources that will help to identify reference materials and other items that might be included in collections. Besides the guides and bibliographies in chapter 10, a good bibliography of the basics is found in Anne Gray's *The Popular Guide to Classical Music* (Birch Lane Press, 1993), pp. 337-40. A bibliography focusing on recorded sound is found in *The Iconography of Recorded Sound 1886-1986* by Michael G. Corenthal (Yesterday's Memories, 1986).

The journal literature is rich with shorter articles describing the current offerings or recommended titles on specific topics. A sampling of articles on diverse topics includes: R. A. Leaver's "Hymnals, Hymnal Companions, and Collection Development," *Notes* 47 (December 1990): 331-54; H. J. Diamond, "The Literature of Musical Analysis: An Approach for Collection Development," *Choice* 27 (March 1990): 1097-99; C. A. Pressler, "Rock and Roll: Dimensions of a Cultural Revolution," *Choice* 29 (April 1992): 1192-1201; and P. Garon, "A Survey of Literature on the Blues," *AB Bookman's Weekly* 89 (February 17, 1992): 619-21. Two more recent entries are R. M. Cleary's "Rap Music and Its Political Connections: An Annotated Bibliography," *Reference Services Review* 21 (1993): 77-90 and the timely article by R. L. Wick, "The Literature of Electronic and Computer Music: A Basic Library Collection," *Choice* 31 (November 1993): 411-14. All of the articles listed here provide bibliographic citations for materials on the focal topics. The journal *Collection Management*, in volume 12 (1990), carried two views of library collection building: W. E. Studwell presented the music researcher's (pp. 92-94) and H. S. Wright the music librarian's view (pp. 95-99).

The journals *Notes* (published by the Music Library Association) and *Fontis Artis Musicae* (International Association of Music Libraries) should not be overlooked. The former carries substantive articles and regularly reviews new publications as well as reference materials and recorded music. The latter, which is multilingual and international in scope, covers activities of the association, proceedings of its conferences, and other topics of broad interest to performing arts librarians.

The selection and use of films is addressed in *InFocus: A Guide to Using Films* by Linda Blackaby, Dan Georgakas, and Barbara Margolis (Cine Information, 1980). Older issues of the now defunct *Film Library Quarterly* may still be of some interest.

Finally, an important special issue for performing arts libraries or general libraries with performing arts collections is copyright. The librarian will do well to know the basics of the issue and to recognize when expert advice is needed. A good introductory publication on the topic is *The Copyright Primer for Librarians and Educators*, compiled by Mary Hutchings Reed and published jointly by the American Library Association and the National Education Association in 1987. Special sections discuss music (pp. 23-26), sheet music (pp. 26-29), and videotapes (pp. 29-39). The *Primer* also offers suggestions about obtaining permissions from publishers and the Copyright Clearance Center (pp. 54-55).

Library Journal, *Library Quarterly*, and other general journals in librarianship include the performing arts by publishing articles on collection development, technical processes, reference services, nonbook materials, and other topics of special interest. These titles should never be overlooked as sources of information for the librarian, student, or general reader.

USE AND USERS OF PERFORMING ARTS INFORMATION

Of the performing arts, music has been the most studied in terms of use and users of information. Malcolm Jones's *Music Librarianship* (Saur, 1979) introduces, very generally, types of music libraries and their users in "Music Libraries and Those They Serve" (pp. 13-23). The chapter on music by Elizabeth Rebman in *The Humanities and the Library*, 2d edition, offers a brief user perspective in the section entitled "The Work of Composers, Performers, and Music Scholars" (pp. 136-37).

More specific studies of the use of the literature of music can be found in the journal literature. The reader will want to see, for example, R. Griscom, "Periodical Use in a University Music Library: A Citation Study of Theses and Dissertations Submitted to the Indiana University School of Music from 1975-1980," *Serials Librarian* 7 (Spring 1983): 35-52; R. Green's "Use of Music and Its Literature Over Time," *Notes* 35 (September 1978): 42-56; and David Baker's "Characteristics of the Literature Used by English Musicologists," *Journal of Librarianship* 10 (July 1978): 182-200. Miranda Lee Pao investigated the behavior of authors and publications in computational musicology in "Bibliometrics and Computational Musicology," *Collection Management* 3 (Spring 1979): 97-109. A more recent study is S. M. Clegg's "User Surveys and Statistics for Music Librarians," *Fontis Artis Musicae* 32 (January 1985): 69-75. Mary Kay Duggan stresses the music scholar's need for information in diverse formats in "Electronic Information and Applications in Musicology and Music Theory," *Library Trends* 40 (Spring 1992): 756-80. The number of electronic resources available to musicologists and other scholars of the performing arts would suggest that they are adopting the new information technologies. The next few years will undoubtedly yield new studies of users in the electronic environment.

COMPUTERS IN THE PERFORMING ARTS

Computers are being used in a variety of ways in the performing arts. As with other aspects of performing arts information, music is the field for which we have the most literature on computer use. In the field, we see computers used in musicological research and analysis, by the creative composer for writing music, and by music educators for the teaching of music. In libraries, information centers, and music archives, computers are used to search and retrieve material via online vendors or CD-ROM databases. Finally, in the 1990s we see musicians, scholars, music librarians, and music historians using the Internet as a resource for machine-readable data, discussion groups, and electronic mail. Music librarians also use computers for the same purposes as other librarians and information specialists, of course.

The most comprehensive article on electronic information in music is Mary Kay Duggan's "Electronic Information and Applications in Musicology and Music Theory," *Library Trends* 40 (Spring 1992): 756-80. The article covers all aspects of computers in music and music librarianship, and an extensive bibliography accompanies the article. It is must reading. Chapter 18, "Music," in *The Humanities Computing Yearbook*, by Ian Lancashire and Willard McCarty (Clarendon Press, 1988), includes a listing of software for the field.

The primary online database for music and related areas is RILM Abstracts. The counterpart to this database in print form is *RILM Abstracts of Music Literature (Repertoire Internationale de Litterature Musicale)*. The database covers all areas of music and some other aspects of performing arts that relate to music; the coverage begins at 1971. A thesaurus is available also. The file is available on DIALOG as file 97, and it has special searchable indexes that enhance the user's ability to home in on very precise topics. The contents of RILM are also available in CD-ROM format; the CD-ROM version covers the entire time span and is entitled MUSE (for *Mu*sic *Se*arch).

Other databases of interest to the music scholar will be *Magazine Index*, *Books in Print*, *Dissertation Abstracts Online*, and ISI's *Arts and Humanities Search*. All have print counterparts. H. W. Wilson's *Readers' Guide to Periodical Literature*, available on WILSONLINE and on CD-ROM, covers the general periodical literature. Special keys can be used in the WILSONLINE files to retrieve performance and book reviews.

Database searches in the performing arts fields of dance, theater, television and radio, and film are usually carried out in what we might term "general" or multidisciplinary" databases. *Magill's Survey of Cinema* is the exception. For appropriate choices for different divisions of the performing arts, consult "End-User Selection of Databases—Part III: Social Sciences/Arts and Humanities," *Database* (October 1990): 59-64, by Den Ruiz and Daniel E. Meyer.

CD-ROM offers great potential for music materials, and a number of CD-ROM products include sound and textual material together in true multimedia personal computer products. Warner New Media, for example, has *Audio Notes: The Magic Flute*. Some general multimedia encyclopedias on CD-ROM also have sound along with text and graphics. A good list of examples of music CD-ROM products is found in Lucy Buck and Paul Travis Nicholls's "Arts and Humanities Sources on CD-ROM," *CD-ROM Professional* (March 1991): 96-99.

Other CD-ROM products in the music area include Chadwyck-Healey's bibliographic *Music Index on CD-ROM* (1981-) and, for recorded music, *Billboard/Phonolog Music Reference Library on CD-ROM*. The latter is a quarterly product begun in 1991. The value of a machine-readable and searchable counterpart to the tradional Phonolog service will not be lost on librarians and retailers of recorded music.

Databases in the Humanities and Social Sciences 4, edited by Lawrence J. McCrank (Learned Information, 1989), contains the following diverse papers on computing in the performing arts: on theater, Margaret Loftus Ranald, "An International Bibliography of Theatre: A History and Description," pp. 543-49, and Neil H. M. Freeman, "Byting the Bard: Databased Shakespearian and Practical Theatre Studies," pp. 231-38; on music topics, Imants Freibergs, "Accessibility of Folksongs Databases," pp. 239-46; Harry E. Price, "Conception, Design, and Implementation of the Orchestra Program Archives and Database (OPAD)," pp. 537-41, and "A FAMULUS Databased Finding Aid for the American Harp Society's Repository," by Lucile H. Jennings and Jodelle Finneyfrock (pp. 367-69). These articles, by their titles alone, illustrate the wide range of subjects in which computers have been applied to database organization and design.

Mary Kay Duggan's article, "Teaching Online Reference for Music Librarians," *Fontis Artis Musicae* 31 (January-March 1987): 44-53 provides additional information on online databases, library catalogs, and CD-ROM resources. "Multimedia Databases for Public Service in Music Libraries," by the same author, in volume 38 (1991) of *Fontis Artis Musicae* (pp. 49-55) is a good introduction to the new multimedia resources.

Electronic music applications are summarized in *Computing in Musicology,* which appears annually (Computer Assisted Research in Humanities), or in earlier years titled as *Directory of Computer Assisted Research in Musicology.* W. B. Hewlett and E. Selfridge-Field are editors. The same co-authors published a comprehensive review of earlier work in the field in "Computing in Musicology, 1966-1991," *Computers and the Humanities* 25 (1991): 381-92. Another resource is D. Davis's *Computer Applications in Music: A Bibliography* (A-R Editions, 1991), a revision of the original 1987 bibliography. All of the bibliographies and directories address multiple topics: printing music, machine-readable music information, computer analysis of music, software, computer-assisted composition, instruction, and notation programs, to name a few.

The Computer Music Association (PO Box 1634, San Francisco, CA 94101-1634) publishes proceedings of its conferences on the subject of computing in music. Journals to consult on the topic include *Computing in Musicology, Array, Computers and the Humanities,* and *Computers in Music Research.* Others are listed in Duggan's "Electronic Information and Applications in Musicology and Music Theory," referenced earlier.

The Internet is a rich source of performing arts material. The music resources are especially numerous, ranging from detailed information about specific artists or particular genres to lists of companies offering hard-to-find sheet music. These resources can be found through the hundreds of music listservs and Usenet news groups. There are also FTP sites that archive files related to music. A simple way to get more information about music resources on the Net is to search for the term "music" in the Usenet newsgroup "news.answers." This search will retrieve FAQs (frequently asked questions files) and lists of Internet resources on music. The gopher file server "Clearinghouse of Subject Oriented Internet Resource Guides" also lists many resources.

Theater resources can also be located through the same gopher. Deborah Torres and Martha Vander Kolk's "Guide to Theater Resources on the Internet" is an exhaustive guide. Ken McCoy's "A Guide to Internet Resources in Theater and Performance Studies" covers dance and cinema as well as theater, and Lisa Wood and Kristen Garlock provide "Film and Video Resources on the Internet." All can be located through the "Clearinghouse of Subject Oriented Internet Resource Guides."

"On-Line Disciplines: Computer-Mediated Scholarship in the Humanities and Social Sciences," by Teresa M. Harrison and Timothy Stephen, in *Computers and the Humanities* 26 (1992): 181-93, gives addresses for several listservs and bulletin boards in the performing arts.

MAJOR ORGANIZATIONS, INFORMATION CENTERS, AND SPECIAL COLLECTIONS

The number of national and international organizations in the performing arts is so great that attention can be given here only to those that are most significant to the librarian. Guides to the specific fields in the performing arts will offer additional information in much greater detail, as will the many directories now in print.

The International Association of Music Libraries has branches in most developed countries. The U.S. branch is located at City College Music Library, New York, NY 10031. It currently sponsors the *International Inventory of Music Sources/Repertoire International des Sources Musicales (RISM)*. Since 1954, it has published *Fontis Artis Musicae*, a journal cited frequently in this chapter. The International Music Council (1 rue Miollis, Paris F750 15 France), one of the first nongovernmental agencies established by UNESCO, studies the development of music and produces many publications. The International Musicological Society (Case Postale 56, CH-4001, Basel, Switzerland) was founded in 1927 to promote research and has published the journal *Acta Musicologica* since 1928.

The Music Library Association (PO Box 487, Canton, MA 02021) supports a wide range of activities, including the publication of *Music Cataloging Bulletin* and, since 1943, *Notes*. Music Library Association activities are tracked and reported in *The ALA Yearbook of Library and Information Services* (American Library Association, annual).

The Association for Recorded Sound Collections (PO Box 75082, Washington, DC 20013) was founded in 1966 and includes in its membership people in the recording and broadcasting industries as well as librarians in the performing arts. It publishes *ARSC Journal* and *ARSC Bulletin*. The Music Educators National Conference (1902 Association Drive, Reston, VA 22091) was founded in 1902 and has over 65,000 members. It publishes *Music Educators' Journal* and the quarterly *Journal of Research in Music Education*. The American Musicological Society (University of Pennsylvania, 201 S. 34th Street, Philadelphia, PA 19104) publishes *Journal of the American Musicological Society* and periodic lists of theses and dissertations in the field. The American Symphony Orchestra League (777 14th Street NW, Suite 500, Washington, DC 20005) was founded in 1942 and has a library pertaining to all aspects of the symphony orchestra. The American Guild of Organists (475 Riverside Drive, #1260, New York, NY 10115) is one of many specialized groups. Like many others, they publish a monthly journal, *Music/AGORCCO*.

Music industry statistics are published annually by the American Music Conference (303 E. Wacker Drive, #1214, Chicago, IL 60601). The publication is entitled *Music Industry USA*.

By contrast, the number of organizations devoted to dance is small; those that do exist seem to be largely concentrated in the areas of ballet and the teaching of dance. The Ballet Theatre Foundation (890 Broadway, New York, NY 10003) appeals to a broad audience for support and publishes *Ballet Theatre Newsletter*. The Imperial Society of Teachers of Dancing (70 Gloucester Place, London, UK) has a branch in the United States (4338 Battery Lane, Bethesda, MD 20814). The Society publishes a bimonthly, *Imperial Dance Letter*. The Dance Educators of America and Dance Masters of America both consist of dance teachers and have regional groups that supplement the activities of the national groups. The Dance Educators can be reached at PO Box 509, Oceanside, NY 11572, and the Dance Masters at PO Box 438, Independence, MO 64051.

The International Federation for Theatre Research (Department of French, University of Lancaster, Lancaster, UK) disseminates scholarly information through *Theatre Research International*. The American Society for Theatre Research (University of Pennsylvania, Philadelphia, PA 19104) issues a newsletter and the semiannual publication *Theatre Survey*. The International Theatre Institute, established in 1948, has a branch in the United States (1860 Broadway, New York, NY 10023) and publishes *Theatre Notes* and *International Theatre Information*.

The American Theatre Association (1010 Wisconsin Avenue, NW, Washington, DC 20007) is concerned with all areas of educational theater. Its publications include *Theatre News*, *Placement Service Bulletin*, and an annual convention program and directory.

The Theatre Library Association (TLA) includes not only librarians, but also actors, booksellers, writers, and researchers in its membership. Located in New York (111 Amsterdam Avenue, Room 513, New York, NY 10023), the Association publishes *Broadside*, a newsletter focusing on performing arts collections; an annual, *Performing Arts Resources*; and *Theatre Documentation*. TLA also has undertaken other publishing projects, especially notable ones in preservation and historical areas.

The University Film and Video Association (University of Southern California, MC2212, Los Angeles, CA 90089-2212), publisher of a journal and digest, was formerly the University Film Association. *Film Society Bulletin* and *Film Critic* are published by the American Federation of Film Societies (3 Washington Square Village, New York, NY 10012). The American Film Institute (30 East 60th Street, New York, NY 10022) supports a wide range of archival, research, and production activities. Publications include *American Film* and *Guide to College Courses in Film and Television*. The Federation of Motion Picture Councils publishes *Motion Picture Rating Preview Reports*. The American Film and Video Association (920 Barnsdale Road, #152, LaGrange, IL 60525) evaluates books and films and publishes *AFVA Evaluations*, *Sightlines*, and *AFVA Bulletin*.

Concern with children's television is the focus of ACT (Action for Children's Television) and the National Council for Children and Television. ACT publishes *RE:ACT*. NCCT publishes a quarterly *Television and Children*.

Because music publishing often occurs outside the usual trade channels, two associations offer information about publishers of music. The National Music Publishers' Association, founded in 1917, was originally established as the Music Publishers Protective Association. Its focus is the publishing of popular music, and it publishes a quarterly, *NMPA News and Views*. The address is 205 E. 42d Street, New York, NY 10017. The Music Publishers' Association of the United States, also located in New York, is concerned with serious and educational music publishing. Its communications vehicle is *MPA Newsletter*, a quarterly.

The American Composers' Alliance (170 W. 74th Street, New York, NY 10023) was founded in 1937. It publishes its catalogues of new music and works for the protection of the rights of its members.

The Committee on Research in Dance (New York University, Department of Dance Education, 35 W. 4th Street, New York, NY 10003) serves as a clearinghouse for research information in the field.

The International Theatre Studies Center at the University of Kansas (Lawrence, KS 66044) publishes *Theatre Documentation* and several other publications. The Wisconsin Center for Theater Research (University of Wisconsin, Madison, WI 53706) concentrates on the performing arts in America. The Institute of Outdoor Drama (University of North Carolina, Chapel Hill, NC 27514) provides advisory and consultation services as well as bibliographic information on the specialty.

The most outstanding music collection in the United States is the Library of Congress, which benefits from copyright deposit. The Music Division, established in 1897, has issued numerous catalogs, several of which are listed elsewhere in this book. Another notable collection is found in the Music Division of the Research Library of the Performing Arts in Lincoln Center (part of the New York Public Library). Music from the twelfth to the eighteenth centuries is a specialty of the Isham Memorial Library of Harvard University, whereas primary sources in early opera scores and librettos are a strength of the University of California Music Library in Berkeley. The Center for Research Libraries has several microform collections of research materials. In Europe, the Austrian National Library (Vienna), the Royal Library of Belgium (Brussels), the Biblioteque Nationale (Paris), the Deutsche Staatsbibliothek (Berlin), the British Museum (London), the Biblioteca Nazionale Centrale (Florence), and the Vatican Library (Rome) all have outstanding collections.

The Dance Collection in the Research Library of the Performing Arts (New York Public Library) includes photographs, scores, programs, prints, posters, and playbills, as well as instruction manuals and other literature on the dance. The Archives of Dance, Music and Theatre (University of Florida Libraries) contains about 20,000 similar memorabilia related to the performing arts in the twentieth century.

The Theater Arts Library (University of California at Los Angeles) has screen plays and pictures in addition to the general collection of English- and foreign-language books on film. The Harvard Theatre Collection (Houghton Library) has rare letters, account books, diaries, drawings, promptbooks, and playbills from the United States, Great Britain, and continental Europe. Similar materials relating to British and American theater from 1875 to 1935 (especially the Chicago Little Theatre Movement, 1912-1917) are found in the Department of Rare Books and Special Collections, University of Michigan. The Theatre Collection in the Research Library of the Performing Arts (New York Public Library) is one of the most notable anywhere. Bibliographic access is provided through its published catalog.

The Free Library of Philadelphia has over 1.2 million items relating to the theater, early circuses, and minstrel and vaudeville shows.

The Library of Congress has several notable film collections, including those received on copyright deposit. The Dell Publishing Company has a collection of over 3.5 million pictures dealing with movie and television personalities.

These represent only a small sampling of the performing arts collections in the United States and Europe that contain specialized information in a rich diversity of formats. Ash's directory and specialized guides to the different areas of performing arts will lead the reader to ample numbers of other libraries, information centers, and archives.

NOTES

[1] Kenneth McLeish, "Performing Arts," in *Key Ideas in Human Thought* (New York: Facts on File, 1993), pp. 548-49.

10 ◆ PRINCIPAL INFORMATION SOURCES IN THE PERFORMING ARTS

PERFORMING ARTS IN GENERAL

Bibliographic Guides

544.   **American and English Popular Entertainment: A Guide to Information Sources.**
Don B. Wilmeth. Detroit: Gale, 1980. 465p. (Performing Arts Information Guide Series, v.7;
Gale Information Guide Series, v.7). ISBN 0-810314-54-1.

The subject matter of this tool is defined as those amusements created and staged by
professional showpeople for unsophisticated audiences in order to turn a profit. There are three
major segments in this useful annotated bibliography of 2,500 books, articles, and dissertations.
Part I lists a number of sources on entertainments prior to the nineteenth century, and general
sources on the topic. The second part covers specific types or forms of entertainment such as Wild
West Shows, minstrel shows, vaudeville, burlesque, dime museums, stage music, lyceum and
Chautauqua, and puppet shows. Also included in this segment are optical and mechanical
entertainments prior to the introduction of cinema. Part II surveys writings on the popular theater.
The emphasis is on nineteenth-century entertainment, although some sources do cover twentieth-
century developments. As might be expected, there is some overlap with the author's *The American
Stage to World War I: A Guide to Information Sources* (Gale, 1978).

545.   **The Performing Arts: A Guide to the Reference Literature**. Linda Keir Simons.
Englewood, CO: Libraries Unlimited, 1994. 230p. (Reference Sources in the Humanities
Series). ISBN 0-87287-982-8.

Another useful literature guide from Libraries Unlimited is this treatment of reference
and information sources relevant to theater, dance, and such related arts as puppetry, mime,
and magic. Excluded from coverage are music, film, and television (which are covered by
other works in the series) as well as those tools dealing primarily with drama as literature
rather than performance. The emphasis is on recent English-language works but old standards
and foreign titles are included. Arrangement of entries is by type of material, with chapter
coverage given to the most important directories, encyclopedias, handbooks, bibliographies,
catalogs, chronologies, etc. These chapters are then subdivided by subject (theater, dance,
etc.), providing easy access for the librarian or student user. Secondary sources such as core
journals, electronic discussion lists, associations and societies, and libraries and archives are
identified and described in additional chapters.

546.   **Popular Entertainment Research: How to Do It and How to Use It.** Barbara J.
Pruett. Metuchen, NJ: Scarecrow Press, 1992. 581p. ISBN 0-8108-2501-5.

Beginning with a fine introduction to the methods of conducting research, including the
searching of databases and employment of interviews, Pruett has produced a useful guide to
the reference literature of the various elements of popular culture. Coverage is given to film,
theater, popular music, and broadcast media. Chapters furnish annotated listings of archive
collections, research centers, databases, journals, and compilations of resources, among
others. Annotations describe the resources and furnish hints on gaining access and making

contacts. Listings of reference materials published before 1990 are given in each chapter. Researchers will find it a good update to the Whalon work (following), as well as the other older tools in this section.

Performing Arts Research: A Guide to Information Sources by Marion K. Whalon (Gale, 1976) is the initial volume of a Gale series which has continued to provide useful bibliographies for specialists and students. It arranges the material in seven parts or segments, identifying guides; dictionaries, encyclopedias, and handbooks; directories; play indexes and finding lists; sources for reviews of plays and motion pictures; bibliographies, indexes, and abstracts; and illustrative and audiovisual sources. Annotations are descriptive and brief but provide information adequate to determine the content and scope of the tools. Coverage embraces a variety of fields and, in addition to theater and film, includes dance, costume, music, visual arts, literature, and rhetoric. Although the tool is showing its age and has been criticized for certain oversights in its organization and index references, it continues to serve a useful purpose.

Bibliographies and Indexes

547. **Index to Characters in the Performing Arts.** Harold S. Sharp and Marjorie Z. Sharp, comps. Metuchen, NJ: Scarecrow Press, 1966-1973. 4v. in 6. ISSN 0072-873X.

Since its publication, this four-volume set has been regarded as an excellent source of information for the identification of characters in the various genres of the performing arts. Volume 1 covers non-musical plays (two volumes); volume 2 treats operas and musical productions (two volumes); volume 3 lists characters in ballets; volume 4 covers radio and television. The established pattern was for two-part coverage, beginning with an alphabetical listing of characters for which cross-references were provided to productions, and a list of citation symbols identifying title, type of production, number of acts, author or composer, name of theater, and place and date of first performance. Thousands of characters, both fictitious and real, major and minor, are treated.

Directories and Biographical Sources

548. **Bibliothèques et musées des arts du spectacle dans le monde/Performing Arts Libraries and Museums of the World.** 4th ed. Andre Veinstein and Alfred S. Goulding. Paris: Centre Nationale de la Recherche Scientifique, 1992. 740p. ISBN 2-222-04604-1.

The first edition of this work appeared in 1960, the next edition seven years later. After seventeen years, the third edition was issued in 1984. Eight years later, the fourth edition was published; the work continues as an outstanding source of information on the collections of performing arts held in museums and libraries all over the world. Traditionally the text is written in both French and English. Entries provide information regarding size and composition of collections, regulations governing their use, and business hours of the various public and private institutions covered. Information is gathered through questionnaires, and arrangement of entries is alphabetical by country, then by city, with place names given in French. There is an index of names and of collections.

549. **Contemporary Theatre, Film, and Television: A Biographical Guide Featuring Performers, Directors, Writers, Producers, Designers ...** Detroit: Gale Research, 1984- . Bienn. v.1- . ISSN 0749-064X.

The first volume of this work expanded and superseded two of the standard long-running serials, *Who's Who in the Theatre* (entry 810) and *Who Was Who in the Theatre* (entry 810n). Since then, it has continued to provide good biographical sketches for hundreds of currently employed personalities as well as prominent retirees from the United States and Great Britain. The subtitle (which is abbreviated in this entry) continues with "Managers, Choreographers,

Technicians, Composers, Executives, Dancers, and Critics in the United States and Great Britain." There is an emphasis on U.S. nationals. Entries provide personal data, education, debut dates, credits, awards, etc., and vary somewhat in length because of the amount of material furnished by the biographee or found in secondary sources. Subsequent volumes each cover some 450 additional personalities, in a manner similar to that of *Contemporary Authors* (entry 988), and update entries for those covered in *Who's Who in the Theatre*, including recently deceased individuals. With the publication of volume 11 in 1993, it brings the total to around 6,500 persons covered. Included is a cumulative index to the entire series as well as *Who's Who in the Theatre* and *Who Was Who in the Theatre*.

550. **Directory of Blacks in the Performing Arts**. 2d ed. Edward Mapp. Boston: G. K. Hall, 1990. 594p. ISBN 0-8108-2222-9.

The initial edition of this directory was issued in 1978, and this replacement effort is welcome. It expands previous coverage by some 150 pages and 300 entries and provides needed updates and revision of previous entries. It is now more comprehensive in its inclusion of musical groups as well as individual performers. All areas of the performing arts are treated and brief biographical information is provided for actors, playwrights, singers, composers, producers, broadcasters, choreographers, agents, and others associated with film, recording, television, and theater. There are some 1,100 entries alphabetically arranged and supplying listings of credits along with identifications. Coverage appears to be up-to-date in terms of the reporting of recent deaths, and the work is especially helpful in identifying figures who have recently been discovered. There is an index classified by field of activity.

551. **Money for Performing Artists**. Suzanne Niemeyer, ed. New York: ACA Books/American Council for the Arts, 1991. 268p. ISBN 0-915400-96-0.

One of several directories of sources of support for artists published under the auspices of the American Council for the Arts, this tool is extremely useful in view of the diminished resources available during the past few years. Listed here are nearly 225 organizations, alphabetically arranged for easy access. Those organizations provide financial support to practitioners of all kinds rather than students, even though there are some awards for fledgling artists. All areas of the performing arts are included with grants, awards, fellowships, residencies, competitions, and technical assistance identified. Entries supply description of types of support and requirements, details of the application process, and types of programs and services. Names of contact persons are given along with their addresses. There are indexes by organization, discipline, geographic area, and type of support offered.

552. **Performing Arts Resources**. New York: Drama Book Specialists, 1974- . Ann. ISSN 0360-3814.

This is an annual publication sponsored by the Theatre Library Association providing, in each issue, articles describing the location, identity, and content of various collections of the performing arts. Earlier volumes covered such diverse units as the research collections in New York City, the motion picture collection of the Library of Congress, and the Federal Theatre Project holdings at George Mason University. The work is intended for the use of serious students, scholars, and archivists in order to facilitate the search for materials on theater, film, broadcasting, and popular entertainments. More recent volumes have tended to emphasize collections on very specific topics as well as performance aspects.

Handel's National Directory for the Performing Arts (5th ed. 1992) is an annual publication which began in 1988 and is issued by Bowker/Reed. It replaces both the *National Directory for the Performing Arts and Civic Centers* and the *National Directory for the Performing Arts/Educational* through its two-part coverage. Volume 1 lists institutions and organizations relevant to dance, instrumental and vocal music, theater, and performing arts in general by state and city, subdivided by specialty. Volume 2 lists educational institutions and their programs in the performing arts. Several indexes provide access.

553. **Sourcebook for the Performing Arts: A Directory of Collections, Resources, Scholars, and Critics in Theatre, Film, and Television.** Anthony Slide et al., comps. New York: Greenwood Press, 1988. 227p. ISBN 0-313-24872-9.

This is a comprehensive directory of the performing arts in terms of scope, but selective in terms of its listings. It is comprised of three major segments, the first a listing of institutions (colleges, universities, libraries, etc.) and historical societies with major research collections. The second lists 200 major personalities involved in scholarly inquiry and/or criticism, whereas the third enumerates bookstores, production companies, journals, studios, and more. Information is brief (considered skimpy by some) and covers little more than the basics of address and telephone number of relatively few persons and units.

The Lively Arts Information Directory: A Guide to the Fields of Music, Dance, Theater, Film, Radio, and Television in the United States and Canada ... edited by Stephen R. Wasserman and Jacqueline Wasserman O'Brien (2d ed. Gale, 1985) is more detailed and thorough coverage. Its magnitude is expressed in the complete subtitle, which goes on to state that it covers national, international, state, and regional organizations; government grant sources; foundations; consultants; special libraries; research and information centers; educational programs; journals and periodicals; and festivals and awards. The first edition appeared in 1982 and it was hoped that the publisher had adopted a triennial frequency. Unfortunately, there has been no subsequent edition. Indexing varies with each component, for the national and international organizations are accessed through a KWIC index, but foundations are approached through subject and geographical indexes. There are more than 9,000 listings, over a third more than in the initial edition, and the work is derived in part from the publisher's database of listings from the *Encyclopedia of Associations* (Gale, 1984), but with enough additional material from a variety of publications to make it a worthwhile purchase.

554. **Variety Obituaries: Including a Comprehensive Index**. Chuck Bartelt and Barbara Bergeron, proj. eds. New York: Garland, 1988- . v.1- . ISBN 0-8240-0835-9 (v.1).

From Garland comes this multivolume compilation of obituaries and related articles of entertainment figures as they appeared in *Variety* (entry 871) over a time span of more than eighty years; the work is of real value to researchers and serious students. Arrangement and format are similar to *Variety Film Reviews* (entry 895) and entries appear in chronological sequence, beginning with volume 1, which contains obituaries published between 1905 and 1928. Much of the material originated as news stories and editorials as well as obituary listings. All aspects of entertainment are represented through listed personalities, who range from performers to business employees in fields from circus to television. No photographs are included. Volume 11 is an index to the first 10 volumes and completes the initial set covering the years 1905-1986. The work continues with separately indexed volumes on a biennial basis. Volume 12 was issued in 1990 and covers the period 1987-1988, and volume 13 (1992) treats the years 1989-1990.

Jeb H. Perry has authored *Variety Obits: An Index to Obituaries in Variety, 1905-1978* (Scarecrow Press, 1980) for those who have *Variety* on microfilm and need only an index to the material.

555. **Variety Who's Who in Show Business**. Rev. ed. Mike Kaplan, ed. New York: R. R. Bowker, 1989. 412p. ISBN 0-8352-2665-4.

This revised issue represents what amounts to the third edition of this well-established biographical dictionary of show business personalities to update earlier volumes published in 1983 and 1985. The intent is for it to become an annual offering. Included here are biographical data for some 6,500 contemporary major figures, including executives as well as performers in the areas of film, television, music, and theater. Also treated are writers and technicians, along with directors and producers. Personalities are selected for achievement and for influence, with inclusions monitored by *Variety* (entry 871). Only living persons and individuals deceased subsequent to November 30, 1988 are considered. International figures are included for the first time. Information is concise for all entries, with listings of credits accompanying simple identifications.

MUSIC

Music in General

BIBLIOGRAPHIC GUIDES

556. **Baroque Music: A Research and Information Guide**. John H. Baron. New York: Garland, 1993. 587p. (Music Research and Information Guides, v.16; Garland Reference Library of the Humanities, v.871). ISBN 0-8240-4436-3.

To address the needs of specialists, students, performers, and others interested in the Baroque period of Western European music, this bibliographic guide cites some 1,400 books, dissertations, anthologies of essays, and, to a lesser degree, periodical articles on the topic. Defining the Baroque period broadly, scope of coverage ranges from 1580 to 1730, with most entries published between 1960 and 1991. They represent various languages of Western Europe, with emphasis on English and German efforts. All aspects of Baroque music are treated, with publications on the stylistic elements, museums, institutions, and instruments, as well as theoretical and philosophical issues. Annotations vary in length from brief identifications of a few sentences to full-page descriptions. Entries provide cross-references and are indexed separately by subject, name, and author.

557. **Bibliographical Handbook of American Music**. D. W. Krummel. Champaign, IL: University of Illinois Press, 1987. 269p. ISBN 0-252-01450-2.

The guide serves as an annotated bibliography of some 700 bibliographies that are described in depth, and help to define the literature of American music. There are four major sections, each of which is divided into chapters. The major sections are "Chronological Perspectives," bearing major national bibliographies; "Contextual Perspectives," treating bibliographies of regions, ethnic elements, and persons; "Musical Mediums and Genres," with bibliographies of concert, popular, and sacred music; and "Bibliographical Forms," identifying and describing bibliographies of collections and writings about music as well as discographies. Books, articles, dissertations, and databases are covered in this work.

558. **Early American Music: A Research and Information Guide**. James R. Heintze. New York: Garland, 1990. 511p. (Music Research and Information Guides, v.13; Garland Reference Library of the Humanities, v.1007). ISBN 0-8240-4119-4.

As part of the publisher's series, this annotated guide adds another important dimension to the organization and control of literature treating early American music prior to 1820. Books, articles, and dissertations are included, with coverage given to both primary and secondary source material. Included are such diverse items as published sermons, church records, and travelers' accounts, along with secondary descriptive matter. Publication dates run through 1987 and entries are placed within two major sections covering reference works (encyclopedias, dictionaries, bibliographic sources, etc.) and historical studies (general histories, topical writings, biographical sources, etc.). Nearly 2,000 entries are furnished, with annotations varying in length and substance. For the most part, coverage of folk, African-American, and Native American music is limited, because of its treatment in other works. Author-title and subject indexes are supplied.

A complementary work by Heintze is *American Music Studies: A Classified Bibliography of Master's Theses*, published in 1989 by Information Coordinators. This effort supplies nearly 2,400 entries organized in a topical arrangement. This material is purposely omitted in the work previously discussed.

559. Information on Music: A Handbook of Reference Sources in European Languages. Guy A. Marco and Sharon Paugh Ferris. Littleton, CO: Libraries Unlimited, 1975-1984. 3v. ISBN 0-87287-096-0.

Originally planned as an eight-volume work to supplement the coverage of reference and research materials provided by Duckles (entry 561) and others, this important series has apparently been concluded with the publication of volume 3, *Europe*, in 1984. The set begins with volume 1, *Basic and Universal Sources* (1975), which furnishes annotated entries for more than 500 tools in the field of music and related areas. Volume 2 (1977) covers the Americas and annotates more than 800 reference sources relating to music in the Western hemisphere. The final volume on Europe appeared seven years after volume 2, and continued the same tradition of providing citations to numerous sources, including individual encyclopedia articles from *MGG* (entry 609) and *The New Grove* (entry 612). Annotations are for the most part brief but informative, and there are references to additional reviews. Each volume is separately indexed, although volume 2 contains a comprehensive index for volumes 1 and 2. An appendix in volume 3 updates materials in the preceding volumes.

560. Music: A Guide to the Reference Literature. William S. Brockman. Englewood, CO: Libraries Unlimited, 1987. 254p. (Reference Sources in the Humanities Series). ISBN 0-87287-526-1.

Designed to supplement the coverage found in Marco's *Information on Music* (entry 559) and the third edition of Duckles's *Music Reference and Research Materials* (entry 561), Brockman has produced a guide that is useful in its identification of important English-language sources issued over the past fifteen years. There are 841 entries describing both current and retrospective sources and providing a valuable perspective of the major reference and bibliographical sources, bibliographies of music literature, as well as music and discographies. There are sections treating current periodicals, associations, research centers, and other organizations in detailed fashion. Annotations are well constructed and informative and vary in length. Generally, they provide ample description and in some cases, evaluation and comparison. The work has been commended for its excellent selection of items. Access is aided by author-title and subject indexes.

Research Guide to Musicology, by James W. Pruett and Thomas P. Slavens (American Library Association, 1985), is the fourth in a series of literature guides edited and co-authored by Slavens, a professor of library science at the University of Michigan. The first part of the two-part format is by Pruett, a musicologist, who provides a series of survey essays on various subjects relating to music scholarship, elements of musicology, and periods of music history. The surveys close with selective bibliographies listing the important sources of information on the topics described. The final section, by Slavens, is an annotated bibliography of reference tools classified by form or type. Although somewhat narrow in conception, the work is still useful.

561. Music Reference and Research Materials: An Annotated Bibliography. 4th ed. rev. Vincent H. Duckles and Michael A. Keller. New York: Schirmer Books, 1994. 740p. ISBN 0-02-870822-9.

The single most important and popular guide for music students, teachers, and librarians, the fourth edition was thoroughly revised and updated in 1988 after twelve years. The basic format remains unchanged, with arrangement by category of tool such as dictionaries, encyclopedias, catalogs, histories, etc. The work provides bibliographic information and annotations for more than 3,200 different reference books, an increase of 1,300 over the previous issue. With Duckles's death in 1985, Keller, who succeeded him as head of the music library at the University of California at Berkeley (and is now at Yale University), is largely responsible for the fourth edition and its revision and has maintained the standard that made the title an indispensable work for students and specialists. There are indexes of persons, subjects, and titles.

Periodicals

562. **International Music Journals**. Linda M. Fidler and Richard S. James, eds. New York: Greenwood Press, 1990. 544p. (Historical Guides to the World's Periodicals and Newspapers). ISBN 0-313-25004-9.

This well-constructed directory supplies useful listings of some 200 mainstream and specialized periodicals. Selections are based on the popularity and importance of the journals in terms of either historical or contemporary impact. Entries are alphabetically arranged by title, and coverage is given to the history and significance of the journal, along with its physical properties, overview of its content, and critical appraisal. Also provided are bibliographic references and locations of buildings. Some fifty contributors, specialists in the field, supplied the well-developed and informative narratives, as well as the bibliographies. The work opens with a concise account of the origins and development of music journals in the Western world. The appendix contains listings of recent journals and indexing/abstracting journals. Chronological, geographical, and subject lists of journals are furnished, along with a name and title index.

563. **Music and Dance Periodicals: An International Directory & Guidebook**. Doris Robinson. Voorheesville, NY: Peri Press, 1989. 382p. ISBN 0-9617844-4-X.

This is a useful and comprehensive (although not exhaustive) directory of music and dance periodicals and annuals currently available. There are 1,867 entries arranged under 19 broad subject categories and supplying detailed information. Given in each entry, in addition to bibliographic identification, are indication of date of inception, frequency, price, format, types of music covered, number and types of reviews, indexing, advertising, and circulation. Annotations describe such considerations as scope, purpose, and reference features. Various types of serials are included, ranging from fanzines to scholarly journals, but membership directories are omitted. Entries represent publications from more than fifty countries, largely from the Western world, making the directory valuable to a wide variety of users. The work is indexed in thorough fashion, supplying access through five approaches: title, publisher or organization, subject, country, and ISSN.

BIBLIOGRAPHIES AND CATALOGS

564. **African Music: A Pan-African Annotated Bibliography**. Carol Lems-Dworkin. Munich/Providence: Hans Zell/K. G. Saur, 1991. 382p. ISBN 0-905450-91-4.

This useful bibliography is comprehensive in scope, as it treats the entire continent of Africa in identifying more than 1,700 books and articles in a variety of languages (European, African, and Middle-Eastern). Annotations are cogent and provide both descriptive narrative and exposition of the documents. Entries are arranged alphabetically by author and are indexed by subject. Selection of entries is highly selective when contrasted to a complementary tool produced by John Gray.

Gray's *African Music: A Bibliographical Guide to the Traditional Popular Art and Liturgical Musics of Sub-Saharan Africa* (Greenwood Press, 1991) supplies more than 5,800 entries in treating a much smaller segment of the Continent. All types of writing, including newspaper articles and unpublished papers, are identified in this exhaustive work. *Indian Music Literature*, by Mohammed Haroon (Indian Bibliographic Bureau, 1991), supplies 4,000 entries representing scholarly efforts and emphasizes the Hindustani and Carnatic systems. Entries are arranged into types of studies (general, biographical, musicological, etc.). The work is useful for its emphasis on Indian literature as opposed to proportional representation of North American or European publications. The work is not annotated, and there is no subject index.

565. **Bibliography of Black Music.** Dominique-Rene De Lerma. Westport, CT: Greenwood Press, 1981-1984. 4v. (Greenwood Encyclopedia of Black Music). ISBN 0-313-21340-2 (v.1).

There has been a recent emphasis on bibliographic coverage of black music, and this work has earned praise from reviewers for its comprehensive nature and ambitious scope. Volume 1 provides a bibliography of reference works (catalogs, bibliographies, encyclopedias, discographies, iconographies, directories, dissertations, etc.). Especially useful is a listing of nearly 200 periodicals related to the topic. Volume 2 represents the Afro-American idiom and covers general histories, and works on spirituals, ragtime, musical theater, concert music, blues, gospel, popular, and jazz. Volume 3 covers geographical studies, including books, articles, dissertations, essays, etc., on the music of various geographic regions; it furnishes a section on ethnomusicology. Volume 4 covers theory and education and enumerates sources on instrumentation, performance, notation, etc. The arrangement of material over the entire set follows the organization established by *RILM* (entry 577n). Volumes 3 and 4 have indexes.

566. **Dictionary Catalog of the Music Collection.** New York Public Library. Boston: G. K. Hall, 1982- . 45v. ISBN 0-8161-1387-4.

One of the leading collections of both music literature and printed music is presented in this set. The first edition appeared in 1964 and was supplemented in 1973 and 1976. Like its predecessor and similar publications from G. K. Hall, this is a photographic reproduction of the catalog, which offers detailed information on books, pamphlets, essays, periodical articles, and micro-materials as well as scores and librettos. The present edition includes imprints through 1971 and represents more than 3.5 million individual documents. Special strengths of this collection are acknowledged to be in the areas of folk songs, Americana, music periodicals, programs, and various elements of printed music, such as operas, historical editions, vocal music, etc. There is also a annual supplement, entitled *Bibliographic Guide to Music* (entry 573).

Music in the Royal Society of London 1660-1806, by Leta Miller and Albert Cohen (Information Coordinators, 1987), is a catalog of journal reports and manuscripts of this eminent scientific society on the subject of music. Acoustics, the ear and hearing, and various instruments and inventions are among the topics covered.

567. **Doctoral Dissertations in Musicology.** 7th North American ed., 2d International ed. Cecil Adkins and Alis Dickinson, eds. Philadelphia: American Musicological Society, International Musicological Society, 1984. 545p. **Ann. Supp.** 1985- . ISSN 1088-4281; **Second Series. 1990-** . ISSN 1088-6238.

This represents the seventh cumulative edition of combined listings of American and Canadian doctoral dissertations, and the second cumulative listing of international doctoral dissertations. It is a comprehensive bibliography of 6,500 dissertations from all over the world, which superseded its predecessors because of its cumulative nature. Most dissertations are North American (nearly 35 percent); the remainder are products of thirty countries (listed since 1972). Arrangement is by period covered and classified by topical subdivisions. There are references to abstracts in *Dissertation Abstracts* (entry 20) and the *RILM* work (entry 577n). Works-in-progress are identified with asterisks, and there are separate indexes for both subject and author. In 1990, the authors issued the first cumulative edition of what is termed the second series of this work. It is a compact volume of 171 pages providing a cumulation of annual supplements published since 1985.

568. **Ethnomusicology Research: A Select Annotated Bibliography.** Ann Briegleb Schuursma. New York: Garland, 1992. 173p. (Garland Library of Music Ethnology, v.1; Garland Reference Library of the Humanities, v.1136). ISBN 0-8240-5735-X.

This recent effort is designed to complement the coverage given to materials on ethnomusicology in earlier bibliographic sources, *Ethnomusicology* by Jaap Kunst (M. Nijhof, 1959) and Bruno Nettl's *Reference Materials in Ethnomusicology* (Information Coordinators, 1973). Schuursma has produced a useful annotated listing of nearly 470 English-language items published since 1960 and organized into five sections. Sections embrace history of the field, ethnomusicological theory and method, fieldwork method and technique, and musical analysis, as well as influential related fields (anthropology, linguistics, folklore, sociology, and psychology). Entries are arranged alphabetically within each section, with cross-references utilized when they belong under more than a single category. Annotations are brief and descriptive rather than evaluative. Both dance and popular music are excluded from coverage, as each area will be covered in a separate volume. Name and subject indexes supply access.

569. **Medieval Music: The Sixth Liberal Art.** Rev. ed. Andrew Hughes. Toronto: University of Toronto, 1980. 360p. (Toronto Medieval Bibliographies, no. 4). ISBN 0-80202-2358-4.

This edition adds more than 250 citations to the 2,000 or so items covered at the time of initial publication in 1974. These documents are listed separately and receive separate indexing. Classification numbers for these materials are interpolated into the main body of the text by use of cross-references. Indexing is thorough and there is exposition in the text to facilitate the search for subject classifications, which are based on twenty-nine main categories with numerous subcategories (geographical, chronological, individuals, genres, etc.). Essentially a bibliography of books and periodical articles on all aspects of medieval music, this work appeals to the relatively unsophisticated user who needs to find out about the topic. Annotations are brief, and there are separate indexes of authors and subjects.

570. **Music Analyses: An Annotated Guide to the Literature.** Harold J. Diamond. New York: Schirmer Books/Macmillan, 1991. 716p. ISBN 0-02-870110-0.

This is a selective listing of some 4,650 citations issued in books, periodicals, doctoral dissertations, and master's theses. Emphasis is on items that provide critical evaluation or exposition of the structural elements that justify and validate the artistic quality of the musical selections treated. The work seeks to update Diamond's initial effort published eleven years earlier under a slightly different title. The present volume is annotated briefly, with indication of level of complexity of analysis presented. The work is intended for a wide audience from advanced students to laypeople, but is limited to analyses in the English language. Arrangement of entries is alphabetical by title under composer's name, with references to general criticism followed by those for individual works. There is an index of distinctive titles.

571. **Music Theory from Zarlino to Schenker: A Bibliography and Guide.** David Damschroder and David Russell Williams. Stuyvesant, NY: Pendragon Press, 1990. 522p. (Harmonologia Series, no. 4). ISBN 0-918728-99-1.

This is an important work serving both as a bibliography of Western music theory and a guide to important theorists. More than 200 works are covered, with entries treating theorists individually. Entries supply brief but informative essays on their writings, providing exposition of the distinctive and unique elements in their scholarship as well as their fit within groupings of musical theory. The essays are followed by a listing of citations to primary source material that includes translations, then by a listing of related works. The scope of the work actually is greater than the title implies, beginning with Glarean's "Isagogue in Musicen" in the early sixteenth century and ending with an analysis by Schoenberg published posthumously in 1967. Access is provided by cross-references along with a set of four indexes, assuring location of desired information.

572. **Répertoire international des sources musicales/International Inventory of Musical Sources.** Munich: Henle, 1960-1980. 15v. in 27. ISBN 3-7618-0512-8 (ser. A, v.1, pt. 5).

This is a joint effort on the part of the International Musicological Society and the International Association of Music Libraries and is commonly referred to as *RISM*. It is a catalog of all bibliographies of music, writings about music, and textbooks on music published up to 1800, with locations where they can be found identified. More than 1,000 libraries worldwide are cooperating in this venture. The two major series are A, alphabetical, and B, systematic or classified. Series A (followed by volume number in Roman numeral) includes individual editions in circulation from 1500 to 1800, which are arranged alphabetically by composer or editor. Series B (followed by volume number in Roman numeral) arranges the materials chronologically by category or genre, such as "manuscripts of polyphonic music." Bibliographical descriptions are generally given in greater detail in the B section. This large-scale effort has earned the respect of music bibliographers everywhere.

Series C has begun as a continuation of a series of directories of international libraries (entry 617). Progress is constant and volumes continue to appear steadily on a wide variety of themes and topics, from Hebrew notated manuscript sources to ancient Greek music theory.

INDEXES, ABSTRACTS, AND SERIAL BIBLIOGRAPHIES

573. **Bibliographic Guide to Music.** Boston: G. K. Hall, 1975- . Ann. ISSN 0360-2753.

A serial bibliography in its own right, this work serves as an annual supplement to the *Dictionary Catalog of the Music Collection* for the New York Public Library (entry 566). Beginning with coverage of the year 1975, it enumerates all types of music materials (including printed music) cataloged by the library during the period under scrutiny (September through August). Additional cataloging is included through use of MARC tapes from the Library of Congress in the areas of music literature (bibliography, history, criticism, and philosophy of music) and music instruction. The age of materials cataloged in any single year varies considerably, with both recently acquired items and older documents cataloged for the first time. Produced by computer, it serves many purposes, including those of reference, acquisition, and cataloging.

574. **Music, Books on Music, and Sound Recordings.** Washington: National Union Catalog, 1973-1989. Semiann. with ann. cum., quin. cum. ISSN 0041-7793.

As part of the National Union Catalog series, with its quinquennial cumulation, this work represented a reproduction of the catalog cards supplied by the Library of Congress and seven other leading music libraries. It covered music in breadth and identified printed music and recordings as well as books about music and musicians. The recordings are not limited to musical works, but represent a vast range of materials (educational, literary, political, etc.). It superseded *Library of Congress Catalog: Music and Phono-records* (Library of Congress, 1953-1972), which appeared semiannually but was limited to entries from LC printed cards. The effort ceased with the 1989 volume, and presently is continued as a microfiche publication, *Music Catalog (Washington, D.C.).* It remains an important serial publication for reference, cataloging, and acquisition purposes.

*575. **The Music Index.** Warren, MI: Harmonie Park Press, 1949- . Mo. with ann. cum. ISSN 0027-4348.

This is the major indexing service for music literature and covers approximately 350 periodicals worldwide, some of which are indexed selectively. Indexing is by author and subject and the work surveys the world of music in comprehensive manner, from musicology to the music industry. Obituaries, reviews of recordings, and book reviews are included. Music reviews are listed under name of performer. The major problem with the print version has always been its tardiness of appearance, with annual cumulations several years behind and monthlies delayed about six months. Recently, however, the publisher has worked to alleviate the problem.

A cumulated index, *The Music Index: A Subject-Author Guide to Music Periodical Literature. 1987-1988* was issued in 1990. The work is well developed, with indexing covering all aspects of the music world, from popular to classical. It is anticipated that the biennial index will become a valuable resource. *Music Index on CD-ROM* has been available since 1991 through Chadwyck-Healey and Harmonie Park Press. It is updated on an annual basis, combining the print editions from 1981 on into a single database easily searched by its users. The 1992 issue covers the period 1981-1989.

576. **Music Library Association. Notes.** Philadelphia: Music Library Association, 1934- . Q. ISSN 0027-4380.

The leading periodical for music librarians is the official publication of the Association. From 1934 to 1942, frequency was somewhat irregular and the publication was suspended during 1939. Since 1943, it has appeared on a quarterly basis and continues to provide excellent comprehensive listings of recently published books and a section of excellent book reviews. Music scores are also identified and reviewed. There is an index to recordings which identifies reviews in other periodicals, and includes both tapes and discs. This is arranged alphabetically by name of composer and provides a list of references which are rated in accordance with the judgment given by the reviewer, similar to what is done in *Book Review Digest* (H. W. Wilson, 1905-). There is also a listing of current music publishers' catalogs and frequent reviews of new music periodicals.

577. **Music Literature International.** New York: International RILM Center, 1967- . Ann. ISSN 0889-6607.

This was formerly known as *RILM Abstracts of Music Literature* and was issued on a quarterly basis. RILM is an acronym for the Center's former name in French (Repertoire International de la Litterature Musicale). Now, as an annual, it is still regarded as a major contribution to the field of music bibliography. It provides abstracts of articles (both in books and periodicals), books, reviews, dissertations, iconographies, catalogs, etc., in the field of music. More than 300 journals in forty-three languages are treated. Each issue is indexed by author and subject, with the fourth issue a cumulative work to the three preceding numbers in the volume. Abstracts are signed and include identification of keywords for purposes of indexing. There are various major divisions, including reference materials, collected writings, ethnomusicology, instruments, etc. It is available online from DIALOG and has a file size of 100,000 items, covering the period 1971-1983 with periodic updating. The CD-ROM version is now known as *MUSE (MUsic SEarch) 1970-1984*. It is available from National Information Services Corporation; the next update will bring the coverage to 1970-1988.

PRINTED MUSIC SOURCES—BIBLIOGRAPHIES, INDEXES, AND CATALOGS

578. **American Music Before 1865 in Print and on Records: A Biblio-Discography.** Rev. ed. James R. Heintze. New York: Institute for Studies in American Music, Brooklyn College, 1990. 248p. (Institute for Studies in American Music Monographs, no. 30). ISBN 0-914678-33-7.

This is a revision and expansion of the useful classified and annotated bibliography of American music issued for the Bicentennial. It lists music originally printed prior to 1865, some of which is still available for purchase through normal channels. Additionally, there is a discography of LPs issued up to 1987. The useful features have been retained and include a segment on music in performing editions, which lists works containing the music as it was conceived by its composers. Another segment on facsimile reprints includes references to music unavailable in other editions. Purchasing information is furnished along with series identification and content of anthologies. It is a reliable and well-constructed work now made more valuable by its more than 1,300 entries, which almost double its previous coverage. Access is aided by an excellent index; the work remains an important choice for reference departments.

579. **Anthologies of Music: An Annotated Index.** 2d ed. Sterling E. Murray. Warren, MI: Harmonie Park Press, 1992. 215p. (Detroit Studies in Music Bibliography, no. 68). ISBN 0-89990-061-5.

The initial edition began as a project for Murray's class and represented a useful pedagogical tool, as it indexed the contents of about forty historical anthologies of musical examples. The second edition indexes some 4,670 pieces (as compared to the previous 3,560) in 66 anthologies. Coverage is given to more than sixty composers (forty in the first edition).

These anthologies are organized chronologically and supply either complete movements or total compositions for music students. They are generally available through college libraries. Selections are arranged alphabetically by title under the composer's name. Entries vary in length and furnish general location information along with additional information of text translations, available recordings, partial signatures, and more. In general, selection of anthologies cannot be faulted and the practical value of the *Index* is evident. A useful feature is the genre index at the end of the work that classifies the entries into correct genres.

580. **A Basic Music Library: Essential Scores and Books.** 2d ed. Pauline Shaw Bayne and Robert Michael Fling, eds. Chicago: American Library Association, 1983. 357p. ISBN 0-8389-0375-4 (pbk).

Originally published in 1978, this work has gained an enviable reputation among music librarians for its excellent coverage of materials useful to a music collection. As such, it represents a good collection development aid as well as reference tool. Designed to provide librarians in small and medium-sized libraries with a selective list of music materials, its coverage includes lists of anthologies of scores, study scores, performing editions, vocal scores, instrumental methods, and studies, as well as music literature consisting of reference books, biographies, periodicals, etc. This edition is an extensive revision of the earlier effort and furnishes a selective listing of music dealers in the appendix. The index is well constructed and provides easy access to material within.

581. **The Book of World-Famous Music, Classical, Popular and Folk.** 3d ed. rev. and enl. James M. Fuld. New York: Dover, 1985. 714p. ISBN 0-486-24857-7 (pbk).

First published in 1966, this work has been a favorite of reference librarians since it first became available. Now in its third edition, it traces the development of 1,300 popular melodies back to their original sources. Included are the various types of music mentioned in the title, along with identification of original singers and interesting commentary. The new edition is essentially a reprint of previous works, but with a supplementary section containing new information and corrections to entries in the main text. Entries provide symbols as cross-references to the supplement for revisions. The work thus has the same scope and remains a listing of musical compositions, both vocal and instrumental, written over a period of 500 years. Arrangement of entries is by title; incipits or opening bars are provided, as are opening words for the vocal compositions. Entries include identification of the earliest publication and information regarding its use and performance. Much of this information is chatty and much is important, such as biographical notes on composers, but all is interesting.

Music and War: A Research and Information Guide, by Ben Arnold (Garland, 1993), is a specialized bibliography identifying relevant art music concerning war developed within the Western tradition. The work is divided into eight chapters, four of which treat music (wars) of the twentieth century. Chapters supply a detailed essay along with annotated listings of selected works and unannotated supplementary listings. Inclusion is appropriate and both familiar and lesser known music is treated.

582. **The Catalogue of Printed Music in the British Library to 1980.** Laureen Baillie and Robert Malchin, eds. New York: Saur, 1981-1986. 62v. ISBN 0-851-57900-0. UK: Bowker-Saur, 1987. ISBN 0-86291-300-4.

Although this set represents a costly investment, it is a vast resource that provides access to about 1 million entries previously found in an array of bibliographic tools utilized by the *British Catalog of Music (BCM)* (slip catalog, accession lists, Royal Music Library catalog, and a catalog of music published between 1503 and 1800). Much of the inconsistency and diversity of cataloging styles has been ameliorated through the computerization process. Of interest to those primarily concerned with printed music is the fact that this tool has a much higher proportion of this material when compared to the New York Public Library's *Dictionary Catalog of the Music Collection* (entry 566). Entries are found under composers' names or under form headings, such as "Songs," in which individual titles are identified.

Two computerized products update this coverage. *Catalogue of Printed Music in the British Library to 1990* is available on CD-ROM through Bowker. It provides many search options, such as composer, title, keyword, arranger, publisher, etc. *British Library Catalogue: Music Library* continues the coverage of the print set by providing both online and CD-ROM access to the *British Catalogue of Music*, a monthly publication listing both popular and classical music scores published in the United Kingdom. The period covered by the computerized source is 1980-1988. Another recent work is *The Catalogue of Music in the Bath Reference Library to 1985*, by Jon A. Gillaspie (Saur, 1986, 4v.), which furnishes a listing of manuscripts and related items. Because Bath served as a center for the performance of music during the eighteenth and nineteenth centuries, the work provides a panorama of musical history.

583. Chamber Music: An International Guide to Works and Their Instrumentation. Victor Rangel-Ribeiro and Robert Markel. New York: Facts on File, 1993. 271p. ISBN 0-8160-2296-8.

Considered to be a practical and up-to-date guide to the repertory of chamber music, this useful tool supplies 8,000 citations to musical works for a variety of instrumental combinations ranging from three to twenty performers. The work is divided into three major segments, the first of which treats composers up to the time of Haydn and Mozart. The second segment covers composers from Beethoven to the present day. The third part supplies an index to combinations of instruments required in the pieces identified. Both vocal and instrumental pieces are included. Entries are well constructed and provide exposition and description of year of composition, duration, and publication elements. Utilizing a grid format, information on alternate scoring is supplied, making it a well-rounded and useful source.

584. Handbook of Early American Sheet Music 1768-1889. Harry Dichter and Elliott Shapiro. New York: Dover, 1977. 287p. ISBN 0-486-23364-2.

This is essentially a reprint of a work published in 1941, with some revision and modification. It was designed to provide an awareness of the more important and more interesting music of a bygone era which is still in existence today, rather than a complete history of every piece of sheet music from that time period. There are three major segments of the publication. The first is the most important, as it lists both vocal and instrumental works in a classified arrangement under headings such as "Music of the American Revolution" and "Uncle Tom's Cabin." These headings are grouped into time periods and organized chronologically. Entries include title, publisher, date, names of individuals associated with the work or for whom it was written, composer, number of pages, first line of the song, and description of cover illustrations and references to plate mark numbers. There are seventy-six reproductions of cover illustrations. The second part provides a directory of publishers, whereas part 3 enumerates lithographers and artists working on American sheet music prior to 1870.

585. Historical Sets, Collected Editions, and Monuments of Music: A Guide to Their Contents. 3d ed. Anna Harriet Heyer. Chicago: American Library Association, 1980. 2v. ISBN 0-8389-0288-X.

First published in 1957, this standard work for music libraries now identifies more than 1,300 sets and collections of music published in the Western world up to 1980. This is a substantial increase over the second edition, which included 900 sets, primarily due to the increased publication of scholarly editions of music over the past two decades. There is an attempt to provide comprehensive coverage of nineteenth- and twentieth-century sets, thus making this an excellent tool for scholars in locating scores. The main part is alphabetical by composer and indicates contents volume-by-volume of these sets and editions, with complete bibliographical information.

Another important work is Sydney Robinson Charles's *A Handbook of Music and Music Literature in Sets and Series* (Free Press, 1972), which treats collected works and major sets as well as monographs and periodicals in series.

*586.   **The Music Cataloging Collection.** Dublin, OH: OCLC, 1991- . Q. (CD-ROM).

For the past few years, the bibliographic records for musical scores and sound recordings in the OCLC Online Union Catalog have been available in CD-ROM format on a quarterly basis. This is of great value to music librarians in their endeavor to stay abreast of collection development in an elusive area of concern. The *LC Authorities Collection* is included automatically with the purchase. The CD-ROM format has become increasingly popular for both new editions of standard information tools and for serial offerings of bibliographic sources. With the enormous cataloging database at OCLC, this resource is proving to be a wise selection. It is issued on two discs each quarter and provides full cataloging data for bibliographic identification.

587.   **Music Library Association Catalog of Cards for Printed Music, 1953-1972: A Supplement to the Library of Congress Catalogs.** Elizabeth H. Olmsted, ed. Totowa, NJ: Rowman and Littlefield, 1974. 2v. ISBN 0-87471-474-5.

The title provides an indication of the content of this work, which was four years in the making under the sponsorship of the Music Library Association, aided by numerous volunteers. What Olmstead (the music librarian at Oberlin) and her fellow workers have done is to identify 30,000 entries of music cataloging which had been submitted to the Library of Congress by cooperating libraries but for some reason had not been entered into the *National Union Catalog*. The volunteers did a good job of editing to provide at least some conformity to acceptable standards of the Library of Congress, although there is some unevenness among the entries. Most deficient is the poor quality of reproduction, with some entries virtually unreadable. Although it serves partially as a supplement to the *Library of Congress Catalog: Music and Phonorecords* (entry 574n), this does not identify the libraries responsible for the cataloging except for New York Public and Harvard University.

LC MARC: Music is an online database available from the Library of Congress, which furnishes bibliographic coverage of monographs of printed and manuscript music as well as nonmusic sound recordings cataloged by the Library from 1984 to the present. It is also available on CD-ROM as part of the Current Cataloging Database project. Updates are provided every month.

588.   **Music-in-Print Series.** Philadelphia: Musicdata, 1974- . Irreg. **Supp.**, 1979- . Ann; also irreg. specialized supps. ISSN 0146-7883.

Corresponding somewhat to *Books in Print* (Bowker, 1948-) are these much-needed listings of available music in print. Individual volumes cover different types of music, both vocal and instrumental, and are compiled from publishers' catalogs in order to provide a continuous record of music available to the performer, instructor, and student. There are seven volumes to date; each is supplemented every few years. Volume 1 covers sacred choral music (2d ed., 1985; supps. 1988, 1992); volume 2, secular choral music (2d ed., 1987; supps. 1991, 1993); volume 3, organ music (2d ed., 1984; supp., 1990); volume 4, classical vocal music (1976; supp., 1985); volume 5, orchestral music (1979; supp., 1983); volume 6, string music (2d ed., 1980; supp., 1984); and volume 7, classical guitar music (1989). An arranger index was begun in 1987; as were a master composer index in 1989, a master title index in 1990, and a master index to both types of choral music in 1991. The continuous record is maintained through these new editions and specialized supplements, as well as a general annual supplement to the whole set. Thousands of pieces have been identified from nearly 1,000 different publishers worldwide. Entries provide title, composer, arranger, instrumentation, and publisher.

Vocal Music

589. **American Oratorios and Cantatas: A Catalog of Works Written in the United States from Colonial Times to 1985.** Thurston J. Dox, comp. Metuchen, NJ: Scarecrow Press, 1986. 2v. ISBN 0-8108-1861-2

This is a work of major proportions and one that was needed by reference librarians, as it identifies 3,450 choral pieces that span the history of our country from its beginnings to the present day. Dox is a professor of music at Hartwick College and used his expertise to construct a tool that received plaudits for both its organization and its detail. There are four sections, beginning with oratorios, followed by choral cantatas, ensemble cantatas, and choral theater. Entries provide publication information, locations for both published and unpublished items, performance requirements, text (source), length, and number of movements. Some annotations are given, as is commentary from composers and critics.

590. **Choral Music Reviews Index, 1983-1985.** Avery T. Sharp. New York: Garland, 1986. 260p. (Garland Reference Library of the Humanities, v.674). ISBN 0-8240-8553-1.

This is a useful source of recent reviews of more than 2,000 pieces of choral music in sixteen English-language journals for a three-year period. Most of the works are Christian sacred hymns, making it especially valuable for religion collections, choir directors, and choir members. The secular music listed is generally intended for schools, and therefore of interest to school libraries and music instructors. Arrangement of entries falls under three main categories—octavos (single compositions), collections, and extended choral works (liturgy, oratories, etc.)—and is alphabetical by title. Entries include titles, composers, arrangers or editors, performers, publishers, vocal ranges, and languages, as well as commentary on accompaniment and use. Separate indexes are furnished for composer, arranger, editor, use, level of group, instrumentation, and voicing.

Sharp has continued his work with *Choral Music Reviews Index II 1986-1988* (Garland, 1990) which follows the same format and indexes fourteen journals. Although there are two fewer journals, the total number of entries has increased substantially.

591. **Musical Settings of American Poetry: A Bibliography**. Michael Hovland. Westport, CT: Greenwood Press, 1986. 531p. (Music Reference Collection, no. 8). ISBN 0-313-22938-4.

Of interest to students of both music and literature is this important source of information that serves as a guide to musical settings of American poetry. Included here are some 5,800 musical settings of 2,400 poems by nearly 100 American writers. The art songs and choral literature represent the efforts of some 2,000 composers. Only published music is listed (both commercial and private), along with recorded music and music in facsimile form. Arrangement is by poet, subdivided by title of poem. Included in the entries are indications of publication information, voice specifications, accompaniment, and collection that contains the song. Information is given on the poet in terms of dates, and for some entries, library holdings are given along with notes of discographies. Access is provided by both a composer index, which supplies dates and names of the poets, and an index of literary titles.

592. **Vocal Chamber Music: A Performer's Guide.** Kay Dunlap and Barbara Winchester. New York: Garland, 1985. 140p. (Garland Reference Library of the Humanities, v.465). ISBN 0-8240-9003-9.

A recent work that has proved to be of value in music libraries, this guide defines *vocal chamber music* as composition for one voice and one instrument (other than keyboard or guitar) up to a dozen solo voices and twelve solo instruments. Compositions for solo voices and chorus also are given when no instrumentation is needed. Works included over 300 years, dating from 1650 to 1980, and generally are available for purchase, making this a practical listing for the music instructor. Entries provide composer, title, publisher, and scoring. There are an index to publishers or collections and one to voice type. Unfortunately, there is no index to instruments identified.

Instrumental Music

593. **Guide to the Pianist's Repertoire.** 2d ed. rev. and enl. Maurice Hinson. Bloomington, IN: Indiana University Press, 1987. 856p. ISBN 0-253-32656-7.

Fourteen years after the initial effort, the second edition of this useful and important title was issued in an enlarged form. Known for its extensive coverage of composers and their works in the past, the new edition assures continued recognition in this regard. Hundreds of composers from countries all over the world are listed and their compositions enumerated. Works have been graded for each composer, and related bibliographic entries of books and periodical articles have been integrated into the main body of the work. The general bibliography includes books, articles, and dissertations, and the appendices include a useful directory of publishers. Several indexes to composers and others conclude the work.

594. **Guitar and Lute Music in Periodicals: An Index.** Dorman H. Smith and Laurie Eagleson. Berkeley, CA: Fallen Leaf Press, 1990. 104p. (Fallen Leaf Reference Books in Music, no. 13). ISBN 0-914913-16-6.

Generally, specialized music periodicals issue supplements that carry original compositions, which then become somewhat fugitive and difficult to retrieve even if the periodicals are covered in *Music Index* (entry 575). This tool indexes the musical compositions appearing in six periodicals devoted to the lute or guitar, three of which have not been treated in *Music Index*. They vary considerably in longevity from the short-lived *Chelys* (1976-1977), *Electric Chelys* (1977-1978), and *Guitar and Lute* (1974-1983), to the still-current *Lute Society of America Journal* (1968-), *Lute Society of America Newsletter* (1966-), and *Guitar Review* (1946-). Cut-off date is December 1988 for the continuing publications, resulting in a listing of 780 musical pieces. Arrangement is under four categories: composer, title, medium, and source/arranger. Entries under composer are full and supply information regarding notation, format, and presentation.

595. **Instrumental Music Printed Before 1600: A Bibliography.** Howard Mayer Brown. Cambridge, MA: Harvard University Press, 1965. 559p. ISBN 0-674-45610-6.

This scholarly work attempts to include all known publications in the field prior to 1600, beginning with the period of the 1480s, shortly after the development of the printing press. Arrangement is chronological, and under each year publications are listed alphabetically by author or publisher. The contents are described and references are provided to modern editions which contain the entries. Much of the music included has been lost or was never published, making the work of great value to music historians. Vocal music is included only if it contained instrumental parts or segments. Although the work has been criticized for omissions (the inevitable challenge to an all-encompassing bibliography), Brown has succeeded in providing a work admired by those it was designed to serve.

596. **Music for Oboe, 1650-1800: A Bibliography.** 2d ed. rev. and exp. Bruce Haynes. Berkeley, CA: Fallen Leaf Press, 1992. 432p. (Fallen Leaf Reference Books in Music, 16). ISBN 0-914913-15-8.

This specialized bibliography of Baroque oboe music was developed by a scholar/performer with the purpose of treating every solo and chamber piece that was intended to be played by that instrument. The oboe has been broadly interpreted to include the English horn and certain variant forms. Within the 3,000 entries are included some 10,000 musical pieces. Entries are arranged alphabetically by name of composer and coded for instrumentation. Enhancing its utility for scholarship is coverage given to national origin and information furnished with respect to manuscripts, original publications, library locations, and contemporary editions. The first edition of this work was issued in 1985, and the second issue represents a more expansive approach in terms of supplying greater detail and refined treatment of the entries.

597. **Organ Literature: A Comprehensive Survey.** 2d ed. Corliss Richard Arnold. Metuchen, NJ: Scarecrow Press, 1984. 2v. ISBN 0-8108-1662-8 (v.1); 0-8108-1663-6 (v.2).

The initial edition was issued as a single volume in 1973. It was organized into two major parts treating (1) the historical survey and (2) the biographical catalog. The new edition simply represents the first part, with slight modification of tables but no updating of chapter bibliographies or text, as volume 1. Volume 2, however, represents a revised and expanded dictionary of composers and their works (originally part 2). Volume 1 offers a chronological overview of the various periods of musical history and development of the organ and its music. Chapters cover different periods and developments and conclude with bibliographies. The biographical catalog (now volume 2) has doubled in size and presents a detailed but not exhaustive listing of individual works and anthologies under the composer's name. This source is excellent in terms of its inclusion of the primary literature, although certain entries may be faulted for omissions.

Harpsichord and Clavichord Music of the Twentieth Century, by Frances Bedford (Fallen Leaf Press, 1993), supplies listings of about 5,600 compositions by 2,700 composers. Like others in the Fallen Leaf line, there is hope that such a compilation will inspire renewed interest in study and performance of the instruments. The first section treats harpsichord music and the second covers the literature of the clavichord. Appendices supply directories of composers and of publishers, music centers, and libraries. Various indexes assure access.

598. **Subject Guide to Classical Instrumental Music.** Jennifer Goodenberger. Metuchen, NJ: Scarecrow Press, 1989. 163p. ISBN 0-8108-2209-1.

This guide provides educators and radio, television, and film production people with a handy and convenient index to classical instrumental music classified by topic or subject, such as "wind," "occupations," and "Shakespeare." Subject headings are conceived by the author and lack the uniformity of a standard thesaurus, but appear to be functional. Entries provide composer's name and dates, title and nickname of composition, along with opus number, translation, and type. Goodenberger's experience as a radio programmer enabled her to select a core body of instrumental music primarily from the nineteenth century. Operas are included when it is felt that they have a central theme. Selection criteria are unclear, as there are many omissions of appropriate musical pieces under the 200 nonmusical subject headings chosen. Availability is a major factor, because entries are thought to be accessible as recordings in libraries and stores. The work suffers somewhat from the lack of a composer index.

THEMATIC CATALOGS AND ANTHOLOGIES

Thematic catalogs are those highly specialized reference tools used by musicologists and trained music librarians to identify compositions. They provide listing of incipits (beginnings or opening bars up to twelve notes). An important contribution to music reference since their initial appearance in the eighteenth century, they are developed on a variety of subjects (single composer, form, style, historical period, or school). Only a few are given here, along with a few anthologies of musical compositions, for which the numbers are legion.

599. **Dictionary of Musical Themes.** Rev. ed. Harold A. Barlow and Sam Morgenstern. New York: Crown, 1975. Repr., London: Faber, 1983. 642p. ISBN 0-571-11998-0.

Called by Sheehy and others the "Bartlett" for musical themes, this has been a vital work which evolved from Barlow's earlier efforts in the 1940s and subsequent years. The first few notes from 10,000 themes of instrumental music are listed (rather than the notation from the initial lines most typical of thematic catalogs). Arrangement is by composer, followed by titles. The notation index is what makes this work a useful identification source, because it arranges the themes alphabetically by notation after having transposed them to the key of C. The tune or melody of the theme can be played on a keyboard or vocalized for ready identification. An index of titles provides easy access if a title is known and one wishes to check its theme. There is a companion volume, *Dictionary of Opera and Song Themes* ... (entry 600).

600. Dictionary of Opera and Song Themes, Including Cantatas, Oratorios, Lieder, and Art Songs. Rev. ed. Harold A. Barlow and Sam Morgenstern. New York: Crown, 1976. 547p. ISBN 0-517-52503-8.

Originally published in 1950 under a different title, this is a companion work or complementary volume to *Dictionary of Musical Themes* (entry 599). Over time, it has changed only slightly except for the title. It lists notations from themes of vocal composition of all types (operas, oratorios, cantatas, art songs, and miscellaneous vocal works). Its basic approach and format are similar to *Dictionary of Musical Themes*, and the initial notes of some 8,000 themes are enumerated alphabetically by composer, then by title of work. Opera themes are identified by act and scene and words are included with the musical bars. The notation index is similar to that of the companion volume, with transposition to the key of C and alphabetical arrangement of notes. There are also indexes of first lines and of songs.

601. National Anthems of the World. 8th ed. W. L. Reed and M. J. Bristow, eds. New York: Blandford Press; distr., Sterling, 1993. 561p. ISBN 0-3043-4218-1.

This is a new edition of this anthology or collection of both music and words of the national anthems of various nations. A new edition generally appears about every five years, although necessity dictates change, as in the case of the seventh edition which was issued only two years after the sixth. During that time there were changes in lyrics, vocal scores, and even language for twenty-five countries. In the past it has not only documented such changes, but also has introduced the anthems of newly created countries. Generally, both words and music are included, with the language in the original text. English translations are furnished, and both authors of texts and composers are identified. In addition, there are brief historical descriptions which include the dates that the works were officially designated as national anthems. More than 170 nations are represented in alphabetical order.

602. Thematic Catalogues in Music: An Annotated Bibliography. Barry S. Brook. New York: Pendragon Press, 1972. 347p. ISBN 0-918728-02-9.

Barry Brook of New York University has been one of the most respected names in music bibliography and has been one of the influential figures in the creation of *RILM Abstracts* ... (entry 577n). This work received excellent reviews and was warmly received by music librarians. Essentially, it is a bibliography of thematic catalogs, which have been the most useful and at the same time the least controlled category of reference tool. This is a listing of 1,450 such catalogs, many of which were unpublished or in process at the time of publication of Brook's work. It is without a doubt the most comprehensive source of its kind, and supersedes earlier, less-detailed efforts. It is of inestimable importance to the music librarian, with its full bibliographic descriptions and references to related works. There is a good exposition on thematic catalogs, as well as an index of subjects and authors at the end.

DICTIONARIES, ENCYCLOPEDIAS, AND HANDBOOKS

603. Dictionary of Terms in Music: English-German, German-English. Worterbuch Musik. 4th ed. Horst Leuchtmann, ed. Munich/New Providence, NJ: K. G. Saur, 1992. 411p. ISBN 3-598-10913-X.

The third edition of this bilingual music dictionary was published in 1981, continuing in the style and format of the earlier issues. It has been regarded as a useful tool for those seeking a bridge to link English and German terminology, and the fourth edition continues the tradition. There is about a 10 percent increase in size and number of entries, with slight format changes including the use of columnar display. The dictionary opens, as did its predecessors, with a preface and instructions for users that remain unchanged—evidence of careless editing because some of the features mentioned are no longer incorporated in the present text. The English segment is treated first, followed by the section on German terminology. A special feature is the listing of musical works in both languages at the end; these contain references to the form in the other language.

604. **Encyclopedia of Music in Canada.** 2d ed. Helmut Kallman et al., eds. Buffalo, NY: University of Toronto Press, 1992. 1524p. ISBN 0-8020-2881-0.

This is a timely expansion of what had already been the largest, most comprehensive, and most detailed reference source on Canadian music. The initial edition was published in 1981 and received a warm reception from both reviewers and librarians. The new issue continues to fulfill its purpose to describe music in Canada and to help define the country's musical relations with the rest of the world. There are several thousand entries, with numerous and extensive survey-type articles on such topics as ethnomusicology. Biographies are provided which include living persons as well as those deceased. Music of all types is treated, although the emphasis is on art music. Performing groups, institutions, organizations, manufacturers, and musical compositions are covered as well. There are many cross-references and bibliographies as well as discographies. An interesting feature is the index of persons, places, and things that did not receive a separate entry.

605. **Encyclopedia of Recorded Sound in the United States.** Guy A. Marco and Frank Andrews, eds. New York: Garland, 1993. (Garland Reference Library of the Humanities, v.936). ISBN 0-8240-4782-6.

In what represents a unique effort, the editors have created a compendium of information on the recording industry in this country from its beginnings with the Edison cylinders to the CD era today. All related aspects and topics are treated with entries on companies, organizations, personalities, societies and associations, sound archives and libraries, laws, technologies, issues, etc. As its title indicates, the primary focus is recorded sound in the United States, but some coverage is given to Canada, Europe, Australia, and New Zealand. The major emphasis is on the two early periods relevant to the 78-rpm era (1877-1948) and to the LP era (1949-1982). Entries are written by the editors and contributor-specialists; a board of experts reviewed and approved them. Illustrations accompany the entries. A bibliography is provided, and a subject-person index is provided.

606. **The Guinness Book of Music.** 4th ed. Robert Dearling and Celia Dearling. London: Guinness Books, 1990. 256p. ISBN 0-85112-363-5.

This is a revised and somewhat expanded edition of the author's earlier volume (1986). Like other works from Guinness, this is a highly readable and interesting survey designed both to appeal and to enlighten. There is a topical arrangement beginning with instruments of the orchestra, followed by non-European instruments. The typical Guinness touch is seen in the listings and approaches provided for the various topics, such as groupings of composers who lived to be ninety, those who had the same last name, and those who committed suicide. Various chronologies are included, such as one on vocal music and another on instrumental music. There is even a chapter on keys that lists popular works by their respective keys. There are name and instrument indexes.

607. **The International Cyclopedia of Music and Musicians.** 11th ed. Oscar Thompson, ed. New York: Dodd, Mead, 1985. 2609p. ISBN 0-396-08412-5.

This is regarded as one of the most comprehensive one-volume reference books in the field and has maintained this reputation since its initial appearance 1939. It is a useful source of information, providing brief articles but also some lengthier survey-type essays. It gives accurate and reliable data on a variety of topics, issues, individuals, and developments. Included are entries on music history, criticism, folk music, opera, compositions, etc. Extensive articles are signed by contributors, many of whom are known scholars of the subject. Biographical coverage of composers is excellent and the narratives are accompanied by calendars of their lives and a listing of their works. The new edition contains an addendum of nearly 100 pages recording the developments in music from 1975 to the present. It adds significant bits of information to entries from the main text as well as entirely new entries on individuals, topics, and organizations.

608. **The Musical Woman: An International Perspective.** Judith Lang Zaimont et al., eds. Westport, CT: Greenwood Press, 1984- . v.1-3. ISSN 0737-0032.

This is designed as a continuing series targeting women's achievements in music. Volume 1 covers the year 1983 and volume 2 treats events and happenings in 1984 and 1985. The most recent volume, issued in 1991, is the most comprehensive and suggests future continuation on a quinquennial basis with its coverage of 1986-1990. Volumes are divided into two principal segments; the first identifies performances, awards, festivals, commissions, recordings, films, books, and more for the period of time covered. The second consists of a series of essays by different authors on a variety of subjects. The 1986-1990 volume contains nineteen such articles under such topical headings as "The Music Profession" and "Music Education." There is value in the mixture of information offered both within the unique listings of part 1 and in the variety of topics treated in part 2. A general index is furnished.

609. **Die Musik in Geschichte und Gegenwart.** Kassel, Germany: Barenreiter-Verlag, 1949-1986; repr. 1989. 17v. ISBN 3-423-05913-3.

Known by all who are involved in any way with music reference, the *MGG*, edited by Friedrich Blume, is considered the most scholarly and comprehensive work of its kind. Not until publication of the *New Grove Dictionary ...* (entry 612) was there anything even approaching it in the English language. The work is international in scope and the product of a team of experts who contributed signed articles covering individuals and compositions. Serious music is covered in depth and popular elements are treated more concisely. There are extensive bibliographical notes and numerous illustrations. A product of nineteen years of labor, the alphabetical arrangement is covered in volumes 1-14. More recently, the supplements have been issued in volumes 15-16, also covering the entire alphabet. The valuable index was recently published as volume 17; it provides access to more than 330,000 names and terms.

Soon to appear from Garland is a planned ten-volume musical encyclopedia with emphasis on ethnomusicological treatment. *Garland Encyclopedia of World Music* is edited by Timothy Rice and James Porter and will supply individual volumes on the major areas of the globe such as Europe, Africa, regional segments of Asia, the Middle East, the Pacific, North America, and Latin America. Each volume will provide an overview of music in the region along with treatment of musical issues and music of the cultures or nations. The final volume will examine global perspectives and furnish a cumulative index.

610. **The New American Dictionary of Music.** Philip D. Morehead and Anne MacNeil. New York: E. P. Dutton, 1991. 608p. ISBN 0-525-93345-X. Repr., New York: Meridian, 1992. ISBN 0-452-01100-0 (pbk).

Recognized for its great scope of coverage, this handy dictionary supplies information on personalities, events, terms, concepts, instruments, etc. All periods and forms of music are covered, from early to contemporary and from popular to classical. Entries are generally quite brief, although there is lengthier coverage of especially important topics. Translations are given for foreign terms; there is a glossary of terms in English, French, German, and Italian. There are some illustrations of musical instruments and musical examples. It is a useful source for quick identification. The reprint version was renamed *The New International Dictionary of Music*.

The New College Encyclopedia of Music, edited by J. A. Westrup and F. L. Harrison (Norton, 1981), basically is a reprint in paperback of the 1976 edition, which had been revised by Conrad Wilson. A British work, it was first published in this country in 1960. It has earned an excellent reputation as a useful reference source emphasizing the coverage of major contemporary figures and their work. It contains about 6,000 entries on a variety of topics, including composers, musical instruments, genres, operas, performers, etc. Terms are defined in a clear and concise manner, and there are illustrations to accompany a good proportion of the entries. Short bibliographies are furnished with some of the descriptions given. Although there are notable omissions of some popular American figures, the work is successful in providing a useful resource for nonscholarly interests.

611. **The New Grove Dictionary of American Music.** H. Wiley Hitchcock and Stanley Sadie. New York: Grove's Dictionaries of Music, 1987; repr. 1992. 4v. ISBN 0-943818-36-2.

This is the most recent effort to be published in the Grove's series, and, like the major twenty-volume publication (entry 612), it has earned the respect of those who minister to the information needs of both scholars and nonspecialists. With four volumes, it is by far the most comprehensive and detailed work on the subject and provides good expositions, descriptions, and identifications of both personalities and subjects in the realm of American music. Known to music librarians as "Amerigrove," it describes the whole range of American musical culture, from acid rock to serious concert music, and, naturally, embraces grand opera as well as country and western contributions. There are 2,500 entries, two-thirds of which are biographical. Articles vary in length from 200 to 10,000 words depending upon the importance of the subject.

612. **The New Grove Dictionary of Music and Musicians.** Stanley Sadie, ed. London: Macmillan; Washington, DC: Grove's Dictionaries of Music, 1980; repr. with minor corrections, 1993. 20v. ISBN 0-33-323111-2.

Possibly the single most valuable title in the reference department, this multivolume tool has had a distinguished history in terms of its recognized quality. A British work first published at the turn of the century, it has continued to grow in stature with each succeeding edition. The most recent issue is basically a reprint with minor corrections of the monumental 1980 publication, which made it the closest competitor to the *MGG* (entry 609) in depth and comprehensiveness. Its coverage is timely and authoritative, with about 23,000 articles, 8,000 cross-references, 3,000 illustrations, and 17,000 biographies of all types of personalities associated with music. This is a masterful publication which is useful to both specialists and nonspecialists and has succeeded in providing an international perspective through purposeful elimination of its former British bias. Arrangement is alphabetical and articles are signed by their distinguished authors, with more Americans than Britons serving as contributors. Definitely an outstanding item and a must for the music library collection.

The Norton/Grove Concise Encyclopedia of Music, edited by Sadie and Alison Latham (Norton, 1988; repr. with corr. 1991), is a spinoff of the multivolume work and is intended to provide quick and easy access to important information for all levels of users. There are some 10,000 brief entries derived from material in the larger work covering a variety of topics: performers, composers, instruments, terms, musical works, etc. Major topics are given lengthier treatment, up to a page or more. The work provides a useful one-volume reference source that compares favorably with any of the others.

613. **The New Harvard Dictionary of Music.** Don Michael Randel, ed. Cambridge, MA: Belknap/Harvard University Press, 1986. 942p. ISBN 0-674-61525-5.

This tool earned an excellent reputation under its original editor, Willi Apel, with its initial publication in 1944 and the revision that followed twenty-five years later. This new edition with a new editor should retain its status as an indispensable reference tool. There are nearly 6,000 entries contributed by seventy distinguished scholars, all specifically commissioned to update, rewrite, or add material. The result is a complete overhaul that makes a notable work all the more useful. Continuing the established pattern, there are no biographies, but instead, excellent definitions and descriptions of a wide range of topics embracing all aspects of music, including individual compositions. It is recommended that the earlier edition be retained, because much material was deleted or revised to include more modern concepts. As in the earlier work, there are a number of good illustrations.

The New Everyman Dictionary of Music, now in its sixth edition, and edited by David Cummings (Fitzhenry & Whiteside, 1988), is based on the 1971 edition edited by Eric Blom. Cummings has refurbished, renewed, and updated this old favorite into a timely and useful new source by introducing some 1,500 new entries and revising some 1,000 more. Alphabetical arrangement is given to composers, performers, orchestras, and musical terms. Listings of major works are given for composers; there has been a special concern for inclusion of singers (who were not well covered in previous editions). Cross-references provide access to related entries; there is a table of abbreviations and a listing of operatic roles.

614.   **The New Oxford Companion to Music.** Denis Arnold, ed. New York: Oxford University Press, 1983; repr. with corr. 1990. 2v. ISBN 0-19-311316-3.
      The 1983 edition is a thorough revision of *The Oxford Companion to Music* by Percy Scholes (10th ed., 1970), and is essentially an entirely new work. The Scholes volumes, which began in 1938, were known for their anecdotal style and inherent charm, but the new publication is far more comprehensive in coverage, and provides greater breadth and precision. There is a certain uniformity or evenness of coverage lacking in the original work, and this one, therefore, is a far better reference tool. Coverage is international, with an acknowledged emphasis on Western culture. Entries cover composers and their works, opera plots, terms, and institutions as well as theory, form, notation, etc. Bibliographies are included. Contemporary music receives much better coverage than in the past. There are many illustrations to enhance the text, and the work should appeal to a varied audience. It is primarily aimed at the interested layperson.
      Michael Kennedy's *The Oxford Dictionary of Music,* 2d ed. (Oxford University Press, 1994) covers personalities, compositions, instruments, and terms in brief fashion, although it should be considered a condensed version of *The New Oxford Companion.*

615.   **Selected Musical Terms of Non-Western Cultures: A Notebook-Glossary.** Walter Kaufmann. Warren, MI: Harmonic Park Press, 1990. 806p. (Detroit Studies in Music Bibliography, no. 65). ISBN 0-89990-039-9.
      The author, who died in 1984, was a former academic who spent a lifetime researching, studying, and, in effect, collecting terms relevant to music in Eastern cultures, with emphasis on the terminology of India. This source represents a wordbook of personal rather than comprehensive nature, but it is useful to students and researchers in the field for the uniqueness of its subject. Coverage is especially noteworthy for India, but there is ample treatment of other parts of Asia and of Africa. About 12,000 terms are defined in entries that are generally concise but vary in length from one or two sentences to a half-page. Terms were selected at random through the author's vast experience, and origins are indicated in the entries along with references to additional sources listed in the bibliography of more than 300 items at the end.

DIRECTORIES, ANNUALS, AND CURRENT AWARENESS SOURCES

616.   **Directory of Music Faculties in Colleges and Universities, U.S. and Canada.** Binghamton, NY: College Society, 1967- . Bienn. ISSN 0098-664X.
      Both the title and frequency of this important computer-produced tool have varied in the past. The first three editions (1967-1970) were entitled *Directory of Music Faculties in American Colleges and Universities* and appeared on an annual basis. The fourth edition (1970-1972) initiated the change in title, which signalled an expansion of the scope to include Canadians, and in frequency, to a biennial publication. The most recent edition is the thirteenth (1988-1990), published in 1990. The tool furnishes a listing of music faculty members in colleges and universities and provides several approaches. There are an alphabetical listing by state of colleges and universities, accompanied by a listing of faculty members with area of interest; a listing of faculty members alphabetically arranged; and a listing of schools by type of degrees offered.

617. Directory of Music Research Libraries. Kassel, Germany: distr., New York: Barenreiter, 1967- . Irreg. (Repertoire international des sources musicales, Series C). 5v; 2d rev. ed. 1979- . ISBN 3761806841 (v.1).

This outstanding directory began publication with the first edition in 1967, furnishing the student and scholar with an international guide to the holdings and practices of music research libraries all over the world. It was developed as a Series C of *RISM* (entry 572). Volume 1 (1967) covered libraries in the United States and Canada that had been inventoried in series A and B (pre-1800 material). Volume 2 (1970) covered thirteen European countries (Austria, Belgium, Switzerland, East and West Germany, Denmark, Ireland, Great Britain, Luxembourg, Norway, the Netherlands, Sweden, and Finland). It included sources for the nineteenth century and some libraries not inventoried in *RISM*. Volume 3 (1972) treated Spain, France, Italy, and Portugal and provided increased depth in descriptions of the collections. These early volumes were published by the University of Iowa. The German publisher, Barenreiter, took it over from the University of Iowa and issued a set of the previously published parts as volumes 1-3 in 1975. Volume 4 appeared in 1979 as part of the second revised edition and covers Australia, Israel, Japan, and New Zealand. This was the first volume to be issued directly under the auspices of *RISM* as part of its recently created series C. A change of editorial policy established the directory as dealing with the total problem of gaining access to the collections described, and information is given regarding not only library collections but also such important aspects as public holidays, names of *RISM* contacts, copyright information, library systems, etc. Most recently, volume 5, covering Czechoslovakia, Hungary, Poland, and Yugoslavia, appeared in 1985. A second edition of volume 1 was issued in 1983.

618. Directory of Record and CD Retailers. 1990-1991 ed. Keith Whelan. Wharton, NJ: Power Communication Group, 1990. 368p. ISSN 1057-7181.

This is a useful listing of significant record and CD stores located in this country. It is limited to stores that carry specialty recordings or deal with rare items, making it an important tool for serious collectors, specialists, and librarians. The popular chains (Musicland, Goody, etc.) therefore are not listed. The work is divided into several sections, the first of which identifies locations, hours, formats carried, music categories, and services provided. This is followed by a listing of stores by recording format (CD, LP, etc.); finally, there is a segment containing county maps for each state, which aid in establishing location.

619. Music Festivals in America: Classical, Opera, Jazz, Pops, Country, Old-Time Fiddlers, Folk, Bluegrass, Cajun. 4th ed. Carol Price Rabin. Great Barrington, MA: Berkshire Traveller Press, 1990. 271p. ISBN 0-930145-01-1.

For the music lover who is willing to travel as well as for students of performance, this directory of music festivals treats all types of musical styles. The guide is organized into six musical categories beginning with classical and continuing with opera; jazz, ragtime, and Dixieland; pops and light classical; folk and traditional; and concluding with a mixed offering of bluegrass, old-time fiddlers, country, and Cajun. These sections are then divided by state, with other locations (Bermuda, Puerto Rico, and Canada) treated at the end of each one. Entries supply name, location, and time of year, along with historical background of festivals and past performances, and ticket information. The work is well illustrated with maps and drawings; there is an index of festival names.

A complementary work is *The Music Lover's Guide to Europe: A Compendium of Festivals, Concerts, and Opera*, edited by Roberta Gottesman and Catherine Sentman (John Wiley, 1992). Cogent, paragraph-long descriptions of specific festivals are furnished along with listings of recent performers. Coverage of Eastern Europe is scanty.

620. Musical America: International Directory of the Performing Arts. New York: ABC Leisure Magazines, 1969- . Ann. ISSN 0735-7788.

Originally appearing as a special directory issue of *High Fidelity* magazine and bearing separate pagination, this work is now an independent and essential reference tool. During its formative period, it was published under the auspices of *Billboard* magazine (entry 683), but it now appears under the masthead of ABC Leisure, which continued to publish *High Fidelity* until 1989 when it ceased. The directory furnishes names and addresses by state, then city, of solo performers, orchestras, performing art series, dance companies, opera companies, choral groups, festivals, music schools, contests, foundations and awards, music publishers, service and professional music organizations, artist managers, music periodicals, and music critics. Coverage is international, with the inclusion of a foreign listing of companies and organizations. The tool also serves as a yearbook, with a section of articles covering the events in music and dance for the previous year.

The American Music Handbook, by Christopher Pavlakis (Free Press, 1974), is an old standard whose value surely diminishes with increasing age. Nevertheless, it has remained on reference shelves as an important tool. Although it shares many areas and topics with *Musical America*, as in most cases where similar sources are available, coverage tends to be complementary as much as it may be redundant. All areas of musical activity in this country are given adequate coverage, and Pavlakis (a composer, teacher, and publisher) has provided more than 5,000 entries. Included are service institutions and organizations, performing organizations, individual musicians and composers, instrumental ensembles with founding dates, conductors and concert masters, bands, vocal groups of all kinds, summer theaters, festivals, contests, awards, grants, schools and their degrees, fellowships, managers, and suppliers. The information appears in thirteen sections and is accessed through a name index.

621. **The Schirmer Guide to Schools of Music and Conservatories Throughout the World**. Nancy Uscher. New York: Schirmer Books/Macmillan, 1988. 635p. ISBN 0-02-873030-5.

This is a useful tool for students planning to choose an educational institution for either graduate or undergraduate programs. Some 750 schools from all over the world are given detailed treatment regarding their history, enrollment, number of faculty, entrance requirements, admission procedures, degrees, and areas of study. Coverage extends to types of facilities, specialized programs, and financial aid, with commentary given to especially noteworthy or important considerations. To be included, a U.S. or Canadian department, school, or conservatory must have either a minimum of ten full-time faculty members above the instructor rank or offer a master's degree. European institutions must prepare students to become professional musicians rather than theorists or researchers. Guidelines vary somewhat for non-European institutions outside the United States or Canada. Three indexes are supplied, providing access by institution, program area, and instrument.

HISTORIES AND CHRONOLOGIES

622. **A History of Western Music.** 4th ed. Donald Jay Grout and Claude V. Palisca. New York: W. W. Norton, 1988. 910p. ISBN 0-393-95627-X.

Now in its fourth edition, this highly acclaimed historical survey of Western music was originally published in 1960. It has been considered an outstanding textbook for music history classes and represents one of the fine contributions of the W. W. Norton Company. The fourth edition represents a substantial change from the critical interpretations given by Grout in the past. After Grout's death in 1987, Palisca rewrote and modified many of the articles in line with current thinking and recent research. This is especially noticeable in the segments on early musical periods. There are a glossary and a bibliography, along with a chronology of musical development. A number of illustrations help to define and explain the musical character and development of the various periods. Title, subject, and name indexes are furnished.

An earlier work from Norton is Paul Henry Lang's *Music in Western Civilization* (W. W. Norton, 1941), which treats musical development within a social, political, and cultural context.

623. **Music History from the Late Roman through the Gothic Periods, 313-1425: A Documented Chronology.** Blanche Gangwere. Westport, CT: Greenwood Press, 1986. 247p. ISBN 0-313-24764-1.

This is an outline or chronology of musical history covering early musical developments over a period of more than 1,100 years. Greenwood has planned a series of these, which eventually will cover the entire history of music in Western civilization. This work identifies important elements with respect to contributions and theoretical influences, and covers terms, notations, and musical instruments. References to sources provide exposition and interpretation and furnish examples of the technique, form, or style under scrutiny. Many of these references are to encyclopedia articles as well as separate monographs. Information is given regarding geographical regions; maps are included. This should become one of the most frequently used tools for answering historical inquiries.

Continuing the coverage is Gangwere's *Music History During the Renaissance Period, 1425-1520: A Documented Chronology* (Greenwood Press, 1991). This chronological sourcebook identifies personalities, events, documents, etc. relating to this brief but important musical period. Arrangement is broadly under two chronological segments; 1425-1450 and 1480-1520. Source references are given for listed events and individuals, along with brief exposition. The index furnishes adequate access for scholars and serious students.

624. **Music Since 1900.** 5th ed. Nicholas Slonimsky. New York: Schirmer Books, 1993. 1280p. ISBN 0-02-872418-6.

First published in 1938, this has been one of the standard historical chronologies providing a day-by-day treatment of musical developments in the twentieth century. The author, a 100-year-old Russian-born musicologist, has been the editor of *Baker's Biographical Dictionary* (entry 629) through the past four editions and is considered one of the experts in the field. The current effort is primarily a listing and exposition of stylistic developments from 1900 to 1991, thus updating the 1971 fourth edition and its 1986 supplement. It includes letters and other primary source material as well as the dictionary of terms, while supplementing the previous coverage with an additional 500 new entries on events of the past six years (1986-1992). Treatment is cogent and well developed and presents trends, styles, and tastes in both serious and popular music. Included are dates of performances, debuts, and more. Indexes are clear and effective.

625. **New Oxford History of Music.** London: Oxford University Press, 1954-1990. 10v. 2d ed. 1990- . ISBN 0-19-316329-2.

Carrying the name of Oxford University, this multivolume history of music has earned an excellent reputation for detailed coverage and scholarly bearing. Its overall effectiveness has been limited in the past by its lack of promptness, as it took about thirty years to complete the set (with several reprints and reissues of various volumes along the way). Individual volumes, all by scholars of distinction, have proved to be valuable tools in their own right, but finally the entire set represents a powerful reference history. In its entirety it represents a comprehensive and detailed survey of music from the earliest times to the present. The set consists of ten volumes, each by distinguished scholars: volume 1, *Ancient and Oriental Music*, by Egon Wellesz (1957); volume 2, *Early Medieval Music up to 1300*, by Dom Anselm Hughes and Gerald Abraham (1954), and in its second edition by Richard Crocker and David Hiley (1990); volume 3, *Ars Nova and the Renaissance, c. 1300-1540*, by Dom Anselm Hughes and Gerald Abraham (1960, 1977); volume 4, *The Age of Humanism, 1540-1630*, by Gerald Abraham (1968, 1988); volume 5, *Opera and Church Music, 1630-1750*, by Nigel Fortune and Anthony Lewis (1975, 1986); volume 6, *Concert Music, 1630-1750*, by Gerald Abraham (1986); volume 7, *The Age of Enlightenment, 1745-1790*, by Egon Wellesz and Frederick W. Sternfield (1973, 1981); volume 8, *The Age of Beethoven, 1790-1830*, by Gerald Abraham (1982, 1985); volume 9, *Romanticism, 1830-1890*, by Gerald Abraham (1990); and volume 10, *Modern Age, 1890-1960*, by Martin Cooper (1974).

626. **The Norton History of Music Series.** New York: W. W. Norton, 1940- .
Norton Publishing has long been associated with quality histories in the field of music. Most of that recognition may be attributable to this group of individual monographs, which are recognized as the Norton History of Music series. These independent works (none has a volume number) all cover different time periods, and were done by scholars and specialists on each topic. When taken collectively, they do, indeed, constitute a history of music from the earliest times to the present, although there are notable gaps in the coverage. The emphasis in these works is on the style, characteristics, and development of musical thought rather than an account of happenings or descriptions of a biographical nature. The titles, listed chronologically by period of coverage, are *The Rise of Music in the Ancient World: East and West*, by Curt Sachs (1943); *Music in the Middle Ages*, by Gustav Reese (1940); *Music in the Renaissance* (1959), also by Reese; *Music in the Baroque Era: From Monteverdi to Bach*, by Manfred F. Bukofzer (1947); *Music in the Romantic Era*, by Alfred Einstein (1947, 1975); *Music in Our Time: Trends in Music since the Romantic Era*, by Adolfo Salazar (1946); and William W. Austin's *Music in the Twentieth Century: From Debussy to Stravinsky* (1966).

627. **The Prentice Hall History of Music Series.** Englewood Cliffs, NJ: Prentice-Hall, 1965- . v.1- .
Similar in concept to the earlier standardized series from Norton (entry 626) is this more popular and less expensive series of slender volumes, each completed by an American scholar. Coverage is less detailed than that of Norton, but personalities and their careers are given more emphasis. Separate volumes treat historical periods of Western music, along with individual volumes on certain non-Eastern nations or cultures. Thus far the following titles have been issued: volume 1, *Folk and Traditional Music of the Western Continents* (2d ed. 1973), by Bruno Nettl; volume 2, *Music Cultures of the Pacific, the Near East, and Asia* (2d ed. 1977), by William P. Malm; volume 3, *Music in the Medieval World* (2d ed. 1975), by Albert Seay; volume 4, *Baroque Music* (2d ed. 1981), by Claude V. Palisca; volume 5, *Music in the Classic Period* (2d ed. 1973), by Reinhard G. Pauly; volume 6, *Nineteenth-Century Romanticism in Music* (2d ed. 1973), by Rey M. Longyear; volume 7, *Twentieth-Century Music: An Introduction* (2d ed. 1974), by Eric Salzman; volume 8, *Music in the United States: A Historical Introduction* (2d ed. 1974), by H. Wiley Hitchcock; volume 9, *Music in the Renaissance* (1976), by Howard Brown; volume 10, *Music in India: The Classical Traditions* (1978), by Bonnie C. Wade; and volume 11, *Music in Latin America, an Introduction* (1979), by Gerard Behague.

628. **A Twentieth-Century Musical Chronicle: Events 1900-1988.** Charles J. Hall, comp. Westport, CT: Greenwood Press, 1989. 347p. (Music Reference Collection, no. 20). ISBN 0-313-26577-1.
This is an interesting and well-constructed chronicle of musical events and developments placed within a broader sociocultural and political context. It is the first of three volumes; the others are to cover the period from 1750-1900, thus providing a sweeping chronicle of almost 240 years of American musical happenings. Each year is treated individually, beginning with fact-filled segments identifying important world events, followed by similar treatment of nonmusical cultural development, prizewinners, deaths, debuts, and openings pertinent to artistic and literary endeavor. Musical events are then treated in depth, with biographical highlights, musical compositions, and musical literature identified along with demographics and prizes. The year is successfully encapsulated in coverage running about three pages in length. Detailed indexes provide references to events and to musical personalities.

BIOGRAPHICAL SOURCES

629. **Baker's Biographical Dictionary of Musicians.** 8th ed. Nicolas Slonimsky. New York: Schirmer Books/Macmillan, 1992. 2115p. ISBN 0-02-872415-1.

Now in its eighth edition, this standard work has been an indispensable item in reference departments since its initial appearance in 1900. It has established a reputation for comprehensiveness which the new edition maintains, covering more than 14,000 personalities, both living and dead, from all geographic areas and periods of time. It has been criticized in the past for relative weakness in coverage of living performers, and the new edition furnishes an additional 1,100 biographical sketches, with revisions to 1,300 of the existing entries. Many represent contemporary popular crooners, rock singers, etc., and there is greater emphasis on ethnomusicologists and female composers. Along with performers and composers, it includes conductors, scholars, educators, and librarians. Biographies vary in length from a few lines to several pages and include updated bibliographies and lists of composers' works.

An abridged version of the eighth edition was issued by Slonimsky as *The Concise Baker's Biographical Dictionary* (Schirmer/Macmillan, 1993). Some 5,000 major figures from all time periods have been taken from the complete edition and represented in a 1,407-page volume selling at less than half the price of the larger work.

630. **Black Music Biography: An Annotated Bibliography.** Samuel A. Floyd, Jr., and Marsha J. Reisser. White Plains, NY: Kraus International, 1987. 302p. ISBN 0-527-30158-2.

From the same writers who created *Black Music in the United States: An Annotated Bibliography* for the same publisher in 1983, this is a major work for documentation of black musicians of all types and styles of performance. Coverage is given to a relatively small but important segment of eighty-seven composers and performers over a hundred-year period beginning with the 1850s. Nearly 150 monographic works have been identified and described in detail. Performers range in nature from Michael Jackson to Leontyne Price, and there is an excellent detailed introduction providing a summary of the literature.

631. **International Encyclopedia of Women Composers.** 2d ed. rev. and enl. Aaron I. Cohen. New York: Books & Music, 1987. 2v. ISBN 0-9617485-2-4.

With the recent emphasis on documentation of the contributions of minority groups to both culture and progress in society, the decades of the 1970s and the 1980s brought a new interest in the work of both blacks and women. This highly useful encyclopedia provides descriptions of the lives and accomplishments of female composers of all ages and parts of the world. The present edition has more than 6,200 entries providing biographical sketches, listings of contributions, and publications by and about the composer. Separate sections furnish photographs of a number of the individuals. Appendices include a listing of sources from which the biographies were derived, a bibliography of additional reading, lists of operas by women, pseudonyms, and discography. Indexes give access by country and century, profession, instrument, musical form, etc.

An earlier work that documents the contributions of female musicians is *Women in Music: A Biobibliography*, by Don L. Hixon and Don Hennessee (Scarecrow Press, 1975). It presents an alphabetical list of women musicians who are identified briefly; coded references refer to any of the appropriate forty-eight sources from which the entries were derived.

632. **Who's Who in American Music: Classical.** Compiled and edited by Jaques Cattell Press. New York: R. R. Bowker, 1983- . Bienn. ISSN 0737-9137.

This second edition of this work was published two years after the appearance of the first edition, and has taken on the character of a biennial publication. It is a typical Cattell effort, giving great attention to details and covering more than 9,000 individuals associated primarily with classical and semi-classical music in America. Musicians, critics, publishers, and editors are among the various groups represented in the listing. The arrangement of entries is alphabetical, and they furnish addresses, personal data, and information on major accomplishments and writings.

First issued in 1935 is a similar British publication, *International Who's Who in Music and Musicians' Directory in the Classical and Light Classical Fields*, edited by David M. Cummings and Dennis K. McIntire (13th ed., International Biographical Centre, 1992). This provides biographical sketches of 8,000 musicians from the Western world. Entries are concise, furnishing background information on lives and accomplishments of musicians and related personnel such as teachers and librarians. Various indexes are provided.

RECORDINGS

Discographies or lists of recordings are of prime importance to both specialists and aficionados and constitute a prolific segment of the reference literature. They are done on a variety of topics representing musical forms, schools, types, and individual composers and performers. Generally, they are arranged by name of performer or title of composition, possibly in chronological sequence.

633. **Bibliography of Discographies.** New York: R. R. Bowker, 1977- . v.1- . ISBN 0-8352-1023-5 (v.1).

This valuable list of discographies has been planned in five volumes, each of which is dedicated to a different category or type of music. Volume 1, *Classical Music, 1925-1975*, by Michael H. Gray and Gerald D. Gibson, was issued in 1977 and listed more than 3,000 discographies of serious concert music under the names of the composers or performers or subject of the efforts. Entries provide name of compiler and imprint of book or periodical title, whichever is the source, but do not indicate the quality or comprehensiveness of the discography. Coverage embraces works in all European languages. The volume has been supplemented by Gray with *Classical Music Discography, 1976-1988: A Bibliography* (Greenwood Press, 1989). The supplement gives an excellent listing of discographies culled from books, articles, dissertations, and program notes. Volume 2, *Jazz*, by Daniel Allen, appeared in 1981 and identified more than 3,500 discographies of jazz, blues, ragtime, gospel, and rhythm and blues published between 1935 and 1980. Although there are a few variations, the general format and arrangement parallel those of the first volume. Volume 3, *Popular Music*, by Gray, was published in 1983 and covers rock music; motion picture and stage show music; country, old time, and bluegrass music; and finally, the pop music of balladeers and orchestral themes up to 1982. Unfortunately, the other volumes have yet to appear. Volume 4 is to deal with ethnic and folk music, and volume 5 with general discographies. *The Journal of the Association for Recorded Sound Collections* has been supplementing the volumes through its column "Bibliography of Discographies."

634. **CD Review Digest.** Voorheesville, NY: Peri Press, 1987- . Q. with ann. cum. ISSN 0890-0213.

This quarterly digest of reviews of both popular and serious concert music recordings established itself as an extraordinary indexing tool of international proportions. It served the needs of a wide-ranging audience from interested listeners to serious specialists and collectors. In 1989, it split into two separate parts. *CD Review Digest: Jazz, Popular, Etc.* is a quarterly digest of reviews of popular music, both audio and visual; jazz, country, rock and roll, folk, and show tunes are all treated with extracts of reviews published in some fifty magazines. Entries are arranged alphabetically by performer; recordings are listed with information regarding locations and dates of recordings, along with extracts of reviews. Awards for excellence are identified. *CD Review Digest: Classical* is structured in the same way, but with the focus on recordings of serious concert music. Both tools supply separate indexes to recording labels, reviewers, titles, and performers. Their annual cumulations follow the same pattern and organization, each covering some 6,000 audio and visual recordings per year. These annual cumulations are especially valuable for purposes of reference because of their comprehensive listings.

There are two spinoff publications; one is *Best Rated CDs: Jazz, Popular, Etc.* (Peri Press, 1992), designed as an annual guide. This is a selective listing of reviews of the top 10 percent of CDs of popular music contained in the first five volumes of *CD Review Digest*, covering a period from 1983-1991. It contains excerpts for nearly 2,100 recordings, each of which has been reviewed at least twice and has received an award for excellence from at least one of the reviewers. Ratings are assigned on a five-point scale. Indexing follows the pattern set in the host publication. The other is the sister effort, *Best Rated CDs: Classical* (Peri Press, 1992), structured in the same vein and providing its record ratings and critical assessments under eight categories.

635. **Ethnic Music on Records: A Discography of Ethnic Recordings Produced in the United States, 1893-1942**. Richard K. Spottswood. Champaign, IL: University of Illinois Press, 1990. 7v. (Music in American Life). ISBN 0-252-01719-6.

This comprehensive and important discography identifies all foreign-language recordings made in the United States over a period of fifty years, and represents an outstanding effort. The work was sponsored in part by the Library of Congress for which Spottswood had previously edited the series of fifteen records, "Folk Music in America." Volume 1 treats Western Europe; volume 2, Slavic; volume 3, Eastern Europe; volume 4, Spanish, Portugese, Philippine, and Basque; and volume 5, Middle East, Far East, Scandinavian, English-language, American Indian, and international. Volume 6 provides artist and title indexes and volume 7 supplies record and matrix number indexes. Omitted are certain forms of music such as operatic and classical, Hawaiian music, etc. Neither language instruction nor U.S. reissues of foreign releases are included. More than 130 record labels are treated, with entries arranged by performer under thirteen national or language groups.

636. **Opus: America's Guide to Classical Music.** Chatsworth, CA: Schwann Publications, 1990- . Q. ISSN 1047-2355.

The *Schwann* catalogs have been popular guides to available recordings since the initial appearance of the basic guide in 1949, *Schwann Long Playing Record Catalog*. Since that time, the work has undergone several name changes and changes of scope, but has always been highly regarded as the best single source of purchasing information on thousands of sound recordings, both disc and tape, available from hundreds of record distributors and publishers. Classical, popular, rock, jazz, country, opera, ballet, and electronic music recordings were covered in various separate publications at different times. Beginning in 1990, *Opus* was issued as a quarterly guide to all classical recordings in all formats, including CD-videos, and is organized like its predecessor, *The Schwann Quarterly*. Also treated are recordings of electronic music, musicals, New Age, and film/television soundtracks.

The companion publication is *Spectrum*, begun at the same time, which covers all other music: rock, pop, jazz, blues, gospel, religious, and Christmas music, as well as children's and spoken recordings. It also duplicates the *Opus* treatment of soundtracks, musicals, and New Age. Both titles are indispensable to the music library. A similar effort of long standing is *Phonolog Reporter*, issued since 1948 by Trade Service Publications, which provides comprehensive weekly loose-leaf updates of currently available phonograph recordings. The work is divided into classical and popular segments and is accessed by titles of albums and songs, composers, and performers. *Laserlog Reporter* from the same publisher treats current compact disks.

Concert Music and Opera

DICTIONARIES, ENCYCLOPEDIAS, ETC.

637. **Annals of Opera, 1597-1940.** 3d ed. rev. and corr. Alfred Lowenberg, comp. Totowa, NJ: Rowman & Littlefield, 1978. 1756 col. ISBN 0-87471-851-1.

This is one of the standards in the field of music reference and has been regarded as an indispensable source of information on the identification of operas since its initial publication in 1943. The second edition (1955) separated the indexes into a second volume and was somewhat less convenient. The new work joins the basic text to the indexes in a single unit. Several thousand operas are listed in chronological order according to date of first performance. Entries provide name of composer, title of opera, author of text, place of first performance, name of theater when known, number of acts, and history of later performances. References are furnished to translations of text and revivals as well. Four indexes provide access: operas; composers (with dates of birth and death and titles of operas); librettists; and a general index listing other individuals, subjects, and places. This work was edited by Harold Rosenthal, who has prepared a supplementary volume, *Annals of Opera, 1940-1981* (Barnes & Noble, 1983).

638. **The Definitive Kobbé's Opera Book.** Gustav Kobbé. Earl of Harewood, ed. New York: G. P. Putnam, 1987. 1404p. ISBN 0-399-13180-9.

The 1979 edition was an extensive revision of an old standard in the field which had been expanded to include more than 300 opera plots, twice the number of *The Metropolitan Opera Stories of the Great Operas* (entry 642). First published around 1920, the work has undergone frequent revision and substantial change under the Earl of Harewood, who has edited it since 1954. This edition has added twenty-nine operas while dropping twenty, and is considered the most complete source of opera synopses because the storylines are given in great detail. Arrangement is by century, subdivided by country. Brief notes are given on composers, and musical motifs are described. Older operas are included if they are still being performed, and there is good coverage of modern operas as well. Dates of first performance and important revivals are enumerated with names of important singers. The work is especially generous in its coverage of Wagner, Verdi, and Britten.

639. **Great Opera Classics.** Rev. ed. Arthur Jacobs and Stanley Sadie. New York: Gramercy, 1984; repr. 1987. 563p. ISBN 0-517-64108-9.

This is a revision of a work originally issued in 1964, and itself is a reissue of *The Limelight Book of Opera* (Limelight Editions, 1985). It describes in considerable depth the features of eighty-seven major operas by forty-one composers. The operas cover a time span of 400 years; therefore, this tool would be an excellent reference guide in any library serving the needs of both specialists and nonspecialists. The operas are described through a three-part approach: a general introduction placing the opera and its composer in historical perspective, followed by a plot synopsis and, finally, a musical commentary. Although the commentaries are brief, they have been commended for their clarity and use of musical excerpts. Arrangement of operas is by composer within chronological time period groupings, beginning with Purcell in the seventeenth century and ending with contemporaries Britten and Menotti. There is an additional chapter on twentieth-century composers not previously described, as well as a general bibliography.

640. **International Dictionary of Opera.** C. Steven LaRue, ed. Detroit: St. James Press, 1993. 2v. ISBN 1-55862-081-8.

This useful new source furnishes a comprehensive examination of important operas and related personalities. There are more than 1,050 entries treating 400 operas, 200 composers, 300-plus performers, and a number of designers, producers, conductors, and librettists. There are more than 450 illustrations. Entries are alphabetically arranged, with volume 1 covering A-K and volume 2 concluding the alphabet and supplying the indexes. Operas vary in popularity and renown from the most famous of classic stature to contemporary works still somewhat obscure. The entries on personalities supply a brief biography, followed by a signed essay on the importance or significance of the individual's career and body of work. They conclude with a bibliography of additional sources. Entries on the operas provide composition and production information along with a signed critical evaluative essay and bibliography. Indexes in volume 2 give access by nationality and by title.

641. **Metropolitan Opera Encyclopedia: A Comprehensive Guide to the World of Opera**. David Hamilton, ed. New York: Simon & Schuster, 1987. 415p. ISBN 0-671-67132-X.

The editor is a well-known figure who has served as music critic and contributor to various journals. He has produced the most extensive treatment of opera offered by a single-volume reference tool while also providing a distinctive focus on performers of the Metropolitan Opera Guild through the 1986-1987 season. There are 2,500 entries featuring 550 opera synopses, including every opera ever performed at the Met. There are biographies of 800 singers, nearly 300 composers and librettists, and some 300 conductors, producers, designers, and executives. More than 200 relevant musical terms are defined. The work is well illustrated in black-and-white. Entries are alphabetically arranged and supply place, dates, and cast of world premieres and U.S. premieres, as well as Metropolitan productions. There are twenty-four guest essays by such luminaries as Pavarotti, Domingo, and Sutherland. There are an opera chronology and brief bibliography.

642. **The Metropolitan Opera Stories of the Great Operas.** John W. Freeman. New York: W. W. Norton, 1984. 547p. ISBN 0-393-01888-1.

This is an excellent choice for the reference collection because it presents the description of plots of 150 operas, by seventy-five composers, presented at the Metropolitan Opera House. These not only represent the major works which are more readily found, such as those by Mozart, Verdi, Wagner, and Puccini, but more important, lesser-known selections which are on the periphery of the Met's repertoire. For each opera, the source and language of the libretto is furnished, along with information of initial performances at the Met and elsewhere and a listing of characters. Story lines are furnished by scenes and acts, along with titles of the important arias. There is a picture along with a biography for each composer. There are no cast listings.

An important complementary tool is *Annals of the Metropolitan Opera Guild: The Complete Chronicle of Performances and Artists, Chronology 1883-1985.* edited by Geraldine Fitzgerald (Metropolitan Opera Guild, 1989). This title provides a chronological record of the casts of the operas performed from the first season in 1883 to the mid-1980s. It replaces an earlier work begun in 1947 and continuously supplemented since then. Volume 1 provides the chronology of nearly 22,000 performances, and volume 2 furnishes an array of indexes (performances, co-composers, librettists, directors, etc.).

643. **The New Grove Dictionary of Opera**. Stanley Sadie, ed. New York: Grove's Dictionaries of Music, 1992. 4v. ISBN 0-935859-92-6.

This is slated to be the final small-volume set derived from Sadie's comprehensive multivolume effort (entry 612). It contains some 10,000 entries, alphabetically arranged from "Aachen," the headquarters of an important German opera company, to "Zylis-Gara," the Polish-born soprano. The signed articles cover all aspects of opera in the Western tradition and treat not only performers but also composers and directors, as well as companies, theaters, locations, terms, and stagecraft. Plot summaries are provided, along with performance history, for individual operas. Secondary bibliographies are supplied for most of the entries. Included are black-and-white illustrations. Some 1,300 specialists contributed to the work and, in most cases, provided lively and opinionated exposition. Much of the material is newly written since publication of the 1980 large-scale set. Volume 4 contains appendices of role names and first lines.

644. **Opera Plot Index**. William E. Studwell and David A. Hamilton. New York: Garland, 1989. 466p. (Garland Reference Library of the Humanities, v.1099). ISBN 0-8240-4621-8.

This comprehensive information source indexes nearly 3,000 operas and musical productions listed in nearly 170 books written in 10 languages. It is an excellent tool for all types of users, from the general public to the serious student and specialist whose purpose is to identify composers, dates, and themes or to determine plots, nature of criticism, and additional sources of information. Entries supply the title of the work, composer, and date of first performance, with references to sources of information and type of information contained in them. In addition to plots, musical illustrations are identified and historical background is provided. An index of composers aids access.

The Opera Handbook, by John Lazarus (G. K. Hall, 1987; repr. 1990), as part of the publisher's Performing Arts Series, complements the preceding work as a less comprehensive but more detailed source. Treated here are the 200 operas most frequently performed by major companies during the decade of the 1980s. Arrangement is by country or national origin in different sections, opening with an introductory chapter. Entries describe plot, characterization, musical idiom, and influences of other works. Special features include a glossary and several directories and bibliographies.

645. **Operas in German: A Dictionary**. Margaret Ross Griffel. Westport, CT: Greenwood Press, 1990. 735p. ISBN 0-313-25244-0.

This is a unique and valuable resource for a wide range of users, from scholars and professionals to devotees and collectors. The principal segment is composed of alphabetically arranged entries treating 380 major operas composed to German text. Entries supply information on premieres and first performers in Germany, the United States, and Britain; plot summaries; cast listings; major roles; and some historical and analytical commentary. Scores, librettos, recordings, and bibliographic references are treated. Appendices include additional coverage of some 1,250 operas not treated in the first section due to space limitations or lack of information. Appendices then list composers, librettists, and authors whose works inspired operas, as well as sources used by librettists. There is a chronology of German operas from the seventeenth century to the present. The work concludes with a bibliography and indexes of characters and premiere participants.

646. **The Oxford Dictionary of Opera**. John Warrack and Ewan West. New York: Oxford University Press, 1992. 782p. ISBN 0-19-869164-5.

This is an expansion of the previous effort by Warrack and Harold Rosenthal described later. In the Oxford manner, it serves as an excellent one-volume handbook to the subject, and in this case contains 4,500 entries. Coverage is given to 750 composers and 900 performers. There is selective inclusion of current performers; a number of obscure performers of the past have been deleted from the concise work. About 600 operas are described in thorough fashion regarding plot and performance aspects; included are listings of cast and treatment of premiere. There are numerous entries for countries and cities, providing background information on the nature of their involvement with opera. Particular aims may also be found among the entries, along with characters, institutions, companies, and festivals. The work is international in scope, with a British perspective, and describes the major themes and contributions of individuals rather than an extensive listing of their credits.

The Concise Oxford Dictionary of Opera, by Rosenthal and Warrack (2d ed. corr. Oxford University, 1985; repr. 1990), has been a reliable source of information since its original 1964 edition (corrected in 1966 and 1972). This is a comprehensive reference title on the opera. The work represents a complete revision and serves as an excellent first source for brief treatment of operas, performers, composers, and terminology. Obscure singers of the past are included.

647. **The Paris Opera: An Encyclopedia of Operas, Ballets, Composers, and Performers.**
Spire Pitou. Westport, CT: Greenwood Press, 1983- . v.1- . ISBN 0-313-26218-7.

The Paris Opera and Opera Comique are documented thoroughly with every extant work produced and all relevant personalities. Volume 1, issued in 1983, treats the period 1671-1715, and sets the pattern for the encyclopedia. Volume 2 was published in 1985, covering the period from 1715 to 1815. Pitou died before volume 3 was issued in two volumes (1990) treating the pivotal period from 1815 to 1914 when the Paris Opera achieved international recognition and acclaim. Volume 4 will complete the set with coverage from 1915 to 1982; publication is assured since Pitou's widow has organized his manuscripts. Entries describe the operas or ballets with a detailed plot summary; performance history of the work, including its Paris premiere; indication of critical recognition; and bibliography. Biographical entries of singers, dancers, choreographers, librettists, scenarists, and executives are ample. Each volume has its own index.

648. **Recent American Opera: A Production Guide**. Rebecca Hodell Kornick. New York: Columbia University Press, 1991. 352p. ISBN 0-231-06920-0.

The author is an academic who researched this material while preparing her doctoral dissertation; it is published with the intent of updating standard works in the field, *Opera Production I* and *Opera Production II* by Quaintance Eaton (Da Capo, 1974). Eaton covers American opera production through 1972, and most works treated in the present effort premiered after that year. Information is given on 213 productions in American opera and musical theater of serious nature, with no duplication of Eaton's coverage. Entries are arranged by composer and supply brief appraisals, plot summary, production requirements, and references to reviews. Information on genre, acts, scenes, length, and style of music are provided. Value lies in the array of composers and their works, from the well-known to the obscure and from the highly sophisticated to the more popular (Sondheim, Berlin, etc.).

649. **A Short History of Opera.** 3d ed. Donald Jay Grout and Hermine W. Williams. New York: Columbia University Press, 1988. 913p. ISBN 0-231-06192-7.

At long last, after twenty-three years, the third edition of this work was issued. Originally published in 1947, the second edition appeared in 1965, with the purpose of updating the material by bringing the historical coverage to 1960. Biographies were updated and additional illustrative material was included. For the third edition, Grout's failing health placed a large responsibility on co-author Williams, and the pair have produced another excellent textual history up to 1986. The opera is treated in a comprehensive manner, as it was before, beginning with the lyric theater of the Greeks. Arrangement is chronological, with attention given to musical styles. Descriptions are scholarly and the intended audience (specialists and students) continues to derive much value from both the articles and the excellent bibliography. Coverage of twentieth-century opera in the last few chapters is somewhat less successful, as much of the change in style and many of the prevailing influences defy neat chronological categorization by decade.

DIRECTORIES, ANNUALS, AND CURRENT AWARENESS SOURCES

650. **Opera Annual: U.S. 1984-** . Englewood, NJ: J. S. Ozer, 1988- . Ann. ISSN 0899-3645.

This tool is a welcome new source and should not be confused with the earlier serial with the same name issued first in 1954-1955. The current effort is edited and published by Jerome S. Ozer and supplies reprints or excerpts from reviews appearing in local newspapers. Facsimile reproductions of programs and illustrations are included as well. The first issue treats the 1984-1985 season and identifies eighty-six operas performed by thirty-five companies. Arrangement is alphabetical by title of opera and reviews are presented in their entirety when only one or two have been found. When a number of reviews are identified, excerpts are provided along with synthesis and editorial commentary. In all cases, the sources of the reviews are clearly revealed. A work such as this depends upon the cooperation of the opera companies, and therefore listings are not complete. Access is provided by a detailed name index.

651. **Opera Companies of the World: Selected Profiles**. Robert H. Cowden, ed. Westport, CT: Greenwood Press, 1992. 336p. ISBN 0-313-26220-9.

This is a directory of about 140 professional opera companies from different parts of the world generally performing on a regular seasonal basis, although there is selective inclusion of some of the major opera festivals. Arrangement of entries is alphabetical by country and city; entries supply description of the history and current operations along with a bibliography of secondary sources, as well as principal administrator, address, telephone, and fax number. Smaller companies are treated briefly in the appendix.

Another title providing worldwide coverage is *The International Opera Guide* by F. M. Stockdale and M. R. Dreyer (Trafalgar Square/David & Charles, 1990). This tool supplies a directory of opera houses and festivals from all over the globe. Individual opera houses are treated in some detail, providing history and exposition along with maps and seating charts. Facilities are described and transportation is explained. Arrangement is alphabetical by city. The second part is a biographical dictionary of composers with synopses of their most important works, and listings of characters and major arias.

652. **Symphony Orchestras of the United States.** Robert R. Craven, ed. Westport, CT: Greenwood Press, 1986. 521p. ISBN 0-313-24072-8.

This useful directory contains a great deal of information on American orchestras not readily available elsewhere. Descriptions are brief, generally running about three pages, but are well written and describe adequately the significant characteristics of each unit. Selection of orchestras was based on membership in the American Symphony Orchestra League (ASOL), where they were designated as either major and regional orchestral units, or metropolitan orchestras with the highest budgets. In addition, an orchestra was included from each state that was not represented in the previous categories, for a total of 126 orchestras. Coverage includes descriptions of the unit's history, organization, budget, and activities, as well as discography, chronology of music directors, bibliography, and an address and contact person for each orchestra. There are a general bibliography, a chronology of orchestra founding dates, and a detailed index to the contents.

BIOGRAPHICAL SOURCES

653. **Concert and Opera Conductors: A Bibliography of Biographical Materials.** Robert H. Cowden, comp. New York: Greenwood Press, 1987. 285p. (Music Reference Collection, no. 14). ISBN 0-313-25620-9.

As a companion to his works on concert and opera singers (entry 660n) and instrumental virtuosi (entry 659), Cowden employs a similar pattern in this biographical bibliography of conductors. Nearly 1,250 conductors are treated alphabetically, with entries supplying dates and places of birth and death. There are citations to listings in seven major reference books, articles in ten music periodicals, biographies and autobiographies, and any additional books that contain pertinent information. Criteria for selection of the composers were treatment in at least two publications and appointment to a permanent post as conductor. This eliminates guest conductors such as Domingo or others who have had such experiences on different occasions. Other sections provide listings of collective works and related books. Appendices furnish additional reference sources as well as an index to more than 1,600 conductors treated in the seventh edition of Baker (entry 629). There is an author index.

654. **Contemporary American Composers: A Biographical Dictionary.** 2d ed. E. Ruth Anderson. Boston: G. K. Hall, 1982. 578p. ISBN 0-8161-8223-X.

First published in 1976, this work has been revised to omit certain categories of individuals, such as those who have written only one or two compositions and those who did not respond to the questionnaires. Still, the number of entries has increased and presently the tool identifies more than 4,000 composers of concert music. These people were born after 1869 and are American citizens or have resided in this country for an extensive period of time. Entries furnish dates of birth and death, education and training, professional and academic appointments, awards and commissions, and mailing address. Because of the reliance on the questionnaire, some caution should be exercised in reporting the information as accurate, but, all things considered, the tool is valuable for its breadth of coverage.

A more recent work is *A Dictionary of American Composers*, by Neil Butterworth (Garland, 1984), which provides greater depth but sacrifices breadth. It supplies well-developed treatment of 558 composers of serious music from the eighteenth century to the present in detailed fashion.

655. **Contemporary Composers**. Brian Morton and Pamela Collins, eds. Chicago: St. James Press, 1992. 1019p. ISBN 1-55862-085-0.

Some 500 composers living at the time that the project was initiated in 1989 (although some have died since) are treated in this useful biographical dictionary of the contemporary music scene. Coverage is international in scope and includes composers from Japan and Korea, although there is emphasis on U.S. and European nationals. More than 100 specialists contributed the entries. Entries are arranged alphabetically and contain three parts, the first of which is a brief biographical sketch in the *"Who's Who"* style. Next there is a detailed listing, arranged chronologically, of all works categorized by type (symphonic, chamber/instrumental, vocal/choral, operatic, etc.). Dates are given for completion and first performance, and citations refer to works by and about the composer. Concluding each entry is critical-evaluative commentary establishing the position or status of the composer within the broader musical fabric.

656. **A Dictionary of Pianists.** Wilson Lyle. New York: Schirmer Books/Macmillan, 1984. Repr., London: Hale, 1985. 343p. ISBN 0-7090-1749-9.

One of the rare biographical sources devoted to the artists of the piano, this tool provides information on 4,000 classical pianists from the eighteenth century to the present day. Listings are arranged alphabetically and the entries are straightforward, except for the inclusion of occasional editorial comments, which may seem anomalous within the context of the work. Coverage excludes individuals whose performance can be categorized as jazz, ragtime, blues, or pops (but, interestingly enough, embraces an entry on Liberace). There appears to be a slight bias toward inclusion of figures of British or European extraction, but in general the tool should prove of value to music librarians and their patrons.

Another biographical dictionary on instrumentalists of a special type is *Great Masters of the Violin: From Corelli and Vivaldi to Stern, Zuckerman, and Perlman*, by Boris Schwarz (Simon & Schuster, 1983; repr. 1987). This is a highly useful survey of the lives and times of violinists from the sixteenth century to the present day. It is written in an anecdotal and informal style and draws upon a wealth of information derived from a variety of sources, including the author's personal knowledge.

657. **Greene's Biographical Encyclopedia of Composers.** David Mason Greene. Garden City, NY: Doubleday, 1985. Repr., London: Collins, 1986. 1348p. ISBN 0-004-34363-8.

A recent biographical tool, this work covers more than 2,400 prominent composers representing all nations and time periods. Greene is known for his irreverence in the columns he has done as a contributing editor to *Musical Heritage Review* (Paganiniana Publications, 1977-), and these biographical sketches are presented in an interesting, informal, and entertaining manner sure to appeal to the intended audience of nonspecialists. Entries are rich in detail and include information on personal traits and habits as well as the more convenient standard material. They give personal data, analysis of the major works, and a listing of their availability as recordings. Arrangement is chronological to facilitate comparisons within schools or periods.

A narrower time span is covered by Jerome Roche and Elizabeth Roche in *A Dictionary of Early Music from the Troubadours to Monteverdi* (Oxford University Press, 1981). This work provides brief but well-written sketches of 700 early composers whose works appear on recordings, in published editions, or in textbooks, or who are the subject of current scholarship.

658. **Index to Biographies of Contemporary Composers.** Storm Bull. Metuchen, NJ: Scarecrow Press, 1964-1987. 3v. ISBN 0-8108-1930-9 (v.3).

The first volume of this work appeared in 1964 and identifies biographical material on nearly 6,000 composers active between 1900 and 1950 from sixty-nine sources. The second volume, published ten years later, indexes another 108 sources and updates material on 4,000 of the previously covered personalities while adding another 2,000 individuals to their ranks. The massive third volume has listed 13,500 composers, with almost 6,000 new entries culled from ninety-eight biographical sources. Arrangement is alphabetical in all volumes, with brief identification given along with references to listed sources. These individuals are contemporary, in that they were born during this century, were still living at time of publication, or had died after 1949. This work is recognized as a useful source for quick identification of modern personalities.

659. **Instrumental Virtuosi: A Bibliography of Biographical Materials.** Robert H. Cowden, comp. New York: Greenwood Press, 1989. 349p. (Music Reference Collection, no. 18). ISBN 0-313-26075-3.

Completing his trilogy of efforts for Greenwood Press, Cowden has produced this biographical bibliography on instrumental virtuosi to accompany earlier works on singers (entry 660n) and conductors (entry 653). The pattern is the same as that of the earlier efforts, opening with a section listing thirty-seven collective works that treat virtuosi. Following that is another segment identifying nearly 140 related publications. Then follows the major segment listing 1,215 virtuosi alphabetically. Entries supply birth and death dates with references to treatment in books previously identified. Virtuosi represent twenty-six different instruments (woodwinds, brass, strings, organ, percussion, piano, etc.). Most frequent listings are for artists of the cello, organ, violin, and piano. Serious concert musicians along with jazz and pop instrumentalists are included. Appendices supply several indexes to entries as well as indexing to instrumentalists treated in Baker (entry 629) and in *New Grove* (entry 612).

660. **Opera and Concert Singers: An Annotated International Bibliography of Books and Pamphlets.** Andrew Farkas. New York: Garland, 1985. 363p. (Garland Reference Library of the Humanities, v.466). ISBN 0-8240-9001-2.

This is a comprehensive bibliography of 1,500 biographies and autobiographies in twenty-nine different languages. Also included are 300 monographs covering more than one subject, which are listed in a separate section. Annotations are excellent, providing useful information and written in a sprightly style. There is a warning from the author that most libraries do not possess more than half the books listed; therefore, this should serve as a purchasing guide to strengthen the collection. A list of unpublished manuscripts is given at the end. All in all, this is an impressive and complete contribution.

Another bibliography published in the same year is *Concert and Opera Singers: A Bibliography of Biographical Materials*, compiled by Robert H. Cowden (Greenwood Press, 1985). Although personalities are duplicated to a great extent in the two works, the latter includes entries from reference books and periodicals. It has only a small number of annotations. It is the first of three such efforts completed by Cowden for the publisher (entries 653 and 659).

RECORDINGS

661. **International Discography of Women Composers.** Aaron I. Cohen, comp. Westport, CT: Greenwood Press, 1984. 254p. ISBN 0-313-24272-0.

The increased interest in the contributions of females to society and culture has led to the production of several reference sources in the field of music, and Cohen has been a leader in this regard. This discography furnishes listings of the recorded music of 468 women composers of concert music. It is hoped that with efforts like this, there will be an increased awareness, not only of the quantity but also of the quality of much of this work, so that it is more frequently performed. The entries are arranged alphabetically by name of composer, under which the recordings are listed along with performers, instruments, record label and number, and dates and nationality of composer. There is a directory of record companies and a list of composers by country of origin and by instrument and form. Treatment of composers is comprehensive, dating from the twelfth century to the present day. An index of titles provides access.

Popular Music (Jazz, Folk, Rock, Country, Etc.)

BIBLIOGRAPHIC GUIDES

662. **Folk Music in America: A Reference Guide.** Terry E. Miller. New York: Garland, 1986. 424p. (Garland Reference Library of the Humanities, v.496). ISBN 0-8240-8935-9.

This is a selective listing of scholarly articles, books, dissertations, and even encyclopedia articles on the topic of folk music. Annotations, although brief, are informative, and emphasis is given to relatively recent writings from the past three decades. The introduction provides an understanding of what may or may not be considered folk music. Treatment is subsequently given to such elements as the music of American Indians and Eskimos; Anglo-American folk songs and ballads; and the more contemporary bluegrass, country and western, and protest music. There are sections on instruments and instrumental music, such as banjo and dulcimer, as well as black and ethnic folk music. This should prove to be a basic reference tool in the music collection.

663. **Popular Music: A Reference Guide.** Roman Iwaschkin. New York: Garland, 1986-1993. 2v. (Garland Reference Library of the Humanities, v.642). ISBN 0-8240-8680-5 (v.1). (Music Research and Information Guides, v.15). ISBN 0-8240-4449-5 (v.2).

Another of the Garland bibliographies, this two-volume bibliography represents a real contribution to the literature of popular music in all phases. Volume 1 provides coverage of more than 5,000 items, some of which receive annotations. There is comprehensive coverage of the vast field of popular music, with such categories as folk, country, Cajun, black, jazz, and stage and screen, as well as rap music, African pop, Grand Ole Opry, and jazz in Germany. The book includes a section on biographies, another on education and instruments, and another on the music business. Songs and recordings receive separate treatment, as do literary works, including novels and poetry. The listing of periodicals is a useful resource feature. Volume 2 is an update to the coverage of Volume 1, in treating the literature from 1984 to 1990. It contains an improved author and title index.

A timely effort in the series is Judy McCoy's *Rap Music in the 1980s: A Reference Guide*, important for its documentation of a sociological phenomenon as well as a grass-roots style of performance. Coverage is given to 1,000 books and articles published from 1980 to 1991 on the various aspects of rap music. Entries are annotated and serve to provide awareness of the content; as a plus, there is an annotated discography of seventy-six recordings. The work is indexed by artist, album title, and subject.

664. **Rockabilly: A Bibliographic Resource Guide**. B. Lee Cooper and Wayne S. Haney. Metuchen, NJ: Scarecrow Press, 1990. ISBN 0-8108-2386-1.

For enthusiasts at various levels of sophistication, this is a unique resource tool providing documentation of books and articles treating this particular form of popular music of the 1950s. Rockabilly represents a merger of musical elements (country music, rock and roll, and the blues) into what is today regarded as an innovative and distinctive genre. This work contains nearly 1,950 entries, largely citing the popular media (*Rolling Stone* and *Crawdaddy*) as well as historical studies and reviews. Arrangement of entries is alphabetical by name of performers, with such well-known practitioners as Carl Perkins along with those of more questionable linkage to the rockabilly movement. There is a separate discography of more than 200 albums that should be useful to both collectors and students, along with a separate bibliography of general books. An author index is furnished.

BIBLIOGRAPHIES AND INDEXES

665. **Fire Music: A Bibliography of the New Jazz, 1959-1990**. John Gray, comp. New York: Greenwood Press, 1991. 515p. (Music Reference Collection, no. 31). ISBN 0-313-27892-X.

Avant garde or free-form jazz performed in unorthodox and unconventional fashion by a large number of musicians between the 1960s and 1970s abandoned some of the more traditional "roles" of harmony, rhythm, melody, etc. to produce this short-lived variation. Documentation is heavy and this work lists more than 7,100 entries representing all types of literature: books, newspaper and periodical articles, dissertations, videos, films, and tapes. Various Western languages are represented, with emphasis on English and French publication over a thirty-year period. The work is divided into six sections providing a general chronology with reference to relevant material, along with segments on African-American cultural history, county and regional studies, jazz collectives, jazz lofts, and biographical-critical studies. Appendices provide listings of reference works, research centers, and performers by country and by instrument. There are author, subject, and artist indexes.

666. **The Literature of Jazz: A Critical Guide**. 2d ed., rev. Donald Kennington and Danny L. Read. Chicago, American Library Association, 1980. 236p. ISBN 0-8389-0313-4.

Originally published in Great Britain by the Library Association, this bibliography has earned a respected position among the useful reference works in the field of music. Essentially, it is a listing of the important books on jazz and it attempts to enumerate all the significant material in the English language published through 1979. Chapters cover the various aspects of the literature, beginning with general background and following with such categories as histories, biographies, analysis, theory and criticism, reference sources, periodical literature, and organizations. There are full bibliographies at the end of each chapter. Chapters on the blues and jazz education are new to this edition. Emphasis is still on English-language materials. There are name and title indexes.

PRINTED MUSIC SOURCES—BIBLIOGRAPHIES, INDEXES, AND CATALOGS

667. **The Great Song Thesaurus**. 2d ed. upd. and exp. Roger Lax and Frederick Smith. New York: Oxford University Press, 1989. 774p. ISBN 0-19-50548-3.

The first edition of this important index to popular songs was issued in 1984 and was hailed as an "invaluable source." Coverage now has been extended by an additional 1,000 songs popular between 1980 and 1987, for a total of 11,000 popular songs in the English language from the Elizabethan period through 1986. The value of the work lies in the many approaches offered in the ten sections. Included here are: year-by-year inventory of significant songs (1558-1986); listing by performance medium; thesaurus of songs by subject, key word, and category; song-title catalog, identifying composers and lyricists, year, and recording artists; award-winners in chronological sequence for both film and television; themes, trademarks, and signatures; elegant plagiarisms; and more. With the inclusion of an index of lyric keylines, one is able to identify titles when only the important lines are remembered.

668. **Musi*key: "The Reference Guide of Note."** Fort Collins, CO: Musi*Key, 1987- . Bimo. ISSN 0895-1543.
    This serial publication is purchased by yearly subscription and supplies six bimonthly issues, each of which represents an updated complete listing of currently available song sheets and collections of popular music. This is important to those who need to keep abreast of materials in this elusive area. Included here are listings for the songs of Broadway, as well as folk music, gospel, jazz, pop, rock, etc. Purposely omitted are classical music, choral arrangements, band charts, and method works. Each issue treats some 155,000 songs in addition to 10,000 pieces of sheet music, and more than 8,000 anthologies. The work is divided into four sections listing the entries under song title, book title, sheet title, and composer/recording artist. Each of these sections contains complete ordering information along with types of musical arrangement.

669. **Popular Music, 1920-1979: An Annotated Index of over 18,000 American Popular Songs.** 2d ed. Nat Shapiro and Bruce Pollock, eds. Detroit: Gale Research, 1985. 3v. **Supp. 1 1980-1984.** 1986. **Supp. 2-** . 1986- . Ann. ISSN 0886-442X.
    This is a major cumulation of what was an eight-volume set that indexed the popular music of this country in five- or ten-year intervals. This comprehensive work organizes the entries alphabetically by title and describes alternate titles, country of origin for songs from other countries, lyricists, composers, dates, history, performers, and record labels. There are indexes of composers and lyricists, important performances, and awards. There is also a list of publishers. The original eight volumes are still available for those libraries that have collected them and do not wish to invest in the new work, but the new edition facilitates access and provides up-to-date publisher lists. The series continues with subsequent publications that serve as supplements; volume 9 is a cumulation for 1980-1984 (Gale, 1986), followed by annual supplements beginning with 1985 (volume 10- . 1986-). A retrospective cumulation for the early years (1900-1919) was issued in 1988, thus providing extraordinary access and facilitating the search for information.

670. **Popular Song Index.** Patricia P. Havlice. Metuchen, NJ: Scarecrow Press, 1975. 933p. **First Supp.**, 1978. **Second Supp.**, 1984. **Third Supp.**, 1989. ISBN 0-8108-2202-4.
    This is an extensive index of 301 song books, mainly U.S., but also including several British, Canadian, and French works. The emphasis is on folk songs, with coverage from 1940 to 1972. It is complementary to the work by de Charms and Breed (entry 672), beginning its coverage with 1940 imprints and emphasizing popular music rather than classical. Main entries are under titles, with cross-references from actual first lines and first lines of choruses. There is also an index of composers and lyricists. The supplements continue the coverage, with the first supplement adding seventy-two anthologies published between 1970 and 1975. The second supplement covers another 145 song books published between 1974 and 1981, and the third supplement identifies songs in another 181 anthologies published between 1979 and 1987.

671. **Song Index ...** Minnie Sears. New York: H. W. Wilson, 1926. 650p. **Supp.** 1934. Repr., Hamden, CT: Shoe String Press, 1966, 1990. 2v. in 1. ISBN 0-7812-9019-8.
    The complete title of the basic edition indicates that it is "an index to more than 12,000 songs in 177 song collections comprising 262 volumes." This was the original work that many of the other song indexes in this section were designed to supplement. Despite its age, it remains an important index and is still widely used in all kinds of libraries including, of course, music libraries. Sears established an excellent pattern of coverage which represented titles, first lines, and names of lyricists and composers all in one for ease of access. The bulk

of the entries are under title, with added entries provided under author and composer. The supplement adds another 7,000 songs from 104 song collections published up to 1932. More recent song indexes by de Charms and Breed (entry 672), Havlice (entry 670), and Shapiro and Pollock (entry 669) supplement this work but do not supersede it.

672. **Songs in Collections: An Index.** Desiree de Charms and Paul F. Breed. Detroit: Information Service, 1966. 588p.

Designed to supplement to a degree the coverage of Sears's *Song Index* (entry 671), this represents a good companion to the original edition of *Popular Song Index* (entry 670), as they both begin their coverage with 1940 imprints. Anthologies in de Charms range from 1940 to 1957. De Charms concentrates primarily on anthologies of art songs and operatic arias, with less emphasis on traditional folk song collections. (There are just a few popular song books which are, of course, the primary focus of *Popular Song Index*.) Songs in 400 collections are indexed, with separate sections given to composed songs, anonymous and folk songs, carols, and sea chanteys. There is an index to first lines and one to authors, with the collections listed at the beginning of the volume.

673. **Where's That Tune? An Index to Songs in Fakebooks.** William D. Goodfellow. Metuchen, NJ: Scarecrow Press, 1990. 449p. ISBN 0-8108-2391-8.

This index identifies 13,500 songs in sixty-four fakebooks. *Fakebooks* are collections of popular songs for which the words, melody lines, and chord notations are provided; they are utilized by musicians to support and enhance their repertoire. Fakebooks indexed in this source were published generally within the past decade and are available in libraries. There are three major parts or segments to the index, with part 1 listing the fakebooks treated. Citations include OCLC number, along with brief descriptive annotations supplying the number of songs or amount of musical notation. Popular songs of all kinds are included: jazz, pop/rock, children's songs, country, show tunes, Christian music, and more. The second part is a title index to all the songs with coded references to the fakebooks; part 3 supplies an index of composers that lists the song titles but not the fakebooks.

DICTIONARIES, ENCYCLOPEDIAS, AND HANDBOOKS

674. **Encyclopedia of the Blues.** Gerard Herzhaft. Fayetteville, AR: University of Arkansas Press, 1992. 513p. ISBN 1-55728-252-8.

Because blues music represents a crossover form and shares the musicians and certain elements of rock, gospel, soul, etc., this is a useful tool in focussing on the genre. Initially a French work, the translation reads well in providing coverage of personalities, instruments, and places, with entries arranged alphabetically. Treatment of instruments is interesting and geographical locations are described in terms of their influences and styles, and their connection with the development of blues music. There are numerous black-and-white photographs, and the work concludes with a bibliography and discography of selective nature. Access is aided by a general index along with an index by instrument.

Hit Parade: An Encyclopedia of the Top Songs of the Jazz, Depression, Swing and Sing Eras by Don Tyler (Quill/William Morrow, 1985) is an interesting and useful chronology of a variety of popular songs that appeal to a wide audience. Entries are alphabetically arranged by title, in chapters that are classified in chronological order. Each entry furnishes name of composer and lyricist, followed by a fairly detailed description of the song. This normally covers circumstances of its introduction, performers, rivals, etc. Introductory material preceding each chapter describes in a highly informal manner the nature of the period. Some errors have been pointed out but, in general, it is a good purchase for a general audience. There are indexes of song titles and of proper names.

675. **Facts Behind the Songs: A Handbook of American Popular Music from the Nineties to the '90s**. Marvin E. Paymer, ed. New York: Garland, 1993. 560p. ISBN 0-8240-5240-4.

This is a handy source of information on popular music in this country, organized into two major sections. The first part supplies about 325 articles on popular songs, describing their origins (such as classic or film musical); foreign influences, if any; domestic roots or influences, such as Motown or Bluegrass; means of popularization, such as "Your Hit Parade"; genre, such as doo-wop or protest song; subject or topic, such as humor or money; and style, such as harmony or scat. Entries on the "Depression Years" and "Roaring Twenties" treat the musical development of historical periods. The second section lists the songs and identifies year, lyricist, composer, type, source, production, etc., with cross-references to articles in the first segment. Fifteen specialized tables identify various award winners and source listings. Bibliographies accompany some of the entries.

676. **The Guinness Encyclopedia of Popular Music**. Colin Larkin, comp. and ed. Chester, CT: New England Publishing Associates, 1992. 4v. ISBN 1-882267-00-1.

This is the most comprehensive reference work on the topic of popular music and provides alphabetically arranged listings of "every important artist, band, genre, group, event, instrument, publisher, promoter, and musical style." Some 10,000 entries are treated within the massive four-volume work; these vary in length, depending upon the importance of the topic, from about 150 to 3,000 words (as in the case of Duke Ellington). Nearly 100 specialists have contributed their efforts. Popular music of the twentieth century is covered thoroughly, with some emphasis on the more recent era of rock. Artists of all nations are included, including those of the East, such as Ryuichi Sakamoto of Japan. Biographical entries give basic factual data along with interpretation of influences, motivation, and success. Events treated include festivals, along with coverage of organizations. There are a massive bibliography and a detailed index. A one-volume concise edition with the same title was issued in 1993.

677. **Lissauer's Encyclopedia of Popular Music in America: 1888 to the Present**. Robert Lissauer. New York: Paragon House, 1991. 1687p. ISBN 1-55778-015-3.

This is another useful source of information for identification of popular music in this country written by an expert in the field. About 19,000 songs spanning a period of 100 years are listed alphabetically in the first section of the work. Entries may supply lyricist, composer, dates, brief history, musical productions, performers, and recordings in narratives varying in length from about ten to sixty-five words. Academy Award winners are noted. All types of songs are treated, including country, rock, jazz, blues, show tunes, and other forms popular in their eras, with cross-references to alternative titles. A second section supplies a chronology listing titles by year of recording or height of popularity. A third part provides an index of authors. Special features include a glossary of terms and a selective bibliography.

678. **The New Grove Dictionary of Jazz**. Barry Kernfeld, ed. London: Macmillan; New York: Grove's Dictionary of Music, 1988. 2v. ISBN 0-935859-39-X.

This is a comprehensive and well-constructed encyclopedia from a fine publishing house on topics and various personalities related to jazz. All periods and all styles are described, with coverage on an international basis. There are some 4,500 entries covering both soloists and groups, bands, styles, topics, instruments, record labels, organizations, and terminology. Most of the biographical entries treat performers, although coverage is given to composers, writers, producers, arrangers, editors, discographers, and others. There are some 200 entries on jazz theory, with lengthy discourse given to survey articles on such topics as "arrangement" and "beat." Specific musical terms receive briefer treatment, several paragraphs in length; most entries supply detailed bibliographies. Coverage given to instruments emphasizes their use in jazz and contrasts that with other genres. Some 350 recording studios are treated historically, with indication of achievements. There is an extensive bibliography of bibliographies in the appendix.

679. **The Oxford Companion to Popular Music**. Peter Gammond. New York: Oxford University Press, 1991; repr. with corr., 1993. 739p. ISBN 0-19-280004-3.

Defining *popular music* as not serious or classical, this is another of the specialized one-volume handbooks in the Companion series. Like others, it provides one- or two-paragraph descriptions along with articles of several pages on major topics or important personalities. Popular music of the Western world is treated (jazz, blues, ragtime, country, operetta and music hall, folk, military, rhythm and blues, etc.). The emphasis is on music in the English language; coverage runs from 1850 to 1985. There is greater coverage of the first half of the twentieth century; relatively brief coverage is given to the major rock and rollers of the recent past. Entries provide biographical sketches of all types of personalities, from performers to executives, plot descriptions of shows and films, and individual songs. The work is indexed by personalities, shows and films, and albums.

680. **Resource Guide to Themes in Contemporary American Song Lyrics, 1950-1985**. B. Lee Cooper. Westport, CT: Greenwood Press, 1986. 458p. ISBN 0-313-24516-9.

A newer tool that has proved valuable for research on song themes is this handbook covering American song production over the past thirty-five years. Categories are defined in terms of socioeconomic elements of importance today, such as death, education, marriage and divorce, occupations, race relations, urban life, youth culture, etc. These categories are then subdivided into more specific themes. A most interesting sociological study is possible through the linking of these topics with music of our time, and comparisons are surely in order with other decades. Several tables show relationships of songs to various events. Both the bibliography and the discography are lengthy and useful.

681. **Variety Music Cavalcade, 1620-1969: A Chronology of Vocal and Instrumental Music Popular in the U.S.** 3d ed. Julius Mattfeld. New York: Prentice-Hall, 1971. 766p. ISBN 0-13-940718-9.

One of the important works in the field is this highly respected chronology of popular music. It spans a period of 350 years, beginning with the Pilgrims, and provides brief descriptions of various events along with the listings of songs. The events are social, political, and literary and help to provide some idea of the context of the period in which the songs were developed. Songs are of varied types and include hymns, all types of popular secular music, sacred songs, choral compositions, and instrumental and orchestral works. Only musical elements (not social events) are indexed, along with dates that lead the user to the proper year. Songs are listed alphabetically under the year of publication and are accompanied by information on composer, lyricist, publisher, and copyright date.

682. **Year by Year in the Rock Era: Events and Conditions Shaping the Rock Genera-tions That Reshaped America.** Herb Hendler. Westport, CT: Greenwood Press, 1983. Repr., New York: Praeger, 1987. 350p. ISBN 0-313-23456-6.

This is a detailed chronology of the twenty-eight-year period from 1954 through 1981, in which rock music is placed within the context of social events in much the same manner as *Variety Music Cavalcade* (entry 681) treats popular music. The author is a former record company executive and has provided a wealth of information by covering each year individually and listing major performers, dancers, and news of the rock music industry along with social, cultural, and political information gleaned from the news. Statistics, fashions, slang, and the like, are included. In addition, there is an interesting section analyzing the rock era by category such as cost of living, *Time* "Man of the Year" winners, and top television shows. The work concludes with a detailed bibliography.

Another chronology of the same period is *Rolling Stone Rock Almanac: The Chronicle of Rock and Roll* (Collier Books/Macmillan, 1983). The introduction of this work describes the history and development of rock and roll and its relationship to rhythm and blues, country and western, etc. The years 1954-1982 are described individually, first with a brief introduc-tory essay, then by a calendar of events. *Shake, Rattle & Roll: The Golden Age of American*

Rock n' Roll, Volume 1 1952-1955 by Lee Cotten is a recent entry in the field (Pierian Press, 1989). Projected as a four-volume history, beginning with coverage of the early formative years in this volume, it will carry through Woodstock. It furnishes a detailed chronology of daily occurrences, events, and happenings, such as openings and closings of concert runs, stage appearances, details of performance, etc. Several indexes furnish access.

An interesting and unique work is *Doo-Wop: The Forgotten Third of Rock n' Roll* by Anthony J. Gribin and Matthew M. Schiff (Krause, 1992) providing treatment of that distinctive vocal style of the 1950s marked by group harmony and range of voices that may include falsetto. The work opens with several useful introductory essays describing the characteristics of the music, followed by a listing of artists and their recordings for which year and label are given.

DIRECTORIES, ANNUALS, AND CURRENT AWARENESS SOURCES

*683. **Billboard.** New York: Billboard Publications, 1984- . Wk. ISSN 0006-2510.

Considered to be the equivalent to music of what *Variety* (entry 871) is to theater and film, this well-known publication appears in a newspaper/magazine format. With a weekly circulation of nearly 50,000, it represents one of the most popular offerings and provides excellent current awareness of news in the music field. The focus is on publishing, recording, and selling music, and articles cover personalities, recent contracts, and shows recently given or soon to be seen, as well as new albums and tapes. The writing style is snappy and informal, and the publication does an excellent job of keeping readers abreast of developments in rock, pop, country, and folk music. Although there is a rather costly index, all materials including reviews are indexed in *Music Index* (entry 575).

Billboard Information Network is an online database that includes charts appearing in the magazine. The aim is to provide market research data on sales, rentals, and play of popular recordings, videos, and related products for home entertainment. About 700 radio stations and 100 dance clubs are monitored. It is available from the publisher, covers the most recent three weeks, and is updated daily. *Rock Net* is another daily service available online through CompuServe. It furnishes reports on the rock music industry (news, concert schedules, reviews, etc.). The system includes online conferences and interviews with rock stars.

684. **Songwriter's Market: When and How to Market Your Songs.** Cincinnati, OH: Writer's Digest Books, 1979- . Ann. ISSN 0161-5971.

The 1992 edition of this popular guide to the marketplace, edited by Mark Garvey, continues in the same manner as its previous issues and of other titles in the Writer's Digest series. There is an introductory narrative on the profession of songwriting, followed by extensive listings of commercial firms involved in the sale and purchasing of songs. Content of articles varies with the importance of issues in the music industry. More than 850 new listings have been added since the previous issue. General information is given regarding address, description, contacts, etc. for the various firms and individuals. Emphasis is on the American music industry, although there are listings for international firms based in other countries of the world. Music publishers, record companies, and record producers are all included. Appendices provide information on a host of topics such as contracts and management of records. A glossary and detailed index are furnished.

BIOGRAPHICAL SOURCES

685. **American Musicians: Fifty-Six Portraits in Jazz.** Whitney Balliett. New York: Oxford University Press, 1986; repr. 1990. 415p. ISBN 0-19-506088-1 (pbk).

Described by the author as a "highly personal encyclopedia," this collective biography represents a compilation of Balliett's numerous contributions to *The New Yorker* over a twenty-five-year period beginning with the early 1960s. The book begins with biographies of two writers: jazz historian Hughes Panassie and discographer Charles Delaunay. It then treats jazz musicians in chronological sequence. The names are well known to most people who have even a passing acquaintance with jazz: "King" Oliver, Sidney Bechet, Duke Ellington, Coleman Hawkins, etc. The author has used his personal interviews with the subjects or their associates as well as standard biographies and various other accounts, to produce cogent and well-developed narratives as well as biographical highlights. Numerous quotations provide real insight into each subject's nature.

686. **American Women Songwriters: A Biographical Dictionary**. Virginia L. Grattan. Westport, CT: Greenwood Press, 1993. 279p. ISBN 0-313-28510-1.

This work fills a basic need in providing coverage of women songwriters overlooked by such dictionaries of music as David Ewen's *American Songwriters* (Wilson, 1986). This is the first work of this type to target this group, resulting in a biographical dictionary of more than 180 women who have written songs for the theater, film, concert hall, and recording label. Included here are all types of popular music: country, blues, jazz, folk, gospel, and rock. Madonna, Janet Jackson, and Mariah Carey are treated along with now-obscure writers of the nineteenth and twentieth centuries. Issue will be taken with omissions rather than inclusions, and treatment is cursory in nature. Entries supply mostly one-page coverage that includes a biographical sketch with career highlights, listing of most important or famous songs, and a few additional sources of information.

687. **Blues Who's Who: A Biographical Dictionary of Blues Singers.** Sheldon Harris. New Rochelle, NY: Arlington House, 1979. Repr. (supp. by author emendations), Da Capo, 1991. 775p. ISBN 0-306-80155-8.

Considered to be the most substantial and complete source of biographical information on blues singers, this work lists the personalities by their real names. As a result, there are many cross-references from variations and stage names to the proper entries. Hundreds of personalities are covered and (although Mahalia Jackson and Billie Holliday have been omitted) coverage is excellent among those local singers, both urban and rural, who achieved some measure of national or international recognition. Howlin' Wolf, Muddy Waters, and B. B. King are listed, of course, among many others. Entries include a biographical sketch, birthdate and place, marriages, children, instruments, songs composed, influences, and critical comments concerning their work. A detailed list of professional concert appearances, television and radio shows, films, etc., is provided.

Great Guitarists, by Rich Kienzle (Facts on File, 1985), offers lengthy biographical essays on the lives of sixty guitarists, including blues performers as well as jazz and rock people. Suggestions about good recordings for further listening are given.

*688. **Contemporary Musicians**. Detroit: Gale Research, 1989- . Semiann. ISSN 1044-2197.

The first issue of this serial publication appeared in 1989, the intent being to continue it as a semiannual production. Each issue covers from 80 to 100 well-known performers and writers of the popular music scene. Included here are personalities and groups from jazz, rock, blues, folk, country, and rhythm and blues as well as rap, New Age, and reggae. As one might imagine, coverage has been diverse: Anita Baker, the Kingston Trio, Reba McIntyre, and Metallica have all been featured. Entries are signed by their contributors, specialists in the field, and furnish bio-critical essays of about 2,000 words. There is a section of biographical data, a selective discography, and a bibliography as well. Like others in the Gale lineup, this work is regarded as an in-depth biographical resource. There are indexes of musicians and of subjects. The work is available online through NEXIS.

689. **The Encyclopedia of Folk, Country, & Western Music.** 2d ed. Irwin Stambler and Grelun Landon. New York: St. Martin's Press, 1984. 902p. ISBN 0-312-248199.

Generally regarded as one of the leading biographical dictionaries, this edition of the encyclopedia updates and expands the number of entries in the previous edition from 500 to more than 600 names. Many popular and known performers from the contemporary scene are present, with data being derived from responses to questionnaires supplied by them or by their estates, if deceased. In a number of cases, documents and other literature provided the source material. The biographies are lengthy and detailed for the most part, although the material does not seem to go beyond 1980. An excellent section includes music awards from a variety of organizations, and there is a useful and comprehensive bibliography.

Artists of American Folk Music: The Legends of Traditional Folk Music ..., edited by Phil Hood (William Morrow, 1986) is a highly selective biographical encyclopedia which may be considered supplementary to this entry. It covers only thirty-one different groups or solo performers, but it does so in depth. Articles run from three to six pages in length. The selection includes such individuals as the Kingston Trio, Peter, Paul, and Mary, Bob Dylan, Woody Guthrie, Pete Seeger, and Leadbelly, who are considered leaders in the troubadour tradition.

690. The Harmony Illustrated Encyclopedia of Rock. 7th ed. Mike Clifford and Pete Frame. New York: Harmony Books/Crown, 1992. 208p. ISBN 0-517-59078-6.

This work of British authorship has appeared frequently (6th ed., 1988) and is considered a useful biographical source on rock music. It has been a consistent favorite among devotees of the genre for nearly twenty years, and covers approximately 1,000 performers thought to be significant. There is some emphasis on British stars, thus overlooking some reasonably important American contributors. As is true of any work of this type, there are some errors and oversights, but the quality of writing is excellent and the content is well presented in an entertaining fashion with many illustrations. Coverage tends to be mainstream.

Norm N. Nite's *Rock On: The Illustrated Encyclopedia of Rock n' Roll* (Harper & Row, 1982-1985) is a three-volume update of an earlier work published in 1979 and provides revisions and enlargements of the biographies of hundreds of artists. It gives good accounts of their careers and includes good discographies. The volumes cover the solid gold years prior to 1964; the years of change, 1964-1978; and the video revolution from 1978 to the time of publication. *Lillian Roxon's Rock Encyclopedia*, edited by Ed Naha (Grosset & Dunlap, 1978) is a tried-and-true source of information always considered to be authoritative, now spiced up by Naha's flippant style. An old favorite, now in its second edition, is Irwin Stambler's *Encyclopedia of Pop, Rock, and Soul* (St. Martin's Press, 1990). This updates and revises the initial 1975 effort as a biographical dictionary of performers, producers, and others important on the rock scene. Articles are well developed and vary in length with importance of the personalities. The emphasis is on influential persons; coverage is given in depth to 500 figures.

691. The Heritage Encyclopedia of Band Music: Composers and their Music. William H. Rehrig; ed. by Paul E. Bierley. Westerville, OH: Integrity Press, 1991. 2v. ISBN 0-918048-08-7.

Regarded by its makers as a seminal volume on band music and its composition, this important tool attempts to document all editions of all music ever published for concert and military bands. The result is an extensive bio-bibliography treating some 9,000 composers of band music and their works. Entries are arranged alphabetically and supply listings of compositions along with references to source materials. Omitted is brass band music, treated well by other tools, and the continents of South America and Africa, because of the scantiness of their information. The utility of this work lies in its coverage of personalities and compositions not included in standard works of the field. Other specialized sources have not been as comprehensive; therefore, it is becoming the standard reference tool for band music. Numerous appendices provide additional information; a title index provides access.

692. Kingsbury's Who's Who in Country & Western Music. Kenn Kingsbury, ed. Culver City, CA: Black Stallion Country Press, 1981. 304p.

A useful biographical dictionary of country music personalities, this comprehensive source provides brief but informative biographical portraits of 716 individuals. These personalities are not limited to performers, but include country music industry people such as publishers and record company executives. Biographies are brief and highly stylized in length and coverage, but do an adequate job in identifying and describing individuals. Pictures are included as well. Recording artists, studio musicians, disc jockeys, composers, agents, etc., are listed, although the emphasis is, of course, on the performers. There are excellent listings of 2,000 radio stations, record companies, publishers, talent agencies, and award winners.

Updated and revised, the third edition of *The Harmony Illustrated Encyclopedia of Country Music*, by Fred Dellar and others (Harmony Books/Crown, 1994) is a biographical dictionary written in a light fashion that covers approximately 450 performers in satisfactory fashion. It is a chatty, well-illustrated, enjoyable tool, and continues to cover the early stars along with the contemporary performers. Promotional photographs are included.

693. The Literature of Rock, III, 1984-1990: With Additional Material for the Period 1954-1983. Frank Hoffman and B. Lee Cooper. Metuchen, NJ: Scarecrow Press, 1994. 2v. ISBN 0-8108-2762-X.

This work is a continuation of two earlier works by the authors from the same publisher. Hoffman authored *The Literature of Rock, 1954-1978* in 1981, covering a twenty-five-year period of writings on rock music. Then Hoffman amd Cooper added *The Literature of Rock II, 1979-1983*, supplementing the initial effort with additional material omitted in the earlier issue and at the same time extending the coverage a few more years. The present effort continues the pattern. All works furnish a selective annotated bibliography of books and periodical articles, arranged in subject categories reflecting a chronological sequence. Such periods as doo wop, rhythm and blues, soul, etc., are included. Most entries are for individuals, although some subjects are given. Source materials include fanzines, trade magazines, books, undergrounds, etc. Each volume has a detailed index and a useful discography.

694. Soul Music A-Z. Hugh Gregory. London: Blandford/Cassell; distr., New York: Sterling, 1991. 266p. ISBN 0-7137-2179-0.

Gregory, a British writer, has chosen to examine a musical element developed by black Americans but later expanded to include white performers who have operated within that synthesis of rhythm and blues and gospel. The result is a biracial biographical dictionary providing detailed sketches of some 600 performers, songwriters, and producers. The range is great, from early practitioners like Little Willie John to today's Mariah Carey and rapper LL Cool J. Entries are arranged alphabetically and, in addition to biographies, furnish highlights of careers, listings of hits, chartings of both the British and U.S. markets, and discographies for some of the performers. All the big-name performers and groups seem to be treated, but real value lies in the documentation of the lives and efforts of the obscure individuals covered. Numerous cross-references are given; a brief bibliography is included.

695. Who's Who of Jazz: Storyville to Swing Street. 5th ed. John Chilton. London: Papermac, 1989. 375p. ISBN 0333483758 (pbk).

This is a well-developed biographical dictionary of more than 1,000 jazz personalities born before 1920 and raised in the United States. Biographies vary in length with the prominence of the individual and range from a brief paragraph to two full pages. Emphasis is placed on the person's career and musical development rather than his or her personal life. A section with photographs and a list of jazz periodicals arranged by country of publication is included.

Leonard Feather has provided an excellent series of biographical dictionaries keyed to different decades. *The Encyclopedia of Jazz* (Horizon, 1960; repr., Da Capo, 1984) is a revised edition of an earlier work and furnishes biographies and illustrations of more than 2,000 performers of that time, with a guide to their recordings. *The Encyclopedia of Jazz in the Sixties* (Horizon, 1966; repr., Da Capo, 1986) updates its predecessor; and Feather and Ira Gitler collaborated on *The Encyclopedia of Jazz in the Seventies* (Horizon, 1976; repr., Da Capo, 1987). This volume extends the coverage of the series to 1975 and adds lists of jazz films and recordings.

RECORDINGS

696. **Billboard Top 1000 Singles, 1955-1992**. Joel Whitburn, comp. Milwaukee, WI: Hal Leonard, 1993. 143p. ISBN 0-7935-2072-X.

Based on data culled from *Billboard* magazine (entry 683), this slender but useful revision of earlier publications covers the period beginning in 1955. It supplies a listing of the top 1,000 hits over a span of thirty-seven years along with a year-by-year ranking of the top 40. Rankings are based on the highest position attained, and longevity as number 1, top 10, and top 40. These listings and rankings are taken from *Billboard* and are of interest to those who need to examine the field of popular music.

A *Billboard* product is *Billboard's Hottest Hot 100 Hits*, by Fred Bransom (Billboard Books/Watson Guptill, 1991), which identifies thirty-five years of hits, also beginning with "Rock Around the Clock" in 1955 and extending through 1990. This work is much more comprehensive in listing the performers and their top 100 hits. Writers are treated in similar manner along with producers. Descriptive sketches are furnished for each. There is a history of most important chart singles for forty-three different record companies. There are numerous specialized listings, including one for the top 3,000 hits of the rock era. Another *Billboard* effort is *The Billboard Book of Top 40 Albums*, by Joel Whitburn, in its revised edition (Billboard Books/Watson-Guptill, 1991). Lists have been updated to 1990, with focus on the most successful artists and their albums.

697. **The Blackwell Guide to Recorded Blues.** Paul Oliver, ed. Cambridge, MA: Blackwell Reference, 1991. 372p. ISBN 0-631-18301-9.

Oliver has earned a well-deserved reputation as a competent jazz and blues critic and historian and has used his expertise to produce this historical discography and guide for collectors of blues music. The initial issue appeared in 1989. The work is divided into several chapters, each written by noted specialists; the first chapter is authored by Oliver, who describes the origin of blues as a Southern variant of earlier folk music and religious music. Chapters are arranged historically, with each one treating a particular style or time period. In addition to the narrative, each chapter provides a list of ten essential recordings along with a list of thirty basic recordings. The historical discography works well for both collectors and serious students in addressing their information needs. Included are a bibliography and several maps, along with a general index.

A complementary guide is *The Down Home Guide to the Blues*, by Frank Scott and the staff of Down Home Music (A Cappella Book; distr., Independent Publishers Group, 1991). This is a more comprehensive tool supplying more than 3,500 reviews of blues recordings culled from twelve years of a newsletter produced by Down Home Music, a mail-order supplier of blues records. Both individual and group recordings are treated. Arrangement is alphabetical by name of performer; a second section treats prewar and postwar anthologies. Reviews address the quality and style of recordings. There is a listing of 100 essential recordings. Unfortunately, there are no indexes.

698. **The Cash Box/Black Contemporary Singles Chart, 1960-1984.** George Albert and Frank Hoffman. Metuchen, NJ: Scarecrow Press, 1986. 704p. ISBN 0-8108-1853-1.

Formerly called rhythm and blues, black contemporary music appeals to an ever-growing audience of white Americans. *Cash Box* magazine has treated the music in a variety of ways over the past twenty-five years. Its listings were fragmented and scattered in different sections and under different categories. This work follows a format established by these authors in previous publications on pop and country music, and makes the weekly chart information of twenty-five years of listings easy to find and convenient to use. Arrangement is alphabetical by performers, with a list of recorded songs alphabetically organized under their names. Entries provide name of song, date of entry onto the chart, record label and number, weekly position, and total weeks on the chart. Another alphabetical listing of song titles includes cross-references to the performers. Additional interesting information is given in the appendices.

The same authors have produced a companion publication, *The Cash Box Black Contemporary Album Charts, 1975-1987* (Scarecrow Press, 1989), also based on weekly charts from the magazine. There is an extensive artist index, alphabetically arranged, which furnishes dates of chart entry, album, label, and weeks on the chart. An album-title index is also included.

699. **The Decca Hillbilly Discography: 1927-1945.** Cary Ginell, comp. New York: Greenwood Press, 1989. 402p. ISBN 0-313-26053-2.

An important tool from the standpoint of historical documentation is this listing of more than 1,500 discs issued by Decca, the leading record label for country and rural music in those early years. Included here are the recordings in the important and prolific 5000 series, 17000 or Cajun series, 45000 or Champion series, and all Decca productions issued on the Montgomery Ward label. Unreleased recordings are included in the comprehensive coverage given to the 5000 and 17000 series. The compiler, an academic who used his personal collection to begin the study, has provided an opening introductory essay giving historical perspective. Listings are by catalog number and identify artists, titles, and instruments. Adequate indexing is furnished by artist, location, composer, and title.

The Billboard Book of Number One Country Hits, by Tom Roland (Billboard Books/Watson Guptill, 1991), covers the period 1968-1989 and identifies all songs ranked number one by Billboard. Some 825 songs are treated with entries providing descriptions of their stories and their eras. Recordings are identified fully and dates are included. About 150 photographs are furnished. The work is indexed by performer and title.

700. **The Jazz Discography.** Tom Lord. West Vancouver, BC: Lord Reference; Redwood, NY: Cadence Jazz Books, 1992- . v.1- . ISBN 1-881993-05-1 (v.6).

Projected as a twenty-volume work, this comprehensive effort by Tom Lord is scheduled for publication over a period of four years. It is anticipated to cover approximately 100,000 entries in treating every known jazz recording in unprecedented comprehensive fashion from 1898 to date of publication. Jazz in all its forms (early, contemporary, Dixieland, swing, etc.) is covered. As of 1993, six volumes have been issued, with coverage through "E" and into "F" in an alphabetical arrangement by name of leader. Information is given for each recording session (band leader, album title, name of group, performers and their instruments, location and date, names of songs and selections, and album numbers).

A useful foreign contribution that complements this work is *Jazz Records, 1942-1980: A Discography*, by Erik Raben (Stainless/Wintermoon; Jazz Media Aps, 1987-). This is a new edition of a multivolume effort initially published over a seven-year period from 1963 to 1970 and covering the era from 1942 to 1969. Volume 1 of the new edition (A-Barnes) continues in the same tradition, providing a detailed compilation of jazz records and earning respect for its comprehensiveness.

701. **Jazz Records 1897-1942: Fifth Revised and Enlarged Edition.** Brian Rust. Chigwell, UK: Storyville Publications, 1982. 2v. ISBN 0902391046.

Considered the standard source for both music librarians and devotees, the fifth edition of this title is an update, correction, and extension of earlier versions. It lists more than 30,000 jazz recordings by American and British artists in standard format, arranged by name of performer. Entries include personnel, instruments, and listing of recording sessions. Information is given about the matrix number, label, and catalog issue number (78s only), with indication of vocals. A song index covers more than 16,000 titles and an artist index includes more than 10,000 band leaders, musicians, singers, and arrangers. There are numerous cross-references to clarify obscure pseudonyms. Since publication of *The Complete Entertainment Discography from the Mid-1890's to 1942* by Rust and Allen G. Debus in 1973, and its second edition by Rust entitled *The Complete Entertainment Discography, from 1897 to 1942* (Da Capo, 1989), as well as Rust's *The American Dance Band Discography, 1917-1942* (Arlington House, 1975), the jazz discography now more closely restricts the entries to jazz and blues recordings.

A more selective effort is *The Blackwell Guide to Recorded Jazz*, edited by Barry Kernfeld (Basil Blackwell, 1991). As part of a series of discographies for the publisher, this work identifies and describes a starter collection of 125 recordings in eleven stylistic categories. Contributors are specialists in the field who provide a well-developed overview and commentary, some of which is highly subjective.

702. **1900-1965 American Premium Record Guide: 78's, 45's, and LP's Identification and Values.** 4th ed. L. R. Docks. Florence, AL: Books Americana, 1992. 447p. ISBN 0896890880.

This is an especially useful discography and guide to the recordings of popular music over a sixty-five-year period. It gives an additional fifteen years of coverage, dating from 1900 rather than from 1915 as in the third edition. It treats a variety of record types, as enumerated in the title, but is limited to the disc format. Format is similar to the previous effort, with recordings divided into four major styles: jazz/big band, blues, country and western, and rhythm and blues. The jazz/big band section receives the most coverage, followed by rhythm and blues, which includes rock and roll. Entries are listed by name of performer and provide evaluative commentary as well as identification, making this a useful source for record collectors. The guide provides a glossary of terms and valuable hints for collecting and understanding the market.

A popular source, now in its third edition, is *The Rolling Stone Album Guide*, edited by Anthony DeCurtis and others (Random House, 1993). First issued in 1979, coverage is given to thousands of albums—in fact, it claims to have included every essential album and essential artist available in the areas of rock, pop, soul, country, soul, blues, jazz, and gospel. Comprehensiveness is impressive, although coverage of rock and soul is more exhaustive than is true of some of the other areas. Another staple is *The Trouser Press Record Guide*, edited by Ira A. Robbins and in its fourth edition (Collier Books/Macmillan, 1991). Coverage is given to some 9,500 CDs and cassettes from some 2,500 bands in this comprehensive listing of available recordings through March 1991.

Musical Theater and Film

BIBLIOGRAPHIES AND CATALOGS

703. **A Comprehensive Bibliography of Music for Film and Television.** Steven D. Wescott, comp. Detroit: Information Coordinators, 1985. 432p. ISBN 0-89990-027-5.

To complement the earlier efforts by Limbacher (entry 704), this more comprehensive compilation identifies nearly 6,350 books, periodicals, and other materials on the popular topic. Treated in these works is the dramatic aspect of music in film and television, as well as its presence in documentaries, advertising, experimental and innovative applications, and its sociocultural context. Radio music is also included in this broad-based bibliography that contains the works of more than 3,700 authors from twenty-eight countries representing eighteen different languages. The work is divided into three major areas: "history," with nearly 3,000 entries identifying surveys and critiques; "composer" (nearly 1,350 entries), treating personalities; and "themes" (more than 2,000 entries), providing sections in aesthetics, special topics, and research. Entries supply full bibliographic descriptions, with publication dates through January 1984. A detailed general index supplies access.

704. **Film Music: From Violins to Video.** James L. Limbacher, ed. and comp. Metuchen, NJ: Scarecrow Press, 1974. 835p. ISBN 0-8108-0651-7.

Because the area of film music has been relatively overlooked, this book has filled a need in reference work. Although it has been criticized for certain omissions and lack of clarity regarding its selection criteria, it has been used by both serious students and interested laypersons in pursuit of information on the nature of film music up to 1972. Part 1 consists of excellent notes and commentary on film music by composers such as Dimitri Tiompkin and Sir William Walton. Part 2 provides various listings, including an alphabetical list of titles with dates, chronological list of films with composers, composers and their films, and musical scores by film title.

A supplementary work by the same author is *Keeping Score: Film Music 1972-1979* (Scarecrow Press, 1981), which continues the listings in three major sections arranged by film titles, composers, and recorded musical scores. Both of these works are updated and expanded through Limbacher's most recent effort, *Keeping Score: Film and Television Music 1980-1988 (with Additional Coverage of 1921-1979)* (Scarecrow Press, 1991), which furnishes a chronological listing of films and television programs from 1921 to 1988 followed by a listing by composer and date of production. A discography follows.

A comprehensive effort is *Movie Song Catalog: Performers and Supporting Crew for the Songs Sung in 1460 Musical and Nonmusical Films, 1928-1988* (McFarland, 1993), by Ruth Benjamin and Arthur Rosenblatt. The title is self-explanatory in its intent to identify song titles from sixty years of motion-picture making. Entries supply year, country, running time, music directors, writers, and vocalists. The work is accessed through indexes by title, performer, and songwriter.

705. **A Guide to Critical Reviews: Part II The Musical, 1909-1989.** 3d ed. James M. Salem. Metuchen, NJ: Scarecrow Press, 1991. 820p. ISBN 0-8108-2387-X.

This is part 2 of a five-volume set that covers American and foreign drama and the screenplay (entry 818n). The third edition furnishes listings of critical reviews for nearly 2,700 Broadway and off-Broadway shows performed between 1909 and 1989. These reviews appeared in popular magazines or in the *New York Times*, and provide both the researcher and the theater buff with useful information. Arrangement of entries is alphabetical by title of play, and entries furnish openings, closings, and numbers of performances, as well as names of writers, lyricists, choreographers, and others concerned with the production. Cast listings are not given.

DICTIONARIES, ENCYCLOPEDIAS, ETC.

706. **American Musical Theatre: A Chronicle.** 2d ed. Gerald Bordman. New York: Oxford University Press, 1992. 821p. ISBN 0-19-507242-1.

This is an update and revision of Bordman's 1978 and 1986 editions, which covered the musical theater from 1866 to the 1970s and 1980s respectively. Beginning with a prologue that summarizes the development of musical theater in this country from its beginnings to 1866, the new work covers each year in detail through the 1989-1990 season. Developments of the season are described, "hits" are identified, and musicals are arranged by date of opening. Included are plot synopses, names of performers, important songs, and a brief analysis of the impact of the show or its relative position in the context of musical theater. Critical comments from reviewers are included. Biographies are given for various personalities (composers, playwrights, actors, etc.). An index for shows and sources identifies original sources from which the musicals were derived. Also included are a song index and an index of personal names.

More comprehensive listings are found in Ken Bloom's *American Song: The Complete Musical Theatre Companion* (Facts on File, 1985). This is a two-volume collection of information on nearly 3,300 musical productions from 1900 to 1984. Included are musical plays from Broadway, off-Broadway, regional theater, touring groups, burlesque, vaudeville, and even foreign productions by major American composers. There are no plot summaries or critical analysis. Indexing is vast, with more than 42,000 songs and 16,000 personalities. Issued the same year as Bloom is *Broadway Musicals: Show by Show*, by Stanley Green (Hal Leonard Books, 1985). Less comprehensive than either Bloom or Bordman, coverage is given to some 300 hit Broadway musicals from 1866 to 1985. Entries supply a synopsis, list of credits, and miscellaneous interesting facts, along with photographs. Several indexes provide access.

707. **Encyclopedia of the Musical Theatre.** Kurt Ganzl. New York: Schirmer/Macmillan, 1994. 2v. ISBN 0-02-871445-8.

This is a comprehensive encyclopedia by a recognized expert on musical theater, with some 2,700 entries alphabetically arranged. It treats all aspects of the musical theater from the mid-nineteenth century to the present day. Plot summaries are furnished for more than 1,000 musicals and represent a well-chosen array of productions from Broadway, London, and the European continent. More than half the entries are given to coverage of personalities: performers, writers, composers, producers, designers, costumers, arrangers, etc. More than 300 photographs are included. The work is well indexed.

Ganzl's Book of the Musical Theatre is an earlier, more selective effort by Ganzl and Andrew Lamb (Schirmer/Macmillan, 1989) designed to complement the Kobbé work on the opera (entry 638) and provide similar coverage for musical theater. More than 300 musicals, operettas, and comic operas are treated with entries from three to four pages giving synopses and listing productions, cast of characters, and references to songs. Arrangement of entries is in five major geographical segments treating sixty-nine musicals of Great Britain (1782-1987); fifty-three of France (to 1980); ninety-five from the United States (1890-1983); seventy-four from Austria, Germany, or Hungary (1865-1964); and seven from Spain (to 1932). Selection is based on popularity and frequency of performance, historical significance, and the authors' personal preferences. Sections are preceded by introductory essays on the history of musical theater in respective locales. There is a discography, an index of names and titles, and an index of songs.

708. **Film and Television Composers: An International Discography, 1920-1989.** Steve Harris. Jefferson, NC: McFarland, 1992. 302p. ISBN 0-89950-553-8.

Derived somewhat from an earlier work by Harris (described later), the new effort provides updated and more comprehensive coverage of film and television music than did its predecessor. Here are nearly 8,000 entries of phonograph records arranged alphabetically by composer. Entries supply production title, country, record format, label, and catalog number. This effort contains an additional three years' production of films, along with inclusions from earlier dates omitted in the previous effort. Composers from fourteen countries are represented, with special emphasis on the United States, Great Britain, France, and Italy. Treated here is original music as well as compositions adapted for television or film.

Harris's earlier work, *Film, Television, and Stage Music on Phonograph Records: A Discography* (McFarland, 1988), supplies about the same number of entries (8,000). About 1,200 deal with stage music, however, which is omitted in the sequel. Coverage runs through 1986; date of release is included here but not in the more recent title. Entries are labeled by title; emphasis is on U.S. and English recordings.

709. **The Great Hollywood Musical Pictures.** James Robert Parish and Michael R. Pitts. Metuchen, NJ: Scarecrow Press, 1992. 806p. ISBN 0-8108-2529-5.

This recent work identifies about 340 musicals considered to be great by the authors, and provides detailed descriptions of plot, history, and criticism, sometimes citing previous reviewers. Also included are the usual identification data, along with listings of credits for all personalities associated with the production (authors, designers, choreographers, editors, music arrangers, music directors, composers, lyricists, sound and camera people, and of course, cast listings. The work is well illustrated with more than 100 black-and-white photographs. Entries are alphabetically arranged beginning with "Annie" and concluding with "Ziegfeld." Coverage is broad and includes those of classic reputation as well as more contemporary efforts; animated musicals as well as live-action vehicles are treated. The work concludes with a chronology of motion pictures covered, from "The Jazz Singer" (1927) to "School Daze" (1988). There is no indexing.

710. **Opening Night on Broadway: A Critical Quotebook of the Golden Era of the Musical Theatre, Oklahoma (1943) to Fiddler on the Roof (1964).** Steven Suskin. New York: Schirmer Books/Macmillan, 1990. 810p. ISBN 0-02-872625-1.

Suskin, obviously an aficionado, provides treatment of 300 Broadway musicals that played during a twenty-year period identified as the golden era. Entries are arranged alphabetically by title and supply personal credits, date of opening, name of theater, and selections or extracts from opening-night reviews with identification of critic and newspaper. Most interesting is the Broadway scorecard that tallies the types of reviews in terms of their favorability. Profit or loss of the show is similarly indicated. Suskin's evaluative commentary is cogent and useful to the reader. There are numerous illustrations of artwork used in window cards and advertisements. The work opens with an introductory essay on the musical theater from 1943 to its present decline. Appendices supply a chronology of shows and directories of notable careers. A name and subject index provides access.

711. **Songs of the Theater: A Definitive Index to the Songs of the Musical Stage.** Richard Lewine and Alfred Simon. New York: H. W. Wilson, 1984. 897p. ISBN 0-8242-0706-8.

This recent effort updates and expands two previous works by the same authors, and identifies 17,000 songs from 1,200 American musicals on stage, film, or television. Songs are both published and unpublished and span a time period from 1891 through 1983. Selection of songs or selectivity of musicals varies with the time period, with greater selectivity exercised for the early period to the 1920s. Coverage is comprehensive for the professional New York stage from the 1920s, for which songs are identified from every theater production seen on Broadway. It also includes songs of off-Broadway productions if they ran at least fifteen days. There are a chronological listing and an alphabetical listing of shows, and a title listing of songs includes composers, lyricists, and shows. There is a separate index of films and television productions.

712. **Stage It with Music: An Encyclopedic Guide to the American Musical Theatre.** Thomas S. Hischak. Westport, CT: Greenwood Press, 1993. 341p. ISBN 0-313-28708-2.

This is a convenient source of varied information, by a professor of theater history, on the American musical theater from its beginnings in the nineteenth century to the present. Some 300 entries are packed into a one-volume format treating various issues, genres, shows, personalities, musical series, production companies, and institutions. All types of individuals are included: performers, producers, choreographers, orchestrators, composers, lyricists, directors, designers, etc. A useful special feature is a chronology of musical shows; a bibliography is furnished. The work is well indexed to ease access.

Nineteenth-Century American Musical Theater, edited by Deane L. Root (Garland, 1994), identifies and supplies original sources for important musical productions of that period. Each of the sixteen volumes reproduces manuscript scores for one or two productions of historical interest and supplies expository material. Volumes treat such topics as early and later melodrama; British and Italian opera; Irish-American, African-American, and Yiddish theater; operetta; burlesque; grand opera; etc. These play scripts with songs and musical scores are of real value to scholars, performers, and teachers as well as students. Each volume opens with an introductory essay summarizing the careers of the creative personalities, describing plots, and evaluating the historical value.

Musical Instruments and Technology

General technical handbooks have been emphasized. Check the specialized bibliographic guides, especially Duckles (entry 561) for material on particular instruments.

713. **Compendium of Modern Instrumental Techniques.** Gardner Read. New York: Greenwood Press, 1993. 276p. ISBN 0-313-28512-8.

The author is a recognized composer and erudite professor emeritus who has developed an important handbook for music instruction. It codifies and synthesizes those modern techniques utilizing conventional instruments in unconventional ways to produce novel effects. Such applications form the essential character of contemporary art music, and represent an important creative element of recent composition and performance. The work is divided into two segments, with the first part treating techniques applicable to all instruments. The second section covers particular instruments, with representation of all categories of the orchestral setting.

Dictionary of Pipe Organ Stops, by Stevens Irwin, now in its second edition (Schirmer Books/Macmillan, 1983), is a more specialized handbook for organists and students of the instrument. This work first appeared in 1962, and the second version has maintained a high standard for music instruction. Many of the definitions have been modified and enlarged with greater attention to detail; there are twenty-five new plates, a similar number of charts, and seven new appendices. The charts are generally informative, with such topical matters as thirteen famous octaves. Appendices include a list of Baroque stops. There are a list of questions for students and a bibliography.

714. **A Dictionary of Electronic and Computer Music Technology: Instruments, Terms, Techniques**. Richard Dobson. New York: Oxford University Press, 1992. 224p. ISBN 0-19-311344-9.

One of the recent reference tools dealing with music automation and electronic configuration is this well-constructed dictionary. Entries tend to be lengthy, establishing this tool as a combination dictionary and handbook on the new technologies. There are numerous cross-references from specific terms to more general categories, such as "acoustics," that receive full treatment of their various aspects and components. Exposition and narratives are clear and cogent, with technical aspects well defined and explained. The work is indexed by names, and also by product/manufacturer, covering more than 350 products.

A complementary effort is *Illustrated Compendium of Musical Technology*, by Tristran Cary (Faber & Faber, 1992), which supplies more entries but briefer treatment. This is considered a practical glossary to the basic concepts, with much greater emphasis on audio technology. Cary's *Dictionary of Musical Technology* (Greenwood Press, 1992) also provides excellent coverage of audio topics, along with computer music and electronic elements, among the 800 entries treated. Line drawings and flowcharts are included. An earlier work is Bo Tomlyn's *Electronic Music Dictionary: A Glossary of the Specialized Terms Relating to Music and Sound Technology of Today* (Hal Leonard Books, 1988). It contains some 400 terms, with cross-references to related words and to general categories or subjects.

715. **Encyclopedia of Keyboard Instruments**. Robert Palmieri, ed. New York: Garland, 1993- . v.1- . (Garland Reference Library of the Humanities, v.1131). ISBN 0-8240-5685-X.

This is the first encyclopedia devoted to keyboard instruments and is planned as a three-volume effort. Volume I, "The Piano," edited by Robert Palmieri and Margaret W. Palmieri, was issued in Spring 1993. Slated to follow in 1994 are volume II, "The Organ," edited by Douglas E. Bush, and volume III, "The Clavichord and Harpsichord," edited by Igor Kipnis. Each volume supplies some 600 articles alphabetically arranged and dealing with personalities of various types, along with events, topics, companies, instrument technology, culture, discoveries, trends, etc. Articles vary in length from a few sentences to more than 7,000 words. There are illustrations and charts to augment the narratives. Entries contain selective bibliographies for further reading.

A similar effort from Garland is the one-volume *Encyclopedia of Percussion Instruments*, edited by John H. Beck and slated for publication in Spring 1994. Articles are alphabetically arranged and provide details of each instrument, such as manufacturer, designer or inventor, country of origin, musical examples, publisher, etc. All types of percussion instruments are covered (drums, bells, chimes, cymbals, whistles, shakers, etc.). There is a segment of twenty-five survey articles signed by experts exploring various topics in detail. Both a chronology and a bibliography are included. A comprehensive index provides access along with cross-references within the entries.

716. **Musical Instruments of the World: An Illustrated Encyclopedia.** The Diagram Group. New York, Paddington/Two Continents, 1976. Repr., Oxford: Facts on File, 1985. 320p. ISBN 0-84-670134-0.

The strength of this work lies in its illustrations of the musical instruments, for there are over 4,000 drawings which identify every conceivable piece of music-making equipment. The arrangement of this impressive work is by type, with sections on vibrating air instruments, self-vibrating instruments, vibrating membrane instruments, vibrating string instruments, and mechanical electronic instruments. Divisions by geographical areas, time periods, and instrumental ensembles are also given when appropriate. The Diagram Group is an organization of artists, writers, and editors, which promotes understanding of essential features of construction and technique through the publication of highly illustrated works of this type. There is a small section with twenty-five to thirty biographies of important instrument makers, virtuosos, and writers as well as a bibliography and a directory of museums. A name-subject index provides access.

717. **The New Grove Dictionary of Musical Instruments.** Stanley Sadie, ed. New York: Grove's Dictionaries of Music, 1984; repr. with corr. 1991. 3v. ISBN 0-94318-05-2.

More than just a spinoff of the *New Grove Dictionary of Music and Musicians* (entry 612), this specialized survey of musical instruments from all periods and geographical regions expands the coverage given the topic in the magnificent general encyclopedia. Sadie edited both works, and for this specialized set has revised, modified, updated, and in some cases replaced the articles as they appeared in the major work. The attempt here was to achieve complete coverage of the world of musical instruments, whereas the original set, although comprehensive, was still subject to certain limitations in this regard. Especially well covered are non-Western and folk instruments. There has been some criticism of the quality of the illustrations, but there is no argument with the depth and quality of the identification, and description of the history, structure, creation, and use of the various instruments. Several reprints with minor corrections have been issued since 1984.

DANCE

Bibliographies, Catalogs, and Indexes

718. **Ballet Plot Index: A Guide to Locating Plots and Descriptions of Ballets and Associated Material.** William E. Studwell and David A. Hamilton. New York: Garland, 1987. 249p. (Garland Reference Library of the Humanities, v.756). ISBN 0-8240-8385-7.

This collective index to fifty-four reference sources in English, French, German, Danish, Russian, and Polish supplies entries to 1,600 ballets ranging from the well-known to the obscure. Entries cite not only plot synopses but, more importantly, descriptive narrative concerning the creation and performance of the ballet. The *Index* is remarkable for its coded notation that serves to identify not only the presence of bibliography and illustrations, but treatment and historical background, criticism and analysis, and musical themes. Arrangement of entries is alphabetical by title of ballet, and identification includes name of composer and year of first performance. The work is geared to the needs of a varied audience ranging from dance researchers and students to patrons of the performing arts. Access is aided by a well-constructed composer index listing the works by each composer.

719. **A Bibliography of the Dance Collection of Doris Nyles and Serge Leslie.** Serge Leslie and Doris Nyles. Ed. by Cyril Beaumont. London: C. W. Beaumont, 1966-1981. Repr., Dance Books, 1981. 4v. ISBN 0-903102-56-0.

From the time of its original appearance in the 1960s, this small-scale publication of the holdings of a private collection has been regarded as a valuable bibliography. Volume I covers 2,000 items related to the dance. The most recent reprint of this work continues in the earlier tradition of restrictive printing, as it also is a limited edition of only 525 copies. Regardless of the relatively few copies available through the years, the work has been considered a real asset in identifying useful source materials. The emphasis is on the ballet, but folk dancing and social dancing are included as well. The arrangement is alphabetical by author; volume 1 treats A-K and volume 2, L-Z. Each volume has an index that provides subject access. Volumes 3 and 4 were published by Dance Books and cover mainly twentieth-century publications.

720. **The Dance Film and Video Guide.** Deirdre Towers, comp. Princeton, NJ: Dance Horizons/Princeton Book, 1991. 233p. ISBN 0-87127-171-0.
    This is one of the few film and video guides to focus exclusively on dance and represents an important purchase for dance collections in all types of libraries. The work identifies some 2,000 dance performances available commercially. All forms of dance are treated (ballet, folk, ballroom, jazz, and even instructional). Entries are arranged alphabetically by title and furnish information on length, format, distributor, production, company, dancers, etc. Brief scope notes describe content. All types of videos and films that include dance scenes are treated. The work is indexed thoroughly by dance style, purpose of video or film, and geographical region, as well as choreographer, composer, dance company, and director.
    Guide to Opera and Dance on Videocassette, by Robert Levine et al. (Consumers Union, 1989), is a highly selective tool by an opera critic, treating only 175 videos. Of that number, only sixty are targeted to dance, with opera receiving the greater emphasis. Entries are arranged alphabetically and supply performers, distributors, year, running time, language, etc., along with subjective commentary by the author.

*721. **Dictionary Catalog of the Dance Collection.** New York Public Library. Boston, G. K. Hall: 1974. 10v. **Ann. Supp.** 1976- . ISSN 0360-2737.
    The complete title of this work goes on to describe it as "a List of Authors, Titles, and Subjects of Multi-media Materials in the Dance Collection of the Performing Arts Research Center of the New York Public Library." As it has done for other important specialized collections, G. K. Hall has produced a listing of catalog cards based on the cataloging done prior to October 1973. The catalog includes some 300,000 entries for nearly 10,000 items, as well as relevant materials in other parts and divisions of NYPL. Included are books, periodicals, playbills, letters, pamphlets, manuscripts, films, scrapbooks, tapes, and dance scores. Some of the entries have detailed descriptions of contents. This collection is considered to be the most comprehensive of its kind.
    The Bibliographic Guide to Dance has continued the coverage as an annual supplement since 1976, listing material cataloged during the preceding year. As is true of the main set, there are numerous cross-references, along with scope and history notes. The seventeenth supplement (Hall, 1992) was issued in three volumes and covers the period from September 1990 through August 1991. *Dance on Disc: The Complete Catalog of the Dance Collection of the New York Public Library on CD-ROM* was issued early in 1992 and published by Hall. It is a cumulation of the library's entire catalog of dance materials on CD-ROM. It is updated annually and contains both the catalog and the authority file of the Dance Collection.

722. **Index to Dance Periodicals.** Dance Collection, New York Public Library. Boston: G. K. Hall, 1990- . Ann. ISSN 1058-6350.
    Another contribution by the New York Public Library (entry 721) is this recently initiated index to dance periodicals. It represents an extensive project in identifying information on all aspects of the field (biography, performance, news, features, videos, book reviews, television programs, motion pictures, etc.). The work begin with an introductory section explaining the criteria for inclusion and organization, along with a listing of periodicals examined. It represents an important tool for students, specialists, librarians, and aficionados.

Guide to Dance Periodicals (University of Florida, 1931-1962) covered a period through 1956 and was one of the few specialized indexes in the field of dance. It was then incorporated into the *Guide to the Performing Arts* (Scarecrow Press, 1960-1972) as one of the important additions to that more comprehensive publication. It varied in frequency, beginning with a series of four quinquennial editions, 1931/1935-1946/1950. Subsequently, its appearance was biennial from 1951/1952 through 1961/1962. Although it was criticized for lack of promptness, it was a useful index of nineteen periodicals by subject and author, compiled by S. Yancey Belknap. It contains a separate index of illustrations. From 1960 to 1972 Bowker published it on an annual basis providing coverage of 50 periodicals from 1957 to 1968.

723. **Resources in Sacred Dance: An Annotated Bibliography from Christian and Jewish Traditions ...** Rev. ed. Kay Troxell, ed. Lancaster, PA: Sacred Dance Guild, 1991. 55p. ISBN 0-9623137-1-8.

A total of 300 resources are supplied in this slender volume, a specialized tool that would be a good purchase for both religion and dance collections. It has expanded by some 135 new entries and an additional 15 pages over the previous edition of 1986. As before, the target audience is those who are interested in dance as a spiritual expression. Most materials are English-language, relatively recent publications covering Judeo-Christian dance traditions. Annotations describe usefulness to the practitioner and means of acquiring the items. Following the pattern set in the earlier issue, entries are organized by format, with sections on books, booklets and pamphlets, articles, and nonprint media embracing film, audio, and videotapes. Reference sources are treated in a final section that includes bibliographies as well as a list of libraries with important collections and professional associations.

Dictionaries, Encyclopedias, Handbooks

DANCE IN GENERAL

724. **The Book of the Dance.** Agnes De Mille. New York: Golden Press, 1963. 252p.

This is one of the important tools in the field and has been regarded as a real asset to the library collection by both librarians and their patrons. It is a first-rate reference work providing historical background, encyclopedic exposition, and excellent biographies. De Mille has been praised for her style and writing ability in creating a work of high quality and versatile character. It is divided into three major sections: ritual and social dance, theater and ballet, and choreography. Various topics, issues, personalities, and subjects are treated in an interesting and informative manner. All periods of time and many countries are considered, and many definitions are provided. Biographies of performers are brief but informative, and the illustrations are excellent.

725. **The Dance Encyclopedia.** Rev. and enl. ed. Anatole Chujoy and Phyllis Winifred Manchester, comps. New York: Simon & Schuster, 1967. 992p. ISBN 0-67-122586-3.

Originally published in 1949, this title has earned the respect and admiration of both specialists and dance buffs. The revised edition just about doubled the original size, and it furnishes about 5,000 entries covering all phases of the dance. Ballet is emphasized, and there are more features, topics, and personalities relating to this form than is true of the others. The various dance forms are given the most extensive treatment, with longer survey articles written by specialists. Many of the articles are signed. Included in the same alphabetical arrangement are brief biographies of personalities, types of dances, definitions of terms, etc. Individual ballets are covered, and entries furnish synopses, choreographers, designers, composers, original casts, and performance dates. This work is considered especially strong in coverage of American ballet.

726. **The Dance Handbook**. Allen Robertson and Donald Hutera. Boston: G. K. Hall, 1988; repr. 1990. 278p. (Performing Arts Handbooks). ISBN 0-8161-9095-X.

This is a selective information source treating Western ballet and modern dance in eight chronological sections, ranging from ballet's romantic era to innovative experimental techniques of today. Within these sections, exposition is provided regarding the nature and development of dance styles in these eras. Following these introductory essays are entries treating choreographers, dancers, and dance companies. In all, there are 200 main entries providing factual information, critical evaluation and commentary, and bibliographies of books, films, and videos containing additional information. An interesting feature of each entry is the lineage aspect supplying links to related dances or dancers. The work is selective, of course, but treats a broad range of topics; ethnic and social dance are purposely excluded. Special features include a glossary, additional readings, and a directory of international information sources (periodicals, companies, and festivals). There is a detailed general index.

727. **Dictionary of the Dance**. W. G. Raffe, comp. New York: A. S. Barnes; distr., London: T. Yoseloff, 1964; repr. 1975. 583p. ISBN 0498016439.

Always considered a comprehensive source of information on dance and dancing, this continues to be one of the important reference tools. All countries and time periods are included, and coverage is excellent for specific dances and dance types. There are more than 5,000 entries, alphabetically arranged. Information covers development and origin as well as form and technique. It is especially strong on folk and ethnic dances; coverage is aided by a geographical index that arranges the dances by country. No biographies are included, but the work is heavily illustrated with a variety of pictures. There is a comprehensive bibliography of items from the fifteenth century to the present, and a subject index facilitates access.

ASIAN DANCE

728. **Theatre in the East: A Survey of Asian Dance and Drama.** Faubion Bowers. New York: Nelson, 1956. Repr., New York: Books for Libraries, 1980. 374p. ISBN 0836992784.

This is an extensive survey of the dances of fourteen different countries or regions, each of which is treated in an individual chapter. Illustrations are abundant and some are taken from the work of *Life* magazine photographers. Hailed as a great asset to both specialists and laypersons who wish to study or to travel to the Orient, the work provides historical overviews and excellent descriptions of folk, traditional, and modern dances in India, Ceylon (Sri Lanka), Burma, Thailand, Cambodia, Laos, Malaysia, Indonesia, Philippines, China, Vietnam, Hong Kong, Okinawa, and Japan. The author and his wife visited these areas, and have produced an impressive and attractive guide.

BALLET

729. **Ballet Guide: Background Listings, Credits and Descriptions of More Than Five Hundred of the World's Major Ballets.** Walter Terry. New York: Dodd, Mead, 1976; repr. 1982. 388p. ISBN 0-396-08098-7.

Based somewhat on an earlier work by the author, this handbook provides brief synopses and identifications of 500 important ballets. In addition to synopses, the tool furnishes historical information, dates of first performance, choreographers, composers, scenery and costume designers, ballet company, principal dancers in first performances, and major recreations of roles. The synopses themselves are well done and informative, and the additional background information is very useful. The arrangement of entries is alphabetical by the title of the ballet, and the work is well illustrated. It covers ballet on an international level. A glossary of terms and a good index are included.

730. **Classical Ballet Technique**. Gretchen Ward Warren. Tampa, FL: University of South Florida Press; distr., Gainesville, FL: University Presses of Florida, 1989. 395p. ISBN 0-8130-0895-6.

This is a well-constructed and useful manual of ballet technique and process, the idea being to clarify and define ballet theory and tradition as well as movements. Ballet steps and positions are presented in narrative form along with excellent illustrations of professional dancers from major ballet companies who serve as models. More than 2,500 black-and-white photographs help to clarify step-by-step instructions and sequenced movements. Information is presented with the intention of providing instruction with respect to the pattern and artistry of ballet. Steps and positions are arranged by category and are given technical treatment. The theoretical commentary enhances the practical exposition. All major schools of classical ballet are defined. Special features include a pronunciation guide, a glossary, and a selective bibliography.

731. **Complete Book of Ballets: A Guide to the Principal Ballets of the Nineteenth and Twentieth Centuries.** Rev. ed. Cyril William Beaumont. London: G. P. Putnam, 1951; repr. 1956. 1106p.

This has been considered a vital reference work since its initial appearance in 1938. It provides comprehensive coverage of nearly 200 important ballets over a period of 150 years. Entries are arranged alphabetically under the names of choreographers, and furnish excellent descriptions of the stories. Also included is information about the authors of the themes or sources, costume and scenery designers, and composers, as well as a listing of the original casts. A useful feature is excerpts from the reviews of the first performances. Ballets that debuted in London, Paris, or St. Petersburg were given preference for inclusion, and both classic works and contemporary contributions are covered. Supplements to the original work appeared in 1945, 1954, and 1955.

A more recent guide written with a similar purpose is *The Ballet Goer's Guide*, by Mary Clarke and Clement Crisp (Random House, 1981). It applies a British perspective to the coverage of nearly 150 of today's most frequently performed ballets. Included is information on choreography, plot, and historical background, and it contains numerous illustrations, some of which are in color. Descriptions are lively and cogent, and the work is important to ballet enthusiasts.

732. **Complete Stories of the Great Ballets.** Rev. and enl. ed. George Balanchine. New York: Doubleday, 1977. 838p. ISBN 0-385-11381-1.

This is a leading handbook of ballet synopses because of its detailed and comprehensive coverage. Originally published in 1954, with a revision in 1968, none of its three editions have had the same title. The latest edition covers more than 400 ballets, either of classic stature and lasting importance, or significant and written in the past twenty-five years. The main part consists of stories and reviews by Balanchine, followed by sections on history, chronology, and careers; an essay on how to enjoy the ballet; and notes on dancers, dancing, and choreography. There are an illustrated glossary, an annotated section on ballet records, and a general bibliography. A detailed analytical index facilitates access.

Balanchine and Francis Mason have issued a new edition of a less comprehensive work, *101 Stories of the Great Ballets* (Anchor/Doubleday, 1989). Ballets are arranged alphabetically and represent both the old favorites, or historically important, ballets and those identified as the most important to appear between 1968 and 1975.

733. **The Concise Oxford Dictionary of Ballet.** 2d ed. upd. Horst Koegler. New York: Oxford University Press, 1987. 458p. ISBN 0-19-311330-9.

Since its first appearance in English in 1977, this tool (based on an earlier German work) has come to be regarded as a first-rate reference book providing brief and informative descriptions, identifications, and definitions. This is a reprint with corrections of the second edition published in 1982. The second edition does not supersede the first issue, inasmuch as many entries from the original effort were deleted to create a more compact and more convenient volume. New subjects and topics of interest were added, making this the most up-to-date ballet dictionary. Many of the entries furnish biographical references to further reading on the topic, and various personalities are covered. Possibly more coverage could have been given to the younger and recently successful individuals, as the emphasis on established stars duplicates much of what is available elsewhere. Coverage is comprehensive and the whole spectrum of ballet is considered, with treatment given to modern and ethnic dance.

734. **A Dictionary of Ballet Terms.** 3d rev. ed. Leo Kersley and Janet Sinclair. London: A&C Black, 1977. Repr., New York: Da Capo, 1981. 112p. ISBN 0-306-80094-2.
This work has taken a turn toward the more technical side since its initial publication in 1952. At that time, it was meant for popular consumption, but more recently the definitions have appealed to a more sophisticated audience. It remains a compact little volume with several hundred entries; some of the definitions are lengthy and detailed. It brings together related terms, sometimes in its liberal use of cross-references, other times in treating several terms under a single subject heading. The many line drawings illustrate a number of the techniques defined.
Another useful tool is Gail Grant's *Technical Manual and Dictionary of Classical Ballet*, now in its third edition (Dover, 1982). Unlike the Kersley and Sinclair work, this one provides pronunciations as well as definitions of dance terms. It also furnishes line drawings of main positions.

735. **A Dictionary of Modern Ballet.** Francis Gadan-Pamard and Robert Maillard, eds. New York: Tudor, 1959. 360p.
Originally published in French in 1957, the English translation of this work has met with a warm reception from librarians and reviewers. Emphasis is on the ballet in the leading European countries and in the United States, and the purpose of the tool is to provide comprehensive coverage which includes history, repertoire, and personalities. This is done in one alphabetical arrangement that identifies ballets, organizations, companies, dancers, composers, and choreographers. Definitions of terms are not furnished. It has served well as a supplementary source to *The Dance Encyclopedia* (entry 725), but is impressive in its own right for its illustrations, which are numerous and of high quality. There are nearly 700 entries providing good coverage of the field, although some notable omissions of personalities have been pointed out by reviewers.

736. **The Guinness Guide to Ballet.** Oleg Kerensky. Enfield, UK: Guiness Superlatives; distr., New York: Sterling, 1981. 224p. ISBN 0-8511-2226-4.
Kerensky is a noted authority and writer on the subject of ballet and has succeeded in developing an interesting and comprehensive guide. The emphasis is on British and American ballet, although coverage is of international proportions. Brief treatment is given to a broad spectrum of aspects and considerations, such as history, language, training of dancers, careers, stars, music, costume and decoration, choreographers, etc. There are good, colorful illustrations, and a well-developed index provides access.
An older work which has been a familiar reference tool in past years is *The International Book of Ballet*, by Peter Brinson and Clement Crisp (Stein & Day, 1971). The emphasis is on the ballets of thirty-eight major choreographers, under whose names are listed 115 different ballets grouped by period and type. It covers a time period from the seventeenth century to the time of publication. Works in the general repertoire at time of publication have been included. There is a bias toward British choreographers among the contemporary contributors.

737. **International Dictionary of Ballet.** Martha Bremser, ed. Detroit: St. James Press, 1993. 2v. ISBN 1-55862-084-2.
An important recent effort, this two-volume compendium provides comprehensive coverage of the topic on a world-wide scale. Entries treat individual ballets beginning with the period of the Renaissance in the late sixteenth century to contemporary productions. There are more than 800 entries providing detailed exposition and averaging two pages in length.

These are arranged alphabetically for ease of access and include ballets, ballet companies, and personalities (dancers, choreographers, designers, composers, and instructors). These are prepared by contributing specialists, and they supply bibliographies. Accompanying the entries are some 550 illustrations.

A Dictionary of Ballet, by George Buckley Wilson, last issued in its third edition (London: A&C Black, 1974), is still considered a useful tool, furnishing about 2,500 entries on a variety of topics and issues pertinent to the study of ballet. Originally published as a Penguin imprint in 1957, it was revised in 1961. All aspects are treated: history, choreography, individual ballets, stage design, ballet companies, and various personalities. Although coverage includes modern dance as well as Spanish and Indian dances, the emphasis is on classical ballet, and definitions and identifications relate primarily to ballet in Great Britain, France, West Germany, and the United States.

Directories, Annuals, and Current Awareness Sources

738. **Dance Directory 1990**. Beverly J. Allen, ed. Reston, VA: National Dance Association, 1990. 104p. ISBN 0-88314-498-0.

The National Dance Association, an association of the American Alliance for Health, Physical Education, Recreation and Dance, sponsored this directory of schools and colleges in the United States. Institutions are arranged geographically, with entries supplying faculty listings, degrees awarded, performance groups within the schools, and course listings. Coverage of the college credit courses is unique and detailed enough to include credit hours for each offering. Schools are neither compared nor rated. A separate listing for high schools in the performing arts gives addresses and telephone numbers.

National Square Dance Directory 1991, edited by Gordon Goss (National Square Dance Directory, 1991), has varied in frequency since its inception in 1979 from annual to biennial. This effort succeeds the 1987 edition. It provides directory-type information on a variety of clubs: square dance, round dance, contra, clogging, etc. There are more than 10,000 dance and folk clubs from all over the world. Each state in the United States, is treated followed by listings for Canada, Australia, Europe, the Far East, Middle East, Pacific, and South America.

739. **Dancemagazine**. New York: Dance Magazine, 1927- . Mo. ISSN 0011-6009.

This is the most popular and widely known dance periodical in the country, with a circulation of about 65,000. It began life as the *American Dancer* in 1927 and was absorbed into *Dancemagazine* in 1942. Today it is an excellent current awareness tool providing coverage of dance activities throughout the world. An important monthly calendar is impressive in its comprehensiveness and attention to detail. Another important feature for reference work is the directory of dance schools. Articles cover all aspects of the subject, including information on performers, tours, costumes, dance companies, etc. Excellent photographs contribute to the informational qualities of this periodical. In 1986, the magazine issued *Performing Arts Directory* for the city of New York.

740. **World Ballet and Dance 1992-1993: An International Yearbook**. Bent Schonberg et al., eds. Pennington, NJ: Princeton Book, 1993. 329p. ISBN 1-85273-042-0.

This annual publication has gained a wide following for its comprehensive coverage and its value as both a critical-evaluative tool and descriptive or expository volume. It serves as a review of the past year and covers the major performances all over the world. Critical commentary is provided on policies and trends and various parts of the world are analyzed in terms of their developments. The current editon contains the usual listings of personalities and companies, along with nearly forty black-and-white photographs. Special coverage is given to conditions in Cuba and in South Africa, along with obituaries of Nureyev and MacMillan.

Dance World, edited by John Willis (Crown, 1966-1979), had provided an annual survey of the New York dance season before it ceased publication. The fourteen volumes are still regarded as a vital collective resource in reference work. Similar to *Theatre World* (entry 786) in the use of illustration, arrangement, and format, each volume provides an excellent pictorial overview, including much useful information on the season just completed (June 1 to May 31). Although the focus is on the New York stage, there was some coverage of other companies and productions, with a section on regional U.S. companies. There are lists of personnel of various companies, repertoires, opening and closing dates, cast lists for dance events, festivals, and biographies of choreographers and key performers. Both dance scenes and individuals are highlighted in the high-quality photographs.

Histories

741. Ballet & Modern Dance: A Concise History. 2d ed. Jack Anderson. Princeton, NJ: Princeton Book, 1992. 287p. (A Dance Horizons Book). ISBN 0-871-27172-9.

This is the second edition, somewhat expanded, of Anderson's informative and easily comprehended history of dance from classical times to the present. The first edition was issued in 1986 and was well received by its audience of general users and music students. Anderson is a long-time dance critic and writer, whose narrative is informal and appealing. He begins with a segment on the pleasures of dance history, and then takes the reader through an interesting survey of ballet history from its place in the royal courts through its professionalization and its rise in the United States. Contemporary dance is examined on the international level. Selected readings from various historical periods are included along with numerous biographical sketches. A lengthy bibliography is provided.

This work updates Anderson's earlier effort, *Dance* (Newsweek Books, 1979), a slender trade paperback edition based on the 1974 hardbound issue. It was prepared as part of a series covering areas of the arts and humanities (music, theater, painting, architecture, etc.), and traces the development of dance from the ritualistic stages to today's intricate choreography of modern and classical styles. Coverage runs from the latter part of the sixteenth century to the mid-1970s, with a good selection of both artists and techniques. A useful chronology identifies dance events along with historical phenomena.

742. The Dance in America. Rev. ed. Walter Terry. New York: Harper & Row, 1971. Repr., Da Capo, 1981. 272p. ISBN 0-306-76059-2.

This work has been judged to be of exceptional importance. The complete history of the American contribution is chronicled, along with illustrations and excellent descriptions of the work of persons such as Isadora Duncan, Ted Shawn, and Martha Graham. A recognized expert in the field who served as the dance critic of the *New York Herald Tribune*, the author has published widely. Beginning with the earliest developments in this country, he furnishes excellent descriptions of European and Oriental influences and surveys all periods to the present day. There are biographies of leading performers, and coverage is given to ethnic dancers, black dance, and the regional ballet movement. It continues to be a much-used and highly popular work.

743. World History of the Dance. Curt Sachs. New York: W. W. Norton, 1937; repr. 1965. 469p. ISBN 0-393-00209-8.

This has been an important contribution from the Norton Company ever since it was translated in 1937 from a German work completed in 1933. It is a successful attempt to categorize and describe the development of dance through an interpretation of its forms, themes, and steps from antiquity to the present day. Emphasis is on sociological conditions attached to dance origins and the significance of religion, war, fertility, or social dance within the time frames presented.

Another useful tool is Selma Jeanne Cohen's *Dance as a Theatre Art: Source Readings in Dance History from 1581 to the Present* (Princeton Book, 1992), which provides a selection of important writings on dance. First published in 1974, the work has been an important tool for both students and specialists. Introductions have been prepared for each of the documents, the selection of which represents exemplary planning. The new edition furnishes an additional section by Kathy Matheson.

Biographical Sources

744. **Biographical Dictionary of Dance.** Barbara Naomi Cohen-Stratyner. New York: Schirmer Books/Macmillan, 1982. 970p. (A Dance Horizons Book). ISBN 0-02-870260-3.

Nearly 3,000 figures are described in this most comprehensive of biographical dictionaries. Included are individuals representing all aspects of dance and performance, such as performers, choreographers, composers, impresarios, designers, theorists, and teachers. They span a period of more than 400 years in both Europe and America. Entries are alphabetical and furnish personal and career information, including education, training, development, and accomplishments, with special attention given to roles and choreographical productions. All forms of dance are covered in various theatrical styles (opera, ballet, striptease, Broadway musical, etc.) and even include television variety performances. Obviously, the greatest value of a comprehensive work of this type is that it sheds light on some of the obscure and little-known personalities for whom information is difficult to locate.

745. **The Complete Guide to Modern Dance.** Don McDonagh. Garden City, NY: Doubleday, 1976. 534p. ISBN 0-385-05055-0.

The emphasis of this work is on the choreographers, and more than 100 are covered in detail on a variety of levels. Material is arranged in a chronological sequence of five periods, beginning with the forerunners of modern dance and culminating with contemporary contributions. Choreographers are arranged alphabetically within the time frames. Entries furnish a biographical sketch, accompanied by descriptions of one or more of the major works and a chronology of all the person's works. The appendix contains a general chronology of significant dates and events in the development of modern dance. There is also a bibliography with additional readings, and a general index provides access.

THEATER AND DRAMA

Bibliographic Guides

746. **American Theater and Drama Research: An Annotated Guide to Information Sources, 1945-1990.** Irene Shaland. Jefferson, NC: McFarland, 1991. 157p. ISBN 0-89950-626-7.

This slender volume contains 536 entries, with annotations of varying length ranging from a single sentence to a paragraph. These annotations provide factual description along with critical and comparative commentary. Entries are organized within several major sections and subsections, such as general reference sources, major sources after 1945, theater arts sources, alternate theater sources (treating black, Jewish, Hispanic, and musical theater), and other sources that include periodicals, databases, and organizations. The title is somewhat misleading, as the scope or period covered is 1945-1990, with publications dating from 1965-1990. It is intended to cite the most relevant and important sources dealing with the history of American theater and drama and excludes works treating technique, theory, and performance aspects. It is most useful for its currency and timeliness. An author index is supplied; unfortunately, there is no subject or title access.

747. **A Guide to Reference and Bibliography for Theatre Research.** 2d ed. rev. and exp. Claudia Jean Bailey. Columbus: Publications Committee, Ohio State University, 1983. 149p. ISBN 0-88215-049-9.

An annotated guide to a broad range of materials available to students and researchers in the field, this tool is divided into two major sections. The first part represents general reference, standard tools, national bibliography, library catalogs, indexes of periodicals and newspapers, and lists of dissertations. The second section covers theater and drama and furnishes more specialized materials. Emphasis is on British and American theater. Arrangement in both sections is classified with entries by author, geographical location, or chronological sequence. More than 650 titles are included, with publication dates up to mid-1979. There is an author-title index.

PERIODICALS

748. **American Theatrical Periodicals, 1798-1967: A Bibliographical Guide.** Carl Joseph Stratman. Durham, NC: Duke University Press, 1970. 133p. ISBN 0-8223-0228-4.

This guide lists nearly 700 titles of serials of all kinds, from dailies to annuals, and includes directories published over a period of more than 175 years. These represent the publications of 122 cities in 31 states. Locations are given in nearly 140 libraries in the United States and Canada, and even include the British Library. Arranged chronologically by year of initial issue, then alphabetically by title, the entries list original title, editor, place of publication, publisher with address, frequency, notes on missing issues, dates of first and last issue, changes in title, etc. Includes index of titles and names. This is a companion work to *Britain's Theatrical Periodicals, 1720-1967: A Bibliography* (entry 749).

749. **Britain's Theatrical Periodicals, 1720-1967: A Bibliography.** Carl Joseph Stratman. New York: New York Public Library, 1972. 160p. ISBN 0-87104-034-4.

The author was a distinguished bibliographer in the field of theater and drama. His untimely death in 1972 ended a period of extensive productivity in providing researchers, specialists, and students with useful listings in both English and American theater studies. This work serves as a companion to *American Theatrical Periodicals, 1789-1967* (entry 748). It furnishes hundreds of titles of British periodicals over a span of 247 years. It is a compact volume with entries arranged chronologically, giving locations of complete files in both American and British libraries. A variety of periodicals is treated, and for those libraries that have the bibliography, it remains a useful resource item.

Bibliographies, Catalogs, and Indexes

750. **American Theatre History: An Annotated Bibliography.** Thomas J. Taylor. Pasadena, CA: Salem Press, 1992. 162p. (Magill Bibliographies). ISBN 0-89356-672-1.

As part of the Magill Bibliography series, this slender volume supplies entries to about 500 books, dissertations, and society or university press publications covering the history of American theater from its beginnings to the present day. Especially good coverage is extended to autobiography of recent personalities of all types. The work is divided into five sections, the first three of which are chronological; "Beginnings to 1914"; "1914 to 1948," which includes coverage of Federal Theater, musical theater, and playhouses; and "New York: 1945 to the Present." The two concluding sections treat various topical elements such as regional, experimental, ethnic, and community theater, along with periodicals. Entries supply paragraph-long descriptive annotations identifying the content, style, range, and critical capacity of the works. Additional sources are cited. A general index is provided.

751. **Bibliography of Medieval Drama.** 2d ed., rev. and enl. Carl Joseph Stratman. New York, Ungar, 1972. 2v. ISBN 0-8044-3272-4. **Supps. 1969-1972.** 1986. **1973-1976.** 1986. **1977-1980.** 1988.

This is one of Stratman's most important works, updating the initial edition published in 1954. It is arranged in ten sections (primarily geographical) which cover general studies, festschriften, liturgical, Latin drama, English drama, Byzantine drama, French drama, German drama, Italian drama, Low Countries drama, and Spanish drama. Many plays are identified in manuscripts, published texts, and various editions. Works about them from a variety of sources, books, articles, and dissertations are also listed. Devised primarily to aid the student of English drama, it should be considered only supplementary to any specialized bibliographies on any of the countries covered. There are more than 9,000 entries, with library locations given for manuscripts and book material. Entries provide author, title, imprint, pagination, etc., with asterisks marking the most important works. A general index provides access.

Subsequent to Stratman's death in 1972, the work was continued with subsequent publications from the School of Graduate and Professional Studies at Emporia State University. *Bibliography of Medieval Drama, 1969-1972*, edited by Maria S. Murphy and James Hoy, was issued in 1986, as was *Bibliography of Medieval Drama, 1973-1976*. Hoy and Carole Ferguson produced *Bibliography of Medieval Drama, 1977-1980* in 1988.

752. **Catalog of the Theatre and Drama Collections.** New York Public Library. The Research Libraries. Boston: G. K. Hall, 1967-1976. 51v. ISBN 0-685-02808-3 (Part 1 no. 1); 0-8161-0106-X (Part 1 no. 2); 0-8161-0107-8 (Part 2). **Supp.** to Part I *Drama Collection*, 1973. 548p. **Supp.** to Part II *Theatre Collection*, 1973. 2v. **Ann. Supp.** 1976- . ISSN 0360-2788.

Another of the important contributions to reference and research by G. K. Hall is this massive reproduction of the card catalog of an outstanding collection of theater and drama materials, established in 1931. Publication of this catalog has been in several parts, related to different components of the collection. Parts I and II were published in 1967. Part I, *Drama Collection: Author Listing* (6v.) and *Listing by Cultural Origin* (6v.), consists of 120,000 entries for plays published separately or in anthologies and even periodicals. Part II, *Theatre Collection: Books on the Theatre*, has more than 120,000 entries from some 23,500 volumes relating to all aspects of the theater (history, biography, acting, etc.). A 548-page supplement to part I and a two-volume supplement to part II were published in 1973. Part III, *Non-Book Collection*, was published in thirty volumes in 1975 and represents over 740,000 cards on such items as programs, photographs, portraits, press clippings, and the like.

Coverage for parts I and II has been continued by an annual supplement, *Bibliographic Guide to Theatre Arts*, appearing since 1976. This lists materials newly cataloged by the New York Public Library, with additional entries furnished from the Library of Congress MARC tapes.

753. **International Bibliography of Theatre.** New York: Theatre Research Data Center, Brooklyn College, City University of New York; distr., New York, Publishing Center for Cultural Resources, 1985- . Ann. ISBN 0-945419-03-1.

This is a recently conceived, comprehensive annual bibliography of theater on an international basis. The year 1982 was covered initially in the 1985 publication, with 1983 coverage being issued in 1986. The delay persists, as the 1988-1989 volume was published in 1993. Regardless, it is a valuable source of information for students and specialists in locating information about all essential components and personalities related to theater. Aided by the computer, this work identifies periodical coverage in various languages (Catalan, English, French, German, Italian, Polish, Russian, the Scandinavian languages, and Spanish). Books published in Austria, Canada, England, France, East and West Germany, Italy, Poland, the former U.S.S.R., Spain, and the United States are treated. Some 6,000 entries are classified by subject, with references to books, articles, dissertations, and other theater documents.

BIBLIOGRAPHIES AND INDEXES OF PLAYS

754. **American Women Playwrights, 1900-1930: A Checklist.** Francis D. Bzowski. Westport, CT: Greenwood Press, 1992. (Bibliographies and Indexes in Women's Studies, no. 15). ISBN 0-313-24238-0.

This work targets the early years of the twentieth century as a time when women were given opportunity to express themselves alongside a growing little-theater movement affording them production outlets in this country. The onset of the Depression in 1930 marked the decline of women's social freedom and decline in their creative opportunity. Some 12,000 plays by American women were written during this time, and this checklist is an attempt to document those efforts in comprehensive fashion. Entries are arranged alphabetically by name of writer (not all of whom are known to be American or even women). Writings of various types are cited, with operettas and exercises included along with plays. Biographical data is spare; library locations are identified in the entries. Unfortunately, there is no subject or title index.

755. **Gay and Lesbian American Plays: An Annotated Bibliography.** Ken Furtado and Nancy Hellner. Metuchen, NJ: Scarecrow Press, 1993. 231p. ISBN 0-8108-2689-5.

A product of its time is this unique bibliography of more than 700 plays in which either a primary character is gay or lesbian or the primary theme involves homosexuality. The effort signals and is representative of a burgeoning body of work in contemporary theater examining the gay lifestyle and its ramifications on people's lives. Entries supply plot descriptions along with names of playwrights and titles; information is given regarding acts, characters, settings, and music. Such material is most useful for play groups, producers, directors, and actors, as well as researchers and students. Appendices furnish much useful information, such as listings of theaters that produce such plays, names and addresses of playwrights and agents, and related bibliographic references, as well as a chart or matrix identifying plays by certain criteria.

756. **Index to Full Length Plays, 1895 to 1925.** Ruth Gibbons Thomson. Boston: F. W. Faxon, 1956. 307p. **Supp. 1926 to 1944,** 1946. ISBN 0-87305-085-1.

This is another of the landmark indexes necessary to identify authors and titles in the field. An earlier effort by Thomson spanned the period 1926-1944 (F. W. Faxon, 1946). Ten years later, she produced this more extensive volume which preceded it in coverage, establishing the first publication as a supplement. Both titles overlap to some extent the coverage given by Firkins (entry 758). Thomson's focus in both volumes is on full-length plays, and the work provides a title index which includes author, translator, number of acts, number of characters, subject, and scene. There are author and subject indexes, with references to the title index for full information. A bibliography identifies publishers and dates at the end.

Norma Olin Ireland's *Index to Full Length Plays, 1944 to 1964* (F. W. Faxon, 1964) continues the coverage with another twenty years of indexing. There is a dictionary index of authors, subjects, and titles. Both anthologies and separate play texts are included.

757. **An Index to One-Act Plays.** Hannah Logasa and Winifred Ver Nooy. Boston: F. W. Faxon, 1924. 327p. (Useful Resource Series, no. 3). **Supp. 1-5.** 1933-1964. 5v.

Logasa was one of the pioneers of this century in indexing. Her early effort concentrated on one-act plays. Children's plays and adult plays are both included, as are both anthologies and separate publications. The basic volume covers plays published from 1900 to 1924. These are limited to English-language dramas, but do include translations from foreign works. Each supplement continues the coverage, adding another eight to nine years of indexing up to 1964. The third supplement (1941-1948) adds radio plays; the fourth and fifth supplements (1948-1964) include television plays as well. Access is provided by title, author, and subject indexes in each volume.

758. **Index to Plays 1800-1926.** Ina Ten Eyck Firkins. New York: H. W. Wilson, 1927. 307p. **Supp. 1927-1934**, 1935. 140p. ISBN 0-404-02386-X.

An early commitment of the Wilson Company was the indexing of plays, and Firkins was one of the pioneers in this area. Her basic work is a comprehensive index of nearly 8,000 English-language plays by more than 2,200 authors over a period of 126 years. The plays are identified with the name of anthology or other source provided. The first part is the author index, in which complete bibliographic information is provided for each entry and additional description is given of the number of acts and type (comedy or tragedy, etc.). The second part is a title and subject index with references to the author list. Firkins produced a supplement eight years later which identifies more than 3,000 plays by more than 1,300 authors.

A more recent index is Gordon Samples's *The Drama Scholars' Index to Plays and Filmscripts: A Guide to Plays and Filmscripts in Selected Anthologies, Series, and Periodicals* (Scarecrow Press, 1974-1986). With the publication of volume 3 in 1986, coverage of the index is through 1983. This work provides a balanced selection of plays from all periods and various parts of the world. Because of its remarkably comprehensive coverage, it is an extremely important tool in identifying sources of plays that have not been indexed elsewhere.

759. **Index to Plays in Periodicals.** Rev. and exp. ed. Dean H. Keller. Metuchen, NJ: Scarecrow Press, 1979. 824p. ISBN 0-8108-1208-8. **Supp. 1977-1987**, 1990. 391p. ISBN 0-8108-2288-1.

This has been an important reference tool since it first appeared in 1971. The expanded edition is cumulative, as it includes the nearly 7,500 entries from the first edition and its 1973 supplement along with 2,145 new citations. Thus, nearly 10,000 plays from all over the world, appearing in nearly 270 periodicals through 1976, are enumerated. There are two major sections. The first is an author listing, which identifies the author's name and dates, title, brief description, number of acts, and volume and date of periodical. The second is a listing by title, which provides references to the author entries. All types of plays in various languages are covered, and cross-references are given for joint authors, translators, etc. The work continues to serve as a valuable identification tool along with other indexes in the collection. Keller's ten-year supplement treats another 4,000 plays.

760. **Ottemiller's Index to Plays in Collections: An Author and Title Index to Plays Appearing in Collections Published between 1900 and 1985.** 7th ed. John Henry Ottemiller. Rev. and enl. by Billie M. Connor and Helene G. Mochedlover. Metuchen, NJ: Scarecrow Press, 1988. 564p. ISBN 0-8108-2081-1.

An old favorite among reference librarians is this index to plays appearing in anthologies. Since its initial appearance in 1943, the work has gained a position of prominence for those who must identify dramatic titles or authors. The present edition furnishes thousands of citations to several thousand plays and authors. Hundreds of anthologies or collections have been identified, with increased coverage of feminist, ethnic, and gay perspectives. English-language materials from various parts of the world are represented, and foreign translations are identified. Plays are universal in nature, ranging from ancient to modern; excluded from coverage are collections of children's plays, amateur plays, one-act plays, holiday and anniversary plays, and radio and television plays. If plays of this type appear in an anthology that is indexed, however, they are included in the listing. Main entries are listed by author; there is a title index and a list of collections analyzed.

761. **Play Index.** New York: H. W. Wilson, 1949/1952- . Quin. ISSN 0554-3037.

This continuing publication from the Wilson Company is the chief reason why some of the other indexes have ceased publication. Coverage at this point is from 1949 to 1992, and has been handled in eight volumes that have varied in frequency from five to ten years. Basically, it appears as a quinquennial publication, with the last volume issued in 1993 and covering the period 1988-1992. Editorship has changed hands over time, with such names as Dorothy H. West and Estelle A. Fidell giving way to the current editor, Juliette Yaakov. The work itself is comprehensive and includes all types of plays from all types of sources (one-act plays, full-length plays, children's plays), either separately published or parts of collections. All are English-language items, but translations are included, as are publishers from all over the world. Generally about 4,000 plays are covered in each volume (4,397 in 1988-1992), and more than 30,000 plays have been treated overall. The main listing is a dictionary index of authors, titles, and subjects followed by a list of collections indexed. A cast analysis is provided which lists plays under gender of cast and number of characters. Finally, there is a directory of publishers.

Heavily used in the past is Marietta Chicorel's *Chicorel Theater Index to Plays* (Chicorel, 1970-1976). The play index segments of this index series were issued in volumes 1, 2, 3, 8, 9, and 25, published between 1970 and 1976. They utilize more than 3,000 anthologies and 150 periodicals to produce more than 58,000 entries. Plays of all types, times, and countries are included. Volume 21 treats drama literature and identifies books and articles on all aspects of drama. Volumes 7, 7A, and 7B represent indexes to the spoken arts and cover recordings of play readings. A more recent work is Herbert H. Hoffman's *Recorded Plays: Indexes to Dramatists, Plays and Actors* (American Library Association, 1985). This source may be of use to scholars and theater buffs in identifying various types of recorded plays (LPs primarily, but also cassettes, video, film, and other discs).

762. **Plays for Children and Young Adults: An Evaluative Index and Guide.** Rashelle S. Karp and June H. Schlessinger. New York: Garland, 1991. 580p. ISBN 0-8240-6112-8.

Designed for all types of individuals or organizations that select material for youngsters, this tool is a comprehensive index to more than 3,500 plays appropriate for children and young adults ages five to eighteen. The plays identified in this volume are primarily American efforts published between 1975 and 1989. Various types of productions are treated, such as choral readings, scenes, musical reviews, readers' theater, and skits as well as full-length and one-act plays. Entries are arranged alphabetically by title and provide grade level, cast analysis, playing time, and number of acts, as well as plot summary, source of story, subject headings, and evaluation by symbol. Numerous contributors have supplied the plot descriptions, which run several lines, as well as the concluding statements of recommendation. The work is well indexed, giving access by author/original title, cast gender, grade level, subject/type, and playing time.

Dictionaries, Encyclopedias, and Handbooks

GENERAL

763. **The Cambridge Guide to World Theatre.** Rev. and upd. ed. Martin Banham, ed. New York: Cambridge University Press, 1992. 1104p. ISBN 0-521-42903-X.

This is a comprehensive, one-volume handbook of the history and practice of theater around the world. It treats personalities, techniques, issues, and topics of varied nature, some of which are overlooked by other tools of this kind. Much of the topical material is covered by the *Oxford Companion to the Theatre* (entry 771), with both publications complementing each other in dealing with popular culture and contemporary influences. All aspects of theater are covered, from production to theory to legal considerations of copyright. There are more than 100 contributors, all of whom have signed their articles. Bibliographies are furnished for the topical entries; there are several hundred black-and-white illustrations.

The Reader's Encyclopedia of World Drama, edited by John Gassner and Edward Quinn (Crowell, 1969; repr., Methuen, 1975), is targeted to drama as literature and not on the performance aspects of theater. Coverage is given to the written works, authorship, and literary characteristics. A number of survey articles examine the development of drama in individual countries from time of origin to contemporary styles and forms, with brief bibliographies provided. Significant playwrights are treated in separate entries giving biographies, critical evaluations, and listings of important works. Plays are included among the entries and receive brief synopses and some critical comments. All articles are signed, and there is an appendix of basic documents in dramatic theory. No indexes.

764. **The Crown Guide to the World's Great Plays: From Ancient Greece to Modern Times.** Rev. upd. ed. Joseph T. Shipley. New York: Crown, 1984. 866p. ISBN 0-517-55392-9.

Since its initial edition in 1956, this has been regarded as an excellent source of information regarding what the editorship has deemed to be "great" plays. Coverage remains excellent for the total of 750 entries, many of which are newer types of drama, such as the products of the "angry young men" and theater-of-the-absurd pieces. Some older plays have been added when their impact has been noticed in the last few years. Of course, many entries previously listed were dropped; thus, one might wish to retain the earlier edition. One-act plays are included here, as well as the Greek plays that have continued to be performed. For each entry is given story line, play history and production, excerpts from reviews, and notes on cast members. One may quibble with Shipley's definition of *great*, which includes popular plays with lengthy runs, but one must agree that his is an indispensable source for those interested in theater and drama.

765. **Drury's Guide to Best Plays.** 4th ed. James M. Salem. Metuchen, NJ: Scarecrow Press, 1987. 480p. ISBN 0-8108-1980-5.

This standard work by Francis K. W. Drury was first published in 1953, with the latest previous revision in 1978. It has been established, along with Shipley (entry 764), as the best handbooks of their kind. The fourth edition by Salem continues in the excellent tradition of the earlier issues and furnishes approximately 1,500 synopses of plays, ranging from the Greek and Roman classics to recent Broadway hits. Descriptions are brief but interesting and informative. Only plays that appear in English (whether translated or not) are identified, and no musical plays are included. This is a useful reference work for those planning or producing plays, as well as those who purchase them for library collections. Entries provide author, title, date of first production or publication, publisher or anthology, royalty fee, synopsis, and identification of number of acts, sets, and actors. Indexes by cast, subject, and title, with lists of award-winning plays and recommendations, are included.

766. **The Facts on File Dictionary of the Theatre**. William Packard et al., eds. New York: Facts on File, 1988. 556p. ISBN 0-81601-841-3.

This is a well-constructed dictionary providing more than 5,000 definitions, expositions, and biographical sketches. Coverage is given to both performers and playwrights, as well as all other aspects of the theater. Styles, genres, forms, techniques, design technology, and companies are treated; schools, organizations, and major plays are included. Entries tend to be brief, and greater length would have been desirable in some cases.

The Encyclopedia of World Theater: With 420 Illustrations and an Index of Play Titles, by noted theater critic, Martin Esslin (Scribner's, 1977), is an old standard created as an amplified and expanded version of a German reference work published in 1969. The volume presents an excellent overview and furnishes brief entries for various personalities (actors, actresses, playwrights, directors, designers) and various facets of the theater. Although somewhat dated, the 2,000 articles and 400 illustrations furnish useful perspective of scenes, theaters, and individuals. As one might expect, coverage is better for continental Europe than is true of most works of this type.

767. **International Dictionary of Theatre**. Mark Hawkins-Dady, ed. Chicago: St. James Press, 1992- . v.1- . ISBN 1-55862-094-X.

Similar to coverage afforded in the publisher's *International Dictionary of Films and Filmmakers* (entry 881), this projected three-volume compendium treats important plays, playwrights, and performers. Volume 1, "Plays," issued in 1992, covers 620 of the world's most significant or notable plays. Selection of foreign plays is based upon their recognition and performance within the English-speaking world; entries are prepared by a large group of specialist contributors. Information is supplied regarding first date of publication as well as production, and references are given to critical material. There are a critical summary and evaluation of each play's significance. Occasional photographs are provided. Volume 2,"Playwrights," published in 1994, treats 500 playwrights and supplies biographical sketches, chronologies, and bibliographies of critical studies. It includes a title index. Volume 3, "Actors, Directors, and Designers," projected for December 1994, will provide biographical and critical treatment of some 500 personalities.

768. **An International Dictionary of Theatre Language.** Joel Trapido et al. Westport, CT: Greenwood Press, 1985. 1032p. ISBN 0-313-22980-5.
    Considered by reviewers to be an excellent choice because of its scope and depth of coverage, this is the most recent dictionary of theater terminology. Coverage is broad, with approximately 15,000 terms described, two-thirds of which come from the English language. The remainder represent terms derived from sixty foreign languages. Selection of foreign terms was limited to those that have been used in English-language theater publications in a romanized form. The terminology spans theater history from ancient times to the present day. Entries identify language, literal meaning, and definition. Some entries include additional description with references to supporting documents. Cross-references are numerous, and an extensive bibliography concludes the effort.

769. **Masterplots II: Drama Series**. Frank N. Magill, ed. Pasadena, CA: Salem Press, 1990. 4v. ISBN 0-89356-491-5.
    This is the sixth effort in the series of sets supplementing the 1976 edition of *Masterplots* (entry 980). It treats 327 twentieth-century plays by 148 playwrights. Plays have all been issued in the English language, although some are translations from their native tongue. Detailed entries are written by more than 230 contributors and run five pages in length, opening with an overview of production and publication history along with a listing of major characters. Coverage continues with a plot summary, followed by narrative describing themes, dramatic devices, and critical context. Entries conclude with a brief bibliography of additional sources. The work is useful for students at both high school and undergraduate levels with respect to its detail and treatment of a wide variety of themes and subjects. It is highly selective, however, and includes only works of major importance. There is an author index.

770. **McGraw-Hill Encyclopedia of World Drama: An International Reference Work.** 2d ed. Stanley Hochman, ed.-in-chief. New York: McGraw-Hill, 1984. 5v. ISBN 0-07-079169-4.
    This is a most welcome revision and expansion of the 1972 edition, which was received in a lukewarm manner. The revised edition provides more complete coverage of national and ethnic theater traditions and of theater in specific countries, while retaining the pleasant and useful illustrated format. As in the earlier edition, the emphasis is on dramatists, with individuals receiving the majority of the entries. Entries for major personalities include biographies, critiques of their work, synopses of selected plays, and a bibliography of editions that include references to plays in anthologies or collections. Biographical and critical references are given as well. Bibliographies for most entries are useful and up-to-date. Articles on theater companies and title entries for anonymous plays are provided. Articles are signed for the most part. Volume 5 furnishes a general index to facilitate access.

771. **The Oxford Companion to the Theatre.** 4th ed., repr. with corr. Phylliss Hartnoll, ed. New York: Oxford University Press, 1993. 934p. ISBN 0-19-211546-4.
    An old standard in the reference department since the initial edition in 1951, the fourth edition (1983) was forced to cut back its coverage to maintain a suitable price level. The final product is a most worthwhile tool, although it does not supersede the third edition entirely. All peripheral entries (ballet, opera, vaudeville) have been deleted and the survey articles on theater

in individual countries have been shortened considerably. The cuts have been most drastic (50 to 80 percent) in stage management and production articles (lighting, scenery, makeup, etc.). The product does an excellent job in its focus on the "legitimate theater." Scholarship is up-to-date and there is frequent reprinting with corrections. Coverage is given to a variety of new topics, such as "Chicano Theatre." Improved treatment of U.S. and British regional theater is evident, with larger numbers of contemporary personalities and developments included. It remains an indispensable tool.

The most recent effort is an even more abbreviated tool, *Concise Oxford Companion to the Theatre*, edited by Hartnoll and Peter Found (Oxford University Press, 1992). It is considered the second edition, and represents an abbreviated version of the fourth edition. Some of the less important entries have been deleted in order to cover the new personalities and topics.

SPECIALIZED BY TIME PERIOD OR GEOGRAPHIC REGION

772. **A Companion to the Medieval Theatre.** Ronald W. Vince, ed. New York: Greenwood Press, 1989. 420p. ISBN 0-313-24647-5.

Designed to appeal to the general reader or student of the theater rather than the medieval scholar, this is a useful tool providing some 250 entries, alphabetically arranged, on all aspects of medieval theater. Emphasis has been placed on performance considerations rather than literary analysis in treating theater over a 650-year period from 900-1550 A.D. Entries supply factual description and exposition of place names, personalities, technical terms, theater forms, genres, etc. They vary in length from several sentences to survey articles of several pages on such topics as dance, music, art, and secular drama, and to geographic regions such as Iberia, the Low Countries, and the British Isles. Cross-references are furnished, along with bibliographies for many of the entries. A useful and detailed chronology precedes the main text. Four indexes provide access by person, place, play, and subject.

773. **Crowell's Handbook of Classical Drama.** Richmond Y. Hathorn. New York: Crowell, 1967. 350p.

A useful handbook of Greek and Roman drama, this work continues to be frequently used in reference departments. The arrangement of entries is alphabetical and coverage includes biographies of dramatists, summaries of myths and legends, identification of gods and heroes, and definitions of historical and dramatic terms. Place names are identified and described, and an especially useful feature is the inclusion of many characters from the plays. Plays still in existence are identified with date of composition or first performance, and entries include brief synopses and some evaluative commentary. Primarily intended for students and interested laypersons, but specialists will find it useful for some of the author's interpretations of controversial subjects.

774. **Crowell's Handbook of Contemporary Drama.** Michael Anderson et al. New York: Crowell, 1971. 505p. ISBN 0-690-22643-8.

Developed as a guide to trends and issues in drama in Europe and the Americas since World War II, the emphasis of this work is on written drama rather than theater. Therefore, an active playwright like Neil Simon receives only a brief entry, whereas other more literary (but far less popular) talents receive more coverage. Included here are outstanding dramatic works, biographical accounts, theater companies, and national developments in specific countries. Some terms are defined as well. Entries on individual plays are detailed, with much opinion being expressed by the contributors. Especially important is the coverage given to avant-garde dramatists and their work. No index is provided.

775. **Dictionary of the Black Theatre: Broadway, Off-Broadway, and Selected Harlem Theatre.** Allen Woll. Westport, CT: Greenwood Press, 1983. 359p. ISBN 0-313-22561-3.

There are two major sections in this useful work describing theatrical contributions related to the black experience. Part 1 enumerates the shows themselves and describes some

300 plays, revues, and musicals "by, about, with, for and related to blacks," from "A Trip to Coontown" in 1898 to "Dreamgirls" in 1981. Entries furnish information on playhouse, opening date, number of performances, writing and production credits, casts, songs, content, and analysis of critical reception. This analysis is enhanced through the inclusion of excerpts taken from the reviews and press coverage of the time. The second section lists and describes the relevant personalities and organizations. Coverage is given to career developments and achievements as well as stage credits of both individuals and groups. To facitilitate access, cross-references are supplied between the two sections.

776. **The Oxford Companion to American Theatre.** 2d ed. Gerald Bordman. New York: Oxford University Press, 1992. 735p. ISBN 0-19-507246-4.

This is the second edition of this specialized version of the Oxford Companion series, and it provides a comprehensive source of information on the American theater. Especially strong is the biographical coverage of performers, playwrights, composers, librettists, choreographers, producers, managers, directors, and designers, as well as orchestrators, photographers, publicists, critics, scholars, and even architects. Represented in addition to the legitimate stage are various forms of live theater, such as minstrel shows and vaudeville. Excellent coverage is given also to individual plays, musicals, and revues, a feature not included in *Oxford Companion to the Theatre* (entry 771). Entries include production date, plot summary, and commentary. Organizations, companies, unions, clubs, societies, periodicals, and newspapers are included, making this an extremely welcome resource for the specialist and the layperson alike.

Bordman also developed *The Concise Oxford Companion to American Theatre* (Oxford, 1987; repr. 1990), which is a pared-down version of the first standard edition published in 1984. About 40 percent or nearly 300 pages were deleted, thus eliminating coverage of all minor and obscure personalities and topics. Exposition has been reduced and the composition of the work has been altered somewhat by the cuts. A recent effort that promises to rival the *Oxford* is *Cambridge Guide to American Theatre*, edited by Don B. Wilmeth and Tice L. Miller (Cambridge, 1993), which continues in the vein of other Cambridge guides. Coverage is comprehensive in providing a well-developed survey of American theatrical development from its origin to the present day. A number of the entries are based on earlier coverage in the *Cambridge Guide to World Theatre* (entry 763), but have been revised and updated. Entries are signed and arranged alphabetically and provide informed description and identification.

777. **The Oxford Companion to Canadian Theatre**. Eugene Benson and L. W. Conolly, eds. New York: Oxford University Press, 1989. 662p. ISBN 0-19-540672-9.

Another of the Oxford Companions, this one supplies 703 articles signed by their contributors covering all aspects of Canadian theater. Articles vary in length from brief identifications to detailed and extensive narratives. Coverage is given to genres, early ritual ceremonies, personalities (actors, directors, designers, dramatists), theaters, theater companies, movements, regional theater, etc. Like others in the Companion series, entries are arranged alphabetically and furnish description, exposition, and biography. Plot descriptions are given for some fifty major plays. Both English and French Canadian theater are treated. A unique feature of this particular work, compared to that of others in the series, is its inclusion of more than 180 illustrations to accompany the text. Many articles contain bibliographies to additional readings and cross-references to related entries. There is a detailed topical index to aid access.

778. **Theatre Backstage from A to Z.** 3d ed. Warren C. Lounsbury and Norman Boulanger. Seattle, WA: University of Washington Press, 1989. 213p. ISBN 0-295-96829-X.

This dictionary was first published in 1967 and revised in 1972. Lounsbury stepped out of retirement to co-author what was perceived as a needed revision in view of innovations and new technology. It represents an important tool for both novices and theater students in bringing together up-to-date terms and treatments important to the understanding of lighting, sound, scene design, set construction, properties, etc. There is an abundance of new material concerning computers and electronic equipment of varied nature. Most useful is a lengthy and detailed introductory essay providing an overview of historical development of scenery and lighting practices in this country from the seventeenth century to the present. The work is profusely illustrated with line drawings and black-and-white photographs. Also included are an up-to-date bibliography and a directory of manufacturers and distributors.

779.   **Variety Presents: The Complete Book of Major U.S. Show Business Awards.** Mike Kaplan, ed. New York: Garland, 1985. 564p. (Garland Reference Library of the Humanities, v.572). ISBN 0-8240-8919-7.

The focus of this handbook is on awards, and treatment is given to Oscars, Emmys, Grammys, Tonys, and Pulitzer Prizes for plays. All winners and runners-up are listed for each prize from the beginning, with coverage given to the end of the year 1983. The work is well illustrated with pictures of award winners and presenters, and furnishes titles and casts. No evaluative commentary is given, but the tool furnishes many facts on movies, plays, and television, which are accessed by a detailed index. *Variety International Showbusiness Reference* (Garland, 1983) is a more comprehensive (and expensive) Kaplan effort which compiles a great deal of information on show business. It furnishes biographies of more than 6,000 personalities; award listings; film, television, and stage credits; festivals; long-running plays; necrology, etc.

Directories, Annuals, and Current Awareness Sources

For current awareness tools on play productions, there are computerized databases linked to specific cities, providing information on entertainment events.

780.   **Dinner Theatre: A Survey and Directory**. William M. Lynk. Westport, CT: Greenwood Press, 1993. 128p. ISBN 0-313-28442-3.

The author is especially well qualified to examine this topic: he is executive director of the American Dinner Theater Institute, columnist on dinner theater for *Back Stage*, and publicist for the largest dinner theater in the country in Akron, Ohio. His work serves as a handbook or manual of practice, source of historical information, and directory. In an introductory essay, he treats the nature of dinner theater and provides historical perspective of its development. Then follows practical advice on operations regarding food service, play production, and business considerations. Various insights are presented citing the wisdom of practitioners, performers, and others; profiles of successful operations are supplied. A geographical directory then follows that identifies individual units. Illustrations of theaters and productions accompany the text; a selection of menus is included. A bibliography of information sources concludes the effort.

781.   **Directory of Historic American Theatres**. John W. Frick and Carlton Ward, eds. New York: Greenwood Press, 1987. 347p. ISBN 0-313-24868-0.

The editors are academicians who prepared this comprehensive directory of nearly 900 theaters built between 1800 and 1915 for the League of Historic American Theatres. It represents an important tool for the theater historian for its identification and factual descriptions of particular theaters. Entries are arranged by state, then city, and supply, when available, name, address, opening date, opening show, architects, style of architecture, type of building, facade, type of theater, restoration activity, closing date, current status, stage and auditorium dimensions, seating capacity, etc. Sources of information used to compile the work are found in the Gene Chesley Collection at Princeton University, although these sources are not listed. The work expands the efforts of Chesley, the first president of the League, who published two such directories in the 1970s. There is a bibliography along with indexes of theaters and subjects.

782. **Directory of Theatre Training Programs: Profiles of College and Conservatory Programs Throughout the United States ...** 4th ed. Jill Charles et al., eds. Dorset, VT: Theatre Directories, 1993. 203p. ISBN 0-933919-25-5.

This directory has expanded in size and coverage since its first edition in 1987. It represents an important source of information for its treatment of theater schools and their programs. The fourth edition covers more than 200 college and conservatory performing arts programs in this country and provides up-to-date information concerning their composition and practices. Entries are based on written and oral responses to questionnaires and telephone interviews. Arrangement is alphabetical by state; entries supply information on contacts and admission, lists of degrees and classes, faculty, facilities, production, number of graduates, curriculum, professional associations, guest artists, and a statement describing the department's philosophy of training. As in most works of this type, entries vary in terms of completeness. Varied appendices supply information on theater training and the performing arts as a career.

783. **The New York Theatrical Sourcebook.** Association of Theatrical Artists and Craftsmen. New York: Broadway Press, 1984- . Ann. ISBN 0-911747-26-5 (1993).

This is a highly useful directory of sources and services in the New York City area for those involved with the entertainment industry. The largest segment is "Products and Services," which furnishes a classified listing of nearly 2,500 different businesses, organized under such categories as "Books, Fake." Information on props, stage designs, costumes, special effects, puppets, and other paraphernalia is acquired through the listings, which furnish address, telephone number, hours of operation, and sometimes descriptive notes. Cross-references are given between entries. There is an alphabetical listing of these companies with references to the "Products" section. The appendices are useful and provide additional listings, including design collections, unions, concert halls, etc. Especially noteworthy is a listing of services available during odd hours.

The Stage Managers Directory, edited by Cathy Blaser and David Rodger (Broadway Press) was a short-lived but useful periodic source of information that began in 1983 and ended with the 1990 edition in 1989. It carried information on several hundred stage managers, especially those in the New York area, and served as a guide for employers and a communication tool for stage managers. It included resumes detailing their backgrounds and experience. Listings were paid for by those treated, and should be somewhat useful for a few more years.

784. **Regional Theatre Directory: A National Guide to Employment in Regional & Dinner Theatres ...** Jill Charles et al., eds. Dorset, VT: Theatre Directories, 1985- . Ann. ISBN 0-933919-21-2 (1992-93).

The complete subtitle goes on to say "for performers (Equity and non-Equity), designers, technicians & management: with internship opportunities for students." This paperback guide to the employment opportunities in regional theater contains union addresses and Equity contracts, organizations, audition lists, references to useful publications, theater listings with information regarding contracts and hiring practices, and estimated salaries. Applications, apprenticeships, internships, etc. are given by geographical region. Each issue contains thematic articles, such as an evaluation of the computerized casting services in New York City and a narrative on the folly of a scattergun approach to job hunting. The 1993-1994 edition was issued in 1993.

Also available from the same publisher is *Summer Theatre Directory*, which began as an annual in 1984 and is organized along the same lines. Both tools are designed as placement aids for actors seeking employment, and both are recommended for purchase by libraries with an interest in theater. Indexing is excellent in both titles.

785. **Theatre Companies of the World.** Colby H. Kullman and William C. Young, eds. Westport, CT: Greenwood Press, 1986. 2v. ISBN 0-313-25667-5 (v.1); 0-313-25668-3 (v.2).

This is a comprehensive directory of theater companies around the world. The definition proposed in the text for theater companies suggests permanent acting groups under contract for a specific period each year who perform a season of plays that includes nonmusical productions. There is some hedging on the criteria, however, to accommodate the practices in various regions that may be disposed to handle repertory theater in their own way. Thus, part-time companies without contracts are included as well as those who engage in mime, puppetry, dance, etc. Entries provide name, address, significance, history, names of playwrights associated with a company, philosophy of production, facilities, and future plans. Plans are to produce a separate listing for the United States; therefore, representation from this country is limited.

786. **Theatre World.** New York: Theatre World, 1944/1945- . Ann. ISSN 0082-3856.
    This important survey of the year in theater has undergone several name changes, but began life with its present title. From 1950 to 1965 it was called *Daniel Blum's Theatre World*, in honor of its editor, and for a time it was called *John Willis' Theatre World*, in tribute to the subsequent editor. Regardless of the title, it has remained an excellent pictorial and factual record of theater productions in the United States. Its emphasis is on Broadway, but coverage is given to off-Broadway, regional theater, and touring companies. It provides opening and closing dates, cast lists, producers, directors, authors, composers, song titles, theaters, designers, agents, technicians, etc. Biographies of cast members are given in a brief, stylized format, and many pictures are included of scenes and personalities involved. There is an extensive index which expedites access to the information in legitimate plays, solo performances, and musicals. Some of this information (without illustrations) may be found in *Best Plays* (entry 792).

Histories and Chronologies

GENERAL

787. **History of the Theatre.** 6th ed. Oscar G. Brockett. Boston: Allyn & Bacon, 1991. 675p. ISBN 0-205-12868-8.
    From the time of its initial publication in 1968, this work has been regarded as one of the best one-volume general histories of the theater. The new edition continues this tradition and provides an excellent overview of the theater from the primitives to the contemporary stage. Scholarship and attention to detail are apparent in this carefully researched and well-documented survey of theatrical practices all over the world. The emphasis is on European theater, as it has been in the past, and American theater as an outgrowth of those influences. There is secondary emphasis on Oriental theater. Excellent coverage is given to the Greek, Roman, and Renaissance theaters. Such elements as performance practices, architecture, and theatrical conditions are covered. There is a selective bibliography, and an index provides access. Frequently updated (5th ed, 1987), coverage now extends to early 1990. The seventh edition is scheduled for publication in 1995.

788. **Plays, Players, and Playwrights: An Illustrated History of the Theater.** Rev. ed. Marion Geisinger. New York: Hart, 1975. 800p. ISBN 0-8055-1091-5 (1971).
    The author has been part of the world of theater as both an actress and an avid student for a number of years, and has provided this revision of a work completed only four years earlier. The newer edition, like the initial effort, is a heavily illustrated history of the theater with 400 photographs and more than 80 drawings. It is comprehensive in coverage, beginning with ancient Greece and Rome and ending with a separately indexed chapter, "Theater of the 70's." Included in the chronological study are biographical pieces on various personalities and play summaries. Thirteen chapters focus on different time periods and countries. American legitimate theater is well covered, as is American musical theater. The illustrations make this an excellent complementary tool, and it can be used as a text at the high school or college level.

SPECIALIZED BY TIME PERIOD OR GEOGRAPHIC REGION

789. **The American Theatre: A Chronicle of Comedy and Drama, 1869-1914.** Gerald Bordman. New York: Oxford University Press, 1994. 793p. ISBN 0-19-503764-2.

Similar in format and design to Bordman's *American Musical Theatre: A Chronicle* (entry 706), this work provides chronological coverage by opening date of every Broadway comedy and drama over a period of fifty years of early production. Sequence is season-by-season and individual shows are described in terms of their plots, major cast members, and production statistics. Additional commentary treats scenery and costuming; quotations from contemporary critics give indication of literary value. Useful to scholars and theater students are the excerpts taken from the plays, some of which are quite extensive. These provide perspective and insight into the period dialogue and dramatic style characteristics of the past. In addition to plot description, this work supplies brief biographical sketches of the major personalities, such as Booth, Barrymore, and Belasco. An index provides access.

790. **American Theatre Companies 1749-1887.** Weldon B. Durham. Westport, CT: Greenwood Press, 1986. 598p. ISBN 0-313-20886-7.

The first of a three-volume set on resident acting companies in this country, this work covers a most interesting and creative period, 1749-1887. Included are P. T. Barnum's American Museum Stock Company and the Thalia Theatre Company, a prominent and successful German-language theater in New York City. Coverage begins with the first important English-speaking company in the colonies and continues through the beginning of the last company organized and managed in the style of the English playhouse. A total of eighty-one theater groups are treated. Entries provide dates and locations of operations, manager, description of artistic and business practices, performers, designers, technicians, etc. An analytical description of the group's repertory and a bibliography of published and archival resources for further study are included. The excellent factual analysis makes this an important tool.

American Theatre Companies, 1888-1930, again edited by Durham (1987), is the second volume of the series and continues the first-rate coverage, with treatment of 105 more companies ranging over a span of forty-plus years. *American Theatre Companies, 1931-1986* (1989) completes Durham's effort on behalf of Greenwood Press, with coverage given to an additional fifty-five years.

791. **Annals of the New York Stage.** George Clinton Densmore Odell. New York: Columbia University Press, 1927-1949. 15v. ISBN 0-404-07830-3.

This massive set chronicles the period from 1699 to 1894 and remains the legacy of a single individual who persevered in the effort for over twenty years. Unfortunately, Odell was to fall short of his goal of reaching the year 1900, but his scholarship, care, and attention to detail have enabled thousands of scholars, researchers, students, and critics to draw upon a wealth of well-organized information. Each volume proceeds in chronological sequence, covering a period of years (volume 1, to 1798; volume 2, 1798 to 1821, etc.). Included in the record are the actors, plays, theaters, critical commentary, and historical background of the period. Plays are identified along with cast listings and comments from contemporary critics and reviewers. Many portraits of now-obscure performers are included, for which access has been facilitated through the publication of *Index to the Portraits in Odell's Annals of the New York Stage* (American Society for Theatre Research, 1963).

792. **Best Plays of 1894/1899-1989 and Yearbook of the Drama in America.** New York: Dodd, Mead, 1920-1989. Ann. ISSN 0197-6435.

This annual review of play production has been an excellent vehicle for keeping abreast of developments in the world of theater. Although the title has varied in the past, as did the frequency in the early years, it is now simply referred to as the Best Plays series, or "Burns Mantle" after its initial editor. Mantle provided retrospective coverage of the early years with two volumes:

1899/1909 (1944), and *1909/1919* (1933). These volumes identify plays and furnish lists of plays produced, with date, theater, and cast. The annual began in 1920 under Mantle and, after his death in 1948, others who later completed the final retrospective volume, *1899-1909*, in 1955. The annuals provided digests and evaluations of selected plays; title lists of plays produced in New York, including author, number of performances, theater, and cast. Various listings of actors, productions, awards, and statistics were supplied. There are indexes of authors, plays, casts, producers, etc.

Since 1990, the work has been renamed *The Burns Mantle Theater Yearbook* (Applause Theater Book Publishers), edited by Otis L. Guernsey and Jeffrey Sweet. Guernsey's *Directory of the American Theater, 1894-1971* (Dodd, Mead, 1971) is a convenient index to the series by authors, titles, and composers for a period spanning seventy-seven years.

793. **Calendar of English Renaissance Drama, 1558-1642.** Yoshiko Kawachi. New York, Garland, 1986. 351p. (Garland Reference Library of the Humanities, v.661). ISBN 0-8240-9338-0.

This is an important new work for those interested in the study of English drama. It furnishes a detailed chronology, on a day-to-day basis, of the Elizabethan period and carries it to the time of Cromwell, when the theaters were closed. Compiled from a variety of primary and secondary source materials, the calendar identifies all types of staged entertainments, including masques, regardless of whether they were performed by professionals or amateurs. Included in the entry are dates, name of company, place, title of play, type (tragedy or comedy), author, and source of play text. There are indexes to plays, playwrights, and dramatic companies to facilitate access to the contents of this useful tool.

794. **The Encyclopedia of the American Theatre 1900-1975.** Edwin Bronner. San Diego, CA: A. S. Barnes, 1980. 659p. ISBN 0-498-01219-0.

Not an encyclopedia in the true sense, this is a highly useful chronology providing information on nonmusical plays, by American or Anglo-American authors, that were performed either on or off-Broadway during the first three quarters of this century. Arrangement is alphabetical by title, and entries provide date of opening, theater, number of performances, and brief synopses or "capsule reviews." Authors are sometimes listed within the body of comments, with quotations from contemporary reviews as well as critical comments from Bronner. Cast members, producers, directors, and revivals are also noted, as are some set and costume designers. There are six appendices: notable premieres of the century, debut roles, debut plays, 100 longest running productions, statistical records by season, and the listing of four major awards (Pulitzer Prize, *New York Times* Critics, Obie, and Tony). Although some omissions have been pointed out, the work is highly useful to basic research.

A specialized tool is *A History of Hispanic Theatre in the United States: Origins to 1940*, by Nicolas Kanellos (University of Texas Press, 1990). The work describes the development of playhouses and theatrical groups in the United States, Spain, Mexico, and Puerto Rico from the nineteenth century through the first decades of the twentieth century.

795. **The Encyclopedia of the New York Stage, 1920-1930.** Samuel L. Leiter and Holly Hill, eds. Westport, CT: Greenwood Press, 1985. 2v. ISBN 0-313-23615-1.

This is the first issue of a series covering all plays (musical and nonmusical), revues, and revivals staged either on or off-Broadway and reviewed by the press in the decade between 16 June 1920 and 15 June 1930. Included are the productions of ethnic and foreign-language groups, as well as important "amateur" companies like the Princetown Players. Entries provide information on author, director, producer, opening, length of run, plot reviews, and, in some cases, interesting anecdotes about the staging, performance, or writing. There are a number of useful appendices, including a chronology, subject listing, locales, foreign-language productions, ethnic groups, awards, sources of plays (novels), institutional theaters, foreign companies and stars, critics cited, seasonal statistics, and theaters. Indexes by proper name and title and a bibliography are furnished.

Continuing the coverage are subsequent publications, *The Encyclopedia of the New York Stage, 1930-1940* (1989) and *The Encyclopedia of the New York Stage, 1940-1950* (1992), both by Leiter.

796. **Famous American Playhouses.** William C. Young. Chicago: American Library Association, 1973. 2v. (Documents of American Theater History, v.1-2). ISBN 0-8389-0136-0 (v.1); 0-8389-0137-9 (v.2).

The author, who is linked to the field of theater through his acting, writing, and teaching, planned this work as part of a series documenting the history of the American theater. He describes famous playhouses in this two-volume segment, with volume 1 covering the period 1716-1899 and volume 2 treating the years 1900-1971. A variety of interesting materials have been collected, most of which are primary sources. Excerpts are provided from newspapers, periodicals, letters, diaries, journals, autobiographies, reviews, magazines, playbills, publicity materials, and architectural descriptions. Some 200 buildings of historical, architectural, or sociocultural prominence are examined. Sections on New York theaters, regional theaters, and more are arranged within chronological periods. Three indexes provide access by name, geographical location, and personal name.

797. **The Federal Theatre Project: A Catalog Calendar of Productions.** George Mason University. Fenwick Library. Westport, CT: Greenwood Press, 1986. 349p. (Bibliographies and Indexes in the Performing Arts, no. 3). ISBN 0-313-22314-9.

Much has been written in recent years about the Federal Theatre Project, a product of the New Deal through the WPA. It was the only federally funded theater in this country and operated between 1935 and 1939, employing many professionals and helping young people to shape their careers. Hopes for a permanent national theater, unfortunately, were shattered by mounting criticism regarding its moral and political character. The materials from FTP were housed in the archives of George Mason University's Fenwick Library on indefinite loan from the Library of Congress and remained there for ten years between 1974 and 1984. This catalog calendar identifies nearly 2,800 individual productions, arranged alphabetically by title and including date and location of performance, theater, name of director or choreographer, and more. Materials in the collection are identified and indexed and include costume and set designs, playscripts, music, photographs, programs, etc.

798. **Historical Guide to Children's Theatre in America.** Nellie McCaslin. Westport, CT: Greenwood Press, 1987. 348p. ISBN 0-313-24466-9.

McCaslin is an academic specializing in educational theater and has authored an important reference tool for the field. The work opens with a historical essay describing the beginnings of children's theater in 1903 and continuing through various stages, including the enriching element of gradual participation by colleges and universities. The history is followed by an interesting selection of black-and-white photographs of important personalities and productions. The major segment of the work is part 2, which supplies alphabetically arranged entries treating more than 400 production companies and theater associations relevant to children's theater. Articles vary in size but generally are brief accounts of the origin, development, purpose, goals, and physical quarters, as well as touring activities. Useful appendices include a chronology of important events from 1903 to 1986, a listing and brief identification of sixty personalities, and a directory of theaters. A general index provides access.

799. **The London Stage, 1660-1800: A Calendar of Plays, Entertainments and After-pieces ...** Carbondale, IL: Southern Illinois University Press, 1960-1968. 5 pts. in 11v. ISBN 0-8093-0437-6.

Proceeding in chronological sequence in the manner of Odell's *Annals of the New York Stage* (entry 791) is this record of play production in London, covering a period of 140 years. The work furnishes a treasury of information to the scholar and serious inquirer, as expressed in its complete subtitle, which continues "Together with Casts, Box-receipts and Contemporary Comment, Compiled from the Playbills, Newspapers, and Theatrical Diaries of the Time." Much detail is gleaned from the materials presented, and one is able to determine not only the types of plays appealing to Londoners during this time period but also the reception given them by the critics. Each volume is preceded by an introduction that provides monographic treatment of the conditions of the theater and its activity.

Ben Ross Schneider's *Index to the London Stage, 1660-1800* (Southern Illinois University Press, 1979) is a computer-produced index to all names and titles appearing in the set.

800. **The London Stage, 1890-1899: A Calendar of Plays and Players.** J. P. Wearing. Metuchen, NJ: Scarecrow Press, 1976. 2v. ISBN 0-8108-0910-9.

Clearly following *The London Stage, 1660-1800* (entry 799), the compiler has furnished a listing of the plays and players on the London stage during the last decade of the nineteenth century. Derived from a variety of sources, the format is established for the entries as a series of playbills. Arrangement is chronological by date of opening and by theater when there was more than one play opening on the same night. Entries furnish title, author, genre, theater, length of run and number of performances, cast, production staff, and references to reviews of opening night performances. A detailed general index facilitates access.

Wearing's subsequent efforts continue the coverage: *The London Stage, 1900-1909* is a two-volume effort published in 1981; *The London Stage, 1910-1919* was published in two volumes in 1982; followed by *The London Stage, 1920-1929*, issued in three volumes in 1984; *The London Stage, 1930-1939* appeared in three volumes in 1990; *The London Stage, 1940-1949* was published in 1991 as a two-volume effort; *The London Stage 1950-1959* was issued in two volumes in 1993.

801. **The Medieval Stage.** Edmund Kerchever Chambers. London: Oxford University Press, 1903; repr. 1978. 2v. ISBN 0-19-811512-1.

An old standard in the field, this work is still considered the most comprehensive and authoritative history of the period. The medieval stage is considered from the fall of the Roman Empire to the Tudor period. The work is divided into four major sections. Part 1, "Minstrelsy," and part 2, "Folk Drama," are covered in volume 1. Part 3, "Religious Drama," and Part 4, "Interludes (Tudor)," are covered in volume 2. Bibliographies are provided, and appendices contain original documents. A subject index facilitates access.

Another major effort by Chambers is *The Elizabethan Stage* (Clarendon Press, 1923; repr. with corr., 1974). This is a four-volume work which is also a standard in the field, though parts of it, such as the section on the Elizabethan playhouse, have been updated in other histories. The variety of topics includes the Court and control of the stage, companies and playhouses, staging at Court and in the theaters, and various plays and authors. Appendices contain original documents, and a general index is provided.

802. **20th Century Theatre.** Glenn Meredith Loney. New York: Facts on File, 1983. 2v. ISBN 0-87196-463-5.

An attractive and easy-to-use chronological record of theatrical developments in the United States and Great Britain, this work has proved to be a popular choice for librarians and their patrons. The arrangement is year-by-year from 1900 to 1979, classified by topics such as American premieres; British premieres; revivals and repertoires; births, deaths, and debuts; and theaters and productions. Within each topic, the activities are listed chronologically from 1 January to 31 December. Many production photographs are used. A chronology of this type will work as a date finder, personality identifier, and event locator when the indexes are sufficient to provide access. It appears that this is true in this case with a general index of names, production tables, and miscellaneous subjects (awards, companies, schools, etc.).

Biographical Sources

803. **A Biographical Dictionary of Actors, Actresses, Musicians, Dancers, Managers, and Other Stage Personnel in London, 1660-1800.** Philip H. Highfill et al. Carbondale, IL: Southern Illinois University Press, 1973-1993. 16v. ISBN 0-8093-0518-6 (v.1).

Originally projected as a sixteen-volume biographical dictionary to serve somewhat as a companion piece to *The London Stage, 1660-1800* (entry 799), this enormous effort reached its final volume in 1993. Biographical sketches vary in length from a few lines to monographic essays for all persons who were members of theatrical companies, occasional performers, patentees or servants of the patent theaters, opera houses, amphitheaters, pleasure gardens, theatrical taverns, music rooms, fair booths, and other places of public entertainment. The tool is remarkable and extremely valuable for its coverage of the unheralded as well as the famous and is a treasure house of information in this regard. The information is derived from a variety of sources, and there are many fine portraits and illustrations.

804. **British Dramatists Since World War II.** Stanley Weintraub, ed. Detroit: Gale Research, 1982. 2v. (Dictionary of Literary Biography, v.13). ISBN 0-8103-0936-X.

This is a detailed description and analysis of sixty-nine of the most significant or potentially most significant playwrights in modern British play production. Such individuals as Tom Stoppard, Samuel Beckett, Harold Pinter, and Christopher Fry are treated in depth in articles that include production lists, books published, biographical sketches, critical commentary, production photographs, programs, playscript drafts, and bibliographic references. Appendices provide a collection of essays on a variety of topics, such as Britain's postwar theater, theater companies, and stage censorship. There is a general bibliography for further reading. This tool is an extremely useful resource for both students and specialists seeking further information about important dramatists.

805. **Contemporary Dramatists.** 5th ed. K. A. Berney, ed. Detroit: St. James Press, 1993. 843p. (Contemporary Writers of the English Language). ISBN 1-55862-185-7.

Continuing in the tradition and style of the earlier editions, which received considerable praise from critics, is the fifth edition which, like the others, covers in excellent detail the lives and works of some 360 living playwrights writing in the English language. Many previous essays have been revised or rewritten with information updating the contributions and activities of the dramatists. More than just a biographical dictionary, this tool continues to provide excellent evaluative commentary as well as a full bibliography of each dramatist's published works. There are references to critical studies; manuscript collections are identified. In addition, there are separate sections for 300 screenwriters, television writers, radio writers, and musical librettists, limited to listings of their works. An appendix provides an additional listing of playwrights who have died since the 1950s. A title index is included.

806. **Early Black American Playwrights and Dramatic Writers: A Biographical Directory and Catalog of Plays, Films, and Broadcasting Scripts.** Bernard L. Peterson, Jr. New York: Greenwood Press, 1990. 298p. ISBN 0-313-26621-2.

Developed as a companion volume to an earlier work on contemporary black playwrights, described later, Peterson continues his tradition of careful and systematic effort in creating an important tool revealing information not easily found elsewhere. Nearly 220 playwrights, screenwriters, and dramatists are profiled in thorough manner. Entries are alphabetically arranged and provide detailed biographical sketches of individuals dating from the 1820s to the 1940s. Included are the well-known, such as poet and writer Langston Hughes and film writer Oscar Devereaux Micheaux, along with the now-obscure, such as Mister Brown of the Africa Company of the early nineteenth century. Included in each entry are listings of commentary about individual works, a bibliography of other writings, and additional sources. Appendices supply pre-1950 titles, chronology of plays and radio/screen scripts, and musical librettists. There is a general index.

Peterson's earlier work, *Contemporary Black American Playwrights and Their Plays: A Biographical Directory and Dramatic Index* (Greenwood Press, 1988), treats the more recent writers of stage, television, radio, and film subsequent to 1950. Current addresses are supplied along with brief biographical sketches and plot descriptions and identifications. A highly selective work is Doris E. Abramson's *Negro Playwrights in the American Theatre, 1925-1959* (Columbia University Press, 1969), although more in-depth analysis is given to the twenty plays (and playwrights) selected. Biographical coverage and critical appraisals are included.

807. The Great Stage Stars: Distinguished Theatrical Careers of the Past and Present. Sheridan Morley. New York: Facts on File, 1986. 425p. ISBN 0-8160-1401-9.

One of the more attractive biographical dictionaries to come out in recent years, this work covers a period of 400 years, with an emphasis on those who performed in London rather than New York. Of those personalities who are living (definitely in the minority), few could be said to be young, and many are vintage. The author is the son of Robert Morley and has been a critic and an author of biographies of theatrical personalities. His descriptions are excellent and his use of comments taken from reviews blends in well with the quotes from the performers themselves. Approximately 200 personalities are covered, and there are about fifty photographs which help the reader to an informative and enjoyable experience.

808. Stage Deaths: A Biographical Guide to International Theatrical Obituaries, 1850 to 1990. George B. Bryan, comp. New York: Greenwood Press, 1991. 2v. ISBN 0-313-27593-9.

Of most use to a library supporting an extensive theater collection, this is a comprehensive index to obituaries of stage personalities found in any of nine Anglo-American newspapers (*New York Times, Los Angeles Times, Boston Transcript, London Times*, etc.) or in English-language biographies or autobiographies. All types of stage people are represented (actors, playwrights, motion picture actors, directors, composers, etc.). Entries supply brief biographical identification: alternate names, family information, dates, and theatrical work, along with references to obituaries and death notices. There are numerous cross-references to related personalities. The contribution of this title is greatest in study of regional theater and the identification of obscure persons about whom little is known. Although the work is valuable for its inclusiveness, biographies of well-known individuals are more easily accessed directly through other tools.

809. Theatrical Designers: An International Biographical Dictionary. Thomas J. Mikotowicz, ed. New York: Greenwood Press, 1992. 365p. ISBN 0-313-26270-5.

This is a unique and valuable source for its emphasis on theatrical designers, for whom biographical informations is difficult to locate. This work treats 270 designers from various historical periods beginning with the fifteenth century up to the present day. Both practitioners and theorists of the field are included as long as they have made an important or significant contribution. Most of the designers are of the modern era, with about 65 percent of them having been born since 1900. The editor is an academic who has been joined by ten contributors in producing this work. Entries are arranged alphabetically and vary in length from a few sentences to a page or two; a list of productions is included. Appendices list designers chronologically and by country of birth; a selective bibliography is furnished. There is an index of names and play titles.

810. Who's Who in the Theatre: A Biographical Record of the Contemporary Stage. 17th ed. Detroit: Gale, 1981. 2v. ISBN 0-2730-1717-9 (v.1); 0-2730-1718-7 (v.2).

This is the final edition of the long-standing series (begun in 1912) originally published by Pitman of London. The Gale Company has chosen to expand the scope with a new serial publication, *Contemporary Theatre, Film, and Television* (entry 549). *Who's Who* was limited to theater personalities, the original emphasis being on those associated with the

London stage. In recent years, there has been greater coverage of Americans, especially in this edition. About 2,400 people from all areas of theater are included: performers, dramatists, composers, critics, managers, historians, etc. Although the emphasis is on living individuals, a necrology is included. Volume 2, the playbills volume, includes playbills from both London and New York.

Who Was Who in the Theatre, 1912-1976: A Biographical Dictionary of Actors, Actresses, Playwrights, and Producers of the English-Speaking Theatre (Gale, 1978) is an omnibus volume, and again, most likely the final offering in this series, which has also given way to the new publication. This composite volume covers more than 4,000 deceased individuals who had been covered in *Who's Who in the Theatre* between 1912 and 1972. Entries were consigned to *Who Was Who* either through death or inactivity over a ten-year period.

Reviews and Criticism

811. **American Drama Criticism: Interpretations, 1890-1977.** 2d ed. Floyd Eugene Eddleman, comp. Hamden, CT: Shoe String Press, 1979. 488p. **Supp. I.** 1984. 255p. **Supp. II.** 1989. 269p. **Supp. III.** 1992. ISBN 0-208-01713-5.

This work supersedes the first edition by Palmer and Dyson (1967) and its two supplements (1970, 1976). It provides a listing of interpretations of American plays published over a period of nearly ninety years. These interpretations (critiques, reviews, etc.) appeared in 200 books and monographs and in more than 400 periodicals. The arrangement of entries is by playwright and then by title. Only the works of dramatists who are or were citizens of the United States are included, except for a few Canadians and Caribbean writers whose works are performed here. The date of first production is noted and musical plays are included. There are indexes of critics and of adapting authors and adapted works. The supplements, also by Eddleman, furnish listings of hundreds of additional interpretations published between 1978 and 1990.

812. **Chinese Drama: An Annotated Bibliography of Commentary, Criticism, and Plays in English Translation.** Manuel D. Lopez. Metuchen, NJ: Scarecrow Press, 1991. 525p. ISBN 0-8108-2347-0.

This is a comprehensive bibliography of both primary and secondary source material concerning Chinese drama. Books, articles, and dissertations are identified in either of two sections providing a total of some 3,300 citations. The first part provides historical treatment with references to literature covering Chinese drama from its origins to the mid-1980s. Arrangement is topical, such as "background and development" or "comparison with other national theatres," and these topics are in turn is subdivided by format (books, articles, dissertations, parts of books). Part 2 identifies the plays themselves, all of which have appeared in English translation. These are listed alphabetically by title, with citations arranged by type of coverage (summaries, commentaries, etc.). Only about 25 percent of the citations are annotated, and then very briefly, a fact that produce some unfavorable comments from reviewers. Nevertheless, it is a useful tool for students or specialists in theater or Asian studies.

813. **Critical Survey of Drama: English Language Series.** Rev. ed. Frank N. Magill, ed. Pasadena, CA: Salem Press, 1994. 7v. ISBN 0-89356-851-1.

Begun in the early 1980s, with coverage of short fiction (entry 990), poetry (entry 1166), and long fiction (entry 1139), the Critical Survey series treats the different genres in standardized manner with individual writers arranged alphabetically. The initial edition of this work was published in 1985 as a six-volume set, followed by a single-volume supplement in 1987. The current effort provides an update and revision in following the same pattern. Coverage begins with a listing of the author's major works within the genre, and progresses with brief description of the writer's success with other literary forms, an assessment of his or her major achievements, a biography, an analysis of major works in this genre, and a list of publications in other forms, and ends with a bibliography of secondary sources. It treats more than 200 dramatists representing all historical periods, and includes British, Irish, Canadian, Australian, African, and West Indian as well as U.S. nationals. Arrangement is alphabetical by dramatist. In the final volume, there is a collection of essays on the drama in all its phases through different historical periods and various nations.

Critical Survey of Drama: Foreign Language Series (Salem, 1986) is another Magill product in six volumes, which completes the critical survey series. The first five volumes cover 199 dramatists from antiquity to the present. There is a European bias, with 44 percent having written in French or German, 23 percent in Spanish or Italian, 15 percent in languages of central or southeastern Europe, including Russian, and 7 percent in Scandinavian. Asian languages represent 3 percent and Latin American 1 percent. There are no African inclusions. Updating both of the works is *Critical Survey of Drama: Supplement* (1987). It supplies forty-nine additional entries not included in the two major editions. Most of the new entries are from the twentieth century; there is African representation along with the others.

814. **Drama Criticism: Criticism of the Most Significant and Widely Studied Dramatic Works from All the World's Literature.** Lawrence J. Trudeau. Detroit: Gale Research, 1991- . v.1- . ISSN 1056-4349.

This new entry in the Gale line of biocritical series in the area of literature provides a focus on the evaluation and literary merit of plays and playwrights of international consequence and representing various countries of origin. In volume 1 (1991), coverage is given to fourteen dramatists thought to have contributed to a considerable degree to the development of such literature. Among the principals treated are Arthur Miller, Lillian Hellman, Yukio Mishima, and Karel Capek. Entries furnish biographical sketches and critical commentary, from both critics and the playwrights themselves, providing much insight for the student and scholar. Volume 2 (1992) includes Ibsen, Camus, and Aristophanes as well as Wole Soyinka; volume 3 (1993) embraces Dryden, Kyd, and Brecht as well as Ntozake Shange.

An older, but still useful, title in two volumes is *Drama Criticism*, by Arthur Coleman and Gary R. Tyler (Alan Swallow, 1966-1971). This is one of the several checklists of interpretations from the publisher which have become well known in reference collections of literature. The work cites interpretations in English that appeared in books or periodicals, but the plays are from different countries of origin. Volume 1 lists critiques of American or English plays. These interpretations were published between 1940 and 1964. Volume 2 (published five years later) covers classical and continental plays for which the interpretations were published between 1950 and 1968. Arrangement of entries is alphabetical by dramatist, then by title of play. More than 1,000 periodicals have been examined, and there is a useful bibliography of books containing criticism.

815. **European Drama Criticism, 1900-1975.** 2d ed. Helen H. Palmer. Hamden, CT: Shoe String Press, 1977. 653p. ISBN 0-208-01589-2.

This is a companion effort or complementary work to Eddleman's *American Drama Criticism* (entry 811) and represents a useful and convenient source book for critical writings on European plays. This checklist covers a period of seventy-five years and furnishes references to critiques in various languages (although the emphasis is on English materials). This work cumulates the entries from an earlier edition and supplements and adds material. The plays and the dramatists are universal in nature, from every time period of play production from Aeschylus to Yeats. Playwrights included represent major figures with recognized impact, although, as is inevitable for a work of this type, major omissions have been noted. There is a listing of books and journals indexed.

816. **Major Modern Dramatists.** Rita Stein et al., comps. and eds. New York: Ungar, 1984-1986. 2v. (Library of Literary Criticism). ISBN 0-8044-3267-8 (v.1); 0-8044-3268-6 (v.2).

This set is part of the well-known Library of Literary Criticism series, which seeks to provide a collection of excerpts of literary criticism on various literary efforts. In the past, its focus has been on the literary products of a language or a country rather than on a literary genre. Thus, this series departs from its tradition by having established this set on dramatists. Volume 1, issued in 1984, covers American, British, Irish, German, Austrian, and Swiss dramatists, whereas volume 2 (1986) extends European coverage to French, Belgian, Russian, Polish, Spanish, Italian, Norwegian, Swedish, Czech, and Hungarian playwrights. The format and purpose of the set are similar to those of previous efforts, in that it provides an overview of the critical reception given to a dramatist from the beginning of his or her career up to the present time through excerpts from reviews, articles, and books. This is a selective effort limited to playwrights who have established an international reputation, beginning with Isben and late nineteenth-century realism up to the present.

Modern Drama: A Checklist of Critical Literature on 20th Century Plays, by Irving Adelman and Rita Dworkin (Scarecrow Press, 1967), is an old favorite that identifies important and significant critiques of modern plays. These are culled from books and journals from all over the world. One is able to compare the number of reviews furnished for the various playwrights in determining their impact.

817. **The New York Times Theater Reviews, 1870-1992.** Hamden, CT: Garland, 1992. 27v. ISBN 0-8153-0351-3. **Bienn. Supp. 1971- .** ISSN 0160-0583.

The first segment to be published of this chronological collection of reviews, published by the *New York Times* and covering the years 1920-1970, appeared in ten volumes in 1971, with the final volume given to indexes and appendices. The segment covering the early years, 1870-1919, was published in five volumes in 1976. Garland has continued the coverage of the biennial supplements, which began in 1971/1972, and now offers a twenty-seven-volume set through 1992. Thus, we are able to consult reviews, as they appeared in the *New York Times*, for a period of 122 years. Reviews are arranged chronologically and there are excellent appendices of awards and prizes, productions, and runs by season. The work is indexed by titles, production companies, names of performers, and names of others associated with the staging of the play; separate indexes are available for the initial two segments. Biennial supplements are separately indexed. Reviews are detailed and have earned a reputation for quality and perceptiveness. The volume for 1991-1992 was issued in 1993.

New York Theatre Critics Reviews (New York Theatre Critics Reviews, 1940-) is a useful weekly publication which furnishes copies of reviews as they appeared in a variety of New York newspapers, as well as periodicals and even on network television. A useful tool in comparing reviews from different critics.

818. **Selected Theatre Criticism.** Anthony Slide, ed. Metuchen, NJ: Scarecrow Press, 1985-1986. 3v. ISBN 0-8108-1811-6 (v.1); 0-8108-1844-2 (v.2); 0-8108-1846-9 (v.3).

The complete set of three volumes covers the first half of the twentieth century in providing a collection of original reviews of productions of the New York stage. Reviews are reproduced in their entirety from an array of periodicals: *Century Magazine, The Critic, The Forum, The Green Book Magazine, Life, The New York Clipper, The New York Dramatic Mirror, The Red Book Magazine,* and *Variety* (entry 871). Volume 1 covers the period 1900-1919; volume 2, 1920-1930; and volume 3, 1931-1950. All types of shows are included: dramas, revues, comedies, and musicals—more than 500 in all. Arrangement in each volume is alphabetical by title, and production information is given along with the reviews. James M. Salem's *A Guide to Critical Reviews* (Scarecrow Press, 1984-) appears in several parts, each dealing with a different entertainment form. Citations to critical reviews are furnished rather than the reviews themselves. Part 1 covers the American drama 1909-1982, and was last issued in 1984. It is a continuing publication.

Play Production

819. **Producing Theatre: A Comprehensive Legal and Business Guide.** Rev. and upd. ed. Donald C. Farber. New York: Limelight Editions, 1987; repr. 1990. 472p. ISBN 0-8791-0074-5.

Farber, an attorney, had combined and updated the contents of two earlier works published in the 1960s to provide the first edition of this guide in 1981. The second Limelight edition maintains the tool's reputation as a comprehensive and comprehensible guide to the legal documents and procedures involved in play production. It is geared to the business of producing plays anywhere, be it on Broadway, resident theater, stock, etc., and covers all possible and probable aspects. Information on contractual agreements is presented in precise and understandable fashion, and there are samples of actual contracts. Now revised and expanded by some ninety pages, it represents the most authoritative and up-to-date legal and business guide in the realm of theater, with chapter coverage given to all aspects of commercial production. These begin with acquisition of a property to important considerations regarding long runs and tours and even sales of motion picture rights. A general index provides access.

820. **The Small Theatre Handbook: A Guide to Management and Production.** Joann Green. Harvard, MA: Harvard Common; distr., Port Washington, NY: Independent Publishers Group, 1981. 163p. ISBN 0-916782-20-4.

The small theatre is defined as having an annual budget of less than $100,000; this work is a manual of management practice for these theaters. The author has served as the artistic director for the Cambridge Ensemble Theatre and therefore is well equipped to handle the discussion of problems and to provide practical directions. The work is considered most useful in regard to organization and administration, and furnishes many examples on budgeting, fund raising, etc. Information on production, such as choosing the play, directors, actors, etc., is somewhat sketchy. In general, the tool should be helpful to people associated with the business end of play production in colleges, neighborhood theaters, repertory companies, and the like.

Another work written in this vein is *The Complete Play Production Handbook*, by Carl Allensworth et al. (Harper & Row, 1982). This is more focused on the production end in its goal of assisting schools, colleges, and little theaters in mounting creditable productions.

821. **Stage Makeup.** 8th ed. Richard Corson. Englewood Cliffs, NJ: Prentice-Hall, 1989. 411p. ISBN 0-13-840539-5.

This specialized handbook is a standard in the field and has been revised frequently (6th ed., 1981; 7th ed., 1986). It continues as an important aid for instructors, makeup artists, and actors who are responsible for their own makeup. The handbook is well illustrated, as were the previous editions; the pictures facilitate the user's comprehension of the narrative on techniques of application. Consideration is given to such factors as skin tone, facial anatomy, and lighting. Application of grease-paint, beards, wigs, artificial limbs, and appurtenances is described in depth. Treatment given hair styles and fashions is timely and contributes to the importance of the work as a manual of practice.

Another specialized effort, this one dealing with another aspect of stage preparation, is Francis Reid's *The Stage Lighting Handbook*, now in its second edition (Theatre Arts Books, 1982). Geared to the needs of amateurs, this tool describes the purposes, equipment, rigging, etc., and enumerates the basic steps in lighting design. Francis Reid's *The ABC of Stage Lighting* (Drama Book, 1992) provides definitions for terminology employed in lighting. Reid is an expert in the field and provides useful and up-to-date coverage that includes both illustrations and cross-references.

822. **Stagecraft: The Complete Guide to Theatrical Practice.** Trevor R. Griffiths, ed. Oxford: Phaidon Press, 1982; distr., New York: Drama Book, 1984; repr. 1990. 192p. ISBN 0-7148-2644-8.

This British work furnishes a practical handbook to all basic aspects of nonprofessional play production. Its ten chapters cover such considerations as directing, stage management, acting, set design, light design, costumes, makeup, and even the conduct of a workshop. Chapters are contributed by authorities in these topical areas, and the work is heavily illustrated in both color and black-and-white. Although the British terminology may seem awkward at first, the material furnished is useful and in keeping with the overall purpose, which is to achieve the best possible production with the fewest pitfalls. A glossary is provided and a general index aids access.

Theatre Design and Technology (U.S. Institute for Theatre Technology, 1978-) is a quarterly journal for professional technicians and production people. It provides several articles in each issue on stage design, scenery, props, etc., for members of the organization.

FILM, RADIO, TELEVISION, AND VIDEO

Bibliographic Guides

823. **Film: A Reference Guide.** Robert A. Armour. Westport, CT: Greenwood Press, 1980. 251p. ISBN 0-313-22241-X.

This is a useful and well-developed reference guide for the person who is about to undertake a serious study of some aspect of film. It has earned praise from reviewers for both its convenience and its content. Written in essay form, the work is divided into various chapters, each of which covers a topic of interest and importance. These include history of film, film production, film criticism by genre, major actors, directors, etc. A chapter on reference works and periodicals in the field should prove of value. Each chapter contains a bibliography. A chronology of American film and a description of film research collections are included in the appendices.

Fay C. Schreibman's *Broadcast Television: A Research Guide* (American Film Institute, 1983) is a small but useful guide in an area not generally covered by such tools.

824. **On the Screen: A Film, Television, and Video Research Guide.** Kim N. Fisher. Littleton, CO: Libraries Unlimited, 1986. 209p. ISBN 0-87287-448-6.

Coverage is given to primarily U.S. writings from the 1960s to the 1980s furnishing information on film, telvision, and video in all aspects of production. Arrangement of entries is alphabetical within broad-based topical categories, each receiving an entry number and accompanying description. Information includes author, title, imprint, pagination, and ISBN or other identifying number. The value of the work lies mainly in its well-developed annotations, which combine both descriptive and evaluative commentary, and on its scope in treating three different media within a single work. Databases are identified, as are research centers, archives, societies, and associations. There are both author-title and subject indexes.

One of the better sources focussed on motion pictures, although it is aging, is *Guidebook to Film: An Eleven-in-One Reference*, by Roberta Gottesman and Harry M. Geduld (Holt, Rinehart & Winston, 1972). This old standard continues to receive heavy use by film librarians and their patrons, and serves as a good starting point for a variety of searches. It provides an array of useful listings: annotated lists of books, periodicals, theses, and dissertations; museums and archives; film schools; equipment suppliers; film organizations and services; festivals and contests; and awards. There is a glossary of terms as well, which will be useful to the amateur filmmaker. Another effort is *Moving Pictures: An Annotated Guide to Selected Film Literature, with Suggestions for the Study of Film*, by Eileen Sheahan (A. S. Barnes, 1979). It furnishes good annotations for film reference books grouped by type, such as encyclopedias, bibliographies, indexes, and so on. Designed for college students, it is especially useful for that audience.

PERIODICALS

825. **Film, Television, and Video Periodicals: A Comprehensive Annotated List.** Katharine Loughney. New York: Garland, 1991. 431p. (Garland Reference Library of the Humanities, v.1032). ISBN 0-8240-0647-X.

This is a useful and comprehensive listing of about 900 of the most widely used and accessible periodicals in the fields of film, television, and/or video. Emphasis is placed on the inclusion of titles in the English language, although some foreign periodicals are treated as well. The titles represent a wide diversity of interests and audiences, from the scholarly (*Film Criticism*) to the technical (*Broadcast Engineering*) and even popular (*TV Guide*). Arrangement of entries is alphabetical by title, supplying publisher, address, telephone number, frequency, ISSN, LC and Dewey call number, and OCLC number. Annotations vary in size but are generally brief, running thirty to fifty words. Most impressive is the comprehensiveness of the coverage given to video periodicals, with nearly 275 titles. Cross-references are supplied to related entries; there are several indexes providing access by country, genre, level, and title.

826. **Union List of Film Periodicals: Holdings of Selected American Collections.** Anna Brady. Westport, CT: Greenwood Press, 1984. 316p. ISBN 0-313-23702-6.

To facilitate research in the field, this finding list covers the periodical holdings of thirty-five American libraries with important film collections. Periodical titles are from nearly sixty countries and include a broad range of emphases in the field, such as film and art, industry and entertainment, and sociological and psychological perspectives. More than 1,600 titles are listed and country of publication, language, ISSN, publication dates, and title changes are given. Numbers of volumes the various libraries hold are enumerated. There is an index of title changes, which includes titles having undergone at least three changes, and a geographical index lists the titles under country of publication.

Bibliographies and Catalogs

827. **Enser's Filmed Books and Plays: A List of Books and Plays from Which Films Have Been Made, 1928-1991.** Upd. ed. Ellen Baskin and Mandy Hicken, comps. Brookfield, VT: Ashgate Publishing, 1993. 970p. ISBN 1-85742-026-8.

Enser's standard work has been revised by other compilers for the first time and now cumulates the content of the previous issues (first published in 1968) while adding another five years of coverage to the last issue, published in 1988. Basically, it is a list of some 6,000 English-language films derived from books and plays. It provides a unique approach to both film buffs and serious students for identifying such works over a sixty-three-year period beginning with the onset of talking pictures. Never claiming to be a completely exhaustive listing, the bibliography is accessed through excellent indexes. Entries in the title index give the name of the distributing company and year of registration, as well as author, publisher, and book title. The author index lists works by the author which have been made into films and includes publisher as well as film distributor. A "change of original title" index lists original book titles that differ from those of their motion pictures.

A recent effort that complements the coverage is *Books and Plays in Films, 1896-1915: Literary, Theatrical, and Artistic Sources of the First Twenty Years of Motion Pictures*, by Denis Gifford (McFarland, 1991). Gifford lists some 3,000 film presentations derived from artistic or literary works (ballets, songs, operas, and comic strips as well as novels and short stories). Most of these early silent films were relatively short and thus have not received much attention from writers of guides such as this. Arrangement is alphabetical by name of author or creator, after which is listed the films in chronological order. Production companies are given and genre is identified.

828. **The Film Index: A Bibliography.** Writers Program of the Work Projects Administration of the City of New York. Volume 1. New York: H. W. Wilson, 1941. Repr., Kraus, 1988. Volume 2. New York: Kraus International, 1985. Volume 3. New York: Kraus International, 1985. ISBN 0-527-29326-1.

This three-part annotated bibliography has had a long and interesting history since the first volume appeared in 1941. It was not to be completed until forty-four years later, because of cutbacks in the budget of the WPA in 1939. The Wilson Company published the first volume, *The Film as Art*, with the Museum of Modern Art. This is an extensive, annotated bibliography of books and articles on the history, technique, and types of motion pictures, based primarily on the collections of the Museum of Modern Art and the New York Public Library. The remaining cards for the other two volumes have been held in the Archives of the Museum; Kraus has finally arranged for their publication. Volume 2, *The Film as Industry*, covers English-language materials (excluding newspapers) based on the holdings of the New York Public Library, with additional listings derived from periodical indexes. Entries are classified under major subject headings in alphabetical order. Volume 3, *The Film in Society*, identifies books and articles under such topics as education, censorship, moral and religious aspects, etc. All annotations are original from their period of preparation and the complete set is an important contribution to film research.

829. **Film Study: An Analytical Bibliography.** Frank Manchel. Rutherford, NJ: Fairleigh Dickinson University Press; distr., Cranbury, NJ: Associated University Presses, 1990. 4v. ISBN 0-8386-3186-X (v.1).

The author is a knowledgeable academic and writer who has updated and expanded his 1974 effort, *Film Study: A Resource Guide*. The new edition supplies introductory essays and bibliographies to each of six approaches to the teaching of cinema. Individual chapters are given to genres, stereotypes, themes, comparative media, periods, and film history. These chapters are subdivided by various topics with listings of relevant monographs and films. More than 2,000 books are covered with annotations of varying length in the first three volumes; volume 4 supplies various appendices, including directories, along with indexes to authors, titles, and film personalities.

Motion Pictures: A Catalog of Books, Periodicals, Screenplays, Television Scripts and Production Stills (Boston: G. K. Hall, 1976) is a standard tool listing cards in the catalog of a major collection at UCLA. Rich in both primary and secondary sources, the catalog is divided into five major sections, the first of which is an author listing of books, journals, personal papers, archival records, and certain memorabilia. Part 2 is a listing of published screenplays arranged by title of film, and part 3 is a listing of 6,000 unpublished screenplays. Part 4 lists television scripts and identifies about 3,000 works by title of the film and of the script. The final segment identifies not only production stills but also posters, pressbooks, programs, and the like.

830. **The Macmillan Film Bibliography: A Critical Guide to the Literature of the Motion Picture.** George Rehrauer. New York: Macmillan, 1982. 2v. ISBN 0-02-696400-7.

A long-time contributor to the reference literature of film study, the author has served as professor at Rutgers University and has used his expertise to produce his most extensive work. This two-volume set covers, in a profound and analytical manner, the contributions of nearly 6,800 books on the topic. Although a few items are not annotated, most of the entries provide excellent descriptions of the content and an assessment of value. Some of these annotations are quite lengthy and have been praised for their wit and sometimes caustic commentary. Arrangement is alphabetical by title in volume 1; volume 2 provides indexes by subjects, authors, and scripts.

831. **Radio and Television: A Selected, Annotated Bibliography.** William E. McCavitt, comp. Metuchen, NJ: Scarecrow Press, 1978. 229p. ISBN 0-8108-1113-8. **Supp. One: 1977-1981**. 1982. 155p. ISBN 0-8108-1556-7. **Supp. Two: 1982-1986**. 1987. ISBN 0-8108-2108-3.

The basic edition furnishes 1,100 annotated entries representing selections from the literature of broadcasting over a period of fifty years, from 1926 to 1976. There is a classified arrangement of twenty-one broad subject headings, including such topical matter as history, regulation, organization, broadcasting, audience, etc. These categories are generally subdivided further. The work has been criticized in the past for lack of sufficient access because of the fragmentation and scatter of entries on similar subjects, and the general categories are awkward as subject headings for some of the entries. An author index provides access by name when known. The first supplement added six new subject headings (news, advertising, corporate video, home video, etc.) but still contains no detailed subject index. The second supplement, by P. K. Pringle, continues the coverage with another 1,000 entries. The work is recommended for those with a serious interest.

832. **Radio Broadcasting from 1920 to 1990: An Annotated Bibliography**. Diane Foxhill Carothers. New York: Garland, 1991. 564p. (Garland Reference Library of the Humanities, v.967). ISBN 0-8240-1209-7.

The importance of this title lies both in its inclusiveness and its currency. Designed to appeal to a wide audience, from scholar to hobbyist, this bibliography by a communication librarian in academe provides comprehensive coverage of writings over a period of seventy years. Emphasis is on books, although there are government documents and some serials among the 1,704 titles treating radio broadcasting. Theses and dissertations are omitted. Coverage is provided in eleven chapters representing full coverage of the field: history, biography, production concerns, programming, regulations, international and educational aspects, technology, careers, amateur radio, women and minorities, and reference sources. Annotations supply brief but informative descriptions. Unfortunately, there are no cross-references between entries and no subject indexing, which may hinder access to particular entries. Author and title indexes are supplied.

833. **Television & Ethics: A Bibliography**. Thomas W. Cooper et al. Boston: G. K. Hall, 1988. 203p. ISBN 0-8161-8966-8.

This unique work is represented by its authors as a seminal work in a field where it is sorely needed. The authors are academics at Emerson College, where study of television ethics has been emphasized within the communications curriculum. They have utilized the talents of a number of scholars to serve as advisors on the development of this work, which is designed to reveal the influence of television and its ethical implications. Coverage is thorough and embraces 1,171 entries spanning antiquity to the present day, organized under various categories. Criteria for inclusion and strategies of searching out the items are described for the user, affirming the text's scholarly nature and its emphasis on relevance and substance of the documents. Annotations are supplied for nearly half the entries; these are brief and mainly descriptive of content. Author and subject indexes are given.

Film/Video Catalogs and Listings

Film listings and catalogs are extremely valuable to both reference and research in film work. Catalogs of important collections are available, as are numerous filmographies based on genres (horror, western, science-fiction, detective, etc.) or an individual's work. Additional items to verify or identify motion pictures are found in the section "Dictionaries, Encyclopedias, and Handbooks." The "Reviews" section contains evaluative tools.

834. The American Film Institute Catalog of Motion Pictures Produced in the United States. New York: R. R. Bowker, 1971- .

Planned to be completed in nineteen volumes, this work, if and when completed, will be the most extensive listing of films ever compiled. Based in the Library of Congress and funded by grants from both public and private sources, it is to be developed in several series or parts. Part A will cover films 1893 to 1910; parts F1 through F6 will describe feature films from 1911 through 1970; parts S1 through S6 will cover short films from 1911 through 1970; and parts N1 through N6 will identify newsreels from 1908 through 1970. Regarding feature-length films, the most recent issue is the two-volume coverage given to the period 1911-1920, bearing the publication date 1988 and marking the start of a new series. This would correspond to the F1 unit of the F series. Prior to that, two units had been published; F2, covering feature films 1921-1930 (2v.), and F6, 1961-1970 (2v.). The first volume of each unit lists films alphabetically by title and furnishes complete information on physical description, production credits, cast credits, and content (genre, source, summary). There are indexes of credits and of subjects.

The Film Catalog: A List of Holdings in the Museum of Modern Art, by Jon Gartenberg et al. (G. K. Hall, 1985) was published in honor of the fiftieth anniversary of MOMA's film department. The catalog describes some 5,500 titles acquired between 1935 and 1980, ranging from fiction and documentary to television commercials.

*835. Bowker's Complete Video Directory. New Providence, NJ: R. R. Bowker, 1990- . Irreg. ISSN 1051-290X.

This monumental and comprehensive guide to available videos of all kinds was first issued in 1990, then 1992, and again in 1993 and 1994. It appears to have settled on an annual frequency, with coverage in three volumes beginning in 1993. Within the three-volume effort are entries treating more than 100,000 programs from more than 1,500 manufacturers and distributors. There are more than 40,000 entertainment and performance videos and more than 60,000 educational and special-interest videos. Entries generally supply brief annotations along with full purchasing information and identification of formats. Presently it is highly competitive with the well-established *The Video Source Book* (entry 839) as the major tool in the field.

Prior to this, from 1988 to 1989, Bowker had issued *Variety's Complete Home Video Directory* as an annual with quarterly supplements targeting the entertainment, cultural, and general interests of the home video market. **Variety's Video Directory Plus*, which was made available on CD-ROM, provided not only brief annotations of all available home videocassettes and videodiscs but also several thousand full-length reviews from *Variety* (entry 871). It has been updated quarterly.

836. Feature Films: A Directory of Feature Films on 16mm and Videotape Available for Rental, Sale and Lease. James L. Limbacher, comp. and ed. New York: R. R. Bowker. 8th ed. 1985- . Bienn. with Q. supp. ISSN 0037-4830.

Settled into what appears to be a biennial pattern of appearance, this directory has undergone a change of title to eliminate 8mm films from its coverage. Each edition carries more than 20,000 entries for items that are available from leading distributors. They are arranged alphabetically by title and include releasing company, year of release, running time, special information, and distributor's name. A *feature film* is defined as any film more than one 16mm reel long or forty-eight minutes' running time. Most distributors are U.S., but some Canadian films are listed as well. Included are a directors' index, foreign-language index, and a directory of names with addresses. A quarterly supplement appears in *Sightlines*.

837. The International Film Index, 1895-1990. Alan Goble, ed. New Providence, NJ: K. G. Saur, 1991. 2v. ISBN 0-86291-623-2.

Developed as a comprehensive reference tool by a single individual, Goble has devoted twenty years to production of this index. The end product is a massive two-volume listing of more than 177,000 films from 25,000 directors listed under 232,000 titles. Listings were culled from more than 400 reference books listed in the bibliography in volume 2. About 90 percent of all mainstream motion pictures for the United States and Europe have been listed, although accuracy is dependent upon the veracity of the reference books used as sources. Also included are listings for 120 countries outside of Europe. Feature-length films, animated films, art films, documentaries, serials, and shorts are all treated. Volume 2 provides a filmography for directors, identifying their country, dates, and films in chronological order. The work represents a synthesis of the content of numerous reference books; its omissions, gaps, and inaccuracies are representative of past oversights.

Directors and Their Films: A Comprehensive Reference, 1895-1990, by Brooks Bushnell (McFarland, 1993), provides excellent coverage of more than 108,000 films of various types (not limited to those of feature length) along with their directors. The first part supplies alphabetical listings of directors, under which are listed their motion pictures in chronological sequence. Part 2 lists the films alphabetically and supplies name of director and year of release. Variant titles are all included both in English and applicable foreign language. The work does not include films made for television.

*838. **National Union Catalog. Audiovisual Materials.** Washington, DC: Library of Congress, 1983- . Q. ISSN 0734-7669.

This microfiche catalog is the latest entry in a line of resource tools to the cataloging of the national library which began with the *Library of Congress Catalog: Motion Pictures and Filmstrips*. This was issued quarterly and in quinquennial editions between 1953 and 1973. Its identity was established at that time as part of the *National Union Catalog* as well, and it attempted to cover all educational motion pictures and filmstrips released in this country. From 1972-1978, it was known by the title *Films and Other Materials for Projection*, and added sets of slides and other transparencies to its field of coverage. From 1979-1982, it was the *Library of Congress. Audiovisual Materials*, and included video recordings and kits. Presently bearing the masthead of NUC and appearing in microfiche format, its purpose and organization remain much the same. Succeeding issues in a volume cumulate those before it in furnishing indexes by name, subject, title, and series. The work is available online and on CD-ROM as *LC MARC; Visual Materials* beginning with the year 1972, as part of the Current Cataloging Database from the Library of Congress.

839. **The Video Source Book.** Detroit: Gale Research, 1979- . Ann. ISSN 0277-3317.

Begun by the National Video Clearinghouse in 1979 as an annual publication, this comprehensive tool is now issued by Gale Research. It identifies and describes prerecorded video program titles of all types available on videotape and videodisc. Arrangement is by title, and several indexes, including one by subject category, are furnished to provide access to materials of interest to home, business, or educational institutions. As an early entrant in the field of video documentation, it is now in its fifteenth edition and issued in two volumes. The present subtitle reads "A Guide to Approximately 130,000 Programs Currently Available on Video from more than 2,400 Sources." This is an increase of some 4,000 programs over the 1993 edition.

Indexes, Abstracts, and Serial Bibliographies

840. **The Critical Index: A Bibliography of Articles on Film in English, 1946-1973 ...** John C. Gerlach and Lana Gerlach. New York: Teachers College Press, 1974. 726p.

In producing one of the very useful indexes through the years, the Gerlachs have indexed articles from twenty-two English-languages journals over a period of nearly thirty years. Covered are directors, producers, actors, critics, and writers, in a names section alphabetically arranged. A section on topics is classified under a hierarchy explained in the front of the work. Such topics as history, aesthetics, techniques of filmmaking, the relationship of film to society, and various film genres are employed. Annotations are provided in cases where the titles are not descriptive of the contents. Approximately 5,000 articles are enumerated, with access provided through author and title indexes. Appendices include lists of archives, bibliographies, periodicals, etc. This complements the coverage of *Film Literature Index* (entry 841).

*841. **Film Literature Index: A Quarterly Author-Subject Periodical Index to the International Literature of Film.** Albany, NY: State University of New York at Albany Film and Television Documentation Center, 1973- . Q. with ann. cum. ISSN 0093-6758.

This work complements the coverage of *The Critical Index* (entry 840), which limits itself to U.S., British, and Canadian journals. This quarterly publication indexes material from some 300 periodicals which are scanned for pertinent articles. Recently, it has included television periodicals as well. Since it was first issued in 1973, it has developed an excellent reputation not only for its coverage of some 160 journals from thirty countries, but also for its organization and ease of use. Developed originally as a pilot offering at SUNY-Albany, with a grant from the New York State Council on the Arts, the work has continued without interruption and occupies a prominent position among such tools. The work is available online from the publisher.

842. **International Index to Film Periodicals.** New York: R. R. Bowker, 1972- . Ann. ISSN 0000-0388.

An excellent example of a cooperative indexing project of international proportions is this effort sponsored by the International Federation of Film Archives (FIAF). It provides a convenient package of index entries cumulated over the year at various archives in Europe and North America and contributed by them to this effort. These entries originally appeared on catalog cards that were distributed to subscribers of the service from FIAF. About sixty to eighty film periodicals are selected from the index based on their representation of their country's thinking and articles of lasting quality. There are separate sections of reviews, biographies, and studies of individual films. It has been made available on microfiche from the Federation since 1981.

The counterpart to this work in the field of television is *International Index to Television Periodicals: An Annotated Guide* (International Federation of Film Archives, bienn., 1979/1980-), which provides cumulations of entries indexed on cards by a service. It covers important articles from nearly 100 periodicals worldwide. There are separate indexes for general subjects, individual programs, and biography, as well as an author index.

Dictionaries, Encyclopedias, and Handbooks

843. **The American Film Industry: A Historical Dictionary.** Anthony Slide. Westport, CT: Greenwood Press, 1986. 431p. ISBN 0-313-24693-9.

Slide and his team of eight research associates have put together a new and detailed dictionary of the historical development of the film industry in this country. There are about 600 entries, all well written and informative. Such aspects as producing and releasing companies, technological innovations, film series, genres, organizations, and technical terms are treated. Entries vary in length from just a few lines to a few pages, depending upon the importance of the subject. There is a general index of persons, subjects, organizations, etc., and numerous cross-references are included. This work is especially useful for the relative depth of the entries, which provide a great deal of detail.

Early American Cinema, by Anthony Slide, now in its second edition (Scarecrow Press, 1993), furnishes a brief history of the motion picture industry up to 1920. Coverage is given to pre-cinema, independent filmmakers, the star system, and D. W. Griffith, as well as technologies and genres. The new issue represents an extensive revision of the title, which originally appeared in 1970. Benjamin Hampton's *A History of the Movies* (Friede, 1931; repr., Arno, 1970) is a true history of the American film industry and is a classic work regarded as a major contribution even today.

844. **Blacks in Black and White: A Source Book on Black Films.** 2d ed. Henry T. Sampson. Metuchen, NJ: Scarecrow Press, 1993. 800p. ISBN 0-8108-2605-4.

Initially published in 1977, this history of a unique era in motion pictures has been expanded considerably. It remains the only detailed source of information on the origin and development of the genre of motion pictures featuring all-black casts, producers, and directors intended to be shown to primarily black audiences. These theaters were mostly in black neighborhoods in cities and towns, and many were owned and managed by black businesspeople. Coverage begins around 1910 with the introduction of the genre and its preparation and ends in 1950 with its demise. Treated here are the achievements of performers and filmmakers, most of whom are now obscure. The second edition enhances the previous coverage given to black producers, describes more films, and provides expanded listings of film titles and cast members. Photographs accompany the text; a detailed general index is provided.

845.   **Chambers Film Quotes**. Tony Crawley, comp. and ed. New York: Chambers, Kingfisher Graham, 1991. 296p. ISBN 0-550-21024-5.

Of interest to a wide variety of users is this quotation handbook identifying more than 2,000 celebrity quotations. It is unique in its focus on Hollywood and those associated with film and filmmaking. Sources of quotations are actors, directors, producers, etc. whose remarks or comments have been arranged by topic or category. Quotations vary widely in terms of their wit, humor, and profundity; in many cases the abrasiveness, vanity, ego, and jealousy of this part of the entertainment industry are revealed clearly. There are more than 260 topics or categories ranging from the "casting couch" to the "method." Each quote in its own way provides insight into the life and character of its creator, thereby addressing the interests of moviegoers and film buffs. Printed sources of quotations are identified. There is an index of speakers to aid access.

846.   **The Complete Actors' Television Credits, 1948-1988**. 2d ed. James Robert Parrish and Vincent Terrace. Metuchen, NJ: Scarecrow Press, 1989-1990. 2v. ISBN 0-8108-2204-0 (v.1); 0-8108-2258-X (v.2).

This unique two-volume set separates male and female television performers, with volume 1 treating 1,587 actors and volume two covering 1,739 actresses. It serves as an enlargement and expansion of an earlier work by Parrish that, together with its three supplements, covered the years 1950-1985. The term "complete" in the title represents the tool's inclusiveness in covering all entertainment programs broadcast on network and cable television as well as those made in syndication. Experimental television from 1931 to 1946 is treated, as are variety series, specials, and dramatic series. Coverage of performers is selective, in that some but not all cast members are identified. Entries in both volumes are arranged alphabetically by performer, for each of whom the television credits are listed chronologically. Name of show is given along with episode, date, and network.

847.   **The Complete Directory to Prime Time Network TV Shows, 1946-Present**. 4th ed. Tim Brooks and Earle Marsh. New York: Ballantine Books, 1988. 1063p. ISBN 0-345-35610-1.

Defining *prime time* in broad terms as the time period from 6:00 P.M. to sign-off, this now-familiar work furnishes the librarian and patron with a comprehensive listing of all regularly scheduled programs ever aired on network television during the choice hours. First published in 1979, it has been updated three times and has followed a pattern of about three years between issues. In addition to network series, it includes the top shows in syndication. Offerings of the Fox network are furnished in this edition for the first time. Entries are arranged by title of the program and include dates of showing, broadcast history, cast, story line, and memorable episodes. The present work covers series through 1984 and is indexed by names. There are several interesting and useful appendices.

Another work that overlaps in coverage is Vincent Terrace's *The Complete Encyclopedia of Television Programs, 1947-1979* (A. S. Barnes, 1979). Much of the same information is provided for series television, but the two titles can be used together to assure that coverage is as complete as possible.

848. **The Complete Film Dictionary**. Ira Konigsberg. New York: New American Library, 1987; repr. 1993. 420p. ISBN 0-453-00564-0.

A comprehensive tool that provides definitions along with history, theory, technical awareness, and business practice of the motion picture industry. This is considered an excellent resource for all types of inquirers. Definitions are thorough and vary in length with the topic; the work provides clear and well-developed text. Terms are not only of American coinage but include European perspective in the vocabulary covered. Around 3,500 terms are treated. There are numerous line drawings and photographs, making it an especially useful aid in understanding both technical aspects of instrumentation and nature of film genres.

Filmmaker's Dictionary, by Ralph S. Singleton (Lone Eagle, 1986; repr. 1990), is a concise and compact volume filled with the terminology of filmmaking practice. It is written in simple language but provides a useful service in helping the user to become familiar with both technical terms and slang expressions employed by professionals in the field. More than 1,500 terms, representing every aspect of the art, are defined. There are abundant cross-references from the entries to other related definitions, making this a convenient and practical dictionary. Most interesting are the almost anecdotal bits of background information attached to many of the definitions.

849. **An Encyclopedia of Film Festivals**. Robert A. Nowlan and Gwendolyn Wright Nowlan. Greenwich, CT: JAI Press, 1988. 368p. (Foundations in Library and Information Science, v.23). ISBN 0-89232-734-0.

Designed as a manual and planning guide for those who wish to develop thematic film programs or festivals, this tool provides entries for more than 800 films. Entries are arranged under eleven different genres, which themselves are subdivided by more specific subgenres (such as the "psychological western" as a subgenre of "the western"). Each genre or subgenre segment is preceded by an introductory statement identifying additional titles not treated as entries. Entries generally supply plot summary, director, studio, major performers, running time, and designation of color or black-and-white. In addition to the listings, there is a chapter on planning film programs that treats financing, physical facilities, and publicity in a general way. Appendices include a glossary, a select bibliography, and listings of periodicals, associations, film festivals, distributors, and companies. There are indexes of film titles and individuals.

850. **The Facts on File Dictionary of Film and Broadcast Terms**. Edmund F. Penney. New York: Facts on File, 1991. 251p. ISBN 0-8160-1923-1.

Another of the publisher's dictionaries specialized to various fields is this reference tool containing 2,500 definitions of trade words. Definitions are brief and emphasis is given to utilitarian needs in explaining technology, equipment, broadcast formats, audiovisual considerations, production staff/activities, networks, unions, etc. Some coverage is given to film theories and to production companies, but personalities are not included. Definitions are pithy and cogent, albeit brief, and are expressed in a personal manner and casual style. There is no attempt to indicate historical background of the words. There are twelve appendices providing script forms, budget forms, releases, and other examples of practical documentation.

Chambers Concise Encyclopedia of Film and Television, edited by Allan Hunter (Chambers, Kingfisher Graham, 1991), provides more depth in its treatment of some 700 technical terms, personalities, major films, and television programs. Hunter has also provided his own perspective based on his experience and expertise in the field, beginning with the preface describing film and television as symbiotic companions.

851. **Film-Video Terms and Concepts**. Steven E. Browne. Boston: Focal Press, 1992. 181p. ISBN 0-240-80111-3.

Designed for those who have had some experience in film or video in its use of somewhat technical language to define technical words, this slim dictionary provides an excellent blend of film and video terminology. Similarities and differences between the two media are examined through definitions bearing symbols for their status. Such symbols indicate whether a term is applicable only to film, only to video, to both media, to both media with different meanings, or to both media with equivalent or highly similar definitions. Terms are basic to the fields and represent both production and postproduction activity, equipment, and processes. Entries are alphabetically arranged and supply definitions that are clear and comprehensible to the intended audience. Cross-references are supplied, and illustrations enhance the text, along with charts and diagrams.

852. **A Guide to World Cinema: Covering 7,200 Films of 1950-84 ...** Elkan Allan, ed. London: Whittet Books; distr., Detroit: Gale Research, 1985. 682p. ISBN 0-9054-8333-2.

Rather than a guide (a term that implies a certain selectivity or evaluative nature), this is a listing of the thousands of motion pictures shown at the British Film Institute over a thirty-four-year period. With such a huge quantity, naturally a wide variety of films are listed, ranging from the classic to the absurd. This is in part what gives this work strength as a valuable identification tool for all libraries supporting film research and inquiry. The work provides for each film what are referred to in the subtitle as "capsule reviews"—brief but informative commentaries taken from the original program notes. Most entries also include a very small production still. The comprehensive coverage and relative depth of information provided make this a notable purchase for the collection, even though it has been criticized for its small print size.

Screen World (Crown, 1949-) has been appearing annually since it was started by Daniel Blum. Since 1966, it has been edited by John Willis and has continued as a highly regarded resource for its survey of film releases in the previous year. Major films are identified with the cast list and production credits. The volume is profusely illustrated with film scenes. There are no plot summaries, but it does have a useful biographical section. The publisher recently reprinted the first twenty volumes of this notable serial.

853. **Halliwell's Filmgoer's and Video Viewer's Companion: Incorporating the Film-goer's Book of Quotes and Halliwell's Movie Quiz.** 10th ed. John Walker, ed. New York: HarperCollins, 1993. 834p. ISBN 0-06-271570-4.

The name *Halliwell* is a familiar one to librarians and patrons of the entertainment arts for the useful and convenient guides he has produced over the years. The ninth edition of this work (two to three years between issues) was published by Scribner's in 1989, and added much new material covering the period up to the time of publication. With the additional emphasis of video, its value to the librarian was enhanced. After Halliwell's death in 1989, Walker edited the tenth edition, in which he continues the tried-and-true format. Arrangement of entries is alphabetical and coverage is given to films, personalities (actors, directors, writers, and others), and other related elements. It remains a storehouse of information on the cinema.

Halliwell's Film Guide (Scribner's, 1989), now in its seventh edition, has added more than 1,000 new entries, and remains a favorite for locating information and descriptions of films. Video availability is indicated. Coverage of early films from the 1930s is excellent, and critical commentary from the time of the film release is provided. Films are listed alphabetically. *Halliwell's Television Companion* (2d ed., Granada, 1982) provides similar coverage for television films, series, and personalities.

854. **Handbook of Old-Time Radio: A Comprehensive Guide to Golden Age Radio Listening and Collecting.** Jon D. Swartz and Robert C. Reinehr. Metuchen, NJ: Scarecrow Press, 1993. 825p. ISBN 0-8108-2590-2.

This well-developed guide to old-time radio is designed for the nostalgia buff as well as the serious student and researcher. More than 2,000 programs are treated in descriptive narrative highlighting the casts, announcers, network affiliations, length of program, duration or longevity, and availability. Story lines are included for certain programs when appropriate. Programs are categorized by type, with chapter coverage given to each type of program. Guidelines are supplied regarding the comprehensiveness of and research for the various categories. Also treated are the most well-known premiums offered by the various programs to the listening audience. In addition, the work describes the history of the major networks, providing useful background information, and there is a listing of resources available for acquisition of old-time programs. Indexing treats more than 8,000 performers and programs.

855. **The International Film Industry: A Historical Dictionary**. Anthony Slide. New York: Greenwood Press, 1989. 423p. ISBN 0-313-25635-7.

Serving as a companion volume to Slide's effort on the American film industry (entry 843), the present effort has utilized the same basic pattern in providing treatment on an international level. It supplies 650 entries pertinent to both historical and contemporary aspects of filmmaking, with coverage given to directors, films, studios, production companies, theaters, awards, techniques, and organizations. Useful information is given on genres, movements, publications, processes, distributors, and series. Entries were prepared by numerous contributors, although articles are not signed. They vary in length from a single sentence to several pages; many contain bibliographies. Although all nations are covered, there is emphasis on the British film industry. Listings are included for archives and film festivals.

International Film Prizes: An Encyclopedia, by Tad Bentley Hammer (Garland, 1991), supplies information on awards given in forty-two nations, with emphasis on those presented to feature-length motion pictures entered in domestic competitions. Arrangement is by country and entries provide historical overviews of the awards and chronologies of winners. There is a bibliography; the work is indexed by title and by personality.

856. **Motion Picture Series and Sequels: A Reference Guide**. Bernard A. Drew. New York: Garland, 1990. 412p. (Garland Reference Library of the Humanities, v.1186). ISBN 0-8240-4248-4.

With series and sequels so much a part of filmmaking and entrepreneurship, reference tools on the phenomenon are used by all types of audiences. This is a comprehensive effort with 800 entries identifying 936 English-language motion pictures dating from 1899 to the present, including those made for television. These films had one or more major sequels or remakes, and embrace all genres (mystery, comedy, etc.); animated films, documentaries, and short comedies are excluded. Entries supply plot descriptions, studio, year, directors, major performers, and alternate titles. The work is illustrated in black-and-white and indexed by title.

Cinema Sequels and Remakes, 1903-1987, by Robert A. Nowlan and Gwendolyn Nowlan (McFarland, 1989), treats all films (silent or sound) having at least one English-language sound remake or sequel. Although not as inclusive as Drew's work in number of films, coverage is more detailed. Entries supply studio, country, release date, cast, credits, and source of story, along with a summary of the storyline. The work is indexed in extensive fashion. *Haven't I Seen You Somewhere Before? Remakes, Sequels, and Series in Motion Pictures, Videos, and Television, 1896-1990*, by James L. Limbacher (Pierian Press, 1991), is an expansion of an earlier edition published in 1979. The work is divided into three sections, the first of which is on remakes. This is followed by sequels (one or two films that follow on the events of the original). Finally, the series section lists efforts with three or more films using the same characters, ideas, or actors.

857. **The New Video Encyclopedia**. Larry Langman and Joseph A. Molinari. New York: Garland, 1990. 312p. ISBN 0-8240-8244-3.

This is a revised and updated version of an earlier work issued in the mid-1980s, which treats the burgeoning world of video with an expanded offering. It now supplies more than 1,500 entries defining every conceivable term pertinent to the field in treating various aspects of production, equipment, business, and marketing. Additionally, coverage is given to magazines as well as notable personalities like Sarnoff and Zworykin. Entries tend to be brief, at around 50 words, although some survey topics provide descriptions of as much as 200 words. They are alphabetically arranged and many are accompanied by illustrations of line drawings or black-and-white photographs. Cross-references are indicated through use of capitalization. The audience for this tool is specialized, but ranges from the technician to the student and interested layperson.

A more specialized handbook is *Cheap Shots: Video Production for Nonprofits*, by Pat Kardas (Scarecrow Press, 1993), which focuses on reasons and reasoning behind video production. In providing its unique emphasis on nonprofit agencies as a target group, the work examines potential audience, basic equipment needs, sources of funding and free talent, scriptwriting, editing, and polishing the product.

858. **The New York Times Encyclopedia of Film.** Gene Brown and Harry M. Geduld, eds. New York: Times Books, 1984. 13v. ISBN 0-8129-1059-1.

Similar to the *New York Times Film Reviews* (entry 893) in format, this monumental collection of articles from the *New York Times* is arranged chronologically from 1896 to 1979. Included are all types of writings pertaining to motion pictures: news items, features, interviews, reports, and promotional pieces. As one might expect, reviews are studiously avoided, allowing the *New York Times Film Reviews* to retain its uniqueness in that area. Many illustrations are included, although the work has been criticized for the poor quality of the reproductions. Many subjects are covered, with a good proportion of the articles on personalities (producers, commentators, critics, and news correspondents, as well as performers). There is an index volume, alphabetically arranged, providing access to the desired subject. Initially published by the *New York Times*, Garland is marketing the work at a bargain price, as it is going out of print.

859. **Radio Soundtracks: A Reference Guide.** 2d ed. Michael R. Pitts. Metuchen, NJ: Scarecrow Press, 1986. 337p. ISBN 0-8108-1875-2.

The purpose of this revised edition of an earlier work is to identify programs from the golden age of radio (1920s to 1960s) that are available on tapes and records. It is divided into five parts, the largest of which lists more than 1,000 programs available on tape. Entries are arranged by name of program, and include network, length, stars, and brief commentary. Part 2 covers radio specials on tape, and part 3 identifies those available on long-playing records. Part 4 is "Performers' Radio Appearances on Long Playing Records"; part 5 describes compilation record albums composed of radio material. More than 2,700 entries are furnished in all, and the work should be extremely useful both for identification of the historical factual material and for information regarding the recording.

860. **Radio's Golden Years: Encyclopedia of Radio Programs, 1930-1960.** Vincent Terrace. San Diego: A. S. Barnes; distr., London: Tantivy, 1981. 308p. ISBN 0-498-02393-1.

An absorbing compendium of information on the great years of radio programming, this work identifies 1,500 network and syndicated entertainment programs. The arrangement is alphabetical by title of the program; entries include story line, cast lists, announcer and music credits, sponsors, program openings, network and syndication information, length, and dates. A variety of entertainment programs are described (adventure, comedy, crime, drama, game shows, musicals, mystery, science fiction, and westerns). There are a number of good illustrations. A name index provides access.

Another useful tool that overlaps to some degree is John Dunning's *Tune in Yesterday: The Ultimate Encyclopedia of Old-Time Radio, 1925-1976* (Prentice-Hall, 1976). Its arrangement is similar, but Dunning offers more background information, with biographical facts about performers. *Primetime Radio Classics* is a database available online through CompuServe. It provides information on episodes of classic radio programs from the 1930s to the 1950s in a variety of categories. Cassettes may be ordered.

861. **The Television Industry: A Historical Dictionary.** Anthony Slide. New York: Greenwood Press, 1991. 374p. ISBN 0-313-25634-9.

This effort completes what has been referred to as Slide's "trilogy" of historical dictionaries, joining his two works on the film industry (entries 843 and 855). There are more than 1,000 entries on various aspects of television, such as production companies, distributors, organizations, various genres, and themes, as well as technical terms and popular language.

The programs themselves are excluded, as there are many available tools dealing with programming. Emphasis is on the United States rather than Great Britain, although the coverage is international in scope. Entries vary in length from brief identifications of a few sentences to two-page articles treating the major networks. An interesting feature is the inclusion of biographical essays on the three magnates of network television, Sarnoff, Paley, and Golderson.

Another useful tool is *Les Brown's Encyclopedia of Television* (Gale, 1992), now in its third edition. Brown has furnished 800 entries treating performers, programs, and events in alphabetical order. Coverage is international in scope and a bibliography is given. There are numerous listings in the appendices. There is a subject index.

862.　**Variety International Film Guide**. Hollywood: Samuel French. 1990- . Ann.

This familiar effort, once known as *International Film Guide* (1964-1989), continues with the 1993 edition, totalling 528 pages. Since its beginning, it has been regarded as an important offering in its detailed reporting of the state-of-the-art of filmmaking in nearly seventy countries. Peter Cowie has remained steadfast as the editor of this annual throughout its existence and is recognized for his efforts. Countries are arranged alphabetically and the essay-reports are produced by scholars or critics in summarizing the condition of film production and attendance. New films are described and biographical sketches of important personalities are included within those entries. Top box office attractions are listed as well. In addition to the reports, there are various listings such as international film festivals, film archives, journals, and bookstores. Unfortunately, there is no title index to the films described.

Directories, Annuals, and Current Awareness Sources

*863.　**Baseline**. New York: Baseline II Inc. (database).

This is a comprehensive computerized system that contains biographies of creative, technical, and administrative personnel for various segments of the entertainment industry (film, television, theater); listings of more than 40,000 films released in the United States for both theaters and television, theater productions, and television series since 1970; current production information on more than 1,400 films and television series; citations to articles in major entertainment trade journals, including *Variety* (entry 871); demographics on audiences attending opening nights; daily information on the Hollywood entertainment community; and synopses and evaluations of literary properties available for purchase, calendar, stocks, and travel. E-mail and bulletin board services are furnished. It is updated daily.

A daily print publication also available online is *HOLLYWOOD HOTLINE*, edited by Eliot Stein. Online access is through CompuServe, NewsNet, and GEnie, among others. It provides news of the entertainment industry, including films, music, and home entertainment. It covers programming, contracts, movie summaries, soap operas, weekly ratings, record albums, and more from 1983 to the present. It is updated daily.

*864.　**Entertainment Weekly**. New York: Entertainment Weekly, 1990- . Wk. ISSN 1049-0434.

This relatively new entertainment journal is linked to its companion effort appearing as a popular television show. The print version is designed to cover the trends and developments in the entertainment industry in this country, and furnishes feature stories and reviews of books, motion pictures, musical recordings, and television programs of all kinds. This concept is shared by the television program, which highlights developments and happenings in the careers of performers and production people. Like *Variety* (entry 871) and *Billboard* (entry 683), it stands foursquare in the realm of popular culture. The publication is also available online through VU/TEXT Information Services, under the auspices of Time, Inc. The service provides full text of the complete file beginning with inception of the weekly in February 1990 to the present day.

865. **International Directory of Film and TV Documentation Centres**. 3d ed. Frances Thorpe, ed. Chicago: St. James Press, 1988. 140p. ISBN 0-912289-29-5.

This slender volume began under the auspices of FIAF (the International Federation of Film Archives) in 1976, with half the entries found in the present edition. The directory now lists 104 collections representing forty-seven countries. Information is given for each unit regarding available documentation services, nature and availability of holdings, and publications issued. These centers are varied in nature and include film schools, state institutions, and specialized agencies. Collections also vary and include scripts, clippings, stills, posters, programs, scrapbooks, diaries, recordings, slides, and other such items, along with books and periodicals. Most are archival in nature and are available for research purposes. Listings of FIAF members are given; there is an index to special collections.

Footage 91: North American Film and Video Sources, edited by Richard Prelinger et al. (Prelinger Associates, 1991) was issued as a supplement to *Footage 89* (Prelinger Associates, 1989) and identifies services and policies of some 1,600 television stations, film archives, and university collections containing films and videotapes available for use. Entries describe collections and supply contact information.

866. **International Motion Picture Almanac**. New York: Quigley, 1929- . Ann. ISSN 0074-7084.

This has been a leading directory of services and products and an important purchase for film libraries throughout its long history and its issuance under varying titles. It is a treasure house of miscellaneous information and statistical data. Included is a who's who providing brief biographical sketches of numerous film personalities. There are also sections on pictures, corporations, theater circuits, buying and booking, equipment and suppliers, services, talent and literary agencies, organizations, advertising, world market, press, nontheatrical motion pictures, censorship, etc. It also gives information on the industry in Great Britain and Ireland.

International Television Almanac (Quigley, 1956-) is also published on an annual basis. Statistical reporting and information on people and developments make it a useful tool for television study. It identifies television stations, shows, networks, personnel, and feature releases, and provides information on the industry in Great Britain and Ireland as well.

867. **Money for Film & Video Artists**. Suzanne Niemeyer, ed. New York: ACA Books/American Council for the Arts, 1991. 234p. ISBN 0-915400-93-6.

The American Council for the Arts sponsored this directory in response to a need not addressed by established tools. It is a comprehensive guide to resources for film and video artists and identifies 193 organizations that offer assistance or support. Most of these units are found in the United States, but some Canadian agencies are also treated. These vary in size and prominence, as do their grants and awards, and range from the well-known national operations to obscure local and state organizations. Included in these pages is information regarding grants, awards, fellowships, artists' residencies, access to equipment, loan programs, and technical assistance. Entries treat each of the organizations separately and supply pertinent data regarding funding, eligibility, types of awards and assistance, application process, and requirements. Several indexes provide access.

868. **The Nostalgia Entertainment Sourcebook: The Complete Resource Guide to Classic Movies, Vintage Music, Old-Time Radio and Theatre**. Randy Skretvedt and Jordan R. Young, comps. Beverly Hills, CA: Moonstone Press, 1991. 158p. ISBN 0-940410-25-7.

This unique directory targets the pre-television era and provides sources and source listings on a variety of elements within the popular culture. Included here are record shops, film and video dealers, jazz festivals, radio shows, and revival cinemas, representing the interests of bygone eras. More than 1,100 sources are cited in all; also treated are fan clubs, research centers, conventions, and radio stations. Separate sections are given to movies, music, radio, and theater, with their own sequence of entries. Coverage of nostalgia extends from the 1920s to the 1940s; sports are not included. Entries supply the normal directory-type information along with brief annotations. Collectors and nostalgia buffs will utilize the listings of museums as well as the sources of available memorabilia. Appendices contain bibliographies; an index is provided.

869. **Television & Cable Fact Book.** Washington, DC: Warren Publishing, 1982- . Ann. ISSN 0732-8648.

This has proved to be a most useful reference tool for those needing up-to-date information on the television and cable industries. It appears in two separate publications. The "Stations" volume covers technical facilities, ownership, personnel, rate, and audience data for all television stations in the United States. Entries are arranged by state, then alphabetically by city, with separate treatment for Canadian and international stations. The "Cable and Services" volumes provide similar coverage of those aspects related to cable industries. Since 1991, there has been a weekly supplement entitled *Television & Cable Action Update*, reporting actions affecting television stations and cable networks.

From the same publisher comes the weekly current awareness tool *Television Digest*, which covers political, social, industrial, and educational issues and developments pertaining to television, cable, and allied fields. It is available online through NewsNet, and coverage is furnished from March 15, 1982 to the present. Also from Warren Publishing is *Public Broadcasting Report*, a biweekly report also available online and dealing with the financial, regulatory, and programming developments concerning public radio and television. Coverage dates from May 7, 1982 to the present. *The Home Video & Cable Report* (Knowledge Industry Publications, 1982-) is another up-to-date tool providing a weekly service. It is the most current print tool for information on the home video and cable industries. *Bacon's Radio/TV Directory* (Bacon's Information, 1986-) is a well-developed and informative annual directory providing complete programming and format information for all radio and television stations in this country. The seventh edition (1992) treats some 10,000 stations and lists some 70,000 key personnel along with address, network, type of programming, target audience, power, etc.

870. **Television Writers Guide.** 2d ed. Lynn Naylor, comp. and ed. Los Angeles: Lone Eagle Publishing, 1991. 442p. ISSN 0894-8658.

Initially projected as an annual publication, this serial effort was first issued in 1989, and incorporated writers' credits dating from the 1978-1979 season through the 1988-1989 season. The second edition, published two years later, retains the format of the earlier issue while updating the coverage through the 1989-1990 television season. The work is divided into two principal sections, the first providing lists of Emmy awards and nominations along with the listing of writers. Writers are arranged alphabetically, with television credits furnished for the time period covered. Membership in the Writers Guild of America is identified, along with names of co-writers or contact telephone numbers. The second section treats comedy series, daytime, drama, variety shows, etc., with shows listed along with their networks and production companies. There is excellent access through indexes by show, agent or manager, and advertiser.

871. **Variety.** New York: Variety, 1905- . Wk. ISSN 0042-2738.

The leading current awareness journal and official newspaper of show business, for which it is analogous to *Billboard* (entry 683) in the music field. There are sections on movies, radio and television, music, records, and vaudeville, providing information of a varied nature on recent developments, trends, personalities, etc. Theater is covered in detail, with reviews of various shows, information on casting, gate receipts, etc. It is well known for its reviews of top records of the week. Excellent coverage is given to the business aspects of this wide range of performing arts.

Art Murphy's Boxoffice Register (Art Murphy's Boxoffice Register, 1982-) has established itself as an annual publication. It provides financial reporting from *Variety* for film distributors for the box office year. Films are identified and income given; arrangement is alphabetical by title.

872. **The Video Register and Teleconferencing Resources Directory 1989-1990.** 11th ed. White Plains, NY: Knowledge Industry Publications, 1989. Ann. ISSN 0190-3705.

The eleventh edition of this annual directory continues to provide useful listings. Manufacturers, teleconferencing suppliers, service units, dealers, consultants, cable access centers, program distributors, trade association workshops, publications, and more are treated. Since two directories were merged as one publication, it has handled the balance well. Information is furnished on a variety of essential and basic sources, as well as some marginal elements to both video and teleconferencing. Both sections begin with introductory material describing the contents. Each has an index to facilitate access. Much of what is covered is difficult to find elsewhere, especially information on teleconferencing equipment and suppliers.

Histories

873. **American History, American Television: Interpreting the Video Past.** John E. O'Connor, ed. New York: Ungar, 1983; repr. 1985. 420p. (Ungar Film Library). ISBN 0-8044-2668-6.

This is a collection of fourteen essays of a historical and critical nature regarding the role of television in American history and culture. The essays cover a variety of subjects ranging from Milton Berle to the 1980 political campaign. Each article treats programming and production issues and industry and public response. News documentaries and entertainment programming are all covered in this fashion. There is a good annotated bibliography with accompanying commentary. The work will be helpful to students of television, history, and communications in general. Those studying sociology and anthropology will also benefit by the exposition provided. In addition to the bibliography, there is a useful guide to archival and manuscript sources.

874. **A History of Narrative Film.** 2d ed. David A. Cook. New York: W. W. Norton, 1990. 981p. ISBN 0-393-95553-2.

This is an important work focused on the development of narrative film. The first edition (1981) proved to be of use to a variety of patrons from serious students to laypersons. The new edition has expanded its coverage, adding 260 pages; it is presented in scholarly fashion, well documented throughout, and provides good illustrations of major scenes from some of the films described. Detailed information is found on individual filmmakers, and their movies are examined in a critical manner. National cinemas and many films are covered. Film elements are analyzed, and in some cases public reaction and influence on the field are gauged. The layperson will be especially interested in the quantity of production stills taken from a variety of motion pictures over the years. There is a good bibliography of 22 pages and a good glossary as well. Both public libraries and academic libraries are well served by this tool.

875. **Producers Releasing Corporation: A Comprehensive Filmography and History.** Wheeler Dixon, ed. Jefferson, NC: McFarland, 1986. 166p. ISBN 0-89950-179-6.

This is a delightful and thoroughly interesting historical overview of the life of a typical "B" movie production company located in Hollywood's "Poverty Row." These small operations would turn out movies in less than one week using unheralded actors and minimal sets. The budget for an entire production generally did not exceed $20,000, and, although the films were shoddy in every way, they do represent an important segment of the history of the American film industry. This work records the story of PRC through a brief narrative and a good chronology. A survey is given of the westerns produced by the studio; biographical sketches are furnished for personnel. Filmographies are included for the leading directors, as well as a checklist of films from the company. A detailed index helps to provide access.

Biographical Sources

876. **A Biographical Dictionary of Film.** 2d ed. rev. David Thomson. New York: Morrow, 1981. 682p. ISBN 0-688-00132-7.

The first edition of this work was published in 1976 and was praised by reviewers for its literate and witty, albeit opinionated, coverage of actors and directors. Librarians found it to be a vital source that was refreshingly entertaining but at the same time cogent and effective as a critical tool. Thomson is a Briton whose "obsessive work provides a sharp expression of personal taste, jokes, and digressions, insults, and eulogies." The second edition updates material for the entries in the earlier work and adds about forty-five personalities, mainly Americans who have had a strong impact in recent years (Robert DeNiro, Goldie Hawn, Steven Spielberg, Al Pacino, and others). It retains its charm and continues to be a top-rated biographical dictionary.

877. **A Biographical Dictionary of Scenographers, 500 B.C. to 1900 A.D..** Robin Thurlow Lacy. New York: Greenwood Press, 1990. 762p. ISBN 0-313-27429-0.

Although criticized for his personal and unpolished style of writing in developing his entries, Lacy has provided a needed service in creating this biographical dictionary of all known scenographers working in the Western tradition from antiquity to the beginning of the twentieth century. As a group, set designers and scenery painters have received little attention in the past, and efforts to document their achievements are considered useful to both scholars and students. Keying the entries to the bibliography of 435 published sources and archival collections, Lacy has produced a biographical dictionary of 3,000 scenographers. Entries vary in length from a single credit to more extended narratives bearing numerous credits of the artist's work. Of interest are the major artists not generally known to have been scenographers. There is a geographical-chronological list in the appendix.

878. **The Film Handbook.** Geoff Andrew. Boston: G. K. Hall, 1989. 362p. ISBN 0-8161-9093-3.

Andrews is a British film critic who has compiled a useful biographical dictionary of 200 leading directors dating from the silent era to the present day. Entries are detailed and run about 800 words in providing factual information and biographical narrative examining the individual's life and career along with evaluative commentary of his or her work. Also, short critical bibliographies are supplied with filmographies of the major works. In choosing to provide treatment of directors whose films are easily available, the focus is primarily on mainstream cinema, which is covered well. It should be noted, however, that Andrew is more prone to favor the mavericks and social critics among this mainstream. A glossary is supplied, as are a bibliography of film books and a listing of information sources divided by country. A general index provides access.

879. **Hollywood Baby Boomers.** James Robert Parish and Don Stanke. New York: Garland, 1992. 670p. (Garland Reference Library of the Humanities, v.1295). ISBN 0-8240-6104-7.

This work is specialized to the needs of those who are seeking biographical or career information on that particular generation of Hollywood achivers born between 1946 and 1960. This group is dominant in terms of box office and popularity today, with such names as Dan Aykroyd, Arsenio Hall, Meryl Streep, Oprah Winfrey, Sean Penn, and Robin Williams. Detailed coverage is given to eighty actors, singers, and comedians. Entries open with a quotation from the biographee, followed by essays of some six to eleven pages describing the personal life and furnishing a chronology of the star's work, along with a summary of his or her present and future status. Film, theater, television, and recording credits are enumerated. A black-and-white photograph is given for each entry. A detailed general index provides access.

880. **The Illustrated Who's Who of the Cinema.** Upd. ed. Ann Lloyd and Graham Fuller, eds. New York: Portland House, 1987. 480p. ISBN 0-51-764419-3.

More than 2,500 biographies covering people from all areas of the cinematic world are furnished, along with some 1,500 photographs of varied size. Actors, actresses, producers, directors, scene designers, costumers, art directors, composers, screenwriters, cinematographers, etc. are all represented, along with critics and censors. Generally conceded to be a record of the personalities of what may be called "mainstream cinema," there is excellent coverage of people from the 1920s to the 1940s. Less elaboration is given to personalities of the 1950s and 1960s. Biographies are brief and include a short filmography which identifies the person's first and last motion pictures and a representative number in between. This volume upates the previous 1983 edition published by Macmillan.

A quite different work is *The Illustrated Encyclopedia of Movie Character Actors*, by David Quinlan (Harmony Books/Crown, 1985), which supplies more detailed narrative. The work furnishes interesting and informed descriptions of 850 British and American character actors. The glib and witty characterizations make this work a pleasure to read.

881. **The International Dictionary of Films and Filmmakers.** 2d ed. Nicholas Thomas, ed. Detroit: St. James Press, 1990-1993. 5v. ISBN 1-55862-042-7.

The new edition of this work is a thorough revision of the earlier issue for which the first volume appeared in 1984. There are numerous illustrations, which enhance the appeal of the new edition. Volume 1 (1990) provides information on 650 of the world's most frequently studied films. Volume 2 (1991) examines the genius of 480 directors and film-makers of international renown. The arrangement is alphabetical by name and entries provide brief biographies; filmographies; selective bibliographies of books and articles, both by and about the personality; and an informative critical evaluation of the individual's work. Volume 3 (1992) treats 635 actors and actresses of international stature and provides coverage similar to that accorded the directors in volume 2. Volume 4 (1993) covers the contributions of writers and production artists. Volume 5 (1993) furnishes a comprehensive index. As one might expect, there is some variation in the quality of the critical essays, as well as the fullness of the biographical entries, but in general the tool is useful for its depth and detail.

882. **Michael Singer's Film Directors: A Complete Guide.** Michael Singer, comp. and ed. Beverly Hills, CA: Lone Eagle Publishing, 1984- . Ann. ISSN 0740-2872.

This annual biographical directory has continued to serve as a useful resource, and covers more than 1,800 living directors from all over the world. Arrangement of entries is alphabetical by name, and each entry furnishes basic information of interest to those who wish to identify or further examine the work of an individual filmmaker. Included are birthdate and birthplace; agent's name, address, and telephone number; and a chronological listing of films (including television works) with year of release, country of origin, and distributor. The value of this work lies in the comprehensive coverage of contemporary figures that one might not find elsewhere. Directors of the past are given coverage in separate segments. The tenth edition (1993) continues the tradition and contains 584 pages.

Biographical Dictionary of Film (entry 876) or George Sadoul's *Dictionary of Film Makers* (University of California Press, 1972) should be used for greater biographical detail. The latter is a translation of a French work and is a selective biographical dictionary of 10,000 producers, directors, scenarists, photographers, and others associated with filmmaking, but not actors or actresses. Entries are brief but informative and commentary is subjective. More limited in scope, but also important, is Larry Landman's *A Guide to American Film Directors: The Sound Era, 1929-1979* (Scarecrow Press, 1981) in two volumes.

883. **Who Was Who on Screen.** 3d ed. Evelyn Mack Truitt. New York: R. R. Bowker, 1983. 788p. ISBN 0-8352-1578-4.

Since its initial appearance in 1974, this retrospective biographical dictionary has been a popular purchase for reference collections serving the needs of both film buffs and specialists. With each edition, it has enlarged its coverage, and the present work covers no fewer than 13,000 individuals who died between 1905 and 1981. Where needed, entries from the previous editions have been revised. The arrangement of entries is alphabetical. They furnish brief biographical identification along with a complete listing of film credits with dates. The latter contribution especially establishes this tool as a basic reference work. Both shorts and features are identified. Inclusion is not limited to actors alone, but extends to prominent personalities who have had cameo appearances, such as Picasso, Hitchcock, and Maugham. A condensed version of this work was published in 1984 as the illustrated third edition. It covers 3,100 personalities and provides sixteen pages of pictures.

884.   **Who's Who in Hollywood: The Largest Cast of International Film Personalities Ever Assembled**. David Ragan. New York: Facts on File, 1992. 2v. ISBN 0-8160-2011-6.
 This is a comprehensive listing of some 35,000 entries identifying anybody who even appeared in motion pictures from 1893 to 1991. The range is great, embracing the very famous, the near-famous, and the never-famous, from international celebrities to bit players. Living actors are described with date and place of birth, current address, and a sampling of motion picture credits. Deceased performers are supplied with year of death and age, along with a sampling of credits. In some cases brief biographical sketches are included as well as career insights. Entries are alphabetically arranged and range in size from a single sentence to a page. Actors are listed by stage names; a brief general bibliography completes the effort.
 Who's Who in the Motion Picture Industry: Directors, Producers, Writers, ... (Packard Publishing 1981-) began as an annual, then changed to biennial and later triennial frequency. Not limited to performers, the subtitle goes on to include "cinematographers, executives, major studios, production companies, and distribution companies." Arrangement of entries is alphabetical; there is a name index. *Who's Who in American Film Now* by James Monaco (Zoetrope, 1987), now in its second edition, is an update of the initial publication that emphasized the 1970-1980 period. The second edition lists some 11,000 individuals and their credits in thirteen categories of film production, beginning with writers and ending with editors. These personalities were associated with 6,000 films between 1975 and 1986. Data are taken from *Baseline* database (entry 863). Entries are alphabetically arranged within each category and supply film credits in chronological order. Unfortunately, no comprehensive name index is given, a real detriment in locating individuals who appear in several categories.

885.   **World Film Directors**. John Wakeman, ed. New York: H. W. Wilson, 1987-1988. 2v. ISBN 0-8242-0757-2.
 Designed primarily for students and hobbyists, this biographical dictionary provides detailed biographical sketches ranging from 1,500 to 8,000 words on 400 major directors whose films are available in English-speaking countries. Volume 1 treats individuals born prior to 1920; volume 2 covers directors who gained prominence during the latter half of the twentieth century, some of whom were still active at the time of publication. The work contains the contributions of some fifty specialists, who together have produced a useful reference tool. Essays treat highlights of directors' lives and careers and supply production details of their major motion pictures, along with a digest of critical response and popular reception. Quotations from the directors are included providing insight into their personality. A photograph, filmography, listing of published screen plays, and brief bibliography accompany each entry.

Reviews and Criticism

886.   **Film Review Index**. Patricia King Hanson and Stephen L. Hanson, eds. Phoenix, AZ: Oryx Press, 1986-1987. 2v. ISBN 0-89774-153-6.
 Treating nearly 8,000 films, this is the most comprehensive index of reviews in its coverage of more than 100 years of filmmaking. Volume 1 examines the period from 1882

to 1949; volume 2 completes the effort with coverage from 1950 to 1985. Although comprehensive in terms of time covered, the title includes only films established as being of most interest to researchers and students and those lesser efforts that have the potential to attract researchers due to their popularity or their relationship to sociological trends. Arrangement of entries is alphabetical by title of American release, with cross-references from foreign or subsequent titles. Entries supply country, director, and date along with citations to reviews in magazines, journals, books, and trade publications. Indexes of director, country, and year are found in volume 2.

887. **Film Theory and Criticism: Introductory Readings.** 4th ed. Gerald Mast and Marshall Cohen, comps. New York: Oxford University Press, 1992. 797p. ISBN 0-19-506398-8.
  The essential character of this work has remained the same through the years, and it has earned an excellent reputation for the selection of articles and essays by theorists of various traditions and backgrounds. Much of the material is repeated from the third edition (1985). Despite being fifty-five pages shorter than the previous issue, there is similar broad representation of critical theory and well-developed coverage of the new breed of critic who has been schooled in the nature of the film art rather than literary criticism. The categories or sections of the work examine important issues and topics identified as basic to the study of film theory, with groupings of an expository nature relating to film and reality, the medium, audience, etc. The essays generally run from twenty to thirty pages, but vary in length.

888. **Guide to Critical Reviews, Part IV: The Screenplay, Supplement One: 1963-1980.** James M. Salem. Metuchen, NJ: Scarecrow Press, 1982. 698p. ISBN 0-8108-1553-2.
  Since the initial volume of this four-part listing of critical reviews of stage and screen came out more than twenty years ago, the parts or basic four volumes have appeared at different times and in different editions with various supplements. Part I of the main volume is now in its third edition (1984) and covers American drama from 1909 to 1982. Part II (3d ed., 1991) covers the Broadway musical from 1909 to 1989. Part III (2d ed., 1979) treats foreign drama from 1909 to 1974. This supplement is to part IV, which has not been revised since the first edition in two volumes in 1971. Part IV is entitled *The Screenplay from The Jazz Singer to Dr. Strangelove* and covers a period from 1927 to 1962, documenting the critical commentary accorded the first thirty-five years of the talkies. This supplement continues the coverage of that work by adding another seventeen years of reviews. The reviews are generally from well-known periodicals such as *Film Quarterly, Life, Newsweek, Rolling Stone, The New Yorker*, etc., and the reviews should not be difficult to find. All volumes, including this one on the screenplay, continue to be a popular, useful purchase for the reference department.

889. **Magill's Cinema Annual.** Englewood Cliffs, NJ: Salem Press, 1982- . Ann. ISSN 0739-2141.
  This is a handy and extremely useful guide to a select number of films of the previous year. Beginning with coverage of the year 1981, it has served as a supplement to the extensive multivolume *Magill's Survey of Cinema* (entry 890). The reviews are lengthy and well constructed and cover, on the average, eighty films released in the United States. Entries include production credits, direction, screenplay, cinematography, editing, editing, art direction, music, MPAA rating, running time, and principal characters. Foreign films are included if they were released in this country during the time period. There is also a section of additional films which treats briefly the same number of films that appear in the "Selected Films" category. In addition, there are an obituary section and a listing of popular awards. There are a number of indexes providing excellent access, including subject, title, performer, screenwriter, etc.

890. **Magill's Survey of Cinema: Foreign Language Films.** Frank N. Magill, ed. Englewood Cliffs, NJ: Salem Press, 1985. 8v. ISBN 0-89356-243-2.
  This is another of the extensive multivolume sets that are parts of a series bearing the Magill name. This set covers more than 750 foreign films arranged alphabetically by the title

used in the United States. The reviews themselves are new and the result of a fresh viewing of the films by about 180 contributors. The reviews are preceded by identifications that include origin, release date, U.S. release date, producers, directors, screenplay, photographer, editor, art, costume, sound and music direction, and running time. Cast lists are also given.

The original set in the series appeared in 1980 as *Magill's Survey of Cinema: English Language Films, First Series*. This was a four-volume set treating more than 500 important English-language films, followed in the next year by a six-volume set, the *Second Series*, covering another 750 films. The third issue was *Magill's Survey of Cinema: Silent Films*, a three-volume set published in 1982. It covered some 300 silent motion pictures from 1902 to 1936. In all cases, the essays are well written and range from 1,000 to 2,500 words in length, including plot summaries and critical commentaries. *Magill's Cinema Annual* (entry 889) serves as an update each year. A useful convenience tool is *Magill's Survey of Cinema-Title Index, All Series* (Salem, 1987), which furnishes a cumulative index for all series published between 1980 and 1986.

891. **The Motion Picture Guide, 1927-1984.** Jay Robert Nash and Stanley Ralph Ross. Chicago: CineBooks, 1985-1987. 12v. **Ann. Supp. 1986- .** ISBN 0-933997-00-0.

This ten-volume set and two index volumes (vols. xi, xii) form one of the most comprehensive and detailed of all reference tools for the identification and description of films. There are 25,000 entries on English-language motion pictures and notable foreign films, with a separate volume devoted to silent films. Volumes are arranged sequentially in alphabetical order, and entries are arranged by title. Ratings from zero to five stars are provided and included are year of release, running time, production/releasing company, and color status. Cast lists are given, and most importantly, good analytical reviews are provided. The reviews are interesting, with their sometimes incisive and sometimes anecdotal commentary. Interesting background information regarding the performers or the making of the films is also included. The two-volume index, published in 1987, provides access to alternate titles, series, and awards.

The Motion Picture Guide: Annual supplements the *Guide*, and covers all films from the previous year that were released to movie theaters in the United States, and some that have been given straight to video. The 1993 annual (covering the films of 1992) is published by BASELINE and distributed by Reed. It is the eighth annual supplement and provides well-constructed, detailed reviews of 529 feature films.

*892. **Movie Reviews Database.** Middleton, NY: Cineman Syndicate, Inc. (database).

Alternately called *Cineman Movie Reviews*, this computerized database is available online through Dow Jones News/Retrieval Service, America Online, and several other vendors. This service is updated weekly. There are more than 5,000 reviews written by critic Jay A. Brown. Reviews include a summary of nearly 100 words, a list of principal actors, and an evaluation rating ranging from "great" to "poor." Included are new releases, current movies, a coming attractions column (updated biweekly), historical reviews (1920-present) and top box office films. Information on the top ten box office features and top ten videocassette sales and rentals is drawn from *The Hollywood Reporter*. Brown's reviews appear in print on an annual basis in *Rating the Movies: For Home Video, TV, and Cable* (Publications International).

893. **The New York Times Film Reviews, 1913-1992.** Hamden, CT: Garland, 1993. 18v. **Bienn. Supp.,** 1969/1970- . ISSN 0362-3688.

This monumental work is one of the best sources of available reviews for motion pictures. The original six-volume set was issued by the *New York Times* and covered a period of fifty-five years from 1913 to 1968. Garland is now continuing the coverage through biennial supplements as well as offering a complete eighteen-volume set through 1992. For the early years of silent pictures through all the great periods of Hollywood genre films, the reviews are chronologically arranged by date of appearance in the newspaper and are reproduced. Thousands of films are covered in excellent fashion; the newspaper's critics have had a reputation for thoroughness and perceptivity. Volume 6 is an index volume to the first five volumes, and contains appendices of overlooked reviews, New York Critic's Circle Awards, Academy Awards, and many illustrations. This index is detailed and is divided into separate sections for titles, people, and corporations. The series is kept up-to-date with biennial cumulations beginning with the period 1969-1970, generally published a year or two following the period of coverage (1991-1992 supplement published in 1993). These supplementary volumes are indexed individually.

The New York Times Directory of the Film (Arno, 1971; abridged ed. 1974) is a reprinting of the personal name and corporate index sections from the index volume of the main set. It is useful for its references to the date and page of the newspaper.

*894. Roger Ebert's Movie Home Companion. 1984- . Ann. Kansas City, KS: Andrews & McMeel. ISBN 0-8362-6243-3 (1993 ed).

Ebert is a critic for the Chicago Sun-Times, whose insightful commentary, along with that of his colleague, Gene Siskel, of the Chicago Tribune, are enjoyed on national television by millions of motion picture fans. Ebert's annual guide to videocassettes is therefore based on respected authority and represents an important purchase for film buffs and hobbyists. Since its beginning in 1984, this tool has proved to be a well-developed and useful guide to motion pictures on videocassettes. Presently there are more than 1,000 full reviews that were issued initially in the Sun-Times, along with miscellaneous articles and highlights. Ebert's writing simulates his television commentary and provides perceptive commentary in lively manner. A four-star rating system is employed, and entries enumerate running time, year, cast, and credits, along with the review. An index is furnished.

895. Variety Film Reviews, 1907-1980. New York: Garland, 1983-1985. 16v. **Bienn. Supp.** v.17- . 1981/1982- . R. R. Bowker. ISSN 0897-4373.

Using the idea developed for production of the New York Times Film Reviews (entry 893), this is another multivolume collection of reviews from a single source. In this case, the film reviews are taken from Variety (entry 871) and cover a period of seventy-three years in fifteen volumes. Volume 16 is an index of titles. The reviews are furnished in chronological sequence in order of their appearance in the magazine. Because feature-length films and shorts were not distinguished from each other until 1927, both types are included up to that time. After June 1927, only feature-length films are included. The R. R. Bowker Company continues the work with biennial supplements, beginning with volume 17 covering the 1980-1981 period. Volume 21 (1989-1990) was issued in 1991.

Similar to the New York Times Directory of the Film (entry 893n) is Max Joseph Alvarez's Index to Motion Pictures Reviewed by Variety, 1907-1980 (Scarecrow Press, 1982). It furnishes a separately published title index to the reviews and includes short subjects and re-releases.

896. Variety Television Reviews 1923-1992. Howard H. Prouty, ed. Hamden, CT: Garland, 1993. 17v. **Bienn. Supp.** 1989/1990- . ISBN 0-8153-0363-7.

Developed in the same style and pattern as the Variety Film Reviews (entry 895), this is a large-scale attempt to capture the history of television through more than 40,000 reviews published over a seventy-year period. These date from the experimental years through the emergence of color and cable. Arrangement of entries is chronological; facsimile reviews are furnished as they appeared in Variety (entry 871). All types of programming are included, making the set a treasure house of information on otherwise elusive local programs from all regions of the country, foreign broadcasts, and daytime fare, as well as prime-time and syndicated offerings. Volume 15 is an excellent index that identifies even titles of episodes of documentary broadcasts; cross-references are provided. Like other works of its type, the biennial supplements are separately indexed; the 1991-1992 supplement (volume 17) was published in 1993 as Variety and Daily Variety Television Reviews.

11 ◆ ACCESSING INFORMATION IN LANGUAGE AND LITERATURE

WORKING DEFINITIONS OF LANGUAGE AND LITERATURE

Language and literature are treated together in this guide because they are interdependent and because one of the primary ways of organizing literature is by the language of the literary work under consideration. The common definitions of language and literature suggest that language has to do with spoken and written words and the systems for their use, and that literature is comprised of the writings that capture ideas. Although literature, it can be said, is dependent on language for its very essence, it is probably wise to look at the definitions of the two fields separately, at least at the outset. Because language is a requirement of literature, it will be considered first.

Language, according to one commonly used reference tool, is "systematic communication by vocal symbols"[1]; another dictionary says that language is the "form or style of verbal expression"[2]; while a third suggests that it is "communication by voice in the distinctively human manner."[3] All of these definitions, spanning more than twenty years, seem to suggest that language must be spoken, when in fact some languages (notably sign languages and artificial languages) are not vocal and nonetheless constitute a means of communication within a community. Some might argue that sign language is a substitute for spoken language, but other researchers suggest that it is indeed a language in its own right and not a surrogate at all.

Languages are subdivided into families and stocks, based upon the relationships among and derivations of each. Often, but not always, the distribution of languages is of geographic origin: Sino-Tibetan languages, for example, are most often used in a particular Asian region.

Closely involved with the study of language are the fields of linguistics (the scientific study of language) and anthropology (the study of social and cultural constructs and how humans live within them). Language is sometimes claimed as a subdiscipline of both. To clarify the definitions of *language*, the reader should consult Edward Sapir's *Language: An Introduction to the Study of Speech* (Harcourt, 1921; repr. 1955), a classic cited in later textbooks.

Literature is easier to define. Helen Haines, in the now-classic *Living with Books* offers: "Literature, in familiar library classification and definition, embraces the whole domain of imaginative and creative writing as well as the history, philosophy, and art of literary expression and various distinctive forms in which literary art finds anifestation."[4] Although Haines later differentiates literature from science, we can read into her definition that the "distinctive forms" might include writings in the sciences and social sciences, thus constituting the literature of science, social sciences literature, and indeed, the literature of library and information science. These "literatures of ..." refer to writings in a special discipline or field of study.

Some are inclined to define literature by the genres, or forms, that are usually included: fiction, poetry, drama, essays, and criticism. Asheim included oratory, excluded essays, and suggested that "imaginative writings" in those forms should define the area of literature.[5] The same parameters are observed in this guide.

Sometimes definitions of literature suggest a value judgment—that the literature has lasting value or is of permanent interest. The issue of value in literature is an important one. Although the issue is of interest in all fields of the humanities, the fact that criticism of one work may itself ultimately become a part of the body of literature is nowhere more evident than in the area of literary scholarship. The critical literature, then, is subject to subsequent criticism as well.

MAJOR DIVISIONS OF THE FIELD

Both of the two basic approaches to the division of literature, by language and by form, are usually taken into account in the customary divisions of the field. Volume 2 of the *Reader's Adviser*, 14th ed., (R. R. Bowker, 1994), divides literature by language group and form, covering drama and then other literature.

Division of literature on the basis of the language in which it is written may require some refinements and modifications. For example, the volume of literature written in English is so large that further subdivision is desirable. In this case the term *English literature* is restricted to the literary output of the United Kingdom that appears in English, or even to the literature of England alone. Separate provision is customarily made for American literature, Australian literature, and so on. At the other extreme, some of the world's smallest literatures may be grouped together under a parent language.

As suggested earlier in the section on definitions, the basic forms of literature are poetry and prose. Prose is normally divided into novels, short stories, and essays. Poetry is normally treated as a unit, but it can be subdivided by type (lyric poems, epic poems, and so forth). The drama, as a literary record of what is to be performed on the stage, has an independent life of its own and may also be considered a major literary form. Modern drama is ordinarily in prose, but it may also be in verse, or it may consist of both prose and verse.

Another approach to the organization of literature is by historical periods or literary movements. These are often combined with the forms outlined previously. J. B. Priestly's classic on the subject of literature divides the field by form (poetry, drama, and fiction) and by chronological period; see *Literature and Western Man* (Harper & Brothers, 1960).

In addition to the extensive coverage of literature and that on individual language literatures in general encyclopedias (*Encyclopedia Americana* and *Encyclopaedia Britannica* both have excellent articles), Haines's *Living with Books* should be consulted for the classic librarian's view of the fields of literature, drama, poetry, and fiction. A more recent article, also directed to the librarian, is James K. Bracken's "Literature," in *The Humanities and the Library*, edited by Nena Couch and Nancy Allen (American Library Association, 1993, pp. 86-131). The sources in the historical section of chapter 12 of this guide also provide plenty of background reading on literature.

USE AND USERS OF INFORMATION IN LANGUAGE AND LITERATURE

Of all the disciplines covered in this guide, literature is the one in which scholars have been subjected to the greatest scrutiny in terms of their information needs and information-seeking behaviors. Surveys, observational studies, and unobtrusive citation analyses provide an interesting and varied picture of the literature scholar's work habits and literature use.

Because of the number of studies in this area, only those reported after 1980 are listed here; for earlier work, see the third edition of this guide.

R. Heinzkill looked at English literary works in "Characteristics of References in Selected Scholarly English Literary Journals," *Library Quarterly* 50 (July 1980): 352-65. M. Stern's "Characteristics of the Literature of Literary Scholarship," *College and Research Libraries* 44 (July 1983): 199-209, is another frequently cited article. In 1985-1986, three significant studies were published: John Cullars's "Characteristics of the Monographic Literature of British and American Literary Studies," *College and Research Libraries* 46 (November 1985): 511-22; John Budd's "Characteristics of Written Scholarship in American Literature: A Citation Study," *Library and Information Science Research* 8 (April 1986): 189-211; and Budd's "A Citation Study of American Literature: Implications for Collection Management," in *Collection Management* 8 (Summer 1986): 49-62.

John Cullars, in his investigations of the characteristics of other special literatures, has authored the following articles: "Citation Characteristics of French and German Literary Monographs," *Library Quarterly* 59 (October 1989): 305-25; "Characteristics of the Monographic Scholarship of Foreign Literary Studies by Native Speakers of English," *College and Research Libraries* 49 (March 1988): 157-70; and more recently "Citation Characteristics of Italian and Spanish Literary Monographs," *Library Quarterly* 60 (October 1990): 337-56.

Richard Hopkins's doctoral dissertation, entitled "The Information Seeking Behaviour of Literary Scholars in Canadian Universities" (University of Toronto, 1988), confirmed and refined findings of some earlier works, and suggests that constraints of time and cost affect information seeking among scholars. The findings are summarized in Hopkins's "The Information Seeking Behaviour of Literary Scholars," *Canadian Library Journal* (April 1989): 113-15.

Broader studies of humanists' information seeking and use have included faculty members and literary scholars. Two recent reports are: Stephen E. Wiberley, Jr., and William G. Jones, "Patterns of Information Seeking in the Humanities," *College and Research Libraries* 50 (November 1989): 638-45; and "The Humanistic Scholars Project: A Study of Attitudes and Behavior Concerning Collection Storage and Technology," *College and Research Libraries* 51 (May 1990): 231-40.

The next few years are likely to yield more studies on the use of electronic materials, scholars' attitudes toward electronic sources and texts, and studies of new work methods made possible by networks, document delivery services, and other information technologies.

COMPUTERS IN LANGUAGE AND LITERATURE

The area of computing in language and literature has grown tremendously in the past decade. In the fields of language and literature, computational linguistics, language teaching, writing and editing, text analysis, and automated translation are just some of the areas for which we have an extensive literature. The teaching of English can be further subdivided into teaching English and English as a second language (ESL). The *Humanities Computing Yearbook*, by Ian Lancashire and Willard McCarty (Oxford, 1988), lists articles, from introductory to expert levels, on the whole range of topics. Included are lists of articles and software for working with both ancient and modern languages. B. H. Rudall and T. N. Corns, in *Computers and Literature: A Practical Guide* (Abacus Press, 1987), discuss word processing, concording, and analytical uses of computers in the field. Papers on concording, indexing, thesaurus construction, content analysis, and teaching of languages were presented at the Cologne Computer Conference and abstracted in the *Volume of Abstracts* (1988). Text checking is the topic of Elaine and John Thiesmeyers's paper in *Databases in the Humanities 4*, edited by Lawrence J. McCrank (Learned Information, 1989), pp. 629-36. Kevin Roddy's "Meaningful Thesaurus Generation: An Experiment with Sixth-Century Texts" appears in the same volume (pp. 561-69). The use of computers in all fields, especially the literary disciplines, is so extensive that only a few guiding works can be mentioned here. The reader should consult the many bibliographies and reviews for a more complete picture.

Finally, an extensive list of sources and an excellent review of literary text analysis is found in Helen R. Tibbo's "Information Systems, Services, and Technology for the Humanities," *Annual Review of Information Science and Technology (ARIST)* 26 (1991): 287-346.

Electronic texts are the subject of many recent articles. One that will introduce the topic to librarians is Anita Lowry's "Electronic Texts in English and American Literature," *Library Trends* (Spring 1992): 704-23. Here the reader can find information about Shakespeare and other English-language text files and also about basic considerations such as descriptive markup language and encoding. Avra Michelson and Jeff Rothenberg discuss all aspects of electronic text in "Scholarly Communication and Information Technology: Exploring the Impact of Changes in the Research Process on Archives," *American Archivist* 55 (Spring 1992): 236-315. The article has especially clear descriptions of conversion of sources to machine-readable form, and of projects such as the *Thesaurus Linguae Graecae (TLG)* and *American and French Research on the Treasury of the French Language (ARTFL)*, both of which are introduced earlier in the guide. Other sources of information on the availability of electronic text include *The Georgetown University Catalogue of Projects in Electronic Text*, *The Humanities Computing Yearbook* (latest edition), Oxford University Press, and Chadwyck-Healey.

Database searching is also important in the fields of literature and languages. MLA Bibliography (file 71 on DIALOG, also available on CD-ROM) covers 1963 to the present, and provides access to books and journals on language, literature, and linguistics. LLBA (Linguistics and Language Behavior Abstracts), produced by Sociological Abstracts, Inc., covers the period 1973 to the present. Included are articles from more than 1,000 journals. It is file 36 on DIALOG. Other popular databases that literary scholars use include *Arts and Humanities Search* (produced by the Institute for Scientific Information), and *Dissertation Abstracts Online*. Rosa Oppenheim's "Computerized Bibliographic Searches in Literary Studies," *Literary Research Newsletter* 10 (Winter/Spring 1985): 17-34, offers additional insight. More than a dozen CD-ROMs in the area of literature are listed in "Arts and Humanities on CD-ROM," by Lucy Buck and Paul Travis Nicholls, in *CD-ROM Professional* (March 1991): 99.

The Internet resources related to literature and linguists are vast and include listservs and electronic journals on many literary genres, writers, and special topics, some of which were addressed earlier. Electronic text projects, such as Michael Hart's Project Gutenberg and the Online Book Initiative, have made the full text of many great literary works available. Dartmouth's Dante Project provides the full text of *The Divine Comedy*, along with six centuries of commentary on the work, in searchable form. An excellent discussion of Project Gutenberg, including instructions for obtaining information from the Internet, can be found in Paul Gilster's *The Internet Navigator* (John Wiley & Sons, 1993).

Listservs in the areas of language and literature are listed in Harrison and Stephen's article in *Computers and the Humanities* 26 (1992): 185, referenced earlier in this guide. Two examples are Shakespeare (shakesper@utoronto) and a *Finnegan's Wake* discussion (fwake-l@irlearn).

Almost every guide to the Internet will list numerous sources for literature information and text. An example of such a guide is Ed Krol's *The Whole Internet: User's Guide and Catalog* (O'Reilly & Associates, 1992), but the reader will do well to continue to check the most up-to-date guides in print, as new offerings appear daily.

MAJOR ORGANIZATIONS, INFORMATION CENTERS, AND SPECIAL COLLECTIONS

The oldest, largest, and best known of the organizations that promote the study and teaching of languages in this country is the Modern Language Association of America (10 Astor Place, New York, NY 10003). Founded in 1883, it has more than 30,000 members, primarily university or college teachers, and it conducts an immense range of programs and activities. Publications include *MLA Newsletter* (quarterly); *PMLA* (quarterly); *Job Information List—English* and *Job Information List—Foreign Language*. The *MLA International Bibliography*, covered in detail in chapter 12, is among the world's most important bibliographic resources.

The American Council on the Teaching of Foreign Languages (6 Executive Plaza, Yonkers, NY 10701) was founded by MLA in 1967, but now exists as a separate entity. Its publications include *Foreign Language Annals* (6/year) and *Series on Foreign Language Education* (annual).

The International Federation of Modern Language Teachers (Seesr. 247, CH-8038 Zurich, Switzerland) is made up of multi- and unilingual associations. It corresponds at the international level to the National Federation of Modern Language Teachers Associations (659 57th Avenue, Omaha, NE 68132), a federation of national, regional, and state associations in the United States that publishes *The Modern Language Journal*, a quarterly.

The American Association of Language Specialists (Suite 9, 1000 Connecticut Avenue, NW, Washington, DC 20036) is a group of interpreters, editors, and translators. The 200-plus members meet annually and publish a yearbook.

U.S. English (818 Connecticut Avenue, NW, Washington, DC 20006) is an organization active in promoting English as the official governmental language of this country. The group issues a newletter bimonthly to keep members up-to-date on legislation.

There are a wide variety of organizations concerned with specific languages. Example include Esperanto Language Society of Chicago, League for Yiddish, Inc., and the International Association for the Study of the Italian Language and Literature.

The International Comparative Literature Association (Comparative Literature Program, Ballentine Hall #402, Indiana University, Bloomington, IN 47405) promotes worldwide study of the field. The American Comparative Literature Association (University of Michigan, Ann Arbor, MI 48209) promotes the study and teaching of comparative literature in American universities, publishes a newsletter, co-sponsors *Yearbook of Comparative and General Literature*, and assists in the publication of two quarterly journals: *Comparative Literature* and *Comparative Literature Studies*.

The Coordinating Council of Literary Magazines (666 Broadway, 11th Floor, New York, NY 10012) assists "little magazines" in a variety of ways.

Regional interests are served by such groups as the Society for the Study of Southern Literature and the Western Literature Association.

Various library, literary, and children's literary associations serve a host of special clienteles with interests in all aspects of books, literature, and publishing. General association directories will lead the reader to the many organizations that are too specialized to be listed here.

Special collections in language and literature are numerous (they include those in information centers, libraries, associations, and scholarly societies) and there are far too many of them to list here. A good source to use to supplement this section is *Subject Collections*, compiled by Lee Ash and William G. Miller (7th ed., R. R. Bowker, 1993).

Some special collections are especially noteworthy. They include the Folger Shakespeare Library (Washington, DC), which has an active research and publication program in British civilization of the Tudor and Stuart periods and theatrical history as they relate to Shakespeare. The Center for Hellenic Studies in Washington, DC, is an international center associated with Harvard University. It conducts research in such areas as classical Greek literature, philosophy, and history. The Center for Textual Studies at Ohio State University conducts research on definitive texts of nineteenth- and twentieth-century authors, including the publication of definitive editions of Hawthorne and Emerson. Other giant collections are held by the Library of Congress, the British Library, the Bibliotheque Nationale, the New York Public Library, and Harvard University. Besides the guide to subject collections by Ash, publications of the American Library Association, Special Libraries Association, and the Center for Research Libraries will guide the reader to other collections of note.

NOTES

[1] *The Concise Columbia Encyclopedia* (Avon, 1983), pp. 465-66.

[2] *The Merriam-Webster Dictionary* (Pocket Books, 1974), p. 397.

[3] *The American College Dictionary* (Random House, 1961), p. 685.

[4] Helen E. Haines, *Living with Books*, 2d ed. (Columbia University Press, 1950), p. 418.

[5] Lester Asheim, *The Humanities and the Library* (American Library Association, 1956).

12 ♦ PRINCIPAL INFORMATION SOURCES IN LANGUAGE AND LITERATURE

LANGUAGE AND LINGUISTICS

Bibliographies and Guides

897. **Bibliography and Index of Mainland Southeast Asian Languages and Linguistics.** Franklin E. Huffman. New Haven, CT: Yale University Press, 1986. 640p. ISBN 0-300-03679-5.

A comprehensive listing which has proved useful to the field, this bibliography divides languages into five major categories: Austroasiatic, TibetoBurman, Tai-Kadgi, Miao-Yao, and Mainland Austronesian. About 10,000 titles on Southeast Asian languages, published up to 1985, are identified; they represent all forms of published materials as well as informal papers, including conference presentations. Arrangement of entries is alphabetical by author, with cross-references furnished from multiple authors and variant names. Materials written in various languages of the world are identified and English translations are provided for entries in other than the common European language systems. An informative introduction describes the language classifications employed, and a detailed index provides ready access.

898. **Bibliography of Semiotics, 1975-1985.** Achim Eschbach et al., comps. Philadelphia: John Benjamins, 1986. 2 pts. (Library & Information Sources in Linguistics, v.16; Amsterdam Studies in the Theory and History of Linguistics Science, Series V). ISBN 90-272-3739-5.

This is the most recent contribution to this important series, under the direction of E. F. Koerner, which has included bibliographies on various aspects of linguistics. "Semiotics" embraces the study of signs and signaling systems and is interpreted by some to include such areas as pragmatics, semantics, and syntactics. Nearly 11,000 entries are furnished for the ten-year period covered. Books, monographs, dissertations, articles, conference proceedings, festschriften, and reviews are all included. The coverage is international and several countries and languages are represented. Part 1 consists of an alphabetical list of nearly 700 periodicals that publish in this field, followed by the first half of the bibliographical entries; part 2 provides the second half of the bibliographical listings and indexes of reviews, subjects, and names.

Another useful product is *Semantics: A Bibliography, 1986-1991*, by W. Terrence Gordon (Scarecrow Press, 1992). This is the third issue of a continuing series, for which the first one covered 1965-1978 (Scarecrow Press, 1980) and the previous volume treated the years 1979-1985 (Scarecrow Press, 1987). The new work opens with an overview of the divisions and fields of semantics and a glossary of terms. The main text consists of an annotated bibliography of books, articles, and papers organized under topics such as ambiguity, synonymy, idioms, and so on. There is an author index and an index of words treated.

899. **Dictionaries, Encyclopedias and Other Word-Related Books.** 4th ed. Annie M. Brewer, ed. Detroit: Gale Research, 1988. 2v. ISBN 0-8103-0440-6.

This is a large-scale enumerative work treating some 35,000 dictionaries, encyclopedias, thesauri, and other word books. The utility of this work lies in its arrangement of entries under Library of Congress subject classification, permitting the librarian to identify sources of word information relevant to different topics. All types of dictionaries are included—monolingual, bilingual, and polyglot—dealing with all types of specialties and specializations. There is no indication of selection criteria, and various editions appear while other are omitted. There is a detailed subject-title index to aid access.

A recent specialized effort is David E. Vancil's compilation, *Catalog of Dictionaries, Word Books, and Philological Texts, 1440-1900* (Indiana State University, 1993). This is a useful tool for scholars and students in providing a catalog of the holdings of the Cordell Collection at the University. The Cordell Collection of Dictionaries is the largest in the world: it contains more than 5,100 dictionaries issued before 1901 along with thousands of more recent origin. Foreign- and English-language entries are interfiled in this catalog of the early works. Emphasis on the early titles is especially useful to historical research. Access is aided through indexes by date, language, and subject.

900. **Kister's Best Dictionaries for Adults & Young People: A Comparative Guide.** Phoenix, AZ: Oryx Press, 1992. 438p. ISBN 0-89774-191-9.

This excellent guide opens with an informative sixty-one-page introductory essay describing the different uses, history, compilation, and various types of dictionaries as well as the debates between prescriptive and descriptive orientation and inclusion of "four-letter" words. It serves as an update of Kister's earlier work on dictionaries issued in the late 1970s, but in this case omits related tools like thesauri and secretarial handbooks. The present effort is divided into two major sections treating 132 adult dictionaries (unabridged, college desk, family and office, etc.) and 168 young people's dictionaries (high school, junior high, upper elementary, etc.). Entries provide description and evaluation and range from one to ten pages in length. Five appendices provide useful listings of associations and publications; there is an author-title-subject index.

From the British perspective is Brendan Loughridge's *Which Dictionary? A Consumer's Guide to Selected English-Language Dictionaries, Thesauri, and Language Guides* (American Library Association, 1990). Preceded by an introductory description of the seven criteria or checkpoints used in evaluating dictionaries, coverage is given almost exclusively to British publications. Some 300 titles are treated, most of which are of the small and specialized nature. An appendix supplies a list of fifty recommended titles. A title index is furnished.

901. **Linguistics: A Guide to the Reference Literature.** Anna L. DeMiller. Englewood, CO: Libraries Unlimited, 1991. 256p. (Reference Sources in the Humanities Series). ISBN 0-87287-692-6.

Designed to serve the needs of a wide range of users, from undergraduates to specialists and researchers, this useful tool describes more than 700 reference sources published between 1957 and 1989. The work is divided into three major sections, the first of which treats general linguistics and includes morphology, syntax, semantics, and other aspects of theoretical linguistics. Part 2 covers allied arms of sociolinguistics, psycholinguistics, etc., and part 3 deals with languages, treating language groups and their components, such as Indo-European languages subdivided by Germanic and English categories. In all, thirty-one chapters constitute the three parts and treat the major types of reference tools: bibliographies, encyclopedias, indexes, abstracts, and biographies, as well as online and CD-ROM databases, periodicals, and associations. Annotations are detailed and informative. Three good indexes provide access by author, title, and subject.

Indexes, Abstracts, and Serial Bibliographies

902. **Bibliographie linguistique des années.** Comite International Permanent de Linguististes. Utrecht, Netherlands: Spectrum, 1939/1947- . Ann.

With its initial publication covering an eight-year period in two volumes, this service achieved worldwide recognition as a massive work of documentation. It provides coverage of linguistics on an international level and identifies books, reviews, and articles from such diverse countries as South Africa, Belgium (Flemish publications), Czechoslovakia, Finland, France, Italy, the Netherlands, Norway, Poland, Spain, and Switzerland in volume 1. Coverage in volume 2 furnishes listings from Austria, Belgium (French publications), Denmark, England, Greece, India, Ireland, Portugal, the Soviet Union, Sweden, Turkey, and the United States. There is an author index to both volumes. The title continues as an annual publication and is highly regarded for its comprehensive coverage of periodical articles. There is no subject index, but the detailed table of contents facilitates access.

903. **Francis bulletin signalétique 524: Sciences du langage.** Nancy, France: Institut de l'information scientifique et technique, 1947- . Q. ISSN 1157-3740.
    Part of the massive international documentation service undertaken initially by the Centre National de la Recherche Scientifique in Paris, its work has been supervised by the Institute since 1991. It is issued on a quarterly basis and provides listings of periodical articles in the field. It began as an abstract journal, with linguistics covered in *Bulletin signalétique: Philosophie, sciences humaines* from 1947 to 1960; from 1961 to 1966, linguistics was treated in *Bulletin signalétique, Sec. 21: Sociologie, sciences du langage*, and from 1967 to 1968 in *Bulletin signalétique 24: Sciences du langage*. It became the *Bulletin signalétique 524: Sciences du langage* after 1968, at which time it ceased providing abstracts and became a bibliography only. At present, it covers the biology and pathology of language, psycholinguistics, sociolinguistics, ethnolinguistics, historical linguistics, descriptive studies, semiotics, and communications. There is a classified arrangement with author and subject indexes. It is available online from the Institute as *FRANCIS: SCIENCES DU LANGAGE*, providing coverage from 1972 to date. It contains nearly 70,000 citations, adding about 800 records per quarter.

*904. **Linguistics and Language Behavior Abstracts: LLBA.** La Jolla, CA: Sociological Abstracts, 1967- . Q. ISSN 0023-8925.
    Formerly *LLBA: Language and Language Behavior Abstracts*, edited at the University of Michigan Center for Research, this abstract journal changed its title in 1985. It continues to cover an array of disciplines related to language and linguistics and treats a variety of journals, books, and monographs from communications and education as well as linguistics. Included are titles in acoustics, anthropology, comparative literature, ethnology, information science, medicine, psychiatry, psychology, and philosophy. Abstracts are grouped in broad divisions, such as linguistics and philosophy, and are subdivided by more specific topics. The more than 1,000 journals surveyed for articles of potential relevance represent a number of languages and countries. There is an author index. It is available online through BRS and DIALOG, with a file size of some 130,000 records. The file coverage is from 1973 to date and increases by about 6,000 records per year.

905. **Modern Language Review.** Belfast: Modern Humanities Research Association, 1905- . Q. ISSN 0026-7937.
    This is one of the most respected review journals in the humanities and provides reviews of studies of medieval and modern languages and literatures. Known for its lengthy, detailed, and thoughtful book reviews, it is a top priority in those libraries emphasizing or supporting communication and language studies. As in many review journals in the humanities, there is a certain amount of delay following publication of the items prior to their review in the journal. It is being made available in microform by the Association.
    Modern Language Quarterly is an American contribution published through the University of Washington since 1940. Several studies of literary works and literary forms appear in each issue and represent Western European and American scholarship. The publication features comparative reviews on topics and issues in the field. It has issued the *Annual Bibliography of English Language and Literature* since its inception.

906. **Year's Work in Modern Language Studies.** London: Modern Humanities Research Association, 1929/1930- . Ann. ISSN 0084-4152.

The war years witnessed an extended suspension of publications for this useful reviewing source; therefore, volume 11 covers the period 1940 to 1949, in which year it resumed its annual frequency. Language and literature are treated in a variety of settings and time periods, such as medieval Latin, Romance languages, Germanic languages, and Slavonic languages. The focus is on developments from the medieval period to the present day. During the past two decades, general linguistics has been treated and today is regarded as an important component.

Studies in Philology, from the University of North Carolina, is a quarterly journal that began in 1906. It furnishes textual and historical research in classical and modern languages and literature. It is of use primarily to the scholar and specialist, and is available on microfilm through Maxwell House, Microforms International.

Linguistics Dictionaries, Encyclopedias, and Handbooks

907. **The Cambridge Encyclopedia of Language.** David Crystal. Cambridge, UK: Cambridge University Press, 1987. 472p. ISBN 0-521-26438-3.

Developed by a British professor of linguistics, this encyclopedia utilizes a thematic arrangement in achieving its intent to promote an informed awareness and understanding of the importance and complexity of human language. Aided by an excellent team of editorial advisers, Crystal has produced a scholarly but readable tool, well illustrated with maps, diagrams, and photographs. There are eleven major sections or parts treating such topics as popular ideas about language; language and identity; structure of language; medium of language; child language acquisition; language, brain, and handicap; languages of the world; etc. These parts are divided into sixty-five subsections treating the different components of the category. There are numerous cross-references to related sections, along with extensive bibliographic references. Several appendices furnish a glossary and table of world's languages, along with indexing by language, authors and personalities cited, and topic.

908. **Compendium of the World's Languages.** George L. Campbell. New York: Routledge, 1991. 2v. ISBN 0-415-02937-6.

This is a scholarly tool treating more than 300 languages in comparative manner. Both individual languages and families are described in terms of their historical development and structure, providing the reader with treatment of the script, phonology, morphology, syntax, and word order. Entries identify the number and location of language speakers as well as language composition. There is general diversity in the languages selected, including Chinese, spoken by over a billion people, to various African dialects spoken by several thousand at the most. In some cases languages are grouped, with a heading for North American Indian languages along with headings for certain individual tribes. Sources used by the author are listed as a general bibliography at the end of volume 2, along with a chart providing exposition of some forty scripts. There is no general index.

909. **A Dictionary of Linguistics and Phonetics.** 3d ed. David Crystal. Oxford, UK: Basil Blackwell, 1991. 389p. ISBN 0-631-17869-4.

The author, a prominent British linguist and editor of the quarterly journal, *Linguistics Abstracts* (Basil Blackwell, 1985-), has provided an updated and expanded edition of his previous two works issued in 1980 and 1985. These earlier efforts had achieved a prominent position among dictionaries designed for both students and researchers in the field. The new work has added some 300 new words, bringing the total to nearly 2,500 terms used as main entry items. The new words came to prominence during the 1980s and represent recent directions with respect to linguistic theory as perceived through new models. Government-binding theory receives full treatment. Many of the definitions have been reworked or expanded. Entries may include descriptions, examples, diagrams, and references to additional reading. The new edition continues the tradition of high quality established by the earlier efforts.

910. **An Encyclopaedia of Language**. N. E. Collinge, ed. New York: Routledge, 1990. 1011p. ISBN 0-415-02064-6.

This is a comprehensive collection of essays by various scholar-contributors representing their specialties within the study of language. There is a total of twenty-six essays by twenty-eight contributors arranged under three general topics or categories, accompanied by numerous diagrams and illustrations. The first category, "The Inner Nature of Language," contains nine essays treating such topics as phonetics, phonology, grammar, semantics, pragmatics, etc. The second category, "The Larger Province of Language," also has nine essays. Coverage includes psycholinguistics, neurolinguistics, language therapy, anthropological linguistics, sociolinguistics, etc. The final segment, "Special Aspects of Language," supplies eight essays treating such topics as lexicography, history of linguistics, language engineering, and Collinge's contribution on the evolution of language. Each essay furnishes a list of references along with suggestions for further reading. There is an index of topics and an index of names to aid access.

911. **The Encyclopedia of Language and Linguistics**. R. E. Asher and J. M. Y. Simpson, eds. New York: Pergamon Press, 1993. 10v. ISBN 0-08-0359434.

With the rapid development of language studies and linguistics during this century, a profusion of theories, practices, and professional jargon have evolved. The development of a comprehensive work of this kind was seen as necessary in treating the diverse elements and personalities contained in over 3,000 years of history and hundreds of different languages from all over the world. This large-scale effort provides international scope and perspective with an honorary editorial advisory board of fourteen members representing the United Kingdom, United States, Japan, France, Australia, Russia, India, and China. The executive editorial board of thirty-five members shows more British orientation along with members from the United States, New Zealand, Italy, the Netherlands, and Australia. More than 1,000 contributors from fifty countries (primarily the United Kingdom and the United States, but also Asia and Africa) have produced detailed and informative articles on 2,000 subjects. There is a glossary of more than 3,000 definitions, along with indexes by subject, contributor, and name. The tool should become the standard for the field.

912. **Encyclopedic Dictionary of Semiotics**. 2d rev. and upd. ed. Thomas A. Sebeok, ed. New York: de Gruyter, 1994. 3v. ISBN 0-31104-229-5.

Sebeok, a professor of linguistics at Indiana University, has performed an excellent service in coordinating the efforts of numerous individuals who served on the editorial board and the panel of contributors in producing this significant work. The first edition was issued in 1986 and utilized the talents of more than 200 specialists from all over the world who contributed signed articles. This updated effort employs a similar pattern in supplying more than 400 articles that provide well-executed coverage. Exposition includes historical background and present usage of terms, with some recommendations to standardize current conventions; biographies of prominent personalities in semiotics; and appraisal of the impact of semiotics on inquiry in other fields. Articles vary in length from those of a monographic nature (more than twenty pages on semantics) to explanations of one paragraph. The title remains a solid work and represents an important aid to specialists and advanced students.

913. **International Encyclopedia of Linguistics**. William Bright, ed. New York: Oxford University Press, 1992. 4v. ISBN 0-19-505196-3.

This comprehensive and detailed work is intended primarily for the scholar and advanced student in its coverage of all known and extinct languages and language families. There are 750 articles signed by specialist-contributors from twenty-five countries. Articles covering the languages generally supply historical perspective along with treatment of script, pronunciation, grammar, syntax, and relationship to neighboring languages. Articles on language families enumerate specific examples and identify the number of speakers. In addition, technical terms are defined and biographical sketches of important personalities are given. There are numerous cross-references, along with a detailed index of more than 100 pages. A glossary is furnished, as are synoptic outlines of entries to place them in perspective.

The Linguistics Encyclopedia, edited by Kirsten Malmkjaer (Routledge, 1991) is designed for a wider audience, ranging from educated laypersons to scholars. All relevant topics of linguistics are treated in enough detail and with enough clarity to achieve good results. Articles are supplied by a group of scholars from all over the world. There are numerous cross-references and illustrations; both a bibliography and an index are furnished.

914. **Longman Dictionary of Applied Linguistics.** Jack Richards et al. New York: Longman, 1985. 323p. ISBN 0-582-55708-9.

The authors have established a reputation as experts in the field of applied linguistics with their work in the area of language teaching and other aspects. This is what appears to be the first dictionary to specialize in applied linguistics; it furnishes more than 1,500 entries of terms used in the practice. Definitions are lucid and contain related terms within the body of a single entry. British and American pronunciations are given in most cases, and there are many cross-references between entries. Focused primarily on the applied linguistics of language teaching, rather than language planning, lexicology, or translation, the work provides a good overview of the field and includes many of the terms from theoretical linguistics as well. Useful for both the college student and the language teacher.

915. **A Manual of European Languages for Librarians.** C. G. Allen. New York: R. R. Bowker, 1975; repr. with minor corr. 1981. 803p. ISBN 0-85935-028-2.

Especially useful for librarians and scholars is this handbook designed to facilitate the use and understanding of books published in some thirty-eight European languages compiled by the former Superintendent of Reader Services at the British Library of Political and Economic Science. Arrangement is in seven language groups: Germanic, Latin/Romance, Celtic/Greek/Albanian, Slavonic, Baltic, Finno-Ugrian, and Other (Maltese, Turkish, Basque, Esperanto). Coverage of each language group follows a stylized pattern, beginning with general characteristics such as history and word order, followed by "bibliolinguistics" examining the bibliographic elements of books and periodicals. Treatment is given to idiosyncrasies of authors' names, editions, titles, volumes, etc. Grammar and parts of speech then follow, concluding with a glossary of bibliographic terms and grammatical index. The work is accurate and thorough in its coverage of the distinctive problems associated with the various languages.

916. **The Oxford Companion to the English Language.** Tom McArthur and Feri McArthur, eds. New York: Oxford University Press, 1992. 1184p. ISBN 0-19-214183-X.

Another in the line of handy one-volume compendia from the publisher, this particular Companion supplies more than 3,500 signed entries by 100 scholars treating all aspects of the English language. Diverse treatment includes historical considerations, dialects, grammar, style, rhetoric, pronunciation, usage, education, literature, culture, linguistics, politics, technology, etc. Articles tend to be well constructed and concise, but thorough in their coverage and accurate in their treatment. Biographical sketches of important personalities, such as Shakespeare, Noah Webster, James Joyce, and Mary Wollstonecraft, are furnished. Scope ranges from the language of ancient times to contemporary considerations such as sexist language, jargon, political correctness, and Black English. Place names from all over the world are included, affirming the global representation of the language within the work. Arrangement of entries, as in other Oxford Companions, is alphabetical for easy access.

917. **The World's Major Languages.** Bernard Comrie, ed. New York: Oxford University Press, 1987; repr. with corr. 1990. 1005p. ISBN 0-19-506511-5.

This is an important and reliable handbook providing extensive information on particular languages and families of languages. The editor, a respected contributor and noted specialist in the area of Slavic languages, has written the introduction as well as two of the fifty chapters, each of which is devoted to a particular language or family. It is apparent that each chapter received careful and thorough treatment by one of the forty scholars responsible for this text's development. Historical, sociological, and linguistic elements are covered, and detailed treatment is given to such aspects as graphic systems, morphology, word formation, and syntactic patterns. For inflected languages, charts indicate declension and conjugation classes. Most chapters have bibliographical notes and references. A general index provides access. The 1990 issue, in addition to correcting minor errors, updates the bibliography.

English-Language Dictionaries

UNABRIDGED AND SCHOLARLY

918. **The American Heritage Dictionary of the English Language.** 3d ed. Boston: Houghton Mifflin, 1992. 2140p. ISBN 0-395-44895-6.

Somewhat between the size of a desk dictionary and an unabridged edition is this important resource, now in its third edition . This useful tool was developed through the efforts of 175 contributors over a period of four years. It furnishes more than 350,000 definitions for 200,000 main entry words. Also included are 4,000 illustrations. An important feature of this work is the usage panel of about 170 specialists who make decisions on questions of current usage. Notes and commentary are provided in many cases. Word histories are furnished for some 400 selected words deemed to be especially interesting. Coverage is comprehensive, from the language of Shakespeare to that of present-day idiomatic expression. The dictionary had quite an impact in the past in its attempt to provide guidance to proper usage not only with labeling of words, but also with usage notes regarding controversial terms. Etymologies are not so extensive. There are separate biographical and geographical segments, although certain proper nouns appear in the main text. It attempts to retain propriety, but is not reluctant to portray the language as it is. The earlier edition became available on computer disc in 1990.

919. **Funk & Wagnalls New Standard Dictionary of the English Language: Complete in One Volume.** Isaac K. Funk et al. New York: Funk & Wagnalls, 1965. 2816p.

The 1964 edition is the latest in a long line of reprints, remediations, and added-on supplementary issues. In character and personality, it is still a 1913 work, which at the time represented a complete revision of the first edition published in 1893. The style is, of course, that of a prescriptive dictionary, in the manner of the traditional attempt to prescribe the nature of the language in terms of propriety or correctness. Usage labels are employed to show the status of a given term, and examples of usage are taken from the "great" writers of the past, even drawing from classical literature. Known for its excellent coverage in geography and biography, names and places are included alphabetically within the main text rather than placed into separate glossaries.

920. **Middle-English Dictionary.** Hans Kurath et al., eds. Ann Arbor, MI: University of Michigan Press, 1952- . v.1- .

This monumental and definitive effort began in the 1930s at Oxford University, which joined with the University of Michigan to begin production in earnest in 1952. Since that time, progress has been slow but steady, and volumes have been issued in parts of fascimiles. Volume 14 emerged in 1993, bringing coverage to "T" in the alphabetical sequence. Volume 15 is expected to complete the set in 1995. Editorship has changed hands from Kurath to

Sherman M. Kuhn (volumes G-P) and now resides with Robert E. Lewis (volumes Q-T). An interesting description of this lexicographic trip, which involved millions of data slips and six decades of work, appeared in the *Washington Post* (May 27, 1992). More than 100 lexicographers and scholars have been involved in this systematic recording of the language from the Norman Conquest through the fifteenth century (1100-1500 A.D.). Entries supply definitions, variants, grammatical forms, citations, and quotations from numerous sources.

*921. **The Oxford English Dictionary.** 2d ed. J. A. Simpson and E. S. C. Weiner. New York: Oxford University Press, 1989; repr. with corr. 1991. 20v. ISBN 0-19-861186-2.

The original descriptive dictionary, which portrayed the language as it was rather than prescribing what it should be, *OED* is unexcelled as a scholarly and comprehensive historical dictionary. The second edition has been issued fifty-six years after the first effort, which itself was published forty-nine years after the work had begun. The enormous task of updating the earlier version and producing the second edition was conducted through the creation of machine-readable text, allowing for computer access. It has been available on CD-ROM as *OED2 on CD-ROM* from the publisher since 1991. The title now furnishes convenient access to some 2,412,000 quotations which continue to illustrate changes in meaning over time for some 500,000 words (290,000 main entries, or about a 15 percent increase) from their beginnings in the recorded literature. There are 5,000 new words in addition to the contents of the five supplements to the first edition along with revisions and additions to entries. For the first edition, James A. H. Murray had served as initial editor from the beginning until his death in 1915, when William A. Craigie assumed his responsibilities.

A ten-volume set was issued in 1928, entitled the *New English Dictionary on Historical Principles (NED)* (Clarendon Press), followed by a supplementary volume in 1933. Then the set was reissued in thirteen volumes as the *Oxford*, with some corrections of typographical errors. It remains an indispensable tool, the best of its kind in the English language. The second edition has deleted proper names, Anglo-Saxon terms that were not used beyond 1150 A.D., certain dialect words emerging since 1500 A.D., and some slang terms. The second compact edition of *OED* is now available as *The Compact Oxford English Dictionary: Complete Text Reproduced Micrographically.* Published in 1991, the work has been issued in greatly reduced form through a reduction process of 9 pages to 1. The twenty volumes now appear as one 2,416-page effort issued in slipcase with a microprint reader (batteries not included). An excellent seventy-seven-page guide by Donna L. Berg, *A User's Guide to the Oxford English Dictionary* (1991), accompanies the work.

To help users find their way through this magnificent source, Donna Lee Berg has authored *A Guide to the Oxford English Dictionary* (Oxford, 1993) providing systematic instructions. With examples taken from the *Dictionary*, Berg explains the various nuances and elements to more fully utilize its potential.

922. **The Random House Dictionary of the English Language.** 2d ed. Stuart B. Flexner, ed.-in-chief. New York: Random House, 1987. 2478p. ISBN 0-394-50050-4.

Originally published in 1966, this is the most recent of the unabridged dictionaries (although it has been described as lying somewhere between an unabridged and a desk dictionary in size). The work contains about 310,000 terms, which represents an increase of some 50,000 terms over the first edition. There are about 75,000 new definitions, along with increased emphasis on illustrations of usage. There is greater inclusion of synonyms, antonyms, and illustrations, as well as conscious effort to remove gender bias in the definitions. Although not as revolutionary in some respects as *Webster's Third* (entry 924), it is more daring in its decision to appeal to a popular rather than a scholarly audience. (Editors compose usage examples rather than cite the literature.) It is of the descriptive type, but employs usage labels more frequently, and is therefore more prescriptive than *Webster's Third*. It is considered up-to-date in its definitions (*AIDS, new wave,* and so on) and no longer avoids obscenities. It furnishes personal and place names within the body of the listings of foreign words (German, French, Spanish, and Italian) as well as an atlas and gazetteer segment.

923. **Webster's New International Dictionary of the English Language.** 2d ed. William Allan Neilson, ed.-in-chief. Springfield, MA: Merriam, 1961 (1934). 3194p.

Descended from a line of distinguished dictionaries from the Merriam Company beginning in 1828, this edition was an important contribution to the prestige and respect accruing to the Webster name. The first edition of the *New International* appeared in 1909, and this work represented a complete revision in 1934. Subsequent printings and reissues showed slight modifications, such as a new-words section added to the front in 1939. This work remained available for several years following publication of the third edition in 1961 (entry 924). Basically, it remains an excellent dictionary based on the rationale of providing a prescriptive tool for maintaining the integrity of the language. Many usage labels are furnished and examples of usage are quoted from the fine literature of the past. Approximately 600,000 words are included, many of which are obsolete or archaic. Word meanings are in historical sequence, earliest to most recent (a Merriam characteristic), and there are a separate gazetteer and a biographical dictionary. The main volume is retained in libraries along with the newer edition.

924. **Webster's Third New International Dictionary of the English Language.** Phillip Babcock Gove, ed.-in-chief. Springfield, MA: Merriam, 1961; repr. 1993. 2662p. ISBN 0-87779-201-1.

It is difficult to imagine the controversy caused by the publication of this work, which placed the prestige and authority of the Merriam Company on the side of the new linguists as opposed to the traditional grammarians. No longer was this a prescriptive tool, but rather one that described the language as it was, using only a few usage labels. Many words regarded as vulgar, colloquial, or incorrect were not qualified as such. About 100,000 new terms were added, including the raw and racy language of the streets. About 250,000 of the older terms were deleted, furnishing a total of 450,000 words. Quotations include some from popular literature and are taken from modern authors rather than classic writers. The biographical dictionary and gazetteer sections have been dropped, and about all that remains the same from the second edition (entry 923) is the historical sequence of definitions given. This is the preferred dictionary of the American people and is found in every library.

12,000 Words: A Supplement to Webster's Third New International Dictionary (Merriam-Webster, 1986) is an attempt to keep up-to-date with the changes in language and language use. This is not a self-contained dictionary, but must be used in conjunction with the basic work. Of interest is the introductory essay describing the recent growth of English vocabulary.

DESK OR COLLEGE

Desk dictionaries are generally understood to be those which stand on the desk and can be found in the possession of secretaries, college students, professors, businesspersons, and others engaged in normal social routines. They are the dictionaries most frequently purchased for adults.

925. **The American Heritage College Dictionary.** 3d ed. Boston: Houghton Mifflin, 1993. 1630p. ISBN 0-395-66917-0.

The third edition continues the good work of the earlier issues and is based on the 1992 edition of the oversize work (entry 918). The present effort is nearly as comprehensive in providing coverage of 185,000 words and 200,000 definitions. It adds more than 15,000 new words and supplies 2,500 illustrations, both photographs and drawings. Since it contains some 500 fewer pages than its parent, there is smaller typeface. Also, the usage examples have been shortened, abbreviations have been employed in the etymologies, and word histories have been eliminated. Biographical and geographical entries are treated within the main sequence, unlike the Merriam-Webster effort. An essay and a chart on Indo-European languages appear at the end.

The Concise American Heritage Dictionary (Houghton-Mifflin, 1987) is a revision of an earlier effort and furnishes some 60,000 definitions and 400 illustrations. *The American Heritage Illustrated Encyclopedic Dictionary*, also issued in 1987, is a merger of a dictionary and encyclopedia, as it offers lengthier descriptions of some 300 topics of interest to high school students. Numerous small maps and illustrations are included.

*926. The Concise Oxford Dictionary of Current English. 8th ed. R. E. Allen. ed. New York: Oxford University Press, 1990. 1454p. ISBN 0-19-861243-5.

Regarded in the past as a small desk dictionary; the new edition has tripled the coverage of the seventh edition (1982) from 40,000 to 120,000 entry words. Preceding editions were based in large part on the supplements to the first edition of the *OED*; the present work is derived from the second edition (entry 921). With its emphasis on current language, many older terms have been discarded in favor of those in current usage. Like its predecessors, it departs from the historical treatment in its arrangement of definitions in order of familiarity rather than chronological sequence. There is less extensive treatment of words from outside the British Isles, in favor of words used in the United Kingdom. It continues to be like the *OED*, a descriptive rather than a prescriptive dictionary, and it records the language as it exists among English-speaking peoples. Alternative forms of the entry words appear in parentheses. The work has been made available on CD-ROM by the publisher as **Concise Oxford Dictionary* (1993).

A recent effort is *The New Shorter Oxford English Dictionary*, edited by Lesley Brown (1993), a two-volume work that treats every word or phrase in use in the English language since 1700. Entries are well developed in furnishing definitions, origins, pronunciation, and other elements. Unlike the *Concise Oxford*, it adheres to a historical approach, sequencing the 83,000 quotations as illustrations of changes of meaning. It should prove of value to both students and scholars. A more comprehensive work is *Chambers English Dictionary*, now in its seventh edition and edited by Catherine Schwarz and others (Cambridge University Press, 1988), supplying 265,000 definitions of both traditional and newer terms. It achieves comprehensive coverage through its system of "etymological nesting" that treats derivatives from the same root word under the heading for the root word. Definitions for main entries and subentries are given in historical order. There are numerous appendices.

*927. Merriam-Webster's Collegiate Dictionary. 10th ed. Springfield, MA: Merriam-Webster, 1993. 1559p. ISBN 0-87779-708-0.

Comparable in size to the ninth edition, but using smaller typeface, this new edition of what is judged to be the best of desk dictionaries maintains the excellence of its predecessors. The addition of "Merriam" to the title for the first time firmly establishes its publishing identity. Some 10,000 new words (*CD-ROM, E-Mail, glasnost*, etc.) have been added and others have been dropped. Similar to the previous edition, there are about 160,000 entry terms, 211,000 definitions, 35,000 verbal illustrations and illustrative quotations, 35,000 etymologies, 4,400 usage paragraphs, and 700 black-and-white illustrations. Treatment of slang and obscene terms has improved and become more courageous. This series has long been regarded as the top choice among college students and academicians. This edition replaces one done ten years earlier, and issued since then on an annual basis containing only slight modification from year to year. Like the others it is based on the entries in *Webster's Third* (entry 924). There is a separate section for biographical and geographical names in the appendices, along with abbreviations and foreign terms. It is an excellent example of an abridged dictionary. The ninth edition has been computer-accessible since 1986 when Target Software of Miami, Florida, issued it on two disks as part of the *MacLightning* computer file. More recently (1989), a Macintosh CD-ROM version has been made available by Highlighted Data of Washington, D.C.

Because the name "Webster's" is not copyright, Random House issued a collegiate dictionary entitled *Random House Webster's College Dictionary* in 1992, largely based on its unabridged edition (entry 922). This succeeds the previous college dictionary issued in 1975, and furnishes 180,000 entries. There is good coverage of current informal speech, including slang and dialect. *Webster's New World Dictionary of American English*, edited by Victoria Neufeldt (Websters's New World/Prentice Hall, 1988), is another popular choice as a desk dictionary. It contains 170,000 entries and emphasizes words of American origin. It is strong in treatment of usage and of etymologies.

USAGE, SLANG, IDIOMS, AND NEW WORDS

928. **A Dictionary of American Idioms: Based on the Earlier Edition**. 2d ed. rev. and upd. Adam Makkai. New York: Barron's Educational Series, 1987. ISBN 0-8120-3899-1.

The first edition of this work was edited by M. T. Boatner and Makkai and appeared in 1975 from Rowman and Littlefield. It had earned its reputation as being the most significant dictionary of idioms and had been used by a wide-ranging audience. The second edition by Makkai, a professor of linguistics, carries on the tradition and opens with an excellent introduction on the nature and use of idioms. More than 5,000 idioms are treated, having been incorporated into the language through varied elements of our society. Expressions from CB radio, computer technology, and drug or hippie cultures are supplied. Main entries include full information on an idiom; many are accompanied by minor entries derived from the main entry. In addition, there are cross-references aiding access to variant forms of the idioms.

Another source of new coinage is *Acronyms, Initialisms and Abbreviations Dictionary 1992*, edited by Jennifer Mossman and issued in three parts (Gale, 1994). This is no less than the eighteenth edition of this important and popular work and identifies some 520,000 acronyms, contractions, and other shortened forms. About 20,000 new terms have been added from the literature of aviation, business, computer science, science, and the military. Entries supply meaning, source, language and country of origin, and subject category.

929. **Dictionary of American Regional English.** Frederic G. Cassidy, ed. Cambridge, MA: Harvard University Press, 1985- . v.1- . ISBN 0-674-20511-1 (v.1); 0-674-20512-X (v.2).

Volume I, A-C, is the initial effort of an important project in providing what is to become a comprehensive, five-volume dictionary of folk expressions, unused meanings of common terms, regional colloquialisms, and words belonging to ethnic or social groups in the United States. Entries include parts of speech, variant spellings, geographical roots, usage labels, cross-references, and definitions. Etymologies are sometimes covered. A series of computer-generated maps shows geographical distribution of the word and gives some idea of the density of the population affected. The initial volume contains an important essay on language changes in American folk speech, guide to pronunciation, and an explanation of the maps. Volume II, D-H, was issued in 1991 and adds another 11,000 entries, continuing the detailed coverage. Both volumes contain cross-references to the content of subsequent volumes; initially it was hoped that the set would be completed in ten years (1995). *An Index by Region, Usage, and Etymology to the Dictionary of American Regional English, Volumes I and II* was issued by the University of Alabama Press in 1993.

930. **The Dictionary of Cliches.** James Rogers. New York: Facts on File, 1985. Repr., Wing Book, 1992. 305p. ISBN 0-51706-020-5.

An interesting and useful work identifying more than 2,000 commonalities of language usage, this volume embraces idioms, proverbs, and quotations. Not surprisingly, Shakespeare and the Bible are two of the leading sources for the cliches, a language species much despised and denigrated by linguists. Nevertheless, they are important features of language study, and this dictionary provides useful treatment of meanings and definitions, as well as etymologies. Entries are covered in depth, with enough information to provide insight and enlightenment (even though some of the etymologies are speculative in nature). Entries are arranged alphabetically and there is a detailed index of cross-references at the end of the book. The work is thorough and should be of use to a variety of library patrons.

Catch Phrases, Cliches, and Idioms: A Dictionary of Familiar Expressions (McFarland, 1990) is a useful listing of trite phrases and banal expressions for which the compiler, Doris Craig, feels there is a ready market among advertising agency executives, among others. It furnishes a detailed index of keywords that should provide ready access.

931. **A Dictionary of Slang and Unconventional English: Colloquialisms and Catch-phrases ...** 8th ed. Eric Partridge. New York: Macmillan, 1984. 1400p. ISBN 0-02-594980-2.

The standard in the field, the Partridge work was the original slang dictionary from the time of its initial appearance in 1937. Previous editions have reprinted the original and added supplements (addenda) to the back. Now, at last, there is an integrated work which brings together in one alphabetical arrangement the original and subsequent supplements as well as additional new words and corrections. (Cockney is no longer included as a label, and such words have been deleted, as it is now accepted as mainstream English.) Partridge had collected most of this material (5,000 of the 6,000 entries) prior to his death in 1979. The new editor, Paul Beale, initialed the entries he contributed to the volume. The new work maintains the tradition of the old and will continue as the major work of its kind.

Contemporary American Slang, by Richard A. Spears (National Textbook, 1991), is an interesting work in that it is intended for those using English as a second or non-native language. Examples of usage are given for each entry, along with alternative forms to clarify shades of meaning. Pronunciations are given in International Phonetic Alphabet. *New Dictionary of American Slang*, by Robert L. Chapman (Harper & Row, 1986), is another useful entry in this field, focusing on American slang. Hundreds of new terms from the past twenty years are included. This is similar to *The Dictionary of Contemporary Slang*, by Jonathon Green (rev. ed., Pan, 1992), which places the emphasis on current usage. Scope is broad for this work in treating 11,500 entries from most parts of the English-speaking world. It identifies the place of origin for terms other than those that are obviously British.

932. **Harper Dictionary of Contemporary Usage.** 2d ed. William Morris and Mary Morris. New York: Harper & Row, 1985. 641p. ISBN 0-061-81606-X.

The second edition of this dictionary follows the original by ten years, in which time the title has gained recognition as the most comprehensive and up-to-date dictionary of American word usage. A prescriptive work by virtue of its nature and purpose, it features a lively style and interesting commentary on some of the difficult elements of American usage. Experts on the panel were asked to vote and comment. An important consideration is the easy-to-read, large-print format. Such terms as *hot pants* and *house husband* are described, as are more traditional words from the past. This is definitely a needed reference work for most American libraries.

933. **International English Usage.** Loreto Todd and Ian Hancock. New York: New York University Press; distr., Columbia University Press, 1987. 520p. ISBN 0-8147-8176-4.

This highly useful, dictionary-style handbook covers English usage in all parts of the world where English is either the first language or an important second language. Interesting and informative comparisons are made about various practices and pronunciations of different nations and regions. There is an attempt to establish coverage which is balanced between descriptive and prescriptive approaches, with distinctions made between logical regional characteristics and actual errors. Generally the style of writing is lucid, although some passages can be understood only by specialists. This is a scholarly work, but it can be used successfully by the interested layperson. Access is facilitated by a good index and numerous cross-references.

934. **Oxford Dictionary of Current Idiomatic English.** A. P. Cowie et al., comps. New York: Oxford University Press, 1975-1983; repr. 1985. 2v. ISBN 0-19-431146-5 (v.1); 0-19-431151-1 (v.2).

Volume 1 of this work, covering verbs with prepositions and particles, was published in 1975; volume 2, dealing with phrases, clauses, and sentence idioms, appeared eight years later in 1983. The intention of the set is to furnish coverage sufficiently broad to answer various practical questions and inquiries regarding the use of idioms. Both volumes taken together cover some 40,000 idioms. Idiomatic statements are defined clearly, and examples of usage from contemporary literature and speech are furnished. Foreigners learning English will be aided by some of the warnings given to avoid wrong usage or construction. As is sometimes true of Oxford University Press titles, there is a British emphasis or slant.

935. **The Oxford Dictionary of New Words: A Popular Guide to Words in the News**. Sara Tulloch, comp. New York: Oxford University Press, 1991. 322p. ISBN 0-19-869170-X.
Another of the increasingly popular dictionaries of new words, this Oxford product identifies 500 new words and phrases as well as 1,500 new meanings that have entered the language in the 1980s up to the time of publication. These words are treated in 750 articles that are well-written, informative, and interesting to a wide array of users. Emphasis has been placed on terms from the United Kingdom and the United States, with less representation from Canada, Australia, and other parts of the English-speaking world. Origins lie in all walks of life, culture, and subculture, representing politics, the drug scene, and science and technology along with Wall Street and the computer industry.
Jonathan Green's *Tuttle Dictionary of New Words: Since 1960* (Charles E. Tuttle, 1992) is more inclusive but less detailed in its coverage of 2,700 new words and phrases that have entered the language since the 1960s. Emphasis is on British expression, and entries are arranged alphabetically in columns providing identification of part of speech, date, definition, and quotation. Computer terms are represented, but there has been an effort to avoid esoteric scientific language. The *Facts on File Dictionary of New Words*, by Harold LeMay et al. (Facts on File, 1988), is a reprint of a 1985 paperback treating 500 new words and phrases, which gives brief definitions, pronunciations, and quotations. Words are culled from the language of the streets and ethnic cultures as well as sports talk, business, politics, etc.

936. **Third Barnhart Dictionary of New English**. Robert K. Barnhart et al., eds. New York: H. W. Wilson, 1990. 565p. ISBN 0-8242-0796-3.
This is a revision and expansion of the second edition published in 1980 and is intended to replace the previous issues rather than serve as a supplement, as did the second to the first. It treats 12,000 new words, abbreviations, and acronyms that have entered the language within the past thirty years. As might be expected, much of the additional word coinage comes from the advances of science and technology, along with language patterns of cultural groups and recently incorporated slang. The previous edition covered only 5,000 words in its role as a continuation of the first issue. This specialized source represents a supplementary volume to the general-purpose dictionaries and responds to the needs of those for whom current and contemporary language is paramount in importance. Entries supply well-developed definitions and numerous quotations and identify the year in which the terms became current.

937. **Webster's Dictionary of English Usage**. Springfield, MA: Merriam-Webster, 1993. ISBN 0-87779-132-5.
This work continues in the tradition of the 1989 issue in providing historical treatment of the common problems associated with disputed usage of words in the English language. Like its predecessor, it is constructed within a descriptive rather than judgmental philosophy and supplies liberal use of quotations in illustrating points of consideration. Those who are opposed to this style will find little value in such a manual—one reviewer likened the first edition to the Humanist Association's publishing of a catechism. Others see it as a fair-minded presentation of summary comment from various authorities and an enlightened treatment of the debates and concerns over the use of language. From this standpoint, the avoidance of value judgments is a positive rather than a negative characteristic.

ETYMOLOGY, SYNONYMS, PRONUNCIATION, ETC.

938. **The Barnhart Dictionary of Etymology.** Robert K. Barnhart and Sol Steinmetz, eds. New York: H. W. Wilson, 1988. 1284p. ISBN 0-8242-0745-9.

This work is useful for both high school and college students who wish to trace the origins of some 30,000 words and related terms, with emphasis on their development within the vocabulary of American English. All types of words are included, both traditional and contemporary, formal and slang. The tool opens with a rather sophisticated introduction treating Proto-Germanic and Indo-European elements, but the ensuing text and definitions are clear, detailed, and easily comprehensible. Included in the entries are pronunciation for unusual words, part of speech, definition, date, and language of origin, as well as alternative and foreign forms of the term, word history, and cross-references to related entries. Additionally, there are glossaries of linguistic terminology and a bibliography. A revised edition is due in 1994.

Initially published in 1987 by Facts on File, and using that publisher's name in the original title, is Robert Hendrickson's *The Henry Holt Encyclopedia of Word and Phrase Origins* (Holt, 1990). With fewer than 600 pages, it is less than half the size of the Barnhart effort and is designed to entertain as well as inform. Origins of some 7,500 words are described; many of the origins are of doubtful veracity but are supplied for their interest and legendary status. All types of words are used, drawing from the Bible, technology, literature, place names, foreign expressions, euphemisms, slang, and obscenities. Purists will need to verify or confirm the information in other sources.

939. **The Concise Oxford Dictionary of English Etymology.** T. F. Hoad, ed. New York: Clarendon/Oxford University Press, 1986; repr. 1991. 552p. ISBN 0-19-861182-X.

Another of the Oxford dictionaries, this, like the others, is a work of high quality. Its parent work, C. T. Onions's *The Oxford Dictionary of English Etymology* (Clarendon Press, 1966), was the first comprehensive etymological dictionary of the English language since 1910, and established an excellent reputation for scholarship and breadth of coverage. The concise edition was begun by an assistant editor to Onions, G. W. S. Friedrichsen, and finally completed by Hoad. In truth, it shows little change from the style or content of the original, although abridgement is noticeable within the entries. Many abbreviations are employed which require reference to a list. Entries furnish dates and origins of various senses of meaning, all arranged in chronological order for each term. Brief definitions are given, but the dictionary should not be used for that purpose. Not appearing here, unfortunately, is the interesting and helpful introduction summarizing the history of the English language, which was an important element in the original edition.

A supplementary work is Adrian Room's *NTC's Dictionary of Word Origins* (National Textbook, 1991), that in truth is simply a reprint of Room's 1986 effort under another title with different publisher. It identifies origins for about 1,200 words about whose beginnings popular misconceptions exist, and should be considered only as a second source for the library.

940. **Dictionary of Word Origins.** John Ayto. New York: Arcade/Little, Brown, 1991. 583p. ISBN 1-55970-133-1.

Designed to establish the historical connections among English words is this well-constructed etymological dictionary by a British lexicographer. Emphasis here is not on definition, nor is coverage given to part of speech or pronunciation. Instead, there is a fascinating linkage through use of cross-references to a wide variety of related terms and expressions, most of which seem far afield from the original reference. For example, the term *doctor* leads to eleven other entries, including *dainty* and *paradox*; there are similar connections provided between *bacterium* and *imbecile*; *map* and *apron*; and *bishop* and *spy*. In all, some 8,000 words are covered, with emphasis on their status in forming the "central core of English vocabulary." Also included are new words with interesting origins. Arrangement is alphabetical in double columns; either century of origin is indicated or there is designation of "OE" for Old English.

941. **NBC Handbook of Pronunciation**. 4th ed. rev. Eugene Ehrlich and Raymond Hand, Jr. New York: HarperPerennial, 1991. 539p. ISBN 0-06-096574-6.

Initially published in the early 1950s, this unique work has become a standard in the field in providing pronunciation according to a "General American" speech pattern. Originally devised by NBC for use by its broadcasters around the country, a careful survey determined that the speech pattern chosen as amenable to most Americans and identified as "General American" was a cross between Midwestern and Western dialects. The present effort treats more than 21,000 entries used frequently by broadcasters and commonly mispronounced. Emphasis is on proper nouns, such as *Boris Yeltsin* and *Mikhail Gorbachev*, and place names like *Riyadh*. The major change from the third edition is the substitution of simple respelling for purposes of pronunciation instead of the previously used International Phonetic Alphabet (IPA). An interesting introduction by Edwin R. Newman provides perspective of the importance of pronunciation in terms of effectiveness of communication.

Another useful effort is *Pronouncing Dictionary of Proper Names: Pronunciations for More Than 23,000 Proper Names ...* edited by John Bollard and others (Omnigraphics, 1993). Emphasis was placed on the selection of terms that are difficult to handle, and include both current and historical personalities, places, things, and events. Similar to the preceding work, this title employs a simplified phonetic respelling to indicate pronunciation, although in this case it does include the IPA transcription. Variants are given along with cross-references.

942. **The Oxford Thesaurus**. American ed. Laurence Urdang. New York: Oxford University Press, 1992. 1005p. ISBN 0-19-507354-1.

The author is a prominent U.S. lexicographer who has authored an important new work for students of language in supplying treatment of 275,000 words. The text is organized into two principal parts with an alphabetical listing of headwords and synonyms, along with a detailed index that includes words not listed in the first segment. Following the headword, the synonyms are grouped together by similarity of meaning. Variant meanings are illustrated with a sample sentence. Prescriptive labels are used to identify words as colloquial, slang, taboo, archaic, etc. Index entries are followed by headwords from the dictionary section, with the particular connotation identified.

The Random House College Thesaurus, by Jess Stein and Stuart Berg Flexner (Random House, 1984; repr. 1992), was previously issued as the college edition of *The Random House Thesaurus* in 1984, and is based on *The Reader's Digest Family Word Finder* published in 1975. Random House increased the number of entries by 1,000 (10 percent) to its present coverage of 11,000 terms, along with a similar increase in the number of synonyms and antonyms furnished for the entry words. No coverage is given to word origins, pronunciation, or spelling, unlike the earlier *Reader's Digest* publication; usage labels such as slang are provided, however. Entries are alphabetically arranged for easy access; coverage is given to synonyms grouped according to meaning. Examples of usage are supplied with sentences prepared by the editors to illustrate the various contexts. Listings of antonyms conclude the entries for many of the terms. There is no index.

943. **Roget's International Thesaurus**. 5th ed. Robert L. Chapman, ed. New York: HarperCollins, 1992. 1141p. ISBN 0-06-270014-6.

A true standard in the field, this thesaurus was originally produced by Peter Mark Roget in 1852. Since that time, it has established itself as the major tool of its kind, its contribution being the classification scheme developed originally by Roget and expanded by others who served as editors. Knowledge is divided into approximately 1,000 subclasses under several main headings, such as abstract relations, space, matter, and intellect. This edition treats some 350,000 words and phrases under 1,073 subclasses (31 newly added) that fall under 15 major classes. In this way, word relationships are shown within an idea framework, with terms placed under the topics that they represent or express. Other synonym dictionaries simply arrange words alphabetically and provide one-word definitions or alternatives. This edition is especially strong in contemporary language and expressions.

An innovative effort is *Roget's II: The New Thesaurus* (Houghton Mifflin, 1992). Developed by the editors of the *American Heritage Dictionary* (entry 918), this work offers a handy and convenient approach to the language in furnishing "rapid access to synonyms which are grouped by precise meanings." In addition to main entries, there are secondary entries which act as cross-references to main entries. Brief definitions are furnished along with the synonyms and antonyms for all main entries.

Foreign-Language and Bilingual Dictionaries

944. The American Heritage Larousse Spanish Dictionary: Spanish/English, English/Spanish. Boston: Houghton Mifflin, 1992. ISBN 0-395-32429-7.

Continuing in the tradition of high-quality lexicography associated with the American Heritage name is this recent bilingual dictionary, a unique work providing excellent coverage of Latin American Spanish as well as European usage. For this reason, it is especially useful to those in both the Southeastern and Southwestern regions of the United States. The work compares favorably in scope and depth to other dictionaries of its type, with good coverage given to idioms and to scientific and technical terms. Among the special features is a verb table at the beginning of the volume, to which are keyed the entries for all the irregular verbs. This is a real asset for students trying to conjugate verbs.

945. The Cambridge Italian Dictionary. Barbara Reynolds, gen. ed. New York: Cambridge University Press, 1962-1981. 2v. ISBN 0-521-06059-1.

A span of nineteen years passed from the appearance of the first volume to publication of volume 2. With its completion, the librarian and the patron have been given an excellent translation tool. Volume 1 is Italian-English, and volume 2, English-Italian, the rationale behind the dictionary being the development of a word book useful to English-speaking individuals. With this idea in mind, it is understandable that the work provides no explanations of English grammar and includes no guides to English pronunciation. Unfortunately, Italian coverage is also lacking in that treatment, and remains the primary deficiency of an otherwise rich and useful source of words from all time periods and types.

Harper Collins Italian Dictionary: Italian-English; English-Italian (Harper & Row, 1990) provides a useful tool supplementary to the Reynolds work in its inclusion of terms relevant to business and office automation. Treated here are 70,000 entries and 100,000 translations. Also covered are a selection of abbreviations and a list of place names.

946. Deutsches Wörterbuch. Jakob Ludwig Karl Grimm and Wilhelm Grimm. Leipzig, Germany: Hirzel, 1854-1960; 16v. ISBN 3740100001. Repr. 1984. 16v. in 33.

This is the great German dictionary which was finally completed more than 100 years after it was started. It was the first dictionary to promote the idea of a compilation based on historical principles, and was the creation of Jakob Grimm, the great German philologist, who with his brother, Wilhelm, began the arduous process. The brothers Grimm today are probably better remembered by most Americans for their collection of fairy tales, produced early in their careers, but it is the dictionary which has served as their greatest legacy. It influenced the development of the *OED* (entry 921) and others of its type. It was the purpose of this work to give an exhaustive account of the words of new High German, the literary language, from the end of the fifteenth century onwards. Etymologies and senses are illustrated by literary quotations. Since 1965, there has been an ongoing effort to develop a revised and expanded edition incorporating the results of new research.

A more practical purchase for most American libraries is *Cassell's German and English Dictionary*, compiled by H. C. Sasse et al. (Collier Books/Macmillan, 1966; repr. 1986). A small, inexpensive paperback, it provides a concise but useful dictionary for the traveler or student in the initial stages of learning the language. *Dictionary English-German, German-English*

(CD-ROM Verlag Gmbh & Company KG) furnishes access to some 200,000 words and word combinations on CD-ROM. There is a separate file of 3,000 idioms and concepts.

947. **Harrap's New Standard French and English Dictionary.** Rev. ed. J. E. Mansion and D. M. Ledbesert, eds. London: Harrap; distr., Lincolnwood, IL: National Textbook, 1971-1980; repr. 1986-1988. 4v. ISBN 0-8442-1874-4 (v.1).

This has long been one of the leading dictionaries of its kind, and this four-volume edition is the most recent issue of a work that had its beginning in the 1930s. Since then, it has undergone several name changes and modifications. The present edition is a thorough revision designed to provide a work that was reasonable in terms of size and wide scope. Emphasis has been placed on modern, technical, scientific, and industrial elements, as well as the modern language, complete with colloquialisms and idioms. These are labeled for propriety and indicate slang, vulgarism, etc. The work has been criticized for the inclusion of dated material from past editions but at the same time has been praised for the inclusion of modern technical terminology.

Harrap's Shorter French and English Dictionary, initially edited by Peter Collin in 1982 and later by Jane Goldie (1991), represents a condensed version in one volume of the four-volume effort. It is a high-quality title that retains the basic coverage needed by students and others learning the language. Treatment is less full, but adequate for most needs in presenting the common elements of the language. An unusual recent effort is *The Oxford Guide to the French Language*, by William Rowlinson and Michael Janes (Oxford, 1992), which provides both a grammar and a dictionary for its users. Numerous examples from newspapers and magazines are given, along with rules of grammatical construction, in the first segment. Also treated are pronunciation peculiarities and translation problems. The second section contains a useful bilingual dictionary of 45,000 words. The work appeals to a diverse audience from traveler to beginning student.

*948. **Languages of the World**. Lincolnwood, IL: National Textbook, 1990. (CD-ROM).

This unique kit supplies access to eighteen dictionaries in twelve languages (English, Dutch, Danish, Finnish, German, Italian, Norwegian, Spanish, Swedish, Chinese, and Japanese). Produced in Japan, it consists of one CD-ROM disk, three floppy disks for search systems with different CD-ROM devices, and a user's manual of forty pages. Only one of the dictionaries is American, NTC's own *American Idioms Dictionary*. No publication dates are given, which must be considered a negative factor. There is emphasis on the inclusion of Harrap's dictionaries, for which NTC serves as U.S. distributor (*Harrap's Science, *Harrap's Shorter, *Harrap's Data Processing, *Harrap's Business*, and *Harrap's Concise*). The advantage of such comprehensive coverage is evident in the opportunity to find definitions, synonyms, and antonyms in twelve languages. The disadvantage appears to be in the age of the various editions used, because many of the newer terms, such as *CD-ROM*, do not "compute" into all language terminologies.

949. **A New English-Chinese Dictionary**. Rev. and enl. ed. The Editing Group, comp. Seattle, WA: University of Washington Press, 1989. 1769p. ISBN 0-295-96609-2.

This important effort originally was developed during the Cultural Revolution and published in 1975 by the Joint Publishing Company of Hong Kong with the participation of seventy scholars located in the Shanghai area. These scholars were faculty members at Fudan University, Shanghai Teachers' University, Shanghai Institute of Foreign Languages, etc. The University of Washington acquired the rights in 1988 after its publication in Hong Kong in 1987. The original 80,000 entries are furnished with 600 modifications and/or deletions of political references to Mao and the Cultural Revolution. Additionally, there is a 4,000-word supplement to the original edition. This contains both new words and those that have changed in meaning or morphology since 1975. There are nine appendices supplying lists of English verbs, weights and measures, common marks and symbols, conversion tables, etc.

Vietnamese-English, English-Vietnamese Dictionary, by Le-Ba-Khanh and Le-Ba-Kong (Hippocrene Books, 1991), fills a need for a work of this type in view of the exodus and relocation of Vietnamese people in this country following the war. It enables them to better understand the written and spoken English language by providing more than 12,000 entries, a list of modern Vietnamese terms, and an appendix of synonyms and antonyms. For the English user, it is useful for its definitions and may be used for translation of the written word. Pronunciation is not given for Vietnamese terms, however.

950. **New Revised Velazquez Spanish and English Dictionary.** Mariano Velazquez de la Cadena et al. Rev. by Ida Navarro Hinojosa et al. Piscataway, NJ: New Century, 1985. 788p. ISBN 0832902659.

Considered one of the best dictionaries of its kind, this edition replaces the one published in 1974. The tool is comprehensive, with more than 150,000 entries for which information is given on pronunciation as well as translation. About 700 new entries have been added, providing up-to-date coverage which includes regional variations for Latin America and Spain. Always considered strong in technical terminology, obsolete terms, and esoteric language, this dictionary's comprehensive nature exceeds most works of this type. Revisions for terms requiring changes from the previous edition, as well as new entries, are included in the middle of the volume between the two sections of the work. In the appendices are brief grammars of Castilian and English, geographical terms, proper names, abbreviations, and other valuable listings.

Collins Spanish-English/English-Spanish Dictionary. Collins Diccionario Espanol-Ingles/Ingles-Espanol (HarperCollins, 1993), now in its third edition and edited by Colin Smith and others, has added more than 30,000 references and some 50,000 translations since its initial effort in 1971. It treats more than 230,000 entries and presents a new emphasis on Hispanic-American languages. Word treatment is up-to-date, with regional usage and slang identified and labeled. *The Random House Portuguese Dictionary: Portuguese-English, English-Portuguese* (Random House, 1991), edited by Bobby J. Chamberlain, furnishes 38,000 entries, the emphasis being Brazilian Portuguese. It identifies gender, and serves as a practical manual through its numerous tables of basic measures, weights, days of the week, and so on.

951. **NTC's New College Greek and English Dictionary.** Paul Nathanail, comp. Lincolnwood, IL: National Textbook, 1990. 556p. ISBN 0-8442-8473-4.

Regarded as a useful and adequate dictionary since its publication in 1985, this reprint of a relatively inexpensive paperback edition packs a great deal of information into a small space. Related items are brought together while maintaining alphabetical order. The vocabulary is considered to be well chosen and balanced, although there is a tendency to favor the contemporary demotic form. Although it is designed for English-speaking users (British-based), there is no guide to English pronunciation. Some hints in this direction for the Greek language would have been helpful, even though Greek orthography is rather regular. There are more than 50,000 entries.

A comprehensive work is the two-volume treatment provided by D. N. Stavropoulos, which was initiated with publication of *Oxford English-Greek Learner's Dictionary* (Oxford, 1977) and completed more than a decade later with *Oxford Greek-English Learner's Dictionary* (Oxford, 1988). *The Oxford Turkish-English Dictionary*, by A. D. Alderson and Fahir Iz, is now in its third edition (Clarendon Press/Oxford University Press, 1984) and is considered the best existing tool for translation of contemporary Turkish texts. Many technical terms are included, and the complicated Turkish morphology and idiom are handled well.

952. **NTC's New Japanese-English Character Dictionary.** Jack Halpern, ed. Lincolnwood, IL: National Textbook, 1993. 1992p. ISBN 0-8442-8434-3.

A solid publication is this recent effort providing comprehensive coverage of 60,000 definitions for 42,000 words. A central meaning considered to be the most important is supplied along with excellent treatment of *kanji* or Chinese characters by patterns. Entries are treated under four patterns (left-right, up-down, enclosure, and solid), and identify number of strokes, order of strokes, grade, frequency, compounds, synonyms, etc. Various appendices provide insight regarding rules and considerations.

A pocket-sized version is Noah S. Brannen's *The Practical English-Japanese Dictionary* (Weatherhill, 1991), a favorite of travelers and tourists. It supplies romanization of Japanese characters along with excellent examples of usage. Also included is an introduction to Japanese grammar identifying parts of speech, pronunciation, and conjugation tables. There are several CD-ROM versions, not surprising with the emergence of Japan as an industrial and technical power. *English-Japanese, Japanese-English Dictionary* (Sanseido) aids the translation of Japanese to English and English to Japanese. The software producer is Dai Nippon Printing Company, which has prepared this work based on the *Century's English-Japanese Dictionary* and *Crown's Japanese-English Dictionary*. Another CD-ROM issue is *Kojien: A Comprehensive Dictionary of the Japanese Language* from Iwani-Jhaten Publishers, available since 1987, which treats a wide range of dialects as well as slang and technical expressions. Etymology and grammar are identified and quotations from Japanese literature are used. A similar revision is available from Fujitsu using a slightly different spelling in the title, *Kohjien (Japanese Dictionary) CD-ROM*. A comprehensive effort is *Kojien Dictionary*, published by Ayumi Software and Qualitas Trading Company. It supplies 200,000 entry words along with 2,000 graphics and sound. The CD-ROM product is compatible with Macintosh systems.

953. **The Oxford Latin Dictionary.** P. G. W. Glare, ed. New York: Clarendon Press/Oxford University Press, 1982; repr. 1983. 2126p. ISBN 0-19-864224-5.

Another scholarly work in the Oxford line-up of dictionary and word source books developed through scholarly pursuits and careful attention to detail. This dictionary appeared in eight fascicles over a period of fourteen years from 1967 to 1981. A milestone was reached with publication of the complete edition in one volume. The work has replaced an older and outdated standard in the field from Harper & Row as well as a more recent work that falls short in comprehensiveness and detail. There is a rich selection of entry words from the Latin literature; quotations illustrate in historical fashion the various senses or meanings which the words have assumed through time. A thorough, precise, and valuable item for reference work.

954. **The Oxford Russian Dictionary.** Rev. and upd. Colin Howlett. New York: Oxford University Press, 1993. 1340p. ISBN 0-19-864189-3.

This new work represents an expansion and update of the publisher's two volumes issued in 1984, *The Oxford English-Russian Dictionary* and *The Oxford Russian-English Dictionary*. The effort furnishes coverage of more than 180,000 words and phrases, as compared to 160,000 in the earlier volumes, and treats 290,000 translations. It provides a complete approach to the study of the Russian language by identifying the terms derived from various dictionaries judged to be useful and of value. The work includes colloquialisms, idioms, and technical terms as well as general standard terminology. Explanations are given, as are translations, and useful appendices of official abbreviations and geographical names are furnished. Correctness of translation is emphasized in the English-Russian segment; the Russian-English section uses quotations from literature and newspapers. Like its predecessors, this work should be purchased by all libraries needing to provide services to specialists as well as students.

Stephen Marder's *A Supplementary Russian-English Dictionary* (Slavica, 1992) furnishes 29,000 entries not found in the *Oxford* work. Included are recently coined terms along with those for which the meanings have changed substantially, as well as slang, technical terms, obscenities, and abbreviations.

955. **Webster's New World Hebrew Dictionary: Hebrew/English, English/Hebrew.** Hayim Baltsan. New York: Prentice-Hall General Reference, 1992. 827p. ISBN 0-13-944547-1.

This is an interesting and useful addition to the small body of work on Hebrew-English dictionaries and is unique in its use of romanized Hebrew words rather than Hebrew characters for the main headings in the Hebrew-English segment. This is in keeping with the work's intent to serve the needs of those with no prior knowledge of the Hebrew language. Transliteration does not follow standard practices, as identified in the scheme developed by ALA and the Library of Congress, but adopts a new system that appears to be accurate. In the Hebrew-English section, following the romanized entry the term is expressed in non-vowelized Hebrew characters, then defined. This non-vowelized Hebrew form is also used in the English-Hebrew section. Some 60,000 entries are treated in the two sections of the work. Practical in nature, the vocabulary includes sociopolitical terms and names of political parties.

Histories and Directories

956. **The American Language: An Inquiry into the Development of English in the United States.** 4th ed., corr., enl. and rewritten. Henry L. Mencken. New York: Knopf, 1950; repr. 1986. 777p.

This monumental work is the most well-known and respected history of the American language. It was first completed by H. L. Mencken, the famous journalist for the *Baltimore Sun*, over fifty years ago, and has gone through subsequent editions, supplements, and reprints. There is nothing to rival it either in breadth or depth of treatment of the English language in America. The work provides historical treatment of the development of the English language in the United States in eleven chapters covering a variety of topics. Included are such topical divisions as the two streams of English, the beginning and growth of the American language, pronunciation and spelling, common speech, proper names, slang, etc. The work contains an appendix which includes a segment on non-English dialects and a general index to provide access.

957. **A History of the English Language.** 4th ed. Albert Croll Baugh and Thomas Cable. Englewood Cliffs, NJ: Prentice-Hall, 1993. 444p. ISBN 0-13-395708-X.

The initial edition of this work was published in 1935, and since that time it has become the leading reference history as well as textbook for courses covering the historical development of the English language from its beginnings to the present. It includes a segment on the development of the language in this country, but for greater detail on that topic one should consult Mencken's *The American Language* (entry 956). Treatment is given to the evolution of the language within the context of the political, social, and intellectual history of England. This is considered the best one-volume survey history on the topic. Bibliographies are up-to-date to time of publication and are linked to the recent scholarship in the field.

LITERATURE

General Works

BIBLIOGRAPHIC GUIDES AND INTRODUCTORY WORKS

958. **The Art of Literary Research.** 4th ed. Richard D. Altick. Rev. by John J. Fenstermaker. New York: W. W. Norton, 1993. 353p. ISBN 0-393-96240-7.

Since its initial appearance in 1964, this standard source has been regarded as one of the more useful, well-constructed, and interesting introductory guides in the field of literature. The fourth edition carries on the good work of the earlier editions and provides excellent narrative and provocative exposition of the principles and practices involved in literary research. Fenstermaker's revision retains the original character of Altick's contribution, but furnishes a needed modification with respect to modern practice and theory. Bibliographies and exercises have been updated and there is more coverage of computerization in the field. Advice is still relevant regarding the consideration of bibliographic procedures, note taking, library practices, and writing as an art practice requiring high standards and commitment. The title continues as a top choice for reference departments.

959. **Key Sources in Comparative and World Literature: An Annotated Guide to Reference Material.** George A. Thompson, with the assistance of Margaret M. Thompson. New York: Ungar, 1982. 383p. ISBN 0-8044-3281-3.

More than 1,200 reference tools are identified and described in this work, including handbooks, encyclopedias, biographical dictionaries, terminologies, guides, etc. An array of bibliographic tools, bibliographies, indexes, and research reviews is covered, both in sections dealing with general and comparative literatures and in those dealing with national and period literatures. Classical, Romance, French, Italian, Hispanic, German, Oriental, and other European types are included, as well as literature in English. As is inevitable in a work of this sort, certain literatures are given short shrift (Oriental, Latin American, African, etc.) but the work is to be commended for its attempt at comprehensive coverage. The arrangement of entries is classified within chapters and access is provided through three indexes: editor and compiler, title, and subject.

960. **Problems in Literary Research: A Guide to Selected Reference Works.** 3d ed. Dorothea Kehler. Metuchen, NJ: Scarecrow Press, 1987. 227p. ISBN 0-8108-1978-3.

Continuing with the pattern established in previous editions, this effort treats thirty-six basic literary reference works fundamental to literary research. The work is equally at home in the reference collection of a high school or undergraduate library or as a textbook for relevant coursework. Coverage is primarily of English and American literature sources, but other literatures are not excluded. The work employs five chapters designed to promote understanding on the part of its readers. The pattern of coverage for each reference work begins with a brief description, and then follows up with review questions and research problems requiring hands-on experience to resolve. Chapter 6 supplies a listing of 161 supplementary sources. Although a useful tool, certain oversights have been noted by reviewers, such as the failure to mention computerized versions of some of the titles. An index aids access.

Periodicals

961. **The International Directory of Little Magazines and Small Presses.** Paradise, CA: Dustbooks, 1973/1974- . v.9- . Ann. ISBN 0-916685-31-4 (1992).

This annual guide and directory replaces the *Directory of Little Magazines* (1965-1972) and continues its volume numbering. Therefore, the initial volume under this title was volume 9. It continues to provide information of a directory nature for low-subscription literary and art magazines (address, telephone number, scope, editor, subscription price, average length, circulation figures), payment rates, and copyright arrangements, but also includes comments by the editors on the policies and types of material published. Lists of recent contributors are furnished as well. Small presses are covered in much the same fashion, with editor, address, scope, average price for books, production methods, and size of press runs. Editors' comments on the nature of the press are also given. Access is aided through subject and geographic indexes useful to those seeking publishing outlets. The twenty-eighth edition (1992-1993) furnishes information on more than 4,600 markets for writers.

Less comprehensive is *Directory of Little Magazines 1993-1994* by R. I. Wakefield and Moyer Bell (Council of Literary Magazines and Presses, 1992). Information similar to that given by the *International Directory* is supplied for about 500 literary magazines from all over the world.

962. **MLA Directory of Periodicals: A Guide to Journals and Series in Languages and Literatures.** New York: Modern Language Association of America, 1979- . Bienn. ISSN 0197-0380.

A companion volume to the important **MLA International Bibliography* (entry 964), the seventh edition (1993) provides information on more than 3,200 journals and series published in the United States and Canada that have been indexed in that work. This biennial is without a rival in terms of providing up-to-date information on currently available titles of serial nature in the field. Arrangement is alphabetical by title of journal or series, with each entry furnished a sequence number referred to in the indexes. Various indexes provide excellent access: editorial personnel; language other than English, French, German, Italian, and Spanish; sponsoring organizations; subject; journal title abbreviations, etc.

Beginning in 1984, another useful biennial publication based on the preceding was published as a more narrowly based work. *MLA Directory of Periodicals: A Guide to Journals and Series in Language and Literature: Periodicals Published in the United States and Canada* draws from the complete version in furnishing coverage of about 1,200 titles published in the United States and its northern neighbor. It follows the same pattern of organization as does the parent work. There is also Margaret C. Patterson's *Author Newsletters and Journals* ... (Gale, 1979), that identifies and annotates over 1,100 titles devoted to the collection and distribution of criticism, bibliographies, biographical information, and more on the lives and works of single authors.

INDEXES, ABSTRACTS, AND SERIAL BIBLIOGRAPHIES

*963.   **Francis bulletin signaletique 523: Histoire et sciences de la litterature**. Nancy, France: Institut de l'Information Scientifique et Technique (INIST), 1991- . Q.

Similar to other indexes and abstracts previously sponsored by the French Centre National de la Recherche Scientifique (CNRS), this abstract journal has been the responsibility of INIST since 1991. A quarterly publication, it has been issued since the early 1970s and continues to provide references and abstracts of journal articles, monographs, proceedings, and dissertations relevant to the history and science of all types of literature. As part of the enormous database known as FRANCIS, it is available online, with its file dating from 1972 and numbering around 100,000 records. The database is updated on a quarterly basis at the time the print copy is issued; it averages an increase of 4,000 items per year. Coverage includes French literature, African literature, and Anglo-Saxon and German literature, as well as the literature of the Slavs, Italians, Latin Americans, and Caribbeans.

*964.   **MLA International Bibliography.** New York: Modern Language Association of America, 1921- . Ann. ISSN 0024-8215.

This monumental bibliography is known and respected by language and literature students both in this country and abroad. A standard work in the field, it has changed title and scope since its inception in 1921, when it was limited to writings by Americans on the literature of various countries, and known as *American Bibliography*. Since 1956, it has been a more expansive source of bibliographic information and was named *Annual Bibliography* from 1956 to 1962. Since 1963, it has had its present title and includes writers from a variety of other languages, although primarily American and European. Books, articles, monographs, and festschriften are all included. Presently, it appears in five volumes, with volume 1 given to the English-speaking nations; volume 2 to European, Asian, African, and South American literatures; volume 3 to linguistics; volume 4 to general literature; and volume 5 to folklore. The volumes may be purchased separately or in several combinations with author and subject index. The file is available online from MLA or through WILSONLINE and on CD-ROM on WILSONDISC. There are about 1 million records online covering the period from 1963 to the present, and about half that number on CD-ROM, with coverage beginning in 1981. More retrospective coverage is slated for the future.

Available through Research Libraries Group (RLIN) is *RLG Research-in-Progress Database* that furnishes some 2,500 references to articles accepted for future publication by fifty scholarly journals selected by the Modern Language Association, along with NEH-funded research in progress and feminist studies and conference papers from the National Council for Research on Women.

965. The Romantic Movement: A Selective and Critical Bibliography. David V. Erdman, ed. West Cornwall, CT: Locust Hill Press, 1979- . Ann. ISBN 0-9339-5149-3 (1992).

This scholarly annual bibliography, formerly from Garland, is a continuation of a bibliography by the same title which appeared in *ELH*, a quarterly journal of English literary history, from 1936 to 1948; then in *Philological Quarterly*, 1949-1963; and finally in *English Language Notes*, from 1964 to 1978. The present work continues the plan and follows the rationale of the earlier publication in its desire to cover a movement rather than a time period. Time periods of Romanticism vary with different languages (the English section being stabilized between 1789 and 1837). Other languages covered are French, German, and Spanish, and Italian has recently been added.

The Romantic Movement Bibliography, 1936-1970 ... (Pierian Press, 1973) is a compilation in seven volumes with indexes to the contents of the first thirty-four years of the bibliographic listings. It was edited by A. C. Elkins, Jr., and L. J. Forstner.

966. Twentieth-Century Literary Movements Index: A Guide to 500 Literary Movements, Groups, Schools, Tendencies, and Trends ... Laurie Lantzen Harris and Helene Henderson, eds. Detroit: Omnigraphics, 1991. 419p. ISBN 1-55888-306-1.

This is the initial offering of a set or series of volumes designed for use at the high school and undergraduate level in aiding comprehension of world literary movements and related elements. The title goes on to say "covering more than 3,000 novelists, poets, dramatists, essayists, artists, and other seminal thinkers from 80 countries as found in standard reference works." Three volumes are planned for the twentieth century, with the second continuing essays on the literary movements and important personalities within them. The series is designed to cover one era at a time. The present volume indexes twenty-eight standard literary reference sources that contain entries on the movements. Part 1 provides an index to the movements; part 2 supplies a name index to the writers, critics, and theorists associated with them. Brief identification information is given along with citations to coverage in indexed sources.

DICTIONARIES, ENCYCLOPEDIAS, AND HANDBOOKS

967. Benet's Reader's Encyclopedia. 3d ed. William Rose Benet. New York: Harper & Row, 1987. 1091p. ISBN 0-06-181088-6.

First published in 1948, with the second edition issued in 1965, this convenient and valuable handbook has been a standard in the field ever since it first appeared. The work furnishes brief articles on a variety of topics and personalities (scientists, artists, and philosophers, as well as creative writers). Included in the present edition are Stephen King, Lawrence Ferlinghetti, and Irving Stone; many of the previous entries have been updated and revised. The coverage is international and all periods of time are treated, in an impressive attempt at comprehensiveness for a one-volume work. Literature-related entries cover authors, titles, characters from fiction, literary terms, allusions, and movements. Important historical figures and topics are identified, as are terms from the sciences, fine arts, philosophy, etc. Entries for titles furnish plot summaries, and those for literary characters give full identification. Musical compositions and art works are also included. The emphasis on world literature continues in the present edition with coverage of the Orient, Russia, Latin America, and the Near East.

968. Calendar of Literary Facts: A Daily and Yearly Guide to Noteworthy Events in World Literature from 1450 to the Present. Samuel J. Rogal, ed. Detroit: Gale Research, 1991. 877p. ISBN 0-8103-2943-3.

The editor is well-known for his work in producing several reference works, including chronologies on British and American literature (entries 1097n and 1101). With this publication he has broadened the scope to embrace world literature over a period of 440 years from 1450 to 1989. The chronology is divided into two sections, the first of which represents a generic day-by-day treatment of births and deaths of writers and includes their nationality and genre. The second part provides year-by-year coverage, beginning in 1450 with the invention of printing from movable type. Categorical divisions for each year include births, deaths, major publications, and significant events relevant to literary interests. Brief annotations of each entry vary from a single sentence to a paragraph in length. Indexing is thorough for both sections.

969.   **Characters in 19th-Century Literature**. Kelly King Howes. Detroit: Gale Research, 1993. 597p. ISBN 0-8103-8398-5.
    A more recent effort patterned after the earlier publication on the twentieth century described later, Howes's book is designed to aid high school students and undergraduates in their understanding of literary characters. It supplies plot summaries and character analysis for 275 major plays, novels, and short stories written by more than 150 nineteenth-century writers currently being studied in classrooms in this country. Minorities are purposely included. About 2,000 characters are thus identified and are examined critically in terms of their status within the development of theme and plot. A bibliography is furnished. Entries supply author, name, dates, nationality, and principal genres. Arrangement is alphabetical by author's name. There is an index of characters and titles.
    Characters in 20th-Century Literature, edited by Laurie Lantzen Harris (Gale Research, 1990) established the precedent for the title just described in analyzing the characters and describing the plots of more than 500 works from 250 major novelists, dramatists, and short story writers who are either still alive or have died since 1899. Special emphasis is given to the post-1960 period. Arrangement and format are similar to the more recent effort.

970.   **Columbia Dictionary of Modern European Literature**. 2d ed., fully rev. and enl. Jean Albert Bede and William B. Edgerton, gen. eds. New York: Columbia University Press, 1980. 895p. ISBN 0-231-03717-1.
    Published initially in 1947, this was recognized as one of the best one-volume works on the subject of comparative literature of the modern period. The new edition maintains the high standard of scholarship, with excellent biographical sketches, critical evaluations, and survey articles on the various national literatures. "Modern" is defined as beginning with the period "toward the end of the nineteenth century when Europe was swept by a wave of new revolutionary movements, largely inspired by the French symbolists and known by different names ... symbolism, decadence, and modernism." More than 1,850 biographical sketches are given for individual authors, each of which is furnished with bibliographical references. There are excellent survey articles on the various national literatures, and all articles are signed. More than 500 scholars contributed to this comprehensive study. Many of the articles from the earlier edition have been revised and some have been deleted.

*971.   **Cyclopedia of Literary Characters II**. Frank N. Magill, ed. Pasadena, CA: Salem Press, 1990. 4v. ISBN 0-89356-517-2.
    Designed as a companion to *Masterplots II* (entry 980n) in the same manner that the initial issue complemented the original *Masterplots* (entry 980), this work provides treatment of the characters portrayed in all literary works embraced by the *Masterplots II* series since its beginning in 1986 (*American Fiction* [entry 1130], *British and Commonwealth Fiction* [entry 1130n], *World Fiction* [entry 980n], and *Drama* [entry 769]). Also included are a few selected titles from the Short Story series, for a total of 1,437 works with more than 12,000 characters. Format is similar to the initial effort, with articles arranged alphabetically by title of work. Articles provide in-depth coverage, treating characters individually, and pronunciation is given for difficult names. Articles are signed and provide description of the characters' role in plot development and relationship to other characters. Access is available on CD-ROM through *Masterplots II CD-ROM* (entry 980n). The work is indexed by title, author, and character.
    Magill's *Cyclopedia of Literary Characters* (Salem Press, 1963; repr. 1972) was issued in two volumes and treats more than 16,000 characters from the 1,300 novels, dramas, and epics of world literature in the original *Masterplots*. Arrangement is alphabetical by the title of the work and information is given on author, time of action, and date of first publication or presentation.

Characters are described in order of significance. An index by characters and authors facilitates access.

972. Dictionary of Concepts in Literary Criticism and Theory. Wendell V. Harris. New York: Greenwood Press, 1992. (Reference Sources for the Social Sciences and Humanities, no. 12). ISBN 0-313-25932-1.

The author is a well-respected academic and writer who has developed a unique work primarily for scholars and serious students. It complements other work in the field, such as *A Handbook to Literature* (entry 979), in its selectivity in choosing only seventy concepts and then by its depth of analysis in providing exposition of them. Such major concepts in literary criticism as "allusion," "deconstruction," "semiotics," and "imagination" are treated in essays ranging from five to seven pages in length. These include current definition, etymology supported by numerous quotations, annotated references, and a bibliographical essay identifying related sources. The index is detailed and compensates somewhat for the generic organization of the work.

From the same publisher is Leonard Orr's 1991 effort, *A Dictionary of Critical Theory*, providing definitions specific to critical terminology. Terms from all over the world are treated, including those derived from Asian as well as European languages. They represent various schools and thought systems and embrace both general concepts and specific elements of theory. The most likely audiences for the work are scholars and serious students, although the author suggests its utility for undergraduates as well.

973. A Dictionary of Literary Terms and Literary Theory. 3d ed. J. A. Cuddon. Cambridge, MA: Blackwell Reference, 1991. 1051p. ISBN 0-631-17214-9.

First published in 1977 and revised two years later, this detailed dictionary has established itself as a useful source of information for serious students of world literature. The third edition has been expanded to provide more than 2,000 terms from various literary genres and various parts of the world, with more than a dozen foreign languages represented. In this respect, it is more comprehensive than other dictionaries of its type. Especially strong is the coverage of theater and rhetoric. Contemporary theory and critical movements are described. Entries vary in length from a single line to more than ten pages in the case of some survey articles. Literary forms and genres receive detailed exposition treating origin and history, examples from the literature, and important writers. Numerous cross-references link related entries. No bibliographies are furnished.

974. A Dictionary of Modern Critical Terms. rev. and enl. ed. Roger Fowler, ed. New York: Routledge & Kegan Paul/Methuen, 1987; repr. as 2d ed., 1990. 262p. ISBN 0-4150-5884-8.

This is an important and unique work because of the depth of coverage it gives to terms associated with modern literary criticism. Fowler has produced a handbook that is sharply focused on literary criticism and treats in essay-length articles the history and significance of such terms, as well as their relationship to modern criticism. Such topics as poststructuralism, feminist criticism, and Marxist criticism are examined in depth. Originally published in 1973, this edition supplies new essays and has updated the old ones. For more comprehensive coverage (with brief definitions) of literary terms, genres, and authors, it is recommended that the user consult other works listed in this section.

975. Encyclopedia of Literature and Criticism. Martin Coyle et al., eds. Detroit: Gale Research, 1991. 1299p. ISBN 0-8103-8331-4.

This is an important work for scholars and serious students, providing ninety-one well-constructed and erudite essays treating the various concepts and elements of literary criticism. The essays are challenging and provocative and are arranged under ten categories, beginning with introductory essays treating the major issues and nature of literature and of criticism. Following are sections on "Literature and History," describing the development of

Anglo-American literature; "Poetry," "Drama," and "The Novel," treating literary movements and periods with respect to the various genres; "Criticism," providing exposition of the various schools; "Production and Reception," identifying the sociocultural conditions affecting literature, such as censorship, publishing, libraries, etc.; "Contexts," examining literature in relation to the arts; "Perspectives," describing other English literatures (Australian, Canadian, etc.); and finally a provocative afterword. An index provides access.

976. **Encyclopedia of World Literature in the 20th Century.** 2d ed., completely rev. and enl. Leonard S. Klein, gen. ed. New York: Ungar, 1981-1993. 5v. ISBN 0-8044-3135-3(v.1).

Based originally on a German work published in 1960-1961, the first English-language edition of this title appeared in three volumes between 1967 and 1971. This edition represents a thorough revision of the earlier work; approximately 70 percent of the material is new. A strong push toward evenness of entries and uniformity of style, as well as truly international coverage, have produced an extraordinary tool. There are excellent survey articles on national literatures, including Third World countries, but the emphasis is on biographical/critical articles. Critical excerpts and bibliographies are supplied for each person covered, and the variety of international authors treated is truly impressive. The title maintains the tradition and reputation established by the earlier issue. Volume 5 provides survey articles on thirty-five little-researched national literatures, authors, critics, literary movements, and trends and an index to the entire set.

977. **A Glossary of Contemporary Literary Theory.** 2d ed. Jeremy Hawthorn. New York: E. Arnold, 1994. 282p. ISBN 0-340-60185-X.

The appearance of the first edition of this scholarly work in 1992, along with that of Harris (entry 972), bears witness to the increased interest in the field regarding literary theory. Its revision and update only two years later is even more impressive. Hawthorn's effort is in contemporary theory or terminology utilized by critics since 1920. It blends well with the more intensive treatment of major concepts given by Harris, because Hawthorn has provided broad and comprehensive coverage of the modern era. Many of the terms are not found in other literary dictionaries and therefore add to the value of the work. Entries vary in size from a few sentences to several pages on survey topics such as "modernism." They generally define the terms with quotations from the originators and provide reference to sources included in the bibliography at the end. There is no index, but there are numerous cross-references.

Hawthorn's *A Concise Glossary of Contemporary Literary Theory* (Routledge, 1992) is a slimmed-down version of 210 pages providing similar coverage in abridged fashion. Intended for a wider audience beginning at the undergraduate level, the most useful information has remained unaltered; nonessential generic terminology has been deleted.

978. **A Glossary of Literary Terms.** 6th ed. M. H. Abrams. Fort Worth, TX: Holt, Rinehart & Winston, 1993. 301p. ISBN 0-03-054982-5.

The current issue of this established handbook, recognized as an outstanding tool since its initial publication in 1957, the current effort represents a good revision, updating, and slight expansion of material in the fifth edition (1988). It continues the useful added feature of a separate section containing several articles examining important critical movements since the 1920s. There are good illustrations, and a number of references to literary and critical material have been furnished. Rather than a list of entries with definitions, the work is more of a handbook, providing a series of essays bringing together related terms in the body of a textual narrative. There is an alphabetical index at the end to facilitate access to the desired term and related passages. The work is clearly written, comprehensive in coverage, and well developed stylistically and substantively, and is a valuable addition to the reference collection.

979.   **A Handbook to Literature.** 6th ed. Hugh C. Holman and William Harmon. New York: Macmillan, 1992. ISBN 0-02-356420-2.

For more than fifty years students and teachers have relied on this title, originally referred to by the name of its initial author, W. F. Thrall. The new edition follows the established pattern, providing definitions of 1,500 words and phrases important to the study of English and American literature. Entries are arranged alphabetically and vary in length from the briefest of identifications (one line or so) to several pages for the survey articles on movements. Cross-references are furnished between entries. There are a number of new terms and many others show evidence of revision or modification. The well-known and useful feature, the chronological "Outline to Literary History," is still present. Included also are the listings of Nobel and Pulitzer prizes. A new feature is the inclusion of references for many of the entries, indicating from what source the definition or exposition was drawn. This work continues to be a top choice among librarians and their patrons.

The Harper Handbook to Literature, edited by Northrop Frye and others (Harper & Row, 1985), is still regarded as an important tool in defining literary terms in comprehensible fashion. Designed as a supplementary resource for college students, it is valuable to the general public and frequently used at the high school level. A useful feature is the detailed chronology identifying literature and world events from 3500 B.C. to the present.

980.   **Masterplots: Definitive Revised Edition.** Frank N. Magill, ed. Englewood Cliffs, NJ: Salem Press, 1976. 12v. ISBN 0-89356-025-1.

Begun in the late 1940s and early 1950s, this work unfolded in four series over a period of nearly twenty years, covering various forms of literature (fiction, poetry, and essays), at which time it was known as *Masterpieces of World Literature in Digest Form*. Since that time, there have been many spinoffs and variations from Salem Press capitalizing on the popularity and prestige of this work, which was the most highly acclaimed source of plot summaries in the field. It brings together in one multivolume set 1,300 detailed and well-constructed plot summaries included in those first four series, which characteristically provided identification of form, author, period, type of plot, locale, date of first publication, principal characters, themes, and a brief critique. Included in this set are approximately 700 new essay-reviews, which are in-depth, evaluative analyses that have been added to the original coverage. These essay-reviews now characterize the products of Salem Press.

Masterplots Annual Volume appeared from 1954 to 1976, also edited by Magill. It furnished about 100 essay-reviews of outstanding books published in this country. It was succeeded by *Magill's Literary Annual* beginning in 1977, which to date supplies essay-reviews of some 200 new books each year from those appearing in the United States. Another important cumulation from the publisher is *Survey of Contemporary Literature* (rev. ed., 1977) in twelve volumes, furnishing updated reprints of 2,300 essay-reviews from the complete run of *Masterplots Annuals* between 1954 and 1976. It also includes material from the *Survey of Contemporary Literature* supplement **Masterplots II: Short Story Series*, also by Magill (Salem Press, 1986) is a six-volume set describing more than 700 short stories from all over the world. Titles are arranged alphabetically and coverage is given to story, theme, and style as well as setting, major characters, dates, authorship, etc. It is available on CD-ROM through **Masterplots II CD-ROM* (1992), which supplies coverage of thirty-eight volumes from the *Masterplots II* series that also includes American fiction (entry 1130), British and Commonwealth fiction (entry 1130n), world fiction (Salem, 1987), nonfiction (entry 999), drama (entry 769), juvenile and young adult fiction (entry 1238), *Cyclopedia of World Authors II* (entry 991), and **Cyclopedia of Literary Characters II* (entry 971).

981.   **The New Princeton Encyclopedia of Poetry and Poetics.** Alex Preminger and T. V. F. Brogan, eds. Princeton, NJ: Princeton University Press, 1993. 1383p. ISBN 0-691-02123-6.

This work is a major revision and expansion of the *Princeton Encyclopedia of Poetry and Poetics* (Princeton, 1975), which itself was a reissue, with an added supplementary section, of the author's highly regarded *Encyclopedia of Poetry and Poetics* published in

1965. The current effort has revised all previous entries that have been retained and added much new material. More emphasis has been placed on non-Western and Third World poetries, with inclusion of recent scholarship. Individual entries vary in length from descriptions, identifications, or definitions of only a few lines to monographic surveys on the poetry of regions and ethnic groups. The work is the product of some 375 contributors, who have produced a tool to suit a variety of needs ranging from those of the serious student to those of the interested layperson. History, theory, technique, and criticism of poetry are treated from the earliest times to the present. A successful blend of scholarship and lucidity has earned this publication a reputation as a standard work in the past. Its updated focus on such topics as feminist poetics, along with its excellent treatment of poetic traditions, assures its continued status.

Another standard in the field of general poetry is Babette Deutsch's *Poetry Handbook: A Dictionary of Terms* (4th ed., Funk & Wagnalls, 1974). It continues as a useful handbook for the prospective poet, the student, and the general reader. It employs a dictionary arrangement and defines techniques and components of the poetic art through examples of poetry.

982. **Plot Summary Index**. 2d ed. rev. and enl. Carol Koehmstedt Kolar. Metuchen, NJ: Scarecrow Press, 1981. 526p. ISBN 0-8108-1392-0.

A popular tool used to identify location of plot summaries is this index of the contents of 111 reference sources. Literary works of all types are treated and entries are found for summaries of fiction, nonfiction, poetry, and even musical comedy. Emphasis is on American, and then English literature, but coverage is international as long as the synopses are in English. The work is divided into two major sections treating titles and authors. Author entries identify the titles for which plot summaries have been indexed. Title entries supply references to any of the 111 digests, handbooks, and guides containing the summaries. Selection of those tools is somewhat extraordinary in the exclusion of several important and familiar works like the Oxford Companion series in favor of many less common and lesser-known titles. The tool appeals to a wide-ranging audience from serious students to laypersons.

983. **Reginald's Science Fiction and Fantasy Awards: A Comprehensive Guide to the Awards and their Winners**. 3d ed. rev. and exp. Daryl F. Mallett and Robert Reginald. San Bernardino, CA: Borgo Press, 1993. 248p. ISBN 0-80950-200-3.

The present work has increased threefold in size over the initial edition published in 1981, and represents a comprehensive treatment identifying awards and award winners from all over the world. There are two major segments, English and foreign, with the first part covering the United States, Ireland, England, and Canada. The second part identifies foreign-language awards, including those for Japan and Russia as well as European countries. Awards in both segments are listed alphabetically and all winners are listed from the beginning of the award to the time of publication. The awards are described and explained briefly. A third section lists non-genre awards such as the Newbery, American Book, Emmys, and Oscars. Four appendices provide listings of association officers and conventions and indexes of authors and of awards. Also, there are statistical tables identifying outstanding winners.

984. **Science-Fiction, the Early Years: A Full Description of More than 3,000 Science-Fiction Stories ...** Everett F. Bleiler and Richard J. Bleiler. Kent, OH: Kent State University Press, 1990. 998p. ISBN 0-87338-416-4.

Considered by one reviewer to be a "gold mine of detail for researchers," this biocritical work provides excellent and comprehensive coverage along with adequate detail. Some 3,000 science fiction stories "from earliest times to the appearance of the genre magazines in 1930, with author, title, and motif indexes" are proclaimed in the complete title. Treatment is given to short stories, novellas, and novels written in English or in English translation, beginning with ideas represented in Plato's writings; most entries were issued from the seventeenth century on. A fine introductory segment categorizing science fiction motifs and providing historical perspective precedes the text. The stories are arranged alphabetically by author and supply biographical and publication data, extensive plot description, and critical commentary. Numerous indexes provide excellent access by motif, date, publication, title, and author.

BIOGRAPHICAL AND CRITICAL SOURCES

985. **Author Biographies Master Index: A Consolidated Index to More Than 1,030,000 Biographical Sketches.** 4th ed. Barbara McNeil, ed. Detroit: Gale Research, 1994. 2v. ISSN 0741-8655.

This biographical index updates and expands the third edition published in 1989, and now contains nearly 200,000 more citations to biographical sketches than did the previous issue. It represents a massive job, indexing some 300 separate English-language directories and biographical dictionaries in 700 volumes and editions from cover to cover. All time periods and most areas of the world are included, producing a universal index covering all genres as well as children's authors and illustrators. Typical coverage includes name, birth and death dates, and coded references; it is strongest on British and American authors of modern times. The work updates listings from the earlier editions with references to new editions of biographical works. Cross-references are lacking; therefore, a single author may appear in more than one place because of variant forms.

McNeil's *Twentieth Century Author Biographies Master Index: A Consolidated Index to More Than 170,000 Biographical Sketches* (Gale, 1984) is a convenience tool derived from the early editions of the preceding work. It is limited to living authors and those who have died during this century. It appears in paperback and is reasonably priced. Another useful index is Patricia Pate Havlice's *Index to Literary Biography* (Scarecrow Press, 1975) providing references to biographical sketches of nearly 70,000 authors located in fifty collective biographies and literary dictionaries. The first supplement appeared in 1983, identifying 53,000 authors covered in fifty-seven literary dictionaries and biographical sources. Nationality and principal genre are given along with dates and coded references.

986. **Black Literature Criticism: Excerpts from Criticism of the Most Significant Works of Black Authors Over the Past 200 Years.** James P. Draper, ed. Detroit: Gale Research, 1992. 3v. ISBN 0-8103-8574-0.

Designed in the format of Gale's Literary Criticism series, this biocritical tool treats the lives and careers of 125 writers. Eighty-eight of the writers were born in North America, twenty-five in Africa, nine in the Caribbean, two in Martinique, and one in Brazil. There is some question about the selectivity and the selection process in the attempt to treat important writers both established and new, and many omissions have been pointed out by reviewers. Entries are arranged alphabetically and supply normal Gale coverage, beginning with a biographical sketch, followed by listings of principal works, and then a selection of excerpts from critical essays by recognized authorities. These are carefully selected to reveal a broad range of the author's work. There is a photograph along with commentary taken from an interview with the writer. Access is aided by indexes of author, nationality, and title. The work is indexed on CD-ROM through *Gale's Literary Index on CD-ROM* (entry 995).

987. **Caribbean Women Novelists: An Annotated Critical Bibliography.** Lizabeth Paravisini-Gebert and Olga Torres-Seda. Westport, CT: Greenwood Press, 1993. 427p. (Bibliographies and Indexes in World Literature, no. 36). ISBN 0-313-28342-7.

Because of its history of colonial control, the Caribbean region (islands of the Caribbean, Belize, Guyana, and Surinam) reveals linguistic traditions embracing English, French, Dutch, and Spanish, all of which are found among the listings provided for the 150 female authors covered. These writers either were born and raised in the Caribbean or have identified themselves as Caribbean, and have written at least one novel since 1950. Entries are alphabetically arranged by name of writer and provide a biographical sketch and a comprehensive listing of works of all kinds (novels, short stories, poetry, essays, etc.). Novels are annotated. Entries conclude with an annotated listing of critical commentary and reviews. The work opens with a bibliography of general works, and closes with a listing of authors by country; there are indexes by title of novel, critic, and themes/keywords.

988. Contemporary Authors: A Bio-Bibliographical Guide to Current Writers in Fiction, General Non-Fiction, Poetry, Journalism, Drama, Motion Pictures, Television, and Other Fields. Detroit: Gale Research, 1962- . v.1- . ISSN 0010-7468.

The initial series in Gale's massive attempt to keep abreast of biographical coverage of authors in various fields, this work furnishes good biographical sketches of authors from many countries. Personal information, career highlights, previous works as well as those in progress, and sometimes bibliographical references are included in the entries. It generally favors American writers and excludes scientific and technical writers. The work continues, and in 1991 access was enhanced with publication of *Contemporary Authors Cumulative Index: Contemporary Authors Volumes 1-132, Contemporary Authors Revision Series Volumes 1-33*. The work is indexed on CD-ROM through **Gale's Literary Index on CD-ROM* (entry 995).

The *New Revision Series* includes entries from the original series that needed revision; only those entries requiring significant changes are modified. Having begun in 1981, the *New Revision Series* reached its forty-first volume in 1993, and is the favored method of updating the series at present. It replaces the *First Revision Series*, an ill-fated attempt to update whole volumes of the original series begun in 1975 and discontinued after four years and forty-four volumes. Also defunct is the *Permanent Series*, established in 1975 to furnish biographies of deceased personalities and retired individuals removed from the current series. This was discontinued after two volumes. These complicated, expensive, and time-consuming attempts to provide continuous biographical coverage mark Gale as a true leader in biographical publishing. Another contribution is the *Contemporary Authors Autobiography Series*, begun in 1984 and furnishing about twenty autobiographical essays of important creative writers per volume. Volume 18 was issued in 1993; the plan is to include nonfiction writers in subsequent volumes. An annual index to the various series is now issued by the publisher. *Contemporary Authors, Cumulative Index, Volumes 1-140* (1993) indexes entries in *Contemporary Authors, New Revision Series, Permanent Bibliographical Series, Autobiography Series, Something About the Author, Dictionary of Literary Biography*, and more. A recent spinoff is *Major 20th-Century Writers: A Selection of Sketches from Contemporary Authors*, edited by Bryan Ryan (Gale Research, 1991), which gives a selection of biocritical essays culled from the parent work. More than 1,000 well-established and known writers of fiction, poetry, drama, and essay are treated in slightly different format but with the same information provided by *CA*. The work is indexed by nationality and by genre/subject.

989. Contemporary Literary Criticism: Excerpts from Criticism of the Works of Today's Novelists, Poets, Playwrights, Short Story Writers, Scriptwriters, and Other Creative Writers. Detroit: Gale Research, 1973- . v.1- . ISSN 0091-3421.

Around seventy volumes have been issued in this series since its inception in 1973. Presently, it provides selected excerpts from criticism of the work of about twenty-five authors per volume, and is limited to those who are still living or who died after December 31, 1959. There is a heavy emphasis on English-language writers, although others are included if their work is fairly well known in the United States. Almost any authors who have been critiqued are eligible for inclusion; therefore, a good mix of individuals is represented. Each author is treated with about five excerpts taken from books, articles, and reviews. Citations to the source documents are furnished. Each volume contains a cumulative author index covering all CLC volumes as well as twenty-two other Gale series and sets. There is a nationality index which is cumulative to the CLC series and a title index limited to the volume itself. Volume 79 was issued early in 1994. The work is indexed on CD-ROM through **Gale's Literary Index on CD-ROM* (entry 995). *Contemporary Literary Criticism: Annual Cumulative Title Index* is a separately bound publication that can be purchased if desired.

A recent addition to the CLC line is *Contemporary Literary Criticism Yearbook* (Gale, 1985-). The subtitle reads, "The Year in Fiction, Poetry, Drama, and World Literature and the Year's New Authors." The *Yearbook* began in 1985 with coverage of 1984, and was identified as volume 34 of the Contemporary Literary Criticism series. *Yearbook 1993*, published in 1994, is volume 81 in the series. Like other issues in the series, the yearbooks furnish the cumulative index to all author entries in the series. Sections of the yearbook include the year in review, new authors, prize winners, obituaries, literary biography, and literary criticism. There are several essays on the various genres covered during the year and highlights of important activities and developments of notable authors. Critical essays of new writers represent an important contribution to reference work.

990. **Critical Survey of Short Fiction.** Rev. ed. Frank N. Magill. Pasadena, CA: Salem Press, 1993. 7v. ISBN 0-89356-843-0.

This is a revision and expansion of the initial edition published in 1981, and its supplement published in 1987. Although British and American writers are emphasized heavily in this work, non-English-language authors are also covered. The work furnishes nearly 350 articles on major writers (with 65 new entries) and covers the influence, characteristics, and analysis of each individual's work along with biographical information and citations to additional works. All previous entries have been reviewed and revised. These essay-reviews combine both analysis and plot summaries of the short stories, and are characteristic of Magill's efforts at present, unlike *Masterplots* (entry 980), which was primarily concerned with the plot. Volume 7 contains twelve detailed essays on the nature and history of short fiction.

991. **Cyclopedia of World Authors II**. Frank M. Magill, ed. Englewood Cliffs, NJ: Salem Press, 1989. 4v. ISBN 0-89356-512-1.

This is a continuation of the earlier issue described later and provides biographical and critical commentary on 700 authors. With its emphasis on modern writers, there is little overlap with the previous edition and only 20 percent of the previous entries are duplicated and updated. These authors are identified as having continued to publish or having inspired a substantial body of new criticism. Essays run about 1,000 words and are accompanied by a bibliographic narrative describing important secondary sources. In addition, there is a bibliography of the writer's major works divided by genre. The work is considered a companion to *Masterplots II* (entry 980n), as it treats more than 80 percent of the authors included in that series.

Magill's *Cyclopedia of World Authors* was initially published in 1958 and revised as a three-volume publication in 1974. It covers the lives and writings of some 1,000 authors, providing birthplace, dates, biographical sketches from 200 words to 1,000 words, list of works, and references to additional biographical sources.

992. **Detective and Mystery Fiction: An International Bibliography of Secondary Sources**. Walter Albert. Madison, IN: Brownstone Books, 1985. 781p. ISBN 0-941028-02-X.

Albert is an academic who, since 1973, has produced the annual bibliographies of secondary literature for the leading periodical in the field, *The Armchair Detective*. This comprehensive bibliography expands those listings into a four-part coverage identifying more than 3,150 entries. They are numbered consecutively throughout the work. Part 1 provides an annotated listing of eighteen major sources (bibliographies, dictionaries, encyclopedias, and checklists). Part 2 contains annotated listings of 450 books and 850 articles, providing general coverage and treatment. Part 3 lists criticism of dime novels, juvenile mystery series, and pulp magazines. The major segment, Part 4, provides annotated listings of studies of individual writers, with references to treatment in sources listed in Part 1. Collaborators from all over the world contributed to this effort, which accounts for the numerous foreign-language citations. There is an index of authors and one of series characters.

993. **Dictionary of Literary Biography.** Matthew J. Bruccoli et al., eds. Detroit: Gale Research, 1978- . v.1- . ISBN 0-8103-0913-0 (v.1).

A series of consequence, this work was started in 1978 with the purpose of providing information reflecting the changes and scholarship since publication of the *Dictionary of American Biography* (Scribner's, 1928-1937; repr., 1943. 21v.). *DLB* volumes continue to appear with great frequency. Initially, the intent was to cover writers, movements, and periods significant to the literature of the United States, Canada, and England, but in 1987 the focus was extended to include modern European literature (entry 1211n). More recently, the series has issued volumes on modern Spanish poets, modern Italian poets, German writers, Latin-American novelists, Chicano writers, and a first and second offering on modern Caribbean and Black African writers. The present mission is to cover all writers of significance to world literary history. All titles in the series treat a different subject and have different editors, and focus on either a specific period of literary history or a literary movement, beginning with volume 1, *American Renaissance in New England*, by Joel Myerson (1978). Presently, there are some 134 volumes, all of which follow a standard format, with major biocritical essays on the important figures furnishing career chronology, publications list, and bibliography of works by and about the subject. Lesser figures are described in terms of life, work and reputation. The work is indexed on CD-ROM through *Gale's Literary Index on CD-ROM* (entry 995).

The Dictionary of Literary Biography Yearbook (1980-) updates and supplements entries that appeared in any of the volumes, and surveys the year's literary issues and events. There is a section on tributes and obituaries, and a cumulative index to all volumes in the series. *The Dictionary of Literary Biography Documentary Series: An Illustrated Chronicle* (1982-) appears less frequently, but is designed to provide a useful selection of documents, including galley pages, manuscript pages, proofs, and photographs of major literary figures linked to a particular literary movement, period, or genre in each volume. There is a listing of the author's books, as well as relevant biographies, bibliographies, and archival locations. Volume 10 was issued in 1992 and covered the Bloomsbury Group.

994. **European Writers.** George Stade, ed.-in-chief. New York: Scribner's, 1983-1991. 14v. ISBN 0-684-19267-5.

With publication of the last seven volumes, bringing the coverage into the twentieth century, this series was completed. The effort provides lengthy articles on the lives and achievements of European writers, as well as plot descriptions of their works. The essays run about 15,000 words and are written by qualified young scholars, professors emeriti, critics, poets, and novelists. The first two volumes cover the Middle Ages and the Renaissance; volumes 3 and 4 cover the Age of Reason and the Enlightenment. Volumes 5-7 deal with the Romantic century. Volumes 8-13 examine the twentieth century, beginning with Freud and ending with Czech novelist and poet, Milan Kundera, born in 1929. Volumes average about twelve to twenty essay-articles each. They are arranged chronologically and are clearly written. There is a good overview of the periods covered in volume 1 by the late editor, William T. H. Jackson of Columbia University. Volume 14 is an index to the set, and furnishes access by name, birthdate, and language. It contains a general bibliography arranged by time period and nationality.

*995. **Gale's Literary Index on CD-ROM**. Detroit: Gale Research, 1993- . Ann. ISSN 1066-7709. (CD-ROM).

Beginning in February 1993, Gale Research issued a master index to every one of its literary series on a single CD-ROM disc. At the time, this comprised 675 volumes and 32 titles. It is projected as a serial publication to provide needed updates on an annual basis. Such important works as the *Dictionary of Literary Biography* (entry 993), *Contemporary Authors* (entry 988), *Black Literature Criticism* (entry 986), *Nineteenth Century Literature Criticism* (entry 1000), and *Contemporary Literary Criticism* (entry 989) are now easily accessed and searched using the well-designed and user-friendly searching system. This permits one to search by author or title, then print or download the search results. Advanced techniques permit searching by nationality and dates of birth and death. The database contains more than 110,000 authors and 120,000 titles dating from antiquity to the present day. Libraries are able to tag holdings, providing the user with instant awareness of availability of volumes.

996. **International Authors and Writers Who's Who.** 13th ed. Ernest Kay, ed. Cambridge, UK: International Biographical Centre; distr., Detroit: Gale Research, 1993. 1004p. ISSN 0143-8263.

The thirteenth edition follows the pattern established in the earlier editions and represents a useful and predictable source of information. At its high point, the eighth edition carried 14,000 writers, whereas the ninth edition provided 9,600 entries. The current effort, like its predecessor, treats about 8,000 writers, including journalists and magazine editors. There is heavy emphasis on English and American writers. Entries generally provide place and date of birth, profession, education, major publications, and address, although there is some variation in completeness of information supplied. Appendices supply listings of literary agents, organizations, and award winners.

997. **Literary Criticism Index.** 2d ed. Alan R. Weiner and Spencer Means. Metuchen, NJ: Scarecrow Press, 1994. 559p. ISBN 0-8108-2665-8.

This index was initially issued in 1984 to fill a need for access to the vast number of bibliographies and checklists of criticism that have multiplied in recent decades. It provides references to these bibliographies rather than to critical studies directly. The current effort continues the pattern of coverage through its indexing of more than eighty guides that treat bibliographies of criticism, and is arranged by author of the creative work. One would look up an author and be referred to a checklist of bibliographies that contains references to critical studies of that author's work. Under the author's name are listed general works followed by entries for criticism of individual titles. This represents a useful tool for those in need of such information.

998. **Literature Criticism from 1400 to 1800: Excerpts from Criticism of the Works of Fifteenth, Sixteenth, Seventeenth and Eighteenth Century Novelists, Poets, Playwrights ...** Dennis Poupard, ed. Mark W. Scott, assoc. ed. Detroit: Gale Research, 1984- . ISSN 0740-2880.

Another series from Gale, this one serves as a complement to the three others covering the nineteenth and twentieth centuries (entries 989, 1000, and 1011). Each volume of this series covers between seven and nine individuals from nations all over the world, along with one topical entry on a major theme or issue. Volume 1 appeared in 1984; volume 23 was issued in 1993. Such writers as Henry Fielding, Confucius, James Boswell, and St. Augustine are treated in terms of the critical response given to their work. Entries are arranged alphabetically within each volume and critical comments are furnished, beginning with the views of the authors' contemporary critics and proceeding to modern-day reviews. It is useful to see the trend in critical acceptance or rejection and the relationship to time periods. Citations are given to the sources and there is a bibliography of additional references for each author. A cumulative index includes all entries from any of the titles in this series.

999. **Masterplots II: Non-Fiction Series.** Frank M. Magill. Englewood Cliffs, NJ: Salem Press, 1989. 4v. ISBN 0-89356-478-8.

This is the fifth set offered in the *Masterplots II* series designed to complement the original *Masterplots* issue. *Nonfiction* embraces a variety of works, such as autobiography and memoirs of important literary figures, essays, and monographs. Various subjects are treated, such as philosophy, literary theory, linguistics, sociology, and culture. Most of the works were published in the English language or, if foreign, have been issued in English translation. A total of 318 works are covered, with contributions from a diverse group like Marshall McLuhan, G. K. Chesterton, and William Buckley. Entries are arranged alphabetically by title and supply author, title, and date along with a three-page summary or overview treating origin, structure and content, analysis of major themes, ideas and motifs, and historical/critical context. A short bibliography of secondary sources completes the entry.

The tool is indexed by author, by title, and by type of work. The work is available on CD-ROM through *Masterplots II CD-ROM* issued in 1992.

1000. Nineteenth Century Literature Criticism: Excerpts from Criticism of the Works of Novelists, Poets, Playwrights, Short Story Writers ... Detroit: Gale Research, 1981- . ISSN 0732-1864.

Following the same plan as Gale's three other series, which complement the coverage given here (entries 989, 998, and 1011), this work treats authors who died during the nineteenth century. All types of creative writers from Europe, Great Britain, and the United States are included. Each volume covers the works of from eight to fourteen different writers, with every fourth volume devoted to topics rather than individual authors. In 1993, the series reached volume 41. Entries furnish a brief biographical introduction, bibliography of works published, excerpts from the critics, and a suggested reading list for further inquiry. The brief excerpts of critical studies are well chosen and expressive of the critic's thoughts, and adequately convey the sense of the critique. Excerpts are arranged chronologically, beginning with contemporary criticism and proceeding to modern thinking. The first volume each year contains a cumulative title index to the entire series, and the last volume of the year has annual topic, nationality, and author indexes. The work is indexed on CD-ROM through *Gale's Literary Index on CD-ROM* (entry 995).

1001. Poetry Criticism: Excerpts from Criticism of the Works of the Most Significant and Widely Studied Poets of World Literature. Robyn V. Young. Detroit: Gale Research, 1991- . v.1- . ISSN 1052-4851.

With publication of volume 1, the publisher begins another series of literary criticism treating world writers both ancient and modern. This effort has progressed through 1992 and 1993 and now offers seven volumes in two series. It targets English-language poets, although foreign-language poets who have been widely studied and translated into English are also included. Each volume treats some twelve to fifteen major poets. Entries supply an introductory biographical sketch and description of the author's important works. This follows listings of critical analysis with excerpts of commentary concerning major poems. Entries conclude with a brief bibliography of secondary sources for further reading. Volume 1 contains coverage of thirteen poets including Auden, Dickinson, Donne, Ferlinghetti, Frost, Plath, and Poe; subsequent volumes treat Robert Browning, Whitman, Rimbaud, and Garcia Lorca. Cumulative indexes provide access by poet, title, and nationality.

1002. Popular World Fiction, 1900-Present. Walton Beacham and Suzanne Niemeyer. Washington, DC: Beacham, 1987. 4v. ISBN 0-933833-08-3.

Designed as a companion work to *Beacham's Popular Fiction in America* (entry 1134), this biocritical tool treats nearly 180 authors not included in the previous effort. Emphasis is on American and British writers who have achieved during the twentieth century, although other parts of Europe are represented as well. The criterion again is a test of "popularity" or best-selling status, which will invite criticism for its omission of Danielle Steele, Georgette Heyer, and Kurt Vonnegut. Entries supply a brief publishing history along with an overview of the author's critical reception. Analytical commentary is given regarding themes, techniques, and adaptations of the works chosen, along with a list of related titles by the author. Arrangement is alphabetical by name of author. Appendices list titles by social issues and themes; there are indexes by genre and by author-title.

1003. Postmodern Fiction: A Bio-Bibliographical Guide. Larry McCaffery, ed. Westport, CT: Greenwood Press, 1986. 604p. ISBN 0-313-24170-8.

Postmodernism, according to the author, is generally meant to embrace those writers who have established their careers since the 1960s. This places the guide in a unique position in terms of its focus on relatively recent individuals and their works. Most checklists and bibliographies have a much greater time span, and pay little attention to the postmoderns. A variety of writers are treated, ranging from genre specialists, such as Günter Grass, and Latin American contributors like Gabriel García Marquez, to a number of critics and contributors to popular magazines. Part 1 provides 15 general articles analyzing the modes of postmodern fiction and criticism; part 2 furnishes more than 100 biocritical descriptions of individual writers. Also included is a bibliography of additional readings on postmodern criticism.

1004. **Science Fiction and Fantasy Reference Index, 1878-1985: An International Author and Subject Index to History and Criticism**. H. W. Hall, ed. Detroit: Gale Research, 1987. 2v. ISBN 0-8103-2129-7. **Supp. 1985-1991**. Englewood, CO: Libraries Unlimited, 1993. 677p. ISBN 1-56308-113-X.

This is a comprehensive index to expository, descriptive, and evaluative writings on science fiction, as well as fantasy, horror, supernatural, and weird. About 19,000 books, articles, essays, audiovisual items, and news items are identified, dating from an early work treating Jules Verne in 1878 to the mid-1980s. Most of the writings were published between 1945 and 1985, with the great majority being in the English language. Treatment of European writings is more selective or representative than it is comprehensive. A total of 43,000 author and subject references are provided for the 19,000 works. The recent supplementary volume, also edited by Hall, contains some 16,250 new citations representing publications for an additional six years.

Initially the work was derived from the coverage provided in the editor's *Science Fiction and Fantasy Research Index* annuals between 1980 and 1984 and his *Science Fiction Index* published in 1980. Volume 1 supplies introductory material, a list of sources, and an author index. Volume 2 provides a subject index, along with a thesaurus.

1005. **Selected Black American, African, and Caribbean Authors: A Bio-Bibliography**. James A. Page and Jae Min Roh, comps. Littleton, CO: Libraries Unlimited, 1985. 388p. ISBN 0-87287-430-3.

This convenient and useful volume identifies the work of nearly 650 writers of African descent, the primary focus being on the Afro-American literature of the United States. Included also are some representative figures of the mother continent and also some from the Caribbean. To be included, an author must have had at least one book published and must have been covered in collective works or handbooks. Poets must have had more than one book of poems published; playwrights must have had at least one play published or performed; and essayists must have produced a body of works in the arts, biography, criticism, history, and so on. The arrangement of entries is alphabetical by author and each entry furnishes dates, places of birth and death, family, education, address, career information, list of works, comments on career, and a list of sources.

1006. **Short Story Writers and Their Work: A Guide to the Best**. 2d ed. Brad Hooper. Chicago: American Library Association, 1992. 70p. ISBN 0-8389-0587-0.

The second edition retains the diminutive size of the earlier effort in being well under 100 pages in length. Coverage is given to more than 100 short story writers chosen by the author for their importance. Both American and foreign and male and female writers are included. The work is useful in its critical assessment not of individual works, but of the body of a writer's effort. The analysis for each writer is cogent and describes the style, thematic influences, and settings. In addition, there is an assessment of the work and of the writer's impact or influence on the literary world. The tool is divided into different parts, the first treating the early masters of the nineteenth century, the second covering living masters. There is a brief segment on genre writers as well.

1007. **Supernatural Fiction Writers: Fantasy and Horror**. E. F. Bleiler, ed. New York: Scribner's, 1985. 2v. ISBN 0-684-17808-7.

This important biocritical reference tool provides coverage of nearly 150 writers from ancient times to the present. Although not all are well-known, the editor and his sixty-one contributor-scholars have selected them for their influence. Entries provide biographical sketches emphasizing the subject's output and contributions to the supernatural, along with a selective bibliography. The result is the most comprehensive work to date on writers in this distinctive genre; in the case of well-known personalities who have written in other areas, only the supernatural writings are considered. Emphasis is definitely on Anglo-American literature, with only limited coverage given to early French and German authors. Arrangement of entries is primarily by period. The work opens with an introductory essay examining the typology of supernatural fiction and identifies the criteria for inclusion. A general bibliography and general index conclude the work.

1008. **Survey of Modern Fantasy Literature.** Frank N. Magill, ed. Englewood Cliffs, NJ: Salem Press, 1983. 5v. ISBN 0-89356-450-8.

Responding to the obvious need for a work of this type for the genre of fantasy fiction, Salem Press has marshalled its considerable expertise and resources to provide an important and popular product. Fantasy literature includes both high and low fantasy, fairy tales, folklore, and horror dating from Victorian times to the present. Included here are 500 representative works of European and American authors for which are furnished essay-reviews of approximately 1,000 to 3,000 words, depending upon the work's significance. Entries include brief author information, date of book publication, type of work, time period, locale, brief description of essay-review, plot, and bibliography.

An earlier product of the publisher was Magill's *Survey of Science Fiction Literature* (1979), also in five volumes. It follows the same pattern and format in furnishing in-depth analyses of 515 world-famous science fiction novels. Annotated bibliographies are supplied for nearly 300 titles.

1009. **Twentieth Century Authors: A Biographical Dictionary of Modern Literature ...** Stanley J. Kunitz and Howard Haycraft. New York: H. W. Wilson, 1942; repr., 1985. 1578p. ISBN 0-8242-0049-7. **Supp.** 1955. 1123p; repr. with updated necrology, 1990. 1126p. ISBN 0-8242-0050-0.

This is the original "old favorite" for identifying modern authors, a product of the Wilson Company that commissioned Kunitz to develop a line of biographical dictionaries. They were all highly stylized, bearing a portrait and providing bibliographies of the author's work, along with a brief biography highlighting the career. This particular tool treated writers of all nations whose books are familiar to English-language readers. A supplement appeared in 1955 by Kunitz and Vineta Colby.

Kunitz and Colby later collaborated in producing *European Authors 1000-1900* (H. W. Wilson, 1967). This was done in the same general manner. Subsequently, in 1975, the publisher produced *World Authors, 1950-1970*, edited by John Wakeman. This neither duplicated nor updated the main work, but provided biographical sketches of nearly 1,000 additional authors of literary importance or unusual popularity. Continuing in this vein are additional publications: *World Authors, 1970-1975*, edited by Wakeman (1980); *World Authors, 1975-1980*, edited by Vineta Colby (1985); and *World Authors, 1980-1985*, also edited by Colby (1991). Each of the five-year volumes furnishes sketches of more than 300 authors. A useful tool is *Index to the Wilson Authors Series* (rev. ed., H. W. Wilson, 1991), which furnishes quick access to entries in all the volumes mentioned here.

1010. **Twentieth-Century Caribbean and Black African Writers. First Series.** Bernth Lindfors and Reinhard Sander, eds. Detroit: Gale Research, 1992. 406p. (Dictionary of Literary Biography, v.117). ISBN 0-8103-7594-X. **Second Series.** 1993. 443p. ISBN 0-8103-5384-9.

These two volumes cover black writers of Africa and the Caribbean as part of the *DLB* series (entry 993). Similar to other bio-bibliographies in the series, there are separate chapters on thirty-four modern writers, all individually authored. These are arranged alphabetically and treat the lives and careers of African and Caribbean authors. Included here are such well-known and important writers as Jean Rhys, Derek Walcott, and Wole Soyinka, along with the less familiar Richard Rive and Nuruddin Farah. Chapters begin with a bibliography of the writer's works and follow with an essay, ranging in length from four to twenty-three pages, describing the writer's career. A photograph is included along with illustrations of dust jackets and manuscript pages, as are a bibliography of published interviews and critical writings about each author's work. A cumulative index is supplied to this and other works in the *DLB* series. Another volume is planned for white South African writers.

1011. **Twentieth-Century Literary Criticism: Excerpts from Criticism of the Works of Novelists, Poets, Playwrights, Short-story Writers ...** Dennis Poupard, ed. Detroit: Gale Research, 1978- . ISSN 0276-8178.
    The subtitle goes on to indicate that the authors treated had lived (and died) between 1900 and 1960. This complements the coverage of *Contemporary Literary Criticism* (entry 989), for which the major focus is on living authors, and fits nicely with the two other Gale series dealing with the nineteenth century (entry 1000) and earlier centuries (entry 998). Each author entry provides a portrait, an in-depth bibliography, a bibliography of principal work, and, most importantly, a selection of excerpts of literary criticism arranged chronologically from the time of publication of the work to the most recent efforts. Fifteen authors generally are covered in each volume of this continuing publication, with every fourth volume devoted to topics rather than authors. Coverage of entries varies in length from ten to more than thirty pages. Volume 50 was issued in 1993. Like its companion titles, the last volume of the year contains annual topic, nationality, and author indexes; the first volume of the year has a cumulative title index to the whole series.

1012. **World Literature Criticism 1500 to the Present: A Selection of Major Authors from Gale's Literary Criticism Series**. James P. Draper, ed. Detroit: Gale Research, 1992. 6v. ISBN 0-8103-8361-6.
    From the publisher of the classic Literary Criticism series comes this set providing somewhat abbreviated coverage of 231 major dramatists, poets, novelists, and essayists from all over the world. These were selected by a panel of high school teachers and public and high school librarians as those most frequently studied in high school or college curricula. Such luminaries as Hans Christian Andersen, Jane Austen, Gertrude Stein, and Edgar Allen Poe are treated in entries arranged alphabetically by author. Special emphasis has been given to modern writers of European and U.S. origin, although Mexico, Africa, Argentina, New Zealand, and Colombia are represented. Entries supply portraits, biocritical sketches, list of major works with indication of films or adaptations, representative excerpts of critical studies, and bibliography of additional reading. Author, title, and nationality indexes provide access.

WRITERS' GUIDES AND DIRECTORIES

1013. **Fiction Writers Guidelines: Over 260 Periodical Editors' Instructions Reproduced and Indexed**. 2d ed. Judy Mandell, comp. and ed. Jefferson, NC: McFarland, 1992. 337p. ISBN 0-89950-673-9.
    Designed to expedite the process of writing for publication, this guide has established an excellent reputation since its first edition in 1988. The second edition retains the format of the original in its treatment of some 250 periodicals of all types. Included here are general-purpose magazines, literary magazines, and children's periodicals of all sizes and degrees of popularity and importance, as well as a selection of pornographic titles. Entries are arranged alphabetically and supply reprinted guidelines for publication in each magazine. Instructions regarding format, type of manucript, rate of payment, and availability of sample copies are presented in easy-to-read fashion. Reader characteristics are included in some cases. One might wish for more description of content that would be useful to teachers and students as well as writers. A comprehensive index provides access in detailed fashion.

Writer's Yearbook: Your Guide to Getting Published This Year, begun in 1930 by Writer's Digest Books, is an annual, enlarged version of *Writer's Digest* magazine, with a number of feature articles and lists of publishing events for the preceding year. Features generally emphasize important aspects of selling one's writing to publishers and editors. *Writer's Digest*, the monthly magazine, started in 1920 and provides information, advice, tips, and techniques of both writing and selling.

1014.   **Grants and Awards Available to American Writers**. 17th ed. New York: PEN American Center, 1992. 163p. ISBN 0-934638-11-X.

This biennial publication provides awareness of hundreds of grants and support funds for writers to help them continue their writing and to develop their careers. The seventeenth edition treats the period of 1992-1993, and covers various categories such as fiction, poetry, drama, journalism, general nonfiction, and children's literature, not only in the United States but also in Canada and other countries. In most cases, the awards provide cash stipends of $500 or more or result in publication of a manuscript or production of a play. Residencies providing room and board are also included. Entries supply information regarding purpose of grant, nature of the award, eligibility, application procedure, deadlines, and contact person. Arrangement is alphabetical by keywords derived from the name of the granting organization. Appendices supply listings of arts councils; the work is indexed by award and by organization.

1015.   **Literary Market Place: The Directory of the American Book Publishing Industry with Industry Yellow Pages**. New York: R. R. Bowker, 1940- . Ann. ISSN 0075-9899.

LMP is the most well known and frequently used directory of its type on the market. It provides up-to-date listings of organizations, periodicals, and some 2,700 publishing houses, with officers and key personnel, all of which are involved in the placing, promotion, and marketing of literary property. A variety of topical headings are used, including book publishing, book clubs, associations, book trade events, conferences and contests, agents, etc. *LMP 1991* (1990) utilizes eight major sections embracing all the categories. A useful alphabetical listing of names is accompanied by addresses and telephone numbers, as well as references to pages in the directory.

*Writer's Electronic Bulletin Board, issued by WEBB of Branson, Missouri, furnishes online access of certain marketing information provided by *LMP*, along with *Publisher's Weekly*, *Writer's Monthly*, and others. Listings of literary agents, editors, and publishers are supplied along with writing tips, literary announcements, services, and clubs.

1016.   **1994 Guide to Literary Agents & Art/Photo Reps**. Kirsten C. Holm, ed. Cincinnati, OH: Writer's Digest Books, 1994. 284p. ISSN 1055-6087.

First published in 1991 and bearing the 1992 date in the title, this serial publication provides listings of agents and representatives in the United States and Canada. Agents listed here represent authors, artists, or photographers to publishers and purchasers. The format is similar to other *Writer's Digest* publications and opens with several introductory essays about literary agents relative to their activity, selection, and responsibilities to their clients. The work is divided into sections treating fee and non-fee literary agents, script agents, commercial art and photography representatives, and fine art representation. More than 500 agents and representatives are treated, with coverage given to date of inception of agency, member agents, areas of interest, conferences attended, etc. There is a glossary and several indexes.

The West Coast is not treated as thoroughly in the preceding work as it is in *Literary Agents of North America*, which in its fourth edition (Author Aid/Research Associates International, 1991) identifies and provides excellent detail on more than 1,000 literary agents. Initially published in 1984, the work has changed from an annual to triennial publication and concentrates on literary agents in the U.S. and Canadian market.

1017. **Novel and Short Story Writer's Market.** Cincinnati, OH: Writer's Digest Books, 1989- . Ann. ISSN 0897-9812.

Replacing the publisher's previous annual guide, *Fiction Writer's Market*, begun in 1981, this work has been recognized as one of the most comprehensive and thorough in terms of its full treatment of the market for its audience. Several thousand markets have been identified by excellent descriptive entries describing the interests, needs, methods of payment, terms of agreement, and preferred formats when applicable. The 1992 edition supplies an additional 300 new markets, along with extensive updating of previously reported information. There are new listings for conferences and workshops, retreats and colonies, and others to go along with the various indexes that continue to provide access in a variety of ways to the periodicals, publishing houses, organizations, and other units treated. There are introductory essays and profiles of selected publishers and authors.

From the same publisher is *Mystery Writer's Marketplace and Sourcebook*, edited by Donna Collingwood and Robin Gee, initiated in 1993. It represents a specialized source of information for writers of a particular genre. Included are sections on the trends, literary agents, organizations, conventions, contests, awards, glossary, and so on. Marketing information is up-to-date. Indexing is thorough and provides access by twenty categories of mysteries sought.

1018. **Poet's Market: Where & How to Publish Your Poetry.** Cincinnati, OH: Writer's Digest Books, 1986- . Ann. ISSN 0883-5470.

One of the few guides focusing on the needs of the poet, the intention of this work is to help serious poets find the right outlets and derive appropriate rewards for their labor. The ninth annual edition of this work (1994) covers more than 1,700 lisitings of various media of interest to poets for publishing their work. Included here are small-circulation literary journals, mass-circulation magazines, and book publishers, both small press and trade. The editors supply a code to identify what might be the most receptive houses and identify specialties. Additionally, there are listings of greeting card companies, writing colonies, and poets' organizations. The contents are accessed through indexes of various types, including geographic region and subject.

1019. **The Writer's Handbook.** Boston: The Writer, 1936- . Ann. ISSN 0084-2710 (1994).

The fifty-eighth issue of this standard work ("New 1994 Edition"), like earlier volumes, provides a number of essays and articles covering the art, craft, technique, and business of writing for publication, with contributions from significant (popular) authors. Both the writing scene in general and more specialized phases or areas are treated in more than 100 chapters authored by literary agents and writers. Covered are various forms of writing: fiction, nonfiction, poetry, drama and television, and juvenile and young adult areas. Business practices are also described. Possibly the most important feature is the market guide, which covers in up-to-date fashion some 2,500 markets or potential outlets for publication, including magazine articles with various subject emphases; fiction outlets; poetry; college, literary, and little magazines; humor; juvenile; etc. Prizes, organizations, and agents are also treated.

A similar tool, although not an annual, has been *Writer's Encyclopedia*, edited by Kirk Polking and others (Writer's Digest Books, 1986). It furnishes definitions and exposition of business practices, organizations, and general advice for writers. The emphasis is on print publishing, but radio and television are also covered, as are advertising, songwriting, etc. Most useful is the appendix segment, with numerous entries furnishing samples of writing projects and identifying pay rates. The revised edition now appears as *Writing A to Z: The Terms, Procedures, and Facts of the Writing Business.*

1020. **Writer's Market: Where & How to Sell What You Write.** Cincinnati, OH: Writer's Digest Books, 1922- . Ann. ISSN 0084-2729.

This is a no-nonsense, no-frills, let's-get-to-the-business-of-selling-your-work type of tool. In contrast to *Writer's Handbook* (entry 1019), which provides some 100 essays on the craft, art, inherent worth, and personal experiences of writing, *Writer's Market* treats issues of authors' rights, negotiation with publishers and editors, and dealing with agents. The coverage of the markets is detailed as compared to the brief one to two lines offered for each entry in the *Handbook*. The audience, as one might expect, is a more veteran group of writers who no longer need the type of inspirational push provided by the *Handbook*. Access is furnished through several indexes.

A useful manual is *Writer's Resource Guide*, edited by Bernadine Clark (2d ed., Writers Digest Books, 1983). Unlike the host of tools developed to aid writers in the marketing of their craft, this one functions as a manual of execution. The question of researching topics is covered in several chapters and involves such considerations as the library as a research tool, government information sources, researching fiction, finding experts, and conducting interviews. Towards this end, there are a number of articles consisting of interviews with knowledgeable authors and writers. A large segment of the work is divided into research areas or topics such as philosophy and religion. It furnishes bibliographic information for further reading, and lists and describes organizations and clubs in terms of their services and practices. There are separate title and subject indexes.

QUOTATIONS AND PROVERBS

1021. The Columbia Granger's Dictionary of Poetry Quotations. Edith P. Hazen, ed. New York: Columbia University, 1992. 1132p. ISBN 0-231-07546-4.

A reference work derived from the 400 anthologies reviewed for the ninth edition of *Columbia Granger's Index* (entry 1151) is this new quotation book. Selections or quotations are chosen by eight English professors from the 4,000 poems most anthologized in the *Index*. The work opens with a selection from anonymous or unknown poets, alphabetically arranged by title. This is followed by treatment of some 700 alphabetically arranged poets with their poems alphabetically arranged by title. Emphasis is on English-language poetry from all time periods; various countries are represented. This title aids identification of poems and poets through memorable lines from within the poem and complements the first-line access employed by the *Index*. There are subject and keyword indexes.

Victoria Kline's *Last Lines: An Index to the Last Lines of Poetry* (Facts on File, 1991) further complements the identification of poetry with a two-volume treatment of the last lines found in poetry taken from 497 anthologies published between 1900 and 1987. Most are English or American in origin, although foreign poetry in English translation is included. The work is indexed by author and keyword.

1022. A Dictionary of American Proverbs. Wolfgang Mieder et al., eds. New York: Oxford University Press, 1992. 710p. ISBN 0-19-505399-0.

Field work for this tool began in the 1940s with a committee of the American Dialect Society and input from numerous scholars and folklorists who began systematic collection of proverbs and expressions. By the 1980s, some 150,000 examples had been collected and Mieder was appointed editor to do the selection. The total was narrowed down to some 15,000 proverbs by rigorously defining the *proverb* as a "concise statement of an apparent truth which has currency among people." The application of "apparent truth" rather than valid argument is meaningful in that many of the racially or gender-based proverbs are offensive and illogical. Entries have had common usage in the United States and Canada, and may include variant proverbs, historical or interpretative commentary, locations, citations to published sources, and cross-references. A bibliography is provided. Arrangement is alphabetical by keyword from the proverb.

1023. Familiar Quotations: A Collection of Passages, Phrases, and Proverbs Traced Back to Their Sources in Ancient and Modern Literature. 16th ed. rev. and enl. John Bartlett. Ed. by Justin Kaplan. Boston: Little, Brown, 1992. 1405p. ISBN 0-316-08277-5.

This is the standard work of its kind; most searches for quotations or imperfectly remembered lines of poetry begin with Bartlett. The first edition of this landmark title appeared in 1855, and it has been a fixture in libraries ever since. New editions are issued on the average of every seven to ten years, and each one generally adds contemporary authors to the coverage. The sixteenth edition retains the chronological arrangement of authors quoted, " a wonderfully eccentric way to organize a book" according to its new editor, an award-winning biographer of both Clemens and Whitman. Of the new sources quoted, forty-five are women and eighteen are black, in Kaplan's attempt to provide a better cross-section for purposes of representation. Among the new entries are Norman Mailer, Bernard Malamud, Philip Roth, a Burma Shave jingle, and the Watson and Crick paper on DNA. As always, the Bible and Shakespeare remain the leading sources of quotations. There is an author index, but most important for this tool (and others like it) is the detailed concordance index by keyword.

1024.　**The New Penguin Dictionary of Quotations**. J. M. Cohen and M. J. Cohen. Rev. and exp. ed. London: Viking Press, 1992. 726p. ISBN 0-670-82952-8.

　　Initially developed in 1960 by a father-and-son team, the new edition still bears the name of the father, J. M. Cohen, although he died in 1989 shortly before its completion. The elder Cohen was a well-known editor, anthologist, and translator of quotations and, with his expertise in Spanish, was able to translate quotations from the Spanish language. This expanded edition has increased the coverage of modern authors, and there is judicious selection of quotations with the potential to survive. For the great body of known or traditional quotations dating from the Bible and classical period, the authors have relied on previously published works in the field, especially *The Oxford Dictionary of Quotations* (entry 1027). Arrangement is similar to that of the *Oxford* in placing the quotations under the names of the authors, who are alphabetically sequenced. A subject index provides access.

1025.　**The New Quotable Woman**. Rev. and upd. ed. Elaine Partnow, comp. and ed. New York: Facts on File, 1992. 714p. ISBN 0-8160-2134-1.

　　This work has been revised, altered, and expanded on several occasions since the initial publication of two volumes in 1977-1980. Quotations attributed to women between 1800 and 1899 are identified in volume 1; quotations from 1900-1975 are in volume 2. In 1982, two volumes were issued, the first treating the period "From Eve to 1799" and the second from "1800-1981." This revised and updated effort combines and updates the contents of those two volumes and adds 105 new personalities. There is a greater emphasis on cultural diversity and the words of contemporary world leaders are given more exposure. Some 300 quotations have been added, to reach a total of 15,000 chronologically sequenced quotations from about 2,500 women representing all times and locales. There is excellent access with two new indexes by occupation and by nationality/ethnicity joining the subject and biographical indexes.

1026.　**The Oxford Dictionary of English Proverbs**. 3d ed. Rev. by F. P. Wilson. Oxford: Clarendon Press, 1970; repr. 1982. 930p. ISBN 0-19-866131-2.

　　It is difficult to imagine many libraries providing services in language and literature that do not have this important title. It is generally a first choice when searching for proverbs in the English language, with the emphasis, of course, being on the language as employed by Britons. The first edition appeared in 1935 and contained about 10,000 proverbs; since then, the coverage has increased somewhat and there have been slight changes in arrangement. The present edition contains more proverbs than supplied by the second edition, but also includes material from the first edition which had been deleted from the second. Each proverb is dated, with references to its use in the literature from its beginning and subsequent changes of meaning identified.

　　Many of the proverbs are treated in Morris P. Tilley's *Dictionary of the Proverbs in England in the Sixteenth and Seventeenth Centuries* ... (University of Michigan Press, 1950; repr., AMS Press, 1982). The subtitle goes on to say " A Collection of the Proverbs found in English Literature and the Dictionaries of the Period."

*1027. **The Oxford Dictionary of Quotations.** 4th ed. Angela Partington, ed. New York: Oxford University Press, 1992. 1061p. ISBN 0-19-866185-1.

First published in 1941, this has been an important reference tool over the years. Proverbs and nursery rhymes are excluded because they are covered in other Oxford publications (entries 1026 and 1241). The title provides a comprehensive listing of more than 17,500 quotations, all of which are arranged alphabetically. Sources of the quotations are more than 2,500 authors of every description (poets, novelists, playwrights, public figures, etc., both English-language and foreign), as well as the Bible and Prayer Book. Also included are quotes from anonymous authors. Indexing is excellent, although possibly not as detailed as in certain earlier editions. Approximately 70,000 entries are contained in the index, for which there is an indication of the author's name along with a page reference. Retained from earlier editions is a separate Greek index. It has been available online through DIALOG, and in 1993 a disk version was issued that provides electronic access for both PC and Mac to both this work and its companion volume.

The Oxford Dictionary of Modern Quotations, edited by Tony Augarde (Oxford University Press, 1991), furnishes some 5,000 quotations from a variety of sources, including song and motion picture titles. *Modern* is interpreted to be twentieth-century in status and quotes have originated from persons alive after 1900. Format and arrangement are similar to the work cited previously, with sources listed alphabetically. As in the major work, quotations are documented with references to printed sources, an essential characteristic for serious students and researchers. It is available on disk as *Oxford English Reference Library (Oxford, 1992).

1028. **Writers on Writing.** Jon Winokur. Philadelphia: Running Press, 1990. 372p. ISBN 0-89471-877-0.

From a compact little volume of 160 pages in its 1986 edition, this collection of quotations of writers on the art and practice of writing has more than doubled its size. Its primary audience is still the teachers and students of literature from high school to college level. More than 2,000 quotations are classified under broad topics such as plagiarism. The claim is that the work results from twenty years of compulsive collecting in this area. It is a most pleasurable and interesting experience in gaining insight into writers' experience with frustration and their development of stylistic techniques.

Another of the books in this vein, now in its third edition, is *The Writer's Quotation Book: A Literary Companion*, edited by James Charlton (Pushcart Press, 1991). First appearing in 1980, the present edition represents an expansion to several hundred quotations. These treat all aspects of literary production: writing, publishing, editing, and so on. Reference use of the new edition has been enhanced by the inclusion of an index.

Literature in English

BIBLIOGRAPHIC GUIDES

1029. **A Reference Guide for English Studies**. Michael J. Marcuse. Berkeley, CA: University of California Press, 1990. 790p. ISBN 0-520-05161-0.

One of the two important research tools covering both print and computerized sources in American and English literature is this guide to more than 2,700 entries arranged under twenty-four subject sections. These sections treat all periods and genres and supply well-developed descriptive and evaluative annotations of the important reference sources in the field. Designed to meet the needs of advanced students, the work explains use, content, and special features, and identifies complementary tools and related sources. Also furnished are unannotated listings of scholarly journals and of background titles. The work is accessed through detailed indexes of authors, titles, and subjects.

The other important tool is James L. Harner's *Literary Research Guide: A Guide to Reference Sources for the Study of Literatures in English and Related Topics*, now in its second edition (Modern Language Association of America, 1993). The first edition was issued in 1990 as a replacement for the second edition of Margaret Patterson's effort, published in 1984. This work, like Marcuse's, is designed for researchers and serious students. It has fewer entries but provides annotations. Harner's focus is on sources useful to the study of English and American literature, although there is brief coverage of literatures in other languages. Annotations vary in length from a few sentences to a few pages and are arranged under twenty-one sections. The second edition contains about 1,200 entries which cite about that number within the body of the annotations. There are indexes to names, subjects, and titles.

1030. **Reference Guide to American Literature**. 2d ed. D. L. Kirkpatrick, ed. Chicago: St. James Press, 1987. 816p. ISBN 0-912289-61-9.

This is a combined and revised edition of the *St. James Reference Guide to American Literature*, a three-volume 1983 reprint of three 1980 publications from St. Martins Press. Volume 1 treats the history of American literature; volume 2 covers American writers to 1900; and volume 3 describes American writers since 1900. The second edition treats 400 major American novelists, poets, dramatists, and essayists. Part 1 covers the writers and provides biographical and critical sketches and listings of critical studies. Part 2 supplies 120 essays on the most important works of American literature from its origins to the present. There is an index of titles.

Guide to American Literature, by Valmai Kirkham Fenster (Libraries Unlimited, 1983), was developed as a guide for both graduate and undergraduate students, and provides annotated listings of sources considered to be important or essential to the study of American literature. It is divided into two major parts or segments, with part 1 given to general guides and reference sources. Covered are such forms as bibliographic guides; indexes; literary surveys; criticism; political, social, and intellectual history; language; anthologies and series; and other relevant reference tools. Part 2 comprises the major portion of the work and furnishes source materials for the study of 100 important writers. John Dos Passos, W. E. B. Du Bois, and Lillian Hellman are just a few of the names included. Primary sources are listed first, by date of publication, followed by secondary sources classified by type (biography, criticism, bibliography, reference work). Author, title, and subject indexes are included. The third edition, under the editorship of Jim Kamp, is to appear in 1994.

1031. **Reference Guide to English Literature**. 2d ed. D. L. Kirkpatrick. Chicago: St. James Press, 1991. 3v. ISBN 1-55862-078-8.

This revision of the eight-volume *St. James Reference Guide to English Literature* (entry 1108) has changed in coverage and format. All U.S. authors have now been excluded in favor of the publisher's *Reference Guide to American Literature* (entry 1030). Volume 1 opens with twelve essays by scholars on distinct periods; coverage is then given to some 900 of the most important writers of English-language literature from Great Britain, Ireland, Canada, Australia, New Zealand, Africa, Asia, and the Caribbean. Arrangement is simplified to an alphabetical listing rather than the previous organization under twelve literary periods and genres. Entries supply a brief biographical sketch, listings of the author's works in chronological order, bibliography of additional readings, and critical essays from 300 to 1,500 words on the writer's work. Volume 3 supplies individual essays on 600 of the most important poems, novels, plays, and essay collections. A title index is furnished.

1032. **Reference Works in British and American Literature**. James K. Bracken. Englewood, CO: Libraries Unlimited, 1990-1991. 2v. ISBN 0-87287-699-3 (v.1); 0-87287-700-0 (v.2).

This annotated bibliography of reference and information sources serves as a useful guide for college students at various levels. Volume 1 treats "English and American Literature," and volume 2 covers "English and American Writers." In volume 1 are some 500 entries organized by form, genre, or literary period. Annotations are detailed and provide critical analysis as well as description of content. Valuable features and deficiencies are identified in relatively thorough and objective fashion. There are separate sections on core journals and principal research centers. Volume 2 treats information sources on individual writers; three titles have become familiar through frequent use in college classes. Coverage is given to nearly 600 writers representing the full range of literary history. Annotations are similar to those in volume 1 in providing critical comparison and description. Each volume is indexed separately.

1033.   **A Research Guide for Undergraduate Students: English and American Literature.** 3d ed. Nancy L. Baker. New York: Modern Language Association of America, 1989. 61p. ISBN 0-87352-186-2.

This compact little volume has gained popularity among undergraduate students as a useful bibliographic guide since its initial publication in 1982. The present issue was designed to acquaint students with all aspects of library use, including computer technology. Only two chapters have been revised, but the changes are significant, introducing the student to the potential of online search services in solving bibliographic problems. This is also true of the chapter on the library catalog, where the user is introduced to online catalogs. In the chapter on locating periodical literature, the online systems DIALOG and BRS are described and endorsed. Although slightly dated in certain aspects of online searching, it is important that the message be considered not only by students but also by their teachers at every level.

The third edition of *A Guide to English and American Literature*, by Frederick W. Bateson and Harrison T. Meserole (Longman, 1970; repr., 1976), continues the production of an excellent line of guides. Originally entitled *A Guide to English Literature*, the two previous editions from the same publisher (1965-1967) were recognized as important aids to both the graduate and undergraduate student in developing an awareness of existing sources of study. Although dated, it is still used to identify major editions and important commentaries by those who wish to pursue literary topics in a serious manner. It opens with a general introductory section, followed by chapters on literary periods. Included are such studies as Medieval, Renaissance, Augustan, Romantic, and Modern English literature. American literature is given separate treatment, and there is a chapter on literary scholarship. A general index provides access.

BIBLIOGRAPHIES AND CATALOGS

1034.   **American Indian Literatures: An Introduction, Bibliographic Review, and Selected Bibliography**. A. LaVonne Brown Ruoff. New York: Modern Language Association of America, 1990. 200p. ISBN 0-87352-191-9.

Following by several years the earlier MLA publication by Paula Gunn, *American Indian Literature* (1983), Ruoff has provided a real service to students and teachers through identification of materials relating to the literature produced by American Indians. Sources treating both oral and written traditions are included. The work is divided into three sections; the first serves as an introduction to the subject. Excellent and detailed exposition is given to the oral tradition, narrative, oration, drama, and song, as well as the written literature. The second section provides a bibliographic review of the major works on the subject. These include bibliographies, research guides, and anthologies, along with study and criticism. Part 3 provides a more expanded treatment of the second section and includes Native American authors and their works, films, videos, journals, and small press publications. There is a chronology of American Indian history; an index is furnished.

1035.   **American Women Writers: Bibliographical Essays.** Maurice Duke et al., eds. Westport, CT: Greenwood Press, 1983. 434p. ISBN 0-313-22116-2.

This work is considered an important contribution to the body of reference literature developed on female authors in recent years. Much systematic effort is still needed, and publications like this help to develop the continuing body of critical inquiry. The essays cover twenty-four female writers, following the pattern established by James Woodress twelve years earlier in *Eight American Authors: A Review of Research and Criticism* (W. W. Norton,

1971), which itself was a revised edition of a work published fifteen years before that. In all these efforts, the essays describe and analyze a wide range of secondary works on the authors. Bibliographies, editions, manuscripts and letters, biography, and critical studies are covered. Both works treat authors ranging from the colonial period to the present.

1036. **The Annotated Bibliography of Canada's Major Authors.** Robert Lecker and Jack David, eds. Toronto: ECW Press; distr., Boston: G. K. Hall, 1979- . v.1- . ISBN 0-920802-08-7.

Projected as an eight-volume work, this series had been steadily moving toward completion, with the publication of volume 6 in 1985 and volume 7 in 1987. The final volume remains to be completed, however. The series is to be divided evenly, with four volumes given to prose writers and four to poets. Both primary and secondary sources are identified for about six writers in each volume. (Volume 7 treats four authors: Marian Engel, Anne Hebert, Robert Kroetsch, and Thomas H. Raddall.) No biographical information is given. Two sections contain works by the author and are divided between complete publications and contributions to publications. References are given to manuscript collections and audiovisual materials and reprints and individual titles within a work are identified. The other two sections contain works about the authors (articles, books, theses, interviews, audiovisuals, honors, book reviews, etc.). This is a highly useful series bringing together a body of material on significant Canadian writers.

1037. **Articles on American Literature, 1900-1950.** Lewis Gaston Leary. Durham, NC: Duke University Press, 1954. 437p.

Leary first published a bibliography of this sort in 1947; it covered the period 1920-1945. This work supersedes that publication in its coverage of the first half of the twentieth century. The tool is derived from the bibliographies published in two literary journals: *American Literature* (on a quarterly basis since 1929), and *PMLA* (on an annual basis since 1922). Coverage back to 1900 has been accomplished through examination of a number of periodicals and other bibliographies. The work is continued by Leary's *Articles on American Literature, 1950-1967* (1970), which, although operating on the same general plan, gives greater coverage to articles appearing in foreign journals. Following that is *Articles on American Literature, 1968-1975* (1979), which, in addition to providing supplemental coverage to the earlier works, includes additions and corrections to those volumes.

Articles on American and British Literature: An Index to Selected Periodicals, 1950-1977, compiled by Larry B. Corse and Sandra Corse (Swallow/Ohio University Press, 1981), is intended for undergraduates in small college libraries. It indexes forty-eight common literary periodicals, and entries are arranged by nationality, then period, then subject.

1038. **Articles on Women Writers: A Bibliography.** Narda Lacey Schwartz. Santa Barbara, CA: ABC-Clio, 1977-1986. 2v. ISBN 0-87436-252-0 (v.1); 0-87436-438-8 (v.2).

Nine years after this bibliography of articles and dissertations on women writers was published, it was joined by a complementary volume, *Articles on Women Writers, Volume 2, 1976-1984*. In both cases, coverage is limited to women writing in the English language, but from a number of countries of the Commonwealth, United States, and other areas. Volume 1 treats 600 personalities who were subjects of at least one scholarly or popular article published between 1960 and 1975. Volume 2 encompasses more writers—more than 1,000 for a period of only eight years. This reflects both an increased interest and also a broadened search strategy on the part of the author. Schwartz has included feminist abstracting services as well as traditional indexes, giving another dimension and added perspective on women's writing. Sources are varied and range from literary journals to the common and popular periodicals. A most useful reference tool for literature study.

1039. **Bibliographies of Studies in Victorian Literature for the Thirteen Years 1932-1944.** William D. Templeman, ed. Urbana, IL: University of Illinois Press, 1945. Repr., New York: Johnson Reprint, 1971. 450p.

The first in a series of retrospective bibliographic compilations of listings originally published in certain literary periodicals, this work and its continuations have become familiar reference tools. They have been prepared under the auspices of the Victorian Division of the Modern Language Association. The Templeman effort provides a reprint of the bibliographies published in the May issue of *Modern Philology* from 1933 to 1945. Arrangement of the bibliographies is year-by-year, and the work includes an author index of individuals mentioned in section IV of each year.

Austin Wright's *Bibliography of Studies in Victorian Literature for the Ten Years 1945-1954* (University of Illinois Press, 1956) continues the effort for the next ten years, with reprints of the annual "Victorian Bibliographies" section from *Modern Philology*. Robert C. Slack's *Bibliography of Studies in Victorian Literature for the Ten Years 1955-1964* (University of Illinois Press, 1967) divides the coverage between two journals. From 1955 to 1956, "Victorian Bibliographies" appeared in *Modern Philology*, and was then incorporated into the journal *Victorian Studies* (1957-). The next cumulation to appear was Ronald E. Freeman's *Bibliography of Studies in Victorian Literature for the Ten Years 1965-1974* (AMS, 1981), which reprints the bibliographies from *Victorian Studies* (entry 1051). The most recent issue is *Bibliographies of Studies in Victorian Literature for the Ten Years 1975-1984*, edited by Richard C. Tobias (AMS, 1991). Again, each of the annual bibliographies is reproduced in sequence. An author and subject index aid access, although it is time for the Division to consider integration of the entries into a unified single listing.

1040. **Bibliography of American Literature.** Jacob Blanck. New Haven, CT: Yale University Press, 1955-1991. 9v. ISBN 0-300-03839-9.

Originally projected for eight volumes, this monumental but highly selective series has finally concluded its slow journey to completion with publication of the ninth volume some thirty-six years following volume 1. Publication of volume 7 in 1983, ten years after the appearance of volume 6, and volume 8 seven years later in 1990, typify the slow and painful labor that has required grants from both private and public agencies to sustain the effort. Volume 9, however, was issued in uncharacteristically quick fashion the year following, in 1991. The title complements the work of the early American bibliographers Charles Evans and Joseph Sabin. Some 300 American writers dating from the Federal period to moderns who died before 1930 have been thoroughly covered. Arrangement is alphabetical beginning with volume 1, "Henry Adams to Donn Byrne." Volume 9, "Edward Noyes Westcott to Elinor Wylie," includes such luminaries as Whistler, Whitman, and Whittier. About thirty writers are covered in each volume in systematic fashion, including first editions; reprints containing textual or other changes; and a selected listing of biographical, bibliographical, and critical works. Only authors of literary interest (popular in their time but not necessarily recognized today as major writers) are included. Bibliographic listings are organized chronologically under their classifications. Excluded from coverage are periodical and newspaper publications, later editions, translations, and volumes with isolated correspondence.

1041. **Black Authors: A Selected Annotated Bibliography**. James Edward Newby. New York: Garland, 1991. 720p. (Garland Reference Library of the Humanities, v.1260). ISBN 0-8240-3329-9.

Newby is an academic at Harvard University who has compiled a useful bibliography of some 3,000 books, monographs, and essays written by African-Americans, along with a few Africans and Caribbeans who are living and writing in the United States. In some cases, the items are unannotated. When there is doubt about the author being black, an asterisk is used; two asterisks are given to writers who are not black. The author identifies it as a selective bibliography; therefore, there are many notable omissions (Richard Allen, Hallie Q. Brown, etc.) from the coverage given to writings over the period of 217 years from 1783 to 1990. There are nine chapters representing subjects or genres such as history, education, juvenile literature, biographies, etc. Annotations vary in size but generally are brief. They may include brief comments on public reception of a work, as well as description of content. Title and author indexes are furnished.

Black Literature, 1827-1940 (Chadwyck-Healey, 1990-) is a catalog of the source material on microfiche produced by the publisher. It identifies fiction, poetry, book reviews, and obituaries from 900 newspapers and magazines published by black Americans from 1827 to 1940. This is part of the Black Periodical Literature Project directed by Henry Louis Gates and enumerates over 50,000 items. CD-ROM format is planned.

1042. Index to British Literary Bibliography. Trevor Howard Hill. New York: Oxford University Press, 1969- . v.1-2, 4-6. ISBN 0-19-818184-1 (v.1, 2d ed.)

This is an important and highly specialized bibliography initially projected in six volumes, although volume 7 was issued in 1992. Volume 3 still remains unfinished. The set targets bibliographical works, books, or articles, concerning British textual and bibliographic history. Volume 1, *Bibliography of British Literary Bibliographies*, is now in its second edition and covers books, parts of books, and periodical articles written in English and published in the English-speaking world after 1890. The subject of these works is the bibliographical and textual examination of British titles (manuscripts, books, printing, etc., of works published in England or written by British subjects abroad). The second edition of this volume, revised and enlarged, was published in 1987. Volume 2 provides identification and analysis of bibliographies of the work of Shakespeare. Volume 3 will deal with the period prior to 1890. Volumes 4 and 5 consider British literary and textual criticism, and list writings and authors from 1890 to 1969. They describe bibliographical aspects of works printed in Britain from 1475 to the present day. Volume 6 is a combined index to volumes 1-2 and volumes 4-5. Volume 7, the most recent addition, continues the coverage from 1970 to 1979, while supplementing the earlier volumes with works published from 1890 to 1969 that had been overlooked. Upon completion of volume 3, a new cumulative index will be issued.

1043. The New Cambridge Bibliography of English Literature. Cambridge, UK: Cambridge University Press, 1974-1977. 5v. ISBN 0-521-20004-0 (v.1).

The earlier edition of this work, *Cambridge Bibliography of English Literature* (1940, 4v.; supp., 1957) was edited by F. W. Bateson. It established a standard for excellent and authoritative coverage of a larger number of sources relating to the periods and authors of Great Britain, beginning with Old English and Latin literature of the British Isles. The volumes are arranged chronologically for the years 600-1900, with volume 4 being an index volume. The more recent edition continues in the same tradition and is recognized as an indispensable reference and research tool in English literature. The pattern of coverage is similar to the original publication, treating hundreds of major and minor figures with listings of both primary and secondary sources. Each period is covered in terms of important sources of all types. This edition provides coverage to the mid-twentieth century, with volume 4 embracing the period 1900-1950, and volume 5 providing the index. Period studies are not limited to creative literary efforts, but include sections on travel, sport, education, etc. In most cases, this work has superseded the earlier edition, although the latter may be retained for certain background chapters not included in the present issue.

Intended for smaller libraries and for home and office use, *The Shorter New Cambridge Bibliography of English Literature*, edited by George Watson (Cambridge University Press, 1981), is an excellent abridgement of the preceding work. Following the plan of the original, as is usually the case with the "shorter" editions, it provides coverage from 600 to 1950, but eliminates the background material and a number of minor authors that have made the lengthier tool an important work for scholars. The primary section or the major corpus of an author's works have been retained, but the secondary section consisting of books and articles on the author has been reduced considerably. The coverage of periods retains the bibliographies, literary histories, anthologies, and critical surveys.

1044.   **The Pen Is Ours: A Listing of Writings by and about African-American Women before 1910 with Secondary Bibliography to the Present.** Jean Fagan Yellin and Cynthia D. Bond, comps. New York: Oxford University Press, 1991. 349p. (Schoenberg Library of Nineteenth-Century Black Women Writers). ISBN 0-19-506203-5.

Oxford University Press has been active in producing a series of bibliographies identifying the literature authored by black American women. This volume is one of ten published in 1991 providing a focus on the period prior to 1910. These volumes continue Oxford's activity marked by publication of thirty volumes in 1988. This particular work supplies bibliographic coverage beginning in 1773 when Phyllis Wheatley's poetry was first published. There is a foreword by the director of the Schoenberg Center, after which the work is divided into five sections. These identify publications by and about writers of separately published works; by and about female slaves; publications appearing in periodicals and collections; publications on the subject of African-American women writers; and finally a listing of contemporary writings about African-American women. A name index provides access to the first four sections.

1045.   **A Short-Title Catalogue of Books Printed in England, Scotland, and Ireland, and of English Books Printed Abroad, 1475-1640.** Alfred William Pollard and G. R. Redgrave. London: Bibliographical Society, 1926; 2d ed. rev. and enl. W. A. Jackson, F. S. Ferguson and Katharine F. Pantzer. 1976-1991. 3v. ISBN 0-19-721789-3 (v.1); 0-19-721790-7 (v.2); 0-19-71791-5 (v.3).

One of the most important and certainly most well-known reference sources in English bibliography is this standard work, known as *STC*. Its coverage is comprehensive and the initial effort identifies more than 26,500 editions covering a period of time rich in English history and creative thought. The arrangement is alphabetical by author and other main entries. The entries provide author's name, brief title, size, printer, date, reference to Stationers' registers entry for the item, and symbols for libraries possessing copies of the work. A serious attempt was made to locate all known copies of rare materials, and there is a representative listing of libraries for more common materials. Included among the 148 libraries are 15 in this country. The second edition was begun by Jackson and Ferguson and completed by Pantzer some ten years after their deaths. Volume 1 covers A-H; volume 2 treats I-Z; and volume 3 furnishes indexes, addenda, and appendices. The work has been continued by succeeding titles (entry 1046).

A complementary effort is William Warner Bishop's *A Checklist of American Copies of Short-Title Catalogue Books* (2d ed., University of Michigan Press, 1950; repr., Greenwood Press, 1968). This work identifies *STC* items held in more than 110 libraries in this country.

1046.   **Short-Title Catalogue of Books Printed in England, Scotland, Ireland, Wales, and British America and of English Books Printed in Other Countries, 1641-1700.** Donald Goddard Wing. New York: Columbia University Press, 1945-1951. 3v.; 2d ed. rev. and enl. Index Committee of the Modern Language Association. 1972-1988. 3v. ISBN 0-87352-044-0 (v.1).

Developed as a complementary work to *STC* (entry 1045), this effort, known as "Wing," continues the coverage for another sixty years. More than 200 libraries are identified in the initial effort through their holdings of English works published during this period. Common books are limited to five locations in the United Kingdom and five in the United States, with an attempt made to disperse the listings geographically in order to facilitate access for scholars and specialists. Wing devised his own location symbols identifying the various libraries involved. The second edition revised and enlarged the original coverage by identifying the holdings of another 100 libraries; bibliographic information has been enhanced in some cases. The revised edition began with the publication of volume 1, *A1-E2926*, in 1972. Ten years later, volume 2 appeared, covering *E2927-01000*. Volume 3, *P1-Z28*, completes the set. Both *STC* and *Wing* have served as models for a similar project of British holdings in the libraries of Australia, as well as one that covers books printed in France.

Coverage continues with *The Eighteenth Century Short Title Catalogue*, a large-scale online catalog of the holdings of the British Library along with some 1,000 other libraries throughout the world. *ESTC* contains some 315,000 records of books and other materials published in Great Britain and its colonial possessions between 1701 and 1800. Arrangement is by main entry (generally author) and material includes membership lists of societies, advertisements, and transportation time tables. The work is accessed through both RLIN and BLAISE-LINE, and is also available in CD-ROM version from Research Publications, Inc. A microfiche edition available through the British Library furnishes some 300,000 records in the file at time of publication in 1990. *The Nineteenth Century Short Title Catalog*, issued in print in sixty-one volumes, will be available both online and in CD-ROM in the future through Avero Publications Ltd. Coverage is given to British publications dating from 1801 to 1918, and includes books, newspapers, journals, school texts, official documents, and others, reprepresenting all subjects. Sources are the major libraries of England and Ireland as well as the Library of Congress and Harvard University.

1047. **Small Press: An Annotated Guide**. Loss Pequeno Glazier. Westport, CT: Greenwood Press, 1992. 123p. ISBN 0-313-28310-9.
Small press publishing continues to represent an important element in the issuance of original literary effort and is not generally well understood. This slender little bibliography provides a needed resource for students and specialists in the literary arts in its well-chosen sources treating the small press. In straightforward fashion, it identifies nearly 175 sources on the small press and small press publishing since 1960. The work is divided into three major segments representing current information sources (directories, indexes, guides, and trade journals); core sources (writings on major social, historical, and commercial issues); and supplementary sources (catalogs, listings, and bibliographies). Annotations are well developed and informative. Glazier is an academic librarian and subject specialist in the area of American literature who has provided an important tool for research of small presses in the United States.

INDEXES, ABSTRACTS, AND SERIAL BIBLIOGRAPHIES

1048. **Abstracts of English Studies.** Calgary, Canada: University of Calgary, 1958- . Q. ISSN 0001-3560.
This is an important abstract journal which provides abstracts of articles appearing in journals from various countries on the subject of literature in the English language. American, Commonwealth, and English literatures are covered. English philology is also within its scope. More recently, world literature and related languages have received attention. The journal has had an interesting and varied existence, beginning life as the monthly official publication of the National Council of Teachers of English. From 1962 to 1980, it was a monthly except for July and August (10/yr.). Beginning in June 1980, it was taken over by the University of Calgary, and in April 1981 it became a quarterly. Abstracts are taken from hundreds of different journals and represent an excellent selection of contemporary thought.

1049. **American Literary Scholarship.** Durham, NC: Duke University Press, 1963- . Ann. ISSN 0065-9142.
This is one of the important review journals in the field and has earned an excellent reputation since its appearance more than thirty years ago. It consists of a series of bibliographic essays furnishing an analysis of published research on the various aspects of American literature. Each issue of this annual publication provides chapters on individual authors or joint authors; also covered separately is the period of American literature up to 1800. Fiction and poetry as well as drama and folklore are some of the literary genres which receive treatment in a manner similar to that used in *The Year's Work in English Studies* (entry 1057). Each volume or issue carries its own index.

1050. **Annual Bibliography of English Language and Literature.** Modern Humanities Research Association. Cambridge, UK: Modern Humanities Research Association, 1920- . Ann. ISSN 0066-3786.

Located in Cambridge since its initial issue, this title represents one of the important annual bibliographies in the field, and the most significant one targeted to English language and literature. It lists a variety of publications on English and American literature and identifies books, pamphlets, and periodical articles. Also included are reviews of the listed books. The work is divided into two major sections, language and literature. Arrangement of entries in the language section is by subject, but the entries in the literature segment are organized in chronological sequence, an arrangement which has been criticized by reviewers in the past. The work provides indexes of both authors and subjects to facilitate access.

1051. **Annual Bibliography of Victorian Studies.** Edmonton: LITIR Database, 1977- . Ann. ISSN 0227-1400.

The *Victorian period* is defined as the time period from about 1830 to the beginning of World War I in 1914. This annual bibliography contains English-language materials of various kinds, including books, periodical articles, and reviews relating to that interesting period. It is not limited to literary subjects, but attempts to treat the period in its entirety. The work is composed of seven major segments or categories, beginning with general and reference works including fine arts, philosophy and religion, history, social sciences, and science and technology. Most important is the section on language and literature, which includes subsections on individual authors. Reviews are cited after the work itself. Indexing is provided by subject, author, title, and reviewer. There is a cumulative index every five years.

Victorian Studies (Indiana University Press, 1957-), a quarterly journal, has published an annual bibliography of books and periodical articles since its first year. "Victorian Bibliography" serves as a continuation of the list originally published in *Modern Philology* and was a project of a Committee on Victorian Literature of the Modern Language Association of America. Periodic cumulations of these bibliographies have been published (entry 1039).

1052. **Index of English Literary Manuscripts.** P. J. Croft et al., eds. New York: Mansell/ R. R. Bowker, 1980- . v.1- . ISBN 0-8352-1216-5.

This work, designed for scholars and specialists in the field, describes the existing manuscripts of literary works by Irish and British authors who wrote during the period 1450-1900 (following the invention of printing). The choice of authors is based partially on their inclusion in George Watson's *Concise Cambridge Bibliography of English Literature, 600-1950* (2d ed., Cambridge University Press, 1965) but is not limited to that listing. Some 400 libraries, depositories, and archives in a variety of geographic locales were approached regarding their holdings. These units were located not only in England, but also in North America, Russia, continental Europe, Australia, New Zealand, and South Africa. Private collections are included as well. Authors are listed alphabetically within the volumes. The manuscripts are described in detail in terms of ownership over the years. Present locations are given. Presently the following volumes are available: volume 1 in two parts, 1450-1625; volume 2, 1625-1700, in two parts; volume 3 in three parts, 1700-1800; and volume 4 in two parts, 1800-1900. Yet to come is volume 5 providing indexes of titles, first lines, names, and repositories.

1053. **Interviews and Conversations with 20th-Century Authors Writing in English: An Index. Series I-III**. Stan A. Vrana. Metuchen, NJ: Scarecrow Press, 1982-1990. ISBN 0-8108-2352-7 (III).

Series II of this work appeared in 1986 and augments the coverage of the earlier volume by adding more personalities. In Series I and II, the interviews were published betweeen 1900 and 1980. Series III continues the coverage, indexing interviews published between 1981 and 1985. In all the volumes, arrangement is alphabetical by name of the author. Interviews are then listed chronologically. These interviews are taken from a variety of sources (newspapers and periodicals, both general and literary, from the United States and foreign countries). Also included, much to Vrana's credit, are African and Asian titles, as well as those from the Western nations. Monographic sources are also covered, but are listed separately. About 3,600 interviews are identified in the first series, 4,500 in the second series, and 5,600 in the third series, providing an extraordinary and convenient access tool for this important material.

1054. **Shakespeare Survey: An Annual Survey of Shakespearean Study and Production.** Cambridge, UK: Cambridge University Press, 1948- . Ann. ISSN 0080-9152.

This is a highly useful and highly successful annual review of studies in a specialized but foremost area of literary research. In the past, it has been under the combined sponsorship of several scholarly and cultural organizations: the University of Birmingham, University of Manchester, Royal Shakespeare Theatre, and the Shakespearean Birthplace Trust. Volumes are given to specific themes which provide a focus for the articles of that year directed toward a particular element or feature of Shakespearean study. The scope is international and articles are furnished by scholars from a number of countries and regions. Most important in terms of bibliography is the regular feature "The Year's Contribution to Shakespearean Study," which is a critical survey of research and publication in the field.

1055. **The Wellesley Index to Victorian Periodicals, 1824-1900.** Walter E. Houghton, ed. Toronto: University of Toronto Press, 1966-1989. 5v. ISBN 0-4150-3054-4 (v.1).

After more than twenty years of work, this set has been completed, furnishing both students and specialists with an extremely useful resource tool. Providing subject, book review, and author indexing, it is especially valuable for citations to contemporary criticism of Victorian writers. It is the most detailed index of Victorian periodicals in existence and includes certain journals not picked up by other sources. A total of forty-three periodicals are indexed in the set, with volume 1 covering eight major journals. Volume 2 treats twelve titles and volume 3 another fifteen, including *Westminster Review*. Volume 4 concludes the text in its coverage of eight more. The volumes are divided into two major sections, with part A furnishing tables of contents for each issue of the titles and part B providing bibliographies of the contributors arranged by author. Volume 5, edited by Jean H. Slingerland, provides a comprehensive author index and tabular overview with excellent detail to the listings in all four volumes.

1056. **The Year's Scholarship in Science Fiction, Fantasy, and Horror Literature.** Kent, OH: Kent State University Press, 1980-1982. Ann. ISSN 0741-2231.

Beginning as *The Year's Scholarship in Science Fiction and Fantasy*, the work provided annual coverage of the years 1972 to 1979, for which two quadrennial cumulations were published, 1972-1975 and 1976-1979. It changed its title with the 1980 issue, published in 1983. Two more volumes followed, covering the period from 1981 to 1982. In 1985, it was absorbed into the quarterly journal, *Extrapolation: Journal of the Scholarly Study of Science Fiction and Fantasy*, published at Kent State since 1959. Commentary, criticism, and interpretation are included in the works identified and annotated. Annotations are descriptive and indicate the nature of the work, with the narratives running between 50 and 100 words per item. Coverage is comprehensive and includes a wide range of materials: books, periodical articles, dissertations, scholarly reprints, and audiovisual materials. Book reviews are excluded. The materials are divided into various sections, including important coverage of individual author studies.

1057. **The Year's Work in English Studies.** Atlantic Highlands, NJ: Humanities Press, 1919/1920- . Ann. ISSN 0084-4144.

This is one of the leading review journals in the field and was originally published by the English Association through H. Milford and John Murray of London. It covers a wide range of studies of English literature. Similar to the *Annual Bibliography* (entry 1050) in scope, it has the additional feature of evaluating the importance or nature of the items indexed. The studies are drawn from both books and periodical articles published in Great Britain, the United States, and various countries of Continental Europe. Language is also treated as a subject and, since 1954, American literature studies have been included as well. The arrangement of entries is chronological by period covered, and the work is indexed by author and subject.

DICTIONARIES, ENCYCLOPEDIAS, AND HANDBOOKS

1058. **British English for American Readers: A Dictionary of the Language, Customs, and Places of British Life and Literature.** David Grote. Westport, CT: Greenwood Press, 1992. 709p. ISBN 0-313-27851-2.
This work serves as both a dictionary and a "companion" or guide to the understanding of British literature and popular culture. Terms and expressions peculiar to British are defined, making it possible for the novice to comprehend the references and quotations expressed in both literary and broadcast media. Such references include places and commonplace objects used on a routine basis. Slang and idiomatic expressions are treated along with political, legal, and bureaucratic terminology. Social customs and routine existence are not overlooked. Grote is a prolific writer, playwright, and magazine editor who has succeeded in producing an unusual, comprehensive work of practical value to a wide-ranging audience. Six appendices provide well-developed perspectives of the British scene as well as an extensive bibliography.

1059. **The Cambridge Guide to English Literature.** Michael Stapleton. Cambridge, UK: Cambridge University Press, 1983. 992p. ISBN 0-600-33173-3.
This work is similar to the *Oxford Companion to English Literature* (entry 1066) in structure, although it has greater scope, covering English writing in a number of countries including the United States. This handbook treats the various elements associated with English literature over the past 1,000 years or more. The focus is entirely on literature (somewhat unlike the *Oxford*). It appears that only 2 of the 3,100 alphabetically arranged articles were not written by Stapleton, a respected editor and writer. These two are lengthy survey articles, "The English Language," by M. H. Strang, and "The Bible in English," by C. H. Sisson. Entries include authors, titles, characters, and literary terms, and are arranged alphabetically. There are many cross-references between entries. Historical or mythological descriptions are excluded for the most part.

1060. **The Cambridge Handbook of American Literature.** Jack Salzman, ed. New York: Cambridge University Press, 1986. 286p. ISBN 0-521-30703-1.
A rather slender and inexpensive work compared to most Cambridge efforts of this kind, the handbook can best be likened to *The Concise Oxford Companion to American Literature* (entry 1065n). Coverage of this work includes literary movements, periodicals, plot summaries, biographical sketches of writers, and important bibliographical details. Entries are brief but informative and are arranged alphabetically. Personal opinions are avoided in the critical commentary in favor of the presentation of historical attitudes toward individual authors. Chronologies of American history and of American literature are placed side-by-side. Also included is a selective bibliography of important critical works published in the past fifty years.

1061. **Companion to Scottish Literature.** Trevor Royle. Detroit: Gale Research, 1983. 322p. ISBN 0-8103-0519-4.
A specialized handbook to the whole realm of Scottish literature, it has been said to take up the study where *The Oxford Companion to English Literature* (entry 1066) leaves off. Entries are alphabetically arranged and include biographical sketches of various personalities (poets, novelists, dramatists, and critics) who have written in either English or Gaelic and have made solid contributions to the literary tradition. There are more than 1,200 entries of varying length depending upon the importance of the topic or the breadth of the issue. Historical events are included in the lengthy articles. Most important is the coverage of minor figures who may be difficult to find in the standard sources.

1062. **Masterpieces of African-American Literature**. Frank N. Magill, ed. New York: HarperCollins, 1992. 593p. ISBN 0-06-270066-9.

This is another of the famous Magill critical/descriptive efforts in the style of *Masterplots* (entry 980) developed for a different publisher. In response to growing demand for material on the black experience, Magill and his contributors have produced this compilation of summary reviews of 149 literary efforts by ninety-six African-American writers. Entries run about 2,500 words in length, and identify principal characters, describe plot, and provide analysis and critical commentary. Selected works represent the various genres; novels, short stories, plays, poetry, biographies, and essays by writers dating from the nineteenth century to the present. Most of the authors are major in terms of importance and impact (Baldwin, Haley, Hansberry, Morrison, etc.), although a few are lesser known. Several children's authors are included; there is a good selection of female writers. Author and title indexes provide access.

1063. **The New Arthurian Encyclopedia.** Norris J. Lacy et al., eds. New York: Garland, 1991. 577p. ISBN 0-8240-4377-4.

The initial edition, published in 1986, was considered to be an important and comprehensive reference work focused on the world of King Arthur. It was not limited to literary coverage, but included the treatment of Arthur in the arts, history, music, chronicles, archaeology, film, and folklore. The new edition represents an impressive revision and expansion of the earlier effort and results in another significant contribution. The time period for Arthurian themes is of course limitless, and works represent all countries and eras. The tool is handy and easy to use, covering both specific subjects and general categories. There are 1,200 entries (an increase of 500) classified by topics or categories, with a list of entries provided at the beginning of each category. Major characters and themes as well as individual works and authors are treated. Articles are signed by 127 contributors (up from 94) and there are twice the number of illustrations (120). A chronology is included along with a double-page map. A detailed subject index gives excellent access.

Ronan Coghlan's *The Encyclopaedia of Arthurian Legends* (Element, 1992) is a smaller work from a minor publisher that opens with a good summary of literary treatment given the Arthurian legend. The bulk of the text is a listing with definitions or identifications of Arthurian names and places, and some objects and phenomena. Entries vary from a single sentence to three or four columns in length.

1064. **The Oxford Companion to American Literature.** 5th ed. James D. Hart. New York: Oxford University Press, 1983. 896p. ISBN 0-19-503074-5.

This well-known standard in the field has been highly regarded since its first edition in 1941. The fifth edition was a long time coming, since the fourth was issued in 1965. The revision is a thorough one and involves a number of modifications. Nearly 250 authors have been added since the fourth edition, along with 115 new entries summarizing books. Many entries have been deleted, especially those on peripheral topics (although many still remain). Of course, many entries have been revised. As always, the work includes biographies of American authors, with lists of their major writings and brief analyses of style and subject matter; descriptions of significant individual works in various genres; definitions; and identifications of awards, societies, and other features, along with descriptions of various issues and topics relevant to society, politics, science, and so on. It continues to be a leading source of information.

The Concise Oxford Companion to American Literature, also by Hart (Oxford University Press, 1987) is an abridged version (497p.) of the preceding work selling for about half the price. (Similarly, it has been judged to provide about half the information of the older and larger work.) There are approximately 2,000 entries covering biographies of authors, definitions of literary terms, movements, awards, societies, organizations, and summaries of significant works. The focus is on American literature, but certain references to other literatures are given if they have relevance to the study of American literature. The emphasis appears to be on more recent authors, with the more specialized writers omitted in this version. A number of cross-references are furnished between entries. Coverage of women writers has been increased, in keeping with modern trends.

1065.   **Oxford Companion to Canadian Literature.** William Toye, ed. New York: Oxford University Press, 1983. 843p. ISBN 0-19-540283-9.

Another useful work in the Oxford Companion series, this handbook succeeds Novah Story's *The Oxford Companion to Canadian History and Literature* (1967) and its supplement (1973). It updates and expands the coverage, with about 750 entries ranging from short biographical sketches to survey articles on such topics as children's literature or mystery and crime. Titles of individual works and various genres are treated in an attempt to provide an encyclopedic overview of Canadian literary and cultural developments. French-Canadian literature is included. Some entries provide references to additional reading, and many have cross-references to related passages. Coverage appears to be especially strong for the period following World War II.

1066.   **The Oxford Companion to English Literature.** 5th ed. Margaret Drabble, ed. New York: Oxford University Press, 1985; repr. 1991. 1155p. ISBN 0-19-866130-4.

The editor is a novelist who has conducted an extensive revision of the fourth edition (1967) with the idea of providing an up-to-date work. This is the original model and oldest title in the now-extensive Oxford Companion series, having appeared initially in 1932. It is a true standard in the field and has become a fixture in library reference collections, with a reputation for brevity, accuracy, and comprehensiveness. The new edition furnishes biographical sketches of approximately 3,000 authors born before 1939, with special emphasis on twentieth-century writers. Allusions have been deleted, but movements and individual works are covered in detail. There are about 9,000 entries along with useful appendices. Biographies of earlier authors have also been expanded in the amount of detail provided. This work remains a staple for reference departments, and is now available in disk versions for both the PC and Mac.

Drabble and Jenny Stringer produced an abridgement of the larger work, *Concise Oxford Companion to English Literature*, for the same publisher in 1987. Their purpose was to prune rather than delete the content of the earlier work, to provide a reasonably priced tool for less sophisticated needs. Nevertheless, the work has been pared down to 5,000 entries, so the emphasis is on basic information rather than critical appraisal.

1067.   **The Oxford Companion to the Literature of Wales.** Meic Stephens, comp. and ed. New York: Oxford University Press, 1986; repr. with corr. 1990. 682p. ISBN 0-19-211586-3.

Another offering in the Oxford Companion series, this work continues in that tradition of most useful and worthwhile tools. Covering a period from the sixth century to the present, the editor (literature director of the Welsh Arts Council) has compiled nearly 3,000 entries. They are alphabetically arranged and emphasize writers in the Welsh language, but also include those who write or have written in English or Latin, as well as foreign writers who have published works set in Wales. In addition to writers, entries cover historical figures, events, movements, critics, genres, motifs, characters, and titles of major works and periodicals. Related areas generally examined in the Oxford Companions are given as well (customs, folklore, institutions, etc.). Useful features are a pronunciation guide and a chronology of Welsh history.

1068.   **The Oxford Illustrated Literary Guide to Great Britain and Ireland.** 2d ed. Dorothy Eagle and Meic Stephens, eds. New York: Oxford University Press, 1992. 322p. ISBN 0-19-212988-0.

In this, the second edition of an interesting and informative literary travel book, the editors have identified nearly 1,350 place names worthy of consideration when planning a trip. More than 1,000 literary figures are treated in terms of geographic locations of some significance to their lives or art. Cities, towns, villages, and dwellings are identifed and described. Arrangement is alphabetical by place name and easily located. Entries for each vary from a few lines given to some small hamlets to a fifty-page spread on London. There are thirteen maps to help pinpoint grid positions supplied by entries and numerous illustrations, some in color.

The *Oxford Illustrated Literary Guide to the United States*, by Eugene Ehrlich and Gorton Carruth, from the same publisher, was published in 1982. Similar in format to its companion work, it appeals to the same audience of travelers with special interests in literary sites and locales. This work provides links or associations between authors and their towns and cities. The arrangement of entries is by state, then by city or town, then alphabetically by author as subject. Brief commentary is included on the sites and the literary figures associated with it. There are many illustrations and quotations, and a detailed author-as-subject index provides access.

1069. **Prentice Hall Guide to English Literature: The New Authority on English Literature**. Marion Wynne Davies. New York: Prentice-Hall, 1990. 1066p. ISBN 0-13-083619-2.

This was issued by the publisher as the *Bloomsbury Guide to English Literature*, and has been reprinted in paperback under that title (1992). As the product of a distinguished scholar, it lays valid claim to its position as an authoritative source, but is easily utilized by layperson and serious student alike. It provides a comprehensive survey of English literature from *Beowulf* to the present. Most impressive is the opening segment, consisting of twelve monograph-length essays on topics important to the study of English literature, such as political history, medieval literature, Shakespeare, and Victorian poetry. Following that is an encyclopedic treatment of some 6,000 entries, supplying brief but informative descriptions of terminology, personalities, and issues. The text is accompanied by some 200 illustrations. A useful feature is a twenty-four-page chronology of important events in the history of English literature.

BIOGRAPHICAL AND CRITICAL SOURCES

1070. **American Women Writers: A Critical Reference Guide from Colonial Times to the Present**. Lina Mainiero and Langdon Lynne Faust, eds. New York: Ungar, 1979-1994. 5v. ISBN 0-8044-3150-7.

This important work describes the lives and contributions of American women who made literature their career as well as those who wrote seriously about their work in a variety of professions (history, psychology, and theology, among others). The intention was to include all writers of established literary reputation and a representative segment of popular writers, as well as bibliographic references. The biography is critical and furnishes an assessment of the writer's contribution. A recognized deficiency is in coverage of black and lesbian writers, which the editors see as being alleviated with much of the biocritical material being published today. Volume 5 serves as a supplement to the complete work in four volumes (1979-1982). A two-volume abridged edition of this work, edited by Faust, was issued by the publisher in 1983 and reprinted in a single volume in 1988.

1071. **American Writers: A Collection of Literary Biographies.** Leonard Unger, ed.-in-chief. New York: Scribner's, 1974. 4v. **Supp. I-III**. 1979-1991. 6v. ISBN 0-684-19196-2.

This entire collection, including supplements, provides a series of critical studies designed to cover in depth the life and work of 185 notable poets, novelists, short story writers, playwrights, critics, historians, and philosophers from the seventeenth century to the present day. The emphasis is on the style, genre, and literary contribution of the individuals and their place within the literary tradition. The original four-volume set contains the material in a series of pamphlets published by the University of Minnesota; the essays on ninety-seven individuals have been updated bibliographically, re-edited, and newly indexed. The essays are excellent in terms of depth and documentation. The supplementary volumes continue the original plan and add eighty-eight personalities designed to fill in gaps and to continue the coverage of major figures into the twentieth century. Enjoined are such figures as Allen Ginsburg, E. B. White, and Sylvia Plath, along with Henry Adams, T. S. Eliot, and Ralph

Waldo Emerson from the original set. Of the twenty-nine figures treated in the most recent supplement, nine are women and five are black.

That same year (1991), two complementary publications were issued by the publisher to compensate for the limited coverage given to minorities in the past. *African American Writers*, edited by Lea Baechler and A. Walton Litz, treats thirty-four personalities ranging from Olaudah Equiano, an eighteenth-century figure, to still-active Alice Walker. Eight of these writers had been covered in the previous set and/or its supplements. *Modern American Women Writers*, by the same editors, provides coverage of forty-one female writers from Frances Ellen Watkins Harper (died 1911) to Walker. Of that number, twenty-two had been covered previously.

*DiscLit: AMERICAN AUTHORS is a CD-ROM database issued for the first time in 1990 by G. K. Hall consisting of 143 volumes of Twayne's United States Authors Series. There are more than 127,000 citations, drawn from OCLC Subject Bibliographies for the American Authors series and listing the works of American authors dating from the colonial period to the present. Twayne, a Canadian publishing house, started the series of biocritical volumes by various scholars, each generally dealing with a single author, in the 1960s. The series has thrived, and there are well over 600 volumes at this time. There are annual updates to *DiscLit*.

1072. **American Writers before 1800: A Biographical and Critical Dictionary.** James A. Levernier and Douglas R. Wilmes, eds. Westport, CT: Greenwood Press, 1983. 3v. ISBN 0-313-22229-0.

Nearly 800 entries furnish biocritical sketches by 250 scholars who have contributed their talents in developing a useful source of information. Names of prominent individuals were selected by the editors from anthologies, histories, and bibliographies. Unlike many works of this kind, the length of the entries is not correlated with the importance of the individuals, and minor figures are treated as fully as are major ones. This is an important consideration for librarians who are asked to search out information on authors who are difficult to locate. Each entry provides a biographical sketch, including comments on factors that influenced the writer's development, a critical appraisal of writings, and a list of selected reading about the writer. The tool is a worthwhile purchase and is used frequently.

1073. **A Bibliographical Guide to African-American Women Writers**. Casper LeRoy Jordan, comp. Westport, CT: Greenwood Press, 1993. 387p. (Bibliographies and Indexes in Afro-American and African Studies, no. 31). ISBN 0-313-27633-1.

Jordan is a retired librarian and library educator who has compiled the most comprehensive bibliography to date on the writings by and about black female authors. Some 900 writers are treated in alphabetical order and receive two-part coverage of primary and secondary sources. Writers represent all genres, including poetry, long and short fiction, memoirs, biographies, diaries, and more. Works date from the poetry of Lucy Terry to the popular writings of the 1990s by Terry McMillan and Alice Walker. All of the important and recognized writers are covered and many obscure individuals are identified. The comprehensive coverage, therefore, is the great strength of this work, as its listings of sources are representative rather than complete.

Complementing the Jordan work is Ronda Glikin's *Black American Women in Literature* (McFarland, 1989), providing more complete bibliographic coverage of a more selective group of 300 women writers.

*1074. **Black Writers: A Selection of Sketches from Contemporary Authors**. 2d ed. Linda Metzger et al., eds. Detroit: Gale Research, 1993. 721p. ISBN 0-8103-7788-8.

Coverage is given to several hundred black writers representing the most familiar and most studied authors of the Harlem Renaissance as well as sociopolitical activism and cultural expression from abroad. Of course, all the top-drawer individuals are included, such as Baldwin, Hughes, and Martin Luther King, Jr. Utilizing the style and coverage found in *Contemporary Authors* (entry 988), the work is a tool of convenience and is in frequent use by students at both high school and undergraduate levels, who find it an asset in locating needed biographical information. Entries are thorough and contain excellent biographical sketches, addresses, awards, and memberships. Critical responses to the authors' works are included, providing insight into their influence and literary reputation. The work is available online through NEXIS.

1075. The Bohemian Register: An Annotated Bibliography of the Beat Literary Movement. Morgen Hickey. Metuchen, NJ: Scarecrow Press, 1990. 252p. ISBN 0-8108-2397-7.

This bibliography focusses on that anti-establishment literary period spanning the 1950s and early 1960s. It includes such proponents as Kerouac, Burroughs, and Ginsberg. Coverage is given to writings by and about some 200 authors and poets. There are about 700 titles written from the late 1940s to 1989, embracing little magazine publications, interviews, letters, essays, biographies, bibliographies, and book reviews. Entries supply biographical notes along with citations. The work is divided into three major segments, the first one listing fifty-six general works and critical studies. Part 2 identifies forty-two collections and anthologies; the bulk of the work is contained in part 3, which cites titles by and about the beat writers. Annotations are informative, generally accurate, and at times irreverent. A chronology is given, along with indexes by name, subject, and title.

1076. British Writers. Ian Scott Kilvert, ed. New York: Scribner's, 1979-1984. 8v. **Supps. I-II**, 1987-1992. ISBN 0-684-19214-4 (Supp II).

Modeled after *American Writers* (entry 1071), for which this was designed as a companion set, this in-depth collection also originated as a series of separate pamphlets first published by the British Council in 1950. It is a collection of essays, all of which are signed by distinguished contributors, providing a detailed exposition of the life and work of significant authors. Articles range from 10,000 to 15,000 words and are placed into volumes, which are arranged in chronological sequence (volume 1, "William Langland to the English Bible," to volume 7, "Sean O'Casey to Poets of World War II"). Volume 8 is the index. As in the case of *American Writers*, the essays describe the writer's life and period and provide a critical assessment of his or her works. The essays have been updated bibliographically and the content re-edited. The supplements are intended to add significant contemporary writers, such as Tom Stoppard and Graham Greene, not treated in the initial effort. The work is useful to a variety of patrons as well as librarians themselves.

1077. Canadian Writers and Their Works. Robert Lecker et al., eds. Toronto: ECW; distr., University of Toronto Press, 1989. 20v. ISBN 0-9208-0243-5.

This large undertaking is devoted to Canadian fiction and poetry of the nineteenth and twentieth centuries. The work is divided equally, with ten volumes on poetry and ten on fiction. Each volume furnishes an introduction and then covers in detail the work of five authors. The format for these essays, written by various experts in the field, provides for a brief biography, discussion of the tradition in which the author has worked, an analysis of major works, and a selective bibliography of primary and secondary sources. This is a worthwhile effort and merits inclusion in any library that values its coverage of literature north of the border. It is a most helpful vehicle for teachers, undergraduates, graduate students, and interested laypersons. In 1993, separate cumulative indexes were issued to both the poetry and the fiction series.

French-Canadian Authors: A Bibliography of their Works and of English Language Criticism, by Mary Kandiuk (Scarecrow Press, 1990), is a well-constructed bibliography of critical reviews and interpretations of thirty-six major writers. Included here are novelists, poets, and playwrights such as Blais, Hebert, Roy, Hemon, and Brossard. Monographs, parts of books, dissertations, articles, and book reviews are enumerated. An index of critics is supplied, along with a listing of Canadian publishers.

1078. Concise Dictionary of American Literary Biography. Detroit: Gale Research, 1987-1989. 6v. ISBN 0-8103-1818-0.

Designed to meet the needs of smaller libraries, this six-volume tool employs a streamlined style in utilizing the entries taken from the *Dictionary of Literary Biography* (entry 993). Each volume treats a literary period, beginning with coverage from 1640-1865 in volume 1 to the period 1968-1988 treated in volume 6. Each volume provides detailed biocritical essays of some thirty to forty important writers from that period. About 200 writers are treated in the six volumes and represent the authors and poets most frequently studied in high school and college curricula. Entries supply charts or "contextual diagrams" providing a quick overview of places, themes, movements, influences, etc. relevant to the subject's work.

Structured in the same manner is *Concise Dictionary of British Literary Biography* (1992), with each of eight volumes treating some twenty to thirty writers. Volume 1 covers writers prior to 1660; volume 8 treats contemporary writers from 1960 to the present. Materials in both these collections have been updated and presented in full when culled from the larger work. The final volumes of each set provide cumulative indexes of people, places, and titles.

1079. **Contemporary Literary Critics.** 2d ed. Elmer Borklund. Detroit: Gale Research, 1982. 600p. ISBN 0-8103-0443-0.

About 125 British and American critics of modern times are covered in this work, 9 of whom have been added since the earlier edition in 1977. Entries for those previously covered have been updated and revised. Entries furnish brief biographical summaries, bibliographies of major writings by and about the individual, and essays of the critical stance of each one. They run from two to six pages long and include quotations (some rather lengthy) of the subject's writings. The work represents an attempt to determine the objectives of each critic, the assumptions he or she makes, and his or her accomplishments. As is true of a number of Gale Research publications, the critical interpretations include personal judgment on the part of the author, who is willing to point out shortcomings in style or thought.

1080. **Critical Dictionary of English Literature and British and American Authors, Living and Deceased, from the Earliest Accounts to the Latter Half of the Nineteenth Century ...** Samuel Austin Allibone. Philadelphia: Lippincott, 1858. 3v. **Supp.** 1891. 2v. Repr., Detroit: Gale Research, 1965. 5v.

A standard in the field, recognized by scholars of the English-speaking world as an important tool, this old favorite has been criticized through the years on a number of counts, most important of which lies in the realm of accuracy. The most useful feature is the comprehensiveness of the listing, with 46,000 authors covered in the original three volumes. Another 37,000 are added in the supplement, providing a rich source for purposes of identification and verification.

Inaccuracies stem from its reliance on Dr. Robert Watt's *Bibliotheca Britannica: Or a General Index to British and Foreign Literature* (Edinburgh, Constable, 1824; repr. 1990), a four-volume effort for which it serves as a supplement or extension. Watt had provided biographical information of authors, along with a listing of their books, in a massive project aided only by his two sons, who continued the project to completion after Watt's death. Errors in bibliographic detail are not surprising when considering the enormity of the task, which produced a total of nearly 3,200 pages.

1081. **The Critical Temper: A Survey of Modern Criticism on English and American Literature from the Beginnings to the Twentieth Century.** Martin Tucker, gen. ed. New York: Ungar, 1969-1989. 5v. ISBN 0-8044-3303-8 (v.1-3); 0-8044-3307-0 (v.4); 0-8264-0435-9 (v.5).

This work serves as a supplement to Moulton's *Library of Literary Criticism* (entry 1090) in its provision of extracts from twentieth-century criticism of authors who wrote prior to that time. The set is arranged in chronological order from the Old English period to the beginning of the twentieth century. The first three volumes were published in 1969 and carry excerpts from modern literary critics from about 1900 to the 1960s. Volume 1 treats literature from Old English to Shakespeare; volume 2 covers Milton to Romantic Literature; and volume 3 targets Victorian and American literature. Volume 4 was issued ten years later in 1979, as a supplement to the entire set, furnishing excerpts written in the past ten years and bringing the critical coverage to the 1970s. Volume 5 (1989) is another ten-year supplement. In all volumes, critical studies from both books and periodicals are used.

1082. **The Essential Shakespeare: An Annotated Bibliography of Major Modern Studies.** 2d ed. Larry S. Champion. New York: G. K. Hall, 1993. 568p. (A Reference Publication in Literature). ISBN 0-8161-7332-X.

An especially useful tool for a student in identifying relevant and important critical studies is this annotated bibliography of more than 1,500 entries, now in its second edition. The coverage is limited to modern criticism, as it provides references to those published only in the twentieth century, from 1900 to the present. Major sections or categories represented are general works, poems and sonnets, English history plays, comedies, and tragedies. Included in the general works section are bibliographies, editions, studies of sources, and film studies. Each of the specialized sections also contains an opening subsection on general studies. Annotations are detailed and furnish scope notes and dominant themes from each work. Although some oversights have been noted in the past edition, the work remains a useful source of information.

Shakespeare Data Bank is to be an online database operating out of Evanston, Illinois, through the efforts of volunteer scholars (Shakespeare Data Bank, Inc.). It will furnish bibliographic references and bibliographies as well as information on all aspects of the life and work of the Bard. *Shakespeare* (CMC ReSearch, 1989) is a CD-ROM publication offering the complete text of all plays, poems, and sonnets in both Queen's English and American English versions. A similar effort is *Complete Works of Shakespeare* (Animated Pixels, 1991) that provides full text of plays and sonnets along with 1,000 illustrations.

1083. **The Feminist Companion to Literature in English: Women Writers from the Middle Ages to the Present.** Virginia Blain et al. New Haven, CT: Yale University Press, 1990. ISBN 0-300-04854-8.

This is the most comprehensive biographical dictionary of its type in its coverage of some 2,700 female writers, from the Middle Ages to the mid-1980s, who have written in the English language. The work has traded depth for its great breadth, and entries are limited to no more than 500 words. Arrangement is alphabetical by name of writer, with entries providing a biographical sketch, a description of important writings, and a brief list of secondary source material for additional reference. Emphasis has been given to inclusion of British writers, although there is representation from the United States, Africa, Asia, the Caribbean, South Pacific, Australia, and Canada. Novelists, poets, and playwrights are treated along with writers of diaries, letters, biographies, nonfiction, and childrens' literature. Along with the biographical entries, there are about sixty on topics such as black feminist criticism and science fiction.

1084. **Gay & Lesbian Literature**. Sharon Malinowski, ed. Detroit: St. James Press, 1994. 488p. ISBN 1-55862-174-1.

Endorsed by the Gay and Lesbian Task Force of the American Library Association's Social Responsibility Round Table, this tool provides comprehensive coverage of authors who have produced writings with gay themes. Included are two excellent introductory essays, one providing an introduction to gay male literature, by noted writer Wayne R. Dynes, and an introduction to lesbian literature by Barbara G. Grier. Some 200 authors of both fiction and nonfiction who have come to prominence in gay and lesbian culture since 1900 are covered. Entries are arranged alphabetically by name of writer, and include such luminaries as James Baldwin, Oscar Wilde, and Gertrude Stein. Treatment is given to life and career along with bibliographical coverage. Separate appendices identify authors not included as entries as well as writing awards, anthologies, and critical studies. There is a detailed table of contents, along with genre and subject indexes.

1085.   **Great Writers of the English Language.** New York: Marshall Cavendish, 1989; repr. 1991. 14v. ISBN 1-85435-000-5.

Biocritical treatment is accorded to those writers considered to be enjoyable. Of course, such subjective criteria lead to the usual questions regarding inclusion and omission of various important personalities. Only fifty-six authors are treated within the thirteen volumes of text and the index volume. Most volumes treat four authors each within a chronological arrangement for the set beginning with volume 1 and what the editors have arbitrarily labeled as "The Early English Writers" (Shakespeare, Bunyan, Pepys, and Fielding). One volume treats eleven great poets and another treats only Dickens and Hardy. Each entry is divided into four segments: biographical treatment; summary of one of the major works, including characterization and analysis of thematic influences; examination of literary devices; and finally, analysis of contemporary events that shaped the writing. The work is highly illustrated and should be popular with high school students in completing their assignments.

An unrelated three-volume effort with the same title and edited by James Vinson was issued in 1979 by St. Martin's Press. It furnishes a collection of biocritical essays of a selection of important writers from the Anglo-Saxon period to the present day. Each volume contributes biographies of individuals associated with a different genre: volume 1 covers poets; volume 2, novelists and prose writers; and volume 3, dramatists. About 500 personalities are treated in each volume, the pattern being to begin with a brief biographical sketch. This is followed by a list of publications, which appears to be quite detailed and full. There are also lists of bibliographies and of critical studies. Most important is the signed critical essay on each writer's works, which appears to be representative of British literary judgment. (Half of the contributors are from outside the United States.) Coverage of writers is broad-based and includes Commonwealth, American, and even African and Caribbean writers.

1086.   **Index to Black American Writers in Collective Biographies.** Dorothy W. Campbell. Littleton, CO: Libraries Unlimited, 1983. 162p. ISBN 0-87287-349-8.

This is an alphabetical listing of 1,900 black writers whose biographical sketches have appeared in nearly 270 biographical dictionaries and other reference tools, including audiovisual collections and some children's works. These biographical sources were published over a span of nearly 150 years, from 1837 to 1982. Each writer has at least one listing or reference, and each source has at least two individuals from the list. Entries are alphabetically arranged and include dates, field of interest, and variant names as well as reference to a biographical source.

Black American Writers: Bibliographical Essays, edited by Thomas Inge and others (St. Martin's Press, 1978), is a two-volume source of information of important biographical and critical writings on significant black American authors. It also identifies manuscript and special collections for further study. The essays cover individuals, groups, and specific genres.

1087.   **Magill's Survey of American Literature.** Frank N. Magill, ed. New York: Marshall Cavendish, 1991. 6v. ISBN 1-85435-437-X.

Designed to meet the needs of both high school and undergraduate students in search of information on significant authors, Magill has produced a six-volume treatment of 190 writers from the seventeenth to the later twentieth centuries. In keeping with the times, attention has been given to gender, ethnicity, and racial considerations in the selection of writers. They are diverse in nature and represent the various genres (fiction and short story, poetry, drama, and nonfiction). Writers of young adult literature are not overlooked. Entries are arranged alphabetically and identify biographical highlights and literary achievements in boxed formats. Essays ranging from seven to nineteen pages supply a sequential overview of the author's life, an analysis of style, and a treatment of specific titles. A listing of the author's works, is given along with a bibliography of additional sources. There is a glossary and an index.

1088.   Modern American Literature. 4th enl. ed. Dorothy Nyren Curley et al. New York: Ungar, 1969; repr. Continuum, 1989. 3v. **Supp. I-II.** 1976-1985. 2v. (Library of Literary Criticism). ISBN 0-8044-3046-2.

Established as a complementary work to Moulton's *Library of Literary Criticism* (entry 1090n), this tool appeared for the first time in 1960. The fourth edition was issued in 1969 as a three-volume set that updated and enlarged the previous edition (1964). About 115 authors were added in this compilation of excerpts of critical essays on American authors who became prominent after the turn of the century. The essays were originally published in both scholarly and popular books and journals. Citations are given to their locations. Volume 3 furnishes an index of critics. Subsequently, the first supplement appeared as volume 4 in 1976 and brought the criticism up-to-date on about half the authors in the original three volumes, and added forty-nine more. The second supplement recently appeared as volume 5 (edited by Paul Schlueter and June Schlueter) in 1985. It updates criticism of 143 authors previously treated, and adds 31 more to the coverage. There is an earnest attempt to include coverage of contemporary female and black writers.

1089.   Modern British Literature. Ruth Zabriskie Temple and Martin Tucker. New York: Ungar, 1966. 3v. **Supp. I-II.** 2v. 1975-1985. (A Library of Literary Criticism). ISBN 0-8044-3140-X (v.5).

Similar to Curley's *Modern American Literature* (entry 1088) in structure and frequency, this title serves as a companion to that work and also supplements the Moulton effort (entry 1090). Excerpts of critical commentaries are arranged in chronological order, as is customary for these works. This arrangement is useful for the student or specialist who wishes to gauge the reception given the writings of an author over the years. The tool was published as a three-volume set in 1966 to cover the critical reception of the work of twentieth-century British authors. Each volume treats different writers, and volume 3 furnishes a cross-reference index and an index of critics. The first supplement (edited by Martin Tucker and Rita Stein) appeared as volume 4 in 1975, updating the earlier criticism on about one-third of the writers and adding forty-nine more. The second supplement appeared as volume 5 in 1985, and was edited by Denis Lane and Rita Stein. It contains eleven new writers, eleven writers who had not been updated in the previous supplement, and new or updated bibliographies for all entries.

1090.   The New Moulton's Library of Literary Criticism of English and American Authors. Harold Bloom, gen. ed. New York: Chelsea House Publishers, 1985-1990. 11v. ISBN 0-87754-779-3 (v.1).

This is a thorough revision of the classic *Library of Literary Criticism*, by Charles Wells Moulton (Moulton, 1901-1905). Like the original, which has been a library standard since its publication date, it serves as both an anthology of critical comment and an index to critical studies. It set the pattern for a number of works to follow in subsequent years by furnishing a compilation of extracts of quoted materials representing critical commentary. An additional 250 authors (British and American) who died before 1904 have been added to the new edition. Each author is given brief biographical coverage, followed by selected quotations of criticisms. These are classified and grouped as personal or individual works. Extracts can be quite lengthy, and adequately convey the sense of the critique. The period of criticism covered in the Chelsea House work remains the same (680-1904), beginning with Volume 1, "Medieval-Early Renaissance," and ending with coverage of "Late Victorian-Edwardian" in volume 10. Volume 11 furnishes a bibliographical supplement and index.

Another supplementary effort is Martin Tucker's *Library of Literary Criticism of English and American Authors Through the Beginning of the Twentieth Century* (Ungar, 1966; rev. with additions, Continuum, 1989). This is a four-volume update as well as an abridgement of the Moulton work. New material has been added with new authors, and other authors were dropped.

1091. **Research Guide to Biography and Criticism**. Walton Beacham, ed. Washington, DC: Research Publishing, 1985-1991. 6v. ISBN 0-933833-00-8.

Designed for high school and undergraduate students, this series provides biocritical coverage of British and American poets, novelists, and nonfiction writers dating from the Middle Ages to the present. Dramatists from all periods are enumerated as well. Volumes 1 and 2 were issued in 1985 and provide signed articles from three to five pages in length on 300 poets, novelists, and prose writers. Included in each article is a brief chronology, selected bibliography, evaluation of biographical and critical works, and references to biographical sources. Volume 3, published in 1986, embraces dramatists, and volume 4 (1990) provides an update with revisions of many entries covered in volumes 1 to 3. Volumes 5 and 6 were issued in 1991 and supply entries for nearly 130 writers who were not treated previously. Most are contemporary Americans, but there is some inclusion of notables from the past. There is a cumulative index in volume 6.

1092. **Who's Who in Writers, Editors & Poets: United States and Canada**. Highland Park, IL: December Press, 1987- . Bienn. ISSN 1049-8621.

The fourth edition of this recently established biennial biographical directory was issued in 1992 and treats the 1992-1993 period. It contains nearly 550 pages and treats about 10,000 individual writers, editors, and poets. Canadians had been added to the third edition. Entries are brief and supply information regarding education, date and place of birth, family, awards, indication of publications, and current address. Information is gathered through questionnaire and inclusion is based on response; therefore, omissions are evident. An interesting observation is the lack of representation among university press editors. The strength or value of the work lies in the great proportion of relatively unknown writers treated; it would appear that at least half the entries are of personalities not covered in biographical works by Gale Research or St. James Press. An index is provided.

1093. **The Writers Directory.** Detroit: St. James Press, 1971/1973- . Bienn. ISSN 0084-2699.

Now in its eleventh edition (1994-1996), this work lists more than 17,000 living writers who have had at least one book published in the English language. Providing brief biographical sketches of the Who's Who variety, the entries give pseudonyms, citizenship, birth years, writing summaries, appointments, bibliographies, and addresses. Writers represent varied genres and include fiction, nonfiction, poetry, and drama. Coverage is geographically comprehensive, with all areas in which English is spoken or written represented (United States, England, Australia, Canada, South Africa, Ireland, and so on). A most useful feature is the "yellow pages" in which writers are classified and listed under different writing categories. The eleventh edition (1994-1996) published in 1994 continues the pattern.

Who's Who in Canadian Literature, compiled by Gordon Ripley and Anne Mercer (Reference Press, 1983/1984-) is a more specialized biennial directory furnishing about 900 sketches of living Canadian poets, novelists, playwrights, critics, editors, and short story writers. The fourth edition, for 1992/1993, was issued in 1992.

1094. **Writers of the Indian Diaspora: A Bio-Bibliographical Critical Sourcebook**. Emmanuel S. Nelson, ed. Westport, CT: Greenwood Press, 1993. 468p. ISBN 0-313-27904-7.

The author is an academic specialist in the area of Indic literature and has produced an important volume for high school and college students at all levels. A total of fifty-eight authors of noteworthy status who have written in the English language are covered, in the attempt to be as comprehensive as possible. These writers represent a variety of geographical areas embraced within the Indian diaspora from the South Pacific to the Americas, including parts of Europe and Oceania. Entries are arranged alphabetically and supply well-constructed biographical sketches, summaries of major works, perspectives regarding critical reception, and listings of primary and secondary sources.

Nelson's earlier work, *Reworlding: The Literature of the Indian Diaspora* (Greenwood Press, 1992), is a slender volume providing exposition of literary development and achievement within separate chapters given to the different geographic regions. Writers are identified and elements of the literature are examined.

HISTORIES AND CHRONOLOGIES

1095. **American Literary Magazines: The Eighteenth and Nineteenth Centuries.** Edward E. Chielens, ed. Westport, CT: Greenwood Press, 1986. Repr., London: Greenwood/Eurospan. 503p. (Historical Guides to the World's Periodicals and Newspapers). ISBN 0-313-23985-1.

Designed as the first volume of a two-volume set covering the history of little (low-circulation literary) magazines in this country, it covers the period 1774 to 1900 and describes ninety-three of the most important titles of the time. Included for each entry is an extensive history of its publishing and editorial policy. The work is scholarly in nature, providing documentation through notes. Also furnished is a bibliography of additional sources for further reading. Reprint editions are identified, as are existing runs of the periodicals and availability of indexes. Title changes are recorded, and volume and issue data are given along with frequency and names of key figures. Also provided is an opening essay on periodical publishing during this period. The appendices contain listings of literary magazines and a chronology.

American Literary Magazines: The Twentieth Century, also edited by Chielens (1992), continues the coverage into the modern era and completes the two-volume set. The most familiar little magazines, seventy-six in number, are featured and described in the same manner as the initial volume. A chronology is furnished, as is a descriptive analysis of nearly thirty repositories of little magazines in the United States. An appendix furnishes brief descriptions of an additional 100 magazines.

1096. **Annals of American Literature 1602-1983.** Richard M. Ludwig and Clifford A. Nault, Jr., eds. New York: Oxford University Press, 1986; repr. 1989. 342p. ISBN 0-19-505919-0.

Modeled after *Annals of English Literature* (entry 1097), this is a chronology of facts and dates focused on literary productivity. Listings are generally of books published in this country, but include some European titles considered important to an understanding of the pre-colonial and colonial periods and published during that time. Listings are year-by-year, with four genres identified (fiction, nonfiction, drama, and poetry). Authors are listed alphabetically each year in entries that include their birthdates, titles of their works, and genres. Parallel columns identify certain historical and literary events. Identified are the founding of newspapers, births and deaths of authors, and foreign literary works. Although there are a number of omissions in this selective work, it should be of value for quick identifications.

1097. **Annals of English Literature, 1475-1950: The Principal Publications of Each Year Together with an Alphabetical Index of Authors with Their Works.** 2d ed. Oxford: Clarendon Press, 1961; repr. 1976. 380p. ISBN 0-19-866129-0.

Originally published in 1935 and covering the period up to 1925, this work has been a fixture in reference departments interested in providing services in the area of English literature. Recognized as an important chronology, it has served as a model for other works in its organization and format (entry 1096). Arrangement is year-by-year, with listings of authors given under each year. Important titles of their works are furnished. Complete listings are given for major authors, and principal works of minor authors are given. Side columns give dates of birth and death of literary figures and founding of newspapers and important periodicals, as well as foreign events having a bearing on English literary contributions.

Another useful chronology is Samuel J. Rogal's *A Chronological Outline of British Literature* (Greenwood Press, 1980), which furnishes comprehensive coverage of literary events in England, Scotland, Ireland, and Wales. It is similar in style and format to Rogal's *A Chronological Outline of American Literature* (entry 1101).

1098. British Literary Magazines. Alvin Sullivan, ed. Westport, CT: Greenwood Press, 1983-1986. 4v. (Historical Guides to the World's Periodicals and Newspapers). ISBN 0-313-22871-X.

An impressive tool covering several hundred important British periodicals by historical period is this four-volume guide. Volume 1 covers the period of Johnson and the Augustan age from 1698 to 1788; volume 2 covers the Romantic period from 1789 to 1836; volume 3 surveys the Victorian and Edwardian years from 1837 to 1913; and volume 4 brings the coverage to the present, from 1914 to 1984. Entries are arranged alphabetically and each periodical is described in terms of its editorial history and general content. Significant contributors and regular features are listed. A useful bibliography of additional sources is given, and American and British library locations are enumerated. Each volume has an index of topics, titles, and names. Although not a history itself, this directory should prove to be an invaluable resource for the literary historian.

1099. Cambridge History of American Literature. William Peterfield Trent et al., eds. New York: Putnam's, 1917-1921. 4v; repr., Macmillan, 1943, 1978. 3v. in 1. ISBN 0-02-520930-2.

This is the original history of American literature, which, although dated to some extent, is still highly respected and frequently used. Especially good is its coverage of the early period in volumes 1 and 2, for which it is acknowledged to be most thorough and comprehensive. Volumes 3 and 4 treat the later national literature and, of course, need updating. Detailed coverage is provided to literary forms and important writers, but the work also describes in adequate fashion a host of less common considerations. Included are accounts of early travelers, explorers, colonial newspapers, literary annuals, and gift books. Coverage of children's literature, the English language in America, and non-English writings make this a worthwhile tool even today. Chapters are written by specialists and the bibliographies are full, although somewhat out-of-date. The Macmillan reprints omit the bibliographies.

1100. Cambridge History of English Literature. A. W. Ward and A. R. Waller, eds. Cambridge, UK: Cambridge University Press, 1907-1927; repr. 1976. 15v.

Considered for many years the most important general history of English literature, this massive work remains a model of scholarship and distinguished narrative. Individual scholars and specialists have prepared each of the chapters. The work begins with the earliest times and proceeds in chronological fashion, volume-by-volume, to the end of the nineteenth century. This century is given detailed coverage in three volumes, 12-14. The final volume provides an index to the whole set. Bibliographies are given in each volume and are generally extensive; although old, they are still useful. Designed originally for graduate students, the work has been reprinted several times, sometimes without the bibliographies. These cheaper reprints limit the reference value considerably in a literature department.

1101. A Chronological Outline of American Literature. Samuel J. Rogal. Westport, CT: Greenwood Press, 1987. 446p. ISBN 0-313-25471-0.

Similar in format and style to a previous work by the author, *A Chronological Outline of British Literature* (entry 1097n), this chronology begins with the year 1507 and covers important events in American literature through 1986. The usual types of literary events are highlighted, such as births and deaths of literary figures; notable occurrences; and publications of various types, including poetry, fiction, drama, and essays. Both important and not-so-important American writers are treated, with the criteria for inclusion being their significance or representativeness. Although there are many omissions, the comprehensiveness of this chronology is commendable. A work of this type is useful to scholars, specialists, educators, and the general public as well. There is an introductory essay, a bibliography, and an index of authors and events. The lack of a title index might be considered an oversight.

1102. **The Concise Cambridge History of English Literature.** 3d ed. George Sampson. Rev. by R. C. Churchill. New York: Cambridge University Press, 1972; repr. 1979. 976p. ISBN 0-521-07385-5.

This is a reprint with corrections of the 1970 edition, which at that time represented a thorough revision of the work. The first edition of this work appeared in 1941 and was followed by a second edition in 1960. Churchill's revision was undertaken with respect to work of contemporary scholars and modern scholarship. Chapters were added on the literature of the United States from the colonial period to Henry James, and the mid-twentieth-century literature of the Commonwealth and the former colonies. The work has remained a useful and popular tool for its blend of the traditional literature of the early and middle periods with that of the modern era.

1103. **A Concise Chronology of English Literature.** P. J. Smallwood, comp. Totowa, NJ: Barnes & Noble, 1985. 220p. ISBN 0-389-20597-4.

Another useful chronology that attempts to place literary contributions within the context of historical events is this recent work. Coverage begins with the period of Chaucer in 1375 and ends with the year 1975. This makes it a useful tool for libraries that have been operating with the *Annals of English Literature* (entry 1097) and its more limited time span (1475-1950). Two schemes are provided, one a listing of important events in English literature, the other giving important historical events that occurred at the same time. Certain European writers, such as Boccaccio, Erasmus, and Machiavelli, are included because of their significance in the development of English literature. The usual number of omissions or questionable inclusions applies. An index of authors' names provides access.

1104. **A Literary History of England.** 2d ed. Albert Croll Baugh. New York: Appleton-Century-Crofts, 1980. 4v.

This is the second issue of a highly regarded and important reference history in four volumes covering the same time period as the much more detailed *Cambridge History of English Literature* (entry 1100). Like the initial edition in 1967, the style of writing in the present effort is well developed and consistent from volume to volume, each of which is done by an American specialist on the topic. Volume 1 covers the Middle Ages in two parts, the Old English period to 1100, and the Middle English period 1100-1500. Volume 2 treats the Renaissance (1500-1660), and volume 3, the Restoration and eighteenth century (1660-1789). Volume 4 carries the coverage through modern times. The work is especially useful for its excellent documentation, with numerous bibliographical footnotes in the text. At the end of the new edition is a bibliographical supplement giving additional references to books and periodical articles.

1105. **Literary History of the United States.** 4th ed. rev. Robert E. Spiller et al., eds. New York: Macmillan, 1974. 2v. ISBN 0-02-613160-9.

This work, first published in 1948, represented the first comprehensive literary history of the United States since publication of the *Cambridge History of American Literature* (entry 1099) in 1921. It has continued to be a useful and popular work through the years. Volume 1 furnishes well-developed historical narratives covering colonial times to the present in a series of chapters written by various experts. Volume 2 contains bibliographical essays designed to provide additional resource material in support of the text. It is divided into four major sections, consisting of a guide to resources, literature and culture, movements and influences, and finally, individual authors. Nearly 250 individual authors are treated here, with listings of their various contributions. Each of the four parts furnishes useful critical commentary on editions, biographies, etc.

1106.   **Oxford History of English Literature.** Frank Percy Wilson and Bonamy Dobrée. Oxford, UK: Clarendon Press, 1945- . v.1-10, 12.

Similar to the *New Oxford History of Music* (entry 625), in that it is a long-range project, is this multivolume history of English literature. Recognized as an important source for its detailed and authoritative coverage, it is hoped that the work will eventually reach fruition as a useful alternative to the much older *Cambridge History of English Literature* (entry 1100). Each volume or part of a volume is written by a specialist in the field, and each furnishes extensive bibliographies. Still in process are volume 1, part 1, ranging from before the Norman Conquest to Middle English literature, and volume 11, the mid-nineteenth century, as well as a possible second part of volume 4 (part 1, "English Drama, 1485-1585"). Most libraries follow the lead of the Library of Congress in cataloging the volumes separately and linking them together with a series added entry in the catalog.

1107.   **The Oxford History of New Zealand Literature in English**. Terry Sturm, ed. New York: Oxford University Press, 1991. 748p. ISBN 0-19-558211-X.

This is a well-executed survey of the literature of New Zealand, with chapters arranged by literary genre and produced by eleven scholar-contributors. New Zealand has been largely ignored in terms of its literary productivity until the present decade with publication of Patrick Evans's *Penguin History of New Zealand Literature* (Penguin, 1990), a less comprehensive work than the present effort. In addition to traditional elements, the *Oxford* provides chapters on popular fiction, children's literature, and nonfiction. Unfortunately, reviewers have found these to be the weakest parts of the work, mainly in their authors' seeming lack of conviction in establishing their importance. The introductory chapter on Maori literature in Maori is especially useful in revealing information difficult to find elsewhere. The concluding bibliographic essay identifies works as recent as 1990. An index is provided.

1108.   **St. James Reference Guide to English Literature.** James Vinson and D. L. Kirkpatrick, eds. Chicago: St. James Press, 1985. 8v. ISBN 0-912289-18-X.

This work provides a varied information package, including more than 1,200 biographical sketches, useful bibliographies of a comprehensive nature, and well-conceived critical essays. Especially noteworthy are the lengthy period and genre histories. The arrangement is by historical period, with volume 1 covering the beginnings and the Renaissance; volume 2, the Restoration and the eighteenth century; volume 3, the Romantic and Victorian years; and volume 4, the novel to 1900. Volumes 5-7 cover twentieth-century poetry, fiction, and drama, respectively, and volume 8 treats Commonwealth literature. More than 400 scholars from various parts of the English-speaking world have contributed to the work. Considering the comprehensive coverage afforded by this tool and its potential in answering a host of questions, it should be regarded as an important purchase for the reference department. The new edition (entry 1031) is known as the *Reference Guide to English Literature*.

FICTION

Bibliographic Guides

1109.   **Afro-American Fiction, 1853-1976: A Guide to Information Sources.** Edward Margolies and David Bakish. Detroit: Gale Research, 1979. 161p. (American Literature, English Literature, and World Literatures in English Information Guide Series, v.25). ISBN 0-8103-1207-7.

Although this work is not without deficiencies in terms of omissions and inaccuracies, it still is important because of its comprehensive nature, incorporating several features not otherwise found in a single tool. First is a checklist of novels, a comprehensive listing of nearly 730 works dating from William Wells Brown's *Clotel* (1853) through publications in the year 1976. Second is a listing of anthologies of short stories, followed by an annotated list of bibliographies and general studies on black fiction and authors. All fictional works are listed chronologically in the appendix. Although there is little material that is not duplicated in other tools, it is convenient to have these features included in one work. There are indexes by author, title, and subject to provide access.

1110. **Dickinson's American Historical Fiction.** 5th ed. Virginia Brokaw Gerhardstein. Metuchen, NJ: Scarecrow Press, 1986. 352p. ISBN 0-8108-1867-1.

First published in 1958, this standard work has now been updated to include work published to 1984. It is a useful tool for reading guidance, providing a classified listing of more than 3,000 novels published primarily between 1917 and 1984. For historical novels, time, place, and social/historical phenomena are identified. The arrangement of entries is by chronological period, beginning with colonial times and ending with the mid-1970s (the turbulent years). Annotations are furnished but are not evaluative, and describe briefly the setting and plot in order to give historical perspective. Included is a subject index as well as an author-title index.

Another useful source, although not as current, is Leonard Bertram Irwin's *A Guide to Historical Fiction for the Use of Schools, Libraries, and the General Reader* (10th ed., McKinley, 1971). This first appeared in 1930, written by Hanna Logasa, and still represents a standard source of favorably reviewed historical novels classified by geography and time period.

1111. **Science Fiction, Fantasy, and Weird Fiction Magazines.** Marshall B. Tymn and Mike Ashley, eds. Westport, CT: Greenwood Press, 1985. 970p. (Historical Guides to the World's Periodicals and Newspapers). ISBN 0-313-21221-X.

Regarded as an excellent source of information on magazines of this type, this work provides comprehensive coverage of English-language periodicals dating from 1882 to the present. It is divided into several sections, the first of which furnishes listings of magazines published in the United States, Great Britain, Canada, and Australia, which are devoted wholly or in part to genre literature. Entries provide a brief history of origin and development, bibliography and sources of indexing, sources of reprinting, and publication data, and include numerous cross-references. Other sections give English-language anthologies, information on significant fanzines and academic journals, and annotations of an additional 178 titles from twenty-three foreign countries. Appendices furnish an index to cover artists and a chronology of magazine origins.

Another important tool, *Anatomy of Wonder: A Critical Guide to Science Fiction* (R. R. Bowker, 1987), edited by Neil Barron, is now in its third edition. It identifies more than 1,650 novels and short story collections. There are additional chapters on foreign-language contributions, film and television, and illustration as well as the major coverage of the primary literature, magazines, and others. Entries have been modified to include recent sequels and other interesting elements.

Bibliographies and Indexes

1112. **The Afro-American Short Story: A Comprehensive Annotated Index with Selected Commentaries.** Preston M. Yancy, comp. Westport, CT: Greenwood Press, 1986. 171p. (Bibliographies and Indexes in Afro-American and African Studies, no. 10). ISBN 0-313-24355-7.

This is a timely and important contribution identifying more than 800 short stories written in a thirty-two-year period between 1950 and 1982. These years are especially significant to the black experience in terms of its manifestation in the literature following desegregation and the 1954 Supreme Court decision. More than 300 authors are represented in this tool, which is divided into several parts. The first part is a year-by-year chronological listing with titles arranged alphabetically under each year. This is followed by a list of anthologies and collections, then by a section of commentaries on selected stories, classified by type. There is an author index which also provides references to biographical sketches in five biographical encyclopedias.

Helen Ruth Houston's *The Afro-American Novel, 1965-1975: A Descriptive Bibliography of Primary and Secondary Material* (Whitston, 1977) still holds a prominent position in reference departments, with its listing of the works of fifty-six black Americans published since 1964. Critical studies and reviews are identified.

1113. **American Fiction, 1774-1850: A Contribution Toward a Bibliography.** Additions and corrs. appended. Lyle Henry Wright. San Marino, CA: Huntington Library, 1978. 438p. ISBN 0-87328-041-5.

This has become a standard reference tool since publication of the first edition in 1939. Since that time, it has been revised on several occasions, with more than 700 titles added to the second revised edition in 1969. This issue contains additions and corrections. The total of 3,500 entries includes novels, romances, short stories, fictitious biographies and travel, allegories, etc. Copies of these works are located in twenty-two libraries. All works are by American authors, and entries are alphabetical by author. Entries furnish title imprints, pagination, and occasional notes. Juvenile fiction is excluded.

The work has been continued by Wright's *American Fiction, 1851-1875* (Huntington Library, 1965; repr. 1978) and *American Fiction, 1876-1900* (Huntington Library, 1966; repr. 1978). The former enumerates more than 2,800 titles in nineteen locations; the latter identifies copies of the first U.S. editions of 6,175 items in fifteen libraries.

1114. **Crime Fiction II: A Comprehensive Bibliography, 1749-1990.** Allen J. Hubin. New York: Garland, 1994. 2v. (Garland Reference Library of the Humanities, v.1353). ISBN 0-8240-6891-2.

Based on earlier works by the same author, this edition adds another ten years of coverage and identifies some 70,000 titles. Newly added features are a listing of more than 4,000 films based on literary efforts, complete with release information, and a listing of individual short stories from 4,000 anthologies. All types of crime stories are included: mystery, detective, suspense, thriller, gothic, police, and spy. The major segment of the work is an author index followed by titles arranged alphabetically, with cross-references to variant titles and pseudonyms. Access is facilitated through indexes by title, setting (geographical), series, and series character.

Another useful title is Albert J. Menendez's *The Subject Is Murder*, in two volumes, (1986-1990) from the same publisher. Volume 1 identifies more than 3,800 titles published between the 1930s and 1985 by subject or major thematic element, such as medicine or politics, covered in separate chapters. Volume 2 supplies references to another 2,100 mystery titles under twenty-nine broad categories. Most of the titles were published between 1985 and 1989. *Murder ... by Category: A Subject Guide to Mystery Fiction*, by Tasha Mackler (Scarecrow Press, 1991), is an annotated bibliography of mystery fiction published between 1985 and 1990. The author, a proprietor of a mystery bookstore, has supplied a classified arrangement with such subjects as "Getting Away with Murder" and "At Sea."

1115. **Encyclopedia of Science Fiction and Fantasy through 1968: A Bibliographic Survey ...** Donald H. Tuck, comp. Chicago: Advent, 1974-1982. 3v. ISBN 0-911682-27-9 (set).

More of a bibliography than an encyclopedic source, this work was completed in three volumes over an eight-year period. Volume 1, *Who's Who and Works, A-L*, consists of an alphabetical listing of authors, anthologists, editors, artists, etc., with biographical sketches when available. Listings of their works in the science fiction and fantasy area are furnished through 1968 and include all known editions and foreign translations. Tables of contents are given for anthologies and collections. Volume 2 covers the same territory for M-Z and also provides an alphabetical listing by title. Volume 3 covers a variety of topics: magazines in the field, paperbacks, pseudonyms (cross-references by pseudonym and real name), series, and general areas of interest such as publishers or films. Initially, it was planned to issue supplements on a quinquennial basis, but thus far this has not been done.

1116.   **Facts on File Bibliography of American Fiction, 1919-1988**. Matthew J. Bruccoli and Judith S. Baughman, eds. New York: Facts on File, 1991. 2v. (Facts on File Bibliography Series). ISBN 0-8160-2674-2.

This bibliography is useful to libraries unable to afford the *Dictionary of Literary Biography* (entry 993) but who wish to provide a handy reference source for high school and undergraduate clientele. Nearly 225 fiction writers are treated, all of whom were born before 1941 and published their most important work between 1919 and 1988. All types of fiction are represented, including of all genres and children's/young adult literature. Author entries are arranged alphabetically and supply listings of primary works identified by genre, and secondary sources identified by type (bibliography, biography, books, articles, and special journal issues). Reviews and dissertations are listed also. These entries are signed by specialist-contributors. Special features include a chronology of authors and their works, an annotated bibliography of 110 titles considered essential to literature study, and a general bibliography. There is an index to authors of secondary works. A retrospective volume was issued in 1993, covering the period 1866-1918. It was edited by James Nagel and Gwen L. Nagel.

1117.   **Fiction Catalog.** 12th ed. Juliette Yaakov and John Greenfieldt, eds. New York: H. W. Wilson, 1991. 943p. (Standard Catalog Series). ISBN 0-8242-0804-8.

As part of the well-known and highly respected standard catalog series, this work has had a long tradition; its first edition appeared in 1908. Presently, new editions are issued quinquennially with annual updates. Considered a companion work to the *Public Library Catalog* (nonfiction), this tool furnishes a selective annotated listing of more than 5,150 English-language titles of prose fiction. Plot summaries are given in adequate detail, and arrangement and format are highly stylized. The largest proportion of the volume consists of individual entries for specific titles. Arrangement is by author, then title; excerpts from reviews are included. There is a title-subject index providing ready access by topical matter, the subject approach being one of the strong features of this work.

1118.   **Fiction, 1876-1983: A Bibliography of United States Editions.** New York: R. R. Bowker, 1983. 2v. ISBN 0-8352-1726-4.

Another of the Bowker spinoffs from *Books in Print* (1948-) and *American Book Publishing Record* (1961-) is this comprehensive listing of fictional works published in the United States over a period of more than 100 years. Included are novels, novellas, short stories, anthologies, and collections. There are more than 170,000 entries, generally found to be reliable (although not error-free) as is true of other works in the Bowker line. Entries emulate those in *Books in Print* and may give author, editor, title, date, price, publisher, LC number, and ISBN. Volume 1 contains a classified author index listing authors by country and period, as well as a main author index. Volume 2 furnishes a title index. Full publication information is found in entries in both indexes.

1119.   **Index to Crime and Mystery Anthologies**. William G. Contento and Martin H. Greenberg. Boston: G. K. Hall, 1991. 736p. ISBN 0-8161-8629-4.

This is the first comprehensive index to anthologies of crime, mystery, detective, espionage, and suspense stories and appeals to a wide variety of users. The authors are both experienced writers and indexers of the genre and bring expertise in treating 1,031 anthologies published between 1875 and 1990. More than 12,500 short stories, 3,700 novelettes, 500 novellas, 70 novels, and 300 articles represent the literary output of more than 3,600 authors. There are five major sections of the work: author listings of books, author listings of stories, title listings of books, title listings of stories, and a contents listing of anthologies. Entries for author listings supply information on authorship and publication, whereas title listings treat type of story and the source of its initial appearance. Anthology listings enumerate each story in the entry. The work is to be updated with subsequent volumes.

1120.   **A Mirror for the Nation: An Annotated Bibliography of American Social Fiction, 1901-1950.** Archibald Hanna. New York: Garland, 1985. 472p. (Garland Reference Library of the Humanities, v.595). ISBN 0-8240-8727-5.

This is a useful work identifying some 4,000 titles of American fiction written during the first half of this century and showing their connection to social history. The emphasis is on novels, but also included are short story collections, plays, and narrative poems. Entries are arranged alphabetically by author, followed by indexes of subject, title, and illustrator. Subjects such as labor and capital or marriage and family life are used, but place names predominate. Principal subject matter is described in brief annotations, and geographical setting is indicated. Excluded for the most part are the genres of western and detective stories and juvenile literature.

1121.   **Nineteenth Century Fiction: A Bibliographical Catalogue Based on the Collection Formed by Robert Lee Wolff.** Robert Lee Wolff, comp. New York: Garland, 1981-1986. 5v. (Garland Reference Library of the Humanities). ISBN 0-824-09474-3.

This set stands as the most complete bibliography of nineteenth-century English fiction available. Based on the important collection of Victorian fiction belonging to the late Robert Lee Wolff, the work identifies nearly 8,000 titles. They represent the intention of the collector to acquire any English novel published during the reign of Queen Victoria, as well as any other novel published by those authors even though it might fall outside the range of 1827-1901. Volumes 1-4 consist of entries for the major segment of the collection, novels by known authors. Volume 5 covers anonymous works, listed by title, and pseudonymous works, listed by pseudonyms. Volume 5 includes the title index to the entire set, as well as an index to all illustrators mentioned in the notes.

1122.   **Science Fiction and Fantasy Series and Sequels: A Bibliography, Volume 1: Books.** Tim Cottrill et al. New York: Garland, 1986. 398p. (Garland Reference Library of the Humanities, v.611). ISBN 0-8240-8671-6.

Another of the Garland bibliographies emphasizing series publications of a genre is this listing of 6,300 book titles in some 1,200 series. Because this work is identified as volume 1 and is restricted to books, it might have been reasonable to assume that forthcoming volumes would cover series carried in periodicals. Unfortunately, there has been no further activity in this regard. Like the western, science fiction and fantasy are well accommodated in the series format and much important work has appeared in this manner. Arrangement is by author, with entries furnishing series title, publisher, and publication date. Although some omissions are evident, the work is useful to those with an interest in the topic. There are good title and sequence indexes.

1123.   **Science Fiction Book Review Index, 1923-1973.** H. W. Hall. Detroit: Gale Research, 1975. 438p. ISBN 0-8103-1054-6.

This is the lead volume and most comprehensive publication for an annual series cumulated on a quinquennial basis. The initial volume covers a fifty-year period and identifies reviews appearing in selected science fiction magazines. Arrangement is alphabetical by authors of the works. A directory of magazines indexed is furnished, and a title index provides access.

The work has continued annually and has cumulated as Hall's *Science Fiction Book Review Index, 1974-1979* (1981), and most recently as *Science Fiction and Fantasy Book Review Index, 1980-1984* ... by Hall and Geraldine L. Hutchins (1986). The recent title identifies more than 13,800 reviews published in more than seventy magazines. An important addition is a section, "Science Fiction and Fantasy Research Index," providing about 16,000 author and subject access points to books, articles, and essays of history or criticism. The effort has been issued annually under the new title since 1984. A similar work is *Science Fiction & Fantasy Book Review Annual* (Meckler, 1988-), a magazine of opinionated commentary and well-developed, cogent reviews. It supplies more than 500 reviews of books in the genre published the previous year. The work has undergone several title changes since its initial appearance in 1978; *Fantasy Review, Science Fiction and Fantasy Review,* and *Fantasy.*

1124. **Short Story Index: An Index to 60,000 Stories in 4,320 Collections.** Dorothy Elizabeth Cook and Isabel Stevenson Monro. New York, H. W. Wilson, 1953. 1553p. **Supps. 1950-1954, 1955-1958, 1959-1963, 1964-1968, 1969-1973, 1974-1978, 1979-1983, 1984-1988.** ISSN 0360-9774.

A valuable and highly regarded standard tool, this work appeared originally in 1953. As its title indicates, the initial volume indexes 60,000 English-language stories published up to 1949 in several thousand collections. Indexing is by author, title, and subject in typical Wilson dictionary arrangement. Since that time, the work has continued through periodic supplements which are now issued annually and cumulated on a quinquennial basis; they identify several thousand stories in recently published anthologies and periodicals. The most recent cumulation (1984-1988) was compiled by Juliette Yaakov and indexes 22,431 stories. Such subject headings as "AIDS," "Homeless," and "Lesbianism" are newly added. Inclusion of periodicals began with the 1974-1978 supplement. A list of collections indexed and a directory of periodicals appear in the back.

1125. **War and Peace Through Women's Eyes: A Selective Bibliography of Twentieth-Century American Women's Fiction.** Susanne Carter. Westport, CT: Greenwood Press, 1992. 293p. ISBN 0-313-27771-0.

This is a unique and important bibliography due to its treatment of novels and short stories with war themes written by female authors. It is highly selective in its coverage of 374 works from more than 200 authors in its resolve to exclude fiction of more popular than literary nature. This focus on quality makes it an especially useful tool for serious students as well as general readers. It opens with an introductory essay of scholarly nature placing war literature in perspective. The text is divided into five thematic chapters bearing annotated entries: "World War I," "World War II," "Vietnam," "Nuclear War," and "War and Peace." These chapters contain an introduction, separate sections on novels and short fiction, and bibliographies of literary criticism and sources. Annotated entries supply an evaluative plot summary for each work. Author, title, and subject indexes are furnished.

1126. **Western Series and Sequels: A Reference Guide.** 2d ed. Bernard A. Drew et al. New York: Garland, 1993. 304p. (Garland Bibliographies on Series and Sequels; Garland Reference Library of the Humanities, v.1399). ISBN 0-8240-9648-7.

As part of the extensive Garland line of bibliographies, this was introduced in 1986 as useful tool for identifying westerns that appeared in series. This particular form of the genre has been common for decades, and the second edition adds 350 additional series to the 375 entries in the first edition. Series titles imply use of the same lead character in different books, each of which has an episode that is complete in itself. The coverage embraces works set in Canada, the French and Indian Wars, and the Civil War, as well as the American West. Foreign series dealing with the theme are included; both juvenile and adult series are treated. There is a brief introductory history of the genre; a general index and author index provide access.

Dictionaries, Encyclopedias, and Handbooks

1127. **Critical Terms for Science Fiction and Fantasy: A Glossary and Guide to Scholarship.** Gary K. Wolfe. Westport, CT: Greenwood Press, 1986. 162p. ISBN 0-313-22981-3.

As the first literary glossary devoted to the area of fantastic literature, this tool has found a receptive audience among librarians and their patrons. Beginning with a twenty-six-page introductory essay on fantastic literature and literary discourse, it provides a list of nearly 500 terms, alphabetically arranged, complete with definitions and in some cases, expositions and commentaries. Some terms are given multiple definitions—those of the author and those of other experts in the field. Certain broad concepts are defined with short essays. References are given to authors and critics whose efforts are listed in a section on works consulted. Both specialists and laypersons will find this tool to be helpful and rewarding. There is an index of primary authors.

1128.   **Genreflecting: A Guide to Reading Interests in Genre Fiction.** 3d ed. Betty Rosenberg and Diana T. Herald. Englewood, CO: Libraries Unlimited, 1991. 345p. ISBN 0-87287-930-5.

Although the primary purpose of this item is to serve as a text for library school classes in book selection and collection management, it also furnishes the librarian with an interesting and useful handbook of miscellaneous information and bibliography of currently available works by authors in the different genres. Using the rationale that no child or adult need apologize for his or her choice of reading matter, Rosenberg surveys the popular genres (western, thriller, romance, science fiction, fantasy, and horror). There is an introductory chapter on genre literature, with succeeding descriptions of publishers, readers, and the place of such literature in libraries. Included in the coverage of each genre are listings of significant and popular authors, as well as anthologies, bibliographies, biographies, history, criticism, periodicals, and awards. This is an update of the 1986 edition to which more authors and titles as well as subgenres have been added (e.g., technothrillers).

A Handbook of Contemporary Fiction for Public Libraries and School Libraries, by Mary K. Biagini with the assistance of Judith Hartzler (Scarecrow Press, 1989), is a practical, well-constructed listing of fiction titles organized by genre. Emphasis is on authors who have been prominent since World War II, although the classic writers have been included as well. The first part of the book provides the listings under nine different genres (mystery and detective stories, science fiction and fantasy, and so on). The second part categorizes the authors by national origin.

1129.   **Masterplots: Revised Category Edition, American Fiction Series.** Frank N. Magill, ed. Englewood Cliffs, NJ: Salem Press, 1985. 3v. ISBN 0-89356-500-8.

Nearly 350 novels and collections of short stories have been taken from the original *Masterplots* (entry 980) and reprinted here in a work limited to coverage of authors from the United States, Canada, and Central and South America. Thus, we have another spinoff of the monumental work originally begun in 1949. The "Revised Category Edition" has proved to be a useful convenience tool. Coverage is uniform, as we have become accustomed to in the *Masterplots* design: type of work, author and dates, type of plot, time setting, date of publication, and principal characters, a brief critical essay, and an excellent summary of the plot. There has been slight modification and updating but basically this is a remake of the older work in a handy package.

Following the same pattern and rationale and published at the same time is Magill's *Masterplots: Revised Category Edition, British Fiction Series* (Salem Press, 1985). Nearly 400 works by authors from the British Commonwealth, with the exception of Canada, are reprinted in this three-volume set.

*1130.   **Masterplots II: American Fiction Series.** Frank N. Magill, ed. Englewood Cliffs, NJ: Salem Press, 1986. 4v. ISBN 0-89356-456-7.

Another publication in the *Masterplots* line-up from Salem Press is this four-volume edition focused on American fiction not previously treated in the *Masterplots* series (entry 980). More than 350 modern works from the twentieth century are examined. Coverage is not limited to North America, but includes Latin America as well. Of the 198 authors whose works are treated, 34 or 17 percent, are Latin American. Thus, Gabriel García Marquez and Carlos Fuentes appear, as do Algren, Bellow, Faulkner, Vonnegut, etc. This makes it a more valuable resource, because exposition of Latin American literature is not easily found. Entries differ somewhat from the traditional *Masterplots*, for, along with the plot summary, there is far more coverage given the evaluation of narrative devices, characterization, and thematic elements. An interpretive summary is included.

Masterplots II: British and Commonwealth Fiction Series (1987) is in the same mold and covers works of more than 150 authors of modern fiction from England, Ireland, Canada, India, Nigeria, and Australia. There are more than 350 evaluative essays of titles never covered in the previous series. Both the American and British series are accessible on

CD-ROM, along with other volumes in the *Masterplots II* line on **Masterplots II CD-ROM* (entry 980n).

1131. **The Ultimate Guide to Science Fiction**. David Pringle. New York: Pharos Books/St. Martin's Press, 1990. 407p. ISBN 0-88687-537-4.

Although probably not the "ultimate guide," this is a comprehensive listing of some 3,000 novels, short stories, and collections written in the English language and enjoying continued popularity. Works published prior to 1970 and not reprinted since are excluded, as are foreign-language publications, lesser works of lesser writers, novelizations of motion pictures, spinoffs, fantasy, and scientific romance. The work opens with an introductory segment providing a "Bibliography and Acknowledgements" section listing important sources. Entries for individual titles are arranged alphabetically and provide information in keeping with the following pattern: title, date, star rating using four stars, classification, author's name and nationality, and a two- or three-sentence summary and evaluation providing names of sequels and film versions. There are cross-references to variant titles and parent novels of series, and an author index.

Biographical and Critical Sources

1132. **American Short-Fiction Criticism and Scholarship, 1959-1977: A Checklist**. Joe Weixlmann. Chicago: Swallow, 1982. 625p. ISBN 0-8040-0381-5.

This work was initially developed as an update for the American portion of Jarvis A. Thurston's *Short-Fiction Criticism: A Checklist of Interpretation Since 1925 of Stories and Novelettes (American, British, Continental) 1800-1958* (Swallow, 1960; repr. 1963). It has exceeded the original work in comprehensiveness, as it provides not only references to critical and scholarly works on short fiction, but also citations to bibliographic publications, biographical studies, and interviews. There are around 10,000 entries to essays in 5,000 books and 325 serials. Individual authors are entered alphabetically by name, under which specific titles are listed. About 500 authors are treated.

The American Novel: A Checklist of Twentieth Century Criticism, by Donna Lorine Gerstenberger and George Hendrick (Swallow, 1961-1970), is the standard checklist in the field relating to novels or long fiction. Volume 1 identifies criticism published up to 1959. Volume 2 cites critical studies from 1960 to 1968. The arrangement is alphabetical by novelist. Citations to critical studies appear under individual novels. A second section gives general studies by century. Another useful older title is *The Contemporary Novel: A Checklist of Critical Literature on the British and American Novel Since 1945*, by Irving Adelman and Rita Dworkin (Scarecrow Press, 1972). About 180 modern writers are treated, with citations to critiques appearing in books and periodicals.

1133. **American Short Story Writers 1910-1945. Second series.** Bobby Ellen Kimbel, ed. Detroit: Gale Research, 1991. 472p. (Dictionary of Literary Biography, v.102). ISBN 0-8103-4582-X.

Designed primarily for undergraduate students, this work continues the coverage of the Dictionary of Literary Biography (entry 993) series by Kimbel on American short story writers. It is a follow-up to the *First Series* effort published in 1989, in which coverage was given to twenty-five American short story writers active between 1910 and World War II. Pattern of coverage remains consistent, as with other *DLB* offerings; the second series treats thirty-seven writers identified as having been contributors to the development of the short story in this country. Author profiles are written by individual contributors and supply name, dates of birth and death, cross-references to other *DLB* volumes, bibliography of primary source material, and, most importantly, a seven- to ten-page summary review and evaluation.

Earlier efforts by Kimbel cover the historical past with *American Short Story Writers Before 1880* (1988), supplying a useful essay on the development of the American short story along with treatment of thirty-six notable writers. *American Short Story Writers, 1880-1910* (1989) is edited by Kimbel and William E. Grant and provides treatment of thirty-one authors.

1134. **Beacham's Popular Fiction in America.** Walton Beacham and Suzanne Niemeyer, eds. Washington, DC: Beacham Publishing, 1986. 4v. ISBN 0-933833-10-5.

Similar in design and purpose to the Magill efforts, this work focuses on what is termed popular fiction. The criteria for inclusion of an author is that he or she be of the "best-selling" variety and that his or her works reflect social concerns. About 200 contemporary novelists of varied type are treated. These are primarily American, although some British writers are included. Most are living or recently deceased, and most are actively publishing, although this is not true of all. Contributors are primarily college professors. The entries follow a set pattern, covering publishing history as well as the critical reception of each writer. Individual titles are analyzed in terms of social concerns, themes, techniques, literary precedents, etc. Although constrained by the required brevity of the individual articles, the work should prove useful to a variety of patrons.

1135. **Contemporary Authors Bibliographical Series. Volume 1: American Novelists.** James J. Martine, ed. Detroit: Gale Research, 1986-1989. 3v. ISSN 0887-3070.

This series from Gale was designed to furnish a selective guide to the best critical studies done on major writers. Each volume covered ten personalities representing a particular genre. These were to complement the biographical sketches given in *Contemporary Authors* (entry 988), primarily on English and American authors. Indexes to critics and writers were cumulative within each succeeding volume. Volume 1 treats such well-known personalities as James Baldwin, John Bart, Saul Bellow, John Cheever, Joseph Heller, Norman Mailer, Bernard Malamud, Carson McCullers, John Updike, and Eudora Welty. Entries furnish a listing of works by the author and a listing of works about the author, which include bibliographies, biographies, interviews, and critical studies. There is also a detailed bibliographical essay comparing and evaluating the critical studies. Volume 2 covers American poets (entry 1164). Unfortunately, the series expired after publication of volume 3, *American Dramatists*, in 1989.

1136. **Contemporary Fiction Writers of the South: A Bio-Bibliographical Sourcebook.** Joseph M. Flora and Robert Bain, eds. Westport, CT: Greenwood Press, 1993. 571p. ISBN 0-313-28764-3.

This work retains the original format used by the editors in their two previous works described later. The present effort focusses on forty-nine current authors (all but three of whom are still alive) who have received critical recognition and wide review transcending regional status. Pat Conroy, Alice Walker, and Alex Haley are included; Anne Tyler is the only repeat from the earlier volumes. All authors are known novelists; short stories are perceived as additional pursuits. Entries provide detailed biocritical essays ranging from nine to sixteen pages in length and following pattern coverage of life, themes, and critical assessment. A detailed index provides access. A second volume is planned to cover poets, playwrights, and essayists.

Covering the earlier period is the editors' *Fifty Southern Writers Before 1900* (Greenwood Press, 1987), treating fifty writers of varied renown (Mark Twain and William Alexander Carruthers) whose careers ended before 1900. *Fifty Southern Writers After 1900*, also published in 1987, treats the Southern renascence writers who published between 1917 and the 1950s. Such luminaries as Thomas Wolfe, Richard Wright, and Eudora Welty are included.

1137. **Contemporary Gay American Novelists: A Bio-Bibliographical Critical Sourcebook.** Emmanuel S. Nelson, ed. Westport, CT: Greenwood Press, 1993. 421p. ISBN 0-313-28019-3.

This work provides biocritical analysis and bibliographical coverage of fifty-seven male novelists, from the widely read James Baldwin, William S. Burroughs, and Christopher Isherwood to those of less prominence such as John Fox and Peter Weltner. There is a conscious attempt to limit inclusion to serious writers (although several have been omitted by their own request). Entries supply biocritical coverage ranging from four to nineteen pages in length depending upon the influence of the subject; most have been prepared by gay scholars who are sensitive to the issues—although they are, in a few cases, overly exhortatory. Critical reception of the subject's work is treated, and is most useful in furnishing insight into the literary existence or plight of a gay novelist. Bibliographies by and about the writers conclude the entries. The work fills a need in the growing interest in study of the work of gay writers.

1138. **Contemporary Novelists.** 5th ed. Lesley Henderson and Noelle Watson, eds. Detroit: St. James Press, 1992. 1053p. ISBN 1-55862-036-2.
First published in 1972, this work is considered an important resource on the lives and contributions of the best-loved and most frequently studied current English-language novelists. Authors are carefully selected, with about 20 percent of the 600 entries in this edition being new to the series. A number of entries from the previous edition have been dropped, as popularity and critical reception change with time. The arrangement is alphabetical by author, and entries provide a brief biographical sketch, a bibliography of published works arranged chronologically by type (novels, plays, verse, and others), and a signed critical essay on the author's work with references to additional reading. Information is given on other published bibliographies and locations of archival collections. Responses from the novelists are encouraged. There is a title index furnishing authors and dates of all novels and short stories. The work continues to maintain a high standard.

1139. **Critical Survey of Long Fiction: English Language Series. Revised Edition.** Rev. ed. Frank N. Magill, ed. Pasadena, CA: Salem Press, 1991. 8v. ISBN 0-89356-825-2.
Another of the Magill offerings from Salem Press, this work furnishes nearly 350 critical essays on important writers. The volumes contain long biographical sketches of a wide range of writers, from Samuel Richardson to John Irving. The *Revised Edition* contains an additional twenty-five writers over the earlier 1983 issue. Such luminaries as Ray Bradbury, Joseph Wambaugh, and Salman Rushdie are now included. More than 150 articles have been revised and many have been completely updated. Critical assessments of each writer's contributions and an exposition of themes are rendered. Bibliographies are updated and annotated. Volume 8 completes the text (Wel-Z), and furnishes the index and fifteen background essays on various aspects of the novel.

1140. **English Fiction, 1900-1950: A Guide to Information Sources**. Thomas Jackson Rice. Detroit: Gale Research, 1979-1983. 2v. (American Literature, English Literature, and World Literatures in English, v.20-21). ISBN 0-810312-17-4 (v.1); 0-810315-05-X (v.2).
Some forty influential British writers are treated in depth in this two-volume work. Volume 1, published in 1979, provides a general bibliography and covers individual authors alphabetically from Aldington to Huxley. Volume 2 treats individual authors from Joyce to Woolf. Each entry furnishes an annotated list of all fictional works by the author and includes a representative selection of other writings. There is also a bibliography of secondary sources identifying journals, biographies, critical studies in books and articles, bibliographies, and studies of individual works. The cut-off date for volume 2 is 1980.
Part of the same series from Gale is S. K. Heninger's *English Prose, Prose Fiction and Criticism to 1660* (1975), which lists about 800 primary and secondary works by type, including fiction. Jerry C. Beasley's *English Fiction, 1660-1800: A Guide to Information Sources* (1978) continues the sequence of coverage.

1141. **The English Novel, 1578-1956: A Checklist of Twentieth Century Criticisms.** Inglis Freeman Bell and Donald Baird. Denver: Alan Swallow, 1959. Repr., Hamden, CT: Shoe String Press, 1974. 169p. ISBN 0-208-01442-X. ISBN 0-208-02231-7 (Supp IV).
The English novel has been covered well in a series of publications providing citations to critical studies published in the twentieth century. This is the first of these checklists,

giving a selective listing of critical studies that appeared in books and periodicals between 1900 and 1957 treating long fiction written over a period of 400 years. The arrangement of entries is alphabetical by name of author, followed by specific titles of his or her works.

This tool is supplemented by *English Novel Explication: Criticisms to 1972*, by Helen H. Palmer and Anne Jane Dyson (Shoe String Press, 1973), which lists criticism published between 1958 and 1972. This supplementary work is followed by its own *Supplement I*, by Peter L. Abernethy et al. (Shoe String Press, 1976), which covered the years 1972 to 1974. *Supplement II*, compiled by Christian J. W. Kloessel and Jeffrey R. Smitten (1981), extended coverage to 1979, and *Supplement III*, also by Kloessel (1986), covers the period from 1980 to 1985. The most recent offering, *Supplement IV* (1990) treats the period from 1986 to mid-1989. Another useful checklist, *The English Novel: Twentieth Century Criticism* (Swallow, 1976-1982) appeared in two volumes. Volume 1 identifies critical writings on the works of about forty-five novelists, from Defoe to Hardy; volume 2 covers eighty writers of the twentieth century.

1142. **English Renaissance Prose Fiction, 1500-1660: An Annotated Bibliography of Criticism**. James L. Harner. Boston: G. K. Hall, 1978. 556p. ISBN 0-8161-7996-4. **Supp. 1976-1983**. 1985. 228p. ISBN 0-8161-8709-6. **Supp. 1984-1990**. 1992. 185p. ISBN 0-8161-9088-7.

The initial volume, issued in the late 1970s, provided a bibliography of 3,000 critical items relevant to the study of fiction produced during the Renaissance period in England over a period of 160 years. The criticism, published between 1800 and 1976, is well chosen, and this tool and its supplements have gained a solid reputation among students and scholars. The basic volume identifies editions and studies (both original works and translations) written in England between 1500 and 1660. Included here are the various forms eventually leading to the development of the English novel, such as novelle, romances, histories, anatomies, and jest books. Listings are supplied of bibliographers, anthologies of Renaissance texts, and general studies. The major segment lists authors, translations, and titles. Entries supply informative annotations for the majority of critical books, parts of books, journal articles, and dissertations. The supplements continue to provide similar treatment of hundreds of additional critical works issued during the period of coverage. Indexes are supplied.

The subsequent literary period is treated in *The Eighteenth-Century British Novel and Its Background: An Annotated Bibliography and Guide to Topics*, by H. George Hahn and Carl Behm III (Scarecrow Press, 1985). This complements the previous source and supplies listings of nearly 3,200 books, chapters, and articles in English furnishing criticism, exposition, or bibliographical coverage of five major and thirty-nine minor novelists, as well as Johnson and Swift.

1143. **Jewish-American Fiction Writers: An Annotated Bibliography**. Gloria L. Cronin et al. New York: Garland, 1991. 1233p. (Garland Reference Library of the Humanities, v.972). ISBN 0-8240-1619-X.

This annotated bibliography fills a void in the coverage of nineteenth- and twentieth-century Jewish-American writers of lesser literary status who have attained popularity among the reading public. The acknowledged greats, such as Bellow, Mailer, Malamud, and Roth, are purposely excluded, but coverage is given to such familiar personalities as Asch, Calisher, Ferber, Fiedler, Hecht, Jong, Ozick, Potok, Sontag, Uris, Wouk, and others. In all, sixty-two writers are given detailed bibliographic treatment. Entries are arranged alphabetically and supply listings of primary sources representing the author's own works (novels, short stories in anthologies and periodicals, and collected works) and of secondary sources written about them (books, book chapters, articles, biographies, bibliographies, and dissertations). The latter segment is annotated in a brief but informative manner. For the most part, these writers, although prominent, are not well covered in the biocritical reference literature.

1144. **The Modern American Novel: An Annotated Bibliography**. Steven G. Kellman. Pasadena, CA: Salem Press, 1991. 162p. ISBN 0-89356-664-0.

This bibliography of criticism and commentary is designed for the use of high school and undergraduate students in providing treatment of sixteen important American novelists of the early twentieth century who produced their major works between 1900 and 1940. Included among these luminaries are Cather, Dreiser, Fitzgerald, Hemingway, Hurston, Lewis, Steinbeck, Wilder, and eight others of equal rank. They are recognized for their contribution to the development or creation of a distinctive American expression among the literatures of the world, and represent a sample of regional, ethnic, and expatriate writers. The tool begins with an introductory section treating general works on the American novel. This is followed by an alphabetical arrangement of authors. Each author entry supplies a bibliography of general studies followed by a listing of sources about individual works. Annotations are brief but informative. An index to authors of critical works is provided.

1145. **Short Story Criticism: Excerpts from Criticism of the Works of Short Fiction Writers**. Laurie Lanzen Harris and Sheila Fitzgerald, eds. Detroit: Gale Research, 1988- . v.1- . ISSN 0895-9439.

This series was initiated in 1988 to survey critical response to major writers. The initial volume treats fourteen important authors of short fiction issued in English or in English translation. Included in the inaugural edition are de Maupassant, Poe, Cheever, and Thurber. Entries are arranged alphabetically and some have been culled from the Gale Literary Criticism series (entry 995). They supply biographical and critical description along with a listing of the authors' major works. Critical sources are listed chronologically to provide a historical perspective. Subsequent volumes have appeared in irregular fashion, with the twelfth volume being published in 1993. This volume devotes about fifty pages to each of seventeen authors. Background on the authors' careers and critical commentary have maintained high quality, and the format remains unchanged. Entries are prepared by scholar-critics who are described in explanatory notes.

1146. **Twentieth-Century Crime and Mystery Writers**. 3d ed. Lesley Henderson, ed. Chicago: St. James Press, 1991. 1,294p. ISBN 1-55862-031-1.

During the past few years, St. James Press has been active in producing updated versions and new editions of useful biocritical tools. Several of these tools treat the realm of modern genre fiction. The third edition of this work on crime and mystery writers provides coverage of nearly 700 of the most important English-language writers. Entries supply brief biographical treatment of each author followed by a complete listing of his or or her works, a listing of critical studies, and location of manuscripts. There is commentary from each author about his or her work and a critical essay signed by its contributor. A title index aids access.

Twentieth-Century Romance and Historical Writers, also edited by Henderson and now in its second edition (1991), treats 500 English-language writers of romance and historical romance. The third edition is to appear in 1994. The third edition of *Twentieth-Century Science Fiction Writers* (1992), edited by Noelle Watson and Paul E. Schellinger, provides coverage of more than 600 modern writers of this genre. *Twentieth-Century Western Writers*, now in its second edition (1991) and edited by Geoff Sadler, examines nearly 500 writers whose works are set in or relate to the American frontier.

1147. **Twentieth-Century Short Story Explication: Interpretations 1900-1975 of Short Fiction since 1800**. 3d ed. Warren S. Walker. Hamden, CT: Shoe String Press, 1977. 880p. ISBN 0-208-01570-1; **Supp. 1-5**, 1980-1991. ISBN 0-208-01813-1 (Supp.1).

Originally published in 1961, the Walker effort is recognized as a standard in the field. The third edition cites interpretations since the turn of the century in books, monographs, and periodicals of short fiction published since 1800. For this series, a *short story* is a work not exceeding 150 average-sized pages. Explications describe or explain the meaning of the story and include observations on theme, symbols, or structure. The arrangement is by author, then story title. About 850 authors are covered by interpretations published through 1975. The supplements, numbered I-V, issued in 1980, 1984, 1987, 1989, and 1991, add hundreds of authors as they progress in time.

Twentieth-Century Short Story Explication: An Index to the Third Edition and Its Five Supplements 1961-1991, by Walker and Barbara K. Walker (Shoe String Press, 1991), furnishes an index to all citations to explications identified in the entire series. Nearly 16,750 stories by 2,300 authors are treated. Authors are listed alphabetically; their stories are listed alphabetically with references to the appopriate volume and page number in the series where explications are cited. *Twentieth Century Short Story Explication: New Series, with Checklists of Books and Journals Used* is Walker's most recent offering (1993). It furnishes some 5,700 entries providing interpretations for short stories by 815 authors published between 1989 and 1990.

POETRY

Bibliographic Guides

1148. English Poetry, 1660-1800: A Guide to Information Sources. Donald C. Mell. Detroit: Gale Research, 1982. 501p. ISBN 0-810312-30-1.

Recently the Gale Company has developed a series of guides in the area of English poetry; individual titles cover different chronological periods. This work covers poetry of the period 1660-1800 and furnishes annotated entries of critical research of the twentieth century through 1979. It is divided into two parts, the first of which furnishes a bibliography of general reference sources, such as histories and guidebooks, as well as collections of poetry and criticism. Also included are bibliographies, checklists, and background studies in related areas. The second part treats thirty-one poets, with listings of standard editions, collected works, bibliographies, and critical studies.

English Romantic Poetry, 1800-1835: A Guide to Information Sources, by Donald H. Reiman (Gale Research, 1979), identifies important studies relating to the work of five major poets (Wordsworth, Byron, Keats, Shelley, and Coleridge) and twelve secondary poets. Emily Ann Anderson's *English Poetry, 1900-1950: A Guide to Information Sources* (Gale Research, 1982) covers the modern period, with detailed coverage of sources of information on the work of twenty-one influential poets.

1149. Middle Scots Poets: A Reference Guide to James I of Scotland, Robert Henryson, William Dunbar, and Gavin Douglas. Walter Scheps and J. Anna Looney. Boston: G. K. Hall, 1986. 292p. (A Reference Guide to Literature). ISBN 0-8161-8356-2.

King James I, Henryson, Dunbar, and Douglas constitute what has been termed a group of "Scottish Chaucerians" who until the twentieth century had been dismissed as minor figures. More recently, however, their stature has grown and their "Scottishness" has been treated more seriously rather than as a curiosity. This work identifies a variety of materials on each individual who is given separate treatment in the guide. All items are annotated. A fifth section lists general works treating the four poets collectively or providing background material. Each of the five sections has a separate index. The criticism covers a span of 450 years from 1521 through 1978, making this a useful tool for the serious inquirer.

Bibliographies and Indexes

1150. The Bibliography of Contemporary American Poetry, 1945-1985: An Annotated Checklist. William McPheron. Westport, CT: Meckler, 1986. 72p. ISBN 0-88736-054-8.

This slender little volume provides a wealth of information on published collections of poetry that include the work of American poets of our time. Coverage actually goes back to the early 1940s. The first section of this annotated bibliography lists multiauthor sources arranged alphabetically by compiler, editor, or title. Only anthologies that furnish significant coverage of individual poets and of the small presses that have published much of their work are included. The second section furnishes a list of 122 single-author studies of leading contemporary poets, arranged alphabetically by name of poet. There is a useful introduction describing key anthologies and problems in bibliographic control.

Contemporary American Poetry: A Checklist, by Lloyd Davis and Robert Irwin (Scarecrow Press, 1975), identifies 3,300 single-author collections of poetry published between 1950 and 1973. This work is continued by Davis's *Contemporary American Poetry: A Checklist, Second Series, 1973-1983*, which lists 5,000 collections published during that ten-year period. Arrangement is by name of poet, and again coverage is limited to single-author works.

1151. The Columbia Granger's Index to Poetry. 10th ed. Edith P. Hazen, ed. New York: Columbia University Press, 1994. 2150p. ISBN 0-231-08408-0.

Since 1904, *Granger's* has been the preeminent work in the field, indexing poems in anthologies by title, first line, author, and subject. The pattern of coverage and scope changed with the seventh edition (1982), no longer providing cumulative coverage of preceding issues. Instead, the seventh edition indexed nearly 250 anthologies published between 1970 and 1981, thereupon supplementing the coverage of the sixth edition, published in 1973. The eighth edition returned to the cumulative format, indexing anthologies published throughout the twentieth century and indexing more than 400 titles. Of these, eighty-two were either new or indexed for the first time in this work. The ninth edition, the first to bear the imprint of Columbia University, added more than 150 new anthologies. Of these, fifty have been translated from other languages. The tenth edition may be indicative of increased frequency under Columbia and follows the ninth by only three years. It supplies coverage of anthologies published through 3 June 1993.

1152. Index to Black Poetry. Dorothy H. Chapman. Boston: G. K. Hall, 1974. 541p. ISBN 0-8161-1143-x.

This work received numerous accolades when it was published as a landmark or first-of-its-kind index, and was included among "Reference Books of 1975" (*Library Journal*, 15 April 1976). It remains a useful access tool for poems focused on the black experience, regardless of the racial origin of the poet, as well as works by black poets. Thus, *black poetry* is defined in broad terms, and about 5,000 poems from 1,000 poets are listed. They span a period of time dating from the efforts of Lucy Terry, the earliest known eighteenth-century black slave poet, to the 1970s. There are three sections in the work: a title and first line index, an author index, and a subject index. A total of ninety-four single-author works and thirty-three anthologies are covered, thus furnishing the means of identifying numerous obscure poets and poetry.

Chapman's *Index to Poetry by Black American Women* (Greenwood Press, 1986) is another important access tool to a specialized type of poetry not easily located in standard sources.

1153. Index to Poetry in Popular Periodicals. Jefferson D. Caskey, comp. Westport, CT: Greenwood Press, 1984-1988. 2v. ISBN 0-313-22227-4 (v.1); 0-313-24810-9 (v.2).

The initial volume of this tool was issued in 1984 and treated poetry published in American general periodicals indexed in the *Readers' Guide to Periodical Literature* (Wilson, 1900-) between 1955 and 1959. It was recognized as a well-constructed and useful index providing access to poems published in forty-five mass-circulation magazines by author, title, first line, and subject. Volume 2 provides an additional five years of coverage, from 1960 to 1964. The work does not duplicate the *Readers' Guide*, because *RGPL* did not index poetry during this period; therefore, most of the poems would be inaccessible otherwise. As one might expect, there is a wide range and diverse group of poets represented, from such stalwarts as e.e. cummings, Robert Frost, Ogden Nash, and Sylvia Plath to the less familiar James Merchant and Helen Singer. The strength of the tool lies in its inclusion of light verse not found in more scholarly indexes.

Index of American Periodical Verse, issued by Scarecrow Press, is an annual index to poems published in participating periodicals from the United States, Canada, and Puerto Rico. It began in 1973 with indexing of the year 1971. Coverage has increased each year and the twentieth annual volume, issued in 1992 and treating the year 1990, analyzes 289 participating periodicals. There are more than 7,000 entries for individual poets and more than 20,000 poems are indexed by title and first line.

1154. Poetry by Women to 1900: A Bibliography of American and British Writers. Gwenn Davis and Beverly A. Joyce, comps. Toronto: University of Toronto Press, 1991. 340p. ISBN 0-8020-5966-X.

This is the second volume of a series designed to provide bibliographic identification of the wealth of poetry by American and British women over a period of 425 years from 1475 to 1900. Poetry published only in the periodical literature is excluded, as this work targets poems appearing in printed books. More than 6,000 books are treated; the poets are arranged alphabetically, with a supplementary appendix providing a chronological listing. The valuable introduction by the compilers provides exposition and analysis of the literary situation, refuting certain misconceptions about the historical paucity of female poets and offering a rationale for the relative oblivion of the great majority. The subject index is especially useful for its topical treatment of poetic themes; it provides the framework for potential comparative study.

Poetry by American Women, 1900-1975: A Bibliography, by Joan Reardon (Scarecrow Press, 1979), provides coverage of nearly 9,500 single-author volumes of poetry written by 5,500 women over a span of seventy-five years. The work is comprehensive, the idea being to provide as complete a listing of those elusive publications as possible. Arrangement of entries is chronological, with access aided by a title index. Entries supply complete bibliographical identification. *Poetry by American Women, 1975-1989: A Bibliography*, also by Reardon (Scarecrow Press, 1990), continues the coverage through identification of nearly 2,900 volumes by 1,565 women published over a recent fifteen-year period. Format and treatment are the same as in the base volume.

1155. Poetry Index Annual: An Author, Title, First Line and Keyword Subject Index to Poetry in Anthologies. Great Neck, NY: Roth Publishing, 1982- . Ann. ISSN 0736-3966.

Rounding out the coverage given to poetry initially by the Granger Book Company (now Roth) is this annual index to English-language poetry appearing in anthologies. The purpose of this work is to index all anthologies published in a single year (including new editions of older works). This supplements the less frequent publication of *Granger's* (entry 1151), now published by Columbia University, and complements the coverage of single-author collections and periodical literature in *Roth's American Poetry Annual* (entry 1156). Indexing is by author, title, and subject, with all entries in a single alphabetical arrangement. From thirty to fifty anthologies are indexed per issue, providing access to several thousand poems. This is a useful resource for librarians and their patrons.

1156. Roth's American Poetry Annual: A Reference and Guide to Poetry Published in the United States. Great Neck, NY: Roth Publishing, 1987- . Ann. ISSN 1040-5461.

When Roth Publishing took over the products of the Granger Book Company in 1989, one of its first acts was to combine *The Annual Survey of American Poetry*, begun in 1982, *American Poetry Index*, begun in 1983, and *Annual Index to Poetry in Periodicals*, which started up in 1982. The result was this important serial that furnishes a "unified index" identifying poems in books of poetry by a single poet, and periodicals issued that year. Entries for several thousand poems published in several hundred collections and standard magazines easily available to libraries make this a useful location tool for reference service. Arrangement of entries is alphabetical by poet and title in one alphabetical sequence. The work opens with the annual survey segment furnishing a state-of-the-art essay, anthology of selected poetry, and several directories of grants, awards, schools, organizations, and publishers. It serves to complement the coverage of *Poetry Index Annual* (entry 1155), which indexes poetry in published anthologies. The list of periodicals indexed shows a wide range of works both well known and relatively obscure.

The Granger Company had begun retrospective indexing in this area. *Index to Poetry in Periodicals: American Poetic Renaissance, 1915-1919* ... (1981), *Index to Poetry in Periodicals, 1920-1924* ... (1983), and *Index to Poetry in Periodicals, 1925-1929* ... (1984) cite poems appearing in magazines and newspapers offering a wide range in terms of quality and popularity. Included are the products of top-notch poets as well as unknown versifiers who have written for both children and adults. More than 300 periodicals are indexed in each volume by name of poet, furnishing about 9,000 poems by more than 2,000 poets per issue.

Anthologies and Collections

1157. **The Columbia Granger's Guide to Poetry Anthologies**. 2d ed. William Katz and Linda Sternberg Katz. New York: Columbia University Press, 1994. 231p. ISBN 0-231-10104-X.

Developed as a companion to the *Columbia Granger's Index to Poetry* (entry 1151), this work is useful to students and librarians. The work identifies, describes, and evaluates all the anthologies used by the *Index* from its seventh through its tenth editions. It succeeds its earlier issue (1991) because of the recent publication of the Granger tenth edition. The Katz publications are well known in the literature of library science and the authors now demonstrate an excellent knowledge of poetry, especially that of American or British origin. Entries are classified by subject and supply detailed exposition of the anthology's comprehensiveness, ease of use, authority, and auxiliary features such as introduction, indexes, and notes. Critical commentary is reasoned and well constructed, and is effective in revealing excellence, oversight, omission, bias, or doubtful veracity of poetic text. As is true of other Katz works, the text is lucid and lively. The work is indexed by author and title.

*1158. **English Poetry Full-Text Database**. Cambridge: Chadwyck-Healey. CD-ROM.

This CD-ROM source consists of four discs and represents a sourcebook of poetry by 1,350 poets listed in the *New Cambridge Bibliography of English Literature* (entry 1043). The tool treats a broad survey of English poetry dating from the Anglo-Saxon period to the end of the nineteenth century. The work is divided into three chronological segments, all of which can be purchased separately. They represent the periods 600-1660, 1661-1800, and 1801-1900. CD-ROM is an especially useful format for retrieval of material in full text, and this work has been coded in a variety of ways. Included in addition to the poetry are epigraphs, dedications, notes, and bibliographical details pertinent to the edition used in the database. Boolean operators "or, not, and" may be employed to locate imagery, language, dates, and names.

Available since 1991 on CD-ROM is the complete text of an array of Columbia Granger products entitled *The Columbia Granger's World of Poetry*. It contains complete text of 8,500 classic poems, quotations from 3,000 additional poems, and anthology citations to some 60,000 poems. These have been culled from *The Columbia Granger's Index to Poetry* (entry 1151), *The Columbia Granger's Guide to Poetry Anthologies* (entry 1157), and *The Columbia Granger's Dictionary of Poetry Quotations* (entry 1021).

1159. **The New Oxford Book of American Verse**. Richard Ellmann, ed. New York: Oxford University Press, 1976. 1076p.

This is the standard anthology in the field and has been recognized as such since its first appearance in 1927. Both the 1927 and 1950 editions were compiled by Bliss Carman and F. O. Matthiessen and earned the respect of teachers and librarians for their excellent representation of both classic and modern poets. This edition continues in that tradition, listing the poets chronologically, beginning with seventeenth-century poet Anne Bradstreet and ending with Imamu Amiri Baraka (Leroi Jones), born in 1934. Inclusion is highly selective, and about seventy-five poets are treated. The intention is to include poems of intrinsic merit while at the same time representing the principal directions of modern poetry. The poems, like the poets who created them, appear in chronological sequence. There is an index of authors, titles, and first lines.

1160. **The New Oxford Book of Australian Verse.** Exp. ed. Les Murray. New York: Oxford University Press, 1991. 420p. ISBN 0-19-553362-3.

One of the recent anthologies in the Oxford line which made its appearance during 1986 is this collection of poems chosen by Les Murray, an important contemporary poet. His anthology is carefully developed and representative of the various elements within Australian poetry over a span of time beginning with the colonial period and running to the present day. This is a reprint with additional poems, resulting in twenty-one additional pages. Criteria for inclusion reflect his judgment of the amount of "poetry" found in a poem, as well as its liveliness and readability. Standard poems are not always included and have given way to "untypical" works of high quality and expressive nature. Included are some titles of aboriginal origin, which have not been included in standard anthologies. This is a most useful source for its unorthodox means of selection, which results in the inclusion of much obscure poetry.

1161. **The New Oxford Book of English Verse, 1250-1950.** Helen Louise Gardner. New York: Oxford University Press, 1972; repr. with corr., 1986. 974p. ISBN 0-19-812136-9.

The Oxford Book of English Verse is the oldest anthology in the Oxford line, first appearing in 1900 under the guidance of Sir Arthur Quiller-Couch. He was also responsible for the second edition in 1939. The first edition covered poetry up to 1900, the second edition to 1918. The present work is not a revision but a new anthology, and furnishes comprehensive coverage up to 1950. It contains nearly 900 poems. Whereas earlier editions had emphasized lyric verse, the new work represents the total range of English nondramatic poetry. American poets Ezra Pound and T.S. Eliot are also included. There are brief notes and references located at the back of the book, and access is furnished by indexes of authors and first lines. There are a number of Oxford anthologies of a specialized nature devoted to a particular period or century of English poetry which complement this general tool.

1162. **The New Oxford Book of Irish Verse.** Thomas Kinsella, ed. New York: Oxford University Press, 1986. 423p. ISBN 0-19-211868-4.

This recent Oxford anthology of Irish poetry takes on a new challenge in covering the period from the beginnings to the fourteenth century. It thus represents a complementary work to the earlier edition, which covered the seventeenth to the twentieth centuries. Kinsella is a master poet in his own right and has not only selected the works, but also translated them faithfully, always keeping in mind the musical quality of the ancient verse. The anthology furnishes a well-balanced collection of Irish art, with representation of various elements of high quality as well as popular culture. The work of Swift, Goldsmith, Sheridan, Yeats, and Synge blends with the numerous folk poems, songs, prayers, and other contributions from lesser known but equally expressive poets.

Biographical and Critical Sources

1163. **American Poets 1880-1945.** Third Series. Peter Quartermain, ed. Detroit: Gale Research, 1987. 2v. (Dictionary of Literary Biography, v.54). ISBN 0-8103-1732-X.

This is the third segment of a series which itself is part of the extensive *Dictionary of Literary Biography* (entry 993). The first series appeared in 1986, the second series followed later that same year, and this, the third series, was first issued in two volumes in 1987. All volumes are in the same format, in keeping with the pattern of the parent series. In each volume, about forty-five American poets are listed alphabetically by name, followed by dates of birth and death, then by name of the author of the entry. There is a bibliography of each poet's publications, followed by a detailed biocritical essay of the poet's life and work.

Concluding the entry is a bibliography of writings on the poet and library locations where manuscripts and letters may be found. One of the attractive features is the inclusion of photographs and copies of title pages and manuscripts.

Continuing the coverage is *American Poets since World War II. Third Series*, edited by R. S. Gwynn (1992). Treatment is given to sixty-seven contemporary poets such as Heather Miller and Bin Ramke.

1164. **Contemporary Authors Bibliographical Series. Volume 2: American Poets.** Ronald Baughman, ed. Detroit: Gale Research, 1986. 387p. ISSN 0887-3070.

This was designed as a companion series to the monumental Gale effort *Contemporary Authors* (entry 988). The first volume covered American novelists (entry 1135) and set the pattern for the series in covering about ten major writers in a particular genre and nationality. In this work, eleven important poets of the post-World War II era are treated, including James Dickey, Randall Jarrell, Robert Lowell, and Anne Sexton. They are covered in separate chapters, each of which is written by a specialist, in a pattern providing bibliographic coverage of major works, followed by a listing of works about the authors and their work. Finally, there is a bibliographic essay analyzing the contribution of the critical studies. There are two indexes which are cumulative to volumes 1 and 2, an index of authors, and an index of critics. The series ceased with volume 3, *American Dramatists*, in 1989.

1165. **Contemporary Poets.** 5th ed. Tracy Chevalier, ed. Chicago: St. James Press, 1991. 1179p. ISBN 1-558-62035-4.

Information on about 900 living poets is furnished in this new edition of a standard reference tool. Individuals are carefully selected for inclusion by a panel of internationally known specialists. There are 120 newly added poets in this edition, such as Wendy Cope, Sharon Olds, and Benjamin Zephaniah. The pattern of coverage for each entry renders a brief biographical chronology; followed by a full bibliography of the poet's writings, arranged chronologically by type, including poetry, criticism, and biography; and finally, a fine signed critical essay on the poet's work. There are listings of other published bibliographies and archival locations. There is also opportunity for the poets to provide their own comments on their work. A title index provides access to poems described in the main body of the work.

1166. **Critical Survey of Poetry: English Language Series**. Rev. ed. Frank N. Magill, ed. Pasadena, CA: Salem Press, 1992. 8v. ISBN 0-89356-834-1.

Initially published in 1982 as an eight-volume set, and supplemented in 1987 (entry 1173n) with a volume designed to give more detailed coverage to contemporary poets, the new edition serves as an excellent update and revision meeting the needs of high school and undergraduate students. A total of 390 entries are provided, with biocritical essays on 368 outstanding poets and 22 comprehensive essays on periods and critical approaches to the genre. A number of minor poets have been dropped in favor of twenty-seven completely new entries (Rita Dove, Carolyn Forche, Raymond Carver, etc.). Forty-four entries have been completely rewritten; all entries have updated bibliographies. Entries average five to ten pages in length, with treatment of poets providing sections on principal works, achievements, biography, and analysis. Entries are prepared by specialists and supply mainstream perspective. A detailed subject index provides access.

1167. **The Great American Poetry Bake-Off, Fourth Series**. Robert Peters. Metuchen, NJ: Scarecrow Press, 1991. 296p. ISBN 0-8108-2410-8.

The author is a witty and insightful poet and critic who initiated this series of critical handbooks in 1979. The second series was issued in 1982 and the third in 1987. With these previous efforts the series established an enviable reputation for its no-nonsense approach in examining strengths and weaknesses and in providing fresh perspectives with regard to poetry and the work of poets such as Ginsburg, Cohen, and Creely. The fourth series continues in that tradition and Peters continues his controversial, iconoclastic commentary on the genre. Treatment is given to various poetry anthologies in a thorough and frank manner, and a number of poets writing outside the genre mainstream, such as Sharon Doubiago and James Broughton, are assessed. An important contribution to the critical literature for its penetrating and sometimes definitive exposition, its access is aided by a general index.

1168. **Guide to American Poetry Explication**. Boston: G. K. Hall, 1989. 2v. (Reference Publication in Literature). ISBN 0-8161-8919-6 (v.1); 0-8161-8918-8 (v.2).
     This is the first part of a two-part, multivolume expansion of the Kuntz work (entry 1170), citing North American poetry explication from 1925 to 1987. Volume 1 is compiled by James Ruppert and treats "Colonial and Nineteenth Century" poems. Volume 2 is compiled by John K. Lee and covers "Modern and Contemporary" poems. The expansion is more comprehensive than was Kunst in its inclusion of explications drawn from critical works on individual authors and of poems of more than 500 lines. All appropriate entries from the 1980 edition are incorporated in both volumes. There is a purposeful inclusion of diverse elements (gay and lesbian, African-American, and Native American poems) in volume 2.
     Guide to British Poetry Explication continues the update and expansion of Kuntz in the same manner and format. Authored by Nancy C. Martinez and Joseph G. R. Martinez, the first two volumes of what is now seen as a four-volume effort were issued in 1991. Volume 1 treats "Old English-Medieval"; volume 2 examines the "Renaissance"; and volume 3, published in 1993, treats "Restoration-Romantic." Again, all appropriate entries from the Kuntz 1980 edition have been incorporated. Still to come is volume 4, which will consider the modern and contemporary period.

1169. **Masterplots II. Poetry Series**. Frank N. Magill, ed. Pasadena, CA: Salem Press, 1992. 6v. ISBN 0-89356-584-9.
     This is the eighth series developed as part of the *Masterplots II* set (entry 980n) and follows the pattern established in previous efforts. Emphasis is placed on English and American poetry, although a number of works in English translation are included among the 760 poems by 275 poets. Poems are well chosen and represent the most popular and most frequently studied works. Arrangement is alphabetical by title across the six volumes, and entries supply header information with poet's name, dates, type of poem, and initial year of publication, followed by a section on "the poem" treating structure, plot, and setting. A "forms and devices" section covers form and technique, while "themes and meanings" provides a useful summary. Entries are signed by the 200 scholar-contributors; coverage is even-handed and suitable at the high school or undergraduate level. Bibliographies and indexes are furnished in volume 6.

1170. **Poetry Explication: A Checklist of Interpretation since 1925 of British and American Poems Past and Present**. 3d ed. Joseph Marshall Kuntz and Nancy C. Martinez. Boston: G. K. Hall, 1980. 570p. ISBN 0-8161-8313-9.
     Originally published in 1950, and revised in 1962, the third edition has retained a prominent position among reference librarians who must conduct searches for critical interpretations of poetry. The 1980 edition incorporates the checklists of the earlier works and has added references to explications published up to 1977. The explications have been published in selected composite works and literary periodicals. An *explication* is defined by the authors as an examination of a literary work for knowledge of each part, for the relationship of these parts to each other, and for their relations to the whole. Kuntz and Martinez are limited to explications considering poems of 500 lines or less. A revision and expansion, also edited by Martinez, et al. is in progress, and when finished will replace this tool (entry 1168).
     Similar to Kuntz in scope and purpose is *American and British Poetry: A Guide to Criticism, 1925-1978*, by Harriet Semmes Alexander (Swallow, 1984). It identifies critical studies in books and articles on a wide range of poetry, which treat poems up to 1,000 lines in length.

Literature from Other Languages

GENERAL WORKS

1171. **Contemporary World Writers**. 2d ed. Tracy Chevalier, ed. Detroit: St. James Press, 1993. 686p. ISBN 1-55862-200-4.

Initially entitled *Contemporary Foreign Language Writers* (St. James Press, 1984), the new edition continues its focus on important living writers of various genres (fiction, drama, poetry) who write in languages other than English and who have been translated into English. A total of 358 writers are treated, having been selected by a panel of twenty academic literary specialists. The entries represent a diverse group, ranging from writers who are recognized and established to those who are relative newcomers. Of the total, just over 100 are Western European, along with representation of Central and Eastern European, Latin American, and Oriental. The work follows the format previously established in the other titles in the publisher's series and supplies for each author a biographical sketch, bibliography citing English translations of his or her other works, listing of critical studies, and a critical essay of 800 to 1,000 words evaluating the writer's work.

1172. **Critical Survey of Long Fiction: Foreign Language Series**. Frank N. Magill, ed. Englewood Cliffs, NJ: Salem Press, 1984. 5v. ISBN 0-89356-369-2. **Supp.** 408p. 1987. ISBN 0-89356-368-4.

Another of the Magill *Critical Surveys* from Salem Press (entries 1139 and 1173), this work follows the pattern set by the others. Volumes 1-4 cover 182 writers judged to be important contributors to the development of long fiction (novels or novel-like prose) in languages other than English. Entries for each writer furnish a list of principal long fiction, description of the writer's contribution to other literary forms, principal long fiction, description of the writer's contribution to other literary forms, assessment of his or her major achievements, a short biographical sketch, analysis of his or her major works of long fiction, a selective list of writings other than in the long fiction genre, and a brief bibliography of biographical and critical sources about the writer. There is a useful set of essays on the history of the novel in various areas of the world in volume 5. An author-title index provides access. The 1987 supplement adds another fifty novelists to the critical coverage.

1173. **Critical Survey of Poetry: Foreign Language Series**. Frank N. Magill, ed. Englewood Cliffs, NJ: Salem Press, 1984. 5v. ISBN 0-89356-350-1.

Similar in format and style to other Magill works in this series (entries 813n and 1172), this work covers all major poetry of the world not in English. Nearly 200 poets are covered in the first four volumes. Each one is treated in signed articles divided into several sections: principal poems and collections, other literary forms, achievements, biography, analysis, major publications other than poetry, and a brief bibliography. More than 100 contributors were involved with the project, so the coverage is somewhat uneven in quality. The idea is to provide introductory information; most of the articles run less than ten pages in length. Volume 5 provides twenty essays on various aspects of the genre, including the oral tradition and linguistics.

Magill's *Critical Survey of Poetry: Supplement* (Salem Press, 1987) adds to the treatment of both the preceding work and the previous edition of its counterpart, *Critical Survey of Poetry, English Language Series* (entry 1166), by supplying more detailed coverage of contemporary poets from all over the world. Entries on nearly fifty eminent individuals, including ten women, are arranged alphabetically and critiqued in a uniform manner in terms of principal poems and collections, achievements, biography, and more. Additionally, there is a section updating information on poets in earlier volumes.

1174. **An Encyclopedia of Continental Women Writers.** Katharina M. Wilson, ed. New York: Garland, 1991. 2v. (Garland Reference Library of the Humanities, v.698). ISBN 0-8240-8547-7.

Designed as a companion piece to the publisher's *Encyclopedia of British Women Writers* (Garland, 1988), this work follows a similar format in providing biocritical treatment of more than 1,800 European (but not British) writers from ancient times to the current scene. All types of writers are included and there is a good sample of novelists, dramatists, poets, and essayists from all parts of Europe and representing various languages such as Yiddish and Arabic. Entries supply quick identification of dates and places of birth and death, genre, and language. Biocritical essays are brief but informative and run from a half-page to a page in length, treating major works, literary impact, and themes of the various authors. A two-part bibliography concludes each entry and provides a listing of the writer's major works along with a selective list of secondary sources. The lack of indexing is unfortunate.

1175. **Hoffman's Index to Poetry: European and Latin American Poetry in Anthologies.** Herbert H. Hoffman. Metuchen, NJ: Scarecrow Press, 1985. 672p. ISBN 0-8108-1831-0.

A recent work useful to students and teachers is this index, which excludes the poetic output in the English language. It treats about 14,000 important poems in about 100 anthologies published since the mid-1930s. Nearly 1,800 poets are represented, with poems written in a number of languages: French, German, Spanish, Italian, Portuguese, Polish, Russian, and Ukrainian. Selection of anthologies is in part based on their availability in the English-speaking world, and adds considerably to the practical value. The main section is arranged by name of poet, alphabetically, with poems listed alphabetically by title. First lines are also given. A title listing and a first-line listing are both grouped by languages.

1176. **Women Writers in Translation: An Annotated Bibliography, 1945-1982.** Margery Resnick and Isabelle de Courtivron. New York: Garland, 1984. 272p. (Garland Reference Library of the Humanities, v.288). ISBN 0-8240-9332-1.

The idea for this tool grew out of a meeting of the Modern Language Association, where foreign-language teachers had discussed the difficulty of locating good translations of works by women writers. The compilers coordinated this project while professors at MIT; it required the expertise of more than fifty contributors and specialists in Portuguese, French, German, Italian, Japanese, Russian, and Spanish. The relatively slender product reflects a disappointing situation of international proportions, which permits work of women writers to go out-of-print in a relatively short time. The annotations vary in quality, as is true of most compilations, but on the whole they are informative regarding theme, genre, and literary significance. This is a valuable tool for both teachers and librarians.

CLASSICAL LITERATURE, GREEK AND LATIN

1177. **Ancient Writers: Greece and Rome.** T. James Luce, ed.-in-chief. New York: Scribner's, 1982. 2v. ISBN 0-684-16595-3.

This is a highly useful biocritical tool because of its depth of coverage of the writers. It consists of forty-seven essays by specialists from the United States, the United Kingdom, Canada, and Israel. The articles range in length from ten to more than fifty pages, and are devoted primarily to individual authors, and in some cases to groups such as Greek lyric poets. The pattern of coverage renders a brief biographical sketch, followed by an extensive critical interpretation of the writer's works. There is a bibliography of currently available editions in the original language, as well as major contemporary translations, along with a list of selected critical studies primarily in English. It is an important purchase for academic and secondary school libraries.

Greek and Roman Authors: A Checklist of Criticism, by Thomas Gwinup and Fidelia Dickinson (2d ed., Scarecrow Press, 1982), is a useful checklist of English-language criticism of the work of seventy classical authors. Critical studies are identified in both books and periodicals. It employs the normal checklist arrangement, with authors listed alphabetically, and with listings of general criticism followed by criticism of individual works.

1178. **Classical and Medieval Literature Criticism: Excerpts from Criticism of the Works of World Authors ...** Jelena O. Krstovic, ed. Detroit: Gale Research, 1988- . v.1- . ISSN 0896-0011.

This represents an important and comprehensive survey of Classical/Medieval literature and its criticism. Coverage ranges from the pre-biblical epics of the ancient world to the end of the fourteenth century. The volumes are well executed and follow an established pattern in providing extensive coverage of five or eight authors or major works per volume. Initiated in 1988, the series reached its eleventh volume in 1993. Such luminaries as Homer, Plato, Cicero, St. Augustine, and Seneca are treated, along with such important works as the Koran, the Bible, *Beowulf,* and the Talmud. Entries open with vital statistics, along with a picture and biographical treatment of the subject. There is a listing of English translations of the work, followed by what is most important, the extracts of criticism through time. An annotated bibliography concludes each entry. There is emphasis on criticism of the past 100 years.

1179. **The Classical Epic: An Annotated Bibliography.** Thomas J. Sienkewicz. Pasadena, CA: Salem Press, 1991. 265p. (Magill Bibliographies). ISBN 0-89356-663-2.

As is true of others in this Magill series, this retrospective bibliography of critical and expository materials on three classical epics is useful to high school and undergraduate students. Treatment is given to writings on *The Aeneid* by Virgil and *The Iliad* and *The Odyssey* by Homer. Listings are provided of books, book chapters, and essays within books; periodical literature is excluded. This is a retrospective bibliography and covers materials written from the turn of the century to the mid-1980s. Treatment is well developed and most of the important English-language book material is included. Information is given on historical background of the societies producing these epics, along with excellent representation of pertinent sources providing biographies, plot summaries, character studies, and studies of particular episodes or passages. A detailed table of contents and author index provide access.

1180. **The Oxford Companion to Classical Literature.** 2d ed. M. C. Howatson, ed. New York: Oxford University Press, 1989; repr. with corr. 1990. 615p. ISBN 0-19-866121-5.

This is the latest edition of a true classic begun in 1937 and edited by Sir Paul Harvey. It is regarded as one of the important tools in the field for use by students and general readers, and is a treasure house of information on a variety of topics and subjects relevant not only to literature but also to the study of classical antiquity. The work has been heavily revised and expanded due to the advances in scholarship made possible by the breakthroughs in deciphering the Linear B script. Entries are furnished not only for classical writers, literary forms and subjects, and individual works, but also for historical events and figures, institutions, and religious observations. The rationale is that knowledge of these elements is necessary in understanding the plots and themes of classical literature. There are cross-references in place of an index; maps but no bibliography.

The Concise Oxford Companion to Classical Literature, edited by Howatson and Ian Chilvers (Oxford, 1993), is a somewhat revised as well as shortened version. It omits background articles on general cultural topics and provides abbreviated treatment of historical, geographical, and political conditions, along with appendices. Little new material has been added, although there is some reorganization of content. *The Oxford Classical Dictionary,* edited by N. G. L. Hammond and H. H. Scullard (2d ed., Clarendon Press, 1970), is a useful resource, although not focused on literature per se. It is a scholarly dictionary covering biography, mythology, religion, science, geography, etc., as well as literature. It includes good survey articles on topics such as music, and bibliographies accompany the articles.

ROMANCE LANGUAGES

French

1181. **The Concise Oxford Dictionary of French Literature.** Joyce M. H. Reid. New York: Oxford University Press, 1976; repr. 1985. 669p. ISBN 0-19-866118-5.

This is a successful condensation of *The Oxford Companion to French Literature*, by Paul Harvey (entry 1183n). Abridgement was achieved through compression in terms of style, format, and type size rather than elimination of articles. Several new articles have been added where needed and older ones have been updated and in some cases expanded. Articles of French-Canadian literature have been deleted, in view of their treatment in *The Oxford Companion to Canadian Literature* (entry 1065). Like others in the Companion series, this volume is extremely useful, providing information on both major and minor writers, genres, plots, and literary movements. Contemporary figures and modern trends are adequately treated.

1182. **A Critical Bibliography of French Literature.** D. C. Cabeen, ed. Syracuse, NY: Syracuse University Press, 1947- . v.1-4, 6.

Considered a work of major importance, this bibliography was originally edited by D. C. Cabeen and in most cases is still referred to as "Cabeen." Presently five volumes and various supplements, revisions, and parts have been published. Each of the volumes is done by specialists in the field and treats a different time period. Volume 1, on the medieval period, was published originally in 1947 and enlarged in 1952. Volume 2 covers the sixteenth century, with the first edition appearing in 1956 and the revised edition in 1985. Volume 3 treats the seventeenth century (1961); 3A, a supplement, was issued in 1983. Volume 4 covers the eighteenth century (1951), with a supplement in 1968. Volume 6 covers the twentieth century in different parts devoted to various genres (1980). Volume 5, covering the nineteenth century, has not yet been published. The series represents a selective, evaluative, and annotated bibliography of books, dissertations, and periodical articles with references to reviews. Each volume is separately indexed.

1183. **Dictionary of Modern French Literature: From the Age of Reason through Realism.** Sandra W. Dolbow. Westport, CT: Greenwood Press, 1986. 365p. ISBN 0-313-23784-0.

This is a detailed and thorough dictionary of French literature specialized in its coverage of the eighteenth and nineteenth centuries from 1715 to 1880. It identifies and describes all major writers and many minor figures of the period. Included among the number of writers are philosophers, historians, novelists, dramatists, and poets. Also covered are literary movements and individual works. Biographical entries furnish sketches of some length and render information adequate for identification and understanding. Similarly, good synopses and descriptions of significance are rendered for individual works. Bibliographies are included for most entries, identifying English-language sources published between 1980 and 1985. A second volume or complementary work is to continue the coverage of postmodernism from 1880 to the present.

Continuing as a useful source, although getting older, is *The Oxford Companion to French Literature*, by Sir Paul Harvey and Janet E. Heseltine (Clarendon Press, 1959; repr. with corrections, 1961, 1984). This is a broader-based and more comprehensive tool covering French literature from medieval times to the late 1930s. Entries furnish information on individuals, titles, places, and institutions. There are general survey articles on movements and phases of French literary development.

1184. **French Women Writers: A Bio-Bibliographical Source Book.** Eva Martin Sartori and Dorothy Wayne Zimmerman, eds. Westport, CT: Greenwood Press, 1991. 632p. ISBN 0-313-26548-8.

Designed for a wide-ranging audience from general reader to scholar, this biographical dictionary provides coverage in depth of fifty-one writers identified with a substantial body of work in the French language. Certain omissions may be questioned, but in general the coverage is comprehensive of female writers in a variety of genres: novels, letters, memoirs, plays, and poetry. One additional entry is generic in its treatment of women troubadours of the twelfth and thirteenth centuries. Entries are approximately ten pages in length and provide treatment in a standard format that includes a biography, discussion of major themes, survey of criticism, and bibliography of primary works, along with a list of English translations and a selection of critical studies. Arrangement of entries is alphabetical by name of writer. Special features include a chronology of women writers in French history and a listing of writers by birthdate. There are detailed title and subject indexes.

1185. Guide to French Literature: 1789 to the Present. Anthony Levi. Chicago: St. James Press, 1992-1994. 2v. ISBN 1-55862-086-9.

This two-volume effort provides a well-constructed comprehensive survey of French literature. Volume 1 was the first volume published, but is actually the concluding volume in terms of its coverage of the period from 1789 to the present. Volume 2, the more recent issue, examines the beginnings to 1789. Levi is an eminent scholar and specialist in French literature and has produced a useful tool for a variety of users ranging from serious students to the general public. Entries supply informative, detailed, and sometimes lengthy treatment of personalities and literary works and movements. Entries on writers provide a full biography, critical analysis and evaluation of all major works, plot summaries, listing of publications, and selective listing of secondary sources. Entries on a movement describe fully its aims, achievements, and major contributors. There is a detailed index providing excellent access.

As volume 119 of the DLB series from Gale Research (entry 993), Catharine Savage Brosman has edited *Nineteenth Century French Fiction Writers: Romanticism and Realism, 1800-1860* (1992), providing biographical coverage of nineteen major French writers whose work was issued during that sixty-year period. As is true of other numbers in the series, the essays provide detailed coverage of the authors' careers and literary styles and influences. This is especially useful for undergraduate users.

1186. Guide to French Poetry Explication. Kathleen Coleman. New York: G. K. Hall, 1993. 594p. ISBN 0-8161-9075-5.

Explications or interpretations are important to students and scholars in providing bases for their teaching, learning, and research activity, and reference works of this kind are common to the study of poetry in the English language. This is the first G. K. Hall venture of this type with poetry in a foreign language, and it represents a milestone in that regard. Like other checklists and guides, the current effort is designed to locate and reveal these critical interpretations on the work of major poets. Emphasis is given to poets generally included in French studies and explications found in standard indexes and bibliographies available in this country. The poetry dates from the Middle Ages to the present, and explications were written between 1960 and 1990. Arrangement of entries is alphabetical by name of poet; titles of poems and their explications then follow in alphabetical sequence. An index of critics and several bibliographies complete the work.

1187. Research and Reference Guide to French Studies. 2d ed. Charles B. Osburn. Metuchen, NJ: Scarecrow Press, 1981. 532p. ISBN 0-8108-1440-4.

The first edition of this work received much acclaim when it was published in 1968, and it was followed by a useful supplement in 1972. The second edition represents a complete revision of the earlier one, with 6,000 entries of value to the study of French language and literature. The earlier edition was more comprehensive and was intended to cover the whole range of French studies. A variety of reference books are covered in the present work: concordances, dictionaries, iconographies, filmographies, encyclopedias, and more, primarily in English, French, and German. The coverage of bibliographies is excellent and critical surveys are identified. This effort was intended as a link between the earlier edition and the machine-readable database of the *MLA International Bibliography* (entry 964).

A *Bibliographical Guide to the Romance Languages and Literatures*, by Thomas Rossman Palfrey and others (8th ed., Chandler, 1971), is a comprehensive and well-respected guide to the Romance literatures such as French, Italian, Portuguese, and Spanish. First published in 1939, it has been the first choice of students and specialists in identifying important studies and literary contributions.

Italian

1188. **Dictionary of Italian Literature.** Peter Bondanella and Julia Conaway Bondanella, eds. Westport, CT: Greenwood Press, 1979. 621p. ISBN 0-313-20421-7.

A useful dictionary and guide to Italian literature, which contains more than 350 entries, alphabetically arranged, covering authors, genres, periods, movements, and related general topics. Most entries are on authors and provide informative sketches of their lives and achievements. Both major and minor writers are covered from the twelfth century to the present. Many of the articles are signed by the contributors. Bibliographies include English translations of important primary texts and critical studies in books and articles in various languages. Although a few errors have been detected by reviewers, they appear to be slight, indicating a carefully prepared work. There is a useful chronology in the appendix enumerating events in Italian literature, world literature, and philosophy.

Spanish/Latin American/Hispanic/Chicano

1189. **Bibliografia de la literatura hispanica.** Jose Simon Diaz. Madrid: Consejo Superior de Investigaciones Cientificas, Inst. "Miguel de Cervantes" de Filologia Hispanica, 1950- . v.1-11, 13, 15. ISBN 8400052021.

Beginning in 1950, this comprehensive bibliography covers all Hispanic literatures and identifies studies and critical works in books, articles, theses, and lectures. In some cases, reviews of books are identified and library locations are given. The last volume to be issued was volume 15 in 1992. Volume 2 identifies more than 2,000 general bibliographies, bio-bibliographies, and indexes in the field. Volume 3 provides coverage of specific time periods for Castillian literature, the Middle Ages from the eleventh to the fifteenth centuries. Volume 4 continues the time coverage and begins the alphabetical coverage of authors from A-Augustin. Volumes 5-13 continue the alphabetical coverage up to the middle of the alphabet. A volume correcting and augmenting the earlier work (volumes 1-3), and another doing the same for volumes 5-6 and adding appendices, were issued. In addition, volumes 1-2 of the third edition were published during 1983-1986.

1190. **Chicano Literature: A Reference Guide.** Julio A. Martinez and Francisco A. Lomeli, eds. Westport, CT: Greenwood Press, 1985. 492p. ISBN 0-313-23691-7.

At time of publication, this filled a void through its coverage of Mexican-American authors and their works written since 1848. It is used frequently by librarians, scholars, students, and laypersons seeking to understand the careers and literary quality of nearly thirty important authors. Also included are ten thematic articles treating important subjects. Entries are arranged alphabetically, with author entries running from 2,500 to 5,000 words in proportion to the subject's importance. These entries supply biographical data relating to date and place of birth, background, and family; followed by a scholarly signed essay describing career highlights and achievements and assessment of contribution. A bibliography of works by and about the writer concludes the entry. There are four appendices that supply a chronology and a glossary as well as a bibliography. An index is furnished.

1191. **Contemporary Spanish American Poets: A Bibliography of Primary and Secondary Sources.** Jacobo Sefami, comp. New York: Greenwood Press, 1992. 245p. (Bibliographies and Indexes in World Literature, no. 33). ISBN 0-313-27880-6.

This is a useful bibliography in its treatment of eighty-six poets born between 1910 and 1952. Selection is based on coverage in national bibliographies and in the MLA *International Bibliography* (entry 964), and treatment is divided between works by and about the poets. Included among the primary sources are poetic works, compilations and anthologies, and even other genres such as fiction and essay. Translations, for the most part, are not identified. Included among the secondary sources are bibliographies and critical studies of the subject's poetry. Although there is quarrel with certain omissions due to bias toward countries with national bibliographies, there was no intent to be comprehensive; the work plays well as a selective survey of contemporary Spanish-American poets. A well-constructed and useful bibliography of general sources concludes the effort. An index is furnished.

1192. **Dictionary of Mexican Literature**. Eladio Cortes, ed. Westport, CT: Greenwood Press, 1992. 768p. ISBN 0-313-26271-3.

As the first of its kind, this dictionary of the literature of Mexico provides coverage needed by students and others in comprehending this body of work. Some 550 entries follow a nineteen-page introductory essay providing an overview of Mexican letters and literature. Entries treat authors primarily; a few cover literary schools and cultural movements spanning Mexican literary history from the sixteenth century to the present day. Emphasis is given to the current scene and more than 80 percent of the writers chosen are either alive or have died during the twentieth century. Entries run from one page to sixteen pages in length and provide a biography and analysis, listing of works, and bibliography of secondary sources. Cross-references are given within the entries. A bibliography of general sources and an index conclude the tool.

1193. **Dictionary of the Literature of the Iberian Peninsula**. German Bleiberg et al., eds. New York: Greenwood Press, 1992-1993. 2v. ISBN 0-313-21302-X.

This is an update and expansion of the editor's 1972 publication bearing a Spanish-language title that earned a reputation as an excellent work for students and specialists. The present effort continues its tradition under Bleiberg (a noted academic Hispanist), his co-editors, and his pool of 140 experts who contributed the well-constructed informative articles. Entries treat all elements of the major literatures of the Iberian peninsula (Spanish, Catalan, Galician, Portugese) in a balanced manner. Included here are descriptions of literary figures, movements, genres, themes, styles, and forms, along with definitions of terms. Entries generally conclude with listings of primary and secondary sources and English translations. Personalities are all Iberian-born, and Spanish-American writers are excluded. Coverage spans a period of about 1,000 years from the tenth century to the mid-1980s. Cross-references are provided along with an index.

1194. **Handbook of Latin American Literature**. 2d ed. David William Foster, ed. New York: Garland, 1992. 799p. (Garland Reference Library of the Humanities, v.1459). ISBN 0-8153-0343-2.

The initial edition of this useful work, issued in 1987, attempted to bring an idealogical approach to the description and analysis of the national literatures of twenty-one Latin American countries, including Puerto Rico. Information was presented through in-depth descriptive and analytical essays on each of the countries and covered a period dating from the colonial times to the time of publication. The second edition continues in the same tradition and supplies essays that have been thoroughly revised, expanded, and updated. Thematic aspects, major literary figures, and literary traditions are treated. Newly added chapters examine the literature of principal Hispanic groups in the United States, film, and para-literature. Annotated bibliographies conclude each entry. A name index provides access.

Literatura Hispanoamericana: Una Antologia, also edited by Foster (Garland, 1994), is designed as a companion volume to the *Handbook* and serves as a sourcebook or anthology of selections of the work of forty-five Spanish-American authors. Although the selections date from the colonial period, emphasis is placed on important twentieth-century authors. Two complete novels and two complete dramas are included, along with a complete slave narrative.

1195. **Hispanic Writers: A Selection of Sketches from Contemporary Authors.** Bryan Ryan, ed. Detroit: Gale Research, 1991. 514p. ISBN 0-8103-7688-1.

About 40 percent of the 400 entries for twentieth-century authors treated in this biographical dictionary have been drawn from *Contemporary Authors* (entry 988) and updated; the rest have been prepared specifically for this tool. *Hispanic* in this case refers to writers from Mexico, the Spanish-speaking countries of Central America and South America, the Caribbean, and the United States. There is broad interpretation of *writers*, with inclusion of major literary figures, such as F. Garcia Lorca and Octavio Paz, and sociopolitical personalities, such as Che Guevara, as well as scholars, historians, journalists, and media personalities. Entries supply personal information, address, career data, memberships, awards, writings, works in progress, biographical sketch, critical reception and personal commentary, and bibliography of secondary sources. All Spanish-speaking countries are represented; there is strong coverage of U.S. authors. An index by nationality of author is provided.

1196. **Latin American Literary Authors: An Annotated Guide to Bibliographies.** David Zubatsky. Metuchen, NJ: Scarecrow Press, 1986. 332p. ISBN 0-8108-1900-7.

This is considered to be the most thorough and complete bibliography of bibliographies on Latin American authors of all types of literature. Novelists, dramatists, poets, essayists, literary critics, and others from all regions of Spanish-speaking America are included. A variety of sources are represented, including books, magazines, journals, dissertations, and festschriften. All major writers seem to be represented, as are scores of lesser known figures. Although there are some omissions, the work is commendable both for its inclusiveness and for its attention to detail. Entries are annotated and appear in two major parts, the first of which provides an alphabetical listing by author. Part 2 gives additional bio-bibliographical sources, arranged by country or region.

Zubatsky's *Spanish, Catalan, and Galician Literary Authors of the Twentieth Century: An Annotated Guide to Bibliographies* (Scarecrow Press, 1992) is developed within the same context and supplies an index to both primary and secondary published bibliographies of the work or criticism of the work of several hundred novelists, playwrights, poets, short story writers, linguists, literary critics, and historians who have published in Spanish, Catalan, or Galician during the twentieth century.

1197. **Latin American Literature in the 20th Century: A Guide.** New York: Ungar, 1986. Repr., Harpenden: Oldcastle Books, 1988. 278p. ISBN 0-948353-15-5.

Based on the four-volume *Encyclopedia of World Literature in the 20th Century* (entry 976), this one-volume work provides a compact but useful survey of literature written in Spanish and Portuguese from twenty countries of South and North America. Each country is treated separately and there is an introductory essay on literary trends and developments. This is followed by biographical sketches of a number of writers, discussion of their works, and a bibliography. There is a summary of each writer's accomplishments. The coverage in all cases has been praised for its high quality and clarity, especially important in examining some of the more complex and difficult works. This is a reliable source and one of the mainstays on the topic in most libraries providing reference services to students and interested laypersons.

1198. **The Latin American Short Story: An Annotated Guide to Anthologies and Criticism.** Daniel Balderston, comp. New York: Greenwood Press, 1992. 529p. (Bibliographies and Indexes in World Literature, no. 34). ISBN 0-313-27360-X.

The work opens with a well-developed introductory essay on the nature and role of anthologies. *Latin America* is here defined as Spanish America and includes the Spanish-speaking countries of the Caribbean and Brazil. This well-constructed tool provides both a bibliography of anthologies of Latin American short stories and a listing of criticism and interpretations. The anthologies section is organized into separate segments treating general anthologies, regional anthologies, and anthologies from particular countries. More than 1,300 anthologies are cited in Spanish, Portugese, or English translation and briefly described. The second section contains an annotated bibliography of criticism divided into segments on theory, general criticism, literary history, bibliography, regions, and particular countries. Annotations are brief but informative. There are more than 375 entries in this segment. The work is indexed by authors, critics, and titles of anthologies.

1199. **Latin American Writers.** Carlos A. Sole and Maria Isabel Abreu, eds. New York: Scribner's, 1989. 3v. ISBN 0-684-18463-X.

This important biocritical tool begins with a useful essay providing exposition of Spanish-American and Brazilian literature that places in perspective the information that follows on particular authors. A total of nineteen countries are represented by 176 writers of all genres (poetry, fiction, drama, journalism, biography, etc.). Writers are treated in chronological sequence by date of birth, beginning with the late fifteenth century and ending with the contemporary scene. Essays are detailed and range from 2,500 to 10,000 words depending upon the importance of the subject. Selective bibliographies of primary and secondary sources are given. Sixteen of the writers are women and contribute to the panoramic view of the literary history of Mexico, Central and South America, and the Spanish-speaking countries of the Caribbean. The articles are written by 135 specialist-contributors (academics, writers, critics, and diplomats). Most entries include quotations from the writer's work. A special feature is a chronology of literary and other events. A detailed index provides access.

1200. **Literatura Chicana: Creative and Critical Writings through 1984.** Roberto G. Trujillo and Andres Rodriguez, comps. Oakland, CA: Floricanto Press/Hispanex, 1985. 95p. ISBN 0-915745-04-6.

This slender volume was completed in response to a need to help document the writings of an important American minority group which up to now has not received much attention in the area of bibliographic control. Limited to material found in books, the work is divided into various forms and genres, with headings such as poetry, novels, short fiction, theater, literary criticism, "literatura chicanesca," oral tradition, anthologies, literary periodicals, unpublished dissertations, bibliographies, autobiographical works, and video and sound recordings. The compilers are librarians at Stanford University and have used their bibliographic skills well in identifying nearly 800 items. Each entry furnishes the author's name, the title of the work, imprint, and pagination. There is a useful introductory essay by Luis Leal on bibliographies in the field. Indexes are by author and title.

1201. **The Oxford Companion to Spanish Literature.** Philip Ward, ed. Oxford: Clarendon Press, 1978. 629p. ISBN 0-19-866114-2.

Another useful resource in the Oxford line-up, this one follows the pattern of the Companions to other literatures by providing an alphabetical approach to articles on a variety of individuals, works, and topics. Of the personalities covered, most are authors, but also included are critics, historians, and philosophers, among others. Plot summaries are given for important books, and good identifications are furnished for journals, libraries, publishers' series, literary movements, groups, and forms. All elements of Spanish literature are included: Basque, Catalan, Galician, and Castillian, but Portuguese is excluded. The literature of many countries is covered, representing most nations of Central and South America as well as Mexico. Although no general bibliography is given, there are references to additional reading materials in many of the entries.

1202. **A Sourcebook for Hispanic Literature and Language: A Selected Annotated Guide to Spanish, Spanish-American, and Chicano Bibliography** ... 2d ed. Donald W. Bleznick. Metuchen, NJ: Scarecrow Press, 1983. 304p. ISBN 0-8108-1616-4.

First published in 1974, the second issue of this guide for both students and scholars furnishes more than 1,400 entries in a classified arrangement. Individual chapters cover style guides, bibliographies and dictionaries, translations, scholarly periodicals, and publishers. Although criticized for certain deficiencies (annotations too general in some cases, incomplete bibliographic data in some entries, and misspellings), this has been acknowledged as a useful introductory work. Author and title indexes are furnished to aid access.

Another title, also in its second edition, is *Argentine Literature: A Research Guide* (Garland, 1982), compiled by David William Foster. It has two major sections: general references, with thirty chapters; and the authors segment, with nearly seventy-five writers. Each of the writers is given extensive bibliographic coverage (in some cases, more than 1,000 citations to studies in books, articles, and theses). Foster has also written *Mexican Literature: A Bibliography of Secondary Sources* (2d ed., Scarecrow Press, 1992). This is a useful bibliography of articles, monographs, dissertations, criticism, and review articles, the emphasis being on eighty-three writers of the nineteenth and twentieth centuries. With access to many catalogs and bibliographic tools, Foster has maintained the excellence of the first edition, and produced a valuable verification and identification tool.

1203. **Twentieth-Century Spanish Poets. First Series.** Michael L. Perna, ed. Detroit: Gale Research, 1991. 400p. (Dictionary of Literary Biography, v.108). ISBN 0-8103-4588-9.

This volume is part of the DLB series (entry 993) and follows the format and pattern of coverage established in that series, well known for its excellent biocritical and bibliographical coverage. In this volume, twenty-nine of the most important twentieth-century Spanish poets are treated in essays ranging in length from seven to almost thirty pages. This is the first volume in the series to treat Spanish-language writers, and such luminaries as Federico Garcia Lorca and Miguel de Unamuno are included. Certain omissions from this work are notable, especially that of Nobel prize winner, Juan Ramon Jimenez. Only three of the poets are female. As is true of other works in the series, the information is accurate and describes the ideology, contribution, and poetic technique of the subject. Included along with the essays are illustrations and listings of both primary and secondary sources for further study.

1204. **U.S. Latino Literature: An Essay and Annotated Bibliography**. Marc Zimmerman. Chicago: MARCH/Abrazo Press, 1992. 156p. ISBN 1-877636-01-0.

This is the second edition of a work initially commissioned and published by the Chicago Public Library in 1990, evidence of the growing interest in Latin American clienteles. The new publisher is a cultural arts organization. This work was designed to provide needed enlightenment and initial orientation to readers and researchers regarding the complexity of Latino cultural identity and its expression in literature. The work opens with an introductory essay on this topic and examines the theories and strategies behind current critical approaches. Entries are thoroughly annotated and placed within several categories or sections treating "Chicano Literature," "U.S. Puerto Rican Literature," "U.S. Cuban Literature," "Latino-tending U.S. Latin American Writing," "Latino Children and Young Adult Books," "Chicanesque Literature," and "Secondary Materials." Emphasis has been placed on English-language publication or translation.

1205. **Women Writers of Spain: An Annotated Bio-Bibliographical Guide.** Carolyn L. Galerstein, ed. Westport, CT: Greenwood Press, 1986. 389p. (Bibliographies and Indexes in Women's Studies, no. 2). ISBN 0-313-24965-2.

A comined effort of eighty contributors is this bio-bibliographical dictionary documenting the contributions of female writers in Spanish, Basque, Galician, and Catalan. In attempting to develop a useful tool for research, it was decided not to include writers for whom no material could be found other than what has already been identified in a comprehensive standard bibliography by Manuel Serrano y Sanz, *Apuntes para una biblioteca de escritoras espanolas desde al ano 1401 al 1833* (Establecimiento ..., 1903; repr., Atlas, 1975). Each author is given a biographical sketch with an annotated listing of her belles lettres contributions in book format. Several listings appear in the appendices: author by birthdate, authors in Catalan, authors in Galician, and translated titles. A title index supplies access.

Women Writers of Spanish America: An Annotated Bio-Bibliographical Guide, edited by Diane E. Marting (Greenwood Press, 1987), is no. 5 in the same series. The pattern of coverage is similar in treating the Spanish-language contributions of Spanish-American women writers from twenty-one countries, including the United States. Some seventy contributors have joined to provide a useful listing of entries, some fully annotated, furnishing the country of origin, dates, biographical information, and selective bibliography. *Women Authors of Modern Hispanic South America: A Bibliography of Literary Criticism and Interpretation*, by Sandra M. Cypess and others (Scarecrow Press, 1989), is a useful resource tool for students and scholars in the areas of Hispanic literature and women's studies. It provides an unannotated listing of studies and critical interpretations of the work of 169 female writers from nine countries. Arrangement is first by country, then by name and literary genre. References are included for books, articles, dissertations, and other materials.

1206. **Writers of the Caribbean and Central America: A Bibliography**. M. J. Fenwick. New York: Garland, 1992. 2v. (Garland Reference Library of the Humanities, v.1244). ISBN 0-8240-4010-4.

This tool is especially valuable for its inclusiveness in examining the literary production of forty-three geographical areas bordering on the Caribbean. Coverage is given to nearly 6,500 personalities writing in the Spanish language, nearly 1,350 English-language writers, and some 700 in French, 100 in Dutch, etc. Arrangement is by country, with entries duplicated under various countries where the authors have lived and worked. Entries supply a listing of the writer's works in chronological sequence, along with a listing of magazines and anthologies in which the works appear. Information is generally provided regarding vital years, genres, and major works, although entries vary considerably in treatment, with some providing only skeletal identification. With such comprehensive coverage, omissions are expected and have been pointed out by reviewers. Nevertheless, the work is unique for its breadth. An index is furnished.

GERMANIC/SCANDINAVIAN LANGUAGES

1207. **A Companion to Twentieth-Century German Literature**. Raymond Furness and Malcolm Humble. New York: Routledge, Chapman & Hall, 1991. 305p. ISBN 0-415-01987-7.

The authors, academics and specialists in the field of German culture, have compiled a useful bio-bibliography for students at various levels. A total of 414 twentieth-century writers of imaginative texts are treated, but there is little consideration for the work of editors, publishers, producers, or critics. Instead, the focus is on poets, dramatists, and writers of fiction from the turn of the century to the 1980s. Included here are all the well-known and most frequently studied German writers, with excellent representation of females, those of Jewish faith, and those from the former German Democratic Republic. Entries take the form of bibliographic essays and run from a few sentences to a page in length. They provide biographical identification, analysis of historical and literary context, and critical judgment. Unfortunately, there is no index.

1208. **Dictionary of Scandinavian Literature**. Virpi Zuck et al, eds. New York: Greenwood Press, 1990. 792p. ISBN 0-313-21450-6.

Specialists from several countries contributed to this tool, which provides coverage of five Nordic countries (Denmark, Norway, Sweden, Iceland, and Finland), producing an important work for students and scholars interested in further study. Articles are arranged alphabetically, employing English convention, and supply biocritical essays ranging from 200 to 1,600 words on 380 writers. Their works are described within the essays or are listed at the end, along with secondary publications, to conclude each entry. In addition, there are numerous topical entries on such subjects as Old Norse poetry, library resources, literary journals, and children's literature. Especially useful are such articles on the literature of the Faroese, Inuit (Greenland), and Sani (Lappland). Special features include a chronology comparing literary history in Scandinavia with that in other countries and an appendix of bibliographical sources. An index is supplied.

1209. **Grundriss zur Geschichte der deutschen Dichtung aus der Quellen.** 2 ganz neubearb. Aufl. Karl Goedeke. Dresden, Germany: L. Ehlermann, 1884- . v.1- .

This is acknowledged to be the most complete bibliography of German literature, a necessary purchase for large reference libraries and those operating in a university environment. Bibliographical and critical comments are included regarding authors and their works, as well as extensive listings of various editions, treatises, histories, biographical and critical works, and sources. Each volume is separately indexed, and an alphabetical index of authors covered in the first fifteen volumes was published in 1975. There is a third edition of volume 4 dealing primarily with the work of Goethe, published in five parts over a period of more than fifty years (1906-1960). Since Goedeke's death in 1887, the work has continued under various editors. Volumes 14-17, edited by Jacob von Herbert, have added "aus der quellen" to the original title. Volume 17 was issued in 1989.

A convenient and informative guide is Michael S. Batts's *The Bibliography of German Literature: An Historical and Critical Survey* (P. Lang, 1978). This work provides a brief overview of bibliographical tools available, with a critical review of current sources.

1210. **Introduction to Library Research in German Studies: Language, Literature, and Civilization.** Larry L. Richardson. Boulder, CO: Westview Press, 1984. 227p. (Westview Guides to Library Research). ISBN 0-86531-195-1.

A useful resource tool for students, because of its detailed coverage of the use of libraries and bibliographic searching techniques, this has become a popular guide to the field. It embraces not only the literature but also related studies of history, art, philosophy, politics, religion, and film. About 250 reference sources are identified and described in a helpful manner. Designed for the student who is studying German literature, it provides many helpful definitions of the types of tools listed, such as usage dictionaries. Works of literary criticism are included, as are major periodicals in the field. Supplementary reference works, guides to research papers, and computerized databases are also covered. There is a glossary, and a comprehensive index covers authors, titles, and subjects.

German Literature: An Annotated Reference Guide, by Uwe K. Faulhaber and Penrith B. Goff (Garland, 1979), is an older but more extensive annotated bibliography of more than 2,000 reference tools, works of literary criticism, and periodicals important to the study of German literature. There is a checklist of pertinent works in related fields such as art or music, but it is not annotated.

1211. **The Oxford Companion to German Literature.** 2d ed. Henry Garland and Mary Garland, eds. New York: Oxford University Press, 1986. 1020p. ISBN 0-19-866139-8.

This edition is a considerable update of the earlier work, published in 1976 and covering the field through the early 1970s. Employing the general format of the previous work (and, indeed, the pattern used in the entire Oxford Companion series), entries are alphabetically arranged and treat a variety of relevant topics. The book's coverage spans the entire history of German literature, from its beginnings to the present, in a well-balanced manner, describing events, writers, plot summaries, genres, literary movements, characters, historical figures, artists, philosophers, and periodicals. Major contemporary writers are included from both Germanies existing at time of publication. Furnished here is the information needed for background understanding and interpretation of German literature.

A new twist for the *Dictionary of Literary Biography* (entry 993) began with the fifty-sixth volume of the series, *German Fiction Writers, 1914-1945*, edited by James Hardin (Gale, 1987). Formerly restricted to coverage of British and American authors, with this volume the series embraced modern European writers. Included are German and Swiss authors whose first important work appeared during the time period specified. Coverage is given to thirty-three individuals, from the obscure to the renowned. As usual, biographical essays provide basic bibliographies for each author.

Work continues in this direction with the publication of *German Fiction Writers, 1885-1913*, also edited by Hardin, as volume 66 in two parts of the same series (1988). Treatment is accorded thirty-eight fiction writers of the late nineteenth and early twentieth centuries. Length of coverage varies from the nearly fifty pages given to Thomas Mann to around five pages for lesser figures.

1212. **The Twentieth-Century German Novel: A Bibliography of English Language Criticism, 1945-1986.** Michael T. O'Pecko and Eleanore O. Hofstetter. Metuchen, NJ: Scarecrow Press, 1989. 810p. ISBN 0-8108-2262-8.

This is an important tool of convenience for scholars and students in providing references to critical coverage published in books and periodicals after World War II on twentieth-century German novels. Coverage is comprehensive, with nearly 6,500 entries to these English-language studies. The work opens with a general section identifying histories and surveys of the German novel prior to World War II and general works on West German, East German, Austrian, and Swiss novels. The bulk of the text is given to individual authors and their novels, with arrangement alphabetical by name of author. Entries supply birth and death dates and references to bibliographies, general criticism, criticism of individual works, and book reviews. Coverage given to individual novels includes publication data, translations in English, and listings of criticism (alphabetically by critic). Unfortunately, there is no index.

SLAVONIC LANGUAGES

1213. **Handbook of Russian Literature.** Victor Terras, ed. New Haven, CT: Yale University Press, 1985. 558p. ISBN 0-300-03155-6.

This work has received much praise from reviewers, who are impressed with the amount of information, precision of language, comprehensiveness of coverage, and the interesting and enjoyable style. More than 100 contributors furnished one or two major articles and a number of minor ones within their areas of expertise. There are more than 1,000 entries, predominantly articles on individual writers. Also covered are literary terms and movements, historical events and figures, periodicals, societies, genres, and other topics relevant to the study of Russian literature. There is an emphasis on pre-revolutionary subjects, a period that has been slighted by recent sources. Bibliographies accompany most articles and emphasize English-language publications.

1214. **Nineteenth-Century Russian Literature in English: A Bibliography of Criticism and Translations**. Carl R. Proffer and Ronald Meyer, comps. Ann Arbor, MI: Ardis, 1990. 188p. ISBN 0-88233-943-5.

In treating that important era of Russian literature marked by the contributions of Turgenev, Pushkin, Tolstoy, Chekhov, and Dostoevsky, this tool provides a real service to students at all levels. It serves as an excellent beginning source in its concentration on English-language translations and English-language study and criticism of sixty-nine important writers of that remarkable period. The work opens with a segment of general works on the topic, and then proceeds with treatment of individual authors. Arrangement is alphabetical by name of author, and entries supply references to bibliographies as well as translations and critical interpretations in books, articles, and doctoral dissertations. Both collective works and monographs are included, and thirty-four different journals are examined to produce the critical publications issued between 1890 and 1986. No annotations are given, nor is an index provided.

1215. **Women and Writing in Russia and the USSR: A Bibliography of English-Language Sources.** Diane M. Nemec Ignashev and Sarah Krive. New York: Garland, 1992. 328p. (Garland Reference Library of the Humanities, v.1280). ISBN 0-8240-3647-6.

This work is useful to both researchers and students at all levels as a starting point for acquiring information on Russian women and their literary efforts. English-language works by and about women writers and about Russian and Soviet women in general are cited in four different sections. The first covers primary sources and lists works by female Russian and Soviet writers; the second segment furnishes listings of biographical and critical sources; supplementary sources are treated in the third section; and the fourth part provides listings of bibliographies. The writings by the women writers are generally belletristic in nature, whereas the writings about women are issue-oriented and represent societal concerns such as education, health, religion, ethnicity, etc. Citations are up-to-date and run through 1990. Unfortunately, there is no index.

ARABIC LANGUAGES

1216. **Modern Arabic Literature**. M. M. Badawi, ed. New York: Cambridge University Press, 1992. 571p. (The Cambridge History of Arabic Literature Series) ISBN 0-5213-3197-8.

This is a revised and expanded version of the 1987 publication issued through another publisher. It continues to furnish excellent coverage of the authors chosen for their importance and influence on post-neoclassical Arabic literature. The emphasis is on twentieth-century writers, with better representation from different parts of the Arabic world. A highly informative introductory essay furnishes a lucid summary of the highlights and important developments in Arabic literature. The following material is organized into thirteen chapters. Some bias was reported by one reviewer regarding a possibly Eurocentric attitude toward Arabic literary creativity. There is a selection of critical analyses from a group of sources both Arabic and English in origin. (Arabic works are in English translation.) Specific works are analyzed, including collections and anthologies of poems and stories.

ASIAN LANGUAGES

1217. **Asian Literature in English: A Guide to Information Sources**. George Lincoln Anderson. Detroit: Gale Research, 1981. 336p. (American Literature, English Literature, and World Literatures in English, v.31). ISBN 0-8103-1362-6.

This is a useful guide to translations into English and to critical studies and histories of the literature written in English. There are nearly 2,225 entries in the annotated bibliography, representing translations from a number of Asian countries (China, Japan, Korea, Burma, Cambodia, Indonesia, Laos, Malaysia, Singapore, Thailand, Vietnam, Mongolia, Tibet, and the Turkic regions of central Asia). Each literature section includes general bibliographies, anthologies, reference works, literary histories, literary forms, individual authors, and critical studies. Indian literature is excluded because it is treated in another volume in this series.

Indian Literature in English, 1827-1979: A Guide to Information Sources, by Amritjit Singh (Gale Research, 1981), is a bibliography of creative writing in English. It includes works that have been translated from Indian languages by their authors.

1218. **Guide to Japanese Prose**. 2d ed. Alfred H. Marks and Barry D. Bort. Boston: G. K. Hall, 1984. 186p. ISBN 0-8161-8630-8.

Another of the G. K. Hall bibliographies, this work was published initially in 1975 and was acknowledged as a useful source of information focusing on a subject that has not received a great deal of attention from Western writers. The second edition, similar to the earlier issue, identifies literary prose available in English translation. A good essay opens the work by examining the historical and literary context. There are two major sections of the work: pre-Meiji literature, which covers the beginnings to 1867; and Meiji literature (1868 to the present).

Also issued by G. K. Hall is Richard J. Lynn's *Guide to Chinese Poetry and Drama* (rev. ed., 1984). First published in 1973, this has proven to be a valuable critical guide to works in English translation for students and interested laypersons.

1219. **The Princeton Companion to Classical Japanese Literature**. Earl Miner et al. Princeton, NJ: Princeton University Press, 1985. 570p. ISBN 0-691-06599-3.

The classical era designated in the title represents the time prior to the Meiji Restoration of 1867-1968, a lengthy and productive term. Within this time span, there are a number of distinctive literary periods, which are introduced with a brief history at the beginning. Many charts, maps, pictures, and figures help to supplement the narrative. Several chronologies are given, as are descriptions of social groups. There are segments on arts, clothing, housing, and other aspects. A section of major importance to reference work covers important authors and their work, with some biographies achieving essay length. Literary allusions are covered well in the glossary of literary terms.

The Indiana Companion to Traditional Chinese Literature, edited by William H. Nienhauser, Jr., and others (Indiana University Press, 1986), is divided into two major sections. The first provides a series of ten essays on Buddhist and Taoist literatures and various genres. Part 2 contains more than 500 entries on writers, individual works, genres, styles, and so on. Each entry is accompanied by a bibliography.

1220. **Writers from the South Pacific: A Bio-Bibliographic Critical Encyclopedia**. Norman Sims. Washington, DC: Three Continents Press, 1991. 184p. ISBN 0-89410-594-9.

This is a useful work treating some 2,000 writers from a geographic region covered only infrequently by sources of this kind. Coverage includes Malaysia and Singapore but excludes the Philippines and Indonesia. As one might expect, there is a diverse collection of ethnic groupings in this region, and there is representation from the aboriginals in Australia, the Maori of New Zealand, the Vanatu of the New Hebrides, and native influences of the Wallis and Fortuna Islands. Emphasis is placed on Singapore and Malaysia, which together comprise about a third of the entries, although the entries in many of these cases are spare in terms of the information provided. Coverage runs from a single sentence to more than two pages in length, with the longer entries providing useful insight into the relationship of the writers to their society. An index is provided.

Children's and Young Adult Literature

BIBLIOGRAPHIES AND INDEXES

1221. **Best Books for Junior High Readers**. John T. Gillespie. New Providence, NJ: R. R. Bowker, 1991. 567p. ISBN 0-8352-3020-1.

This is one of three literature guides produced by Gillespie during this time period and provides brief annotated entries to about 5,675 books deemed worthy for students in grades seven through nine. Because the work was designed as a practical guide for purposes of selection, availability is an important consideration, and all items were in print in 1990. Entries are arranged under broad categories corresponding to discipline or subject area, such as history or music. They are then arranged alphabetically by author under subheadings. Listings are taken from four retrospective bibliographies, including the *Junior High School Library Catalog* (Wilson, 1990), and are appropriate and well-chosen.

Best Books for Senior High Readers, also by Gillespie (R. R. Bowker, 1991), complements the preceding effort in identifying more than 10,800 titles under sixty-seven major subject categories. These are culled from review journals and standard sources such as *Senior High School Library Catalog* (14th ed., Wilson, 1992). *Best Books for Children* is the earliest of Gillespie's trilogy and is now in its fourth edition (R. R. Bowker, 1990). It treats several thousand books suitable for grade-school youngsters and dramas from such sources as *Children's Catalog* (16th ed., Wilson, 1991).

1222. **The Best in Children's Books: The University of Chicago Guide to Children's Literature, 1985-1990**. Zena Sutherland et al. Chicago: University of Chicago Press, 1991. 492p. ISBN 0-226-78064-3.

Sutherland is a professor emeritus of the University and former editor of its *Bulletin of the Center for Children's Books*. This is the fourth volume in a series for which earlier issues covered the periods 1966-1972, 1973-1978, and 1979-1984, maintaining the tradition begun by the initial work, *Good Books for Children 1950-1965* (1966). The present volume provides

1,150 reviews selected from those published in the *Bulletin* between 1985 and 1990. Reviews run from 75 to 225 words and provide summary and criticism of the fiction and nonfiction selections that are generally suitable for youngsters from preschool to junior high school level. There is a fine introductory essay by Sutherland describing the importance of book selection for children and identifying the criteria used. Six indexes provide access.

1223.   **The Best of Bookfinder: A Guide to Children's Literature About Interests and Concerns of Youth Aged 2-18**. Sharon Spredemann Dreyer. Circle Pines, MN: American Guidance Service, 1992. 451p. ISBN 0-88671-440-0.

Preceded by three earlier volumes, this work has been recognized for its excellent treatment of books suitable for youngsters at different levels of emotional and mental growth. The present effort identifies and describes more than 675 books classified under 450 psychological, behavioral, and developmental topics. Many of these works were culled from the earlier volumes, which provided a well-constructed source of available materials. A few items of real value are labeled as out-of-print. It is the intent to provide books that are timely, representative of a universal theme, or are possibly the only work on a subject. Entries supply bibliographic description, primary themes, synopsis, reading level, availability in film, cassette, etc. Indexing is by author, title, and subject.

Sensitive Issues: An Annotated Guide to Children's Literature K-6, by Timothy V. Rasinski and Cindy S. Gillespie (Oryx Press, 1992), is designed especially for use by schools and their personnel involved in whole language programs. It cites juvenile titles treating such social issues as child abuse, cultural differences, death, disability, etc. Entries identify grade levels and provide annotations, along with suggested activities.

1224.   **Books by African-American Authors and Illustrators for Children and Young Adults**. Helen E. Williams. Chicago: American Library Association, 1991. 270p. ISBN 0-8389-0570-6.

The author is a librarian and professor of childrens' literature who has supplied a representative selection of books for young people written and illustrated by black writers and artists. A total of 1,200 titles published between 1900 and 1989 are identified within four chapters. The first three chapters treat books for very young children (picture books, concept books, folk and fairy tales, biographies, etc.); books for intermediate readers (folk literature, mystery, adventure, poetry, fiction and nonfiction for grades 5-8); and books for young adult readers, with more sophisticated works aimed at the senior high school level and above. Entries supply brief annotations describing content and identifying review sources. The fourth chapter treats illustrators and their works; entries describe style and technique of the illustrators and listings of their efforts. A bibliography, appendix of awards, glossary, and index are furnished.

1225.   **Children's Book Review Index, Master Cumulation, 1965-1984 ...** Gary C. Tarbert and Barbara Beach, eds. Detroit: Gale Research, 1985. 5v. ISBN 0-8103-2046-0. 1975- . Ann. ISSN 0147-5681.

This is a twenty-year cumulation of what, in 1975, became an annual publication.It is a convenience tool, listing materials in *Book Review Index* (Gale, 1965-) that are identified as children's books. The subtitle of the cumulation goes on to say "a Cumulated Index to More Than 200,000 Reviews of Approximately 55,000 Titles." The work represents a treasure house of information for those doing retrospective selection for purposes of collection development. It is also of importance to those in reference who are seeking to identify, verify, and locate critical reviews of children's materials for their patrons. The reviews cited have appeared in more than 370 periodicals, for which references are provided. Listings are by author, then title. The 1992 annual cumulation furnishes more than 26,000 citations to reviews of more than 11,000 books for children up to ten years old.

1226. **Fiction, Folklore, Fantasy & Poetry for Children, 1876-1985.** New York: R. R. Bowker, 1986. 2v. ISBN 0-8352-1831-7.

Another of the comprehensive bibliographies produced from the Bowker database, this massive work identifies works of fanciful children's literature by author, title, and illustrator over a period of 110 years. Introductory sections on children's books and a history of the R. R. Bowker Company are furnished in volume 1. Author and illustrator indexes follow. Volume 2 contains the title index and a section on book awards. Entries furnish author/illustrator dates and pseudonyms as well as title and imprint. The awards section seems to be less successful and has been criticized by reviewers. Newbery and Caldecott award winners are listed with date of publication rather than date of award. The first award winners in each of these categories have been omitted, and there are some misspellings. Despite these faults, the work must be considered a useful convenience tool.

1227. **Index to Children's Poetry: A Title, Subject, Author, and First Line Index to Poetry in Collections for Children and Youth.** John Edmond Brewton and Sara Westbrook Brewton. New York: H. W. Wilson, 1942. 965p. **Supps.** 1954, 1965, 1972, 1974, 1984, 1989.

The original volume of what is now a continuous series, this work indexed 130 collections of poetry for young people published up to the late 1930s. Title, subject, author, and first lines are indexed in a manner similar to that of *Granger's Index* (entry 1151). More than 15,000 poems by 2,500 poets are classified under a variety of subjects. The first supplement to this work appeared in 1954 and indexed more than sixty-five collections published between 1938 and 1951. The second supplement was published eleven years later and covered eighty-five collections published between 1949 and 1963.

Index to Poetry for Children and Young People, 1964-1969, by Brewton and G. Meredith Blackburn (H. W. Wilson, 1972), began the series of six-year supplements which placed increased emphasis on books at the seventh to twelfth grade levels. This was followed by *Index to Poetry for Children and Young People, 1970-1975*, by Brewton and Blackburn (H. W. Wilson, 1978). The same title and authorship continued with the supplement covering the period 1976-1981 (H. W. Wilson, 1984). The most recent issue, covering the period 1982-1987 (H. W. Wilson, 1989) was compiled by Blackburn and indexes 125 collections with 8,500 poems.

1228. **Our Family, Our Friends, Our World: An Annotated Guide to Significant Multicultural Books for Children and Teenagers.** Lyn Miller-Lachmann. New Providence, NJ: R. R. Bowker, 1992. 710p. ISBN 0-8352-3025-2.

This is an important tool identifying some 1,000 books, published between 1970 and 1990, that are useful in providing understanding of multicultural elements and diverse ethnic groups all over the world. It is the product of twenty-one contributor-specialists who bring expertise to the development of the eighteen geographic/ethnic segments into which the work is divided. Included here are the four leading minority groups in the United States (African-Americans, Asian-Americans, Hispanic-Americans, and Native Americans), along with the peoples of Great Britain and Ireland, sub-Saharan Africa, Eastern Europe and the Soviet Union, etc. Introductory essays provide a clear overview to the work itself and to each of the segments. Maps and statistical data are included. Entries follow the introductory passages and are annotated briefly. There is an appendix of professional sources, series titles, and publishers. A detailed general index is supplied.

1229. **Peoples of the American West: Historical Perspectives through Children's Literature.** Mary Hurlbut Cordier and Maria A. Perez-Stable. Metuchen, NJ: Scarecrow Press, 1989. 230p. ISBN 0-8108-2240-7.

This is a highly selective guide to reading for youngsters of all ages, providing historical perspective of the United States west of the Mississippi River from the sixteenth century to the early 1900s. Among the 100 items chosen for inclusion in this annotated bibliography are both imaginative and factual works treating a variety of regional and social settings. Included here are several of the works of Laura Ingalls Wilder and Patricia Beatty. Fiction entries are divided into thematic sections on homesteading and settling, overland journeys and major train trips, immigration, Native Americans, American Southwest, and West Coast. Additionally, there is a nonfiction segment embracing the factual items. Both sections are then subdivided by grade levels K-3 and 4-9. Entries supply geographic location, dates, characterization, half-page synopses, and summaries of strengths and points for class discussion. Readability levels as determined by four formulas are included.

1230. Portraying Persons with Disabilities: An Annotated Bibliography of Fiction for Children and Teenagers. 3d ed. Debra E. J. Robertson. New Providence, NJ: R. R. Bowker, 1992. 482p. (Serving Special Needs Series). ISBN 0-8352-3023-6.

This useful guide continues to identify books for youngsters from kindergarten through senior high school chosen to help sensitize them to the problems of the physically and mentally disabled. Earlier editions were entitled *Notes for a Different Drummer* (1977) and *More Notes for a Different Drummer* (1982). More than 450 books portraying disabled characters in realistic fashion are identified in the third edition, with inclusion of picture books, suspense novels, adventure novels, historical fiction, etc.; folklore is excluded. All types of disabilities are embraced (physical, sensory, cognitive, behavioral, etc.). Entries are arranged under category of disability and supply bibliographic data and reading level along with an extensive annotation of plot summary and critical analysis. Additionally, there are well-constructed essays on stereotyping and publication trends in fiction.

A companion effort is *Portraying Persons with Disabilities: An Annotated Bibliography of Nonfiction for Children and Teenagers*, by Joan Brest Friedberg and others, now in its second edition (R. R. Bowker, 1992). This tool identifies 300 biographies, case histories, and other sources published between 1980 and 1991.

1231. The Young Adult Reader's Adviser. Myra Immell, ed. New Providence, NJ: R. R. Bowker, 1992. 2v. ISBN 0-8352-3068-6.

Based on *The Reader's Adviser* (14th ed., R. R. Bowker, 1994), this new tool for reading guidance is designed to help students, teachers, and librarians in their quest for good reading material on subjects and authors. Materials are suitable for youngsters from the middle grades through the high school years and are organized into four topical areas of the curriculum: literature and language arts, mathematics and computer science, social science and history, and science and health. Each segment contains entries on personalities, which supply a biographical sketch as well as listings of primary and secondary source material. Along with the personalities, entries also treat major topics and issues, such as adolescence and aging, for which annotated bibliographies are furnished. In serving as both a critical bibliographic guide and a biographical encyclopedia, the work has earned a reputation as an important tool. It is indexed by author, title, and publisher.

An annual listing of value is *Young Adult Annual Booklist*, published by the Los Angeles Public Library since 1983. It identifies some 250 books and supplies reviews from library staff members. Arrangement of entries is under subject categories such as science, literature, etc. Overall evaluations are indicated by symbol.

1232. Young People's Books in Series: Fiction and Non-Fiction, 1975-1991. Judith K. Rosenberg and C. Allen Nichols. Englewood, CO: Libraries Unlimited, 1992. 424p. ISBN 0-87287-882-1.

This is an update and expansion of Rosenberg's earlier efforts in the 1970s, and supplies listings of series books for children in grades 3-12. The segment on fiction is arranged alphabetically by author and provides numbers for titles within each series. Treatment in this section is comprehensive and all series published during the sixteen-year period are included. Listings within each series appear to be complete in cases where the series has been included for the first time. Annotations tend to be brief, providing plot summaries but little more in many instances; age-level recommendations are indicated. The nonfiction segment is organized alphabetically by series title, and entries also supply brief evaluations and age-level recommendations. An index is furnished.

Vicki Anderson's *Fiction Sequels for Readers 10 to 16: An Annotated Bibliography of Books in Succession* (McFarland, 1990) identifies some 1,500 titles by 350 authors listed in sequence to identify sequels. Most were published after 1960; series such as Nancy Drew and the Hardy Boys have been excluded, because sequels are distinguished from series in their greater emphasis on character development. Annotations are based on material provided on book jackets, catalog cards, reviews, and the books themselves.

DICTIONARIES, ENCYCLOPEDIAS, AND HANDBOOKS

1233. **Award-Winning Books for Children and Young Adults, 1990-1991.** Betty L. Criscoe and Philip J. Lanasa, III. Metuchen, NJ: Scarecrow Press, 1993. ISBN 0-8108-2597-X.

Criscoe authored the initial edition of this guide in 1990 and covered award-winning books for 1989. It was to continue as an annual publication, but policy changes ensued and thus this second number was issued three years later and covers a two-year period. It would appear that either a biennial or triennial pattern of frequency is to follow. The title has been received enthusiastically by reviewers, who consider it "a wonderful book for collection development, reading guidance, and research" and "invaluable in selecting the best from a year's publications." Its value is obvious to teachers, school librarians, and public librarians who deal with the needs of children and young adults, as it provides a valuable selection tool and purchasing guide. Awards are listed, with entries supplying background history of each award along with method and criteria of selecting winners. Winning books are identified and described; a reproduction of the book cover is given. For awards given to personalities, a biographical sketch and listing of credits are provided. Useful appendices include listings of publishers, authors and titles, and genres. Several indexes supply excellent access.

1234. **The Black American in Books for Children: Readings in Racism.** 2d ed. Donnarae MacCann and Gloria Woodard, eds. Metuchen, NJ: Scarecrow Press, 1985. 298p. ISBN 0-8108-1826-4.

This is a valuable collection of essays for librarians and teachers who work with young people, written by specialists in children's literature, sociology, education, and history. Intellectual freedom is described in many of the essays, all targeted to the presentation of the black experience in literature for children. Titles such as *Sounder* and *Dr. Doolittle* are described and analyzed and trends are explained. Both illustrations and picture books are also treated. Originally published in 1972, the second edition provides information in helping to establish an informed perspective on the portrayal of the black experience. This work is extremely useful as a resource tool for courses in book selection and acquisitions.

1235. **Characters from Young Adult Literature.** Mary Ellen Snodgrass. Englewood, CO: Libraries Unlimited, 1991. 229p. ISBN 0-87287-883-X.

Hundreds of characters, both major and minor, are identified from seventy-one works of fiction, drama, biography, and nonfiction dating from the sixteenth to the twentieth centuries. The works are listed alphabetically by title, and all are English-language writings that have been popular with this age group and may have been included within school curricula. Entries furnish date of work, author's name and dates, genre, setting, and a brief plot synopsis. Characters are then described in terms of their gender, age, social circumstances, and nature. More extensive treatment is given to the major characters, but the reader is apprised of the role and situation of even the minor players. In this regard the tool is unique, and its in-depth introductory material regarding the characters is a welcome touch. An index is provided.

1236. **Children's Literature Awards and Winners: A Directory of Prizes, Authors, and Illustrators.** 3d ed. Dolores Blythe Jones. Detroit: Neal-Schuman/Gale Research, 1994. 678p. ISBN 0-8103-6900-1.

This is a revision of the second edition, issued in 1988 and identifies some 7,000 prize-winning authors and illustrators, along with 5,000 books. Arrangement is in three parts, with part 1 being an alphabetical list of awards presented to works of children's literature by organizations in the United States and abroad. Entries include name of award, address, founder, history, criteria, purpose, time of presentation, and full citations to all award winners and runners-up, in chronological sequence. The second part furnishes an alphabetical arrangement of authors and illustrators, with indication of their books and the awards they won. Finally, there is a bibliography of source materials on children's literary awards.

Another useful tool is *Children's Books: Awards & Prizes, Including Prizes and Awards for Young Adult Books* (Children's Book Council, 1986). This guide groups the entries (awards) in four categories: U.S. awards selected by adults, U.S. awards selected by youngsters, British Commonwealth awards, and international awards. Entries describe the awards briefly and furnish listings of winners in chronological order. There is an award classification section which provides "subject" access, as well as a title index and a person index.

1237. Dictionary of American Children's Fiction, 1859-1959: Books of Recognized Merit. Alethea K. Helbig and Agnes Regan Perkins. Westport, CT: Greenwood Press, 1985. 666p. ISBN 0-313-22590-7. **Supp. 1960-1984.** 1986. 914p. **Supp. 1985-1989.** 1993. 368p.

This is an interesting and useful tool that provides historical information on award-winning books of children's fiction covering a period of 100 years. Entries are listed alphabetically by title, with related entries for authors and significant characters. Settings are also included in the index when important. Title entries furnish basic bibliographic data as well as an informative synopsis of the work and references to specific awards received. Cross-references are also provided. Most valuable is a detailed subject approach in the index, which identifies numerous specific subjects or topics relevant to the listed works. The index also provides access by age of protagonist, time period, and ethnic customs.

The work is continued by these two authors with publication of *Dictionary of American Children's Fiction, 1960-1984: Recent Books of Recognized Merit* (Greenwood, 1986). It identifies an additional 489 meritorious books written during that time period. Format remains the same in publication of *Dictionary of American Children's Fiction, 1985-1989: Books of Recognized Merit* (Greenwood, 1993), the first of what is projected to be a series of five-year supplements. This one reveals 134 award-winning and significant books.

1238. Masterplots II. Juvenile and Young Adult Fiction Series. Frank N. Magill, ed. Pasadena, CA: Salem Press, 1991. 4v. ISBN 0-89356-579-2.

As part of Magill's *Masterplots II* series (entry 980n), this set provides a focus on fiction of interest to youngsters from the middle grades through high school. Picture books are excluded in this treatment of nearly 550 titles, all alphabetically arranged for easy access. Variety of selection is apparent, with inclusion of such general classics with appeal to youngsters as *Animal Farm* and *The Count of Monte Cristo* as well as popular children's works like *The Chocolate War*. Nearly 450 of the selections are new to the series and about 100 titles have been included in other sets. They have been completely rewritten and updated. Entries generally supply brief header information identifying dates, settings, principal themes, and recommended ages, along with plot synopsis and exposition of the story, themes and meanings, and context. Author, title, and subject indexes are in volume 4.

1239. Newbery and Caldecott Medalists and Honor Book Winners: Bibliographies and Resource Material through 1991. 2d ed. Muriel Brown et al., comps. New York: Neal-Schuman, 1992. 511p. ISBN 1-55570-118-3.

Somewhat of a cross between a bibliography and a handbook is this interesting compilation of material on the Newbery and Caldecott medalists and Honor Book winners. A good introduction describes the medals. This is followed by the main listing of award winners, authors and illustrators, alphabetically arranged with dates provided. Listed for each illustrator and author are their award-winning books and other works. Also included are indications of media formats developed from their works, library collections, exhibitions, and additional readings. The time span covered is from the beginning of their careers to 1992.

A companion title is *Newbery and Caldecott Medal and Honor Books in Other Media*, compiled by Paulette B. Sharkey and Jim Roginski (Neal-Schuman, 1992). Listings of media publications based upon the award-winning books include audio, film, filmstrip, software, television, video, and so on. There is a useful directory of producers and distributors and a good bibliography of resources. Another useful work is *The Newbery and Caldecott Awards: A Guide to the Medal and Honor Books*, issued annually by the American Library Association. The 1992 volume contains annotations along with excellent essays on the history and terms of the awards. There is a listing of the media used in each of the award-winners and honor books. There are author/illustrator and title indexes.

1240.   **The Oxford Companion to Children's Literature.** Humphrey Carpenter and Mari Prichard. New York: Oxford University Press, 1984; repr. with corr., 1985. 586p. ISBN 0-19-211582-0.

The authors are a husband-and-wife team working in much the same manner as Iona Opie and Peter Opie did in developing their *Oxford Dictionary of Nursery Rhymes* (entry 1241). This work covers children's literature on a broad scale and in a comprehensive manner, covering literature in all languages and countries where information could be found. There are approximately 2,000 entries in all, of which 900 are biographical sketches. Summaries are given for hundreds of children's titles and various topics, most of which are timely and of importance, such as "television and children." Articles vary in length in proportion to the importance of the topic, with lengthy descriptions given to Lewis Carroll and to *Alice in Wonderland*. The work is used frequently by writers whose interests parallel the topical coverage.

1241.   **The Oxford Dictionary of Nursery Rhymes.** Iona Opie and Peter Opie, eds. Oxford: Clarendon Press, 1951. Repr. with corr., New York: Oxford University Press, 1991. 467p. ISBN 0-19-869111-4.

Working together, this husband-and-wife team produced the most comprehensive and authoritative work ever developed on the English nursery rhyme. A useful introduction begins the work, after which about 550 nursery rhymes are described. All of them are in current use or have been used in the recent past. The arrangement is alphabetical by the most significant word; when nonsense language is employed, the entry is listed under the opening phrase. (This strategy has worked well and most rhymes are easily located.) Along with numerous illustrations from the early published works, the earliest recorded version of the rhymes and the familiar or standard phrasing are included. Two indexes are given, the first of notable individuals associated with the nursery rhyme. There is also an index of first lines of both standard and original versions.

BIOGRAPHICAL AND CRITICAL SOURCES

1242.   **American Writers for Children Since 1960: Fiction.** Glenn E. Estes, ed. Detroit: Gale Research, 1986. 488p. (Dictionary of Literary Biography, v.52). ISBN 0-8103-1730-3.

This is one of the recent publications in the Dictionary of Literary Biography series (entry 993). Like other volumes in the series, this one covers individuals determined to be influential in their genre. Nearly forty-five authors of children's fiction who have been productive since 1960 are included, thus providing useful information on some contemporary realistic writers. The coverage is of high quality, with well-developed entries providing good biocritical essays and furnishing career chronologies, publications lists, and bibliographies of works by and about the subject. Individuals represent the entire realm of children's fiction popular during this time in realism, historical fiction, fantasy, among others. Included are Judy Blume, Robert Cormier, Paul Zendel, and Katherine Paterson.

A more recent and more specialized effort is *Science Fiction for Young Readers*, edited by C. W. Sullivan (Greenwood Press, 1993), providing a collection of well-developed essays on a full range of topics relevant to science fiction for youthful readers. Leading writers such as Asimov and Heinlein are examined in terms of their contributions, and particular titles and series are analyzed.

1243. **Biographical Index to Children's and Young Adult Authors and Illustrators**. David V. Loertscher. Castle Rock, CO: Hi Willow Research & Publishing, 1993. 320p. ISBN 0-931510-47-3.

This easy-to-use, comprehensive tool now indexes more than 13,000 writers, illustrators, poets, filmmakers, and cartoonists covered in both collective and single biographies. This represents an increase of 6,000 personalities over the number treated in the 1992 edition. Individuals are from all over the world and are linked to biographical sketches appearing in more than 1,500 biographical works, both print and audiovisual. The initial edition (1992) grew out of an earlier publication designed as a state-by-state guide and limited to U.S. authors. Entries supply name, dates, country or state, and citations. The strength of this work lies not only in its extensive listing of children's and young adult authors, but also in its inclusion of authors for adults whose works have appealed to high school students. An interesting aspect of this tool is its plan for continous updating, which initially projected a publication frequency greater than that of an annual.

1244. **Black Authors & Illustrators of Children's Books: A Biographical Dictionary**. 2d ed. Barbara Rollock. New York: Garland, 1992. (Garland Reference Library of the Humanities, v.1316). ISBN 0-8240-7078-X.

Rollock is retired head of children's services at New York Public Library, who in 1988 published the initial edition treating the lives and careers of 115 writers and illustrators. Since that time, the contributions of black authors and illustrators have continued in a fashion commensurate with the nation's increased sensitivity to its multicultural composition. The new edition has added thirty-five new authors and has updated and revised the original entries by providing biographical treatment of 150 writers and illustrators of children's books that have been published in the United States between 1930 and 1990. Biographees are from the United States, Africa, the Caribbean, Britain, and France, providing an array of life-view perspectives important to intellectual development of youngsters. There is a good introductory essay along with appendices containing award winners and listings of series.

Bookpeople: A Multicultural Album, by Sharron L. McElmeel (Libraries Unlimited, 1992), provides a selective treatment of fifteen authors and illustrators who either are members of a minority culture or who have produced books about such persons. Entries supply biographical sketches, photographs, and description of works. Suggestions to teachers and media specialists include discussion questions along with identification of related books by other authors.

1245. **Children's Literature Review. Excerpts from Reviews, Criticism, and Commentary on Books for Children and Young People.** Detroit: Gale Research, 1976- . Irreg. ISSN 0362-4145.

Another of the Gale efforts, this work has built a following, although the frequency of publication has been sporadic. Volumes 9-11 were issued during 1985-1986, which marked a period of increased activity. Since then publication has been steady, with volume 31 produced in 1993. Each volume contains excerpts from criticism and reviews published in books and periodicals on the writings of a dozen or so children's authors from all over the world, both past and present. Each author is treated in a separate section of the work; each entry begins with a description of the writer's literary background and style along with a photograph. In some cases, there is an author's commentary, permitting the writer to reflect on his or her own work. A general commentary by a reviewer is followed by extracts of reviews of individual titles. There is a cumulative title index for the various volumes, along with those of authors and of nationality.

*1246. DISCovering Authors: Biographies & Criticism on 300 Most Studied Writers. Detroit: Gale Research, 1992- . Ann. ISSN 1066-7792. (CD-ROM).

A total of 305 authors are treated in Gale's first CD-ROM product, containing much bibliographical, biographical, and critical information drawn from its various print series. Selections were made on the basis of popularity and familiarity and include the most studied authors from ancient times to the present. Some thirty-five nationalities are represented from the time of Aristotle to the present. Entries supply introductory information, biographical sketch, personal and career information, bibliographies of primary and secondary sources, identification of media adaptations, and several excerpts of criticism with references to sources. Approximately 30 percent of the entries are original to this work; the remainder were revised and updated prior to their inclusion. There are a variety of search options permitting access by author, title, subject-term/character, and personal data (birth date, death date, nationality, etc.). The work is offered either as a package or on disk only.

1247. Homosexual Characters in YA Novels: A Literary Analysis, 1969-1982. Allan A. Cuseo. Metuchen, NJ: Scarecrow Press, 1992. 516p. ISBN 0-8108-2537-6.

Cuseo initially began his literary investigation of the depiction of homosexuality in novels for young adults while earning his doctorate at Columbia University. This tool provides an analysis of sixty-nine realistic novels published between 1969 and 1982. In providing an assessment of their literary quality, the treatment given to their homosexual characters is examined in terms of the degree of realism and possible negativity or stereotyping present. It represents an earnest effort to determine whether such realistic literature in effect promotes myths about the gay/lesbian experience. Various elements are examined, such as the language, setting, image, violence, cultural diversity, relationships, and roles, with interpretation based on quotes from the literature. For this period, it was found that authors did indeed buy into a socially prejudiced view of homosexuality through their representation of stereotypes in these "realistic" novels.

1248. The Junior Book of Authors. 2d ed. rev. Stanley Jasspon Kunitz and Howard Haycraft. New York: H. W. Wilson, 1951; repr. 1991, 310p. ISBN 0-8242-0021-7; ISBN 0-8242-0777-7 (Sixth).

The second edition of this work by Kunitz and Haycraft furnishes biographical sketches of nearly 270 writers and illustrators, 160 of them repeated with revisions from the first edition in 1934. Of the 108 names deleted, most are of classic stature and are covered in other Wilson publications. This work marked the beginning of another series: it was supplemented by Muriel Fuller's *More Junior Authors* (H. W. Wilson, 1963), which provided 268 biographical sketches of authors and illustrators. *Third Book of Junior Authors & Illustrators*, edited by Doris De Montreville and Donna Hill (H. W. Wilson, 1972), continued the coverage with more than 200 biographical sketches, as did the *Fourth Book of Junior Authors and Illustrators*, edited by De Montreville and Elizabeth D. Crawford (H. W. Wilson, 1978). The most recent issues have been Sally Holtze's *Fifth Book of Junior Authors & Illustrators* (H. W. Wilson, 1983), treating nearly 240 individuals who "have come to prominence since 1978," and her *Sixth Book of Junior Authors & Illustrators* (H. W. Wilson, 1989), examining the contributions of another 250 personalities. There is a cumulative index to all volumes in the back.

1249. Something About the Author: Facts and Pictures about Authors and Illustrators of Books for Young People. Anne Commire, ed. Detroit: Gale Research, 1971- . ISSN 0276-816X.

Since 1971, this has been a prolific series, with seventy-seven volumes published through 1994. Each of the volumes provides illustrated biographies of between 100 and 125 juvenile and young adult illustrators and authors. Both well-known and less popular individuals are treated, with several writers selected for lengthy treatment and the rest receiving brief entries. Emphasis is on contemporary writing, with more than 7,000 authors treated thus far. Primarily written for the youngster to read, the articles are lucid, well developed stylistically, and contain complete names and pseudonyms; date of birth; career information, including awards, titles of works, publication dates; and indication of genre. Numerous illustrations are reproduced from the works. Descriptions are noncritical, similar to the series from the Wilson Company (entry 1248). There is a two-part cumulative index in each volume, along with an illustrations index identifying volumes where art work is furnished, and the author index. Obituaries are included. The series is now edited by Donna Olendorf and Diane Telgen.

Something about the Author Autobiography Series, edited by Joyce Nakamura, began in 1986 and furnishes biographical sketches and commentary from the authors themselves. Treatment may include important events in their lives, sources of inspiration, or exposition of their style and method of writing. Each writer has been covered in *Something About the Author* prior to being selected for inclusion here. Volume 17 was issued in 1993, with coverage of about twenty authors per volume. *More Authors and Illustrators for Children and Young Adults*, edited by Nakamura and Laurie Collier (Gale Research, 1992), is a six-volume selection of updated entries initially appearing in *Something About the Author*. Intended for the small library, it supplies biographical sketches and bibliographies of the most popular and widely read authors. Emphasis is on contemporary writers, but there is a good selection of those of classical importance. *Children's Authors and Illustrators: An Index to Biographical Dictionaries*, also edited by Nakamura (Gale, 1987), is now in its fourth edition. It identifies biographies of 25,000 individuals appearing in 450 biographical dictionaries.

1250. **Twentieth-Century Children's Writers.** 3d ed. Tracy Chevalier, ed. Chicago: St. James Press, 1989. 1288p. ISBN 0-912289-95-3.

First published in 1978, and revised in 1983, this work is considered a useful source of information on modern children's writers of fiction, drama, and poetry. The third edition covers more than 800 individuals (an increase of 100 over the last issue). Of the total, 150 appear for the first time. Authors are selected carefully for inclusion. Entries are arranged alphabetically and treated with a short biography, a bibliography of published writings, and an informative critical essay about one page in length. The essay treats their works and their significance. Locations of manuscripts are provided and references to critical studies are given. Writers in the main text have published primarily in the twentieth century, but an appendix contains sections on several figures of the nineteenth century (Lewis Carroll and Robert Louis Stevenson). A listing is provided of foreign-language writers of prominence. A title index also includes the author's name amd year of publication.

AUTHOR AND TITLE INDEX

This index generally refers to entry numbers found in chapters 2-12, not to page numbers. Additional sources mentioned in the annotations are indexed with the letter "n" following the entry number. Authors and titles identified or described in the access chapters are indexed by page numbers and are located inside parentheses.

The following guidelines were used in alphabetizing index entries: Articles that occur at the beginning of titles have been omitted in the index. Lengthy titles have been shortened in most cases where this could be done without ambiguity. Entries have been arranged in accordance with the word-by-word or "nothing before something" method of filing. Names beginning with "Mc" or "Mac" are treated as spelled; those with prefixes such as de or De are treated as a single word. Acronyms and initialisms such as UNESCO or LLBA are treated as single words. Numbers (including dates), when part of the title, are arranged as though written in word form except when they are part of a sequence or series. In such cases, the titles in the sequence are listed in numerical order from lowest to highest. Finally, all sources available online or in CD-ROM format are marked with an asterisk (*).

SUBJECT INDEX

The purpose of this index is to provide access to broad topics. Consequently, only those organizations associated with more than one discipline are listed here. More specialized organizations will be found in the "Accessing Information" chapter for each discipline, as will bibliographic citations to works about the topics included here. Reference is first to entry numbers; page number entries are preceded by the letter "p".